INSTRUCTOR'S MANUAL TO ACCOMPANY

MARKETING RESEARCH

AN APPLIED APPROACH

FIFTH EDITION

Thomas C. Kinnear
Professor of Marketing
School of Business Administration
The University of Michigan

James R. Taylor
Professor of Marketing
School of Business Administration
The University of Michigan

The McGraw-Hill Companies, Inc.
New York St. Louis San Francisco Auckland Bogotá Caracas
Lisbon London Madrid Mexico City Milan Montreal
New Delhi San Juan Singapore Sydney Tokyo Toronto

McGraw-Hill
A Division of The McGraw-Hill Companies

**Instructor's Manual to Accompany
MARKETING RESEARCH An Applied Approach FIFTH EDITION**

Copyright © 1996 by The McGraw-Hill Companies, Inc. All rights reserved. Printed in the United States of America. The contents or parts thereof may be reproduced for use with
**MARKETING RESEARCH An Applied Approach FIFTH EDITION
by Thomas C. Kinnear and James R. Taylor**
provided such reproductions bear copyright notice, but may not be reproduced in any form for any other purpose without permission of the publisher.

ISBN 0-07-034800-6

1234567890 BKM BKM 909876

PREFACE

This manual has been prepared for use with the fifth edition of the textbook, Marketing Research: An Applied Approach. It is designed to serve three purposes--first to aid the instructor in designing a course structure, second, to provide answers to discussion and objective questions for use in the classroom or on examinations, and third, to provide commentaries on the classroom use of the cases and the computer data on the disk enclosed with the book.

The manual is divided into six parts. The first part includes suggestions for alternative uses of the material in developing a course structure. The second part presents suggested answers to the discussion questions appearing at the end of each chapter. The third part contains true-false and multiple-choice questions for each chapter. The fourth part presents teaching notes for the cases. The fifth part provides instructions and associated questionnaires for three data sets provided on disk with the book. The first computer data set is for the Milan Food Cooperative case (case 4-1) in the text. The second computer case, the Ann Arbor Metro Times (case 5-1), is a new case not included in the main text. The last computer case is based on the Midwest Marketing Research Associates (A) and (B) cases (cases 3-8 and 5-2). An improved questionnaire and codebook, along with an associated data set are provided. The sixth presents a more detailed discussion of the cost and value of marketing research information based on Bayesian decision theory. Finally, the seventh part presents transparency masters of the figures, tables, and exhibits which appear in the chapters and cases.

The authors wish to thank Ms. Pamela Downie for her excellent assistance in wordprocessing this manual.

TABLE OF CONTENTS

	Page
PART I--COURSE STRUCTURE	1
PART II--DISCUSSION QUESTIONS	5

Chapter

1	MARKETING RESEARCH ROLE IN MARKETING MANAGEMENT	6
2	THE MARKETING RESEARCH BUSINESS	13
3	THE MARKETING RESEARCH PROCESS: CONCEPT AND EXAMPLE	20
4	THE DECISION TO UNDERTAKE RESEARCH	25
5	RESEARCH DESIGN AND DATA SOURCES	32
6	SECONDARY DATA	39
7	THE MEASUREMENT PROCESS	46
8	ATTITUDE MEASUREMENT	51
9	CAUSAL DESIGNS	63
10	DATA COLLECTION: EXPLORATORY RESEARCH	74
11	DATA COLLECTION: CONCLUSIVE RESEARCH	80
12	DESIGNING DATA COLLECTION FORMS	86
13	THE BASICS OF SAMPLING	92
14	SIMPLE RANDOM SAMPLING AND SAMPLE SIZE	99
15	MORE COMPLEX SAMPLING PROCEDURES	108
16	FIELD OPERATIONS	155
17	DATA PROCESSING	158
18	UNIVARIATE DATA ANALYSIS	164
19	BIVARIATE DATA ANALYSIS	169
20	MULTIVARIATE DATA ANALYSIS I: INTERDEPENDENCE METHODS	182
21	MULTIVARIATE DATA ANALYSIS II: DEPENDENCE METHODS	185
22	REPORTING RESEARCH FINDINGS	188
23	DEMAND MEASUREMENT AND FORECASTING	190
24	PRODUCT RESEARCH AND TEST MARKETING	194
25	ADVERTISING RESEARCH	204
26	DISTRIBUTION AND PRICING RESEARCH	211

PART III--OBJECTIVE EXAMINATION QUESTIONS 215

Chapter

1	MARKETING RESEARCH ROLE IN MARKETING MANAGEMENT	213
2	THE MARKETING RESEARCH BUSINESS	223
3	THE MARKETING RESEARCH PROCESS: CONCEPT AND EXAMPLE	226
4	THE DECISION TO UNDERTAKE RESEARCH	229
5	RESEARCH DESIGN AND DATA SOURCES	235
6	SECONDARY DATA	241
7	THE MEASUREMENT PROCESS	244

Chapter		Page
8	ATTITUDE MEASUREMENT	251
9	CAUSAL DESIGNS	256
10	DATA COLLECTION: EXPLORATORY RESEARCH	264
11	DATA COLLECTION: CONCLUSIVE RESEARCH	267
12	DESIGNING DATA COLLECTION FORMS	271
13	THE BASICS OF SAMPLING	275
14	SIMPLE RANDOM SAMPLING AND SAMPLE SIZE	278
15	MORE COMPLEX SAMPLING PROCEDURES	282
16	FIELD OPERATIONS	288
17	DATA PROCESSING	291
18	UNIVARIATE DATA ANALYSIS	294
19	BIVARIATE DATA ANALYSIS	299
20	MULTIVARIATE DATA ANALYSIS I: INTERDEPENDENCE METHODS	303
21	MULTIVARIATE DATA ANALYSIS II: DEPENDENCE METHODS	306
22	REPORTING RESEARCH FINDINGS	313
23	DEMAND MEASUREMENT AND FORECASTING	315
24	PRODUCT RESEARCH AND TEST MARKETING	320
25	ADVERTISING RESEARCH	326
26	DISTRIBUTION AND PRICING RESEARCH	331

PART IV--CASE TEACHING NOTES 335

Case

1-1	NATIONAL MARKETS—NUTRITIONAL LABELING	336
1-2	WESTON FOOD COMPANY	340
1-3	FIELD MODULAR OFFICE FURNITURE	343
1-4	UNITED WAY OF AMERICA	347
1-5	ETHICAL DIMENSIONS IN MARKETING RESEARCH	351
2-1	AGT, INC.	354
2-2	TWIN PINES GOLF AND COUNTRY CLUB (A) AND (B)	359
2-3	AUTOMOTIVE SUPPLY, INC	366
2-4	NESTLE	369
3-1	THE NEW ENGLAND SOUP COMPANY	372
3-2	CHRYSLER CAR LEASING SATISFACTION STUDY	377
3-3	MAINLINE PACKAGE GOODS	382
3-4	UNILEVER'S PERSIL DETERGENT	386
3-5	EUROPEAN ALCOHOL RESEARCH FOUNDATION	390
3-6	KELLOGG'S HEARTWISE CEREAL	393
3-7	PARKSIDE CORPORATION	395
3-8	MIDWEST MARKETING RESEARCH ASSOCIATES (A)	398
4-1	MILAN FOOD COOPERATIVE (A)	402
4-2	CYNTHIA LU, STUDENT COUNCIL CANDIDATE	406
4-3	UNITED AIRLINES	410
4-4	ICE CREAM CASTLE	413
4-5	COSMOPOLITAN	416
4-6	GALLUP	418
4-7	A DAY IN THE CAREERS OF PAMELA PALMERS AND SANDY SANDERS	420

Case		Page
5-1	THE ANN ARBOR METRO TIMES	424
5-2	MIDWEST MARKETING RESEARCH ASSOCIATES (B)	430
5-3	MILAN FOOD COOPERATIVE (B)	435
5-4	BERNIE'S STUDENT CAFETERIA	443
5-5	SOUTHERN ILLINOIS MEDICAL CENTER	447
5-6	THE SOPHISTICATED RESEARCH GROUP	450
6-1	TECHNO FORECASTS, INC.	452
6-2	"NO SWEAT"	464
6-3	EXECUTIVE EXPRESS	467
6-4	THE CUPERTINO GROUP	469
6-5	PARADISE FOODS	472

PART V--COMPUTER CASES—INSTRUCTIONS 475

INTRODUCTION 475
CASE 1—MILAN FOOD COOPERATIVE 477
CASE 2—THE ANN ARBOR METRO TIMES 480
CASE 3—MIDWEST MARKETING RESEARCH ASSOCIATES (C) 483
QUESTIONNAIRE FOR THE ANN ARBOR METRO TIMES
    READER SURVEY 487
CODEBOOK FOR THE ANN ARBOR METRO TIMES
    READER SURVEY 493
REVISED QUESTIONNAIRE FOR NUTRITIONAL
    LABELING STUDY 501
REVISED CODEBOOK FOR NUTRITIONAL LABELING STUDY 509

**PART VI--A DECISION THEORY APPROACH TO MARKETING
    RESEARCH** 519

PART VII--TRANSPARENCY MASTERS 533

PART I

COURSE STRUCTURE

The material presented in the textbook and exercise book is designed for flexibility of use. This is accomplished by having shorter chapters and alternative material of varying difficulty. More complex material can easily be skipped without throwing off the flow of the book. At Michigan, we have followed this approach in using the material at both undergraduate and graduate levels.

Exhibit 1 presents an overview of the relationship among chapters, cases, and computer data disk exercises. By reviewing the teaching notes for the cases and computer exercises, the instructor can develop a perspective as to the nature of this material and how it supports the chapters.

In developing alternative course structures, the authors have visualized three possible usage patterns. These course structures are presented for your consideration with the anticipation that each instructor will formulate a somewhat different course structure depending upon his or her special pedagogical needs.

COURSE STRUCTURE #1

A course oriented to provide a managerial overview with little quantitative material; here one might use Chapters 1, 2, 3, 4, 5, 6, 10, 11, 12, 13, 14, 16, 17, 18, 19, 22, 23, 24, 25 and 26.

COURSE STRUCTURE #2

A course oriented to providing a managerial overview and to providing a good understanding of the basic quantitative concepts; here one might add to the previous list in (1) above Chapters 7, 8, 9, 14, and 15.

COURSE STRUCTURE #3

A course oriented to providing a managerial overview and to providing a somewhat in-depth understanding of quantitative material; here one might add to the previous list in (2) above Chapters 20, 21, and the Appendices to Chapters 19 and 21.

When developing lectures for a chapter, the instructor is encouraged to review the chapter discussion questions and the suggested answers presented in Part II of this manual. The discussion questions have been designed to represent a good summary of the key points covered in each chapter. In addition, you will find that we have included an extensive set of transparency masters for the figures, tables, and exhibits presented in each chapter, case, and exercise (see Part VI).

EXHIBIT 1

RELATIONSHIP AMONG CHAPTERS, CASES, AND EXERCISES

Chapter	Case
PART I: INTRODUCTION TO MARKETING RESEARCH IN MARKETING DECISION MAKING	
1. Marketing Research Role in Marketing Management	National Markets—Nutritional Labeling Weston Food Company
2. The Marketing Research Business	Ethical Dimensions in Marketing Research
3. The Marketing Research Process: Concept and Example	Field Modular Office Furniture
4. The Decision to Undertake Research	United Way of America Twin Pines Gold & Country Club (A)
PART II: DETERMINE RESEARCH DESIGN DATA SOURCES	
5. Research Design and Data Sources	AGT, Inc. Nestle
6. Secondary Data	Automotive Supply, Inc. Techno Forecasts, Inc.
PART III: DEVELOP THE DATA COLLECTION PROCEDURE	
7. The Measurement Process	The New England Soup Company Chrysler Car Leasing Satisfaction Study
8. Attitude Measurement	European Alcohol Research Foundation
9. Causal Designs	Mainline Package Goods Unilever Persil Detergent Kellogg's Heartwise Cereal
10. Data Collection Exploratory Research	Parkside Corporation
11. Data Collection: Conclusive Research	None
12. Designing Data Collection Forms	Midwest Marketing Research Associates (A)

Exhibit I (continued)

Chapter	Case

PART IV: SAMPLING PLAN AND DATA COLLECTION

13. Basics of Sampling — None

14. Simple Random Sampling and Sample Size — None

15. More Complex Sampling Procedures — Milan Food Cooperative (A)
    Cynthia Lu, Student Council Candidate
    United Airlines
    Ice Cream Castle
    Cosmopolitan Magazine
    Gallup Polls

16. Field Operations — A Day in the Careers of Pamela Palmers and Sandy Sanders

PART V: DATA ANALYSIS AND REPORTING RESEARCH FINDINGS

17. Data Processing — The Ann Arbor Metro Times
    Midwest Marketing Research Associates (B)

18. Univariate Data Analysis — (See data analysis discussion questions at end of chapter)
    The Ann Arbor Metro Times—Computer Case (see disk)

19. Bivariate Data Analysis — (See data analysis discussion questions at end of chapter)
    Bernie's Student Cafeteria
    The Ann Arbor Metro Times—Computer Case (see disk)
    Midwest Marketing Research Associate (C)–Computer Case (see disk)

20. Multivariate Data Analysis I: Interdependence Methods — Southern Illinois Medical Center
    The Sophisticated Research Group

21. Multivariate Data Analysis II: Dependence Methods — Milan Food Cooperative (B)
    Milan Food Cooperative—Computer Case (see disk)
    Midwest Marketing Research Associate (C)–Computer Case (see disk)

22. Reporting Research Findings — The Ann Arbor Metro Times—Computer Case (see disk)

Exhibit I (concluded)

Chapter	Case
PART VI: APPLICATIONS	
23. Demand Measurement and Forecasting	Techno Forecasts, Inc. Executive Express The Cupertino Group
24. Product Research and Test Marketing	"No Sweat" Paradise Foods
25. Advertising Research	Advertising Testing Services, Inc. Paradise Foods
26. Distribution and Pricing Research	Executive Express The Cupertino Group

PART II

DISCUSSION QUESTIONS

This section contains comments and suggested solutions for the discussion questions appearing at the end of each chapter. There are three types of discussion questions presented.

The first type of discussion question can be answered directly from the chapter. Questions of this type serve two purposes: 1) they lend themselves nicely as examination short answer questions, and 2) they can be used by the student as a study review in that failure to answer the questions implies that the essential points in the chapter have not been comprehended. The instructor may wish to make the answers in this manual available to students as a means to check the adequacy of their answers.

The second type of discussion question is less specific and often controversial. Obviously there is no correct answer specified in the chapter. The purpose of this type of question is to challenge the student's understanding of the issues presented and to broaden their perspective by confronting the differing student viewpoints. Our comments in regards to these questions are designed to stimulate the instructor's thinking on the issues and are not intended to present a comprehensive overview of the potential viewpoints. Discussion questions of this type are intended for use in the classroom setting to supplement a chapter lecture or review.

The third type of discussion question can best be described as a problem situation. Questions of this type present the student with a problem situation which requires the student to demonstrate knowledge regarding the process involved in solving the problem. Typically, the solution requires an analytical approach such as conducting a test of significance. This type of question can be used to supplement a chapter lecture or used by the student in studying a chapter. The student can be required to hand in solutions for grading and/or the solutions can be posted for purposes of solution feedback. Alternatively, these questions can be used on an examination.

The proportion of discussion questions in these three categories will vary depending on the content of the chapter. For example, Chapter 2 has several questions of a general and controversial nature, Chapter 4 has many questions which can be answered directly from the chapter, while Chapter 18 has several questions which require an analytical solution.

As an additional aid for the instructor, this edition contains "probe" questions as follow ups for most discussion questions found in the textbook. Probe questions can be used as additional discussion questions, exam questions, or substitutions for the original discussion question. Probe questions are generally designed to force the student to think more broadly about some of the discussion questions found in the text. Some discussion questions may not have a probe question due to their nature or complexity.

CHAPTER 1 – MARKETING RESEARCH ROLE IN MARKETING MANAGEMENT

1. What effect has the increasing adoption of the marketing concept by organizations had on marketing research?

   More and varied demands have been placed and will continue to be placed on marketing research. The implementation of the marketing concept is contingent upon the clear delineation of consumer needs and wants which the organization is capable of satisfying. The key role which marketing research occupies is evident. Also, the broadening of the marketing concept and subsequent adoption by diverse groups call for a correspondingly broader application of marketing research. Consumption, in the most basic sense, encompasses much more than the traditional concept, e.g., membership, patronage, etc. Marketing research must be sufficiently flexible to address the various facets of behavior falling within the expanding domain of marketing organizations.

   Instructor's Further Probing: What effect has the recent increase in development and marketing to foreign markets (like China and India) had on marketing research?

   Suggested Probe Response: Answer should focus on key concepts of awareness of cultural differences and flexibility of marketing research to accommodate and take advantage of these differences. The inserts found in this chapter and the rest of the text highlight issues dealing with this global theme.

2. Present the four essential components of the marketing system and examples of each.

   I. Situational factors
   1) Demand
   2) Competition
   3) Legal/Political
   4) Economic Climate
   5) Resources of the Organization
   6) Technological

   II. Marketing Mix
   1) Price Decisions
   2) Promotion Decisions
   3) Distribution Decisions
   4) Product Decisions

   III. Behavioral Response
   1) Awareness
   2) Knowledge
   3) Liking
   4) Preference
   5) Intent-to-buy
   6) Purchase

   IV. Performance Measures
   1) Sales
   2) Market Share

3) Costs
4) Profit
5) R.O.I.
6) Cash Flow
7) Earnings/Share
8) Image

Instructor's Further Probing: In the context of the Jacksonville Symphony Orchestra insert in the text, what situational factors existed, what marketing mix components were used, and what behavioral responses and performance measures resulted in the marketing research that was done for them?

Suggested Probe Response:
Situational factors: 1) demand of the type of entertainment
                       2) competition among other types of entertainment

Marketing mix:

1) price - insert does not provide information to indicate this as a significant factor

2) promotion - use of "product oriented" promotion techniques such as billboard advertising and direct mailings

3) distribution - the assortment of various series to cater to different types of people lead to five different series in three different halls

4) product - the product is the performance itself

Behavioral Response:

1) awareness - since there were subscribers there was a certain level of awareness of the Jacksonville Symphony Orchestra; this was a key area that was targeted in the marketing campaign (to increase this level of awareness)

2) liking - Ben West of West and Company summed up this concept by saying "we want to portray some of the romance and sensuality of the symphony as well as the emotional quality..."

3) purchase - the goal was to increase this level of purchasing of tickets

Performance measures:

1) Sales - nearly doubled as a result of the marketing research

2) Image - as West and Company indicated, they tried to add emotion to classical music, which enhanced the symphony's image

3. In what aspects of the marketing system is marketing research of limited applicability?

While undoubtedly employed more widely in some aspects than others, marketing research has proven useful in every aspect of the marketing system.

Instructor's Further Probing: When would marketing research be inefficient or not useful? Could this situation occur in an organization that had a marketing system? How?

Suggested Probe Response: Since the goal is for a manager to make an effective decision, if the manager's experience is reliable, and can help make that effective decision, then marketing research may be an inefficient use of time and money. Since marketing research may be used more in certain parts of the marketing mix than in other parts, the manager's experience may render marketing research unnecessary for certain areas of the mix.

4. Outline the steps in the research process for marketing managers considering introducing a new formulation of a laundry detergent.

   The general approach to a decision making process:
   1) Recognition of a decision situation.
   2) Definition of the decision problem.
   3) Identification of alternative courses of action.
   4) Evaluation of alternatives.
   5) Selection of a course of action.
   6) Implementation of the selected course of action.

   Specifically for this example:
   1) Recognition: The managers realize they need to make a decision on whether or not it would be worthwhile to launch a new detergent.

   2) Definition: Would the introduction of a new formulation of laundry detergent X generate sales and profits in this country that would give us at least a 25% profit margin within one year of its introduction?

   3) Identification:
      a. Launch product
      b. Delay launching of product for Z number of years
      c. Dismiss idea as not strategically beneficial

   4) Evaluation: Based on research, launching product now would produce only 5% profit margin, 35% profit margin could be expected when some competitors pull out of market in 2 years, and not implementing the idea would allow another competitor to use it to their advantage.

   5) Selection: Wait 2 years and launch product in this country.

   6) Implementation: Layout plan to prepare engineering, manufacturing, and sales teams for product launch in 1997.

Instructor's Further Probing: How does the decision-making process when a new product or service is introduced differ from when action needs to be taken because an existing product or service shows a change in a performance measurement?

Suggested Probe Response: The decision making process is used to make non-routine decisions, that is, to make decisions in situations where experience or judgment are irrelevant. Since an existing product has some history, there may be fewer non-routine decisions to be made than in the case of a new product with no history. The process following the decision making process is otherwise the same in both cases.

5. What factors determine the relative importance of a managerial experience versus marketing research in a given situation?

1) The nature of the decision situation, i.e. repetitive or atypical.

2) The degree of uncertainty and magnitude of the various outcomes associated with decision alternatives.

3) The ability of the manager to draw pertinent information from his his/her own experience.

4) The extent to which marketing research can effectively improve decision-making in a given instance.

5) The immediacy of the situation.

Instructor's Further Probing: If you were the hiring manager of a consumer goods company and were looking for a new marketing manager, which of these two candidates would you choose, and why: a marketing veteran who has enormous experience, but has never had education in the formal marketing research steps or concepts; a new marketing manager, who has a solid grasp through education on the steps and concepts of marketing research, but lacks the experience of a veteran?

Suggested Probe Response: As in most cases, this is very situation dependent. If the hiring firm needs someone to be able to make major decisions quickly, a veteran is the most likely choice. On the other hand, a newcomer to the marketing field has the structure and tools to analyze a situation and present an analysis to others, if time and money allows him/her to do so.

6. A marketing manager responsible for CD-ROM based video games for personal computers has received a copy of ten new books on this industry and five new industry reports prepared by industry consultants. These items total over three thousand pages. "All this data will be a great help with the new games we are planning," noted the analyst who delivered the documents. Comment on this quote, and describe how the manager should proceed.

The distinction between data and information is that data refers to observations and evidence regarding some aspect of the marketing system, while information refers to data which reduce the uncertainty in a decision situation. Since the marketing manager is in a decision situation, he needs information not just data. The manager should first proceed to review with the analyst what data from all the three thousand pages received can be used as information. Once the information has been located, the manager can then use the decision making process steps to make a decision based on that information. For example, reports about war games may not be useful if the company is looking at planning an adventure game.

Instructor's Further Probing: Of the following data obtained from a cashier at a grocery store, what is useful for determining which product sells the most: date and time of sale, cashier name, product name, product price, coupons used, register number, and register computer model number.

Suggested Probe Response: The following would be useful in determining the best selling product in the store: data and time of sale (to obtain the time frame of the sale) and product name.

7. One of the key marketing trends of the 1990's is that organizations are trying to become more market driven. What role should marketing research play in the process? Some

legendary business people, such as Charles Revson of Revlon, have had great success without using marketing research in any systematic way. **(probe question)** How is this possible?

While such success is not common, many times the experience of the marketer or manager can be almost as effective as marketing research itself. In addition, the market that Revlon dealt in was not new at all and so it was possible to see the rise and fall of other cosmetic companies and learn from their mistakes.

Marketing research helps companies understand the needs of the customer. Marketing research should play a key role in every phase of the business so that the needs of the customer are always focused on.

8. How might the following organizations effectively utilize marketing research?

   A. Walmart
   - Monitor customer awareness of special promotions (e.g. shelf tags for "environmentally friendly" products).
   - Measure effect of such promotions on sales.
   - Measure level of customer satisfaction with all aspects of store's physical layout and service.
   - Conduct ongoing research to stay abreast of changing consumer needs that may affect shopping habits
   - Site location potential studies.

   B. Diet Pepsi
   - Test new advertising campaign before it airs.
   - Measure effect of price reduction or increase on sales.
   - Generate ideas for new commercials.
   - Better understand reasons consumers would choose Diet Pepsi instead of Diet Coke, or vice versa.
   - New product development.

   C. National Museum of Art
   - Determine popularity of various permanent and temporary exhibits.
   - Find ideas for new exhibits.
   - Better understand reasons people choose to attend or not attend the Museum.

   D. American Airlines
   - Determine appropriate market segmentation scheme.
   - Examine differing needs and purchase decision criteria of various segments.
   - Determine appropriate pricing structure for various segments.
   - Test new advertising or promotional campaign.
   - Find ways to encourage infrequent flyers to fly American Airlines more.
   - Measure level of customer satisfaction with all aspects of airline service.

E. Dell Computer
- Get feedback on new market segments.
- Determine appropriate pricing levels.
- Test advertising copy.
- Test various sales techniques.
- Test product configuration preferences (hardware and software).

F. Your favorite restaurant
- Determine segment of population that eats there.
- Find ways to encourage people who do not normally eat out to eat there.
- Determine if varying the price of popular entrees affects volume of customers.
- Test advertising copy.
- Determine level of quality of service customers expect.

G. Sysco Food Services—a food wholesaler
- Study price/volume relationship to determine how quantity discounts will affect total sales volume and revenues.
- Measure effect of increased trade advertising on sales.
- Test new trade advertising copy.

Instructor's Further Probing: A good marketing plan for a company is derived from effective use of the marketing system and thus from the effective use of marketing research. Design an outline of such a marketing plan for Dell, a computer products wholesaler, based on Exhibit 1-1 on p. 18 in the text.

Suggested Probe Response:
(answer should be structured similarly to the sample below)
I. Situational analysis
   A. Demand analysis
      1. Buyer behavior and characteristics
         a. Customer purchases computer and peripherals
         b. 80% of customers are between 17-30 years old

9. Swatch watch's management (A Swiss Company) was considering simultaneously launching a new line of women's watches in the USA, Canada, UK, France, Germany, Italy, Spain, Switzerland, Japan, Hong Kong, and Korea. How might marketing research be useful to the planning of all marketing aspects of this launch: product design, advertising, consumer and trade promotion, and price points?

Due to the global nature of this launch, marketing research could be very beneficial to the marketing managers. Marketing managers in Switzerland may lack the experience and insights of markets outside of their country, so that marketing research can help them make informed decisions. This concept can be applied to all aspects of the launch by the fact that the design of the product, the type of advertising, consumer and trade promotion opportunities, and price points will all vary throughout all these different countries.

Instructor's Further Probing: Are there alternatives to marketing research when trying to make an informed decision with such a global launch as described in the above question? Does the additional cost of marketing research on a global scale outweigh the benefits?

Suggested Probe Response: If a marketing manager is experienced in launching a product globally, then many decisions become routine and thus do not need formalized marketing research. However, since some marketing errors may not be reversible, it is most likely worth taking the time to do marketing research. Therefore a common alternative to marketing research is to find someone with experience to make judgments without formalized marketing research. An example of this is the Chevy Nova automobile. This car was marketed very unsuccessfully in Mexico. A major reason for this flop was that "Nova" translated into "no go" in Spanish. Of course, this error could have been detected through marketing research in Mexico.

CHAPTER 2 — THE MARKETING RESEARCH BUSINESS

1. What is the institutional structure of marketing research business?

    Organizations may fall into one of three classifications:

    1) Users include manufacturers, wholesalers, retailers, service organizations, trade associations, and government agencies.
    2) User/doers include advertising agencies and advertising media.
    3) Doers include marketing research supply firms of ad hoc studies, syndicated data sources, universities, and research institutes.

Instructor's Further Probing: Categorize the following business into users, users/doers, and doers: Walmart, a retail chain, Marriott Corporation, described at the beginning of this chapter, and a local advertising agency.

Suggested Probe Response:

Walmart--a user; they use marketing research information from other sources to respond to the market

Marriott--user/doer; since their marketing research division is in-house, it is both a user and doer of its marketing research

Ad agency--user/doer; since they perform research for their clients and the agency performs research for itself to locate more potential clients

2. What type of person would make a good research analyst?

    According to studies, good qualities for a researcher include: high intelligence, high analytic ability, imagination/creativity, interpersonal skills, curiosity, writing proficiency, and drive/ambition. Beyond this, knowledge of marketing, plus some statistics and/or economics and/or business and/or psychology is considered useful.

Instructor's Further Probing: What is the function of a research analyst and what responsibilities does the analyst have?

Suggested Probe Response: The research analyst, also known as a research generalist, does the bulk of the designing and supervision of the actual marketing research studies. The analyst responsibilities include defining problems and opportunities, identifying management alternatives, proposing profit-oriented research to close information gaps, and balance risks with research costs to obtain high payoff research. For a more complete description of these responsibilities, see Table 2-2.

3. How can the marketing research function be organized?

    Either centralized, decentralized, or integrated.

Instructor's further probe: What marketing research function would be best suited for a consumer goods company, like Procter and Gamble, which produces scores of different types of products and has numerous divisions?

Suggested Probe Response: Since this company has numerous products and many divisions, a centralized organization would most likely make effective use of its resources. The shared services, effective coordination, increased objectivity, and cross-fertilization of ideas through a single marketing research organization, would allow this company to effectively use its resources. To prevent the organization from isolating researchers from day-to-day activities and problems as well preventing the marketing organization from diverting all its energies to corporate problems and not division problems, a division representative would be needed. The division representative can oversee the interests of each division. This setup is similar to the one described in the insert at the beginning of the chapter about Marriott Corporation's marketing organization.

4. What are the advantages and disadvantages of each organizational alternative?

   Centralized Organization:

   1) Advantages
      a) effective coordination
      b) effective control
      c) more efficient
      d) increased usefulness for corporate executives
      e) increased visibility

   2) Disadvantages
      a) possible isolation of researchers
      b) potential lack of adaptability to diverse divisional needs
      c) difficulty in measuring performance

   Decentralized Organization:

   1) Advantages
      a) improved ability to react
      b) increased usage by divisional personnel

   2) Disadvantages
      a) may be viewed as biased
      b) potential for insufficient control
      c) potential for inefficiency

   Integrated Organization:

   1) Advantages
      a) better coordination
      b) more effective research

   2) Disadvantages
      a) potential conflict of control
      b) possible duplication of effort

Instructor's further probe: What type of organization best describes Marriott Corporation's Central Market Research (CMS)?

Suggested Probe Response: CMS, as described in the insert at the beginning of the chapter, appears to be an integrated organization. CMS is available to the entire organization, but its reporting structure of reporting to individual units makes it an integrated organization not just a centralized organization.

5. On what basis should an organizational structure be selected?

   1) The marketing research function should reside where the marketing decision-making power resides.

   2) The researcher should be free from undue influence or manipulation by those areas or people for whom the research is conducted.

   3) The research function should be placed so that the process can be implemented quickly and efficiently.

   4) The research department should report to an executive who is genuinely interested in marketing research.

Instructor's further probe: Review Marriott Corporation's Corporate Marketing Services, as mentioned in the beginning of the chapter, using the above criteria for picking an organizational structure. Based on the above criteria, is CMS the appropriate organizational structure for Marriott?

Suggested Probe Response: Reviewing each criteria step-by-step, here is an analysis of Marriott's CMS...

   1) Marketing research function resides where marketing decision-making power resides

   Since the vice president of CMS reports directly to the senior vice president for strategic and business development, the research work in CMS resides where the marketing decision-making power resides. In addition, each business unit has a vertical "reporting relationship" with CMS. This further supports that marketing research resides where the marketing decision-making power resides.

   2) Researcher should be free from influence by the people for whom the research is being done.

   The insert makes no statements explicitly addressing this issue; however, with the reporting procedure of having the researchers report to the senior managers of each individual business unit and a vice president of research, the extent of influence is minimized.

   3) The research process should be placed so that the process can be implemented quickly and efficiently

   With CMS as a corporate wide service and researchers directly reporting to individual business units, the research process is very well streamlined.

4) The research department should report to an executive who is genuinely interested in marketing research

Since the researchers report to a vice president of CMS, this criteria holds.

Therefore, based on the above analysis, Marriott's CMS has been well designed and implemented and thus is suitable for Marriott Corporation.

6. How should a research supplier be selected?

A pool of potential suppliers may be screened on the basis of such criteria as: 1) the capabilities of personnel; 2) degree of specialization needed and provided; 3) technical competence; 4) facilities; 5) experience; 6) location; and 7) cost. The firms passing the screening may be asked to submit a proposal, which the client then incorporates into the decision to select the supplier.

Instructor's further probe: If you were the CEO of a small company looking to do research on a single product, based on the above research supplier selection guidelines, would you pick The Arbitron Company (see Table 2-1), one of the largest marketing research firms, or choose a much smaller marketing research supplier?

Suggested Probe Response: To make a qualified judgment, extensive research must be done on all suppliers being considered; however, we can make some basic analysis based on the differences between large and small suppliers. Arbitron Company has many qualified personnel, different areas of specialization, sufficient technical competence, adequate facilities, a history of experience, and may charge quite a bit more than a small company. In comparison, a smaller company will provide more one-on-one consulting and attention, but may lack the resources, personnel, and experience needed for the project at hand.

In this case since this is a small company looking for a marketing research supplier, there may not be a need for a vast amount of resources or expertise. A routine task may be done more suitably and more cheaply through a smaller supplier.

7. What should the buyer and supplier of research expect from each other?

The supplier should expect:

1) A statement of the background of the problem.
2) A statement of the management problem.
3) A statement of the research problem and objectives.
4) An opportunity to discuss these statements.
5) Budget range.
6) Desired timing.
7) That they will be approached only when there exists a reasonable expectation that they will be selected.

The buyer should expect a research proposal containing:

1) Problem (or opportunity) definition.
2) A statement of objectives.
3) A list of alternative courses of action.
4) The information needs.

5) The qualifications of the personnel who will be assigned to the project.
6) An evaluation of the project, including how data will be handled, the potential for duplicating the project in other parts of the company, and the likelihood of its success.
7) A budget (cost estimate).
8) An accurate timetable.

Instructor's further probe: Give some examples of complications that may arise if the buyer and supplier of marketing research services fail to establish their expectations clearly.

Suggested Probe Response: Some examples are: the buyer may not communicate the problem statement properly and the supplier may produce a meaningless set of information as a result; the supplier may not use qualified personnel if the supplier fails to include personnel as a concern; without preset guidelines regarding cost, the supplier may spend more money than the buyer may be able to afford.

8. Should legal action be taken to regulate marketing research activity? If so, state specifics.

Again, this question is designed to give students a free hand at an ambiguous area of marketing research.

The student should focus on the areas of ethics, competition, economics, and consumer protection. Regulation is designed to ensure businesses compete in a "fair" environment and that consumers are protected in so far as possible.

Instructor's further probe: Give some examples of legal action taken to regulate marketing research activity. The student may have to do research outside the scope of this text.

Suggested Probe Response: The student's answer should include relevant laws and cases that show the limitation of the practices of market research. For example, in some areas of the U.S., automated calling devices (that use a computer with a pre-recorded message to phone people) to solicit information or business are illegal.

9. For the Marketing Research in Action that began this chapter, evaluate Marriott's use of a centralized marketing research function.

Marriott successfully avoids some of the potential downfalls of centralization. Marketing research at Marriott is efficient, highly visible, supported by upper management, and helpful to divisional level decision makers. Marketing research works effectively because there is sharing of information and expertise through the centralized organization. At the same time, there are strong relationships between research directors and the functional areas that they support, which implies more specialized research and better communication between researcher and manager.

Instructor's further probe: What problems may Marriott face even with its current setup?

Suggested Probe Response: Since Marriott's CMS is focused based on individual business units, changes in the units will affect CMS. If more units are added, or some are dismantled, CMS will undergo changes as well.

10. What type of marketing research organization would the following organizations logically have?

   a) A large multi-division packaged goods company such as Procter & Gamble ...

   Would likely have an integrated organization, with a central staff available to carry out projects with company-wide implications, undertake projects for departments without their own research staff, advise and support divisional research staff. Product and category specific research would be decentralized, to allow researchers to develop expertise and keep marketing information close to where the brand decisions will be made.

   b) A local pizza company with 15 locations ...

   There is probably a main location or office where "corporate" affairs such as payroll, purchasing and administration are handled. Marketing research would be best handled at this central location.

   c) A large multi-division chemical company such as Monsanto Chemical ...

   Would likely divisionalize its research function, because end uses of chemicals are highly diverse. Monsanto has separate marketing research organizations for its NutraSweet, Searle (pharmaceutical), Agricultural and Chemical Divisions.

   d) An industrial supply house that provides over 2,000 items to industrial buyers ...

   Would probably find it most economical to centralize the marketing research function, perhaps grouping researchers by product or industry specialization.

11. What role does central marketing research services play in marketing planning at Digital Equipment Corporation (see marketing research in action)? What limits the effectiveness of this central service marketing research group?

   Central marketing research services (CMS) at Digital acts as a communications center. CMS offers fee-based primary and secondary research services for client managers. CMS's effectiveness might be limited in its effectiveness due to the disadvantages generally found in a centralized organization. CMS's structure can isolate researchers from day-to-day activities, some of Digital's divisions may suffer by CMS's focus on corporate problems, and the action of the research may be separated from the research itself--leaving the researchers with minimal responsibility for their recommendations.

Instructor's further probe: How can Digital's CMS perform marketing research on itself to find out if its internal clients are satisfied with CMS's services?

Suggested Probe Response: To keep objectivity, CMS will most probably need to contract an external supplier of marketing research. This supplier will need to provide CMS with some industry standards of the level of service other types of organizations like CMS have. Also the supplier can objectively solicit feedback from CMS's clients.

12. How might the life of a marketing researcher change from an assignment in the USA, to the Middle East, and to Asia? Be as specific as possible. (See the global marketing research dynamics insert.)

    In the United States of America, marketing research is highly structured and strict. Information resources are also well defined and readily accessible. In addition, technology allows researchers to collect more data faster.

    In the Middle East, one-on-one interactions are emphasized. The less structure leads the researcher to take into account many different factions: customers, suppliers, government officials, and internal buyers to name a few. The researcher needs to research the clients first and needs to establish credibility.

    In Asia, the lack of homogeneity forces the researcher to take a different perspective and realize there is not significant marketing cross-fertilization among Asian countries. The researcher will have to deal with: differing attitudes among different countries towards research; research capabilities and techniques that are inconsistent among various countries; due to different standards and resources, database information can not always be compared from country to country; and due to higher rates of change, future forecasting is difficult.

Instructor's further probe: What steps can a marketing research firm take to minimize the effects of the wide range of research practices and resources in various areas of the world?

Suggested Probe Response: Here are just a few: One method would be to hire researchers native to the area of the region in interest. Another, more cost effective method would be to train a marketing researcher in the various aspects of the research assignment, as well as the culture the researcher will be operating in.

CHAPTER 3 – THE MARKETING RESEARCH PROCESS: CONCEPT AND EXAMPLE

1. Specify the sequence of steps in the research process.

   1) Establish the need for information.
   2) Specify research objectives and information needs.
   3) Determine sources of data.
   4) Develop the data collection forms.
   5) Design the sample.
   6) Collect the data.
   7) Process the data.
   8) Analyze the data.
   9) Present research results.

Instructor's Further Probing: What is the most complex and time consuming step in the research process?

Suggested Probe Response: Depending on the specific research project, any one of the research process steps could potentially be complicated and time consuming; however, if we can guess that as an estimate, the second step ("Specify research objectives and information needs") would be the most time consuming and intricate. Since a research project must have a clearly defined and accepted goal, it is essential to define that goal explicitly. Many of the other steps are procedures that can be very mechanical in nature.

2. Why is it essential that a researcher anticipate all of the steps of the research process?

   The interdependence of the steps requires the researcher to anticipate the remaining ones at each phase of the process. For instance, in stating research objectives, the ability to gather and analyze the data must be considered in order to insure consistency and feasibility. Likewise, the format of the research results is dependent on the mode of data analysis.

Instructor's Further Probing: What are the possible consequences if a researcher fails to adequately anticipate all of the steps of the research process?

Suggested Probe Response: There are some forms of data that can not be obtained and thus if the ability to gather and analyze the data required for a particular objective is not considered, then the research project will not be able to be completed successfully. For example, if an objective stated "To determine the secret recipe of soft drinks of our competitors", it can be stated that obtaining this information, legally, will be extremely difficult if not impossible.

3. How did the marketing research firm ascertain the information needs of SPI?

The research firm gathered preliminary information at an initial meeting with SPI representatives. After reviewing that information, the firm requested a formal statement of objectives and potential courses of action available for reaching those objectives. Then, together with SPI, the research firm generated the information needs relevant to the decision problem so explicated. This joint effort insured that the research objectives would be consistent with the information needs at hand.

Instructor's Further Probing: In question #2, it was mentioned that it is important for a researcher to anticipate the remaining steps of the research process. For instance, in stating research objectives, the ability to gather and analyze the data must be considered in order to insure consistency and feasibility. How did the marketing researchers working with SPI anticipate this?

Suggested Probe Response: "The Problem Setting in Perspective" section describes considerations and concerns that went into the development of the courses of actions stated in response to the objective set by SPI. Each approach considers the type of data sought, either qualitative or quantitative; the possible complexity and number of data sources needed; and the possibility of requiring specialized research projects.

4. What type of research did the Study of Packaging Markets involve? Why?

   This study was exploratory in nature, since its purpose was to identify specific alternative courses of action to reach the SPI objectives previously discussed. Note, this question and the next help serve as a lead-in to Chapter 4 where types of research are defined formally.

Instructor's Further Probing: What type of data sources did the marketing researchers use?

Suggested Probe Response: The researchers used a combination of internal and external sources of data. The internal sources included internal reports, publications, and records. External sources included trade magazines, industry surveys done by other firms, and interviews with industry experts.

5. What type of research did the Study of Consumer Acceptance involve? Why?

   This study involved both exploratory and conclusive research. The initial phase (exploratory) was designed to identify relevant dimensions of consumer attitudes toward plastic containers, which were then examined in a conclusive mode of research.

Instructor's Further Probing: Could the exploratory research here have been eliminated since there was conclusive research being done?

Suggested Probe Response: Quite often exploratory research is used to determine how to obtain quantitative data. In this case, the marketing researchers used the exploratory research to design a questionnaire to be used for a consumer acceptance survey. Without the exploratory research to give guidance on the feasibility of a line of research at the quantitative level, the quantitative research may not prove as effective as it could have been.

6. Evaluate the manner in which the group discussion phase of the Study of Consumer Acceptance was carried out.

A number of steps were taken to enhance the interpretability of the group discussion findings:

1) controlled environment
2) recorded sessions
3) reasonable length of sessions
4) discussion groups which could be characterized on attributes of interest (marital status, usage of product, etc.)
5) groups led by trained moderators
6) moderator directed by a "guide"
7) final tape edited for presentation

As characteristic of exploratory research, however, the sample was small and not representative. Hence, no inferences to the general population are possible.

These are trade-offs associated with exploratory research. Again, this type of research is designed for a specific type of information need. As long as the two are consistent, the benefits of exploratory research far exceed the shortcomings.

Instructor's Further Probing: What conclusions did the exploratory research in the Study of Consumer Acceptance lead to?

Suggested Probe Response: In general, the researchers gained a better idea of what consumers thought of containers and the consumers' preferences for the type and use of a container. This information was then used to help design quantitative research that focused in on these key areas to determine if problems or opportunities presented themselves through the attitudes of consumers about containers. For example, the research showed that consumers generally viewed plastic containers in positive terms as opposed to the drawbacks consumers found in paper containers.

7. What is nonsampling error?

    Nonsampling error includes all of the errors that may occur in the research process except the sampling error.

Instructor's Further Probing: What is sampling error? Give an example.

Suggested Probe Response: Sampling error is the statistical error that results in a survey. Since it is not always possible to survey the entire universe for a survey, a subset that yields an acceptable confidence level is surveyed and the results are then interpolated for the entire universe. The error that occurs by measuring the subset of the universe and applying it to the whole universe is the sampling error.

8. What are the properties of nonsampling errors?

    They tend to be of unknown direction and magnitude.

Instructor's Further Probing: Give an example from the SPI case of a nonsampling error.

Suggested Probe Response: In the SPI case, the "round robin" approach to coding the collected data showed errors in the coding scheme, which can be labeled as a data analysis error, one type of nonsampling error.

9. Define and then give an example of each type of nonsampling error listed in this chapter.

   1) Defective population definition
   2) Unrepresentative frame
   3) Nonresponse errors
   4) Faulty problem definition
   5) Poor questionnaire design
   6) Measurement error
   7) Interviewer-related errors
   8) Improper causal inferences
   9) Data processing errors
   10) Data analysis errors
   11) Interpretation errors
   12) Auspices bias

   We leave it to each student to suggest an example of each type of error.

10. A major marketing research firm once declared one of its survey-based services to be "free of all error, except sampling error." Do you think this could be a true statement?

    The student should run down the list of nonsampling errors and ask for each one whether it is possible to be sure that no error has occurred. Clearly, it is impossible to make such a statement and be correct.

Instructor's Further Probing: What are some possible ways to minimize nonsampling error?

Suggested Probe Response: Since there are many types of nonsampling errors, there are many factors and variables that need to be taken into account when trying to minimize nonsampling errors. In the SPI case, the moderator for the exploratory discussion groups was given a guide, so as to force a standard direction for questions. This would help minimize the interview-related nonsampling error. In a similar manner, standards and cross-checking can help minimize other nonsampling errors.

11. *MINICASE:* The Wool Producers Board of New Zealand wants to stimulate the primary demand for wool in the world. What marketing research could they do to facilitate the development of such a primary demand stimulation campaign? Describe a program of marketing research in detail. Explain how potential errors in marketing research will be controlled in this marketing research.

As an overview, we can see some key areas that will need to be addressed in this case: global marketing research, error minimization, and developing a program using the marketing research process.

Types of marketing research that could be performed in this case include trend analysis, demographic analysis in each segment of the world, and exploratory research with various major consumers of wool around the world. This type of research would lead researchers to the factors influencing the purchase and use of wool. With these factors identified, marketers can then focus on using this knowledge to stimulate demand for wool.

The approach in developing a program of marketing research for wool in this case is very similar to the program described in the text for the SPI case. The student should follow that example as he/she answers this question. The following is an example of the various issues involved in creating a program for marketing research in this case:

1. The first step is to establish the problem recognition and definition. In this case, the problem is finding a way to stimulate the primary demand for wool in the world. Further definition is needed to identify what areas of the world have the potential to use wool (e.g.: areas with continual warm climates will have far less demand for wool than cooler regions).

2. Once the need for information has been established through problem recognition and definition, the research objectives and information needs must be determined. TO stimulate the demand for wool, research must determine who uses wool, why they use it, and how they use it. So information needed includes demographics and industry trend analysis, on a global scale.

3. Research design and data sources include interviews in various countries with industry experts, focus groups (discussion groups as described for the SPI case), and access to reference information regarding consumer buying patterns (both from wool manufacturers and from reports done by outside firms)

4. Data collection procedure can be complex when performing marketing research on a global scale. Researchers will have to use the expertise of local firms and people to plan the collection of the data.

5. Sample design will have to be planned carefully since there are many variances in the sample population on a global scale. Segmented research may have to be performed.

6. Data collection, data processing, data analysis, and the presentation of results all will be very similar to the SPI case.

    Potential errors in this marketing research program could result in sampling errors and nonsampling errors. To minimize errors, it will be important to carefully regulate the data collection process (especially since data from various sources around the world will be collected), provide standards for the various procedures used in analyzing and coding the collected data, and provide verification procedures to ensure that the data is accurate.

CHAPTER 4 — THE DECISION TO UNDERTAKE RESEARCH

1. Why is the analysis preceding the decision to undertake research so crucial to the success of the project?

    It is this analysis which determines the necessity of the research and, when deemed necessary, ensures that the research satisfies the requirements of the decision process.

Instructor's Further Probing: What is the marketing researcher's role at this stage?

Suggested Probe Response: The researcher should be attempting to establish an effective link between the early stages of the decision and research process.

2. Discuss the types of marketing research appropriate for various stages of the decision-making process.

    Exploratory research is appropriate during the recognition and identification stages. Characterized by flexibility, it is designed to obtain a preliminary investigation of the situation with a minimum of cost and time delay.

    Conclusive research is appropriate during the evaluation and selection stages of decision making. It is characterized by clearly defined research objectives and information needs as well as more formal research procedures.

    Performance monitoring research is designed to improve control of marketing programs. It involves monitoring performance measures, marketing mix variables, and situational variables.

Instructor's Further Probing: How are these three types of research interrelated?

Suggested Probe Response: Exploratory research aids in the design and development of an effective conclusive research study. Conclusive research provides information needed to make a decision. Performance monitoring research reviews conclusive research results and monitors and adjusts the research focus.

3. Distinguish among problems, opportunities and symptoms.

    Problems: Factors (independent variables) that impede an organization's performance from meeting its objectives. They require corrective action.

    Opportunities: Situations where performance could be improved by undertaking new activities. Can arise from problems.

    Symptoms: Conditions (dependent variables) that signal presence of problems or opportunities.

Instructor's Further Probing: U.S. based Amway Corporation, a successful user of multi-level marketing, targeted Japan as a new market to be developed. Japan is known for its lack of formal and rigid distribution channels. Should Amway marketing managers consider the lack of an effective distribution system in Japan a problem or an opportunity?

Suggested Probe Response: Since Amway uses multi-level marketing, which relies on personal selling more than formal distribution channels, Amway could use this as a competitive advantage. Most firms rely on formal distribution channels, but Amway viewed this as an opportunity to utilize multi-level marketing. As a result of this strategy, Amway is now the second largest U.S. company in Japan.

4. What are the essential elements of a decision problem?

    1) Management has an objective to accomplish.

    2) There are two or more alternatives under consideration which may enable the firm to achieve its objective.

    3) Uncertainty exists regarding the best course of action.

Instructor's Further Probing: What are two methods for formulating a decision problem?

Suggested Probe Response: Two methods mentioned in the text are: 1) the analysis of existing information, and 2) the use of exploratory research to aid in defining the decision problem.

5. What are the implications for marketing research of a decision situation characterized by primary (organizational) and secondary (personal) objectives?

    The researcher must first identify the relevant objectives and determine from which source they stem. This is no easy task since organizational objectives are often not explicit, personal objectives even less so, and the decision may be the responsibility of a group rather than a single individual. Effective research will serve organizational objectives while maintaining a sensitivity to the personal objectives of the decision maker.

Instructor's Further Probing: What are some ways to minimize the conflicts between organizational objectives and personal objectives?

Suggested Probe Response: Two approaches are given in the text to minimize conflicts between these two goals: have the organizational goals explicitly stated to everyone in the organization; and develop explicit decision criteria for the selection among alternative courses of action.

6. What is the purpose and nature of a situational analysis?

    The purpose of a situational analysis is to identify those variables that cause poor performance or represent opportunities for future growth for a firm. The analysis focuses on the past and future situation facing an organization, relies on a diversity of information sources, and is characterized by flexibility.

Instructor's Further Probing: In a situational analysis there are two types of factors: internal factors, describing the influences within the organization; and external factors, describing the environment the organization operates in. Give some examples of internal and external factors in a situational analysis for a computer chip manufacturer.

Suggested Probe Response: Internal factors: financial resources to build facilities to produce computer chips, cost structure of products, advantage of being able to produce a chip that no one else can.

External factors: A multitude of competitors who also produce similar computer chips, increase in the use of electronic devices that contain the company's chips, and new legislation restricting the patent coverage of the design of a chip.

7. What is the basic criterion in deciding whether or not to conduct a research project?

Cost-benefit; the cost and time delay associated with the study must be weighed against its benefits--namely, the extent to which research findings are likely to reduce management uncertainty regarding selection of a course of action.

Instructor's Further Probing: Would a marketing research project be cost effective if it were implemented after a marketing decision had been made, to verify the value of the decision?

Suggested Probe Response: The value of marketing research is reduced when there is reduced uncertainty. Once a decision is made, there is no uncertainty. So research done after the fact has very little value.

8. What are the responsibilities of the researcher in establishing the need for marketing research information?

The researcher must be certain that the information is needed and that research will provide it. To this end, the researcher should strive to:

1) Understand the problem situation from the perspective of the decision maker.

2) Identify the relevant objectives, both organizational and personal.

3) Accurately define the problem or opportunity at hand.

4) Ascertain that the relevant courses of action have been identified and approved by management.

Instructor's Further Probing: Since a marketing researcher knows the issues involved in a research project so well, even formulating alternatives, why should the researcher not make a recommendation to the decision maker?

Suggested Probe Response: A researcher should not be involved in making the final decision because the objectivity of the research process could be influenced due to the researcher's personal involvement. In addition, the researcher would most likely weigh the research findings heavily in choosing a course of action and not necessarily consider broader policy considerations.

9. What characteristics should research objectives possess?

1) The research objectives should be precisely stated in order to communicate exactly why the study is being conducted.

2) The objectives should be in writing.

3) The objectives should be agreed upon by both the researcher and the decision maker.

4) The objectives should be attainable.

Instructor's Further Probing: Should the researcher attempt to eliminate the personal objectives in a research project as much as possible?

Suggested Probe Response: Since every manager has some set personal objectives, attempting to eliminate them would cause conflict with the organization's goals, thus leading to discourse in the results of the research.

10. Should the decision maker be involved in formulating research objectives and listing information needs? Why or why not?

    Yes. Only the decision maker has the perspective necessary to specify the type of information needed to reduce the uncertainty surrounding the decision situation. Such involvement assures that the research will satisfy the requirements of the decision maker.

Instructor's Further Probing: What steps of the decision making process should the decision maker be involved in?

Suggested Probe Response: The decision maker is crucial in the beginning of the process to define the goals and at the end of the process to evaluate the information presented by the research findings. Ideally, the decision maker should monitor every step of the process, but not necessarily get involved at all stages of the decision making process.

11. Of what use is a mock-up of potential research findings?

    Such a simulation serves at least three purposes:

    1) The decision maker, when presented with the mock-up, can identify voids in the original list of information needs.

    2) The researcher and decision maker may be better able to determine whether the data so collected would serve to reduce the uncertainty surrounding the decision situation.

    3) The manager can often specify more clearly how the data should be analyzed and presented after seeing a mock-up of the potential findings.

Instructor's Further Probing: At what stage in the decision making process should the mock-up of potential findings be done?

Suggested Probe Response: The mock-up of potential findings is most useful after the information needs and goals of the research project have been specified. At this point, the manager can more clearly specify how the data should be analyzed and presented.

12. What are decision criteria? When should they be developed?

Decision criteria are rules for selecting among alternative courses of action given various research findings. They should be developed before research results are obtained in order to maintain a healthy balance between the weight assigned to information existing prior to the research and the research findings.

Instructor's Further Probing: Generating decision criteria before research results are shown can avoid what specific conflict?

Suggested Probe Response: Decision criteria stated specifically before research results are obtained can help avoid conflicts between organizational goals and a manager's personal goals.

13. Why is the evaluation (a priori) of marketing research inherently subjective?

The objective criterion of cost-benefit is not very useful because the benefits to be derived from a research project are very difficult to quantify. Lacking a more precise measure, the evaluation remains subjective. A procedure for doing so is presented in Chapter 27.

Instructor's Further Probing: What other criterion, mentioned in the text, serves as an aid in the evaluation of marketing research?

Suggested Probe Response: The level of confidence a manager is willing to accept in a research project can help evaluate that research project.

14. How might an organization assure that marketing research is being used effectively in the decision-making process?

A number of organizational designs enhance the research decision-making interface. One such design is to assign management responsibility for the initial and final stages of the research process. Another is to give the researcher a more powerful role in dealing with management. Yet another is the employment of a research generalist to serve as a middle person.

Research request forms are also used and ensure that the basic concerns of management regarding the utilization of research are being addressed.

Research proposals serve essentially the same purpose when research is contracted out.

Instructor's Further Probing: What kind of marketing research would be involved in identifying the use of marketing research in an organization, as was done in "Marketing Research in Action" insert at the beginning of this chapter?

Suggested Probe Response: This type of marketing research would generally be considered performance monitoring research, which gives feedback to the organization's managers on the effectiveness of their marketing program.

15. What are some of the factors which impinge upon the management-research relationship?

One factor is the diverse backgrounds of the two groups. Researchers tend to be specialists in terms of knowledge and skills, oftentimes technique-oriented. On the other hand, management may have little training in research and therefore a limited perspective as to the nature and role of research in the decision-making process.

Research is sometimes used for purposes other than originally intended. This abuse renders the interface even more tenuous.

Organizational factors, including objectives, structure, etc., have an important impact on the link between researchers and management.

Instructor's Further Probing: Why is the management-researcher interaction so important?

Suggested Probe Response: The management-research interaction is so important because this interaction has highest total influence on research use, of all the variables studied.

16. What actions should Melissa Molloy (see chapter starting Marketing Research in Action) take related to her perceived misuse of marketing research results?

    Let us address each of the questions in the survey that concerned Ms. Molloy:

    "Managers often request marketing research in order to have power and knowledge over other managers"

    As mentioned in the text, when a clear organizational objective has not been defined for the managers, managers will substitute their own personal objectives for their work, hence creating conflict. To resolve this problem, Ms. Molloy needs to set organizational goals so that the various managers can work together and need not be in a power struggle.

    "Managers often request marketing research in order to support a decision that has already been made"

    More lead time and planning needs to be performed by managers, well before a decision is made. Lack of planning and forethought may lead to marketing research being performed after a decision has been made.

    "Managers often request marketing research reports in order to appease their superiors"

    Good horizontal relationships are more important than vertical relationships. An effort should be made to enhance the marketing researcher - marketing manager relationship. With clearly defined organizational goals, their is no need to appease supervisors.

    "Managers often request marketing research studies because it is a policy requirement"

    A policy of requiring marketing research for decisions will not be needed if the organization and its marketing managers utilize the principles discussed above and in the text. The policy can be removed after marketing managers, marketing researchers, and top management all view marketing research as an effective tool in the decision making process.

Instructor's Further Probing: What action should Ms. Molloy take if the survey mentioned that the majority of marketing managers mentioned that they do not use marketing research because the marketing researchers do not come up with innovative solutions?

Suggested Probe Response: In this case, the researchers need to be involved more in the strategy formulation stage. In this manner, researchers can effectively assist in developing innovative solutions that could lead the marketing managers in to an effective decision.

17. It is reported that General Motors expended over $500,000 on marketing research for the 1995 Oldsmobile Aurora. Why would this much expenditure be justified?

    If we base the answer to this question on the material discussed in the "Cost and Value of Research" section, we can see that we can get a contribution margin of about $100 per automobile. If we take the figure given in the text of the sales reaching 500,000 units, we then have a total contribution of $50 million. Therefore $500,000 is about 10%, a small percentage of the overall revenue from the benefits of the research. As long as this percentage is low, as it is in this case, we can justify marketing research.

    Instructor's Further Probing: At what point is the marketing research done for a product or service no longer justifiable, in terms of cost?

    Suggested Probe Response: While each situation will differ, generally the marketing manager will have to put some type of quantifiable limit on how much can be spent on marketing research. If the product is relatively new and early in its life cycle, then a higher percentage of total revenue can be dedicated to marketing research, say for example 20%. However, if a product is in the mature or a later stage in the product life cycle, then a lower percentage is needed to justify marketing research, say under 10%.

18. MINI CASE: Proctor & Gamble is considering the simultaneous launch of a liquid detergent in ten European countries. This product is based on a successful product introduction in the U.S.A. What marketing research program would you recommend that P&G undertake?

    While a complete and thorough answer to this question would, in effect, require a marketing research plan, we can generalize and outline the key parts of such a marketing research program. Due to the global nature of such a product, intensive research needs to be done in each of the targeted countries. Since each country will have differing languages, customs, and laws, marketing research will need to find the information needed to determine how to make launches in those countries successful. Hence, the goals and objectives may differ for the marketing research performed in each individual country.

    While key product features and successful product promotions may be used as a starting point in the marketing research in the European countries, the success in the U.S. may not be applied directly to the foreign markets.

CHAPTER 5 — RESEARCH DESIGN AND DATA SOURCES

1. Discuss the nature and role of research design in marketing research.

    A research design is the basic plan which guides the data collection and analysis phases of the research project. The design specifies the type of information to be collected, the sources of data, and the data collection procedure. The research design selected is generally a function of the objectives of the research project, determined by the information needs of the decision maker.

   Instructor's Further Probe: What determines the characteristics desired in the research design?

   Suggested Probe Response: Research objectives, dependent on the stage of the decision-making process for which the information is needed, determine the characteristics desired in the research design.

2. What type of research design is associated with exploratory research?

    The design is best characterized by flexibility and lack of structure since exploratory research is appropriate in the initial stages of the decision-making process.

   Instructor's Further Probe: Exploratory research is mainly used to develop what other type of research?

   Suggested Probe Response: Exploratory research allows the researcher to develop a focus and direction for conclusive research.

3. Why is exploratory research often utilized in the initial steps of the decision process?

    Exploratory research is flexible enough to bring insight and ideas to a decision situation where limited knowledge exists. Hence, it is most useful in uncovering problems and opportunities, identifying the relevant variables in the decision situation, etc.

   Instructor's Further Probe: What is the purpose of exploratory research?

   Suggested Probe Response: The purpose of exploratory research is to formulate a hypothesis regarding potential problems and/or opportunities present in the decision situation.

4. What is descriptive research?

    Descriptive research is a mode of research whose purpose is to characterize marketing phenomena, identify associations among selected variables, and/or make predictions regarding the occurrence of marketing phenomena.

   Instructor's Further Probe: Descriptive research can not be used to describe causal relationships. Does the marketing researcher always need to determine causal relationships?

Suggested Probe Response: No, the researcher does not always need to determine causal relationships in order to make an accurate predictive statement. A predictive statement without an identified causal relationship can help determine future events, thus it is useful for forecasting data.

5. How does the research design in descriptive research differ from that in exploratory research?

    The design in descriptive research is necessarily more structured. This follows from the nature of the decision situation with which descriptive research is associated--clear statement of the problem, specific research objectives, and detailed information needs.

Instructor's Further Probe: When is descriptive research more appropriate to use than exploratory research?

Suggested Probe Response: Generally, descriptive research can quantify the characteristics and behavior of a market or the market variables. Thus, as a type of conclusive research, descriptive research is more appropriate when a hypothesis needs to be tested. Exploratory research helps in creating that hypothesis used in the conclusive research phase.

6. How does the cross-sectional design differ from the longitudinal design?

    A cross-sectional design involves taking a sample of population elements at one point in time. It is generally associated with descriptive research.

    A longitudinal design involves measuring a fixed sample over different points in time. It is generally conceded to be the more powerful of the two designs.

Instructor's Further Probe: Which design is more accurate?

Suggested Probe Response: Cross-sectional designs, when properly constructed, can give a good indicator of the general population; however, trends in consumer behavior can not be captured in cross-sectional designs as they can be noted in longitudinal designs. Longitudinal design, thus, can give a more accurate representation of a given situation.

7. What role does an implicit causal model play in descriptive research?

    Descriptive research presupposes that an implicit causal model exists--i.e., in the mind of the decision maker. It is only when descriptive evidence is incorporated into the decision maker's personal model of the marketing system that the research evidence contributes directly to the decision-making process.

Instructor's Further Probe: What is this implicit causal model based on? What are the advantages and disadvantages of such a basis?

Suggested Probe Response: The implicit causal model is based on the researcher's experience and judgment. If the researcher's experience is broad, then this model can be quite accurate; however, if the researcher has limited experience in the specific area under investigation, then the model may not be as accurate.

8. What are the objectives of performance-monitoring research?

The purpose of performance-monitoring research is to signal the presence of potential problems or opportunities. This is done by monitoring performance measures, such as sales and market share, sub-objectives, such as attitudes and distribution penetration, and situational variables such as competitive and regulatory activity.

Instructor's Further Probe: What are two sub-types of performance-monitoring research mentioned in the text?

Suggested Probe Response: Ad hoc performance monitoring research consists of research programs designed to monitor new or special marketing programs of the organization or competitor. Another type of performance monitoring is the continuous performance measure. The continuous performance measure is designed to monitor the dependent variables in the marketing system in a formal manner.

9. What advantages does the longitudinal design offer relative to the cross-sectional design?

   1) Analytical in nature.
   2) Yields more data.
   3) Yields more accurate data.
   4) Yields comparable data at a lower cost.

Instructor's Further Probe: If longitudinal designs offer all these advantages over the cross-sectional design, why then use the cross-sectional design?

Suggested Probe Response: A key advantage the cross-sectional data has over the longitudinal study is that cross-sectional data can be compiled much faster, thus yielding quicker results.

10. What problems are associated with longitudinal designs?

Since longitudinal designs require that panel members serve on the panel for some period of time, there may be a problem as to the representativeness of the persons actually willing to serve. Also, there exists the problem of response bias, which involves inaccuracies due to the respondents' boredom or fatigue, desire to give the "right" answers, etc.

Instructor's Further Probe: How can response bias be minimized in longitudinal designs?

Suggested Probe Response: Some methods of minimizing response bias include providing anonymity for sensitive questions and avoiding questions that force an answer that conforms to the social norms.

11. Discuss the four basic sources of marketing data.

Respondents constitute an important source of data. Information is acquired through the observation of and communication with respondents.

Analogous situations include the study of case histories and simulations. The former is an intensive investigation of situations relevant to a particular problem setting and is used primarily early in the decision process. Simulation involves creating a model of the real world in order to explicate the dynamics of the variables operating therein.

Experimentation involves assessing the effect of an independent variable on a dependent variable while controlling for "competing" causal variables.

Secondary data are data collected for purposes other than the research needs at hand. The data may be obtained from internal and/or external sources.

Instructor's Further Probe: What types of data are required for descriptive research designs?

Suggested Probe Response: Descriptive research designs require interrogation of respondents, secondary data, and simulation.

12. What is the primary distinction between qualitative and quantitative research?

    Qualitative research involves a smaller number of individuals within a longer time span (i.e., 1 or 2 hours) while quantitative research involves a larger number of respondents within a relatively brief time span (i.e., 15 to 45 minutes).

Instructor's Further Probe: Marketing research has been classified into three types of research: exploratory research, conclusive research, and performance monitoring research. Which type of research is qualitative in nature? Which type of research is quantitative in nature?

Suggested Probe Response: Exploratory research is qualitative in nature, using many sources of data to formulate a hypothesis. Conclusive research is quantitative in nature, leading the researchers to present information to be used to make a decision.

13. What are the benefits and limitations of simulation?

    Benefits:

    1) Simulation allows the evaluation of alternative marketing strategies, changes in the marketing environment, etc., at a relatively low level of cost and risk.

    2) Encourages creativity in the formulation of strategic options.

    3) May be used as a training device for members of the organization.

    Limitations:

    1) A valid model is difficult to develop and maintain.

    2) The model is useful only to the extent that it parallels the dynamics of the corresponding system.

Instructor's Further Probe: What are the advantages of simulations over other types of data sources?

Suggested Probe Response: Simulations can be less expensive and quicker than conducting a survey or test marketing and compiling and analyzing the data. In addition, simulation offer other benefits such as: secrecy-simulations can be conducted without the knowledge of other competitors, whereas other sources may not guarantee this secrecy; various strategies can be tested to provide a type of "proof" of the validity of a particular strategy; the risks are minimal in running various situations in a simulation as opposed to a higher degree of financial risk in test marketing; the ability to provide sensitivity analysis; and finally, simulations can be used as a training device for other members of the organization.

14. What is meant by a "syndicated source?"

    A predominantly profit-making organization which provides standardized data to an array of clients is known as a syndicated source.

Instructor's Further Probe: What is the most common use for syndicated sources?

Suggested Probe Response: Syndicated sources are most commonly used to provide information for performance-monitoring research.

15. What types of data are available from syndicated data sources?

    A multiplicity of data is available, classified broadly into the following categories:
    1) Consumer
    2) Retail
    3) Wholesale
    4) Industrial
    5) Advertising Evaluation
    6) Media and Audience Data.

Instructor's Further Probe: Give an example of a syndicated source for each type listed above.

Suggested Probe Response: From the text, here are examples of syndicated sources:

> Consumer - National Menu Census (done by Marketing Research Corporation of America)
> Retail - A.C. Nielsen's Retail Index
> Wholesale - SAMI (Selling Areas-Marketing, Inc.)
> Industrial - Dun & Bradstreet's "Market Identifiers"
> Advertising Evaluation - Starch Message Reports
> Media and Audience Data - Simmons Market Research Bureau

16. Describe and evaluate the concept of single sourcing.

    Single sourcing represents the idea that a user of marketing research can get access to a single, comprehensive, and integrated database from a marketing research provider, containing all the data the user needs. Through technology, the user can get information to achieve real-time decisions. This real-time technology can aid in making the identification of a cause and effect relationship easier.

While single sourcing has a number of advantages, its main focus is in the collection of data. Successful use of marketing research is the analysis of data to produce meaningful information to make an effective decision. User-friendly systems and decision support systems will continue to thrive as will custom marketing research.

Instructor's Further Probe: Give an example of a single sourcing technology.

Suggested Probe Response: Bar code scanning technology has been an effective and prevalent example of single sourcing technology in the retail environment. Using this type of technology, data can be compiled at the point-of-sale regarding consumer purchasing habits and behaviors. Some systems can even print out coupons at the time of purchase (in a grocery store for example) for a comparable brand of a product just purchased.

17. What is the role of a marketing information system within an organization?

An MIS is designed to gather, analyze, and report data for decision-making purposes. Hence, it occupies a key role in the organization.

Instructor's Further Probe: Why is it necessary to use an MIS in today's business environment?

Suggested Probe Response: Due to the availability of technology, many companies are using systems that allow them to forecast sales or predict the results of changing the marketing mix based on very recent data. It is no longer acceptable to wait a month to determine the results of a marketing program, since competitors may have already taken new action.

18. What attributes should MDSS output possess?

MDSS output should be:
1) Timely.
2) Flexible.
3) Convenient.
4) Accurate.
5) Inclusive.

Instructor's Further Probe: What is the current state of the MDSS concept?

Suggested Probe Response: The MDSS concept has met with only partial success. The ideal MDSS is rare, with most systems operating at the monitoring or linking system stage. There is a growing acceptance of more customized decision support systems, but limited acceptance of the idealized MDSS concept. Evolution beyond the marketing research system hinges on the ability of marketers to develop and implement marketing information systems attuned to the needs of decision makers at various levels within the organization.

19. What could cause MDSS to be more utilized by marketing managers in the future?

    Data sources are the backbone for MDSS. As the technology to collect, store, and organize these sources become cheaper and more prevalent, MDSS will be utilized further. Furthermore, flexibility and ease of use can be increased with the introduction of faster and more portable computers and electronics devices.

Instructor's Further Probe: What factors are integral in a marketing managers decision to implement a MDSS?

Suggested Probe Response: MDSS requires support from all parts of the company. Since data sources will need to be overhauled, the time and money needed to update these sources to use a MDSS are key factors. Other factors include the current state and cost of technology needed to implement the MDSS.

20. *Minicase:* The marketing department of a major U.S. fast food retailer has hired you to develop a set of research designs and data sources to assist them with the performance monitoring, and with problem and opportunity identification. What research designs and data sources would you recommend? How would your recommendation change if the company expanded into the Korean and Hong Kong markets?

    The objectives in performance monitoring research are to monitor and report changes in performance measures, subobjectives, and situational variables. This case lends itself to the development of continuous performance monitoring approach. Continuous monitoring will allow the retailer to monitor future performance more effectively than will an ad hoc performance monitoring design. The data sources to be used include units sold, sales volume, and market share. This data can be derived from secondary data and interrogation of industry experts. Secondary data can be obtained from internal data collected by the retailer as well syndicated sources such as data published by the Marketing Research Corporation of America (MRCA). From these sources of data, continuous performance monitoring can be achieved, revealing problems and opportunities when objectives are not met.

    If the company expanded into Korea and Hong Kong, then the sources of secondary data would change. Syndicate sources from U.S. companies may not be readily available at a reasonable cost. Customized marketing research may have to be performed along with surveys of end users and distributors. Internal data, showing items like sales and volume, will still be available.

CHAPTER 6 — SECONDARY DATA

1. What is the role of secondary data in the research process?

    Secondary data represent the focus of initial efforts at gathering information. An efficient complement to primary research, secondary data sources should be exhausted before primary research is undertaken.

    Instructor's Further Probing: What are some examples of secondary data?

    Suggested Probe Response: Some examples of both internal and external secondary data, include sales reports, accounting records, industry reports, periodicals, and books.

2. What are the advantages of secondary data relative to primary data?

    Secondary data are available at a lower cost and involve substantially less time than comparable data collected by primary research. Often at times, the scale of the data required precludes primary research by a given firm--for example, data collected by the Bureau of the Census.

    Instructor's Further Probing: What are some functions that secondary data performs?

    Suggested Probe Response: Secondary data can aid in the formulation of the decision problem, suggest methods and types of data for meeting the information needs, and serve as a source of comparative data by which primary data can be interpreted and evaluated.

3. Discuss the shortcomings of secondary data.

    Secondary data may not fit the information needs of the research project. The degree of fit is a function of 1) units of measurement, 2) definition of classes, and 3) publication currency.

    The second problem relates to the accuracy of the data. The lack of involvement by the researcher in the study which generated the secondary data makes it more difficult to assess its accuracy. Nevertheless, the following criteria are useful: 1) source, 2) purpose of the publication, and 3) evidence regarding quality.

    A third problem with secondary data is the timeliness of the data. Since secondary data is normally collected over a period of time and then published, the researcher has to rely on data that may be years old (for example as in census data).

    Instructor's Further Probing: Distinguish between the types of sources for secondary data and which is more preferable.

    Suggested Probe Response: Secondary data may be secured from two types of sources: an original source or acquired source. An original source is the source that originated the data. An acquired source is data that is procured from an original source (e.g.. *Statistical Abstract of the United States*) An original source is more desirable since it is usually the only place where the details of the data collection and analysis process are described. In addition, an original source is generally more accurate and detailed than the acquired source. Errors in transcription and failure to reproduce footnotes and other textual comments can seriously influence the accuracy of the data.

4. Suggest some examples of census data useful to marketers.

   Census data involving housing patterns, demographic profiles, appliance ownership, etc. are particularly relevant for marketing purposes.

Instructor's Further Probing: What recent technological innovations have made the use of census data easier and more practical?

Suggested Probe Response: The development of CD ROM drives and discs has allowed researchers to use computers to search through and retrieve volumes of information in a relatively short amount of time. This type of technology also minimizes the amount of time lag between when the data was compiled and the time the researcher can access it, since CD ROM allows for quicker publication of secondary data.

5. Indicate the main components of the hierarchy of geographic units in descending order of level of aggregation.

   Nation, region, division, state, MSA, county, tract, and block are the most common units.

Instructor's Further Probing: What new type of zip coding method has been developed to assist in the identification of more accurate geographic units?

Suggested Probe Response: The introduction of geocoded Zip+4 codes allows users to create customized boundaries, enabling them to target individual streets, neighborhoods, or specific geographic areas. This type of geographic information system (GIS) is a major step in allowing marketing research users more flexibility in target market and behavior identification.

6. Using the most recent edition of General Social and Economic Characteristics published by the Bureau of the Census for your state, compare the United States, your state and your county. Include analysis of the total population, general level of education, income and employment in each population unit. Write a short paragraph describing how your county compares with your state and the nation.

   There is no one answer to this assignment as it will vary by state and county.

   To use this exercise, be sure that the appropriate publication is available to students in the library. It is PC80-1-C, **General Social and Economic Characteristics** for your state. Also, be sure the library can handle the number of students involved. If you have too many students to have each one do this, you can assign specific individuals to do this assignment. They can then report to the class. If the 1990 Census data are available, use the relevant 1990 report.

Teaching Strategy: There are worksheets in this manual (see page 23) for these problems which can be distributed when the assignment is made.

7. Using the U.S. Bureau of Census' most recent edition of Census Tracts report on the MSA of your choice. Compare the totals for the MSA to the two tracts within the MSA. Select and compare two tracts that will provide significant contrast in areas that interest you such as racial makeup, age population, industries employing residents, education level or income of population. Write a short paragraph comparing the two tracts and the MSA for each area you studied.

What was said for Question 6 also holds for Question 7 except that the required publication is PHC80-2 Census Tracts reports for a SMSA of choice. If the 1990 Census data are available, use the relevant 1990 report.

The answer to the three questions in this exercise will be situation specific and will require the instructor to be flexible in terms of the profile of his or her area and the implications of this profile. They make a good hand-in assignment. A worksheet is also available (see pages 24-25).

8. *MINICASE:* You have been hired by an electronics automobile parts marketer to research the market in Europe for its products. The company has tentatively targeted SAAB and Volvo in Sweden, Fiat in Italy, Renault in France, and Audi in Germany as its prime prospects. Outline an approach to the use of secondary data to help assist the marketers in the assessment of these prospects.

The "Global Marketing Research Dynamics" insert gives an overview of the various sources of data on foreign companies.

In this case, in order to research the market in Europe, it is important to get an overview of the data available by the use of European Regional Directories, The European Directory of Marketing Information Sources, and The European Directory of Non-Official Statistical Sources, among other general directories of information.

With some specific sources identified for Europe, it is feasible to move on to other secondary sources of marketing information. These sources would include Chambers of Commerce for each of the countries involved in the research; foreign brokerage houses' reports on each of the companies in their respective countries; and corporate information databases.

It is then the task of the researcher, once these sources have been identified, to determine what data can be used as information for the marketers.

9a) What type of geographic areas are shown in Table 6-3 and in Figure 6-5?

The table and figure feature the counties, urban areas, and central city of the Washington, DC MSA.

9b) Using the data in Table 6-3, analyze the changes in the population. Which areas experienced the greatest growth or decline? Do the areas of growth and decline share any significant characteristics?

To determine what areas experienced the greatest growth or decline in population, look at the percent change and index of population change between 1980 and 1986. Those figures are provided in the following chart:

Population Growth for Washington D.C. MSA

Political Unit	1980 (A)	1986 (est) (B)	% Change $\left(\dfrac{A-B}{A}\right)$	Percentage of Total Population 1980 $\left(\dfrac{a}{\Sigma a}\right)$	Percentage of Total Population 1986 $\left(\dfrac{b}{\Sigma b}\right)$	Index of Population Change[1] $\left(\dfrac{\frac{b}{\Sigma b}}{\frac{a}{\Sigma a}}\right)$
District of Columbia	637,651	626,000	-1.8%	.208	.188	.904
Maryland:	1,316,875	1,435,600	+9.0%	.430	.430	1.0
Montgomery Co.	579,053	665,200	+14.9%	.189	.199	1.053
Prince Georges Co.	665,071	681,400	+2.4%	.217	.204	.940
Charles Co.	72,751	89,000	+2.2%	.024	.027	1.125
Virginia:	1,105,714	1,276,000	+15.4%	.361	.382	1.058
Arlington Co.	152,599	158,700	+4.0%	.050	.048	.96
Alexandria City	103,217	107,800	+4.4%	.034	.032	.94
Falls Church City	9,515	9,700	+1.9%	.003	.003	1.0
Fairfax City	19,930	19,900	+2.6%	.006	.006	1.0
Fairfax Co.	596,901	710,500	+19.0%	.195	.213	1.092
Loudon Co.	57,427	66,800	+16.3%	.019	.020	1.053
Prince William Co.	144,703	175,400	+21.2%	.047	.053	1.128
Manassas Park City	6,524	7,100	+8.8%	.002	.002	1.0
Manassas City	15,438	20,100	+30.1%	.005	.006	1.2
Total	3,060,240	3,337,600	+9.1%	1.0	1.0	1

As the figures show, the overall size of the MSA grew by 9.1%. The only area where population declined was the District of Columbia, with a 1.8% decrease in population. The areas of greatest increase in population in Virginia were Manassas City, Prince William, Loudon and Fairfax Counties. In Maryland, Montgomery County experienced the greatest growth. Looking back at the map, notice that the fastest growing areas were those farthest from the center city.

Looking again at the indices of population change, notice that the areas closest to the District of Columbia (Arlington, Alexandria, Falls Church, Prince Georges County) have indices less than or equal to 1.0. This indicates that while the District was the only area that experienced a population decline, the areas close to the city grew at a rate less than or equal to the area as a whole.

---

[1] Population growth within a subunit (e.g., county) that has not kept up with the unit's (e.g., MSA) percentage of growth will have an index less than 1.00; however, those areas that have experienced a percentage increase that exceeds that of the unit will have an index greater than 1.00.

Name _____

WORKSHEET FOR PROBLEM 6-6

COMPARING A COUNTY WITH ITS STATE AND THE NATION

Publication needed: PC80-1-C, *General Social and Economic Characteristics,* for your state.

Compare the nation, the state, and a county by completing the following table, then answer the question at the end.

Subject	*U.S.*	*State*	*County*
RESIDENCE			
Total population	226,504,825	_____	_____
Percent rural	_____	_____	_____
Percent of the native population residing in state of birth	_____	_____	_____
EDUCATION			
Median school years completed by persons 25 years old and over	_____	_____	_____
Percent high school graduates of persons 25 years and over	_____	_____	_____
INCOME			
Median family income	_____	_____	_____
Percent families w/income less than poverty level	_____	_____	_____
EMPLOYMENT			
Percent in labor force of persons 16 years old and over	_____	_____	_____
Percent workers in county of residence	_____	_____	_____
Percent workers in white-collar occupations	_____	_____	_____
Percent workers employed by government	_____	_____	_____

Name _____

WORKSHEET FOR PROBLEM 6-7

COMPARING NEIGHBORHOODS IN A METROPOLITAN AREA

Publication needed: PC80-2, *Census Tracts* report for the SMSA of your choice.

Census data are often used to compare the characteristics of different population groups. For this exercise, use a census tract report for an SMSA you live in or in which you are interested. Pick two tracts to compare, basing your selection on characteristics of interest to you. Consider possibilities such as one you have lived in, one with a large minority population, one which is outside the central-city limits, one with a high median family income, one with a large proportion in group quarters, or one with a relatively large elderly or young population. Fill in the table with the appropriate summary statistics for each tract and the SMSA as a whole.

Census Statistics for Selected Tracts (Data from PHC80-2 Reports)

Subject	SMSA	*Tract No.* ___	*Tract No.* ___
Total population	_____	_____	_____
Percent black	_____	_____	_____
Number of persons other than white or black	_____	_____	_____
Number of persons age 65 and over	_____	_____	_____
Percent of all persons who are age 65 and over	_____	_____	_____
Average number of persons per household	_____	_____	_____
Percent of children under 18 years who are *not* in husband-wife families	_____	_____	_____
Percent of persons 16-21 years old, not high school graduates and not enrolled in school (dropouts)	_____	_____	_____
Median years school completed for persons 25 and over	_____	_____	_____
Number of persons who went to work by private auto	_____	_____	_____
Number of persons who went to work by public transportation	_____	_____	_____
Number of working mothers of children under age 6 with husband present in household	_____	_____	_____
List the two industries employing the most persons	_____	_____	_____

Census Statistics for Selected Tracts (Data from PHC80-2 Reports) – *Continued*

Subject	SMSA	Tract No. ___	Tract No. ___
Median family income	_____	_____	_____
Percent of families below poverty level	_____	_____	_____
One-person households	_____	_____	_____
Number of housing units with more than one person per room	_____	_____	_____
Median monthly rent of renter occupied units	_____	_____	_____
Number of single-family houses	_____	_____	_____
Number of families who had lived there more than 20 years	_____	_____	_____
Number of households without an automobile	_____	_____	_____

Write a short description comparing the two census tracts and the SMSA. (Look for interrelationships in the data—don't just catalog the numbers.)

CHAPTER 7 — THE MEASUREMENT PROCESS

1. What is measurement?

   Measurement is the assignment of numbers to characteristics of objects or events according to rules. The nature of the relationships existing in the empirical system determines the type of numerical manipulations permissible.

   Instructor's Further Probing: What are some examples of measurement that marketing researchers are interested in?

   Suggested Probe Response: Marketing researchers are interested in measuring, for example, the market potential for a new product, psychographics, and the number of competitors for a certain brand.

2. What is the objective of the measurement process?

   Measurement is intended to develop a correspondence between the empirical system (which includes marketing phenomena) and the abstract system (which includes the numbers used to represent the marketing phenomena).

   Instructor's Further Probing: Explain what level of involvement research specialists and the marketing manager have in the measurement process.

   Suggested Probe Response: The research specialist takes the primary role in the measurement process. The marketing manager rarely becomes directly involved in the actual measurement process.

3. What role does measurement play in marketing?

   Measurement occupies a fundamental role in marketing and marketing research. The measurement of a broad range of variables is essential to effective planning and control.

   Instructor's Further Probing: What are some possible ethical issues involved in the designing of a measurement method to collect marketing research data?

   Suggested Probe Response: Here are a sample of some ethical issues:

   1) Even though a researcher may feel that he/she knows the outcome of the survey, great care must be taken not to bias data collection or respondents to reach that assumed conclusion.

   2) The researcher may run into a high number of non-willing candidates in a study and thus the researcher may feel the need not to include those results in the study; however, even no answers or "poor" answers must be noted in a survey.

4. Why is measurement so difficult in marketing?

The phenomena of interest are typically behavioral in nature. Current measuring devices, such as the questionnaire, are subject to substantial measurement error.

Other factors of interest are concepts or constructs thought to exist in the minds of people, such as brand loyalty, attitudes, etc. Often the people are not even aware of these constructs. Therefore, marketing researchers must first define the construct operationally and then devise a means by which it can be measured.

Instructor's Further Probing: Measurement error and its control is a large part of the measurement process. What are the five main sources of measurement error discussed in the text?

Suggested Probe Response: The five main source of measurement error are :

1) Short term characteristics of the respondent may influence the measurements--personal factors such as mood may influence the measurements

2) Situational factors--variations in the environment in which the measurements are reached

3) Data collection factors--variations in how the questions are administered and the influence of the interviewing method

4) Measuring instrument factors--the degree of ambiguity and difficulty of the questions and the ability of the respondent to answer them

5) Data analysis factors--errors made in the coding and tabulation process

5. What are the four characteristics of the number system?

   1) Each number in the system is unique.
   2) The ordering of the numbers is given by convention.
   3) Equal differences can be defined.
   4) Equal ratios can be defined.

Instructor's Further Probing: What is a result of being restricted to follow only the above characteristics that describe the number system?

Suggested Probe Response: Often the restriction of using only the characteristics in the number system hampers the sophistication of data analysis that can be properly performed.

6. Distinguish among the four scales of measurement. Give examples of the types of marketing phenomena which each scale might be used to measure.

   A nominal scale is one where numbers serve only as labels to identify or categorize objects or events. Marketing applications include identification of store types, brands, sales territories, sex, etc.

   An ordinal scale defines the ordered relationship among objects or events. This scale is used in measuring preference, social class, attitudes, etc.

An interval scale involves the use of numbers to rank objects or events such that the distances among the numerals correspond to the distances among the objects or events on the characteristic being measured. Attitudinal, opinion, and predisposition judgments are often treated as interval scaled data.

A ratio scale has all of the properties of an interval scale plus an absolute zero point. Sales, market share, ages, and number of customers are measured on the ratio scale.

Instructor's Further Probing: What type of scale(s) would be most appropriate for a marketing research study trying to determine which brand of cookies consumers prefer the most and why?

Suggested Probe Response: A nominal scale could be used to note identification data of the consumer. An ordinal scale could be used to measure the consumers' preference of a brand. Finally, the interval scale could capture attitudinal and opinion data.

7. What is measurement error?

Measurement error is the lack of correspondence between the number system and the phenomena being measured. It consists of two components: systematic error and random error.

Instructor's Further Probing: What three major issues should the marketing manager be concerned with in order to effectively control measurement error?

Suggested Probe Response: The three main issues the manager needs to focus on to control measurement error are:

1) Specification of information needs should recognize the difficulty in obtaining accurate measures.

2) The alternative measurement procedures for obtaining the information should be recognized.

3) The cost of measurement versus the accuracy of measurement should be evaluated.

8. Distinguish between the validity and reliability of a measure.

The reliability of a measure refers to the extent to which the measurement process is free from random error.

The validity of a measure refers to the extent to which the measurement process is free from both systematic and random error.

Reliability is a necessary but not a sufficient condition for validity.

Instructor's Further Probing: Describe systematic error and random error.

Suggested Probe Response: Systematic error and random error together make up the total error. Systematic error refers to error that causes a constant bias in the measurements. Whereas, random error refers to influences that bias measurements that are not systematic.

9. Discuss the major ways in which the validity of measurement is assessed.

Construct validity involves understanding the theoretical rationale underlying the obtained measurements.

Content validity involves a subjective judgment by an expert as to the appropriateness of the measurements.

Concurrent validity involves correlating two different measurements of the same marketing phenomena which have been administered at the same point in time.

Prediction validity involves the ability of a measure of marketing phenomena to predict other marketing phenomena.

Instructor's Further Probing: What type of validity would be needed to be checked if a marketing research study wanted to determine what people think about Japanese manufactured cars?

Suggested Probe Response: A content validity check could be used by an expert to determine the relevance of the items used in determining the relevance of the measurements to the underlying construct.

10. How may the reliability of a measure be evaluated?

The researcher can repeat the measurement using the same measuring device under conditions which are judged to be very similar (test-retest). Low discrepancies imply higher reliability.

The alternative forms method involves giving the subject two forms judged equivalent but not identical. The degree of discrepancy between the two scores is again the indication of reliability.

Split-half reliability involves dividing a multi-item measurement instrument and correlating the item responses from each section to estimate reliability.

Instructor's Further Probing: What are some of the issues involved in implementing some of these reliability methods?

Suggested Probe Response: Due to the increased complexity of the tests as a result of these methods, more time and perhaps money will be needed to appropriately implement these methods. Also, some of these methods expose the study participant to more complex and perhaps more time consuming research, possibly affecting the availability of the participants.

11. *MINICASE:* In its domestic US operations, the Gillette Company makes extensive use of consumer measures about advertisements that it is considering using on television. These measures include: awareness, brand association, recall, and believability. Gillette has standard measures for each entry into Korea, Japan, Singapore, and Indonesia. Concern has been raised about the appropriateness of these standard measures.

(a) How could each of these constructs be measured?

Each type of measurement can be constructed utilizing standard survey methods. The survey would most likely need to be conducted by natives of each of the countries via personal research collection.

(b) What scale level would these constructs be?

Awareness, recall, and believability can all be measured using interval scales, whereas brand association can be measured using a nominal scale.

(c) What steps could Gillette take to determine the appropriateness of these measures in new markets? Be specific.

First a thorough understanding of the various cultures must be undertaken through either primary or secondary sources. Information needed through these sources include any possible biases for or against marketing research, attitudes toward various types of scales (for example, the Japanese culture feels strongly against describing situations in extremes--so a strongly polarized question may not be effective in that country), and data collection methods. Next, the concepts of validity and reliability must be applied to ensure the data collected is usable. Finally, it is essential to realize that comparisons across cultures will inherently be inaccurate, even with some type of normalization, due to the intangible differences in the cultures.

CHAPTER 8 — ATTITUDE MEASUREMENT

1. What is an attitude?

    An attitude is an individual's enduring perceptual, knowledge, evaluative, and action-oriented processes with respect to an object or phenomena.

Instructor's Further Probing: Why is it important to study attitudes?

Suggested Probe Response: Attitude measurement can be central to a marketing plan. Often attitude measurement becomes the basis for evaluating the effectiveness of an advertisement campaign. In addition, finding a correlation between attitudes and behavior can assist in the prediction of product acceptance and in the development of marketing programs.

2. What are the three main components of attitudes?

    The three main components of attitudes are:

    1) The cognitive component—concerned with **beliefs** about an object or phenomenon.
    2) The affective component— concerned with **feelings**.
    3) The behavioral component—concerned with a person's **readiness to respond behaviorally**.

Instructor's Further Probing: Give three examples, one for each type of component of an attitude.

Suggested Probe Response:

    Cognitive: "I believe that type of car should last 10 years."
    Affective: "I don't think that color is any good."
    Behavioral: "If that was sold in my hometown, I would buy it immediately."

3. Describe the stages of the hierarchy-of-effects model.

    In the hierarchy-of-effects behavioral model, six stages corresponding to the three attitude components are hypothesized:

Components	Hierarchy of Effects Model
Cognitive	1. Awareness
	2. Knowledge
Affective	3. Liking
	4. Preference
Behavioral	5. Intention to-buy
	6. Purchase

Instructor's Further Probing: The hierarchy-of-effects model is only one behavioral model of many. What do you think might be missing or is needed to be added to the model? Why?

Suggested Probe Response: Some missing elements possibly could be: retention (of knowledge), since many messages are received by people and the ones that are retained have a higher likelihood of affecting behavior even after the message has been given; post-purchase evaluation, since all people review to some level the satisfaction with a choice made (this can affect future behavior and modify the knowledge of the product or service).

4. What questions must the researcher always be concerned with when measuring attitudes?

    1) What are the characteristics of the construct being measured?

    2) What properties of the number system properly relates to this construct?

Instructor's Further Probing: What level are attitudes measured at?

Suggested Probe Response: Typically, attitudes are measured at the nominal or ordinal level, although several more complex scaling procedures allow measurement at the interval level.

5. What general methods of attitude measurement exist?

    The general methods of attitude measurement, including examples of each, are as follows:

    1) Communication techniques
        - self reports
        - responses to unstructured or partially structured stimuli
        - performance of objective tasks

    2) Observation techniques
        - overt behavior
        - physiological reactions

Instructor's Further Probing: What ethical issues may arise for the researcher that is involved in attitude measurement?

Suggested Probe Response: Here are a sample of possible ethical issues involved in attitude measurement:

- Sometimes respondents may react negatively to a particular research purpose. Without deception how does the researcher conduct a self-reporting study?

- Certain images or situations are offensive to certain people. For example, an advertisement that may depict partial nudity may offend certain respondents and cause them not to continue with the measurement process. How does the researcher present the advertisement for a survey of attitudes without offending the respondent?

- Many view unsolicited request for information as an intrusion of privacy. How does the marketing researcher obtain information without pressuring a respondent or intruding on a person's privacy?

6. What self report techniques are used in marketing research?

1) Nominal scales.
2) Rating scales.
3) Rank order scales.
4) Paired comparison scales.
5) Semantic differential scales.
6) Stapel scales.
7) Indirect scales (to a lesser extent), including the Likert scale method.

Instructor's Further Probing: Table 8-1 in the text shows that the most frequent type of scale used is the rating scale. The least used scale is the Stapel scale. What are some of the reasons that the rating scale is so much more favored over the Stapel scale? Does the Stapel scale have any advantages over the rating scale?

Suggested Probe Response: The rating scale measures situations involving ordinal, and interval levels of measurement. The Stapel scale on the other hand is a modification of the semantic differential scale, which is generally used to measure company and brand image studies. Rating scales are applicable to virtually all marketing variable circumstances, and thus are most broadly utilized. One key advantage of the Stapel scale over the rating scale is the ability to avoid polarized response scale. In some foreign cultures, for example, it is not customary to describe attitudes in extreme terms.

7. Discuss some of the issues involved in constructing a verbal rating scale.

1) How many categories? -- typically 5 or 6 are used in practice; a 5 or 6 category scale is easy to administer and adds precision over scales with fewer categories.

2) Odd or even number of categories -- if even, there is no neutral category and the respondent is forced to take a position expressing some feeling.

3) Balanced vs. unbalanced scale -- if distribution of feelings lies heavily to one side of the continuum, an unbalanced scale could be used, but at the risk of biasing the results.

4) Extent of verbal description -- clearly defined categories may increase the reliability of the measurements

5) Category numbering -- should be done if researcher believes the data can be treated as interval scaled.

6) Forced vs. nonforced scales -- nonforced scale is best if a large proportion of respondents have no opinion.

7) Comparative vs. noncomparative scales -- depends on the given research situation; noncomparative scales allow respondent to choose own reference point.

Instructor's Further Probing: What are the issues involved in the following sample verbal rating question:

Choose the phrase that best describes how you view the reliability of Japanese cars as compared to American cars:

Much more reliable   more reliable   same   less reliable   much less reliable

Suggested Probe Response: The following issues must be addressed in order to decide if this is an appropriate rating scale question: the number of categories (does the number of choices reflect an appropriate spectrum), the fact there is an odd number of categories (do we need to force a non-neutral response), is the balanced scale appropriate (do we expect more positive responses, so that we need more choice on the positive end of the spectrum), comparative scale (is it appropriate to set American cars as the base reference point).

8. What are the advantages and disadvantages of rank order scales?

   1) Advantages
      a) Simple in concept
      b) Easy to administer
      c) Less time-consuming to administer than other comparative methods
      d) Instructions easily comprehended.
      e) Realistic since techniques are similar to purchase decision process.
   2) Disadvantages
      a) Forced choice.
      b) Only ordinal data.

Instructor's Further Probing: Give an example of a question that utilizes the rank order scale.

Suggested Probe Response: An example of a rank order question:

Rank the following symbols in order of which best symbolizes the image of a computer:

     !   # $ &   *
    __ __ __ __ __

9. Describe the methods by which ordinal and interval scales can be derived from paired comparison data.

   1) Ordinal scaling: Convert data matrix to one containing 0-1 scores and sum by column to determine ranking.

   2) Interval scaling: Analyzed by Thurstone's Law of Comparative Judgment.

Instructor's Further Probing: Why is it useful to derive ordinal and interval scales from paired comparison data?

Suggested Probe Response: Interval and ordinal scales provide higher level scales for analysis.

10. What advantages and limitations exist for the paired comparison technique?

    1) Advantages
       a) Judgment task simple.
       b) Comparative nature of task.
       c) Availability of interval scaled data methods.

    2) Limitations
       a) Use confined to small number of objects to control respondent fatigue.
       b) Order of presentation of objects may bias results.
       c) Task not realistic.
       d) Simpler methods may yield similar results.

Instructor's Further Probing: What are some possible applications or situations in which the paired comparison technique may be appropriate?

Suggested Probe Response: Since the paired comparison technique allows a great number of items to be compared, brand comparisons would be useful. In addition, this technique allows the researcher to determine relatively easily what strengths and weaknesses a product has over other products of a similar type. This technique is a more complex method than the one dimensional ordinal scale of measurement.

11. Explain the profile analysis method of evaluating data from semantic differential scales.

    The arithmetic mean or median is calculated for each set of verbal phrases or opposites for each object. These measures are then plotted on the original scales to allow comparison of each object's profile.

Instructor's Further Probing: What is the major limitation of the semantic differential scale?

Suggested Probe Response: In a semantic differential scale, the scales must be composed of bipolar adjectives or phrases. It is argued that the pilot testing required to meet this bipolar requirement is expensive and time consuming. Thus many times pilot testing is never performed, possibly compromising the integrity of the scale.

12. How does the Stapel scale differ from the semantic differential scale?

    Several differences exist:

    1) Unipolar ten-point scale (+5 to -5).
    2) Measures direction and intensity of attitudes simultaneously.
    3) Scale values indicate how close the descriptor fits the evaluated object.

Instructor's Further Probing: What one feature does allow the Stapel scale to be more widely used and faster implemented than the semantic differential scale?

Suggested Probe Response: The Stapel scale has been shown to be easily administered over the phone. With the advent of new technologies in computer assisted telephone surveying, the Stapel scale is very appealing when trying to get quick results.

13. When may an indirect scale offer advantages to marketing research over other self-reporting methods?

    If a respondent is unwilling or unable to express an attitude, or otherwise may not accurately self report an attitude, indirect scale methods may be of assistance.

Instructor's Further Probing: What are some disadvantages to the indirect scale over the direct scale?

Suggested Probe Response: The indirect scale is subject to the researcher's bias and influence. In addition, it is more difficult and more costly to obtain useful data through indirect scales.

14. Prepare a set of attitude measurement questions that Walmart could have used in its attitude research in Hong Kong. (See the "Marketing Research in Action" at the beginning of the chapter.) Be sure to include an example of each of the following types of scales: a nominal scale, a verbal rating scale, a numeric scale, a graphic rating scale, a rank-order scale, a paired-comparison scale, a semantic-differential scale, and a Stapel scale.

    Here is a sample set of attitude measurement questions that Walmart could have used...

    <u>Nominal Scale:</u>
       Have you heard of Walmart? (answer YES or NO)

    <u>Verbal Rating Scale:</u>
          How often do you shop ?
      very often often on occasion   rarely

    <u>Numeric Scale:</u>
       How many items do you purchase when you shop? (circle one)
       <5   5-10   10-15   15-20   >20

Graphic Rating Scale:

How satisfied are you with your current grocery store? (mark an "X" on the scale below)

```
      -         0         +
      |_____|_____|
```

Rank Order Scale:

Rank the following items in order of need:
Bath Soap   Milk   Candy   Toilet Paper   Liquid Soap
_____   _____   _____   _____   _____

Paired Comparison Scale:

Pick the soap in each line that you feel has the most lather :

Zest   Ivory
Zest   Irish Spring
Ivory   Irish Spring

Semantic-Differential Scale:

How do you view your current grocery store? (mark an "X" on the scale below)

Reliable	___ ___ ___ ___ ___	Unreliable
Friendly	___ ___ ___ ___ ___	Unfriendly
Modern	___ ___ ___ ___ ___	Old fashioned

Stapel Scale:

How do you view your current grocery store?

```
                    +5              +5
                    +4              +4
                    +3              +3
                    +2              +2
                    +1              +1
    Fast service            Friendly
                    -1              -1
                    -2              -2
                    -3              -3
                    -4              -4
                    -5              -5
```

15. *MINICASE:* For each of the scaling problems, answer the specific questions asked in each situation.

   a. Verbal rating scale construction: Construct a verbal rating scale to measure high school students' attitudes toward attending your college. Briefly discuss the issues involved in constructing the verbal scale, and identify the appropriate level of measurement (ordinal, interval, or ratio).

b. Image measurement: Construct a scale to measure the image high school students have of your college and your top three competitors. Design the scale and briefly discuss the issues involved in constructing the scale.

c. Measuring the hierarchy of effects: Develop questions to measure each level of the hierarchy of effects, awareness, knowledge, liking, preference, intention-to-buy and purchase, for *National Geographic* magazine. Obtain responses to your questions from two respondents. What do you conclude about *National Geographic* from your results?

A. VERBAL RATING SCALE CONSTRUCTION

Here the task is to construct a verbal rating scale on which high school students can indicate their position regarding attending a specific college by selecting among verbally identified categories.

Construct to Measure

One important issue that students should address is: what construct is to be measured? Using the hierarchy of effects concept, the choices are:

Cognitive   - awareness
                - knowledge

Affective   - liking
                - preference

Behavioral   - intention-to-buy
                  - purchase.

Clearly, this problem is one that is beyond awareness and knowledge. The issue is one of students' likely choice of a school. Therefore, preference or intention seem more appropriate. The latter construct is better because preference may have little to do with choice. This is so because other factors such as ability to get in, cost, peer pressure, parents' attitude, etc. affect intention greatly and are much less involved in preference. For example, a student may prefer College A, but be unable to attend due to grades, finances, etc. His or her intention then is a better construct to measure than preference.

The Scale

The verbal labels on categories of the scale can identify the construct or the lead in statement or the question can identify the construct. For example, using the latter procedure, the question might be:

"How likely are you to attend College X?"
    ___ Very likely
    ___ Somewhat likely
    ___ Indifferent
    ___ Somewhat unlikely
    ___ Very unlikely.

This is an ordinal scale, but would probably be close enough to interval to be treated that way in data analysis.

Many other question formats are possible. The instructor should be flexible to student suggestion. No matter what verbal scale students select, they must be prepared to address seven issues in the construction of the scale.

Issues in Construction

These issues as discussed in Chapter 8 are: 1) number of categories, 2) odd or even number of categories, 3) balanced versus unbalanced scale, 4) extent of verbal description, 5) category numbering, 6) forced versus nonforced scales, and 7) comparative versus noncomparative.

Student should be prepared to address why they picked a particular combination of these seven aspects in forming their scale.

B. IMAGE MEASUREMENT OPTIONS

The first thing that should be understood about image is that it is likely a multidimensional construct. Therefore, more than one question is likely to be needed to measure the images of the schools.

Two options seem appropriate for measuring image. They are: 1) the semantic differential scale, and 2) the scale.

The choice between these scales may depend on the type of interviewing used in the study. The semantic differential is appropriate for personal and mailed questionnaires but is virtually impossible to use on the phone. The scale can be used with any interviewing mode.

C. MEASURING THE HIERARCHY OF EFFECTS

One possible scheme for measuring the hierarchy of the effects is presented below in Table 15C.

The instructor must be flexible to allow students to have different operational definitions (questions) for the levels in the hierarchy.

D. PAIRED COMPARISON SCALE

This problem parallels the one presented in Table 8-2 of the textbook. The solution involves converting the paired comparison data in Matrix A to a dominance matrix of 0-1 scores. To do this, a one is assigned to a cell if the column brand dominates the row brand (1 if the proportion >.5) and a zero is assigned to a cell if the column brand does not dominate the row brand (0 if the proportion ≤ .5). The ordinal relationship among brands is determined by totaling the columns of the dominance matrix.

Table 15D of this note presents the original matrix (Matrix A) and the dominance matrix (Matrix B) (also see Transparency Masters). The ordinal scaling of brands is thus:

D > B > A > C > E

TEACHING STRATEGY FOR QUESTION 15A-D

We have found it useful to have a student or group of students come down to the front of the class to present their scale and their resolution of the issues related to this scale. This gives the class a specific scale to talk about in bringing out the issues. You may want to identify specific students ahead of time so that they have overhead transparencies available for the class to see. A different student or group would deal with each part of the question.

The instructor should then guide the discussion through each part of the question. Be sure not to let the students slide by the issues surrounding their choice of scale. This is more important than just having the scale to look at.

Students selecting specific scales should be prepared to address certain issues related to their choice. For the semantic differential the issues are: 1) the choice of single-word adjectives versus descriptive phrases and why the particular ones chosen were used, 2) polar opposite versus phrases with less extreme positions, 3) maintenance versus elimination of negative portion of the scale, 4) inclusion of ideal point or not, and 5) the nature of numbers assigned to the scale. For the scale the main issue is the rationale for the domain of descriptive phrases used.

TABLE QUESTION 15C

THE HIERARCHY OF EFFECTS

Level	Definition	Possible Questions
1. Awareness	Consumer's ability to remember a brand name. This can be either when given no prompting about brands (unaided awareness), or when given prompting (aided awareness).	1. Unaided awareness: Please name some consumer magazines. 2. Aided awareness: Have you ever heard of *National Geographic*?
2. Knowledge	Extent that consumer can accurately describe the salient attributes of a product. It is the belief held by a consumer about a product.	1. What types of articles appear in *National Geographic*? 2. Describe the nature of the photography in *National Geographic*. 3. How often is *National Geographic* published?
3. Liking	This is an overall appraisal of how the consumer feels about the product. It is what we loosely refer to as the attitude.	1. Check the response on the following scale that best describes your feelings about *National Geographic*. _____ Like very much _____ Like somewhat _____ No opinion _____ Dislike somewhat _____ Dislike very much
4. Preference	A consumer may like many products. Preference gives value to the level of liking relative to other products for a given use.	1. For possible purchase, please rank-order the following magazines from most preferred to least preferred: _____ *Omni* _____ *National Geographic* _____ *Discover* _____ *Time* _____ *Sports Illustrated*
5. Intention to buy (conviction)	A consumer may prefer one product but not intend to buy it due to circumstances such as lack of money or family pressure. Conviction measures the intent one has to purchase a product.	1. On a scale from 0 to 100 - where 0 means no chance and 100 means you are absolutely certain - indicate the possibility that you will purchase *National Geographic*.
6. Purchase	Here the actual purchase or nonpurchase of the item is recorded.	1. What magazines do you purchase?

TABLE QUESTIONS 15D
PAIRED COMPARISON AND DOMINANCE MATRICES

Matrix A

	A	B	C	D	E
A	–	.60	.44	.59	.25
B	.40	–	.42	.52	.37
C	.56	.58	–	.52	.13
D	.41	.48	.48	–	.43
E	.75	.63	.87	.57	–

Matrix B

	A	B	C	D	E
A	–	1	0	1	0
B	0	–	0	1	0
C	1	1	–	1	0
D	0	0	0	–	0
E	1	1	1	1	–
TOTAL	2	3	1	4	0

Ordinal scaling: D > B > A > C > E.

CHAPTER 9 — CAUSAL DESIGNS

1. What is the fundamental question that should be asked when searching for causality?

    The fundamental question to be asked is "Are there some other possible factors that could have caused the changes you observed?"

Instructor's Further Probing: Say, for example, a local supermarket installed a new automated self checkout system to speed up the purchasing part of a shopper's task. One month following this improvement, the supermarket's sales increase by 20%. If we ask the fundamental question, what other factors could have contributed to the increase in sales? Can it be concluded that the increase in sales was due to the new checkout system?

Suggested Probe Response: Some factors contributing to the increase in the supermarket's sales may include improved management, seasonal factors, decreased competition, price fluctuations, better service by experienced employees, change in customer attitudes, among others. As shown here, there are a myriad of possible factors so that it is very difficult to make any kind of inference based on just the situation as listed above without more formal research.

2. What are the necessary conditions to infer causality?

    Three conditions are necessary:

    1) Concomitant variation.

    2) Time order of occurrence of variables.

    3) Elimination of other possible causal factors.

Instructor's Further Probing: Can we ever prove 100% causality? Why or why not?

Suggested Probe Response: Marketing research follows the scientific model in regard to causality. Both marketing research and the scientific model believe in inferring causality, where there is always some degree of uncertainty in regards to the conclusion arrived at regarding causality. Therefore, we can never prove, with 100% confidence, a causal relationship.

3. What is an experiment?

    An experiment is a procedure in which one or more independent variables are controlled or manipulated by the experimenter, with measures taken on one or more dependent variables. These measures indicate the effect of the independent variables.

Instructor's Further Probing: Give an example of a marketing research experiment a computer retailer may perform in its outlets.

Suggested Probe Response: One possible experiment would be the relocation or repositioning of where the computers or accessories are physically located in the store, while keeping all other factors, like price and service, constant. This will help in making some general inferences in whether the physical location of some products helps them sell better. Remember, there are other factors, so this is only a weak inference.

4. How does an experiment differ from surveys or observational studies?

The fundamental difference between surveys or observational studies (nonexperimental research) and experiments concerns the manipulation of independent variables. In experimental research, independent variables are manipulated. In the case of surveys and observational studies, an **ex post facto** procedure is used, in which an effect is observed and a search for a cause follows.

Instructor's Further Probing: In what way are experimental studies superior to nonexperimental studies?

Suggested Probe Response: Experimental studies allow the researcher to know the time order of occurrence of variables and the effects of other possible independent variables that have been excluded from consideration.

5. What scale of measurement must the independent and dependent variables form in an experiment?

In an experiment, dependent variables must form an interval scale, while independent variables may be as weak as nominally scaled.

Instructor's Further Probing: What are some examples of independent variables? of dependent variables?

Suggested Probe Response: Some examples of independent variables include price and location. Some examples of dependent variables include sales and return on investment (ROI).

6. How may one control the effects of extraneous variables?

Four different approaches are possible for controlling the effects of extraneous variables:

1) Physical control.
2) Randomization of assigning treatments to test units.
3) Use of specific experimental designs.
4) Analysis of covariance.

Instructor's Further Probing: Physical control is a preferred approach to controlling the effects of extraneous variables. Where can physical control not be used?

Suggested Probe Response: Many times experiments must be conducted while a product or service is currently being offered to consumers. As a result, there are variables, such as price, that may be unable to be changed. The other approaches to controlling extraneous variables must be considered in this case. Physical control can work optimally with new products or services that have not yet been offered.

7. What is internal and external validity?

   Internal validity is concerned with whether the experimental results obtained have been caused by the treatment (independent) variables as opposed to extraneous variables. External validity refers to the generalizability of the experimental results to test units or circumstances other than those used.

Instructor's Further Probing: When is an experiment determined to be confounded?

Suggested Probe Response: An experiment is labeled as being confounded when there is a lack of internal validity.

8. Describe seven different types of extraneous variables.

   Seven different types of extraneous variables can be listed: (1) history; (2) maturation; (3) testing; (4) instrumentation; (5) statistical regression; (6) selection bias; and (7) test unit mortality.
   1) History concerns events which are concurrent but external to the experiment and which may affect the dependent measure.
   2) Maturation is an extraneous variable concerned with changes in the experimental units that occur over time.
   3) Testing involves the effects on the experiment of taking a measure on the dependent variable prior to presenting the treatment.
   4) Instrumentation concerns changes in the calibration of the measuring instrument used or changes in the observers, or scorers used.
   5) Statistical regression concerns the phenomenon that outliers tend to move toward a more average position over time.
   6) Selection bias concerns the assignment of test units or treatment groups such that the groups differ on the dependent variable prior to the presentation of the treatment.
   7) Test unit mortality refers to test units' withdrawal from the experiment before its completion.

Instructor's Further Probing: What is direct or main testing?

Suggested Probe Response: Direct or main testing occurs when the first observation in an experiment affects the second observation. Direct and interactive testing make up the two testing effects discussed in the text.

9. What is the interactive testing effect?

   The interactive testing effect, also known as the reactive testing effect, occurs when the test unit's pre-treatment measurement affects the reaction to the treatment. This effect can decrease external validity.

Instructor's Further Probing: Give an example of interactive testing in an experimental situation that could occur for, say, a firm trying to determine if people prefer their brand of cola over leading competitors.

Suggested Probe Response: In the process of pretesting, the cola manufacturer may ask what brands of cola the respondent likes. This type of question may invoke positive images of the respondent's favorite cola. The treatment may be affected since the respondent may no longer have an unbiased frame of mind.

10. How can a design described as $R\ O_1\ X\ O_2$ be confounded?

    A design described as $R\ O_1\ X\ O_2$ could be confounded by all sources of invalidity except selection bias. Thus, history, maturation, testing, instrumentation, statistical regression, and test unit mortality could all serve as confounding variables.

Instructor's Further Probing: Describe a design that is vulnerable to be confounded by all the seven extraneous variables mentioned in the text.

Suggested Probe Response: The following design can be potentially confounded by all the mentioned extraneous variables: $O_1\ X\ O_2$.

11. What design could control these confounding variables?

    One possible true experimental design which could be used to control these variables is the pretest-posttest control group design:

    $$R\ O_1\ X\ O_2$$
    $$R\ O_3\ \ \ \ O_4$$

    In this case, $O_2 - O_1 = TE + H + M + T + I + R + TM$

    $$O_4 - O_3 = H + M + T + I + R + TM$$

    Therefore, $(O_2 - O_1) - (O_4 - O_3) = TE$.

Instructor's Further Probing: Even with the above design, what remaining variable still can confound the experiment?

Suggested Probe Response: The variable that can still confound the experiment is the effect of interactive testing (IT). Other designs can eliminate both TE and IT.

12. Under what circumstances is it impossible for even the best design to control an extraneous variable?

    One of the basic principles of experimental design is that all extraneous variables operate equally on all treatment and control groups. To the extent that they do not, even the best design will fail to control extraneous variables.

Instructor's Further Probing: What does the text suggest as the design that is the best in both eliminating confounding variables and remaining relatively inexpensive?

Suggested Probe Response: The text suggests the posttest-only control group design, minimizes the confounding variables and still remains economically feasible, as relative to other designs.

13. What is a quasi-experiment?

    A quasi-experiment is an experimental design in which the researcher has control over data collection procedures but lacks complete control over the scheduling or randomization of the treatments. Examples of quasi-experimental designs include time series experiments, multiple time series designs, equivalent time-sample designs, and nonequivalent control group designs.

Instructor's Further Probing: Give an example of a quasi-experiment that a retailer might perform.

Suggested Probe Response: A classic quasi-experiment is the measuring of the effects of running an advertisement series. The retailer can control when and how the media message is released, but the retailer can not control the randomization of the treatments (i.e., the ads being shown to the viewers) or even if the treatments were given at all (i.e., the selected people even saw the advertisement).

14. How does a time-series experiment allow for the control of extraneous variables?

    A time-series experiment, which may be represented as $O_1\ O_2\ O_3\ O_4\ x\ O_5\ O_6\ O_7\ O_8$, is similar to the pre experimental one-group pretest-posttest design. Control of extraneous variables in the time series design results from the multiple observations which are taken. Maturation effects, main testing, instrumentation, and statistical regression can be assessed through the multiple observations. The remaining extraneous variables, selection bias and test unit mortality, can also be controlled if the experimenter exercises proper care.

Instructor's Further Probing: Why is the time-series experiment considered a quasi-experiment?

Suggested Probe Response: The above design shows the control over the time period when the measurements are taken ($O_1\ O_2$...) and who is subject to the treatments (x). However, the design shows no randomization (R) or control of when the treatments are administered. These characteristics make the time-series experiment a quasi-experiment.

15. Compare laboratory and field experiments.

    Laboratory experiments are those done in an artificial setting designed for the purpose of the experiment. Such settings offer maximum possible control over confounding variables, and thus have high internal validity. However, the generalizability of results obtained in such a setting may be difficult, resulting in low external validity. Laboratory experiments are generally smaller (in terms of subjects used), shorter, more tightly defined graphically, and generally simpler, thus resulting in lower cost and shorter time requirements than field experiments.

Field experiments, which are conducted in actual market conditions, offer less control over confounding variables but are more easily generalizable. Thus, by comparison to laboratory experiments, they offer lower internal but higher external validity. As noted above, their cost and time requirements are higher.

Instructor's Further Probing: Give an example of both a laboratory experiment and a field experiment.

Suggested Probe Response: A laboratory experiment would perhaps be the pretesting of an advertisement in a magazine. The physical environment and distractions could be controlled by the researcher in a research room. A field experiment would perhaps be to run those advertisements on a small scale and to gauge through secondary sources what consumers thought of those ads.

16. How does one choose between these two environments?

   Ultimately, the choice becomes one of judgment on the part of the experimenter. What must be done is to trade-off the factors of internal validity, external valid, cost, and time to arrive at a design which best satisfies the requirements of the given situation.

Instructor's Further Probing: Which environment would be more favorable for a candy manufacturer looking to determine what design would be most appealing on their candy packages? Why?

Suggested Probe Response: Considering that the design of a candy package can be shown to a respondent in a laboratory environment relatively easily. This would be more cost efficient and faster, considering the infrequentpurchase interval and unpredictability of candy purchases.

17. Outline the limitations of experimentation in marketing.

   Three major limitations exist:

   1) The effects of extraneous variables may not always be controlled. Field experiments are particularly susceptible to differential effects among treatment groups.

   2) Lack of cooperation among wholesalers and retailers can pose problems in field experiments.

   3) Lack of knowledge among marketing personnel concerning experimentation may result in limited use of experiments and/or dismissal of experimental conclusions.

Instructor's Further Probing: What other limitations exist on experimentation in marketing?

Suggested Probe Response: Two other possible limitations exist on experimentation: the cost and time involved; and the unpredictability and difficulty in minimizing test bias from the researcher when using people as units in an experiment.

18. What steps should be taken in executing an experiment?

    The eight steps in executing an experiment are:

    1) Stating the problem.
    2) Formulating an hypothesis.
    3) Constructing an experimental design.
    4) Ascertaining that the design allows the problem to be answered.
    5) Checking that the possible types of results can be analyzed by available statistical procedures.
    6) Performing the experiment.
    7) Applying statistical analysis procedures to the results to determine whether the results are real or random error.
    8) Drawing conclusions concerning internal and external validity.

Instructor's Further Probing: While all aspects of the experiment are important, what is the most critical step in the eight steps listed above?

Suggested Probe Response: The problem statement determines the direction of the entire experiment, and thus becomes the most important step to do correctly.

19. What is a CRD (completely randomized design)?

    A completely randomized design, CRD, is the simplest type of designed experiment. It involves measuring the effect of one independent variable, which may be scaled at the nominal level of measurement. Experimental treatments are randomly assigned to test units.

Instructor's Further Probing: Give an example of a CRD designed experiment that a computer chip manufacturer may perform.

Suggested Probe Response: A computer chip manufacturer may perform a CRD designed experiment by setting a nominal independent variable as "type of training performed", with several categories: on-the-job, classes, no training. Each category represents a treatment, with the last category representing the control group (no service). In this manner, the manufacturer can determine the causal effects of the various types of training.

20. How does a RBD (randomized block design) aid the experimenter?

    The randomized block design, RBD, is an experimental design in which test units are blocked on the basis of some external criterion variable. The advantage to this procedure is that it allows a smaller sampling error to be obtained than in the absence of the blocking (i.e., under the CRD). This results from the fact that the variable of interest is more homogeneous within the groups than across all groups, and that some of the variation is assigned to the blocking factor.

Instructor's Further Probing: We saw in question #19, the computer chip manufacturer perform a CRD designed experiment. If the chip manufacturer wanted to do a similar experiment but with an RBD design, what would that experiment look like?

Suggested Probe Response: The manufacturer could look at the size of the sales territory, hypothesizing that the size may affect the experiment results. So, the manufacturer would then possibly break up the sales territories into several blocks, based on, say, sales potential.

21. Why are LS (Latin Square) designs so utilized in marketing field experiments?

    Latin Square designs are often utilized in marketing field experiments since they help control extraneous sources of variation which frequently can pose difficulties. Specifically, the LS design is capable of controlling and measuring the effects of two extraneous variables simultaneously, making it more useful than the RBD.

Instructor's Further Probing: What are some possible drawbacks to the LS design?

Suggested Probe Response: As is the issue with most marketing experiments, cost and time are always key issues. The LS design requires some more work (as compared to other designs) to plan out the treatments in the experiment to conform to a design that conforms with LS design requirements.

22. What is a factorial design?

    A factorial design is an experimental design which is useful for measuring simultaneously the effects of two or more independent variables. The factorial design allows the measurement of each of the main effects for the independent variables separately as well as the interaction effect between the independent variables.

Instructor's Further Probing: Describe the concept of "levels" in factorial design.

Suggested Probe Response: In a factorial design the categories of each of the independent variables are called *levels*. In the design, each level of each independent variable appears with each level of all other independent variables.

23. **V-8 Experiment**

    (a) This is a basic before-after design with control groups in a factorial design. In general it is as follows:

    $$R\ O\ X_i\ O$$

    where X_i represents the different treatments including the control treatment.

    The X_i are:

    X_1: old budget; old mix; old creative (control)
    X_2: new budget; television/radio; new creative
    X_3: new budget; television/radio; old creative
    X_4: new budget; television prime; new creative
    X_5: new budget; television prime; old creative

X_6: new budget; television fringe; new creative

X_7: new budget; television fringe; old creative

X_8: new budget; radio; old creative

(b) Extraneous variables are handled by the random assignment of markets to treatment conditions, and by the use of a control condition.

(c) An extraneous factor that differently impacts treatment markets in a systematic way could confound the experiment. For example, a competitor could increase its advertising budget in a selected treatment market.

(d) A Latin Square design is not appropriate here as the number of treatments cannot equal the number of blocking factors. In addition, the interaction effects that the factorial design measures could not be measured with a Latin Square design.

Navy Experiment

(a) Like the V-8 experiment, the Navy experiment is a basic before-after design with control group, in a factorial design. Again the R O X_i O applies where each treatment condition, X_i, represents the combination of treatment levels in Figure 9-7.

For example:

X_1: AD + 100%; recruiters same

X_2: AD + 50%; recruiters -20%

The student should easily be able to complete the X_i definition by following the cells in Figure 9-7. They should note the control condition as expected is: AD same; recruiters same.

(b) Same as in the V-8 experiment.

(c) Same as the V-8 experiment in principle. For example, the recruiters in the minus conditions may have become demoralized and acted with less effort than desired.

(d) Same as in the V-8 experiment.

24. Here the objective is to measure the influence of price of foreign cars on attitudes about foreign cars. One possible design follows.

Treatments

This is a one-way ANOVA design situation. The design has one nominally scaled independent variable whose categories form the treatments. With price as the independent variable, the treatments could be:

T_1	$70,000	(high)
T_2	$50,000	(medium)
T_3	$30,000	(low)

where T_2 could be the control treatment (current price).

Of course, the exact definitions of high, medium, and low would depend on the type and make of car involved. The design may have to control for this price spread. The spread from $30,000 - $70,000 may be far too much for certain types of cars.

The instructor should press the students to specify a particular car--Honda, BMW, etc., in order to realistically set treatment levels.

Dependent Variable

The situation clearly calls for the use of some attitude scale as the dependent variable. An argument could also be made for using more than one attitude scale. Most likely a verbal rating scale would be used. The students should clearly indicate that the attitude scales must form an interval scale.

Test Units

The test units would be people exposed to the different treatments. They should be selected in some random manner based upon a population definition deemed relevant to this problem. Students should state their assumption on the relevant population definition.

Control of Extraneous Variables

There are a number of choices here. Most important is randomization. That is, the treatments will be randomly assigned to test units. The assumption will be that extraneous variables will act evenly on all groups.

It may also be necessary to block on some extraneous factors to get better measure of experimental error in ANOVA. Such factors as income and type of car may be contributing to extraneous variation in the dependent variable (attitude).

Students should also note that a laboratory situation will provide better control than a field study.

Symbolic Representation

One possible symbolic representation is:

R	O_1	X_1	O_2
R	O_3	X_2	O_4
R	O_5	X_3	O_6

where X_1, X_2, and X_3 are the three treatments. If one is concerned about testing effects and can be confident in randomization, then the design might be:

```
R        X₁        O₁
R        X₂        O₂
R        X₃        O₃
```

25. *MINICASE*: Find an organization's new marketing program or activity described in a newspaper or magazine--Business Week or Advertising Age, for example. The program might be a new advertising theme, distribution plan, pricing strategy, and so on. Your assignment is to design an experiment or quasi-experiment to measure the effectiveness of this new program or activity. Be sure to address the following six terms.

    (a) Describe the new marketing program or activity.
    (b) Describe the treatments.
    (c) Describe the dependent variable(s) and how it (they) will be measured.
    (d) What or who are the test units?
    (e) How will extraneous variables be controlled?
    (f) Using the symbols R, O, and X, describe the experiment.

This situation requires flexibility on the part of the instructor as each student will have a different program or activity. Just make sure the following aspects are present:

1) A nominal independent variable or variables defining the treatments.
2) An interval dependent variable.
3) A set of test units.
4) Randomization.
5) A control group.
6) Other possible controls--blocking if needed.

CHAPTER 10 — DATA COLLECTION: EXPLORATORY RESEARCH

1. What is the role of exploratory research in a research project?

    Exploratory research is an initial or preliminary stage in the research process. Information is collected from either primary or secondary sources in order to provide insight into the management problem and identify courses of action. Generally, exploratory research allows focused quantitative research to be developed and performed.

    Instructor's Further Probing: Can the researcher skip the exploratory phase and go directly to the quantitative research?

    Suggested Probe Response: If experience and other sources provide a direction and focus for the quantitative study research design, then the researcher may be able to skip the qualitative phase altogether. Generally, though, for new products, services, or ideas, the qualitative phase is needed to provide an area for further exploration through the quantitative phase of the research project.

2. Why are the on-line focus groups, discussed in the example at the beginning of this chapter, a good medium for qualitative data?

    On-line focus groups, as described at the beginning of the chapter, allow the researcher to conduct a qualitative study with minimal cost; ability to use small convenient sample sizes (and ability to electronically control that size); use an open-ended data collection format; record data that is given across the electronic system; maintain anonymity of respondents to a greater degree and conduct the research on an international basis, again with minimal cost. Of course, the on-line focus groups do not allow the researcher to visually see the person, so that some information is lost from the respondents non-verbal signals (e.g.. body language) and fluctuations in the voice.

    Instructor's Further Probing: Are there any other ways that technology could be used to improve marketing research for qualitative data (for example, using the Internet)?

    Suggested Probe Response: Developments on the Internet have led to the creation of the World Wide Web (WWW), a dynamic method of interchanging information on the Internet. Many companies have used this visually oriented interface to take surveys, including the use of open-ended questions. Responses filled out using the WWW are then electronically mailed directly to the research organization. Future developments include the use of virtual reality interfaces to use the Internet to further improve marketing research potential

3. What are the characteristics of qualitative data?

    Qualitative data have the following characteristics:

    1) Small convenient samples are used

    2) Information sought relates to the respondent's motivations, beliefs, feelings, and attitudes.

3) An intuitive, subjective approach is used in gathering the data.

4) Data collection format is open-ended.

5) Approach is not intended to provide statistically or scientifically accurate data.

Instructor's Further Probing: Which of the following questions would be considered questions that solicit qualitative data:

1) *Describe your experiences with using an electronic can opener.*

2) *What stores do you normally buy chocolate bars from?*

3) *Have you ever heard of the Power PC brand computer chip?*

4) *Detail what you feel are the advantages of owning a snow blower.*

Suggested Probe Response: Based on the characteristics of qualitative data, as described above, questions 1 and 4 would be considered questions that elicit qualitative data. Questions 2 and 4, while open-ended, do not focus on the respondents motivations, beliefs, feelings, or attitudes.

4. Why are focus groups important in marketing?

As primary sources of information, focus groups provide a valuable resource for current data on customer buying behavior, perceptions, attitudes, and motivations. Strategic marketing decisions can be made from the use of focus groups in conjunction with conclusive research.

Instructor's Further Probing: Specifically, what uses in marketing can focus group interviews serve?

Suggested Probe Response: Several uses of focus group interviews have been suggested, including:

1) Generating hypotheses for subsequent quantitative testing.
2) Generating information helpful in structuring consumer questionnaires.
3) Providing overall background information on a product category.
4) Getting impressions on new product concepts for which little information is available.
5) Stimulating new ideas about older products.
6) Generating ideas for new creative concepts.
7) Interpreting previously obtained quantitative results.

5. Discuss some of the problems that may arise in designing or conducting a focus group.

Some potential problems that may arise in the designing or conducting of a focus group include:

- finding participants that fit the criteria established as needed for the group (especially adhering to the idea that the participants should be homogenous within a particular session)
- the variable expense in physically having to find people and bring them together (this is especially difficult in trying to conduct internationally oriented focus groups)
- participants who fail to volunteer information or allow free flowing of thoughts (the moderator can play a role in encouraging people to talk, but only to a degree)

Instructor's Further Probing: What are some issues that need to be considered when carrying out focus groups?

Suggested Probe Response:

1) Composition of respondent group: homogeneous characteristics best.
2) Size of respondent group: 6-7 for nonconsumer goods 10-12 for consumer goods.
3) Selection of respondents: careful screening essential to find people with sufficient knowledge, who have not participated previously, or do not know others in group.
4) Physical setting of interview: living room environment, either actual or created in a lab.
5) Length of interview: 1-1/2 - 2 hours typical.
6) Number of sessions conducted: variable with nature of research, number of market segments, cost constraints.
7) Client observation of interviews: typically do, but best if behind two-way mirror.
8) Importance of monitor to success of technique: essential.
9) Sex of monitor: Arguments for either same or opposite sex from the group.

6. What are some of the desirable characteristics for focus group moderators?

    Some of the desirable characteristics for moderator are:

    1) Kind but firm.
    2) Permissive.
    3) Involved.
    4) Appearance of incomplete understanding.
    5) Encouraging.
    6) Flexible.
    7) Sensitive.

Instructor's Further Probing: According to the text, what kind of educational or work background is common for a position of a focus group moderator?

Suggested Probe Response: Since the position of a focus group moderator requires significant ability in dealing with people and understanding group dynamics, the moderator often has a background as a psychologist with supplementary developed moderator skills through special training.

7. Discuss the advantages and disadvantages of focus groups.

Advantages:

1) Synergism - group produces wider range of material than sum of individuals.
2) Snowballing - one comment may trigger chain of responses.
3) Stimulation - individuals open up as group excitement over topic increases.
4) Security - individuals in group find their ideas similar to others.
5) Spontaneity - individuals can address issues that most concern them.
6) Serendipity - some idea "drops out of the blue."
7) Specialization - use of more highly trained, more expensive interviewers possible.
8) Scientific scrutiny - closer scrutiny of data possible with group interview.
9) Structure - more flexible than individual interviews concerning topics, depth.
10) Speed - increased speed over individual interviews.

Disadvantages:

1) Evidence from focus groups not projectable to a target segment, but decision makers may use evidence in conclusive research manner.
2) Individuals may compromise proper procedures for personal gain.

Instructor's Further Probing: What are some of the variations found based on the traditional one moderator focus group?

Suggested Probe Response: Since different research projects have different goals, there are several variations on the single moderator focus group theme. These variations include:
1) Mini-groups - include a smaller number of participants (4-5) than usually found in a focus group
2) Two-way focus groups - one group explains an issue to a second group, which then discusses the information learned
3) Dual-moderator group - a typical focus group format with two moderators instead of just one
4) Client-participant groups - a focus group in which the client of the focus group study actually is involved in the discussion, as opposed to remaining an unseen observer, as is the typical format

8. When would a depth interview be more useful than the focus group method?

A depth interview has the advantage over the focus group method of being able to explore ideas to a greater degree. A depth interview would be more useful than the focus group method in developing hypotheses, defining decision problems, and formulating courses of action. Issues that are confidential, sensitive, or susceptible to group peer pressure make the depth interview a more comfortable medium in that regard than the focus group method.

Instructor's Further Probing: Give an example of a situation where the depth interview would be preferred over the focus group method.

Suggested Probe Response: Since depth interviews are well suited for probing for answers on sensitive issues, a pharmaceutical company may, for example, ask females one-on-one about their perceptions and sexual habits to determine what females think about oral contraceptives. In a focus group method, the sensitivity to such an issue would prevent people from saying what they might say in private.

9. What are the issues and steps in the analysis of qualitative data?

   The main steps and issues involved in the analysis of qualitative data are:
   1) Reviewing the research purpose.
   2) Thoroughly study the group discussions. Verbatim transcripts or video tapes are very useful for this step. Understanding group dynamics (in the case of focus groups) is essential at this stage.
   3) Create categories. It is important to develop a demographic profile of the respondents and then develop a respondent profile.
   4) Identify potential relationships. Here the researcher looks for informal relationships between variables and various inferences.

Instructor's Further Probing: Why is it so important for the research to obtain verbatim transcripts or video tapes of the focus group or depth interview sessions?

Suggested Probe Response: Since due to the nature of the group or topic people may not verbalize all they feel, it is important to note word choice, body language, sentence phrasing, among other characteristics to determine fully what a person perceives or feels. Again, this is why many moderators have a background in psychology, so that they are able to interpret people's response, verbal and nonverbal.

10. *MINICASE:* Discuss the issues in determining when and where an automobile tire manufacturer should conduct focus groups to determine feedback from customers on its line of winter tires. Give a brief description of who would be a good candidate for this type of focus group.

    The student's response should focus on the following key ideas:

    First the automobile tire maker must decide what the purpose of this qualitative research will be. If the manufacturer will eventually, through further quantitative study, decide on which products to market or decide the location of its distribution centers, then the moderator's guide should appropriately reflect these issues.

    Next, to determine where the focus group will be held, it is important to, again, look back at the purpose of the research--does the tire maker want to find out about attitudes from people who do not use the tires very much, or find out from people who live in cold and snowy environments and use winter tires all the time. Say, for example, the tire maker decides it wants people who use winter tires extensively. If this is the case, then the group will probably be held in snowy and cold regions like North Dakota or parts of Colorado, for example (in the U.S.). Focus groups conducted in other countries, for example, like Canada would have other issues involved, including the prevalence of automobiles, the amount of disposable income, etc..., before the location in a specific country can be determined acceptable.

    Given the premise that the tire maker wants to talk to people who use winter tires extensively, the group should consist of 30-40 year old males, in the income range of

$60,000-$80,000 per household, owning a pick-up truck or van. This homogenous group should give the client a good idea of what extensive users think of the line of winter tires since they have both the experience with the tires and the disposable income to be purchasers.

The group probably will yield best results if it were to be held right after the end of winter. At this point in the year, the participants will have used winter tires through the entire winter and will have a good idea of what they like and do not like regarding their tires.

CHAPTER 11 — DATA COLLECTION: CONCLUSIVE RESEARCH

1. What is the objective of conclusive research and what approaches are used?

   The qualitative phase of the marketing research process, as described in Chapter 10, generates various alternatives for management to consider. Conclusive research aids in determining which of the generated alternatives will yield the most favorable results.

   In order to evaluate the various alternatives, two main approaches are used: communication method and observation. The communication method involves the participant directly soliciting his/her cooperation to express their thoughts. The observation method requires less involvement from the participant and uses external means, such as visual observation or mechanical observation to collect data.

Instructor's Further Probing: Describe the four types of communication approaches available for obtaining data from respondents.

Suggested Probe Response: The four communication approaches are:

   1) personal interview
   2) telephone interview
   3) mail interview
   4) computer diskette interview

2. What types of respondent data exist?

   Three major types of respondent data can be distinguished:

   1) Past behavior--using past experience as a predictor of future behavior.
   2) Attitudes--determining the extent of the assumed relationship between attitudes and behavior.
   3) Respondent characteristics--finding correlations between various characteristics and associated behavior.

Instructor's Further Probing: A popular way of describing respondents is in terms of life-style. A broader term which includes this life-style concept is psychographics. Describe the term psychographics.

Suggested Probe Response: As described in the text, psychographics is a quantitative research procedure which seeks to explain why people behave as they do and why they hold their current attitudes. It seeks to take quantitative research beyond demographics, socioeconomic and user/non-user analysis, but also employs these variables, of which life-style is one. The others are psychological and product benefits.

3. List the most common communication media used in respondent data collection; what criteria are used to select which media to use?

The telephone interview is used by 94% of business, making it the most popular communication approach. The reason for the telephone interview's popularity stems from its efficient and economical procedures and its application to a wide range of information needs. In addition, new technologies in the area of computer assisted telephone surveys have further made the telephone interview more appealing.

Criteria used for selection:

1) Versatility.
2) Cost.
3) Time.
4) Sample control.
5) Quantity of data.
6) Quality of data.
7) Response rate.

Instructor's Further Probing: The discussion on international marketing research discusses traits of the implementation of three major communication methods. For each of the three major communication methods (personal, telephone, and mail interviews) describe how the implementation of these methods is similar or different as compared to the U.S.

Suggested Probe Response: Due to lack of technology or infrastructure, personal interviewing is popular in many foreign countries, with the majority of the interviews taking place in the respondent's home or through intercept interviews, as is done in the U.S.

Due to the lack of availability or lack of use of the telephone, telephone interviewing use varies widely among countries.

In Europe, Canada, and Japan, mail interviews are used extensively due to high literacy rates, well-developed postal systems, and address listings for target markets. This is not true in other countries, where the postal system is not as developed or as efficient.

4. Identify and explain the techniques used for estimating nonresponse error when communication approaches are used.

1) Sensitivity analysis--the determination of how different each successive callback group is from the previous respondent group.

2) Trend projection--based on the results of successive waves of callbacks, a trend may be used to estimate the characteristics of the nonrespondent group.

3) Subsample measurement--a specially designed survey or interview to estimate the results of the nonrespondent group (and then the results are incorporated into the data set of those who already responded to the survey).

4) Subjective estimate--the researcher uses experience and judgment to estimate the degree of nonresponse error.

Instructor's Further Probing: How can nonresponse error be minimized?

Suggested Probe Response: To minimize non-response error, several steps can be taken:

1) Provide a series of callbacks. Callbacks are correlated to high response rates.
2) Focus on respondent motivation.
3) Provide an advance letter or telephone call before the actual survey is done to request cooperation.
4) Use first-class postage in mailings and include hand stamped return envelopes.
5) Consider the use of monetary incentives.
6) Use a postcard, letter, or phone call as a follow-up requesting completion of the survey.

5. What are the advantages and disadvantages of observation methods?

Advantages:

1) Does not depend upon the respondent's willingness to provide the desired data.
2) Potential bias as a result of the interviewer and interviewing process is either reduced or eliminated.

Disadvantages:

1) Not all things are observable (awareness, beliefs, feelings, etc.).
2) Personal and intimate activities may be very difficult to observe.
3) Data collection cost and time requirements are such that the behavior to be observed must be of short duration, occur frequently, or be reasonably predictable.

Instructor's Further Probing: Describe a situation where the use of the observation method is more favorable than the use of the communication methods.

Suggested Probe Response: For example, in a situation where a marketing researcher is trying to determine what types of sales techniques work best on potential customers of used cars, the customer may not be receptive to helping the researcher. In this case, the research could observe the customer-salesperson interaction and note what techniques or methods improve the chances of a sale.

6. Discuss the classification of observational techniques. For each technique, give a case for which it would be best suited.

   Five classifications are suggested:
   1) Natural or contrived observation.
   2) Disguised or undisguised observation.
   3) Structured or unstructured observation.
   4) Direct or indirect observation.
   5) Human or mechanical observation.

Natural observation techniques observe behavior in its normal environment as opposed to in a simulated artificial environment (contrived observation). Natural observation works best when all variables affecting a person can be simulated (or are not economical to stimulate), for example, in the case the of a shopper's behavior in a supermarket. A contrived observation would work best when there are only a few variables affecting a situation, as is in the case of observing someone reading a magazine with various types of advertisements to determine which ads they focus on.

Disguised observation is designed to observe behavior without the respondents' knowledge that they are being watched, and thus undisguised behavior is observation with a respondent's knowledge. Disguised behavior works best if the involvement of the researcher may bias the respondent, as in the case of a shopper in a department store looking at personal items such as toiletries or undergarments. Undisguised behavior works best if the researcher would like the participant to focus on a specific area or if a sensitive issue is being addressed, for example, if the buying behavior ofcustomers in only the clothing department of a department store is of interest. Of course research must maintain a high standard of ethics in the case of disguised observation.

In structured observation, the researcher specifies what is to be observed and how to record the measurements. By comparison, in unstructured observation, the observer is free to observe what appears to be the relevant behavior. Structured observation works well if there is a specific target of research, developed through past observations, data, and experience. For example, structured observation would work well in the case that the researcher wanted to examine the number of times a person walked by an advertisement sign to determine the value of that location for the ad. Whereas, unstructured observation would be suited if the researcher wanted to examine what types of toys toddlers liked given a selection to choose from.

Direct observation observes behavior as it occurs, rather than observing a record of past behavior (indirect). Direct observation is most efficient if lots of data are to be gathered in a short amount of time, for example in observing people in stores. Indirect data are best suited for a situation that does not occur very often or where substantial data has already been collected in that area. Indirect data could be applied in the case of consumer buying behavior based on price levels (price sensitivity) of computers.

Mechanical observation techniques involve the use of some sort of mechanical device. Mechanical observation is helpful in determining data in areas where the researcher could not observe with the naked eye alone. The various mechanical devices can all be used in a number of different applications as described in the text

Instructor's Further Probing: Say, for example, a computer keyboard manufacturer wants to determine what the best design is for their newest product line. What type of observation would be most appropriate for this type of situation?

Suggested Probe Response: The manufacturer could prototype several designs and place them in an office or home setting and perform natural observation techniques. In this manner, the manufacturer would have a very good idea of how the product would be used in the actual place of use. In addition, mechanical observation may be used to record the research subject for later analysis.

7. What major mechanical devices are employed in observation techniques in marketing and how are they used in marketing research? (Instructor's Probe) Give examples of where each device would be best suited for a particular type of marketing research.

    1) The motion picture camera
    2) The Audimeter.

3) The psychogalvanometer.
4) The eye-camera.
5) The pupilometer.

The motion picture camera-- can be used to record shopping behavior, etc. ; best suited for complex situations or situations where detailed analysis is necessary and an observation takes many passes at the same scene to record.

The Audimeter--can be used to measure TV and radio viewing. Best suited for mass media monitoring, for example, in determining ratings for advertisement rates on TV or radio.

The psychogalvanometer--can be used to measure perspiration changes in response to verbal messages or images such as in advertisements or in selling techniques. Very well suited for measuring involuntary or minute reactions to stimuli, as in the case of visual or auditory stimuli in advertising.

The eye-camera--can be used to measure eye movements for determining the best placement of advertisements in print media. Useful for determining the focus of a person's view, and not readily visible by an observer.

The pupilometer, measuring pupil diameter--can also be used in determining the effectiveness of placement of print media. It is best suited for applications similar to the eye-camera.

8. *MINICASE:* Give an example of a case where the communication method techniques would be more efficient than the observation method techniques. Give a case where the observation method techniques would be more efficient than the communication method techniques.

Communication Method Case:

If ABC Toys, Inc. wanted to determine whether or not their customers were satisfied with the quality of toys that they purchased through ABC's distributors, the communication method would be most favorable over the observation method. Several reasons lead us to choosing the communication method: due to the nature of the study, a large number of samples must be taken, done far cheaper and faster through communication methods; observation alone may not capture the feelings and thoughts not shown by the respondent and the researcher's involvement may bias the response received; and the satisfaction study could be conducted throughout the country, not just in regional areas, as would have to be done due to the nature of observation studies.

Observation Method Case:

NipCar, Inc., an automobile manufacturer, wanted to do a marketing research study to determine how passengers using their cars use their seat belts (how far do they have to reach, how long does it take, etc...). The purpose of the study is to design safer, easier to use, and cheaper seat belts based on the user's current method of use of the belts. While a communication study could reach many users and capture some data, the nature of the study demands that the researcher examines the actual process, visually, of many different people. Communication methods may not allow researchers to accurately capture important criteria such as weight, build, and height of the user. A motion picture camera would be one of the mechanical devices that would greatly assist the researcher in capturing the needed data to perform the study.

CHAPTER 12 — DESIGNING DATA COLLECTION FORMS

1. What role does the questionnaire play in the research project?

    The questionnaire occupies a central role in the research project. As a formalized schedule for collecting data from respondents, the questionnaire must be free from measurement error to insure the accuracy of the data so obtained.

Instructor's Further Probing: Why is there a need for careful construction of a questionnaire, even to the level of deciding on word choice?

Suggested Probe Response: As seen from the examples in the text, the construction of a questionnaire can greatly affect the outcome of the survey. As a result, it is important to take care in the design of a questionnaire to avoid measurement error.

2. What are the typical components of a questionnaire?

    A questionnaire may include the following components:

    1) Identification data.
    2) Request for cooperation.
    3) Instructions.
    4) Information sought.
    5) Classification data.

Instructor's Further Probing: Why is classification data generally sought at the end of the questionnaire and not asked with the identification data?

Suggested Probe Response: Due to the generally personal data requested in this section, some respondents may be reluctant to answer such questions. Putting these questions on the questionnaire may immediately bias the respondent for the rest of the survey and may even increase test unit mortality.

3. What decisions precede the questionnaire design stage?

    Prior decisions include:
    1) The type of research design.
    2) Sources of data to be utilized.
    3) Selection of target population.
    4) Details of the sampling plan.
    5) Mode of data analysis.

Instructor's Further Probing: What important aspect in the decisions is listed here and time and time again appears at the beginning stages of most marketing research processes?

Suggested Probe Response: The type of research design incorporates knowledge of the purpose and focus of the research. Most marketing research processes or steps involve the initial review or development of such a purpose.

4. What criterion governs the inclusion of questions in the questionnaire?

   Questions should address a specific information need. Otherwise, the questionnaire will be lengthier than necessary and relatively inefficient in terms of time and costs.

Instructor's Further Probing: Why is it that the addition of "interesting" questions adds cost? For example, estimate the added cost for the addition of the following question, asked by phone interviewers, to 1,000 people: "How many extension cords or other similar devices do you own in your household?"

Suggested Probe Response: Consider that the question takes 5 seconds to read, and is most likely repeated, making the time to read the question about 10 seconds. The respondent may take, on an average, about 15 seconds to respond. The interviewer will take about 2 seconds to record the information. The total time in the interview phase for this question takes about 17 seconds (10 sec + 15 sec + 2 sec). This does not include analysis and presentation time for that specific question. Thus, if it costs $8/hr to pay an interviewer to ask the questions, each 17 second question will cost 4 cents. 4 cents times the 1,000 respondents makes that question cost $40! With the additional analysis costs and design costs, it is easy to see how such a small study can increase in costs even from one question.

5. How does the respondent affect the content of the questions?

   The respondents' ability to answer accurately and willingness to respond influence the content of questions.

Instructor's Further Probing: What two main sources can inaccurate data result from?

Suggested Probe Response: Inaccurate data can result from two sources: the respondent is uninformed or the respondent is forgetful.

6. How can a researcher overcome the problems associated with collecting data about unimportant or infrequent events?

   The researcher may interview persons most likely to remember, e.g., recent purchasers. She/he may also use techniques which stimulate the respondent's recall of the event, e.g., aided recall.

Instructor's Further Probing: What problems may be associated with asking recent purchasers a survey question?

Suggested Probe Response: Some potential problems with seeking recent purchasers of a product or service is that these people have not seen the product or service through its entire life. In addition, persuasive techniques are often used by merchants to reassure a buyer, especially of large purchases such as cars. Such biasing may not yield a spectrum of opinions.

7. Why may a respondent be unwilling to respond accurately to a given question?

   1) The situation is not appropriate for disclosure of the data.
   2) Disclosure of the data would be embarrassing.
   3) Disclosure may be a potential threat to the respondent's prestige or normative views.

Instructor's Further Probing: When is the unwillingness-to-respond potential highest (with which communication medium)?

Suggested Probe Response: Given that studies have shown people are most influenced by others in person and from our own experiences, the personal interview and telephone interview are most likely to affect the respondent from yielding accurate data to a particular question.

8. What approaches are available for dealing with the bias resulting from respondents' unwillingness to respond accurately?

   1) Counterbiasing statement.
   2) Indirect statement.
   3) Labeled response categories.
   4) Randomized response technique.

Instructor's Further Probing: Develop a counterbiasing statement for a question that seeks to find out how many times a respondent has had severe (lasting more than 4 days) hemorrhoids.

Suggested Probe Response: A typical counterbiasing statement would be something to the effect of: "Many people suffer from severe cases of hemorrhoids, a well-known ailment, due to various changes in diets. How many times have you experienced a severe (lasting more than 4 days) case of hemorrhoids in the past year?" The question acknowledges the respondent is not alone and that it is not uncommon for people to get a severe case of hemorrhoids. In this manner the respondent will feel more comfortable answering truthfully.

9. What are the advantages and disadvantages of open-ended questions?

   Advantages:

   1) Permit divergent responses.
   2) Help establish rapport.
   3) Yield helpful insights, side comments, and explorations.

   Disadvantages:

   1) Potential for interviewer bias.
   2) Time and cost of coding.
   3) Implicit weighting of responses by articulate respondents.
   4) More costly.

Instructor's Further Probing: Develop an open-ended question to seek out why people use oral contraceptives.

Suggested Probe Response: Not only does this topic have to be developed into an open-ended question, but the sensitivity of the issue must be addressed as well. The following illustrates a possibility of such a question:

"Oral contraceptives are the second most common form of birth control used in this country. Some people use oral contraceptives for a number of reasons, not just for birth control. If you use oral contraceptives, why do you use them? "

10. List the advantages and disadvantages associated with multiple-choice questions.

   Advantages:

   1) Minimal interviewer bias.
   2) Minimal cost and time associated with data processing.
   3) Easier to administer.

   Disadvantages:

   1) Potential for bias, either from the specification a priori of a response set or the order in which the response alternatives are presented.

Instructor's Further Probing: What are two key issues that need to be considered in multiple choice questions?

Suggested Probe Response: In developing multiple choice questions, the number of alternatives and position bias need to be examined.

11. What guidelines govern the design of responses to multiple-choice questions?

   Responses should be:

   1) Collectively exhaustive.
   2) Mutually exclusive.
   3) Varied in sequence to reduce position bias.

Instructor's Further Probing: What are these guidelines seeking to accomplish? What are some of the potential difficulties in following these guidelines?

Suggested Probe Response: All these guidelines seek to reduce bias from the way the questions are presented. To be collectively exhaustive requires careful wording of the question or extra coding effort to process an "other" clause, increasing length and cost. Mutually exclusive questions prevent the respondent from picking more than applicable answers (exceptions that include multiple answers then require special data processing needs). Finally, with varied sequence, despite the extra time and effort that is needed to make an answer free from position bias, the respondent may still mentally reorder the items into a potentially biased order.

12. Under what conditions would dichotomous questions be inappropriate?

    If there are more than two grades of response present in the respondent group or indecision predominates, dichotomous questions may yield results which contain substantial measurement error.

Instructor's Further Probing: Are dichotomous questions different than multiple choice questions?

Suggested Probe Response: Actually dichotomous questions can be seen as a subset of multiple choice questions where there are only a few grades of answers.

13. What general guidelines should one utilize in designing the wording of a question?

    1) Use simple words.
    2) Use clear words.
    3) Avoid leading questions.
    4) Avoid biased questions.
    5) Avoid implicit alternatives.
    6) Avoid implicit assumptions.
    7) Avoid estimates.
    8) Avoid double-barreled questions.
    9) Consider the frame of reference.

Instructor's Further Probing: Given these guidelines and other rules of thumb, researchers can scientifically design and implement questionnaires. Is this a true statement...why or why not?

Suggested Probe Response: The text mentions that despite proven guidelines, experience influences the design of a questionnaire significantly. Therefore, questionnaire design is an art form more so than an exact science.

14. *MINICASE:* As the lead researcher on a marketing research team seeking to explore opinions and attitudes of people in the areas of Middle East and Asia on a certain brand of disposable tissues, what are some of the key issues, specifically related to international marketing, that you and your team will need to consider in implementing such a survey? What time frame do you estimate the research to take, on average?

    The answer to this minicase can vary significantly; however, these are the key issues that can be derived from the case:

    - Language may be a barrier, requiring translation and pretesting in each language

    - Word choice and sentence structure, along with various forms of bias, such as position bias, will need to be addressed in detail

    - Interviewing may require the recruitment of natives of each of the countries being examined

    - Cultural differences will need to be noted in the use of the product (all cultures may not view the use of disposable tissues as acceptable or commonplace)

The text estimates that marketing research using questionnaires in the Middle East may take up to six months, and three to four months elsewhere. Given this as an estimate, this research project could potentially take about eight months, including design, pretesting, and analysis of all the data.

CHAPTER 13 — THE BASICS OF SAMPLING

1. Why is sampling so often used in marketing research?

    Sampling offers major benefits over the alternative of taking a census.
    1) A sample is less expensive.
    2) Sampling takes less time than a census.
    3) Sampling may be more accurate.
    4) Sampling does not contaminate the entire population of interest.

Instructor's Further Probing: Considering sampling has several major advantages over a census, why conduct a census?

Suggested Probe Response: In the case where such a diverse population is being examined and the number of people and diverse groups is high, it is difficult to conduct enough samples to generalize for the whole population. In this case it is advantageous to survey each element in the population and thus conduct a survey.

2. Distinguish among the following sampling concepts: element, population, sampling unit, sampling frame, and study population.

    An element is the unit about which information is sought, i.e., individuals, products, stores, etc.

    A population is the aggregate of the elements defined prior to selection of the sample. Properly designated, the population is defined in terms of elements, sampling units, extent, and time.

    Sampling unit is the element or elements available for selection at some stage of the sampling process.

    A sampling frame is a list of all the sampling units in the population. The actual sample is drawn from this list.

    A study population is the aggregate of elements from which the sample is drawn.

Instructor's Further Probing: Can a marketing researcher always find an accurate, up-to-date sampling frame? Why or why not?

Suggested Probe Response: Due to the nature of some research, there may not exist any reference to list all the sampling units in a given sampling frame. The text cites as an example, that there is no list of all people who suffer from a particular allergy, thus making it very difficult to create a sampling frame. However, as discussed in previous chapters, secondary sources and other means can aid the researcher in, at the very least, estimating a sampling frame.

3. Distinguish between probability and nonprobability sampling.

In probability sampling each element of the population has a known chance of being selected for the sample, a characteristic which enables the researcher to determine the degree of sampling error.

In nonprobability sampling the selection of population elements to comprise the sample is partly a function of the judgment of the researcher or field interviewer. There is no known chance of any particular element in the population being selected. Therefore, the researcher is unable to determine the extent of sampling error.

Instructor's Further Probing: A common form of a communication method discussed in Chapter 11 was the intercept interview (a form of a personal interview). What type of sampling is the intercept interview?

Suggested Probe Response: Due to the judgmental and nonprobabilistic nature of the intercept interview, the intercept interview can be considered a convenience sampling method, a form of nonprobability sampling.

4. What is the nature of the error generated by a nonprobability sampling procedure?

It is of unknown direction and magnitude.

Instructor's Further Probing: If the nature of the error generated by a nonprobability sampling procedure is of an unknown direction and magnitude, then how is it possible to account for this error in the analysis of the results of the survey?

Suggested Probe Response: The key point is that it is not possible to do so.

5. Distinguish among three types of nonprobability sampling procedures.

Convenience sampling involves selecting elements from the population on the basis of the convenience of the researcher, i.e., because they are easily accessible. Unfortunately, it is unclear as to the population from which the actual sample is drawn. The inability to measure sampling error renders inference impossible.

Judgment sampling involves selecting elements on the basis of expert opinion regarding those particular elements' potential contribution to the study at hand. Sampling error is immeasurable in this instance as well.

Quota sampling seeks to obtain a sample that is similar to the population on some prespecified "control" characteristic. To properly select a quota sample, the researcher must know two things: (1) the relevant control characteristics, (age, race, region, income, etc.) and (2) the distribution of these characteristics across the population of interest. The specificity of the control characteristics is limited by the rapidly increasing number of sampling "cells" which result. Also, bias may enter the procedure when the interviewer actually selects respondents.

Instructor's Further Probing: The text shows in figure 13-5 that the majority of businesses seldom use judgment sampling, if at all. Why is this the case?

Suggested Probe Response: Judgment sampling requires an expert with sufficient experience to make decisions regarding the sampling. Recruitment and retention of such an expert each time a sampling needs to be performed can be costly and time consuming. In addition, since the error resulting from the sampling is immeasurable, it is difficult to have a high degree of confidence in the results.

6. Why are nonprobability sampling procedures so often used in practice?

   They tend to be less expensive, faster, easier to administer, and can provide useful information when a large error can be tolerated by management.

   Instructor's Further Probing: Give an example of a situation in which nonprobability sampling would be appropriate--where a large error can be tolerated.

   Suggested Probe Response: If a marketing manager wanted some feedback on how the marketing program was performing (in terms of a favorable/unfavorable determination), a nonprobability sample would be appropriate. The manager only wants a general idea of what areas are doing well and what areas are not doing so well. In addition, the quick turn around time for a nonprobability study here is appropriate, since in order to make decisions about the marketing plan, the manager needs to have feedback quickly.

7. Evaluate each of the samples listed in the Marketing in Action entitled "Business Uses Non-Probability Samples." What potential errors could occur in results from these samples?

   A. Convenience Samples

   Insurance Sales — The potential problem here is response bias. Volunteers are likely to differ from non-volunteers in some way (more enthusiastic, perhaps?) The sample is not representative of all sales agents.

   Soft Drinks — Mall intercept studies suffer from several potential problems. First, the sampling frame (people shopping at a particular mall on a particular day) may not be truly representative of the population in question. Second, those shoppers who agree to participate in a mall intercept study may be different in some way from those who do not. This is an example of response bias. Finally, there may also be some selection bias in that interviewers choose to approach certain shoppers and avoid others. One must wonder if there are any systematic differences between those shoppers who appear more approachable and those who do not.

   B. Judgment Samples

   Irish Spring — Could the residents of test market cities differ from the population on some dimension that researchers have not accounted for? There is a potential for sampling frame error.

   Credit Study — There is some selection bias in this study. Compulsive shoppers who recognize their problem and ask for help are probably different in some way from people with a similar problem who do not try to get help.

C. Quota Samples

Female Heads of Household (FHHs) — A great deal of marketing research is done on this group, because in many product categories (e.g. groceries and household cleaning products). FHHs make the vast majority of all purchases. However, research on FHHs provides no insight about the purchase behavior of other groups (e.g. single men, students).

Air Travelers — Groups are based on three variables with multiple levels: nationality (at least 2 levels, but probably more), number of miles flown annually (multiple levels, most likely 3 or more), and sex (2 levels). This could lead to a complicated sampling plan with a minimum of 2x3x2 = 12 cells.

Instructor's Further Probing: Considering the potential for problems and error in the above examples, are these sampling studies useful for making marketing decisions?

Suggested Probe Response: A key goal in marketing research is to reduce the amount of uncertainty in a decision situation. While the above sampling methods have the potential for complexity and error, they do reduce the amount of uncertainty for the decision maker to some degree. Thus, the sampling procedures are useful.

8. Is it appropriate for the Census Bureau to agree to adjust the Census count on the basis of sample results? What are the pros and cons?

It is appropriate for the Census Bureau to make some adjustment to figures that everyone agrees are understated. However, care must be taken in designing the new sampling procedure and making the adjustments in a statistically valid way. The new sample should be fairly representative of the census population. A small sample of New York City, for example, is probably representative of that city as a whole but not the country as a whole. As long as the sampling plan is carefully designed so that a representative sample of the censused population is obtained, the adjustment process will result in a more accurate and fair representation of the nation's homeless and impoverished population.

Instructor's Further Probing: Should the Census Bureau simply replace the process of taking a census with a well-defined series of samples of the population?

Suggested Probe Response: Sampling is meant to provide a snapshot of an aspect of a segment, which then can be interpolated and generalized for the entire population. The error resulting from performing a sample alone can be quite high, depending on the nature of the sample. The Census Bureau needs to perform a census, since its goal is to exhaust all possible elements in the population.

9. GM does some evaluations of car designs and advertising themes using focus groups. These groups consist of from eight to ten potential customers that match the target segment for the car being evaluated. The focus group interviewees are selected by a research firm for GM by telephone solicitation of people who are qualified as matching the required target profile by a series of questions asked over the phone. The phone directories are used to identify individuals to call from geographic areas where cars like the one being evaluated have historically sold well.

a. What sample procedure is being used?

Judgment sampling, with the phone book as a sampling frame.

b. Evaluate the sampling procedure used.

Screening procedure — Subjects will match the target segment on attributes questioned, but not necessarily on other variables. As long as researcher's assumptions about variables important to automobile purchase decision are correct, this is acceptable.

Sampling frame — Higher income people with unlisted numbers and lower income people without telephones are underrepresented in the phone book. As long as these people are not part of the target segment, this is acceptable.

Geographical issues — Researching consumers in regions where GM cars have traditionally sold well does not allow the firm to obtain any information about selling in new regions.

c. What inferences to the whole target segment population can be drawn from this sampling approach?

This procedure is acceptable for obtaining feedback on automobile design and advertising from a group of consumers defined by specific variables and residing in a particular geographic area. However, one should question how applicable this group's opinions are to other demographic or geographic segments.

d. What biases may exist due to the sample selection method?

Some key biases include: people willing to participate in a focus group may differ from those who would chose not to; phone directories inherently contain errors and are not accurate to the day the participants are recruited; the area being surveyed is a historically good market for GM cars, making the opinions of poor geographic regions underrepresented.

Instructor's Further Probing: If there is a potentially large error resulting from this sample, how can this information be useful for GM?

Suggested Probe Response: GM managers may be willing to accept a large margin of error to obtain a general guideline to either base future studies on or in making adjustments on current marketing practices. In either case, an entire marketing plan is not being based on these samples, only a few changes are.

10. Kraft Foods does some mall-intercept interviewing to evaluate new food product offerings. These samples are typically done in only a few malls for any one test. Subjects are recruited as they pass by particular locations in the mall, on the basis of appearing to match certain demographic characteristics: age, sex, etc.

    a) What sampling procedure is being used?

    The procedure being used is quota sampling based on demographic characteristics. The sampling frame is the group of people shopping at the malls where the study is conducted.

b) Evaluate the sampling procedure being used.

While the sampling procedure may result in a sample that mirrors the target population in desired demographic characteristics, it would not be acceptable to a statistical purist. The sample consists of the first people matching the desired demographic characteristics who are approached by field research personnel and who agree to participate in the study. Inherent in this procedure are selection bias (the researcher may perceive some potential subjects as being more approachable than others; hence they are not randomly selected) and response bias (subjects who decline the offer to participate may be different from those who do not.) Also, because the test is conducted in "only a few malls," a truly random sample of the population cannot be obtained.

c) What inferences to the broader population can be drawn?

Researchers make inferences about product preferences and advertising effectiveness, among other things. An example might help illustrate the point. A laundry detergent manufacturer wanted to test which of two fragrances consumers preferred for their brand. They sampled adult women via mall intercept and had them smell two variants of the detergent. A mean score was calculated and a winning fragrance chosen. It was inferred that the majority of American women would agree with the fragrance preference of women sampled in the mall study, and researchers recommended that fragrance to the brand manager.

d) Why has mall-intercept sampling become so widely used in practice?

While mall intercept research may not have the statistical validity that a mathematician would like, it is widely used in practice for several reasons. First, it is relatively low cost and provides very useful information. Second, while the test situation may raise questions about external validity, researchers often know from experience how test results translate into "real world" consumer behavior. For example, they can make adjustments to figures for stated purchase intent that provide accurate predictions of actual trial rates.

e) What biases may exist due to the sample selection method?

Some key biases that exist include: people willing to stop and take the survey differ from those who decline to participate; the judgment of the interviewer biases results; the type of people who shop in a mall are usually within a certain range of economic levels, and the interviewer himself may influence the participants through word choice or approach.

Instructor's Further Probing: Why is it possible that opinions of Kraft products may be solicited in an intercept interview, but the same method would most likely be inappropriate for GM trying to solicit feedback about its cars?

Suggested Probe Response: Due to the diverse nature of the two types of products being surveyed, the intercept interview may not be right for both of them. GM's products cost a substantial amount of money (as compared to Kraft), requiring specific people in their sampling trials. Kraft products on the other hand are more accessible to the general public, making them a good candidate for intercept interviews.

11. *MINICASE:* Xyco Semiconductor supplies computer chips to the aerospace, automobile, major appliance and consumer electronics. Xyco sells to different sizes of companies in each of these industries and to companies in all regions of the world. Historically, Xyco's management has noted sales differences by industry type, size, and geographic region. Xyco desires to select a quota sample to predict the sales level of a new product offering.

   a) What control characteristics should be used for this quota sample?

   Industry type, size, and geographic region.

   b) What would one need to know about these control characteristics for them to be useful in this study?

   The distribution of control characteristics across the population.

   c) Explain how many respondents would be specified for each cell.

   $$\text{Cell Sample Size} = \begin{pmatrix} \text{total} \\ \text{sample} \\ \text{size} \end{pmatrix} * \begin{pmatrix} \text{proportion} \\ \text{in each} \\ \text{cell} \end{pmatrix}$$

   d) What inferences could be drawn to Xyco's whole customer base from such a sample?

   They could predict new product sales for various segments as defined by industry, size, and geographic region. However, the size and direction of the sampling error present is unknown.

CHAPTER 14 — SIMPLE RANDOM SAMPLING AND SAMPLE SIZE

1. What is the difference (if any) between a parameter and a statistic?

   A parameter is a summary description of a measure in the defined population, while a statistic is a summary description of a measure in the selected sample.

   Instructor's Further Probing: Since it is unrealistic to presume that a researcher would know the standard deviation (σ) in a survey, would he/she use statistical values or parameters in the calculations?

   Suggested Probe Response: The researcher would use parameters in the calculations, which are more technically correct than statistical values.

2. Identify the symbols which denote common parameters and statistics of both continuous and dichotomous variables.

		Population	Sample
Continuous	1) mean	μ	$\bar{X}$
	2) variance	σ^2	s^2
Dichotomous	1) proportion answering yes	π	p
	2) proportion answering no	$(1-\pi)$	$(1-p)$ or q
	3) variance of proportion	σ^2	s^2

   Instructor's Further Probing: How are population and sample related?

   Suggested Probe Response: A population is the entire universe of all the possible elements. A sample is a subset of a given population.

3. Define the mean and variance in words and mathematical notation for both a population and a sample, first treating the variable as continuous and then dichotomous.

   Continuous Variable

   1) Population:

      The mean is a measure of central tendency derived by summing the values and dividing the number in the population.

      $$\mu = \frac{\sum_{i=1}^{N} X_i}{N}$$

The variance is a measure of the dispersion of a distribution of values obtained by dividing the sum of the squared deviations about the mean by the number in the population.

$$\sigma^2 = \frac{\sum_{i=1}^{N}(X_i - \mu)^2}{N}$$

2) Sample:

The mean is obtained by dividing the sum of the values in the sample by the number in the sample.

$$\overline{X} = \frac{\sum_{i=1}^{n} X_i}{n}$$

The variance is obtained by dividing the sum of the squared deviations about the sample mean by the number of degrees of freedom in the sample.

$$s^2 = \frac{\sum_{i=1}^{n}(X_i - \overline{X})^2}{n}$$

Dichotomous

1) Population:

The mean is obtained by dividing the number of affirmative answers by the total number in the population.

$$\pi = \frac{\sum_{i=1}^{N} X_i}{N}$$

The variance is obtained by multiplying the mean of the population times one minus the mean.

$$\sigma^2 = \pi(1-\pi)$$

2) Sample:

The mean is the sum of the affirmative responses divided by the number in the sample.

$$p = \frac{\sum_{i=1}^{N} X_i}{n}$$

The variance is the sample mean times one minus the sample mean, multiplied by an adjustment factor for degrees of freedom.

$$s^2 = p(1-p)\left(\frac{n}{n-1}\right)$$

Instructor's Further Probing: What does an increasing value of standard deviation signify (i.e., 1σ, 2σ, 3σ)?

Suggested Probe Response: The higher the deviation, the more elements in the sample that are guaranteed to be within that deviation. Thus nearly all the elements will be contained within 3σ.

4. Why is the Central Limit Theorem critical to measuring sampling error?

The Central Limit Theorem allows the researcher to know: 1) that the one sample mean he or she has calculated comes from a sampling distribution of means that is the shape of a normal curve; and 2) the size of the standard deviation of the sampling distribution. Also, since we know the area under a normal curve as measured in standard deviations from the mean, we can measure sampling error.

Instructor's Further Probing: What is the relationship between the size of the samples (n) and the sampling error, according to the Central Limit Theorem?

Suggested Probe Response: Based on the Central Limit Theorem, we can conclude that as n grows, the sampling distribution curve becomes more and more normal (bell shaped) and thus decreases the standard deviation.

5. What is a confidence interval?

A confidence interval is an interval about a statistic calculated from a sample drawn from a specific population, corresponding to a specific level of confidence and computed for a given sample size. For a given level of confidence (say .95), we state that the confidence intervals constructed in 95 out of 100 random samples would contain the true population parameter.

Instructor's Further Probing: How does the confidence interval relate to the size of the sample population?

Suggested Probe Response: Based on an acceptable level of confidence that the researchers choose, the sample population needed to achieve that confidence level is then determined.

6. What affects the size of a confidence interval?

1) The sample size is related inversely to the size of the confidence interval.
2) The standard deviation of the variable of interest is related directly to the size of the confidence interval.
3) The level of confidence selected is related directly to the size of the confidence interval.

Instructor's Further Probing: The confidence interval, theoretically, is based on the knowledge of the standard deviation (σ). The knowledge of the σ in an actual study is unrealistic. What then is used to account for the unknown σ, in an actual study?

Suggested Probe Response: The t-distribution (aka the Student's t-distribution) is one distribution, for example, used to account for the fact that the σ may not exactly be known.

7. What are the desirable properties of estimators?

   1) Unbiased--the expected value of the statistic equals the parameter.
   2) Consistent--as sample size increases, the statistic converges on the parameter.
   3) Efficient--the distribution of the statistic about the parameter has a smaller variance than that of any other estimator.

Instructor's Further Probing: What is the *most efficient estimator*?

Suggested Probe Response: The *most efficient estimator* is the term used to describe an estimator that provides the minimum variance and thus the maximum standard error for any given sample size.

8. To what extent do confidence intervals increase our certainty with regard to making inferences?

   Confidence intervals are based on a measure of sampling error only. If nonsampling errors are present, a bias of unknown degree and magnitude is introduced, rendering inference somewhat less than accurate.

Instructor's Further Probing: In what practical business situations would a confidence interval be useful? When would a confidence interval be inadequate?

Suggested Probe Response: For management of a manufacturing company, an interval would give management an idea to help forecast demand and production schedules, thus assessing the risk involved in producing a certain amount of goods. Based on this information, the management can decide upon a manufacturing quota and order the manufacturing plant to produce that many items. However, consider that in a manufacturing facility, the plant manager can not be told to produce somewhere between 5,000 and 10,000 items a week. The manager needs to be told an exact figure, thus configuring the line and people to produce that amount.

9. Most political pollsters judged the 1980 Presidential election to be too close to call. Explain how this could happen.

The confidence interval about either candidate being elected overlapped 50 percent. Also, there were a great many undecided voters. It was not clear how to distribute their vote.

Instructor's Further Probing: What is one possible way to account for the undecided voters?

Suggested Probe Response: A separate sampling of the undecided voters with some type of graphic rating scale would measure how much people lean towards one candidate or another. Based on these results, the undecided voters could then be accounted for and an overall predicted winner could be made.

10. What problems are likely to occur in implementing a field study using simple random sampling?

    1) Getting a complete list of sampling elements to select from.
    2) Jumping all over that list in terms of the specific elements selected by random number.
    3) Noncontrol of other variables that might be affecting the values of the elements selected.

    Note that this question is really a lead-in to the approaches to sampling presented in the next chapter.

Instructor's Further Probing: Is simple random sampling free of sampling bias? Why or why not?

Suggested Probe Response: Yes, simple random sampling is free of sampling bias since each sample has an equal chance of being selected. However, in practical situations, such as in the field, the probability of an element being selected may change due to the above stated reasons.

11. Why do some researchers calculate confidence intervals from data generated from nonprobability samples?

    1) They do not understand that it should not be done; or
    2) They believe that it makes results appear more scientific and therefore appear more valid.

Instructor's Further Probing: How should confidence intervals be determined properly?

Suggested Probe Response: The marketing researcher must use probability sampling methods.

12. Since nonprobability samples do not yield a measure of sampling error, why are the procedures so extensively used in commercial and academic practice?

    Time and cost constraints, in addition to the fact that certain decisions can tolerate large errors.

Instructor's Further Probing: Why would institutions use a nonmeasurable method of research, even if it allows for cheaper and quicker studies?

Suggested Probe Response: Many forms of research are intended to give the decision maker an estimate of a situation and to reduce the uncertainty of a situation to a degree. Not all nonprobability samples will lead to major marketing decisions.

13. What is absolute precision? What is relative precision?

    Absolute precision is expressed in terms of units. Relative precision is expressed in terms of percentages of the mean value.

Instructor's Further Probing: What is the purpose in defining how accurate (accuracy is a two-dimensional term consisting of reliability and precision) a sample needs to be?

Suggested Probe Response: By defining the desired level of accuracy, the sample size and the associated resources needed can be determined.

14. What information is necessary in order to calculate a statistically optimal sample size for (1) a continuous variable, and (2) a dichotomous variable?

    For a continuous variable:

    1) confidence level
    2) precision required
    3) coefficient of variation (s/$\overline{X}$)

    For a dichotomous variable:

    1) confidence level
    2) precision required
    3) p

Instructor's Further Probing: What is the key difference between continuous variables and dichotomous variables?

Suggested Probe Response: Basically, continuous variables measure a continuum of possibilities, and dichotomous variables measure specific discrete values.

15. What factors should one consider in determining the sample size for a study?

    1) Study objectives.
    2) Cost involved.
    3) Time requirements.
    4) Type of data analysis planned.
    5) Existence of nonsampling errors.
    6) Statistically optimal sample size.

Instructor's Further Probing: How is the size of the sample selected related to the population from which the sample is drawn?

Suggested Probe Response: The size of the sample study is affected by the variability of the population the sample was selected from. An example of variability is that students generally have low incomes and thus the variability in the student income population is very low. Whereas doctors on the other hand have a large variability of earnings based on specialty, location, etc... The variability of a population is summarized by the population's standard deviation. and therefore must be estimated before conducting the sampling survey.

16. The membership director of a national fraternity wanted to do an attitude study of the fraternity's 2500 currently active members and the 12,000 alumni.

   a) What sampling frame(s) would likely be available for this purpose?

   Fairly accurate lists of current members and alumni would likely be available at the fraternity's national headquarters.

   b) Explain how you would select a simple random sample of current and alumni members.

   Code each member on the list with a number (1 through 14,500). To randomize selection, choose numbers in the order indicated by the random number list.

   c) Most of the questions were to be on a seven point rating scale. For a sample size of 200 members, what is the 95% confidence interval for a rating scale result where the mean answer is 2.4 and the standard deviation is 1.1?

   Given $\overline{X} = 2.4$, n = 200, and s = 1.1. We want to find the numerical range for the 95% confidence interval around x. To do so we use the formula for confidence interval. It is:

   95% confidence interval: $= x \pm 2(s/\sqrt{n})$

   Plug the given numbers into the formulas and solve for unknowns.

   95% CI $= x \pm 2(s/\sqrt{n}) = 2.4 \pm 2(2.4/200) = 2.4 \pm .34 = 2.06$ to 2.74

   d) One question dealt with the proportion of alumni members who attend local chapter meetings. Historically, this proportion has been about 20 percent. The membership director reasoned that an error of ± 5 percent was acceptable for making this estimate. What is the sample size that will yield this quality of estimate at the 95 percent confidence level?

   Given p = .2, CI = 95% and precision is ± .05. To solve this problem, use the formula for precision for dichotomous variables. It is:

   precision $= \pm 2 \sqrt{\dfrac{pq}{n}}$

We can plug in the numbers we have and solve for the unknown variable n.

$$.05 = 2\sqrt{\frac{.2 \times .8}{n}}$$

$$.05\sqrt{n} = 2\sqrt{.16}$$

squaring both sides, we get

$$.0025n = 4 \times .16$$
$$.0025n = .64$$
$$n = 256$$

Instructor's Further Probing: What possible biases lie in this sample in the field?

Suggested Probe Response: Some possible biases that may result in the field include locating up-to-date older alumni and realizing the bias created if active members and nonactive members are treated the same (active members will inherently be more positive or negative than nonactive members due to their proximity to the organization).

17. *MINICASE:* The coffee institute wanted to estimate the number of cups of coffee consumed per day by residents of California. The coefficient of variation on previous studies of this type had been .31. Management wanted a precision of ± 5 percent of the mean, and was willing to use the 95 percent level of confidence.

   a) What is an appropriate sample size?

   There are two ways of finding the appropriate sample size. One is more difficult but more accurate. First the more accurate method:

   To find the appropriate sample size, we need to do a little bit of algebra. Using the formulas for precision and coefficient of variation, we can solve for sample size.

   precision = $\pm 2 s/\sqrt{n}$ = 5% of mean = .05 $\overline{X}$
   coefficient of variation = $s\,\overline{X}$ .31
   We can combine the two equations in the following way:
   $s/\overline{X} = .31$ so $\overline{X} = s/.31$
   Canceling out the s
   $2/\sqrt{n} = .05/.31$
   Cross multiplying
   $.62 = .05\sqrt{n}$
   Then squaring both sides to get rid of the radical
   $.3844 = .0025n$
   Dividing both sides by .0025 to solve for n
   $154 = n$

The easy method is this: Look at the Figure 13-4. It provides an approximate sample size needed for a given precision (relative allowable error), confidence level and coefficient of variation.

b) If management changed the required precision to ± 2 percent of the mean, and a better estimate of the coefficient of variation was deemed to be .4, what would the appropriate sample size be?

precision = $\pm 2 s/\sqrt{n}$ = 2% of mean = .02 X

coefficient of variation = $s/\overline{X}$ = .4

We can combine the two equations in the following way:

$s/\overline{x}$ = .4 so $\overline{X}$ = s/.4

Then, substituting this for $\overline{X}$ in the precision formula, we get

$2 s/\sqrt{n}$ = .02 s/.4

Canceling out the s

$2/\sqrt{n}$ = .02/.4

Cross multiplying

.8 = .02 $\sqrt{n}$

Then squaring both sides to get rid of the radical

.64 = .0004n

Dividing both sides by .0025 to solve for n

1600 = n

Thus, we can see that increasing precision (decreasing the percent deviation) and increasing the coefficient of variation, we need a much larger sample to generate a result at the 95% confidence level.

Instructor's Further Probing: What possible biases lie in this sample in the field?

Suggested Probe Response: Some possible biases that may result in the field include the time period the survey is taken (the weather tends to stimulate or discourage coffee drinking) and certain areas, such as college campuses, have a greater consumption of coffee than other urbanized areas.

CHAPTER 15 — MORE COMPLEX SAMPLING PROCEDURES

1. How is a stratified sample selected?

    Stratified sampling is a two-stage process. First, the defined population is divided into mutually exclusive and collectively exhaustive subgroups or strata using some stratification variable such as sex. Then, an independent simple random sample is drawn from each stratum.

Instructor's Further Probing: Must the stratification be applied always before the sample is taken?

Suggested Probe Response: No, the stratification can be applied after data has been taken; however, due to the control available in the planning and organization of the stratification before the sample is taken, applying stratification before taking the sample is the preferred method.

2. What is the objective of stratified sampling?

    Stratified sampling may yield smaller standard errors of estimators than does simple random sampling. Hence, precision can be gained with no increase in sample size, or equivalently, the same level of precision may be obtained with a smaller sample size.

Instructor's Further Probing: What is necessary for stratification to be effective in the minimization of error?

Suggested Probe Response: In order for stratification to be effective, the strata must correlate highly with the characteristic(s) being estimated. In addition, the means and variance must differ widely by strata for stratification to be effective.

3. What is proportionate stratified sampling?

    Proportionate stratified sampling involves selecting sample elements from each stratum such that the ratio of (1), the number of sample elements drawn from stratum j to the total sample size, is equal to the ratio of (2), the number of population elements within stratum j to the total number of population elements. In the notation of Chapter 9:

$$\frac{n_j}{n} = \frac{N_j}{N}$$

Instructor's Further Probing: What is the purpose of using a proportion for stratified sampling?

Suggested Probe Response: The nature of some experiments requires only relative comparisons be made (proportions) and absolute numbers may not be able to be specified or may not even be desired.

4. What is disproportionate stratified sampling?

    Here $$\frac{n_j}{n} \neq \frac{N_j}{N}$$

    Strata are either under- or over-sampled relative to their population size.

    Instructor's Further Probing: How does variability relate to disproportionate stratified sampling?

    Suggested Probe Response: When strata have differing variability among each other, then the sample sizes required varies from strata to strata, resulting in a disproportionate stratified sampling. The greater the variability, the larger the sample size needed. Likewise, the smaller the variability, the smaller the sample size needed.

5. How are the whole sample mean and standard error calculated from a stratified sample?

    The overall sample mean is simply a weighted average of the stratum means.

    $$\overline{X} = \sum_{j=1}^{A} \left(\frac{N_j}{N}\right) \overline{X}_j = \sum_{j=1}^{A} w_j \overline{X}_j$$

    The standard error is the square root of the weighted combination of the square of the standard error within each stratum

    $$s_{\overline{X}} = \sqrt{s_{\overline{X}}^2}$$

    where

    $$s_{\overline{X}}^2 = \sum_{j=1}^{A} \left(\frac{N_j}{N}\right)^2 s_{\overline{X}_j}^2 = \sum_{j=1}^{A} w_j^2 s_{\overline{X}_j}^2$$

    Instructor's Further Probing: How are strata values represented in calculations involving stratification?

    Suggested Probe Response: Generally, the "ST" subscript is used to denote a strata and a decimal point and a number follow the "ST" signifying which strata that value corresponds to.

6. Under what circumstances does stratified sampling reduce the standard error?

    Variables which are highly correlated with measure of interest are candidates for stratification variables. Such variables yield strata which are relatively homogeneous within, and thus reduce the standard error.

Instructor's Further Probing: If we wished to obtain the same results with an unstratified sample as we could get with a stratified sample, what modifications would be needed to be made to the unstratified sample to obtain the same precision?

Suggested Probe Response: The unstratified sample would need to be a smaller sample.

7. Why does stratified sampling reduce the standard error?

   Only within strata variability is used to calculate the standard error, and these variabilities are smaller than overall variability. This is because certain outlier means on the sampling distribution of the means are not possible.

Instructor's Further Probing: Give some examples of various types of stratifying characteristics a marketing research study may use to setup a stratification sample study.

Suggested Probe Response: Some examples of stratifying characteristics include type, model, sex, age, occupation, and geographical location such, as state.

8. What is cluster sampling?

   Sampling in which clusters or groups of elements are sampled at the same time is called cluster sampling.

Instructor's Further Probing: Give some examples of cluster units.

Suggested Probe Response: Some examples of cluster units include households relative to individual members, a school relative to students, and a shipping container of a product relative to each individual product.

9. What are statistical efficiency and overall efficiency?

   Overall efficiency (or total efficiency) is a measure of both the statistical efficiency and the cost of a sampling procedure. It is the size of standard error per dollar. Statistical efficiency relates to the size of the standard error for a given sample size.

Instructor's Further Probing: How does cluster sampling relate to other sampling procedures in terms of overall efficiency?

Suggested Probe Response: Cluster sampling is often the most overall efficient procedure.

10. How is a systematic sample selected?

    The researcher selects every kth element in the frame after a random start somewhere in the first k elements where k = N/n.

Instructor's Further Probing: What is the one-stage cluster sampling procedure?

Suggested Probe Response: When all the elements in the cluster generated by systematic sampling are used, it is called a one-stage cluster sampling procedure.

11. What is periodicity? How is it caused and cured?

   Periodicity occurs when the list of elements forming the frame forms a cyclical pattern that coincides with a multiple of the size of the sampling interval.

   It is caused by having a frame that has a specific cycle in it. It is cured by reordering the frame.

   Instructor's Further Probing: What does it mean to reorder the frame?

   Suggested Probe Response: Reordering the frame entails rearranging the sampling elements in a different order so as to avoid the periodicity.

12. How does implicit stratification occur?

   If the frame is ordered on what might be used as a stratification variable, then selection of a systematic sample will automatically provide a stratified sample.

   Instructor's Further Probing: Why is implicit stratification advantageous to the researcher?

   Suggested Probe Response: Since ordered frames do occur in systematic sampling, it is very easy and convenient if the ordered frame is ordered on what is used as a stratification sample. In this manner, no extra work is required to stratify the sample.

13. What is area sampling?

   An area sample is a type of cluster sample in which pieces of geography are selected.

   Instructor's Further Probing: Why do researchers use area samples?

   Suggested Probe Response: Since accurate listing of residents and their buying patterns and other data are not available, it is important to survey a geographic region. However, since the researchers can not survey all the area under research, a sample (an area sample) must be taken.

14. What is a multistage area sample?

   Here the process of listing sampling units and random selection from this list occurs a number of times. The number of times this listing and selecting occurs equals the number of stages in the sampling process.

   Instructor's Further Probing: Discuss the potential of error in multistage area sampling.

   Suggested Probe Response: Multiarea sampling is much less statistically efficient than simple random sampling. A n-stage multistage sampling is subject to n sampling errors. In addition, the standard error for this type of sampling is quite complex to compute.

15. How do you get equal probability of element selection using a multistage area sampling procedure?

1) Equal chance selection of sampling units at each stage of the process no matter how big the clusters are relative to each other.

2) Select the first stage clusters by probability proportionate to their size (PPS), and select the same number of sampling units from each selected first stage cluster. For stages beyond the second, select by equal chance methods.

Instructor's Further Probing: What is a common application of the PPS technique?

Suggested Probe Response: As the text suggests, the use of marketing research involving geographic regions is commonly used.

16. Why does one sometimes get unequal probabilities of element selection?

    1) The researcher wants to do detailed subgroup analysis and so purposely over-samples this group.
    2) One is doing disproportionate stratified sampling.
    3) A sample yields a smaller proportion of a particular subgroup than the population proportion.
    4) In a PPS design, the expected cluster sizes were not as realized.

Instructor's Further Probing: Can unequal probabilities of element selection hinder a researcher's efforts in obtaining as accurate as possible data?

Suggested Probe Response: Unequal probabilities present no problems as long as the researcher is interested in doing only within-subgroup analysis.

17. How are whole-sample estimates made when elements have unequal selection probabilities?

    Elements are assigned a weighting factor in proportion to the inverse of its probability of being selected.

Instructor's Further Probing: Demonstrate how this weighting factor is calculated.

Suggested Probe Response: We take the probability of selection, then take the mathematical inverse and multiply that number by the subgroups values. Then we take the sum of the subgroup values and we arrive at the weighted sample size.

18. Outline the steps in random-digit dialing.

    1) Use area sampling procedures down as far as the city or town of interest.
    2) Obtain telephone directories for the selected cities or towns and systematically select a sample of telephone numbers from the directories.
    3) Replace the last one or two digits of these selected numbers with random numbers.
    4) Call the resultant numbers.

Instructor's Further Probing: What are some drawbacks to the random-digit dialing procedure?

Suggested Probe Response: Some possible drawbacks include: reaching the same household due to multiple lines and the chance of reaching computer, faxes, or other electronic communication devices instead of a voice line.

For questions 19-21 prepare a sampling design. Be sure your design includes a description of each of the following and a statement of your reasoning:

a) Population

b) Sampling Frame

c) Sample Size

d) Sampling Procedure (Include a step-by-step description of how the sample will actually be drawn.)

e) Method for determining the accuracy of sample results.

Note that for part c), students should address some of the qualitative issues that come into play in determining the accuracy of sample results.

19. Frank Johnson was the director of student services in the business school of a major university. He wanted to conduct a survey of both BBA and MBA students to determine their attitudes toward course offerings, counseling services, and job opportunities. There were a total of 3000 BBA students and 700 MBA students in the business school. Since a census was not possible, Frank needed to develop a sampling design.

   a) **Population**

   The major issue related to population definition is whether or not BBAs and MBAs are to be considered two different populations. The argument for treating them as separate is that they may hold very different attitudes about courses, counseling, and jobs. They are in different programs with different courses, opportunities, etc. Combining their attitudes may just form a mid-point between two distinct attitude segments.

   The argument for treating the two as one population is that the interest may be in overall attitude. To us this seems like a weaker argument. Two populations seems a better way to proceed.

   The populations could be:

   I. A. Elements--BBA students
       B. Sampling units--BBA students
       C. Extent--the school in question
       D. Time--the current term

   II. A. Elements--MBA students
       B. Sampling units--MBA students
       C. Extent--the school in question
       D. Time--the current term.

Of course it is possible to combine the two populations and just treat BBAs and MBAs as two subgroups or strata. As long as different subgroup results are not combined to give whole sample estimates, this is a proper way to think about it.

b) **Sampling Frame**

A ready-made frame for both populations is most likely available here. They are the list of registered: 1) BBA students, and 2) MBA students.

c) **Sample Size**

The sample size question is one that is hard to be definitive about. However, students must be prepared to give one, and defend it. In doing so, they should discuss: 1) sampling error, 2) nonsampling error, 3) study objectives, 4) time constraints, 5) cost constraints and 6) data analysis plans. All of these aspects are not laid out in the exercise. However, they should state their assumptions and be clear about certain aspects, specifically: time and cost constraints are likely severe, and data analysis will likely be of the simple one-way kind (i.e., the reporting of mean attitude scores).

One might examine the question of sample size from a statistical point of view. Suppose one designated: 1) absolute precision of $\pm .25$ (assuming we will be using a 7-point rating scale which is assumed to provide interval data), 2) at 95% level of confidence, and 3) standard deviation, s, is .75.

Then we solve the following equation for n, the required sample size.

$$.25 = 2 \frac{(.75)}{\sqrt{n}}$$

$$.25 = \frac{1.50}{\sqrt{n}}$$

$$.25 \sqrt{n} = 1.50$$

$$\sqrt{n} = 1.50/.25$$

$$\sqrt{n} = 6$$

$$n = 36$$

Students using this type of procedure should recognize that they had to specify a precision and a confidence level plus assume an "s" value. Also, cost and other factors must be discussed along with the fact that n = 36 would not allow for crosstabular analysis, if any were desired.

d) **Sampling Procedure**

Simple random sampling is possible here given the existence of student lists. However, this procedure is inefficient in terms of work effort. The person selecting the elements would be jumping all over the list as random numbers were selected. A better procedure here would be to select a systematic sample, since there is no reason to expect a problem with periodicity in the list. Also, if a combined sample analysis (both

BBAs and MBAs) is desired, a systematic sample would yield a proportionate stratified sample, since there is no reason to expect a problem with periodicity in the list.

e) **Accuracy**

The only measure of accuracy available is that of size of sampling error. Sampling error could be measured using the confidence interval formula:

$$\overline{X} \pm 2 \frac{s}{\sqrt{n}}$$ for the 95% confidence interval.

In the flow of the class, some students may suggest the use of a nonprobability sampling procedure, usually a quota sample. It should be made clear that this makes little sense given the ease with which one can select a probability sample here, and the problem of error measurement with a quota sample.

20. Sara Ranski is a consultant to the World Church Council. One information need of the Council is to develop a demographic profile of church members in the U.S. Ranski has been asked to develop a sampling design to facilitate the collection of this information.

a) **Population**

One possible population definition is as follows:

- A. Elements--adults on church rosters
- B. Sampling units--regions of the county; cities and towns; sections of cities and towns; churches; adults on church rosters
- C. Extent--the continental U.S.A.
- D. Time--some specified period.

Questions would be raised about the definition of elements. Adults on church rosters do not necessarily attend church and therefore one may not want to include them. However, how does one obtain a list of those who really attend? This would add a stage in the sampling procedure where one would have to qualify those on church rosters as attendees and then select.

The specific sampling units could also vary. The instructor should be open to other reasonable sequences.

b) **Sampling Frame**

At each stage of the multistage sample a list of the available sampling units must be obtained. Thus, a list of regions must be obtained, then a list of cities and towns in the selected regions, then sections of the selected cities and towns, then churches within these selected sections, and finally, adults on the rosters of the selected churches.

c) **Sample Size**

The factors to consider on sample size are again: (1) sampling error, (2) nonsampling error, (3) study objective, (4) time constraints, (5) cost constraints, and (6) data analysis plan. Some of these points are ambiguous in the situation and thus student assumptions should be made clear.

There are two points that should be made. First, statistical formulas presented in the text do not help, as none were presented for a multistage problem. In theory, one could derive the standard error for this sampling process and solve for sample size. The precision and confidence interval levels, expected mean and standard deviations on the attitude scales would have to be designated.

Second, the data analysis here will likely not be just simple univariate analysis. Crosstabulations among demographics and such things as denomination, region of the country, etc. are likely. Thus, the sample size will have to be large enough to accommodate this process, say 400-500 people. If detailed denomination differences are of interest, then the sample size will have to be even larger.

d) **Sampling Procedure**

Clearly, based upon the discussion so far, this problem lends itself to a multistage area sampling procedure. The repeating cycle of listing sampling units and selecting them using a probability procedure will continue through as many stages as necessary. The time and cost of developing a complete list of population elements renders a nonmultistage procedure to be impossible.

Some students may argue for a nonprobability sample due to cost considerations. The cost of obtaining the required lists could be quite high in this situation. The loss of understanding of sampling error is, of course, important and should be discussed. A good argument could be made here for a carefully done quota sample controlling on denomination and region of the country. The big advantage would be in cost. Students suggesting a multistage area sample should be prepared to state how they are going to assure themselves of equal probability of element selection. Selecting an equal proportion of available sampling units at each stage may exclude some large regions or cities deemed to be important in terms of religious profile. Thus, an argument can be made for using probability proportionate to size (PPS) at stage one of selection.

e) **Accuracy**

A confidence interval could be calculated on the demographic measures if a probability sampling procedure is used. To do so one would have to use the relevant formulas available in more advanced sampling books. Also, crosstabular chi-square analysis would be possible to test for significant associations among variables. Neither procedure would be available if a nonprobability procedure was used.

21. Roy Lena was the product manager for a new brand of cereal, named Multi-Vit, that was currently under development by a major package goods company located in New York City. The product offered vitamins and other nutrients not available in other cereals. Lena was in the process of designing an in-home usage test for the product. The object of the test was to measure the reaction of adults to the product's taste. Results of this test would be used to further refine the product before submitting it to additional in-home and market tests. The problem facing Lena was to design the sample for the in-home placement test.

a) **Population**

A local or regional population near the company's offices will likely be fine here, as there is no reason to believe that reactions to taste will vary by region. Therefore, a population definition could be:

  A. Elements--ready-to-eat cereal users
  B. Sampling units--households, ready-to-eat cereal users
  C. Extent--metropolitan Minneapolis
  D. Time--some specific period.

b) **Sampling Frame**

A directory of households in metropolitan Minneapolis would form the frame at the first stage, then households would be qualified as to whether or not a ready-to-eat cereal user is present to form the second stage frame.

c) **Sample Size**

Given the objective of the study, a very small sample size would be used, say 50-150 people. They are just trying out the product, not predicting market share.

d) **Sampling Procedure**

Everything presented thus far argues for a two-stage convenience sample. We would contact households, determine if a ready-to-eat cereal user is present and attempt to solicit cooperation. One would make the argument that a quota sample controlling on target audience demographics (unspecified in the exercise) would be better. To do this the household would be questioned on these dimensions before cooperation is asked for.

There seems little need for complex probability sampling procedures here, given cost and benefit tradeoffs.

e) **Accuracy**

Given the procedures suggested, accuracy cannot be determined.

22. For the STP/Lou Harris Marketing Research in Action, answer the following questions:

 a) What sampling units were defined by this procedure? What was the sampling frame?

  Sampling units were U.S. residents (not including AK and HI residents, prison inmates, students and clergy), states, regions and metropolitan areas, counties, minor civil divisions/towns/cities, and phone numbers. Sampling frames were lists of each unit type.

b) Why was stratification used?

Stratifying the U.S. on a geographic basis enabled them to be sure to take a geographically representative sample of the U.S. population, and to correlate differences among consumers with geographic/demographic information contained in the Census.

c) What purpose was there in selecting cities or towns with probability proportionate to census estimates of their respective household populations? How could this be accomplished?

The purpose was to obtain a sample of people representative of the census population, by giving larger metropolitan areas a higher probability of being selected. The procedure for selecting a PPS sample is clearly presented in the text.

d) What alternative sampling procedures could be used here?

For this type of research, quota, and even convenience sampling are commonly used. They are less costly than the Harris/STP procedure.

23. For the AT&T Marketing Research in Action at the beginning of this chapter, answer the following questions:

a) Why was the sample selected from a stratified population?

To control for any impact on sales forecasts of effects due to market segment and exposure to varying levels for price, promotion and distribution. This enabled AT&T to experiment with varying price, promotion and distribution, to see which combination of marketing mix variables worked best for each consumer segment.

b) Why was the sample size over 2600? Is this the appropriate sample size for this study?

Yes, the sample size was appropriate. With 16 groups and 2600 observations, there were an average of 162 observations per group. To make valid comparisons between groups, most statisticians like to see at least 100 observations per group.

24. *MINICASE:*

a) For the Milan Food Cooperative (A) case in this section of the book, the population mean for weekly food expenditures is $43.20. Select the following samples from this data and calculate an estimate of the mean weekly food expenditures and the associated 95% confidence interval. Use the random number table A-1 at the end of the text to obtain random numbers.
   1) Simple random sample, n = 10
   2) Simple random sample, n = 30
   3) Stratified sample, n = 10
   4) Systematic sample, n = 10
   5) Convenience sample, n = 10
   6) Quota sample, n = 10

b) What conclusions do you draw about each of these sampling methods?

PURPOSE

The purposes of this question are (1) to improve students' understanding of the sampling process and (2) to improve their ability in drawing samples. Following the procedures outlined in class lectures, the student draws samples from a population and compares his or her results with those of other students.

BACKGROUND

The question presents a complete study population ($N = 500$) organized into a sampling frame. The population element is a household. Each household is described with reference to six variables: (1) weekly food expenditures, (2) number of persons in household, (3) annual household income, (4) education of head of household, (5) age of head of household, and (6) age of children.

The examples illustrate the drawing of probability (simple random sampling, stratified, and systematic) and nonprobability (convenience and quota) samples from the study population. A computer program was used to calculate the statistics for a large number of samples drawn by students at The University of Michigan using each of the probability and nonprobability sample selection procedures. The "Sample Selection Computer Results" presents the output from these calculations. Using this computer output, the instructor can compare the statistics calculated from each of their samples with those from a large group of students, and they can also compare each of the sample selection procedures based on the computer results.

TEACHING STRATEGY

Sample calculations, worksheets, and computer output are available in this manual for use with this problem. The instructor can copy and hand out worksheets and have students complete sampling exercises at home, recording the statistics from each sample in the Summary of Calculations section at the end of the worksheet. In class, have several students discuss their results for each type of sample, to illustrate the variation possible among samples selected with the same sampling method. Then use the computer results to make generalizations about the differences resulting from choice of sampling method.

About the Computer Output

For each of the six sampling problems, computer output is available to use in class discussion. The output was generated by taking 60 or more samples using each selection procedure and tabulating the results.

Table 1 contains a summary of the results (number of samples, mean, standard error, and percent in confidence interval) for each sampling procedure.

Figures 1 through 10 present the distribution of sample means for each procedure.

Tables 2 and 3 present more detailed computer output resulting from simple random sampling and convenience sampling.

a) Simple random sample, n = 10

1. Procedure: Systematically select 10 three-digit numbers in the range 001 to 500 from the table of random digits provided in the text. The following illustration shows you how to calculate the mean, standard deviation, and confidence interval for the weekly food expenditure data.

2. Sample of 10 households:

Random Household number	Expenditure ($) X	X²
100	75	5625.00
375	37.5	1406.25
084	30	900.00
128	20	400.00
310	86	7396.00
118	20	400.00
099	40	1600.00
441	30	900.00
125	22.5	506.25
154	75	5625.00
	ΣX = 436	ΣX² = 24758.5

3. Sample mean:

$$\bar{X} = \frac{\Sigma X}{n} = \frac{436}{10} = 43.6$$

(population mean μ = $43.2)

4. Sample standard deviation:

$$s = \sqrt{\frac{\Sigma X^2 - \frac{(\Sigma X)^2}{n}}{n-1}} = \sqrt{\frac{24{,}758.5 - \frac{190{,}096}{10}}{9}} = \sqrt{\frac{24{,}758.5 - 19{,}009.6}{9}}$$

$$s = \sqrt{\frac{5748.9}{9}} = \sqrt{638.8} = 25.27$$

(population standard deviation σ = $20.9)

5. Sample estimate of $\sigma_{\bar{X}}$ (standard deviation of the sample mean or standard error of the mean):

$$s_{\bar{X}} = \frac{s}{\sqrt{n}}$$

$$= \frac{25.27}{\sqrt{10}} = \frac{25.27}{3.16}$$

$$= 8.0$$

6. Interval estimate of μ (95% confidence coefficient; $Z = 2$):

$$\bar{X} - Z(s_{\bar{X}}) \leq \mu \leq \bar{X} + Z(s_{\bar{X}})$$

$$43.6 - 2(8) \leq \mu \leq 43.6 + 2(8)$$

$$43.6 - 16 \leq \mu \leq 43.6 + 16$$

$$27.6 \leq \mu \leq 59.6$$

Note: $\mu(43.2)$ does appear in this interval.

7. Interpretation of confidence interval:

   If one takes a great many simple random samples from this population and constructs a 95% confidence interval for each, about 95% of these statements will be correct.

b) Simple random sample, n = 30

1. Procedure: Systematically select 30 three-digit numbers in the range 001 to 500 from the table of random digits provided in the text. For this example, we continued with the same string of random numbers used for the previous sample. This was done to highlight the differences in the means, standard deviations, standard errors of the mean, and confidence intervals resulting from different sample sizes.

2. Sample of 30 households:

Random Household number	Expenditure ($) X	X^2
100	75	5625.00
375	37.5	1406.25
084	30	900.00
128	20	400.00
310	86	7396.00
118	20	400.00
099	40	1600.00
441	30	900.00
125	22.5	506.25
154	75	5625.00
424	75	5625.00
235	37.5	1406.25
044	12	144.00
005	46.5	2162.25
359	45	2025.00
460	9	81.00
321	30	900.00
195	40	1600.00
451	75	5625.00
331	35	1225.00
186	60	3600.00
116	15	225.00
483	37.5	1406.25
196	45	2025.00
093	50	2500.00
340	22.5	506.25
455	45	2025.00
020	32	1024.00
053	15	225.00
035	34.5	1190.00
	$\Sigma X = 1197.5$	$\Sigma X^2 = 60278.75$

3. Sample mean:

$$\bar{X} = \frac{\Sigma X}{n} = \frac{1197.5}{30} = 39.91$$

4. Sample standard deviation:

$$s = \sqrt{\frac{\Sigma X^2 - \frac{(\Sigma X)^2}{n}}{n-1}} = \sqrt{\frac{60{,}278.5 - \frac{(1197.5)^2}{30}}{29}} = \sqrt{\frac{60{,}278.5 - 47{,}800.2}{29}}$$

$$s = \sqrt{\frac{12{,}748}{29}}$$

$$s = 20.97$$

5. Sample estimate of $s_{\bar{X}}$ (standard deviation of the sample mean or standard error of the mean):

$$s_{\bar{X}} = \frac{s}{\sqrt{n}}$$

$$= \frac{20.97}{\sqrt{30}} = \frac{20.97}{5.48}$$

$$= 3.83$$

6. Interval estimate of μ (95% confidence coefficient; $Z = 2$):

$$\bar{X} - Z(s_{\bar{X}}) \leq \mu \leq \bar{X} + Z(s_{\bar{X}})$$

$$39.51 - 2(3.83) \leq \mu \leq 39.51 + 2(3.83)$$

$$39.51 - 7.66 \leq \mu \leq 39.51 + 7.66$$

$$31.85 \leq \mu \leq 47.17$$

7. Interpretation of confidence interval:

If one takes a great many random samples from this population and constructs a 95% confidence interval for each, about 95% of these statements will be correct.

Comparing this example to the previous one, notice that the larger sample generated a smaller standard deviation, smaller standard error of the mean and narrower 95% confidence interval.

c) Stratified sample (n = 10)

1. Procedure:

    a. The population of households to be sampled is subdivided (or stratified) into groups which are mutually exclusive but which together include all items in the population.

    b. A simple random sample is then chosen independently from each group or stratum.

2. Strata and weights:

Education Group	f	Relative Weight of Stratum %		Stratum	n
1	104	20.8	=	W_1	2
2	102	20.4	=	W_2	2
3	180	36.0	=	W_3	4
4 & 5	114	22.8	=	W_4	2
	500	100.0			10

3. Household number by stratum:

Stratum	Household Number
W_1	001 - 104
W_2	105 - 206
W_3	207 - 386
W_4	387 - 500

4. Random sampling of ten households:

W_1			W_2		
	Random Household Number	$X_{st.1}$		Random Household Number	$X_{st.2}$
(1)	023	37.50	(1)	146	40.00
(2)	086	60.00	(2)	190	37.50
	$\Sigma X_{st.1} = 97.50$			$\Sigma X_{st.2} = 77.50$	

W_3			W_4		
	Random Household Number	$X_{st.3}$		Random Household Number	$X_{st.4}$
(1)	269	50.00	(1)	437	30.00
(2)	251	37.50	(2)	450	57.00
(3)	291	45.00		$\Sigma X_{st.4} = 87.00$	
(4)	314	60.00			
	$\Sigma X_{st.3} = 192.50$				

5. Sample stratum means:

$$\bar{X}_{st.1} = \frac{97.50}{2} = 48.75 \qquad \bar{X}_{st.3} = \frac{192.50}{4} = 48.13$$

$$\bar{X}_{st.2} = \frac{77.50}{2} = 38.75 \qquad \bar{X}_{st.4} = \frac{87.00}{2} = 43.50$$

6. Sample mean ($\bar{X}_{st}$):

Stratum	Sample Mean in Stratum $\bar{X}_{st.j}$	Relative Weight of Stratum (W_j)	$W_j \cdot \bar{X}_{st.j}$
	48.8	.208	10.15
	38.7	.204	7.89
	48.1	.360	17.32
	43.5	.228	9.91
		1.000	$\bar{X}_{st} = 45.27$

d) Systematic (n = 10)

1. Procedure:

   a. Determine the total number of items in the population (N = 500).
   b. Divide this figure by the desired sample size (500 ÷ 10 = 50)
   c. The result is called the sampling interval (50).
   d. Select a random number from 1 through the sampling interval of 50.
   e. This identifies the first element on the list to be included in the sample.
   f. Add to this random number the sampling interval.
   g. The result identifies the second items to be included in the sample.
   h. Continue adding the interval and taking the items so identified until the sample is drawn (n=10).

2. Systematic sampling of ten households:

   a. Random number = 23
   b. Sample

	Random Household Number	Expenditure X
(1)	23	37.50
(2)	73	24.00
(3)	123	45.00
(4)	173	27.00
(5)	223	30.00
(6)	273	50.00
(7)	323	22.50
(8)	373	52.50
(9)	423	75.00
(10)	473	60.00
		ΣX = 423.50

3. Sample mean:

$$\bar{X} = \frac{423.5}{10} = 42.4$$

e) Convenience sample (n = 10)

 1. Procedure: Select 10 household numbers in a manner convenient to you. In the following illustration, selection involved turning to the third page of the enclosed data set and arbitrarily selecting 10 households (119 through 128).

 2. Convenience sample of 10 households:

	Household Number	Expenditure X
(1)	119	50
(2)	120	57
(3)	121	47
(4)	122	48
(5)	123	45
(6)	124	15
(7)	125	22.5
(8)	126	52.5
(9)	127	15
(10)	128	20
		$\Sigma X = 372$

 3. Sample mean:

$$\bar{X} = \frac{372}{10} = 37.2$$

f) Quota sample (n = 10)

 1. Two-control variable quota sample: Population distribution by income and number of persons in family

Annual Income ($)	Number of Persons in Family		
	1 or 2	3 or 4	5 or more
Less than 6000	84	43	25
6000 to 14,999	59	107	81
15,000 and over	26	44	31
			N = 500

 2. Allocation of sample among cells (n = 10)
 For n = 10, one household per cell and the remaining household allocated to the largest cell.

 3. Procedure:
  a. Pick an arbitrary starting point and look for households which meet the requirements of the quota.

4. Quota sample of 10 households:

	Household Number	Expenditure X
(1)	119	50.0
(2)	181	45.0
(3)	282	69.0
(4)	144	40.0
(5)	171	55.0
(6)	187	37.5
(7)	154	75.0
(8)	218	30.0
(9)	257	45.0
(10)	383	<u>54.0</u>
		$\Sigma X = 500.5$

3. Sample mean:

$$\bar{X} = \frac{500.5}{10} = 50.0$$

Using Random Numbers

The probability sample selection procedures use a set of random numbers to select the population elements. This list, as the name implies, is composed of numbers that have no pattern of occurrence. Any number is as likely to appear in any spot on the table as any other.

In the Populations Data Set, each household is identified by a three-digit household identification number ranging from 001 to 500. Thus, we can use the random-digit table to give us a three-digit number in the range of 001 to 500 to select an element for the sample. We would use as many of these three-digit numbers as we wanted in the sample.

An example will help make this clear. Suppose we wish to select a sample with n = 5. If we start on the random-digit table at an arbitrary point in row 11, columns 16 and 17 (first two digits of column 16 and the first digit of column 17) and move vertically down the columns, we would select a sample consisting of elements 294, 184, 211, 455, and 436. These are the first five 3-digit numbers in the range 001 to 500 that we meet. Consequently, we have randomly selected a sample size of 5 from a population size of 500.

Name _____

WORKSHEETS ON SAMPLE SELECTION

Probability Sampling Method

A. Simple random sampling
   1. Sample of 10 households:

	Random Household Number	Expenditure ($), X	X^2
(1)	_____	_____	_____
(2)	_____	_____	_____
(3)	_____	_____	_____
(4)	_____	_____	_____
(5)	_____	_____	_____
(6)	_____	_____	_____
(7)	_____	_____	_____
(8)	_____	_____	_____
(9)	_____	_____	_____
(10)	_____	_____	_____
		$\Sigma X =$	$\Sigma X^2 =$

2. Sample mean:

$$\overline{X} = \frac{\Sigma X}{n} =$$

(population mean μ = $43.2)

3. Sample standard deviation:

$$s = \sqrt{\frac{\Sigma X^2 - \frac{(\Sigma X)^2}{n}}{n-1}} =$$

(population standard deviation σ = $20.9)

Name _____

4. Sample estimate of $\sigma_{\bar{X}}$ (standard error of the mean):

$$s_{\bar{X}} = \frac{s}{\sqrt{n}} =$$

5. Interval estimate of μ (95% confidence coefficient; $Z = 2$):

$$\bar{X} - Z(s_{\bar{X}}) \leq \mu \leq \bar{X} + Z(s_{\bar{X}})$$

Does μ (43.2) appear in this interval?   Yes   No   (circle one)

Name _____

B. Simple random sampling
   1. Sample of 30 households:

	Random Household Number	Expenditure ($), X	X^2
(1)	_____	_____	_____
(2)	_____	_____	_____
(3)	_____	_____	_____
(4)	_____	_____	_____
(5)	_____	_____	_____
(6)	_____	_____	_____
(7)	_____	_____	_____
(8)	_____	_____	_____
(9)	_____	_____	_____
(10)	_____	_____	_____
(11)	_____	_____	_____
(12)	_____	_____	_____
(13)	_____	_____	_____
(14)	_____	_____	_____
(15)	_____	_____	_____
(16)	_____	_____	_____
(17)	_____	_____	_____
(18)	_____	_____	_____
(19)	_____	_____	_____
(20)	_____	_____	_____
(21)	_____	_____	_____
(22)	_____	_____	_____
(23)	_____	_____	_____

Name _____

	Random Household Number	Expenditure ($), X	X^2
(24)	_____	_____	_____
(25)	_____	_____	_____
(26)	_____	_____	_____
(27)	_____	_____	_____
(28)	_____	_____	_____
(29)	_____	_____	_____
(30)	_____	_____	_____
		$\Sigma X =$	$\Sigma X^2 =$

2. Sample mean:

$$\bar{X} = \frac{\Sigma X}{n} =$$

(population mean $\mu = \$43.2$)

3. Sample standard deviation:

$$s = \sqrt{\frac{\Sigma X^2 - \frac{(\Sigma X)^2}{n}}{n-1}} =$$

(population standard deviation $\sigma = \$20.9$)

Name _____

4. Sample estimate of $\sigma_{\bar{X}}$ (standard error of the mean):

$$s_{\bar{X}} = \frac{s}{\sqrt{n}} =$$

5. Interval estimate of μ (95% confidence coefficient; $Z = 2$):

$$\bar{X} - Z(s_{\bar{X}}) \leq \mu \leq \bar{X} + Z(s_{\bar{X}})$$

Does μ (43.2) appear in this interval?   Yes   No   (circle one)

Name _____

C. Stratified sampling

1. Sample of 10 households:

W_1			W_2		
Random Household Number		$X_{st.1}$	Random Household Number		$X_{st.2}$
(1)	_____	_____	(1)	_____	_____
(2)	_____	_____	(2)	_____	_____
	$\Sigma X_{st.1} =$			$\Sigma X_{st.2} =$	

W_3			W_4		
Random Household Number		$X_{st.3}$	Random Household Number		$X_{st.4}$
(1)	_____	_____	(1)	_____	_____
(2)	_____	_____	(2)	_____	_____
(3)	_____	_____		$\Sigma X_{st.4} =$	
(4)	_____	_____			
	$\Sigma X_{st.3} =$				

2. Sample stratum means:

$\bar{X}_{st.1} =$

$\bar{X}_{st.2} =$

$\bar{X}_{st.3} =$

$\bar{X}_{st.4} =$

Name _____

3. Sample mean ($\bar{X}_{st.j}$):

Stratum	Sample Mean in Stratum ($\bar{X}_{st.j}$)	Relative Weight of Stratum (W_j)	$W_j \cdot \bar{X}_{st.j}$
W_1	_____	.208	_____
W_2	_____	.204	_____
W_3	_____	.360	_____
W_4	_____	.228	_____
		1.00	$\bar{X}_{st} =$

Name _____

D. Cluster sampling – Systematic

   1. Sample of 10 households:

      a. Random number = _____

Sample	Random Household Number	Expenditure X
(1)	_____	_____
(2)	_____	_____
(3)	_____	_____
(4)	_____	_____
(5)	_____	_____
(6)	_____	_____
(7)	_____	_____
(8)	_____	_____
(9)	_____	_____
(10)	_____	_____
		$\Sigma X =$

   2. Sample mean:

$$\bar{X} = \frac{\Sigma X}{n} =$$

(population mean μ = $43.2)

Name _____

E. Convenience sample

1. Sample of 10 households:

	Household Number	Expenditure X
(1)	_____	_____
(2)	_____	_____
(3)	_____	_____
(4)	_____	_____
(5)	_____	_____
(6)	_____	_____
(7)	_____	_____
(8)	_____	_____
(9)	_____	_____
(10)	_____	_____
		$\Sigma X =$

2. Sample mean:

$$\bar{X} = \frac{\Sigma X}{n} =$$

(population standard deviation $\mu = \$43.2$)

137

Name _____

3. Sample standard deviation:

$$s = \sqrt{\frac{\Sigma X^2 - \frac{(\Sigma X)^2}{n}}{n-1}} =$$

(population standard deviation $\sigma = \$20.9$)

4. Sample estimate of $\sigma_{\bar{X}}$ (standard error of the mean)

$$s_{\bar{X}} = \frac{s}{\sqrt{n}} =$$

5. Interval estimate of μ (95% confidence coefficient; $Z = 2$):

$$\bar{X} - Z(s_{\bar{X}}) \leq \mu \leq \bar{X} + Z(s_{\bar{X}})$$

Does μ (43.2) appear in this interval?   Yes   No   (circle one)

Name _____

F. Quota sample

1. Sample of 10 households:

	Household Number	Expenditure X
(1)	_____	_____
(2)	_____	_____
(3)	_____	_____
(4)	_____	_____
(5)	_____	_____
(6)	_____	_____
(7)	_____	_____
(8)	_____	_____
(9)	_____	_____
(10)	_____	_____
		$\Sigma X =$

2. Sample mean:

$$\bar{X} = \frac{\Sigma X}{n} =$$

(population mean μ = $43.2)

Name _____

Summary of Calculations

	Sampling Procedure					
	Simple Random Sample		*Stratified*	*Systematic*	*Convenience*	*Quota*
	n=10	n=30	n=10	n=10	n=10	n=10
Sample Mean						
Standard Deviation			✕	✕	✕	✕
Did Confidence Interval Include μ? *(Yes No)*			✕	✕	✕	✕

SAMPLE SELECTION COMPUTER RESULTS

Table of Contents

1. Table 1 — Summary Results
2. Figure 1 — Simple Random Sample (n = 10)
3. Figure 2 — Simple Random Sample (n = 30)
4. Figure 3 — Stratified Sample (n = 10
5. Figure 4 — Stratified Sample (n = 30)
6. Figure 5 — Systematic Sample (n = 10)
7. Figure 6 — Systematic Sample (n = 30)
8. Figure 7 — Convenience Sample (n = 10)
9. Figure 8 — Convenience Sample (n = 30)
10. Figure 9 — Quota Sample (n = 10)
11. Figure 10 — Quota Sample (n = 30)
12. Table 2 — Computer Output: Simple Random Sample (n = 30)
13. Table 3 — Computer Output: Convenience Sample (n = 30)

Table 1 Summary Results

	Number of Samples	*Mean of Samples*	*Standard Error of Mean*	*Percent μ in Confidence Interval*
Simple random sample (n = 10)	64	$42.6	6.45	92.2%
Simple random sample (n = 30)	62	$43.7	3.61	93.5%
Stratified sample (n = 10)	64	$44.0	6.43	92.2%
Stratified sample (n = 30)	61	$43.7	3.79	96.7%
Systematic sample (n = 10)	65	$41.6	5.75	90.8%
Systematic sample (n = 30)	62	$43.4	3.72	100.0%
Convenience sample (n = 10)	65	$43.6	6.05	75.4%
Convenience sample (n = 30)	60	$42.9	3.60	75.0%
Quota sample (n = 10)	63	$44.2	6.07	90.5%
Quota sample (n = 30)	61	$44.0	3.68	100.0%

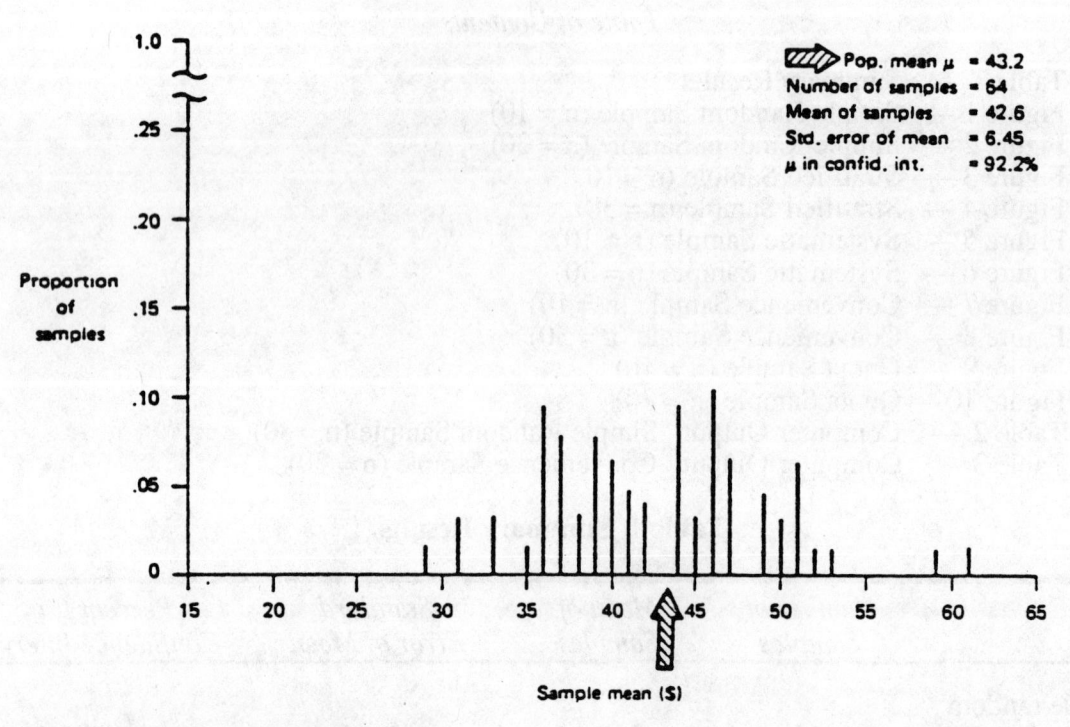

Figure 1   Simple random sample ($n = 10$)

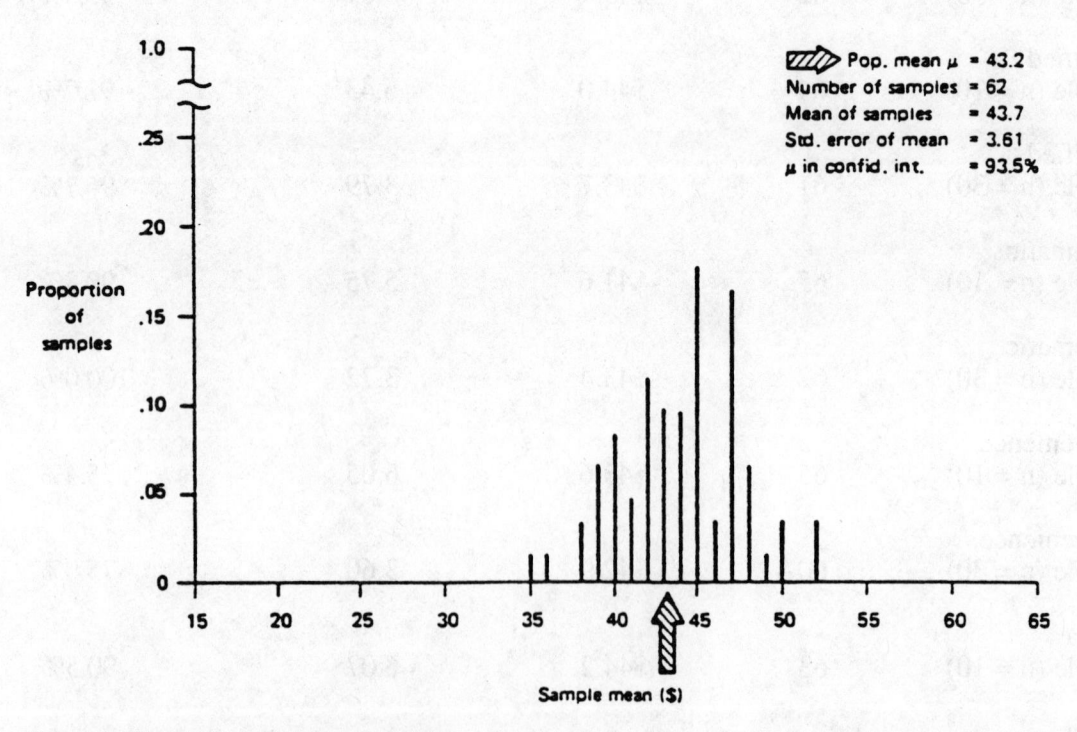

- Pop. mean μ = 43.2
- Number of samples = 64
- Mean of samples = 42.6
- Std. error of mean = 6.45
- μ in confid. int. = 92.2%

Figure 2   Simple random sample ($n = 30$)

- Pop. mean μ = 43.2
- Number of samples = 62
- Mean of samples = 43.7
- Std. error of mean = 3.61
- μ in confid. int. = 93.5%

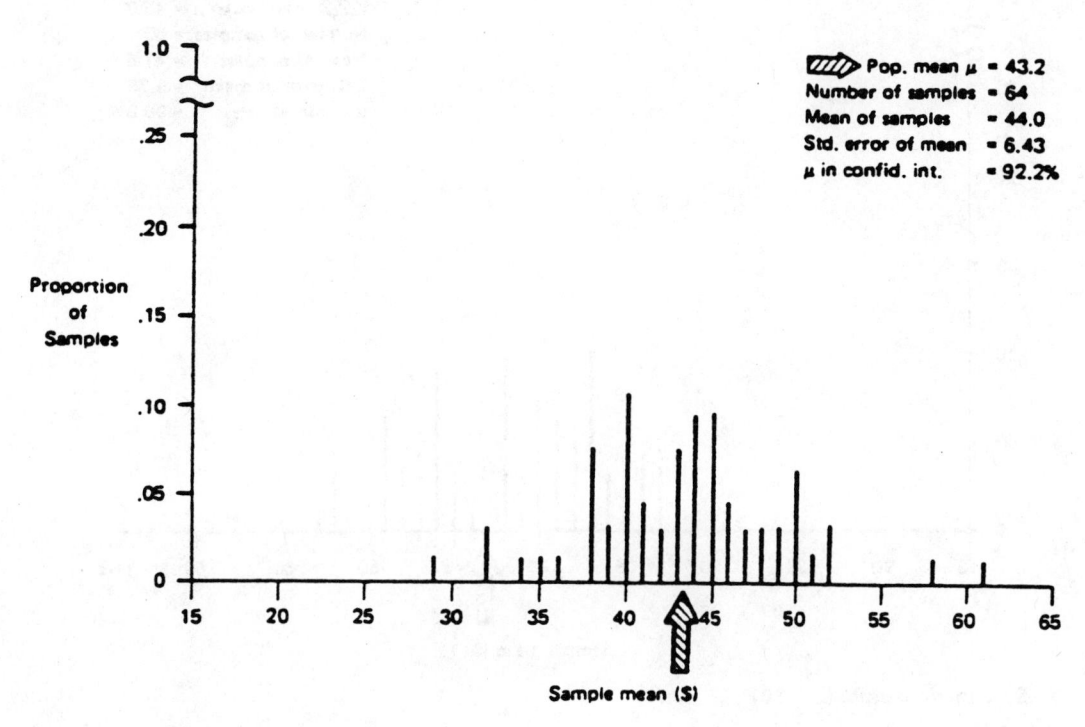

Figure 3 Stratified sample ($n = 10$)

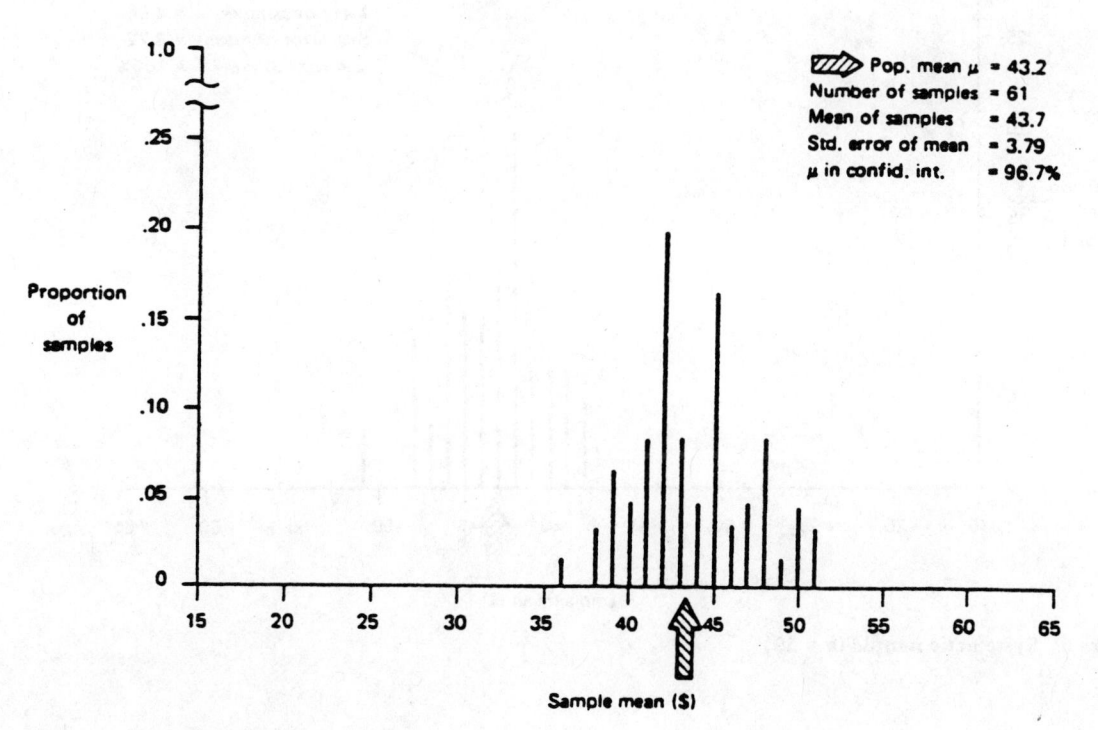

Figure 4 Stratified sample ($n = 30$)

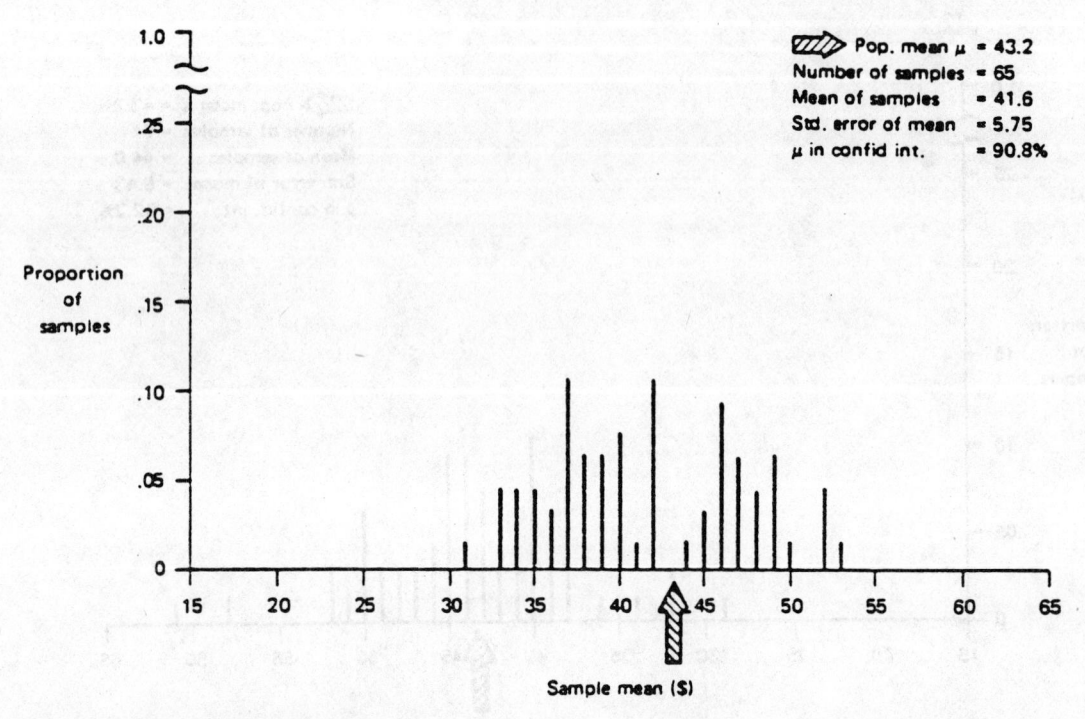

Figure 5 Systematic sample ($n = 10$)

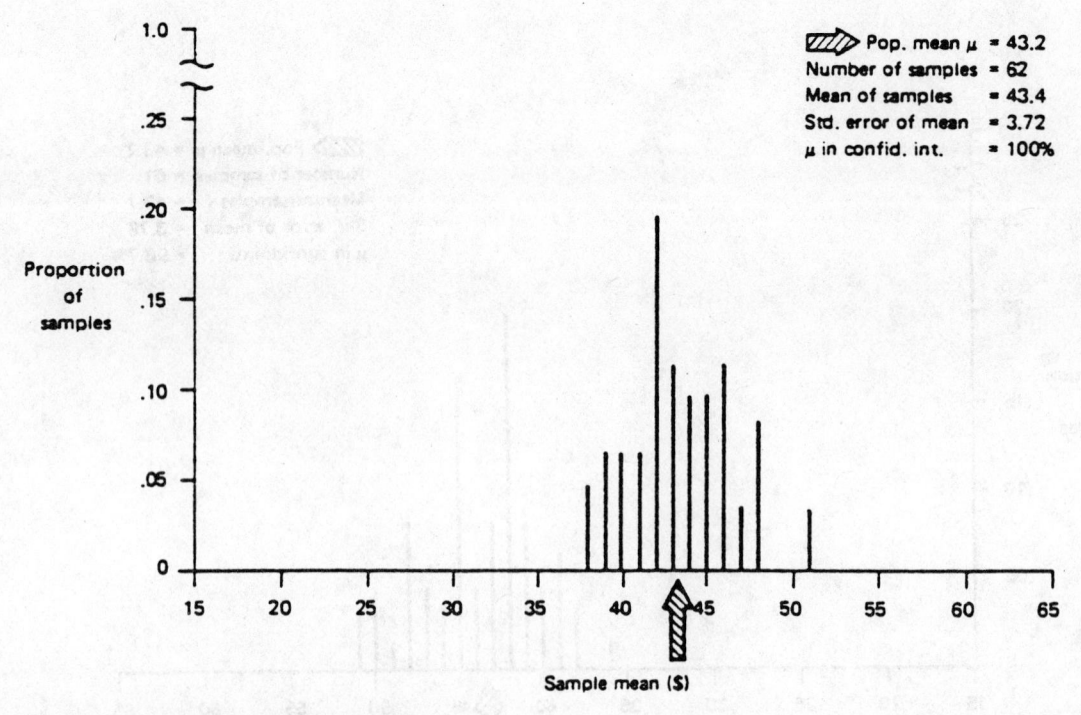

- Pop. mean μ = 43.2
- Number of samples = 65
- Mean of samples = 41.6
- Std. error of mean = 5.75
- μ in confid. int. = 90.8%

Figure 6 Systematic sample ($n = 30$)

- Pop. mean μ = 43.2
- Number of samples = 62
- Mean of samples = 43.4
- Std. error of mean = 3.72
- μ in confid. int. = 100%

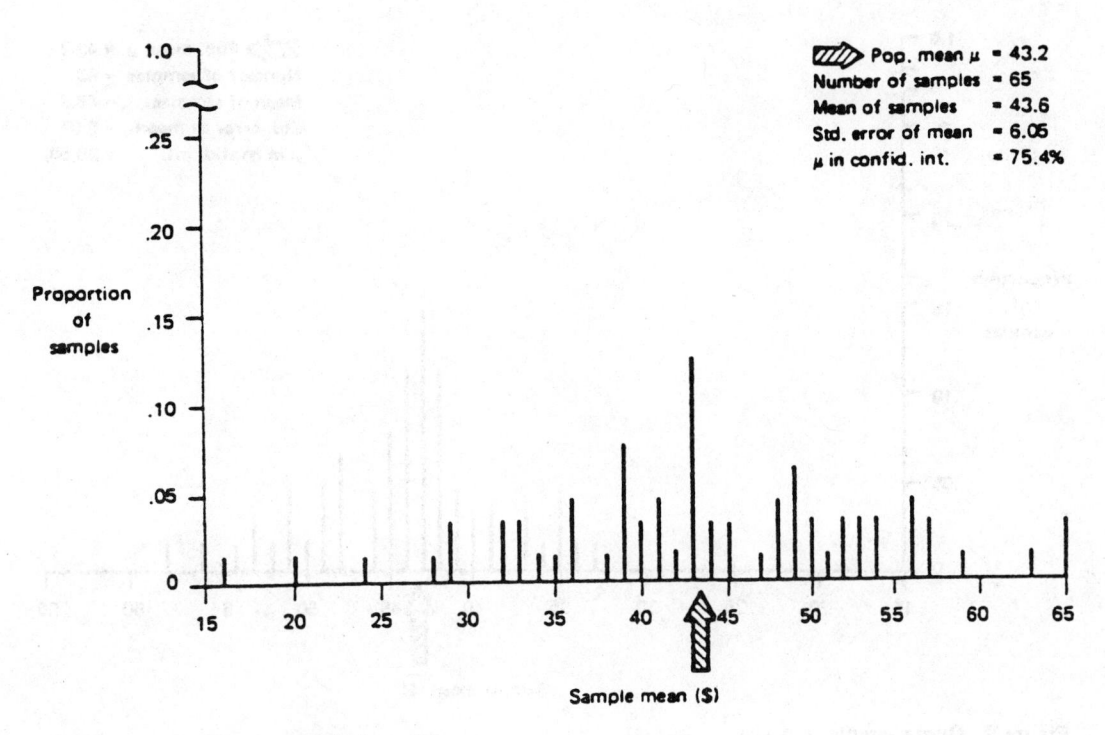

Figure 7 Convenience sample ($n = 10$)

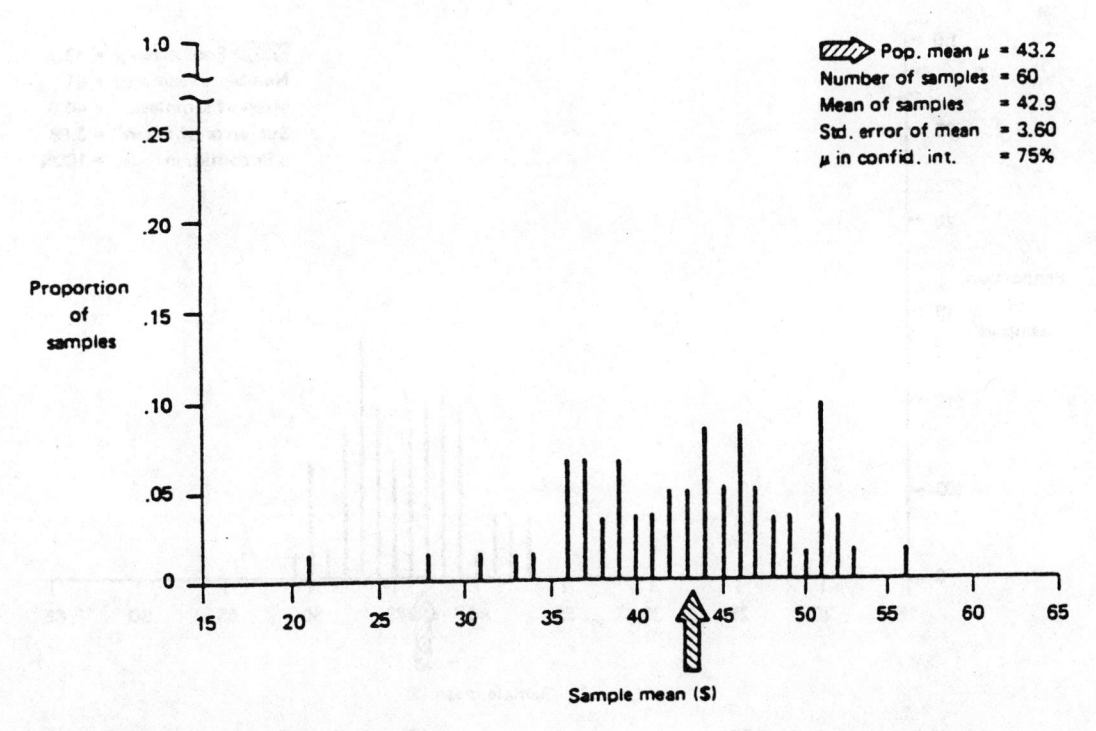

Figure 8 Convenience sample ($n = 30$)

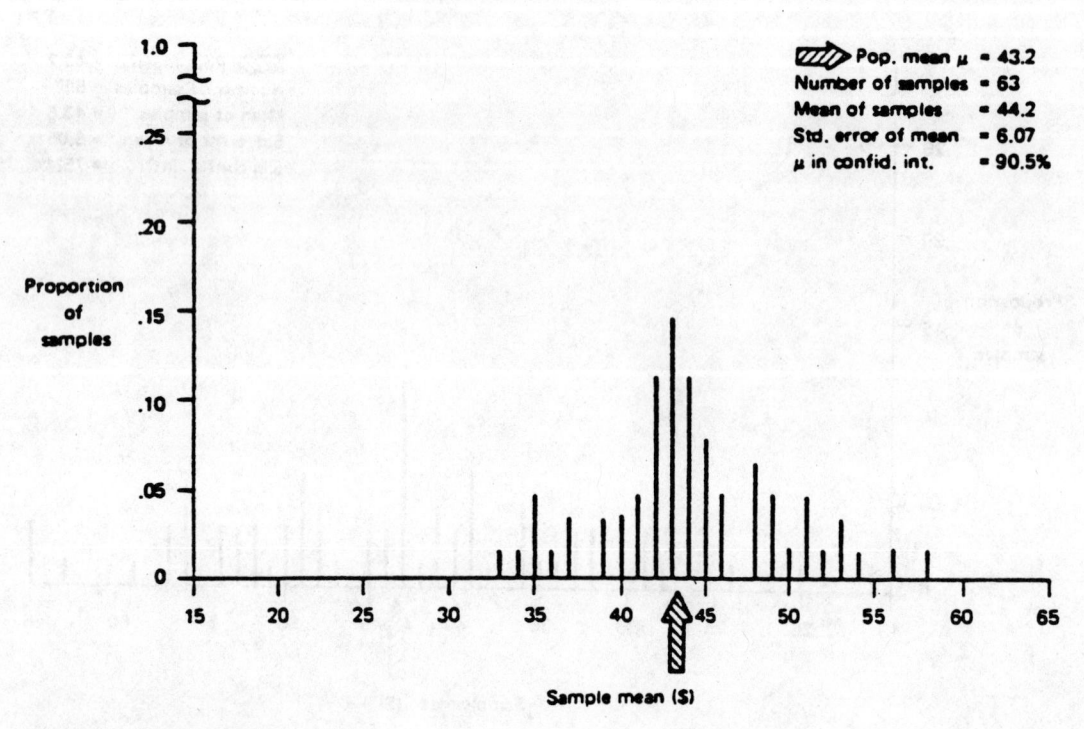

Figure 9 Quota sample ($n = 10$)

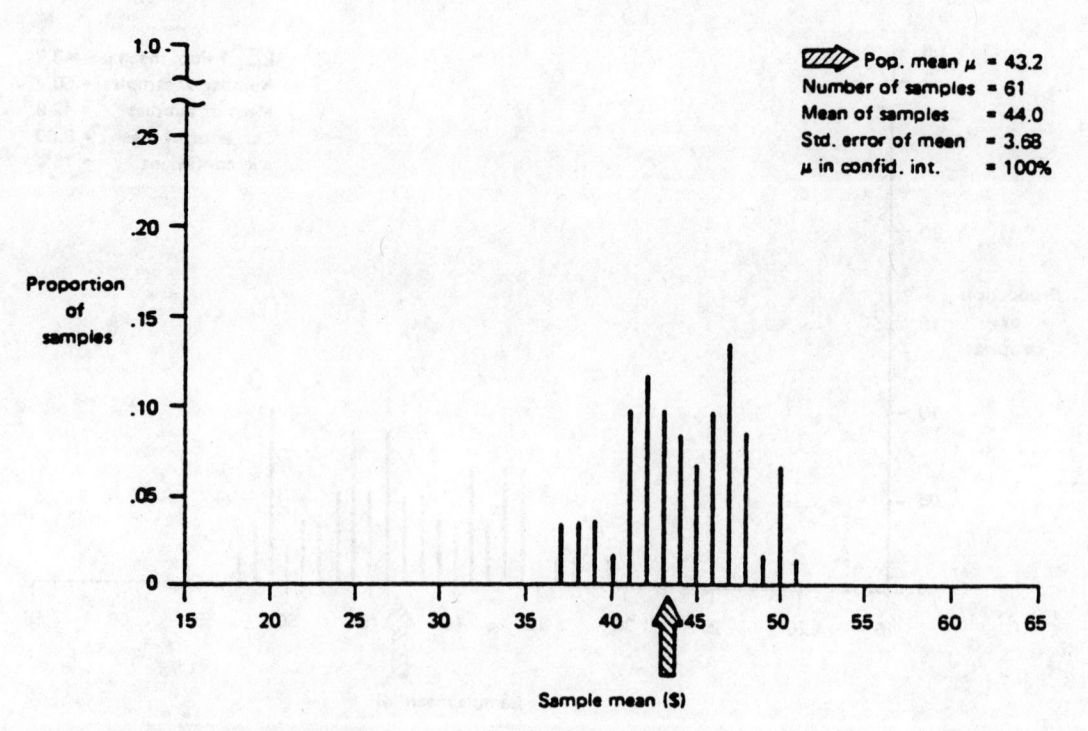

Figure 10 Quota sample ($n = 30$)

Table 2 Simple Random Samples of 30 Cases*

MEAN	MEAN STD. ERR.	CONF. INTERVAL	
43.15	4.2099	34.73-51.57	1
44.90	3.2395	38.42-51.38	1
45.40	4.6985	36.00-54.80	1
49.57	3.4537	42.66-56.47	1
41.45	2.9575	35.53-47.37	1
42.23	2.6683	36.90-47.57	1
48.50	4.7611	38.98-58.02	1
45.05	3.2358	38.58-51.52	1
41.32	2.7417	35.83-46.80	1
51.95	3.6000	44.75-59-15	11111
47.53	3.8684	39.80-55.27	1
42.28	4.3186	33.65-50.92	1
37.68	2.4388	32.81-42.56	11111
45.32	4.7707	35.78-54.86	1
35.13	2.4171	30.30-39.97	11111
49.55	3.8031	41.94-57.16	1
44.17	2.9504	38.27-50.07	1
36.37	3.0412	30.28-42.45	11111
37.50	3.5242	30.45-44.55	1
43.33	3.6012	36.13-50.54	1
47.90	3.7679	40.36-55.44	1
41.38	2.9920	35.40-47.37	1
47.57	3.5630	40.44-54.69	1
40.30	4.0177	32.26-48.34	1
44.12	3.2108	37.70-50.54	1
39.17	2.6162	33.93-44.40	1
39.18	3.3252	32.53-45.83	1
41.92	2.7490	36.42-47.41	1
44.48	2.5028	39.48-49.49	1
46.93	3.7234	39.49-54.38	1
45.12	4.0732	36.97-53.26	1
43.88	3.9478	35.99-51.78	1
44.57	4.1746	36.22-52.92	1
44.13	3.8023	36.53-51.74	1
46.40	3.8566	38.69-54.11	1
43.03	4.6926	33.65-52.42	1
44.57	3.7030	37.16-51.97	1
42.40	3.5064	35.39-49.41	1
46.05	4.4272	37.20-54.90	1
51.83	4.7911	42.25-61.42	1
40.03	4.2141	31.61-48.46	1
45.05	3.5235	38.00-52.10	1
42.03	4.4319	33.17-50.90	1
44.12	4.5250	35.07-53.17	1
49.32	4.6731	39.97-58.66	1
46.93	3.8023	39.33-54.54	1
42.75	3.2364	36.28-49.22	1
45.48	3.5953	38.29-52.67	1
46.50	3.7164	39.07-53.93	1
41.67	2.7407	36.19-47.15	1
39.65	2.7068	34.24-45.06	1
47.00	3.7759	39.45-54.55	1

* 1 indicates that the population mean falls within the interval; 11111 indicates that the population mean does not fall within the interval.

Table 3 Convenience Samples of 30 Cases

MEAN	MEAN STD. ERR.	CONF. INTERVAL	
50.83	3.9337	42.97-58.70	1
52.55	3.6086	45.33-59.77	11111
51.08	3.9171	43.25-58.92	11111
36.92	2.1683	32.58-41.25	11111
50.50	3.9355	42.63-58.37	1
20.77	2.1184	16.53-25.00	11111
42.03	4.2657	33.50-50.56	1
41.62	4.0817	33.45-49.78	1
46.08	4.2997	37.48-54.68	1
35.60	3.9515	27.70-43.50	1
43.24	3.9458	35.35-51.13	1
55.97	4.0798	47.81-64.13	11111
43.53	4.2503	35.03-52.03	1
40.72	3.6191	33.48-47.95	1
46.82	4.0205	38.78-54.86	1
36.88	2.4927	31.90-41.87	11111
48.93	3.0886	42.76-55.11	1
51.77	2.9559	45.85-57.68	11111
38.68	2.4662	33.75-43.62	1
48.93	3.0886	42.76-55.11	1
45.28	3.2817	38.72-51.85	1
28.07	3.6801	20.71-35.43	11111
46.20	3.1253	39.95-52.45	1
48.37	4.7530	38.86-57.87	1
50.50	3.9355	42.63-58.37	1
39.48	3.1492	33.18-45.78	1
39.02	2.8358	33.35-44.69	1
38.62	2.9027	32.81-44.42	1
37.13	4.1017	28.93-45.34	1
43.63	3.9944	35.64-51.62	1
45.95	3.4997	38.95-52.95	1
36.72	2.5162	31.68-41.75	11111
44.50	5.1851	34.13-54.87	1
42.13	3.7422	34.65-49.62	1
46.13	3.2478	39.64-52.63	1
43.63	3.0695	37.49-49.77	1
41.12	3.4571	34.20-48.03	1
34.10	3.7280	26.64-41.56	11111
35.60	3.9515	27.70-43.50	1
44.63	3.3273	37.98-51.29	1
46.63	3.2175	40.20-53.07	1
52.08	3.6474	44.79-59.38	11111
43.63	4.0405	35.55-51.71	1
40.38	4.5304	31.32-49.44	1
50.42	5.6712	39.07-61.76	1
35.60	3.9515	27.70-43.50	1
44.00	5.3473	33.31-54.69	1
51.13	2.9852	45.16-57.10	11111
38.00	3.8845	30.23-45.77	1
47.42	2.8877	41.64-53.19	1

Name _____

WORKSHEETS ON COMPUTER RESULTS

1. Review the summary results in Table 1. Figure 1-10 presents the distribution of sample means for each procedure. What conclusions can be drawn from these results?

2. Under what condition would the stratified sampling procedure exhibit no more efficiency than the simple random sampling procedure?

3. Compare the computer results for the stratified and simple random sampling procedures (Figures 1 to 4). Would you conclude that the efficiency of the stratified sampling procedure was better than that of the simple random sampling procedure? Support your position.

4. In the stratified sampling, education was selected as the stratifying variable. What other variable would be better? Support your position.

5. The 95 percent confidence interval for the systematic sampling (n = 30) included μ for every sample (see Table 1). What characteristics of the population listing contributes to this accuracy?

6. What condition must exist for the convenience sample to be considered a simple random sample?

7. Compare the computer results for the convenience and simple random samples (Figure 1, 2, 7, and 8). Would you conclude that this special condition (see question 6) exists for this data? Support your position.

8. Why did the quota sampling procedure (n = 30) do so well? (See Table 1.)

9. Tables 2 and 3 present individual sample results of a computer program which calculates means and confidence intervals and indicates whether the population mean (μ) was included in the confidence interval. In the right-hand column, a single "1" indicates that μ was included in the confidence interval, while five 1's indicates that μ was not included in the confidence interval. Compare the computer results for the simple random sample (Table 2) and the convenience sample Table (3). What conclusion can you draw regarding the reason some samples failed to include μ in the confidence interval?

Answers to Questions Given on the Worksheets on Computer Results

1. Review the summary results in Table 1. Figures 1 through 10 present the distribution of sample means for each procedure. What conclusions can be drawn from these results?

   a. Mean of samples:

      1) The mean of the samples for n = 30 tends to be closer to μ ($43.2) than for n = 10.

   b. Standard error of mean:

      1) The standard error of the mean for n = 30 is substantially smaller than n = 10.

   c. Percent included in confidence interval:

      1) The confidence interval included the population mean to a higher degree when n = 30 than when n = 10.

      2) The probability sampling methods did better than the nonprobability sampling methods (with the exception of quota, n = 30).

      3) The convenience sample (n = 10, n = 30) was the worst method.

   d. Distribution of sample means:

   Both the probability and nonprobability sampling procedures exhibit somewhat bell-shaped distributions. The samples of n = 30 exhibit better bell shapes than n = 10.

2. Under what condition would the stratified sampling procedure exhibit no more efficiency than the simple random sampling procedure?

   a. Where the stratifying variable (education) is not correlated with food expenditures.

   b. The higher the correlation the more efficient the procedure as compared to simple random sampling.

3. Compare the computer results for the stratified and simple random sampling procedure (Figures 1, 2, 3, and 4). Would you conclude that the efficiency of the stratified sampling procedure was better than the simple random sampling procedure? Support your position.

   a. No.

   b. Support:

      1) The distribution of sample means (standard error of the mean) are similar for the random and stratified procedures.

      2) The percent of μ in the confidence interval is similar for the random and stratified procedures.

3) The correlation between the stratifying variable (education) and food expenditures appears to be low (actual correlation is r = .23).

4. In the stratified sample, education was selected as the stratifying variable. What other variable would be better? Support your position.

   a. Number in the family would be a better stratifying variable.

   b. Support:

   1) Would expect a higher correlation with number of persons in family than with education because of the logical causal association among number of persons to feed, the need for food and amount spent on food. (The correlation for education is r = .23 while for number of persons in family is r = .43.)

5. The 95% confidence interval for the systematic sample (n = 30) included μ for every sample (see Table 1). What characteristic of the population listing contributes to this accuracy?

   a. The population listing contains a useful, although imperfect cycle by number of persons in the family, an excellent stratification variable.

   b. Taking a systematic sample from a stratified population will result in a more efficient sample than a systematic sample taken from a random population listing. This assumes there is some correlation between the stratifying variable and the variable of interest.

6. What condition must exist for the convenience sample to be considered a simple random sample?

   a. The population listing must be random.

7. Compare the computer results for the convenience and simple random samples (Figures 1, 2, 7, and 8). Would you conclude that this special condition (see Question 6) exists for this exercise? Support your position.

   a. No.

   b. Support:

   1) The range of sample means is greater for the convenience samples (n = 10, n = 30).

   2) The percent included in the confidence interval is lower for the convenience samples (n = 10, n = 30).

   3) Population listing grouped by education and somewhat by number of persons in household.

8. Why did the quota sampling procedure (n = 30) do so well (see Table 1)?

   a. The control variables of income and number of persons in family have a logical association with amount of food expenditures. (The actual correlations are: Income r = .38, number of persons in family r = .43.)

153

b. These two control variables rule out many unrepresentative sample combinations.

9. Tables 2 and 3 present individual sample results of a computer program which calculates means, standard error of the mean, confidence intervals and indicates whether the population mean was included in the confidence interval. In the right column, a single one (1) indicates that was included in the confidence interval while five ones (11111) indicates that was not included in the confidence interval. Compare the computer results for the simple random sample (Table 2) and the convenience sample (Table 3). What conclusion can you draw regarding the reason some samples failed to be included in the confidence interval?

   a. Outlier sample mean combined with average or below average standard error of the mean.

   b. Reasonably representative sample mean combined with a below average standard error of the mean.

TEACHING STRATEGY

We have found it useful to begin a class on this question by taking a poll of the class with respect to whether or not the confidence intervals from the samples taken by the class members did or did not contain the population mean. Do this for:

1) Simple random sample, n = 10.

2) Simple random sample, n = 30.

3) Convenience sample, n = 10.

Then quickly note to the class the percentage of confidence intervals from each of (1)-(3) above that contain the true population mean. These percentages could then be compared to the summary results in Table 1 of the Sample Selection Computer Results. Their results will likely be very similar to those in Table 1 with the exception of convenience sample, n = 10. Our experience is that the results here can vary greatly. Thus, your class may find that less than 50 percent of convenience sample (n = 10) confidence intervals contain the population mean.

Once this is done, the class should proceed to answer the questions on the Worksheets on Computer Results one at a time.

This question usually fills most of a full class period. The instructor may wish to save some time at the end for a short review lecture on sampling. This could help solidify the insights about sampling that we have found that always come with the use of this exercise.

Chapter 16 — FIELD OPERATIONS

1. What four areas are important in the planning of field operations?

   The four areas are:

   1) time schedules,
   2) budgets,
   3) personnel, and
   4) performance measurement.

Instructor's Further Probing: What aspect of the research process is a major influence on the planning of field operations?

Suggested Probe Response: The design of the sample, specifically the data collection method employed, highly influences the planning of the field operations.

2. What are the problems peculiar to the use of the personal interview in field operations?

   Qualified persons must be located in the geographic locations required by the sampling plan, trained to insure a high degree of commonalty in the collection of the data, and these persons must be monitored constantly.

Instructor's Further Probing: What is a key issue involved in the compensation of interviewer training?

Suggested Probe Response: Method of compensation is an important factor in determining the quality of work performed by the interviewer. An hourly pay will prevent the possible biases incurred by per interview compensation; however, hourly pay does not reward the interviewer for more efficient and quicker work performed. The research manager must take into account many factors before deciding on a compensation scheme.

3. Evaluate the use of the telephone interview in field operations.

   Training and supervision of telephone interviewers remain essential. However, monitoring and corrective actions are more easily taken here.

Instructor's Further Probing: What has the effect of technology been on telephone interviewing?

Suggested Probe Response: We saw in previous chapters and in the Computer-based Interviewing section that the use of computer assisted telephone interviewing allows more accurate and more efficient data taking by the interviewer. Training and supervision, thus, becomes much easier.

4. What are the main sources of error in field operations?

The main sources of error are:

1) Sample selection errors,
2) Nonresponse errors, and
3) Interviewing errors.

Instructor's Further Probing: Give an example of each type of error in a marketing research study.

Suggested Probe Response: One example of a sample selection error includes the tendency for interviewers to avoid seemingly resistant potential respondents in a quota based study. An example of nonresponse error includes refusals by people to take part in a survey or even "not-at-homes" reached during the course of a telephone survey. Interviewing errors include "cheating" by the interviewer, that is the interviewer fills out or completes surveys, perhaps in order to achieve an incentive offered for the surveys.

5. What is nonresponse error?

Nonresponse error refers to the differences on questions asked between those who respond to a survey and those who do not respond.

Instructor's Further Probing: What is a common technique to reduce the number of nonresponse errors?

Suggested Probe Response: Callbacks are common techniques to reduce the number of nonresponse errors. This technique involves the interviewers calling people back a number of times until a survey has been completed. Usually three to four callbacks is sufficient to reduce the nonresponse error significantly.

6. How can the interviewer contribute to measurement error?

The manner in which the questions are asked and responses recorded presents another "opportunity" for error. Finally, interviewers may falsify some aspects of the interview.

Instructor's Further Probing: What is the purpose of rapport in an interview situation?

Suggested Probe Response: The rapport between interviewer and respondent is essential to obtain complete and accurate information. The interviewer's dress and demeanor affect the chances of obtaining complete and accurate information.

7. What guidelines should an interviewer be given regarding the asking of questions?

1) Be thoroughly familiar with the questionnaire.
2) Ask the questions exactly as worded in the questionnaire.
3) Ask the questions in the order in which they are presented in the questionnaire.
4) Ask every question.
5) Use probing techniques to get the respondent to answer the question.

6) Keep track of changes made in the questionnaire.
7) Provide a logical reason for collecting personal data.

Instructor's Further Probing: What are some neutral probing techniques that an interviewer may use to stimulate a fuller and clearer response?

Suggested Probe Response: Several techniques are available for probing, including: repeating the question, an expectant pause, repeating the respondent's reply, reassurance of the respondent, neutral questions or comments, and a direct request for clarification of a response.

Chapter 17 — DATA PROCESSING

1. How are responses to a questionnaire represented in an ASCII file or on a spreadsheet?

   The spreadsheet or ASCII file contains 80 columns. For each variable, one or more columns of the file are assigned to a particular respondent and one or more rows are assigned for each question the respondent needs to answer. Then within the column(s) assigned, numeric values are assigned to represent the possible responses for that variable.

   Instructor's Further Probing: What other recent advances in technology now facilitate data processing of marketing research data?

   Suggested Probe Response: Recent advances such as computer based optical scanners, which allow hand-written or type-written text to be converted into computer readable format just by "scanning" a document; voice recognition software also allows computer readable format of data by recording a response through a person's verbal communication; and the popular use of the World Wide Web, an Internet interface, allows vast amounts of data to be collected and stored in computer readable format from all over the world.

2. How does one identify data collection instruments that are unacceptable for data processing?

   Although the exact criteria vary from study to study, the following criteria can be suggested:

   1) A significant part or key elements of the instrument are not answered.
   2) Judging from the answers given, the respondent clearly misunderstood the task of filling out the instrument.
   3) The answers show too little variance.
   4) The wrong sample element completed the instrument.
   5) The instrument is physically incomplete.
   6) The instrument is received after an established cut-off date.

   Instructor's Further Probing: Why is it important to establish criteria for unacceptable instruments before they are received?

   Suggested Probe Response: In order to maintain a uniform and unbiased set of criteria, it is important to establish these criteria ahead of time so as not to be influenced by the results (from the received instruments).

3. What should an editor do in examining an instrument?

   The editor has a number of concerns in examining an instrument, including:

   1) Legibility - removing ambiguity from the data.
   2) Completeness - regarding unanswered questions.
   3) Consistency - preliminary check for inconsistencies in the data.
   4) Accuracy - including interviewer bias or cheating.
   5) Response Clarification - particularly regarding open-ended questions.

Instructor's Further Probing: What is the key to resolving many problems with instruments?

Suggested Probe Response: Simply stated, good field work can prevent many problems from even reaching the editor. Good field work will ensure any preventable errors can be avoided or questions clarified before the respondent leaves the interviewer. Good questionnaire design with clear and concise explanations will aid in minimizing mail survey response problems.

4. What are the fundamental rules of code construction?

   Five fundamental conventions can be listed:

   1) Establish mutually exclusive and collectively exhaustive code categories.
   2) Retain as much detail as possible, particularly if uncertainty concerning possible uses for a particular variable exists.
   3) Follow standard card layout conventions.
   4) Be sensitive to the issues involved in choosing breakpoints for continuous variables.
   5) Put a respondent and card identification number on each row in the data matrix.

Instructor's Further Probing: How can open-ended questions be coded?

Suggested Probe Response: Generally the verbatim responses are recorded by the interviewer. Then two approaches can be taken to code the response: develop a well defined coding scheme before field work is performed and place the response into a predefined category; or develop a coding scheme after reviewing all the responses and place the received response in a particular category.

5. How should multiple responses be handled?

   Depending upon whether multiple responses were anticipated when the codebook was developed, several options are possible, including:

   1) Single answer expected:
      a) Select first answer.
      b) Combine multiple answers into additional single categories.
      c) Designate as missing data.

   2) Multiple responses expected:
      a) Treat each response as a separate variable, with separate column designated in the data matrix.
      b) Assign separate columns for each response anticipated (when the number of responses is known in advance).

Instructor's Further Probing: What is an important point in ensuring multiple responses are handled appropriately, especially in large studies?

Suggested Probe Response: It is important for the editors to maintain consistency in dealing with multiple responses from instrument to instrument and from editor to editor. Consistency will decrease further potential error resulting from poor editing.

6. What is a codebook? What should it contain?

The codebook is a listing of the documentation of the coding sequence and other information regarding the variables in a dataset. It should contain:

1) The question number.
2) The variable number.
3) The relevant card columns.
4) The format.
5) The variable name.
6) The category definitions.

Instructor's Further Probing: What are the three main functions of the codebook?

Suggested Probe Response: The three main functions of the codebook include: serve as a guide to the coders; help researchers locate variables they desire to use in a particular data analysis run; and, finally, allow proper identification of variable categories as computer output is generated.

7. How is a dataset cleaned?

Cleaning the dataset attempts to remove errors from the computer datafile. This process usually involves the following checks:

1) Wild code check.
2) Consistency check.
3) Extreme case check.

Instructor's Further Probing Describe potential sources of error that each type of check is attempting to catch.

Suggested Probe Response Wild code checks attempt to flag errors made in the coding or data entry stage. Consistency checks flag errors that are within reason (i.e. responses that are defined) but due to errors in coding, data entry, or poor response, are not valid. Extreme case checks coding, data entry, or poor responses by noting unusually large or small values.

8. Why would one want to create new variables?

Several circumstances may arise resulting in the need for new variables, including:

1) Adding data not collected by the original instrument.
2) Collapsing interval variables into categorical ones.
3) Forming variables as combinations of others already collected.
4) Creating indices representing numbers of variables already collected.

Instructor's Further Probing What is the primary purpose in adding new variables?

Suggested Probe Response The primary purpose in adding new variables is to improve accuracy, flexibility, and usefulness of the survey. The addition of new variables allows flexibility in making changes to the coding to accommodate for unforeseen circumstances.

9. What are the alternative data processing types?

   Six tracks are described in the text. The traditional one is known as Track One Processing, and involves: 1) editing, 2) coding of instruments, 3) transferring of codes to coding sheets, 4) computer entry and verifying of a dataset, 5) preparing the resultant data deck into a computer-readable form, 6) cleaning the data, 7) generating new variables, 8) weighting, and 9) storage. Each of the remaining five tracks sequentially removes one or more parts of these steps through more elaborate data collection procedures, such that the various processing functions become simpler, less time-consuming, and less prone to error. At the same time, these procedures become more expensive and more restrictive in terms of the types of questions and instruments possible.

Instructor's Further Probing PDA's (Personal Digital Assistants) are a new type of computer device that allows hand held, pen based entry. PDA's, while still relatively new, allow quick and easy data entry by the user directly into a data matrix. If an interviewer in the field wanted to use this method for recording responses from respondents (thus eliminating the data entry aspect of the process since the PDA can electronically relay all its information to a central computer), what track would be best for the data processing to follow?

Suggested Probe Response Track six, the direct computer entry, would be most suited for this type of scenario.

10. How does one select a type?

    A number of factors need to be considered, including:

    1) The availability of necessary hardware,
    2) Time and cost constraints, and
    3) The degree of complexity in the data collection instrument.

Instructor's Further Probing The text suggests what type of track would be chosen for a complex instrument?

Suggested Probe Response The text mentions that as the instrument becomes more complex, the more likely it is that the track one processing method will be chosen.

11. You have been assigned the task of preparing a coding manual for a study of personal computer users in fifteen countries: U.S.A., Canada, Mexico, Brazil, Japan, China, U.K., France, Italy, Germany, Spain, Austria, Hungary, New Zealand, and Australia. Outline your approach to this task.

    In this case there are several important factors to note: the large number of countries involved, the high technology aspect (and thus exclusiveness) of the study, and the inherent cost and time constraints.

    The first step in designing this type of codebook is to realize that a combination of international methods must be chosen to accomplish this task. The fourth method suggested in the text for international coding needs to be used, creating a code frame valid for all countries, but translated into the local language. In addition, computerized coding is needed to speed up and instill accuracy in the task, considering the volume of information potentially available.

With this as a framework our codebook (written here in English, but would be translated for other coders in various languages) may look something like this:

Question Number	Variable Number	ASCII File Column	Format	Variable Name	Category Definitions
25	55	72	I1	Sex	1= Male 2= Female 9= Missing Data
26	56	73-74	I2	Age	2 digit num. from 00-98; 99 =Missing Data
.	.	.	.	.	.
.	.	.	.	.	.
.	.	.	.	.	.
57	92	101	I1	Operating System Used	1=Windows 2= DOS 3= Mac 4= UNIX 5= OS/2 6= Other 9= Missing Data

Instructor's Further Probing What are some potential problems in performing this survey, even if a well coded scheme is developed?

Suggested Probe Response While the coding manual can be accurately written and translated as needed, the actual survey itself must undergo pretesting and rigorous quality control in its design before it is used as a valid instrument. In addition, there needs to be a system set up to monitor and track the quality of the interviewers conducting the survey. The use of mail surveys or other nonpersonal means may not be effective since postal services vary significantly among the countries being studied. Furthermore, due to the distances and costs involved, there is very little chance of being able to follow up with a respondent if there is a problem with an instrument response. Thus the sample size must account for inaccurate responses that may result in discarded instruments.

12. *MINICASE:* Presented below are selected questions that were developed for the survey conducted related to the National Markets-Nutritional Labeling case (case 1-1) presented in Part 1 of this book. For each question, give an appropriate scheme.

   One approach to coding these questions is presented next to the question with comments where appropriate. Note MD = missing data.

[1/10] 1. Where do you buy most of the food your family eats?
- [1] ( ) Large supermarket chain
- [2] ( ) Independent grocer
- [3] ( ) Farmer's market
- [4] ( ) Convenience store like 7-11 or Stop-N-Go
- [5] ( ) Other _____

MD [6]

Assumes the "other" does not need to be specified more in coding.

[1/11] 2. Is this store helpful in providing nutritional information?
- [1] ( ) Yes
- [2] ( ) No

MD [3]

6. Which of these sources do you use "Most Often"? (Read list) "Second Most Often"?

	1/21	Most Often	1/22	Second Most Often
Advertisements	1	( )	1	( )
Books	2	( )	2	( )
Doctor	3	( )	3	( )
Food Labels	4	( )	4	( )
Friends or relatives	5	( )	5	( )
Magazines	6	( )	6	( )
Store clerks	7	( )	7	( )
	MD 8	( )	MD 8	( )

(Assume one response to each question)

[1/23-24] 7. What problems do you have finding information about the nutritional content of your food?
Uses 2 digits to allow for more than 10 responses

[1/45-46] 38. How many children live at home?
Allows recording of actual number of children

39. List all the brands of cereal purchased in the last month.

Record all brands mentioned. Set up a binary (yes-no) column code for each brand.)

CHAPTER 18 — UNIVARIATE DATA ANALYSIS

1. What is univariate data analysis?

    Univariate data analysis is the analysis of one variable at a time. It can be contrasted with bivariate and multivariate procedures, which consider two, and more than two variables, respectively.

2. Distinguish between descriptive and inferential statistics.

    Descriptive statistics is the branch of statistics that provides researchers with summary measures for the data in samples. Inferential statistics is the branch of statistics that allows researchers to make judgments concerning the population based on the results generated by samples.

3. Why are (1) measures of central tendency and (2) measures of dispersion necessary to describe a variable?

    Measures of central tendency and measures of dispersion are both descriptive statistics. The objective of descriptive statistics is to provide summary measures of the data contained in the sample. Measures of central tendency (essentially describing the "middle" of the distribution in some sense) do not alone provide enough information to fully understand the distribution. Thus, measures of dispersion (indicating the spread of the distribution) are also necessary.

4. Describe the steps in hypothesis testing in general.

    The general steps for hypothesis testing are as follows:

    1) Formulate a null and alternative hypothesis.
    2) Select the appropriate statistical test given the data.
    3) Specify the significance level.
    4) Find the value of the test statistic in a set of tables for the specified level.
    5) Perform the statistical test chosen in (2) on the data to yield a value of the statistic.
    6) Compare the value of the statistic obtained with the value found in (4). Reject H_O if value (5) value (4).

5. Distinguish between significance level and confidence level.

    The significance level, which equals α, indicates the probability of making a type I error. The confidence level, equal to $1 - \alpha$, indicates the probability of **not** rejecting the null hypothesis when it is true.

6. What are a type I and type II error?

    A type I error, also known as the α error, is the rejection of a true null hypothesis. A type II error, or β error, is the nonrejection of a false null hypothesis.

7. What is the power of the test?

    The power of the test, equal to $1-\beta$, is the probability of rejecting a false null hypothesis.

8. From a sample of Macintosh computer users, the following frequency count was generated for the categories of the variable age:

Age	
55 & over	150
40-54	190
25-39	270
18-24	210
n =	820

Is Macintosh usage spread evenly across the population in terms of age?

$$\chi^2 = \sum_{i=1}^{k} (O_i - E_i)^2 / E_i = 22.22$$

Calculation:

O_i	E_i	$(O_i - E_i)$	$(O_i - E_i)^2$	$(O_i - E_i)^2 / E_i$
150	205	-55	3025	14.76
190	205	-15	225	1.10
270	205	65	4225	20.61
210	205	5	25	0.12
820	820			36.59

Critical χ^2 at 3 df and $\alpha = .01 = 11.3$

Therefore, we conclude that there are significant differences between groups.

9. The manager of a movie theater hypothesized that twice as many of the theater's patrons were under 30 as were 30 and over. A sample of patrons yielded the following results:

Age	
Under 30	310
30 and Over	215
n =	525

Is the theater manager's hypothesis about the population of the patrons correct?

$$\chi^2 = \sum_{i=1}^{k} (O_i - E_i)^2 / E_i = 13.71$$

Calculation:

O_i	E_i	$(O_i - E_i)$	$(O_i - E_i)^2$	$(O_i - E_i)^2 / E_i$
310	350	-40	1600	4.57
215	175	40	1600	9.14
525	525			13.71

Critical χ^2 at 1 df and $\alpha = .01 = 6.63$
$\alpha = .05 = 3.84$

Therefore, we conclude that the observed pattern among patrons is significantly different from that hypothesized by the manager.

10. A sales manager had promised the entire sales force a special trip if average daily sales per salesperson were $6000 or more. A sample of 10 salespersons yielded the following results: Average daily sales per salesperson $6,300; the standard deviation = $900. Can the sales manager conclude that the entire sales force has reached the goal?

One way to set this problem up is:

$H_0 : \mu \leq 5,999$ $n = 10$

$H_1 : \mu \geq 5,999$ $\bar{X} = 6,300,$ $s = 900$

$$t = \frac{\bar{X} - \mu}{s/\sqrt{n}} = \frac{6300 - 5999}{900/\sqrt{10}} = \frac{301}{284.61} = 1.06$$

For a one-tail test, 9 df, critical value of t at $\alpha = .1$ is 1.38.

On this basis, the null hypothesis is not rejected. From this, we cannot conclude that the entire salesforce has reached the goal. The trip is not taken.

Another way to set up this problem is:

$H_0 : \mu \geq 6000$ $n = 10$

$H_1 : \mu < 6000$ $\bar{X} = 63000,$ $s = 900$

$$\frac{\bar{X} - \mu}{s/\sqrt{n}} = \frac{6300 - 6000}{900/\sqrt{10}} = \frac{300}{284.60} = 1.05$$

For a one-tailed test, 9 df, critical value of t at $\alpha = .1$ is 1.38 (as before).

On this basis the null hypothesis is not rejected. Here the trip would be taken.

These types of results show the importance of thinking through how the null and alternative hypotheses are stated. They also present an intuitive view of the workings of beta error.

11. A political research firm undertook a sample of registered voters in a small community to see whether a particular candidate would win the election. The sample size was 50, and the result was that 51 percent of the sample favored this candidate. If the people voted as they say they will, do the results indicate that this candidate will win the election?

$H_0 : \pi \leq .5$ $n = 50$

$H_1 : \pi > .5$ $p = .51$

$$z = \frac{p - \pi}{\sqrt{\frac{pq}{n}}} = \frac{.51 - .5}{\sqrt{\frac{(.51)(.49)}{50}}} = \frac{.01}{\sqrt{.0005}} = \frac{.01}{.071} = .141$$

For a one-tailed test $z = 1.29$ for $\alpha = .1$
    $z = 1.64$ for $\alpha = .05$

In this case, the z value computed is less than the critical level for $\alpha = .1$, and the null hypothesis is not rejected. On this basis, we cannot conclude that the results indicate this candidate will win the election.

12. A company had adopted the following decision rule with respect to introducing a new product: If average monthly consumption is 200 ounces or more, we will enter into test market. An in-home placement test of n = 50 yielded the following results: Average monthly consumption = 196 ounces; standard deviation = 35. Given their decision rule, what decision should they make?

$H_0 : \mu \geq 200$ $n = 50$

$H_1 : \mu < 200$ $\bar{X} = 96$ $s = 35$

$$z = \frac{\bar{X} - u}{s/\sqrt{n}} = \frac{196 - 200}{35/\sqrt{50}} = \frac{-4}{4.95} = -.81$$

For a one-tailed test $z = 1.64$ for $\alpha = .05$

On the basis of this test, at = .05, the null hypothesis is not rejected: we conclude that the true mean is 100. Given the decision rule, the firm should test market.

13. The Lake City chief of police wanted to find out how fast an average car traveled on a particular stretch of highway. To get this information, he placed a hidden radar device beside the highway and clocked speeds for an hour. The following data were recorded by the device:

73	49	70	63
55	61	60	68
52	56	69	60
65	66	59	62

Questions:

A) Calculate the appropriate statistics for central tendency and dispersion.
B) What are the problems with this design?

A) The mean is the appropriate measure of control tendency, and is calculated as follows:

167

$$\frac{\Sigma X_i}{n} = \frac{988}{16} = 61.75$$

Using the computational formula to calculate the standard deviation results in the following:

$$s = \sqrt{\frac{\Sigma X^2 - (X)^2/n}{n-1}} = \frac{61676 - (976144/16)}{15} = 6.67$$

B) There is a major problem with using a design such as this to calculate the speed of an average car. A disproportionately large number of fast cars were included in the sample because more of the faster cars would pass by the radar detector in a one-hour stretch. A "fast" car increases its probability of selection if it is traveling faster than the others, simply because it covers more highway per hour than a slower car. To correctly determine the speed of an "average" car, the officer would have to "freeze" a stretch of highway and then record the speeds of all cars in this sample. From this, he could determine the speed of an "average" car.

Also, radar is often inaccurate; with only one device doing the testing, the reliability and validity are compromised. And, finally, the use of radar detectors by motorists could confound the experiment and render the results useless.

CHAPTER 19 — BIVARIATE DATA ANALYSIS

1. What questions must one answer in order to select the appropriate bivariate statistical procedure?

   Three questions must be answered:

   1) Are two variables to be analyzed at a time?
   2) What is the scale level of these variables?
   3) Is a descriptive statistic or an inferential test desired?

2. What is linear correlation?

   Linear correlation is a measure of the degree to which two intervally scaled variables are associated. One measure of the direction and strength of the relationship between two interval variables is the linear correlation coefficients, defined as:

   $$r_{XY} = \Sigma xy / \left[\Sigma x^2 \Sigma y^2\right]^{1/2}$$

3. What is the coefficient of determination?

   The coefficient of determination, r^2, is the exact percentage of variation shared by two variables, and is calculated by squaring the correlation coefficient, r.

   In the case of simple regression, r^2_{XY} is the proportion of the total variation in Y explained by the regression line.

4. When can simple regression be used?

   Simple regression can be used when one has one intervally-scaled dependent variable and one intervally-scaled independent variable, and is interested in assessing how the independent variable is related to the dependent variable. The method is often used to obtain predictions of scores on the dependent measure based on the independent variable scores.

5. How does one test to see whether a simple regression has explained a significant portion of the variation in the dependent variable?

   The appropriate test is the F statistic, which is the ratio of the variance explained by the regression over the unexplained variance ("error"). In the terminology of the regression analysis,

   $$F = \frac{\left[S\left(\hat{Y}_i - \overline{Y}_i\right)^2\right]}{\left[\Sigma\left(\hat{Y}_i - Y_i\right)^2 / n - 2\right]}$$

This procedure is identical to a one-way ANOVA testing procedure (see Chapter 20-Appendix).

6. When should the z and t tests on the difference between means be used?

    The same decision criteria are used as were applied in univariate analysis. The z test is appropriate if the population standard deviation, is known for both measures or if a sample size over 30 is used for both measures. If neither of these conditions holds, the t test is the appropriate procedure.

7. What is the chi-square test a test for?

    In bivariate applications, the chi-square test is used to determine whether a relationship not attributable to sampling error exists between two variables. As the test is used, the null hypothesis is that the two variables are independent; the alternative hypothesis is that they are not.

8. In what alternative ways may percentages be calculated in a crosstab table? Which way is the best?

    Percentages may be calculated as row percentages, column percentages, and cell percentages. The key consideration in constructing a crosstab table is to cast percentages in the direction of the causal factor.

9. What is elaboration?

    Elaboration is a further consideration of a two-way crosstab, taking into account categories of some other variable or variables.

10. What may be found in elaboration?

    A. The original table led to the conclusion of a relationship.

       1. Retain the original conclusion of a relationship.
       2. Specify a different relationship according to control categories.
       3. Conclude the original relationship to be spurious.

    B. The original table led to the conclusion of no relationship.

       1. Retain the original conclusion of no relationship.
       2. Identify a relationship.

11. A marketing manager was given the following table of frequency counts to show the nature of the relationship between age and attendance at NFL games. What conclusion should be drawn?

Attend NFL Games	Age Under 40	40 & Over	Total
Yes	466	231	697
No	224	323	547
Total	690	554	1244

Set up a chi-square test as follows:

Cell Number	O_{ij}	E_{ij}	$O_{ij} - E_{ij}$	$(O_{ij} - E_{ij})^2$	$(O_{ij} - E_{ij})^2 / E_{ij}$
1,1	466	523.72	-57.72	3,331.60	6.36
1,2	231	314.73	-83.73	7,010.71	22.28
2,1	224	253.78	-29.78	886.85	3.49
2,2	323	151.77	171.23	29,319.71	193.19
Total	1244	1244.00			$225.32 = \chi^2$

For $(R-1)(C-1) = 1$ df, the critical value of χ^2 at $\alpha = .05$ is 3.84. On this basis, the null hypothesis of no relationship between age and attendance at NFL games is rejected.

12. The same marketing manager as in Question 11 also had a table of frequency counts between age and attendance at college football games. What conclusion should be drawn?

Attend College Football Games	Age Under 40	40 & Over	Total
Yes	242	271	513
No	251	265	516
Total	493	536	1029

Set up a chi-square test as follows:

Cell Number	O_{ij}	E_{ij}	$O_{ij} - E_{ij}$	$(O_{ij} - E_{ij})^2$	$(O_{ij} - E_{ij})^2 / E_{ij}$
1,1	242	206.83	35.17	1,236.93	5.98
1,2	271	301.50	-30.50	930.25	3.09
2,1	251	210.95	40.05	1604.00	7.60
2,2	265	309.73	-44.73	2000.77	6.46
Total	1029	1029.00			$23.13 = \chi^2$

For $(R-1)(C-1) = 1$ df, the critical value of χ^2 at $\alpha = .05$ is 3.84 and at $\alpha = .1$ is 2.71. On this basis, the null hypothesis of no relationship between age and attendance at college football games is rejected.

13. In a study of advertising effects, two waves of consumers were interviewed. Wave 1 took place before a new campaign was introduced, and wave 2 a few months after the new campaign had started. As part of the analysis of the data, a comparison was made between the demographic characteristics of the consumers in wave 1 and wave 2. The hope was that the demographics would be the same. Typical of the reported results is the following:

	Sex	
	Male	Female
Wave 1	52%	47%
Wave 2	48	53

(chi-square = 4.16)

What conclusion can be drawn from this result?

First, we note that the critical chi-square at 1 df and $\alpha = .05$ is 3.84. Therefore, we know that the waves and sex distributions are not independent of each other. We are now ready to look back into the table to interpret this relationship. However, we cannot do this given the way information is presented in the table.

The percentages in the table are in the wrong direction. What we are interested in is a comparison of the male/female percentages in wave 1 versus wave 2. This would be directly observable if we had row percentages. What we have instead, for example, is the percentage of all males in both waves that were in wave 1 (52%).

This is not a useful piece of information for comparing the sex composition of the waves. It would be even more of a problem as the difference in size of the waves gets larger.

As an aside, a large set of tables like this one got a marketing research supplier fired from a big project. Casting percentages the proper way is considered an important part of marketing research competence.

14. The same study used in Questions 11 and 12 yielded the following data concerning the number of NFL home games a person attended in a year and the number of years the person has lived in the city.

Case	No. of Home Games Attended	Years Lived in City
1	8	28
2	2	6
3	1	3
4	3	12
5	8	20
6	4	23

What is the relationship between the two variables?

Let Y_i = number of home games attended

X_i = number of years lived in city.

Then set up linear regression of form $Y = a + bX$ as follows:

X_i	Y_i	$x_i = (X_i - \overline{X})$	$Y_i x_i$	x_i^2
28	8	12.67	101.36	160.53
6	2	-9.33	-18.66	87.05
3	1	-12.33	-12.33	152.03
12	3	-3.33	-9.99	11.09
20	8	4.67	37.36	21.81
23	4	7.67	30.68	58.83

$\Sigma X_i = 92 \quad \Sigma Y_i = 26 \quad \Sigma X_i = 0 \quad \Sigma Y_i x_i = 128.42 \quad \Sigma x_i^2 = 491.34$

$\overline{X} = 15.33 \quad \overline{Y} = 4.33$

$a = \overline{Y} = 4.33$

$b = \Sigma Y_i x_i / \Sigma x_i^2 = 128.42/491.34$

$= 0.26$

$\hat{Y}_i = a + bx_i = 4.33 + 0.26\, x_i$

$= 4.33 + 0.26\, (X_i - \overline{X})$

$= 4.33 + 0.26\, (X_i - 15.33)$

$= 4.33 + 0.26\, X_i - 3.99$

$\hat{Y}_i = .34 + 0.26\, X_i$

This represents the line fitted by regression analysis.

Test of significance of equation:

Y_i	$\overline{Y}$	$\hat{Y}_i$	$\hat{Y}_i - \overline{Y}$	$(\hat{Y}_i - \overline{Y})^2$	$Y_i - \hat{Y}_i$	$(Y_i - \hat{Y}_i)^2$
8	4.33	7.62	3.29	10.82	.38	.144
2	4.33	1.90	-2.43	5.90	.10	.010
1	4.33	1.12	-3.21	10.30	-.12	.014
3	4.33	3.46	-.87	.76	-.46	.212
8	4.33	5.54	1.21	1.46	2.26	6.052
4	4.33	6.32	1.99	3.96	-2.32	5.382
			$\Sigma = 0$	$\Sigma = 33.20$	$\Sigma = 0$	$\Sigma = 11.814$

	SS	df	MS	F
SS explained	33.20	1	33.20	11.25
SS unexplained	11.81	4	2.95	
SS Total	45.01	5		

For 1,4 df at $\alpha = .05$, the critical value of F = 7.71.

Thus, it is concluded that at $\alpha = .05$ a significant relationship exists between the number of home games attended and the number of years lived in the city.

15. Mark Schwinn and Jennifer Grier were advisors assigned to the first coed hall at Montana College. A welcome party was scheduled to take place the weekend after classes started, and the RAs had the responsibility of ordering the soft drinks. They couldn't, however, agree on kinds of soft drinks they should order (diet cola vs. regular cola vs. other assorted flavors). A total of 30-40 cases was to be ordered, and any unopened cans could be returned. Mark wanted 16 cases of regular cola, 6 diet cola, 6 regular non-cola, and 2 diet non-cola. Jennifer wanted to order, respectively, 11, 6, 9, and 4 cases. To avoid running out of anything, they decided to get the highest estimate of each kind, making a 35 case order (16 cases regular cola, 6 diet cola, 9 regular non-cola, and 4 diet non-cola). The actual consumption at the party was 12 cases of regular cola, 4 diet cola, 8 regular non-cola, and 1 diet non-cola.

Questions:

A) Is there a difference in preferences between regular vs. diet pop? Cola vs. non-colas? Are the two variables independent?

Because there was soda of every type left over, one can assume that consumption was not a function of a beverage's availability. The first two parts of question A require univariate analysis.

Calculation:	O_i	E_i	$(O_i - E_i)$	$(O_i - E_i)^2$	$(O_i - E_i)^2/E_i$
Cola vs.	16	12.5	3.5	12.25	.98
non-cola	9	12.5	-3.5	12.25	.98
					1.96
Regular vs.	20	12.5	7.5	56.25	4.50
diet	5	12.5	-7.5	56.25	4.50
					9.00

The critical value of chi-square at 1 df and $\alpha = .01 = 6.63$
$\alpha = .05 = 3.84$
$\alpha = .10 = 2.71$

We can conclude that there is no difference in preference between cola and non-cola at $\alpha < .10$. However, there is a difference in preference between regular and diet sodas, with more people preferring regular. This is significant at $\alpha < .01$.

Independence of the two variables cannot be determined since neither of the expected cell sizes are large enough: regular cola = 12.8, diet cola = 3.2, regular non-cola = 7.2, and diet non-cola = 1.8.

16. In a recent study on American travel habits, the following data were obtained:

Case	Sex	Children at Home	Respondent's Age	Vacations Per Year
1	M	Y	25	1
2	M	N	52	16
3	F	N	34	8
4	F	Y	33	1
5	F	Y	51	5
6	F	Y	29	0
7	M	Y	35	2
8	F	N	27	8
9	M	Y	46	4
10	M	N	30	10
11	F	N	45	14
12	M	Y	38	3

Questions:

A) Is there a relationship between the presence of children at home and the sex of the respondent?

B) What is the relationship between age and the presence of children at home? (Hint: Create nominal age categories.)

C) What is the relationship between age and number of vacations per year? Calculate r-squared. (Hint: Plot the data points before doing a regression analysis. Look for the interaction of an extraneous variable, and calculate your least squares regression line(s) accordingly. Is one equation appropriate? Would two explain the data better?)

D) (From chapter Appendix.) Is (are) your answer(s) to Question C significant? (i.e., was a significant proportion of the variance in the dependent variable explained by the regression?)

E) Using the equation(s) you computed in the previous problem, complete the following data set:

Case	Sex	Children at Home	Respondent's Age	Vacations Per Year
a	M	Y	40	?
b	F	N	40	?
c	M	Y	65	?
d	F	N	18	?

A. The first question cannot be answered because of the small expected values in the cells. The usefulness of data such as this is questionable. The instructor may wish to have students evaluate the usefulness of this type of data and under what circumstances it may have value (e.g., if the study population were single or divorced persons).

B. As in the first question, the expected values in each cell are not five or larger, so a chi-square test is inappropriate and no conclusions can be drawn.

C. Obviously, two "clumps" of data points exist here. They are differentiated by the variable "children present at home." R-square for the whole data set is only .24. Compare this to the r-squares of the clumps: both of them are .89. This illustrates the importance of "rough-sketching" the data before performing analyses. For regression solutions and calculations see below in Tables.

D. Students can use either a t-test or an F-test to check for significance.

T-TEST:

Whole Data Set:

$H_0: \beta = 0$

$H_1: \beta \neq 0$

s_{YX}: standard error of the estimate

$$s_{YX} = \sqrt{\frac{(Y_i - \hat{Y}_i)^2}{n-2}} = \sqrt{\frac{232.53}{10}} = 4.822$$

s_b: standard error of the regression coefficient

$$s_b = \frac{s_{XY}}{\sqrt{\Sigma(X_i - \overline{X}_i)^2}} = \frac{4.822}{\sqrt{952.96}} = .1562$$

$$t = \frac{b}{S} = \frac{.27}{.1562} = 1.73$$

at $\alpha = .10$; n - 2 = 10 degrees of freedom: critical value = 1.812

Therefore, results are not significant at $\alpha = .10$.

One cannot reject the null hypothesis that $\beta = 0$. This means that knowledge of the X variables (age in this case) does not make a significant contribution to the explanation of the Y variables (the number of vacations taken per year).

"Children at Home" Data Set:

$H_0: \beta = 0$

$H_1: \beta \neq 0$

s_{YX}: standard error of the estimate

$$= \sqrt{\frac{2.11}{5}} = .6496$$

s_b: standard error of the regression coefficient

$$= \frac{.6496}{\sqrt{505.40}} = .0289$$

$$t = \frac{b}{s_b} = \frac{.185}{.0289} = 6.401$$

at $\alpha = .01$, n - 2 = 5 degrees of freedom: critical value = 4.032

Therefore, results are significant at $\alpha = .01$.

"No Children at Home" Data Set:

H_0: $\beta = 0$

H_1: $\beta \neq 0$

s_{YX}: standard error of the estimate

$$= \sqrt{\frac{5.98}{3}} = 1.412$$

s_b: standard error of the regression coefficient

$$= \frac{1.412}{\sqrt{445.20}} = .0669$$

$$t = \frac{b}{s_b} = \frac{.324}{.0669} = 4.843$$

at $\alpha = .02$, n - 2 = 3 degrees of freedom: critical value = 4.541

Therefore, results are significant at $\alpha = .02$.

E. Using the appropriate equations, the answers for parts a and b are as follows:

a. $\hat{Y}_i = 4.50 + .185X_i$

$= -4.50 + .185(40)$

$= 2.9$

Whole data set:

X_i	Y_i	$X_i - \bar{X}$	$Y_i(X_i - \bar{X})$	$(X_i - \bar{X})^2$	$\hat{Y}_i = -4.01 + .27 X_i$	$Y_i - \hat{Y}_i$	$(Y_i - \hat{Y}_i)^2$	$Y_i - \bar{Y}$	$(Y_i - \bar{Y})^2$
25	1	-12.08	-12.08	145.93	2.74	-1.74	3.03	-5	25
52	16	14.92	238.72	222.61	10.03	5.97	35.64	10	100
34	8	-3.08	-24.64	9.49	5.17	2.83	8.01	2	4
33	1	-4.08	-4.08	16.65	4.90	-3.90	15.21	-5	25
51	5	13.92	69.60	193.77	9.76	-4.76	22.66	-1	1
29	0	-8.08	0.00	65.29	3.82	-3.82	14.59	-6	36
35	2	-2.08	-4.16	4.33	5.44	-3.44	11.83	-4	16
27	8	-10.08	-80.64	101.61	3.28	4.72	22.28	2	4
46	4	8.92	35.68	79.57	8.41	-4.41	19.45	-2	4
30	10	-7.08	-79.80	50.13	4.09	5.91	34.93	4	16
45	14	7.92	110.88	62.73	8.14	5.86	34.34	8	64
38	3	.92	2.76	.85	6.25	-3.25	10.56	-3	9

$\Sigma X_i = 445$ $\Sigma Y_i = 72$ $\Sigma(X_i - \bar{X}) = 0$ $\Sigma Y_i(X_i - \bar{X}) = 261.24$ $\Sigma(X_i - \bar{X})^2 = 952.96$ $\Sigma(Y_i - \hat{Y}_i) = 0$ $\Sigma(Y_i - \hat{Y}_i)^2 = 232.53$ $\Sigma(Y_i - \bar{Y}) = 0$ $\Sigma(Y_i - \bar{Y})^2 = 304$

$\bar{X} = 37.08$ $\bar{Y} = 6$

$a = \bar{Y} = 6$

$b = 261.24/952.96 = .27$

$\hat{Y}_i = 6 + .27 (X_i - 37.08) = -4.01 + .27 X_i$

SST = SSR + SSE

304 = SSR + 232.53; SSR = 71.47

r^2 = SSR/SST = 71.47/304 = .24

With children at home:

X_i	Y_i	$X_i - \bar{X}$	$Y_i(X_i - \bar{X})$	$(X_i - \bar{X})^2$	$\hat{Y}_i = -4.50 + .185 X_i$	$Y_i - \hat{Y}_i$	$(Y_i - \hat{Y}_i)^2$	$Y_i - \bar{Y}$	$(Y_i - \bar{Y})^2$
25	1	-11.71	-11.71	137.12	.13	.87	.76	1.29	1.66
29	0	-7.71	0.00	59.44	.87	-.87	.76	-2.29	5.24
33	1	-3.71	-3.71	13.76	1.61	-.61	.37	-1.29	1.66
35	2	-1.71	-3.42	2.92	1.98	.02	.00	-.29	.08
38	3	1.29	3.87	1.66	2.53	.47	.22	.71	.50
46	4	9.29	37.16	86.30	4.01	-.01	.00	1.71	2.92
51	5	14.29	71.45	204.20	4.94	.06	.00	2.71	7.34
$\Sigma X_i = 257$	$\Sigma Y_i = 16$	$\Sigma(X_i - \bar{X}) = 0$	$\Sigma Y_i(X_i - \bar{X}) = 93.64$	$\Sigma(X_i - \bar{X})^2 = 505.40$		$\Sigma(Y_i - \hat{Y}_i) = 0$	$\Sigma(Y_i - \hat{Y}_i)^2 = 2.11$	$\Sigma(Y_i - \bar{Y}) = 0$	$\Sigma(Y_i - \bar{Y})^2 = 19.40$
$\bar{X} = 36.71$	$\bar{Y} = 2.29$								

$a = \bar{Y} = 2.29$

$b = 93.64/505.40 = .185$

$\hat{Y}_i = 2.29 + .185 (X_i - 36.71) = -4.50 + .185 X_i$

SST = SSR + SSE

19.40 = SSR + 2.11; SSR = 17.29

r^2 = SSR/SST = 17.29/19.40 = .89

179

Without children at home:

X_i	Y_i	$X_i - \bar{X}$	$Y_i(X_i - \bar{X})$	$(X_i - \bar{X})^2$	$\hat{Y}_i = -.98 + .324 X_i$	$Y_i - \hat{Y}_i$	$(Y_i - \hat{Y}_i)^2$	$Y_i - \bar{Y}$	$(Y_i - \bar{Y})^2$
27	8	-10.6	-84.8	112.36	7.77	.23	.05	-3.2	10.24
30	10	-7.6	-76.0	57.76	8.74	1.26	1.59	-1.2	1.44
34	8	-3.6	-28.8	12.96	10.04	-2.04	4.16	-3.2	10.24
45	14	7.4	103.6	54.76	13.60	.40	.16	2.8	7.84
52	16	14.4	230.4	207.36	15.87	.13	.02	4.8	23.04
$\Sigma X_i = 118$	$\Sigma Y_i = 56$	$\Sigma(X_i - \bar{X}) = 0$	$\Sigma Y_i(X_i - \bar{X}) = 144.4$	$\Sigma(X_i - \bar{X})^2 = 445.20$		$\Sigma(Y_i - \hat{Y}_i) = 0$	$\Sigma(Y_i - \hat{Y}_i)^2 = 5.98$	$\Sigma(Y_i - \bar{Y}) = 0$	$\Sigma(Y_i - \bar{Y})^2 = 52.80$
$\bar{X} = 37.6$	$\bar{Y} = 11.2$								

$a = \bar{Y} = 11.2$

$b = 144.4/445.2 = .324$

$\hat{Y}_i = 11.2 + .324 (X_i - 37.6) = -.98 + .324 X_i$

$SST = SSR + SSE$

$52.80 = SSR + 5.98; \; SSR = 46.82$

$r^2 = SSR/SST = 46.82/52.80 = .89$

b. $\hat{Y}_i = -.98 + .324X_i$

$= -.98 + .324(40)$

$= 11.98$

The answers for parts c and d cannot be computed using the regression equation from question 3. The ages 18 and 65 are outside the range of data from which the regression was calculated. It is incorrect to extrapolate the equation to data points beyond the range of 25-51 years for those with children at home, and beyond 27-52 years for those without.

CHAPTER 20 — MULTIVARIATE DATA ANALYSIS I: INTERDEPENDENCE METHODS

1. Why is multivariate analysis becoming more used in marketing research?

   Several reasons help explain this trend:

   1) The use of one or two variables alone usually will not completely describe marketing problems.
   2) More advanced computing equipment facilitates the solution of multivariate procedures.
   3) Marketing researchers and managers have an increased knowledge of statistical concepts.

2. Distinguish between dependence and interdependence methods.

   The point of distinction is whether or not some variables in the analysis are dependent on others. In dependence methods, some variable or variables are dependent; in interdependence methods this is not the case.

3. What is the overall objective of factor analysis?

   The overall objective of factor analysis is to identify a small number of common factors which account for the intercorrelation of a larger number of variables or objects. In marketing, this technique is useful for purposes of:

   1) data reduction;
   2) structure identification;
   3) scaling; and
   4) data transformation.

4. Describe the nature of the input and output of factor analysis.

   The input to factor analysis is a set of correlations between all combinations of variables of interest, which must be assumed to be intervally-scaled, i.e., a correlation matrix.

   The output is a series of matrices, including the initial (unrotated) factor matrix and the rotated solutions (either orthogonal or oblique). The rationale for rotating the initial factor matrix is to increase interpretability of the factors generated.

5. What are R- and Q-type factor analysis?

   R- and Q-type factor analysis differ according to the basis on which correlations are calculated. R-type factor analysis calculates correlations between variables, whereas Q-type factor analysis calculates correlations between cases (people, products, etc.).

6. What is the objective of cluster analysis?

   The objective of cluster analysis is to take a set of variables or objects, form subgroups or clusters, and place the original variables or objects into these subgroups.

7. Describe the nature of the input and output of cluster analysis.

   The input to a cluster analysis is a matrix of associations between variables or objects. Depending upon the algorithm used, the input matrix may be formed using nominal, ordinal, interval, or ratio-level scaled variables.

   The output includes identification of the objects of interest by cluster. Additionally, alternate groupings of objects into clusters may be presented.

8. What is the objective of multidimensional scaling?

   Multidimensional scaling is a multivariate data analysis method that takes as input a matrix of relationships between objects with unknown underlying dimensionality, determines the minimum dimensionality of the relationships between the objects, and positions each object on each dimension.

9. What is nonmetric multidimensional scaling?

   Nonmetric multidimensional scaling is the type of multidimensional scaling which is most widely used in marketing applications. It differs from other types of multidimensional scaling on the nature of the input and output data. Specifically, it takes ordinal measures of relationship as input and gives interval relationships among the input objects as output.

10. Describe the nature of the input and output of nonmetric multidimensional scaling.

    Nonmetric multidimensional scaling uses ordinally-scaled input data and generates an intervally-scaled set of relationships among the objects.

11. How does one name factors, clusters, and dimensions for interdependence methods?

    Once the computer output of the various procedures is in hand, it is up to the market researcher or manager to use his best judgment based on experience, intuition, etc., to attach meaningful labels to the factors and dimensions, and to properly explain clusters. It is a risky business.

12. If you were the marketing vice president of a major bank, how might you use the factor analysis results given in the Marketing Research in Action at the beginning of this chapter?

    The study's purpose was to identify strategic dimensions upon which banks compete. Having done so, the marketing vice president could further investigate how the bank is doing in these areas in the eyes of customers, in comparison to competitors, etc. The results could also be used as a guideline for allocating marketing dollars in proportion to their importance in the factor analysis.

13. It is standard practice in the automobile industry to use multidimensional scaling representations of automobile brands in marketing planning. Why would this be so? How could an automobile marketing person use the scaling results given in Figure 19-5?

    Multidimensional scaling provides a graphical representation of consumers' perceptions of similarities and differences between automobile brands. Its potential uses include:

- Identification of important attributes upon which consumers differentiate automobile brands.

- Identification of segments/competitive groups/potential substitute brands. Those which are mapped closely together are perceived as being similar.

- Determine which combination of attributes consumers perceive to be "ideal." Also determine where current brands fall in relation to "ideal"

- Find gaps in the market which can be filled with new product.

- Determine effectiveness of automotive advertising in achieving desired positioning.

CHAPTER 21 — MULTIVARIATE DATA ANALYSIS II: DEPENDENCE METHODS

1. How are dependence methods classified?

   Dependence methods are classified according to

   1) The number of variables designated as dependent, and
   2) The scale levels of the dependent and independent variables.

2. What is the coefficient of multiple determination? How is it calculated from a regression printout?

   The coefficient of multiple determination is the proportion of the variation in Y explained by the multiple regression equation. It can be calculated as:

   $$SS_{explained}/SS_{total}$$

3. What does a coefficient mean in multiple regression?

   A coefficient in multiple regression has meaning both in terms of size and direction. The size of the coefficient shows the amount of change in the dependent variable associated with a one-unit increase in that independent variable, assuming that all other independent variables are held constant. The sign of the coefficient indicates either a direct or inverse relationship between that independent variable and the dependent variable.

4. How does ANCOVA work?

   The following steps are incorporated in ANCOVA:

   1) A regression is carried out with the covariates as independent variables and the dependent variable from the experiment as the dependent variable.
   2) Regression estimates $\hat{Y}_i$'s are calculated for each covariate observation.
   3) Estimated Y_i's are subtracted from the observed experimental data Y_i, the result being a set of experimental data (defined as $Y_i' = Y_i - \hat{Y}_i$) with the effects of the covariates removed.
   4) An ANOVA is performed using the Y_i' values.

5. How are nominal independent variables handled in a regression?

   Nominal independent variables are handled in a regression through the creation of a series of binary variables coded 0-1. Specifically, each nominal variable can be represented by n-1 of these binary variables, known as dummy variables.

6. How is AID related to ANOVA?

   AID performs a series of one-way ANOVAs in breaking down the total sample into a number of subgroups which are more homogeneous on the dependent variable than the total sample.

7. What is a discriminant function? What criterion is used to derive its coefficients?

As used in discriminant analysis, the discriminant function, defined as $DF = v_1X_1 + v_2X_2 + ... + v_nX_n$, is a linear combination of the independent variables such that the mean scores across categories of the dependent variable on this linear combination are maximally different.

The coefficients are derived using the ANOVA F test, such that $F = (SS_{between}/SS_{within})$ is maximized.

8. How could conjoint measurement be used to predict market share?

The technique could be used to determine the total utility a consumer places on various attribute combinations for a product. Extending this to a sample of consumers would allow the prediction of market share based on the combination of attributes a product offers.

9. The regression coefficients expressed in standardized form, and with the sign removed (the impact of units of measurement have been removed) for the service quality Marketing Research in Action at the beginning of this chapter are:

Predictor Variable	Regression Coefficient
Physician Interaction	.6155
Doctor Interest	.1616
Emergency Availability	.1096
Professionalism	.1104
Reasonable Fees	.1122
Medical Competence	.2044
Latest Technologies	.1443
Diagnostics Available	.0866
Staff Interactions	.0757
Brochures Available	.0688

a. What do these coefficients indicate?

A variable's coefficient indicates its relative importance to the dependent measure (service quality rating.) In this example, physician interaction, medical competence, doctor interest, and latest technologies are the most important variables. Staff interactions, diagnostics available, and brochures available are the least important variables.

b. What other information would you like to have about the regression coefficients?

It would be helpful to know the t and p values for each coefficient, to determine their significance in the regression equation. It would also be helpful to know the sign of each coefficient. This would indicate whether each variable adds to or subtracts from the overall service rating.

10. Prepare a tradeoff matrix that Marriott could have used in the development of the Courtyard Concept. Hint: use a maximum of three attributes at a time.

The four attributes mentioned were size of room, nature of meal service, price of room, and nature of surroundings. One of several possible tradeoff matrices Marriott could have used is this:

Variable	Level 1	Level 2	Level 3	Level 4
Room Size	150 sq. ft.	200 sq. ft.	250 sq. ft.	300 sq. ft.
Meal Service	room service	snack bar	dining room	vending machines
Price/Night	$50	$75	$100	$125

CHAPTER 22 — REPORTING RESEARCH FINDINGS

1. Why is the research report important?

   The research report communicates findings to the management group responsible for utilizing marketing research. Management's evaluation of the project as a whole is influenced greatly by the effectiveness of the written and oral presentation. Thus, it is imperative that the research report be of high quality.

Instructor's Further Probing: The Marketing Research in Action insert at the beginning of the chapter showed a key element that must be incorporated into the presentation of research reports. What is that element?

Suggested Probe Response: The insert example showed that just facts and figures are not enough to provide reliable findings. Human psychology must be taken into account during the presentation of research findings. The presentation must be tailored to the audience, with certain negative reactions anticipated ahead of time.

2. What general guidelines exist for the preparation of written research reports?

   1) Consider the audience.
   2) Address information needs.
   3) Be concise yet complete.
   4) Be objective yet effective.
   5) Use an appropriate writing style.

Instructor's Further Probing: Is it true that a thick report packed with details and conclusions is better than a thin report with only a few remarks? Why?

Suggested Probe Response: No, not necessarily. Presentation does not mean expressing all possible results and conclusions. Presentation means tailoring the findings to what is relevant for the audience. The point of a presentation is to transmit and convey findings, anything else during the presentation should only support that purpose and not distract from that purpose.

3. How might an oral presentation supplement a written research report?

   An oral presentation may be used to highlight the research report, permit the audience to raise questions, and allow the researcher to clarify points of concern.

Instructor's Further Probing: What dynamics may be different for an oral presentation versus a written research report?

Suggested Probe Response: Written research reports must convey all the information and answer any doubts or questions the audience may have--very quickly. In addition, the written report must be well planned since the writer can not guide the reader based on any feedback. The oral presentation can be dynamic and change the information presented as the audience changes or as the audience requests it.

4. What components are typically included in a research report?

   1) Title Page.
   2) Table of Contents.
   3) List of Tables (or figures, graphs, etc.).
   4) Management Summary.
   5) Body.
   6) Conclusions and Recommendations.
   7) Appendix.

Instructor's Further Probing: What is perhaps the most important component in a research report?

Suggested Probe Response: The management summary is usually read first, giving an idea to the reader whether the rest of the report is worth reading. If the summary is not appealing, then the rest of the report may never be read, thus making the management summary the most important component in a research report.

5. What are the alternative means of displaying data graphically?

   Data may be displayed either in pie charts, bar charts, or line charts. Dressier versions of the above graphs include exploding pie charts and cluster bar graphs.

Instructor's Further Probing: What recent uses of technology have enhanced the presentation of data graphically?

Suggested Probe Response: With the prevalence of laptop computers and projectors for computer displays, graphs can be generated, and even animated, by a computer. This allows the presenter to dynamically choose which graphs to show based on audience feedback. Some technology even allows the presenter to use a laser pointer on the projected screen to control the computer, allowing for an impressive, and seamless presentation of a host of data.

CHAPTER 23 — DEMAND MEASUREMENT AND FORECASTING

1. Develop four alternative definitions of market demand for television sets.

    1) The market demand for black and white televisions is the total unit volume that will be sold to discount distributors in the state of Michigan.

    2) The market demand for color televisions is the total unit volume that will be sold during the Christmas season to all buyers in the continental United States.

    3) The market demand for all color and black and white portable televisions is the total unit volume that will be sold that are made in the United States and sold through department stores to consumer buyers.

    4) The market demand is the total unit volume for all televisions, domestic or imported, to be bought by all buyers, consumer, government and business, in the United States.

    Note that the definitions contain and vary the product type, customer group, time period, and geography, plus assume a specific environment and marketing programs.

Instructor's Further Probing: Why is the market demand important knowledge for a marketing manager?

Suggested Probe Response: The market demand gives the marketing manager an idea of what is the greatest possible number of sales feasible in a given time period. As a result, combined with marketing research, an appropriate marketing plan can be developed.

2. What is the difference between market potential and market forecast? Why is this difference important?

    Market potential establishes an upper limit to market demand as industry marketing effort increases. On the other hand, market forecast refers to the expected market demand at a given, expected level of industry marketing effort. In both cases, the market demand is estimated given a specified time period and an assumed marketing environment. The difference between market forecast and market potential is important because a forecast refers to a particular level of demand and market potential establishes the upper limit to market demand as industry marketing effort increases without bound.

Instructor's Further Probing: What does "assumed marketing environment" mean?

Suggested Probe Response: When referring to an "assumed marketing environment", we are referring to marketing goals and limitations set on reaching those goals. This includes budget and time constraints, strategy, research, and efforts associated with advertising and promotion. It is always important to understand the environment we are working in.

3. What is the difference between a market forecast and company sales forecast?

A market forecast refers to the level of market demand expected as a result of an expected level of industry marketing effort, given an assumed environment. A company sales forecast is the expected level of company sales based upon a chosen marketing plan and an assumed environment. Therefore, a market forecast applies to an entire industry and a company sales forecast applies to a particular company within a given industry.

Instructor's Further Probing: How would the concept of market share relate to market and company sales forecasting?

Suggested Probe Response: Since market share defines how much a company will compose of the total industry sales, company sales forecasting is directly related to the market share a company has within the industry.

4. Compare and contrast the breakdown and buildup method for estimating current demand.

While the breakdown method begins with aggregate market or industry data and breaks it down into units that the firm is interested in, the buildup method aggregates data from the customer or account level to the industry or market level. The breakdown method utilizes either the direct data method, which estimates market and sales potential from total industry or market data, or the indirect data method which relies on the development and use of an index of market or sales potential from one or more statistical series to determine an area's market potential. In using the breakdown method, a firm must have an estimate of total potential. The buildup method does not require a total potential estimate but instead involves the collection of data on customer past purchases or probable future requirements. It often involves the use of Standard Industrial Classification (SIC) data.

Instructor's Further Probing: What are the two approaches in the breakdown method?

Suggested Probe Response: Two approaches that can be used in the breakdown method include the direct data method and the indirect data method.

5. Why is accurate sales forecasting important to an organization?

Many plans and budgets made by an organization are based upon the sales forecast. Functional areas such as finance, production, personnel and marketing rely upon the information contained in a sales forecast. Because of the economic climate of the 1990's, shortages and excesses resulting from inaccurate forecasts can be devastating to both a firm's financial and competitive position. Since a sales forecast is an estimate, it can never be 100 percent correct. However, by employing systematic and objective procedures that show sensitivity to statistical and nonstatistical sources of error and by utilizing valid data sources, the accuracy of a forecast may be maximized.

Instructor's Further Probing: What does marketing research have to do with forecasting?

Suggested Probe Response: As we have seen in the text and in earlier questions, marketing research can be used in determining important elements for a forecast. Research is essential to producing a realistic forecast, since experience and past knowledge cannot give an accurate picture of the market and industry at the present time.

6. How would you determine a proposed forecast's accuracy?

There is no direct measure of a forecast's accuracy before the forecasted period. However, there are several ways to ensure that a forecast comes as close to actual sales as possible. Forecasts should be made by individuals with a level of training and experience appropriate to the requirements of the task. Some forecasting techniques require special knowledge and techniques. All techniques should utilize systematic and objective procedures that are sensitive to statistical and nonstatistical sources of error and employ valid data sources that will provide timely information, containing the adequate detail needed for the forecast. Guidelines that can help ensure an accurate forecast include: define the purpose for which the forecast is intended; define the products and product segments; prepare an initial forecast; relate the forecast to company capabilities and objectives; and review trends in the environment.

Instructor's Further Probing: How can previously made forecasts assist in making a present forecast more accurate?

Suggested Probe Response: By the assessment of a previous forecast, in terms of accuracy, methods used to develop that old forecast can be evaluated and adjusted accordingly for the current forecast.

7. Compare and contrast the three classifications of sales forecasting techniques: (a) qualitative methods, (b) time series methods, and (c) causal methods. (**Probe question**) Why is this distinction important?

Under the appropriate conditions, each type of sales forecasting technique can provide a firm with reliable, accurate forecasts. However, they do differ in their levels of sophistication and the degree to which they can anticipate turning points. Qualitative methods rely upon the judgments or opinions of knowledgeable individuals. A given judgment is based upon all the information deemed relevant to the situation. As a group, qualitative methods are the most frequently used forecasting technique. They can be very accurate but are also subject to inaccuracies resulting from their reliance upon human judgment. Time-series methods involve extrapolating historical sales data forward. Accuracy is enhanced if the environment is stable and if there are discernible trends or patterns to the historical data. Time-series forecasting may be as simple as using visual extrapolation or it may employ various statistical techniques. Causal methods are the most sophisticated and they involve the identification of the forces that affect sales. Accuracy is maximized when historical sales data is available. They are best able to predict turning points and explain the variation in sales data because they understand the causal relationships involved.

Because of the differences in expense, effort and expertise involved, different sales forecasting techniques may be appropriate for different forecasting situations. Furthermore, a company's capabilities and objectives determine what technique is employed. It is more accurate to use a simple forecasting technique well than to utilize a complicated technique without the necessary expertise.

8. Evaluate the forecasting approach used for the wallpaper and band-aids examples in Morocco in the Global Marketing Research Dynamics insert.

We saw in this example that the sources of information for forecasting may not be the same from country to country. This type of "guerrilla marketing research" showed the necessity of using multiple sources of information and comparing them to give an idea of the accuracy of those sources. This approach was mainly in the research for the wallpaper and proved to be effective.

Also shown in this example was the application of marketing research to develop a forecast. In the band-aid example, researchers used exploratory research to determine what sources of data to pursue. This approach proved valuable and indicated some definitive trends.

In both the wallpaper and band-aid examples, the researchers' main wild card was the economic climate of the country. Would the trend of the economy continue to support the forecast? Would future political events change the economy? In lesser developed countries, these basic issues are important, even for marketing researchers.

9. *MINICASE:* Outline an approach that Debra Clipper should use to prepare a sales forecast for the Network Connect product of Tele Turbo, Inc. (See chapter opening Marketing Research in Action.)

Here is an example of how Debra should approach the task of creating a forecast:

1. Define the purpose for which the forecast is intended.

The purpose of this forecast is to create a report to forecast the sales of a new product called "Network Connect."

2. Define the products and product segments.

In this case the product is the Network Connect and the product segment is telecommunications products.

3. Prepare an initial forecast.

Based on the data available to Debra, she should develop a "first run" forecast as a starting model.

4. Relate the forecast to company capabilities and objectives.

Since Debra's company has particular financial goals and marketing objectives, this must be taken into account to give meaning to the forecast.

5. Review the trends in the environment.

Since any forecast must take into account the trends in the field of relevance, Debra must survey the telecommunications field to see what future trends are. This will help determine the future outlook for the Network Connect product.

CHAPTER 24 — PRODUCT RESEARCH AND TEST MARKETING

1. Why are focus groups used for both idea generation and concept testing?

   Focus groups are commonly used for exploratory research purposes, examples of which are both idea generation and concept testing. While the amount of direction provided by the moderator differs between idea generation and concept testing, the objective in each case is to gain insight and ideas from the frank responses and reactions of individuals. In idea generation, where the moderator directs discussion from general to specifics, the goal is to generate and improve ideas regarding new products or product improvements. In concept testing, where the moderator provides more direction, the group addresses specific concepts that the firm is evaluating.

Instructor's Further Probing: Discuss synetic sessions.

Suggested Probe Response: Synetic sessions (or brainstorming sessions) are a special type of focus group where the respondents are experts. As in all focus groups, the synergy and creativity is guided by a moderator to produce ideas that the client can then consider doing further research on. Brainstorming sessions are less rigid and guided than standard focus groups, since a free flow of ideas is the goal of the sessions.

2. What are monadic ratings?

   Monadic rating is a concept testing technique for evaluating a product concept. Respondents are divided into as many groups as there are concepts to test. A respondent group is given only one product concept and each respondent in the group rates it, along specified dimensions, on some sort of rating scale. The scores for each product concept are averaged and compared. Those concepts with the highest scores receive further evaluation. Since the respondents do not compare product concepts, it is important to control for differences between groups of evaluators.

Instructor's Further Probing: Discuss the major objectives of product testing in general.

Suggested Probe Response: Monadic ratings are a form of product testing. The major objectives of monadic ratings and product testing in general include (1) to get a first-cut reaction as to consumers' views of the product idea, (2) to give direction to future development of the project, (3) to select the most promising concepts for further development and (4) to get an initial evaluation of potential commercialization prospects for the product. In general the objectives of product testing center around seeking a direction for further exploration or research.

3. Describe the structure of a usage test for a new cake mix.

   A usage test for a cake mix could consist of several parts. First of all, the mix would be tested in-company by laboratory testers. They would evaluate the mix along many dimensions and under several conditions including taste, different baking temperatures, flavor, lightness and texture. The objective is to discover and anticipate problems that consumers may run into as a result of product problems or failure to follow the exact instructions. A second phase of the test would involve consumer usage tests. A sample of consumers would be given a mix (or mixes) to prepare normally at home and then evaluate along specific performance and taste dimensions.

Instructor's Further Probing: Would a standard focus group consisting of experts as respondents be appropriate for evaluation of the new cake mix?

Suggested Probe Response: As always, the purpose of research must be defined and the research must be appropriate for that purpose. If the goal of the focus group is to determine trends and possible changes to the new mix, then the expert panel would be useful since the experts could use their knowledge and gauge the mix with other products they have used in the past. However, if the goal of the focus group was to find out how consumers would react to the mix, then experts would give a biased opinion that would therefore not be appropriate.

4. What is test marketing?

   Test marketing can be defined in any number of ways, ranging from "trying something out" to a highly defined controlled piece of marketing research. The definition which we prefer is: the implementation and monitoring of a marketing program in a small subset of the target market areas for the product in question.

Instructor's Further Probing: What is the goal of test marketing and why is it preferable to simply trying out the product on a production scale and monitoring the results?

Suggested Probe Response: The goal of test marketing is similar to the goal in any experiment, to make inferences or conclusions based on a smaller subset or model of the population. Sometimes the production of a product can be costly or require a large overhead in capital, thus full scale production could be costly if the product fails to meet anticipated marketing research expectations. After all, marketing research can only provide indications, not facts about how people will react to a product. Test marketing, when performed properly, adds further value to previous marketing research by trying out hypotheses.

5. On what basis would you select alternative courses of action for use in a test market?

   Through the use of personal judgment, prior experience of the company, and strategy research prior to test marketing, one defines a small number of alternatives for possible testing from a larger number of price, promotion, product, etc. alternatives.

Instructor's Further Probing: A common theme is used repeatedly in making decisions in marketing research, as shown by the criteria in selecting alternative courses of action for use in a test market. What is this common theme used time and time again?

Suggested Probe Response: In most aspects of marketing research personal judgment and past experience weighs heavily in the decisions a manager will make. Marketing research results alone can not determine a course of action. Test marketing can aid in providing some of this experience, through actual field testing.

6. What are the two fundamental uses of test marketing?

   Two fundamental uses exist:

1) Serving as a managerial control tool, and
2) Serving as a predictive research tool.

Thus, from test marketing one derives information or experience concerning possible alternatives in addition to predictions concerning outcomes of these alternatives.

Instructor's Further Probing: Discuss the two situations in which test marketing serves as a predictive research tool.

Suggested Probe Response: Two situations in which test marketing serves as a predictive research tool include the new-product or new-brand introduction and the evaluation of alternative marketing programs for existing brands. Of course the implementation of the test marketing may differ based on which purpose the researcher has in mind. New-product testing may require finding new consumers whereas evaluation of alternative marketing programs may require seeking an established base of consumers.

7. How can test market results be projected to national results?

   A number of methods of projection exist:

   1) Buying-income method, based on relative income levels.
   2) Sales-ratio method, based on sales of another brand.
   3) Share-of-market method, based on product category sales.

Instructor's Further Probing: What is another possible method for projection to national sales?

Suggested Probe Response: Another possible method for projection includes panel methods, based on consumer panels' repeat purchase patterns, and product penetration levels.

8. What information can a test market provide?

   In summary, a test market can provide such information as:

   1) Sales in units and dollars.
   2) Market share.
   3) Profitability and return on investment.
   4) Consumer behavior and attitudes concerning the product.
   5) Effectiveness of alternative marketing strategies.
   6) Reaction of the trade to the product and the marketing program.

Instructor's Further Probing: What are some sources that allow a company to determine the above information from a test market?

Suggested Probe Response: As mentioned in the text, syndicated as well as customized research services are some possible ways of obtaining results from a test market.

9. What are the costs of test marketing?

Direct Costs:

1) Pilot plant to manufacture the product (if product is new).
2) Commercials.
3) Payments to advertising agency for services.
4) Media time at a higher rate because of low volume.
5) Syndicated research information.
6) Customized research information and data analysis costs.
7) Point-of-purchase materials.
8) Couponing and sampling.
9) Higher trade allowances to obtain distribution.

Indirect Costs:

1) Opportunity cost of lost sales from successful national introduction.
2) Cost of management time on test market.
3) Diversion of sales force from money-making products.
4) Possible negative impact on other products with same family name.
5) Possible negative trade impact on other products if test product consistently fails.
6) Cost of letting competitors know what you are doing.

Instructor's Further Probing: The Marketing Research in Action insert "Cyanamid Tests Combat" quoted Cyanamid's product manager as saying "test market success gives a margin of comfort for the national plan." What did the product manager mean by this?

Suggested Probe Response: As shown by the advantages of test marketing, a firm can interpolate or project the results of the test market onto the general population. This projection can help estimate and plan for a national rollout. But since the test market can not, of course, guarantee success, it only provides a margin of comfort.

10. Why do test marketing results often give poor projections?

Several reasons can be given, including:

1) Stimulation of salespersons beyond normal activity levels.
2) Trade is aware of test and gives artificially high distribution and retailer support.
3) Special introductory offers and promotions are made in the test area which are not available on a national level.
4) Competitive efforts, either deliberate or accidental, are disproportionate in the test area to their national levels.
5) Measurement accuracy problems yielding ambiguous data.
6) Competitors can use your test market activities and beat you to the national market with a similar product.

Instructor's Further Probing: Can firms always use the test market strategy as planned from the beginning?

Suggested Probe Response: No, due to competition monitoring a firm performing test marketing, there is a danger of rushing or eliminating a part of the test to avoid being beat by competitors to a full scale rollout of a new product. For example, Proctor and Gamble rushed its Crest pump toothpaste dispenser to market without testing to catch up with Colgate's pump toothpaste dispenser, already on the market.

11. Under what circumstances should a company undertake test marketing?

    Circumstances which would weigh heavily in favor of test marketing include:

    1) Costs and risks are high.
    2) Large incremental plant investment is necessary for a national introduction.
    3) Competitors are not likely to be able to copy one's program quickly.
    4) A failure is likely to have a major long-range consequence on the company's reputation.

Instructor's Further Probing: Can you name some examples of products that would be ideal for test marketing?

Suggested Probe Response: Some examples of products that would be good candidates for test marketing include automobiles, electronic products, and extensive advertising campaigns.

12. What type of cities should be used in test marketing?

    A number of guidelines exist, including:

    1) The market should not be overtested.
    2) They should have normal historical development in the product class.
    3) They should represent a typical competitive advertising situation.
    4) They should not be dominated by one industry.
    5) Special resident profile markets should be avoided.
    6) Each region should be tested if sales differ by region.
    7) Little media spillover should occur between test markets and outside areas.
    8) Markets should have media usage patterns similar to the national one.
    9) Markets should be large enough to provide meaningful results but small enough to be of manageable cost.
    10) Distribution channels should be representative.
    11) The competitive situation should be similar to the national one.
    12) Sales auditing and other research services should be available.
    13) Product shipping costs to the test area should be reasonable.
    14) The city should have a "representative" demographic profile.

Instructor's Further Probing: Of the following cities, which would be good cities for a test market of a new type of toothpaste, such as Listerine toothpaste, given a small budget: New York City, NY; Boulder, Colorado; Princeton, New Jersey; Cleveland, Ohio; Oklahoma City, Oklahoma.

Suggested Probe Response: Of all the cities listed, perhaps only Cleveland, Ohio meets the most number of guidelines listed above. The other cities are either too large, thus increasing exposure outside the region or have too specific resident profile (such as Oklahoma City where religion is heavily prevalent).

13. What is a control market?

    A control market is a test market city in which a research supply house has paid retailers for a guarantee that they will carry products designated by the supply house.

Instructor's Further Probing: Why would a control market be used?

Suggested Probe Response: Control markets allow more control over the test market, thus decrease the cost and improve the speed with which results can be obtained from the test market. However, it is important to realize that control markets, due to their structured nature, do not necessarily accurately reflect the situations that may arise in an actual rollout.

14. What are the pros and cons of control markets?

    Advantages:

    1) Speedier access to distribution and results gathering.
    2) Reduced cost per market.
    3) No distraction of sales force attention from other lines.
    4) Greater secrecy.

    Disadvantages:
    1) True trade reaction to the product cannot be obtained.
    2) National projections more difficult due to smaller test market size.
    3) Isolated media typically unavailable, resulting in advertising spillover effects.

Instructor's Further Probing: What is the more common type of test market used by most firms?

Suggested Probe Response: Standard markets, where the company must fight for trade support in the same fashion as a national roll-out, are more commonly used.

15. How long should a test market run?

    Several factors should be taken into account:

    1) The test should be long enough to measure repurchase activity.
    2) The faster the competitors react, the shorter should be the test.
    3) The value of additional information beyond some time point will be outweighed by costs--thus costs must be considered.

Instructor's Further Probing: Essentially, what must be done to make effective use of a test market run?

Suggested Probe Response: Basically, continuous monitoring is essential to determine how long to keep a test running. Only continuous marketing can tell a firm when repurchase takes place, what the competitors are doing, and at what point costs are outrunning the benefits of the test.

16. Outline the steps in a simulated test market.

    1) A group of respondents, usually about 300, is recruited at shopping malls to match the target segment of the test product.
    2) Respondents are taken to a nearby laboratory facility to complete a questionnaire. They are asked about whether or not they purchase any brand in the product

category, unaided brand awareness, advertising awareness, brand preference, importance ratings of product attributes, and ratings of brands on these attributes.

3) Respondents are then exposed to advertisements for the new brand and the leading competitive brands in the category.

4) After the advertising presentation, respondents are taken to a simulated retail store where the test product is on a shelf display with a complete set of competing products. They are given $2 to use to buy a brand from the category if they wish. Those not wanting to buy any brand are given free samples of the new brand as a way of simulating free samples in the market place.

5) After the simulated shopping trip, respondents are interviewed as to what brand they purchased, if any, and their reactions to the product and its advertising.

6) The respondent then returns home with the test product with instructions to use it. A follow-up interview is conducted by telephone several weeks later. The measures taken are similar to the pre-exposure to advertising measures taken (preference, importance of attributes, and brand ratings), except that the new brand is now included in the brand set. Additionally, usage of the test product is determined, and the respondents are offered a chance to repurchase the new brand using their own money and having it delivered by mail. Those not wanting to repurchase in this way are asked to indicate their intention to purchase the new brand on a five-point scale if the brand were available in a store in the future.

Instructor's Further Probing: Why use a simulated test market?

Suggested Probe Response: As a result of the costs associated with test marketing using either standard test markets or control markets, simulated test markets are a cheaper alternative.

17. How could simulated test market procedure be applied to consumer durables such as dishwashers or personal computers? Be specific.

    Simulated test marketing could be used to test various aspects of the marketing campaign and to predict sales potential of a new dishwasher or personal computer. Techniques used by packaged goods and automobile manufacturers could be adapted, such as:

    - Potential buyers could be recruited via mall intercept. Their knowledge and experience with product category could be determined via questionnaire.

    - Subjects could be exposed to advertising and display material for the brand in question and competing brands.

    - Subjects could then be placed in a simulated purchase situation or their purchase intent could be determined through a survey.

    - Purchase behavior for various levels of advertising and display could be compared to determine most effective approach.

    - Purchase behavior could also be compared to historical test market data to determine potential sales. If historical data is available, a regression equation with test market ratings as independent variables and sales as dependent variable could be used for prediction.

Instructor's Further Probing: If potential buyers are recruited via mall intercepts, what problems or biases does this introduce into the test?

Suggested Probe Response: In past chapters we have seen that intercepts can lead to biases due to interview bias, for example. As always, the researcher must be careful to take into account any possible biases introduced at various stages in the test marketing.

18. Kenner Toys uses the following procedure to test new toys. Evaluate this approach:

    Ouija Boards, the Magic 8 Ball and dart boards are three popular toys that have enjoyed long lived success. These toys, however, are not used to try to predict the next big winner in the very fast moving and unpredictable toy industry, even though they may prove more accurate than trying to perform marketing research with 5-year olds!

    Kenner has developed a method for testing toys. Mock stores are set up in several locations around the country with a wide variety of toys, including the new test concepts, and the company's existing product as well as current competing products. A sample of 200 children are individually shown videos depicting the concepts and product demonstrations for each of the toys under research. Following the video each child is escorted into the mock store and given tokens to make the purchase.

    The simulated purchase situation is believed to be necessary because observation is a much more reliable measure of behavior of young children than focus groups, interviewing, or other more conventional and less expensive marketing research methods.

    Good Things About Kenner's Approach

    - Generous sample size.

    - Wise decision not to rely on verbal techniques such as interviewing and focus groups to determine five year olds' interest in new toy concepts.

    Problems with Kenner's Approach

    - Test does not account for parents' influence in toy buying process.

    - Is a mock purchase situation the best or most economical way of assessing interest in a new product? There are certainly other ways of doing so. A few ideas appear below:

    Alternative Approaches

    - Develop a model to forecast sales potential based on childrens' interest rating after exposure to commercial for a new toy. Commercials could be embedded in a segment of cartoons or other childrens' programs. Children could be asked questions that they could relate to, such as, "Would you ask Santa Claus to bring you this new toy for Christmas?"

    - A more exploratory approach that might work well for concept evaluation is a "play group." A group of children could be placed in a room with lots of toys, including the new toy concepts and existing products. The new concepts' potential could be assessed simply by observing the childrens' degree of interest in the new toys.

19. Coca-Cola is considering entering the bottled, fruit-based drink market in direct competition with Snapple. Outline a complete program of marketing research for the development and commercialization of this new drink product at Coca-Cola. Describe specific marketing research activities and studies.

20. *MINICASE* This question gives students a chance to conduct an in-depth or focus group interview to evaluate a product concept and guide their revision of the concept. We find it an insightful way to show the usefulness of qualitative research in marketing.

Since this is a class oriented activity, there will not be a single right answer. Encourage class discussion and presentations if time allows.

TOWARD A REVISED CONCEPT

In working toward a revised concept, one needs to understand just what message is being communicated by the original concept. The class could develop a list of problems with the original concept. These include: the convenience claim is too weak, it sounds like medicine, and it's just for fat people. The message seems to be "hey fatties-- we have something for you."

It should be noted that when this focus group was asked to taste the product all members said "not me; I won't taste it." Also, when rice with this gravy on it was brought into the room reactions included: "smells like a cafeteria," "an army smell," "poor color," and "looks like you spilled it on the floor and then put it on the rice."

The instructor may wish to point out to the class that these reactions occurred despite the fact that 500 homemakers in a blind taste test rated the gravy as excellent. That is, the product is actually a good one. The problem is perceptual. Expectations based on past experience with "diet" products are biasing responses.

TYPES OF SOLUTIONS

To solve these problems, some changes in descriptors are needed. Dropping the word diet in the name seems appropriate (e.g., Freska, Tab, etc.), plus changing "brown" to "beef." Students will suggest others.

THE REVISED CONCEPT

The table below presents the revised concept actually used in the study. This concept generated a positive response in the group sessions. People readily ate this gravy (it is physically the same as before) and described it in superlatives.

TABLE

THE REVISED CONCEPT THAT ULTIMATELY TRIGGERED

A POSITIVE RESPONSE

GRAVY SUPREME

Here's a delicious new gravy mix that not only tastes great, but it also helps you look great. It's Gravy Supreme, an entirely new gravy that comes in five mouth-watering flavors--Prime Au Jus, Southern Chicken, Buffet Roast, Country Mushroom, and Bermuda Onion.

This gravy not only has a wonderful flavor, but it also keeps you slim. It contains only six calories per tablespoon which is much less than regular home-made gravy, yet it tastes every bit as good.

Just add to one cup of water, bring to boil, simmer for four minutes, and serve.

So, the next time you want to give your family a delicious new gravy, try Gravy Supreme--costs only 19 cents a packet. Each packet makes a one-cup serving of gravy.

To discuss this question, have students present problems with the original concept and possible solutions. If necessary, tell students that the physical product has tested well.

Then ask a number of students to read their first revised concept and describe the focus group or in-depth interview they conducted. Ask them to explain how the results of these interviews were used to develop a second or third, etc. concept. Have them read the revised concepts.

It is the experience of the interviews and the types of insights that can be generated from this process that are important here. The emphasis of the class session should then be on the students' experiences.

It is usually an interesting session. However, after hearing 5-10 revised concepts and the process of interviewing, it does become redundant. Therefore, the exercise should be run for about half a class session in combination with lecture or video tape materials on focus group interviews if available.

CHAPTER 25 — ADVERTISING RESEARCH

1. Why is advertising research used so much in practice? Why is this true given the great experience base among marketing managers in advertising?

    Advertising research is widely used in practice because advertising expenditures on a product are usually very high. Research may be applied to many aspects of advertising including measuring audience size, media vehicle distribution and message effectiveness.

    The experienced manager would have little in his or her experience base to allow good estimates of either audience size or media vehicle distribution. Also, audience interest changes quickly and the manager cannot easily guess which message will best reach this moving target.

    Because of the large amounts of money spent, and the risk involved in an advertising campaign, managers prefer to have research information to base their decisions upon, rather than relying solely on past experience. Advertising research allows managers to test ads on a current, representative sample of the target population. By engaging in research, problems may be detected before a full campaign is undertaken and modifications may be made.

    Instructor's Further Probing: Discuss the various risks associated with advertising, beyond cost. Such a discussion should help further understanding of the importance of advertising research.

    Suggested Probe Response: While cost is indeed the biggest risk in advertising, there are other risks that could potentially require careful attention before launching a large advertising campaign. Some of these risks include: brand or company image, which may go up or down depending on how the public perceives the advertiser's message; legal liabilities , which may be an issue if regulatory agencies or the public feel the advertisement message is misleading or false; and finally an advertiser risks not being able to pick up trends without advertising research.

2. What different types of data would advertisers like to have about media vehicles?

    Advertisers would like to have six different types of data about media vehicles:

    1. Media vehicle distribution, which provides circulation numbers for print media and the number of TV's and radios for broadcast media .

    2. Media vehicle audience data, which reports the number of people who are exposed to a media vehicle.

    3. Advertising exposure data, which reports the number of people exposed to a specific advertisement in a specific media vehicle.

    4. Advertising perception data which reports the number of people who perceived a specific advertisement.

5. Advertising communication data which reports the number of people who comprehend specific things about the ad.

6. Sales response data, which reports the number of people who buy as a result of exposure to an ad.

Instructor's Further Probing: Discuss why the last four categories of data are difficult to assign numbers related to the media alone.

Suggested Probe Response: These four categories involve the media and the message interaction. Because of this, media vehicle data are typically obtained for only two of the above categories: media vehicle distribution and media vehicle audience.

3. Why are some of these data (from the categories in question 2) difficult to obtain? Be specific.

   Data involving numbers of people who are exposed to a media vehicle or specific ads are difficult to obtain because more than one person may read one copy of a magazine or watch a particular TV set. On the other hand, a TV may be on and no one is watching it, or the viewer may leave the room during the commercials. When respondents report what they have watched or read in a diary or interview, the answers are subject to forgetfulness or falsification. When researchers attempt to measure advertising perception and communication and sales response, the numbers are generally smaller than audience size and advertising exposure figures. Since the goal of much research is to estimate an ad's effectiveness, it becomes quite difficult to generate from data and draw relationships between the measure and desired buying behavior. For example, an individual may notice an ad and be able to remember the message and yet not be motivated to purchase it. Often other factors intervene in the sales response. Therefore it is often difficult to interpret and generalize from data. In addition, cost and time considerations impact an advertiser's ability to collect data.

Instructor's Further Probing: How has technological advancement helped in increasing the ability to gather advertising data in television?

Suggested Probe Response: The new developments of people meters, which can track when programs are being watched, have greatly advanced the ability to more accurately estimate viewership.

4. Why do the Simmons Market Research Bureau and Mediamark Research, Inc. obtain estimates of magazine audience size that differ? Which method of measurement is better?

   Audience size measures taken by Simmons Market Research Bureau (SMRB) and Mediamark Research, Inc. (MRI) differ because of differences in sampling procedures and in audience measurement procedures. SMRB uses a cluster sample and asks respondents to pick from a group of magazine logos those they may have looked at or read in the last six months. MRI asks respondents to indicate which publications they have read in the last six months and more precisely in the last publication interval. One method is not necessarily better; the differences lie in methodology, not execution. The problem is that the differences may affect advertising rates and there is a need to make the two scores adjustable to each other.

Instructor's Further Probing: What are some possible methods of adjusting the scores so that a valid comparison may be made between the scores of SMRB and MRI?

Suggested Probe Response: This answer may take some creative thinking on the student's part, as the answer may not be found in the text. One possible answer includes creating a rating scale that incorporates the various errors associated with each method available for taking measurements for audience size measures. This rating scale can then be applied to the methods a firm uses and this objective scale number can be used for comparison.

5. What methods may be used to measure the size of television audiences? Evaluate each.

   TV audience data is collected by four methods: 1) diaries; 2) meters; 3) coincidental telephone recall; and 4) personal interview recall. Diaries are relatively inexpensive. Viewers record the shows they watch and mail the diaries back to the researcher. Unfortunately, data is subject to distortion because respondents forget to record which shows they watch or forget which shows they watch or do not tell the truth. During the time when Arbitron uses diaries, or during "sweeps" months, networks try to "hype" their ratings with specials and movies.

   Meters measure and record when a television is on and to what channel it is tuned. The Nielsen Television Index audimeter is connected to a computer. NTI calculates the share of households watching a show and the share of total households watching a particular program out of the total number of households watching any program. Meters are expensive and cannot measure whether anyone is watching the television or not. However, they do not rely upon respondent-reported data.

   In the coincident telephone recall method, a sample of households is contacted and asked what show, if any, is being watched at that particular time. Respondents are also asked to identify the product being advertised or the sponsor. Although the method is inexpensive and lessens errors, as the measure is taken while the show is being viewed, respondents may try to indicate that they are watching socially acceptable programs. Also, nontelephone homes are excluded and rural homes are under-represented. Therefore it is difficult to accurately estimate the total audience size. Furthermore, this method may only be used for programs shown during certain hours (8 AM to 10 PM).

   Use of the personal interview recall method involves conducting in-home interviews with respondents. Recall is aided by producing a listing of shows by the quarter hour and respondents are asked to indicate which shows they watched. Problems include the time and cost of personal interviews and respondent error of forgetfulness and untruthfulness.

Instructor's Further Probing: What is the main problem with methods that require the respondent to track his/her viewing or reading habits?

Suggested Probe Response: Since a respondent may forget or give only socially acceptable answers, methods requiring respondents to note their habits can be inherently biased. However, there is no way of determining the extent of the bias, or even if any bias exists at all.

6. What are the characteristics of an ideal copy testing procedure? Why does practice not follow the ideal?

An ideal copy testing procedure incorporates several important characteristics. They are represented by PACT principles, Pomerance's Idealized Copy Testing Procedure and the Idealized Measurement Procedure. Characteristics include: the measurements are relevant to the advertising objectives; the usage of results are agreed upon in advance; multiple measures representing all intended media are taken; the measures are based upon a model of human response to communication and the ideal measure is natural purchase or profit; consideration is given to whether the stimulus should be repeated; recognition that a finished ad is most desirable; provides controls to avoid the biasing effects of the exposure context and recognizes the desirability of a natural exposure environment; as unobtrusive a measure as possible; the test takes into account bias considerations of sample definition with probability samples being preferred and the size is great enough so that similar results could be obtained if the test were replicated and the measures demonstrate reliability and validity.

In practice, constraints such as time and cost prevent these principles from being rigidly adhered to. Deviations should be justified and researchers must be cognizant of the effects on the test measurements when they attempt generalizations. Often it is impossible or impractical to prepare ads in finished form or to measure natural purchase behavior or to present ads or groups of ads for comparison, in a natural environment.

Instructor's Further Probing: What is the basis of the PACT principles?

Suggested Probe Response: The basis of the PACT principles is a model of human response to communication. Essentially based on perceived operation of the mind, we can propose several important criteria in being persuaded by an ad copy.

7. How can you measure the reliability and validity of a copy testing procedure? Why is this important?

   The same test could be readministered to a group of respondents several days after the first test. Alternate forms of a copy test may be given to different respondents. Predictive validity may be measured by relating rating scores to desired behavioral responses. Multiple measures are important in copy testing and can help demonstrate concurrent and discriminate validity. Assessing reliability and validity are important because if the measures cannot relate advertisement or message effectiveness to the advertising objective, they are relatively meaningless. Additionally, the results must be generalizable to some target population to be useful. A major question to be resolved with many copy tests is whether the results are affected by the environmental context and if they are generalizable to natural viewing situations where the number of advertising stimuli is substantially larger.

Instructor's Further Probing: What is a good benchmark procedure from which to measure new copy testing procedures?

Suggested Probe Response: The IMP (idealized measurement procedure) is a good benchmark representing an ideal procedure.

8. How are ads pretested? Evaluate each method.

   Ads are pretested by a variety of methods. Consumer juries have 50-100 members who are interviewed individually or in small groups. Ads are usually presented in rough, unfinished form and respondents are asked to rank order, compare, or numerically rank them along several dimensions. Rating scales allow the use of standards and norms for comparison. The reliability and validity of jury systems is often questionable because of the artificial exposure environment and the use of rough ads.

Portfolio tests expose respondents to a package of test and control ads through which they are to look and read anything of interest. Ad effectiveness is measured by recall. One problem with them is that recall often differentiates product interest rather than creative presentation. However, the exposure context may be quite natural.

Physiological methods are not widely used because of the difficulties in interpreting physical reactions and establishing causal links. Methods include eye cameras, galvanic skin responses, and tachistoscopes.

Dummy advertising vehicles utilize test and control ads inserted into a dummy magazine. The magazines are randomly distributed and the respondents are interviewed about editorial and advertising content. The environmental context is quite natural. However, since ads are not compared, differentiation may not reflect creative presentation.

When consumer response is measurable by an inquiry or sale, inquiry tests may be used to evaluate ad effectiveness. No interview or other follow-up is required of the researcher and artificiality problems are minimized. However, the presence of a coupon may mask creative differences between ads; also, interested individuals may not respond or a response may not lead to desired behavior.

Ads may be tested in actual broadcast presentations by a method called on-the-air-tests. They are quite similar to their print counterpart, dummy vehicles. Both recognition and recall measures may be taken. Well-known services include Day After Recall, Total Prime Time, AdTel Cable System, IRI's Behavior Scan, and Nielsen's ERIM. Differences in methodology and measurement exist. Cost for these tests is high.

Theater and trailer tests show recruited respondents ads alone or in a program context and immediate measures are taken. Artificiality of the viewing context is a concern and recruiting methods may yield a nonrepresentative sample.

Laboratory stores utilize a simulated shopping environment and suffer from problems associated with artificiality. They may be extremely costly but may be used in conjunction with other marketing research.

9. In post-testing recognition and recall are two different measures taken? Give an example of each and evaluate the two.

An example of recognition is the Starch Readership Service Tests. Respondents in a sample are asked about specific periodical readership. For those read, recognition measures of noted, seen-associated and read most are taken. Several useful scores and ratios can be calculated, including cost ratio and norm scores, which allow for comparisons. Disadvantages include possible differentiation by product interest rather than creative presentation and respondent errors such as forgetfulness, confusion or untruthfulness.

Recall tests require respondents to recall specifics about ads. Gallup and Robinson's Magazine Impact Readership Service is an example of such a test. Respondents are asked to read test magazines in a normal fashion and then are interviewed the next day. They are asked to identify advertisements from a list. Since the cue stimulus is not strong, recall tests may understate an ad's impact. Furthermore, there is not a causal relationship between recall or recognition and the desired response.

Instructor's Further Probing: Basically what is a key factor that distinguishes between the recognition test and recall tests?

Suggested Probe Response: Recognition tests rely more heavily on cues, whereas the cue bias in recall tests are relatively small.

10. Why aren't sales tests the most common form of post-testing?

    Because of the difficulty in establishing a direct relationship between an ad and its impact on sales, and because many additional factors affect sales, sales tests are not a common form of post-testing. They are used in an experimental or quasi-experimental setting, in test marketing and with AdTel and other panels. Measurement difficulties also preclude the use of sales tests since the context is either unnatural or subject to respondent errors.

Instructor's Further Probing: What are some factors that affect sales?

Suggested Probe Response: Sales is not a common form of post-testing due to the fact that sales can be affected by promotions, changing trends magnified by popular media, and even by the quality of sales staff.

11. Sometimes marketing research can reveal feelings about products that might easily have been overlooked. When the Timberland company wanted a new print campaign for its shoes, the rugged footwear was riding a new wave of popularity as a fashion item. Research showed, however, that consumers actually bought the shoes because they were durable and they thought they improved with age. As a result, Timberland's agency resisted a campaign that presented the shoes as fashion accessories and instead developed one which emphasized how long the shoes lasted.

    a) What research design could have been used to determine these conclusions?

    The initial idea probably came unexpectedly from an exploratory technique like a focus group, an open-ended survey question or a perceptual map. The hypothesis was likely verified through a large sample survey with closed-ended questions administered to previous Timberland buyers.

    b) How should one measure the level of success of the advertising campaign that was actually implemented?

    The measure of success depends on the goals of the campaign. Most likely, the goals of this campaign were to change consumers' perceptions of the brand and ultimately increase sales.

    Measuring the effect on sales could be done. Simply record the level of sales for a period before and after the new campaign aired. If there is a difference, it can be attributed to the new campaign. The only difficulties with this method are accounting for potentially confounding variables like price reductions and local/store promotions. These would affect sales independently of the new advertising campaign. Care would have to be taken to remove the effects of these covariates.

If changing perceptions is the goal, some measure of consumer perceptions of the brand must be taken pre- and post-exposure to the new advertising. Most research of this type involves forced exposure to advertising in a laboratory situation, but could also be field based. Again proper controls are necessary.

12. What are the research limitations of the passive people meter described in the Marketing Research in Action at the beginning of this chapter? How might the passive people meter change the pricing and buying of advertising space on television?

Limitations

- The fact that meters cannot distinguish guests is more troublesome for measuring viewership of events such as the Super Bowl, where people are more likely than usual to watch with a larger group of people.

- With all forms of panel research, one has to wonder if people who agree to participate are somehow different from those who do not.

Changes in Pricing and Buying Advertising

- Media pricing structure will reflect position within commercial break as well as program ratings.

- Demographic characteristics of a particular program's audience will be more accurately measured. This may also affect media pricing structure. If the networks can find a way to price discriminate based on this information, they will.

13. *MINICASE*

   1. Evaluate the procedure used by ATSI.

   2. Evaluate the measures taken by ATSI.

   3. In comparing test results against the norm, is the stated significant difference level in scores appropriate? From a statistical testing point of view, is type I or type II error more important here?

   4. How should the reliability and validity of ASTI's results be determined?

   5. What conclusions for the advertiser would you draw from the results reported?

CHAPTER 26 — DISTRIBUTION AND PRICING RESEARCH

1. A marketer of industrial electronic components such as switches and wire sells these items through electrical distributors to hardware stores. How could marketing research be used to determine support of the marketing effort?

   Performance measures could be taken to compare actual with desired sales, customer service, inventory, display and advertising activity, and sales personnel performance. This could be done by comparing recent performance with historical records (e.g. sales), surveying customers to determine their satisfaction with store services, or observing in-store personnel, monitoring advertising and display activity.

   Instructor's Further Probing: What is the key aspect in making marketing research work in conjunction with the marketing effort of a firm?

   Suggested Probe Response: It is essential that the goals of the marketing team and marketing research team are coordinated and work together to solve particular problems. As always a clear purpose is the first step in any activity.

2. How may scanner data and demographic data be combined to provide useful information to the local retailer and the packaged goods marketer?

   Scanner data and demographic data are becoming more and more widely used by both retailers and packaged goods manufacturers. Scanner data enable both parties to see the correlation between sales of particular brands and product categories with demographic factors. This enables the manufacturer to choose distribution channels with the most potential for their products. It also enables the retailer to customize purchases, floor and shelf space allocations based on local market demographics. The result is less homogeneity and more local character in distribution outlets.

   Instructor's Further Probing: In the Marketing Research in Action insert at the beginning of the chapter, scanner data and demographic data was used in conjunction in the evaluation on category sales of minorities. Why was this a useful application?

   Suggested Probe Response: With the ability to monitor trends of specific ethnic groups, firms can target promotions and product features to the local consumer in various regions of the world. Ethnic populations tend to vary more than the general population, thus it is important to be able to track trends in a particular ethnicity.

3. Design and "image" study for your favorite local restaurant.

   This study was designed to assess customers' perceptions of Zingerman's, a popular New-York style deli in Ann Arbor, Michigan. Below is a portion of the questionnaire designed, using a semantic differential scale to measure attitudes:

friendly	___	___	___	___	___	___	unfriendly
progressive	___	___	___	___	___	___	not progressive
healthy	___	___	___	___	___	___	unhealthy
inexpensive	___	___	___	___	___	___	expensive
high quality	___	___	___	___	___	___	low quality
ethnic	___	___	___	___	___	___	non-ethnic
great food	___	___	___	___	___	___	lousy food
fun	___	___	___	___	___	___	not fun

Instructor's Further Probing: Who are the main users of attitude/image studies, such as the one done in the question above?

Suggested Probe Response: Wholesalers and retailers can utilize attitude measurement procedures to determine the perception that current and potential customers have of them over a host of various attributes.

4. Ford Motor Company is trying to determine the location for a new dealership in the Santa Clara area of California. Describe what marketing research you would do to help pick the appropriate location.

   The appropriate steps are 1) define the relevant market trading area or areas, 2) identify population characteristics within trading areas; 3) determine the competitors locations; 4) determine shopping patterns within the trading area; 5) develop a store patronage forecasting model based on the above factors.

Instructor's Further Probing: Discuss from your experience and knowledge of the business world how franchisers might use marketing research to pick out locations or zones for selling their franchises (for example, some firms do not let people buy and set up franchises in certain areas).

Suggested Probe Response: Generally franchises face the same problem as Ford Motor Company did in the above question. Franchises need to be located not only with the above list of criteria, but also they need to take into account the location of other franchises. This shows an example of how pervasive this type of research is.

5. Design a conjoint study to determine an appropriate set of attributes for the student lounge at your business school.

   One possible design is as follows. Assume that students are very concerned with the cleanliness of the lounge, the snack bar's hours of operation, and prices on snack bar items relative to prices at neighboring establishments. The lounge management would like to see how improving cleanliness, increasing hours, and lowering prices might affect sales. They are particularly interested in knowing if a small price cut will increase their sales volume. They have asked a group of market research students to do a study for them.

The attributes to be tested are:

cleanliness (3 levels)
hours (3 levels)
prices (4 levels)

There are 3x3x4 = 36 possible combinations of items. The researchers could decide to have subjects rate all 36 combinations on a 10 point scale. Data analysis would show the overall importance of each attribute and the value that respondents place on each level of each attribute.

Instructor's Further Probing: What are some possible problems with implementing this study? (e.g., what biases lie in this study?)

Suggested Probe Response: Factors include the proximity of neighboring establishments (i.e., can students go elsewhere easily for other choices?) to determine elasticity may not be measured; finding an appropriate number and cross section of the student population may be difficult and expensive since students generally have little time for volunteering in such studies and thus may need monetary incentives.

6. A food manufacturer has developed a new frozen dessert. Design a research study which would determine the price sensitivity of this product to prices of $.99, $1.09 and $1.19.

    There are a number of options available, ranging from indirect measures with low control to direct measures with high control. The choice always involves weighing trade offs between experimental control, cost, response rate, internal and external validity, reliability, etc.

Alternatives

Survey Research — Indirect measure with low experimental control. Advantages are low cost, fast results, flexible format can be tailored to meet many product/market requirements. Disadvantage is lack of external validity.

Historical or Syndicated Data — Direct measures with low control. Advantages are low cost and speed of results. Disadvantage is extreme lack of control — too many other factors besides its price may affect a product's sales. Internal validity of measures is questionable.

Simulated Purchase Survey or Conjoint Study — Indirect measures with high control. Advantage - more similar to actual purchase situation than measures previously discussed. Disadvantages - higher cost. External validity is an issue.

Laboratory or Field Experiment — Direct measures with high control. Advantages - measuring real or at least very realistic purchase behavior. Disadvantages - higher cost and time commitment.

Instructor's Further Probing: Given that the firm has a limited budget and limited time, which is the best alternative?

Suggested Probe Response: The firm will most likely need to use survey research due to time and cost constraints. However, the host of other factors may influence another decision in an actual marketing decision.

7. A manufacturer of consumer light bulbs has historical sales and price data on its line of soft white bulbs. They would like you to determine the price elasticity of this product line based on historical changes in manufacturers' selling prices and shipments data. Can you do this? Why?

   Historical data about manufacturers selling prices and sales volume can yield information about **retailers** price sensitivity, but not about consumers'. Data on trade shipments bears little or no relation to actual sales, and wholesale prices do not correlate perfectly with retail prices. An increased shipment with a lower wholesale price may just indicate that the retailer is stocking up on reduced price products. The consumer may never see that discount.

Instructor's Further Probing: In general, what impacts the price of goods?

Suggested Probe Response: Several factors influence the price of goods, including: demand sensitivity to price changes, costs, competitive price levels, and organizational objectives.

8. A new apartment building is interested in pricing the apartments based on market demand. The apartments are one and two bedrooms, basement through 8th floor, half with river view and half with parking lot view. Design a conjoint study to measure the price elasticity.

    bedrooms (2 levels)

    floor (9 levels)

    view (2 levels)

    price (5 levels)

   There are 2x9x2x5 = 180 possible combinations of attributes to test. A mix of at most 30 combinations should be selected for testing using a statistically valid procedure for data reduction.

   Subjects should be asked to rate each test combination on a scale of 1 to 10. Data analysis will show the overall importance of each attribute and the value that respondents place on each level of each attribute. We would be most interested in knowing the relative importance of price as a factor, and the changes in utility that result at each price point tested.

Instructor's Further Probing: In an actual situation what other factor may limit the flexibility in pricing for this apartment building?

Suggested Probe Response: Some laws in some areas prohibit property from being sold or rented at more than a certain price, determined by some formula. Thus legal and regulatory problems and consideration arise in determining pricing for a product or service.

PART III

OBJECTIVE EXAMINATION QUESTIONS

This section presents true-false and multiple-choice questions for each chapter. The questions from this section plus those presented in the previous section (Part II) give the instructor several options in designing the mid-term and final examination. The instructor can develop an examination composed entirely of objective questions from this section, develop an examination composed entirely of short answer questions from the previous section, or develop an examination which is a combination of both objective and short answer questions.

The distinction between the questions in this section and those in the previous section involve the nature of the memory task required of the student. Objective questions require the student to recognize and apply the material covered while discussion questions require the student to recall the material and present it in a clear and concise manner.

To give the instructor flexibility in the creation of exams, many chapters presented here have a surplus of questions for an exam, thus allowing the instructor to pick and choose the most appropriate questions to test the students with.

While there are several approaches to constructing multiple-choice questions, the approach chosen here is the more standard approach of having the student select one "best answer" from among the five alternatives presented. The students should clearly understand that they are to pick the "best answer" from among the alternatives presented. It is important to note that this "best answer" is best in the context of the response opinions presented. In this regard, the following instructions are used at Michigan and are offered as a guide for the instructions to accompany your multiple-choice examination.

> Each question has one best answer. There is no penalty for guessing, so answer each question. Be sure to **circle** your answer to each question in the examination. At the end of the examination, transfer your answers to the machine-graded answer form. Watch for mistakes in recording your answers.

The following are some suggestions and reminders regarding the selection and use of the true-false and multiple-choice questions for your examinations.

1. The questions vary substantially from a focus on detailed points and specific facts to questions which draw on the student's broader understanding of concepts and relationships. Our experience has been that questions which target on specific facts and points are more appropriate for the mid-term examination where the student is concentrating on a narrower domain of material. The broader questions may be more appropriate for the final examination where the objective is to have the student review previously examined material and integrate various sections of the course together.

2. At times, two or more questions have been prepared which cover the same material. Within the true-false and multiple-choice sections, similar questions have been placed next to each other. The instructor should note those questions which are similar across the true-false and multiple-choice sections. The purpose for having similar questions is to (1) allow for instructor's preference regarding question wording, and (2) allow for the need to have similar, but not identical questions on the mid-term and final examination plus the need for alternate versions of the examination when the course has multiple sections meeting at different time periods.

3. There is always the problem that the wording of one question tips off the student to the answer to another question. The instructor can eliminate this problem by not including such questions on the examination. If one desires to use such questions, they should be widely separated in the examination to minimize this problem.

CHAPTER 1 — MARKETING RESEARCH ROLE IN MARKETING MANAGEMENT

True - False

T   1.   In the marketing system, the marketing mix variables are independent variables.

F   2.   In the marketing system, the situational variables are dependent variables.

F   3.   In the marketing system, behavioral responses are independent variables.

T   4.   In the marketing system, performance measures are dependent variables.

F   5.   Due to the nature of most marketing information systems, opportunities are generally recognized by managers more readily than are problems.

F   6.   The vast majority of decisions made by managers are nonroutine.

T   7.   Managers should follow the formal decision-making steps when confronted with a nonroutine decision situation.

F   8.   Marketing research is most appropriate for routine decision situations.

F   9.   Marketing research is a valuable tool for marketing managers because it eliminates the uncertainty typically associated with situations calling for a decision.

F   10.   In the interest of efficiency, marketing research should be utilized only after the key issues underlying a problem or an opportunity have been clearly delineated.

F   11.   Contingency planning specifies the broad principles according to which the marketing program will operate in achieving objectives.

F   12.   "Information" refers to observations and evidence regarding some aspect of the marketing system.

F   13.   Given the difficulty in determining precisely the information needs of the marketing manager, the marketing researcher should provide more than enough data from which the manager may glean the needed information.

F   14.   The marketing research system should be viewed as an ad hoc data gathering and analysis function.

F   15.   The primary purpose of marketing research is to provide data to management.

F   16.   The characteristics which define marketing research are equally applicable to managerial experience and judgment.

F   17.   The definition of marketing research is completely different from that of management experience and judgment.

T   18.   Basic research findings are often applicable to applied research.

F   19.   Applied research seeks to extend the boundaries of knowledge regarding some aspect of the marketing system.

T   20.   Conclusive research differs from exploratory research not only in its intent but in its character as well.

T   21.   Rarely does the manager's initial request for help adequately establish the need for research information.

T   22.   A researcher should generally attempt to utilize existing data, from either internal or external sources, prior to collecting new data.

T   23.   Marketing research projects are sometimes undertaken for purposes unrelated to decision making.

T   24.   In a marketing research system, marketing research plays a major role in the marketing management and decision making process.

F   25.   Marketing research has not yet become popular with the majority of companies, as less than 50% of companies undertake any type of research.

F   26.   Marketing managers use the decision making model for routine decisions and their experience for non-routine decisions.

T   27.   Secondary data availability and reliability in other countries is a problem facing market researchers.

T   28.   International marketing research may lead to logistic problems that result in high costs.

Multiple Choice

E   1.   Which of the following characterize the marketing concept?

   A.   Focus on consumer needs and wants.
   B.   The provision of information pertinent to marketing decision making.
   C.   Marketing research is a key component in the marketing management process.
   D.   A and B above.
   E.   A, B and C above.

E   2.   Which of the following would have no reason to employ marketing research?

   A.   A hospital.
   B.   A restaurant.
   C.   The grocery store at which you shop.
   D.   The vendor who sells souvenirs outside of the football stadium on Saturdays.
   E.   None of the above.

E   3.   The increasing adoption of the marketing concept by organizations will most likely:

   A.   Decrease the utilization of marketing research in the short term.
   B.   Increase the utilization of marketing research in the long run.

C. Affect the use of marketing research, but the direction cannot be predicted a priori.
D. Increase the utilization of marketing research in the short run.
E. B and D above.

E 4. The marketing system may be depicted as a model composed of four parts: marketing mix, situational factors, behavioral response, and performance measures. Marketing research is most appropriate for which of the components.

A. Marketing mix.
B. Situational factors
C. Behavioral response.
D. Performance measures.
E. All of the above.

D 5. A(n) _____ is a property that takes on different values at different times.

A. Model.
B. Equation.
C. Symbol.
D. Variable.
E. None of the above.

D 6. Identify the statement(s) which accurately reflect(s) the relationship between a manager's experience and marketing research.

A. There are instances in which the manager's experience alone may be relied on.
B. No decisions should be made by a manager without using marketing research.
C. Marketing research and a manager's experience are best used conjunctively.
D. A and C above.
E. None of the above.

E 7. Which of the following typify a nonroutine decision situation?

A. Marketing research information is generally a key input.
B. The level of uncertainty regarding the correct course of action is relatively low.
C. A manager's past experience and judgment are less relevant.
D. All of the above.
E. A and C only.

A 8. Ideally, marketing research should enter into the decision-making process at what point?

A. Recognition and formulation of problems or opportunities.
B. The identification of specific alternatives.
C. The evaluation of alternatives.
D. The selection of an alternative.
E. The implementation of the selected course of action.

A 9. The _____ stage of the decision-making process relies heavily on creativity.

   A. Identify alternative courses of action.
   B. Evaluate alternative courses of action.
   C. Select a course of action.
   D. Implementation.
   E. Control.

C 10. Many marketing decisions involve limited input from marketing research. Why?

   A. Marketing researchers often fail to appreciate the complexity of marketing problems. Therefore, marketing managers prefer to rely on their own experience and judgment.
   B. Marketers have traditionally preferred to act on their own intuition. The increasing sophistication of marketing research has not dampened this tendency.
   C. Many decisions, particularly those of a repetitive nature, are such that the manager's experience and judgment provide adequate input.
   D. A and C above.
   E. B and C above.

B 11. Which factor would **decrease** the importance of managerial experience and judgment relative to the use of marketing research in a given decision situation?

   A. Repetitive decision situation.
   B. High degree of uncertainty exists as to the decision outcome.
   C. Funds available for research.
   D. Need for an immediate decision.
   E. All of the above.

C 12. Four essential elements are embodied in a definition of marketing research. Which one of the following was not proposed?

   A. Objective.
   B. Systematic.
   C. Valid.
   D. Information.
   E. Decision making.

B 13. _____ refers to the requirement that the research project should be well organized and planned.

   A. Objective.
   B. Systematic.
   C. Information.
   D. Decision making.
   E. None of the above.

C 14. Which pair of terms in the definition of marketing research does **not** apply to the definition of management experience and judgment?

   A. Objective and Information.
   B. Decision Making and Systematic.

C. Objective and Systematic.
D. Systematic and Information.
E. All of the above.

D 15. Which of the following is **not** characteristic of applied research?

   A. Aimed at assisting managers in decision making.
   B. Guided by the requirements of the decision making process.
   C. More organization specific.
   D. Typically broader in purpose than basic research.
   E. Concerned with the cost and value of information.

A 16. Applied and basic research can be differentiated in regard to the _____ of the research.

   A. Thoroughness.
   B. Design.
   C. Accuracy.
   D. Reliability.
   E. None of the above.

The following questions relate to the "Marketing Research in Action" about General Motors insert from the text...

E 17. The following helped GM reduce its market share loss:
   A. Marketing research was employed in various aspects of the manufacturing and design phases.
   B. Managers used marketing research to target the actual audience of customers and methods to reach them.
   C. GM spent most of their marketing budget in advertising.
   D. GM hired more marketing managers.
   E. A and B.

C 18. The most significant impact management made in reducing losses was:
   A. More assembly lines were added to production.
   B. Additional safety training was given to workers.
   C. Allowing the marketing researchers to influence the design of vehicles.
   D. Raising the price on all vehicles to make up for the losses.
   E. Adding more layers of management.

The following questions relate to the "Global Marketing Research Dynamics" insert in the text:

B 19. The large, U.S. based carbonated soft drink firm failed to sell in Indonesia successfully because they did not use marketing research early enough. What could marketing research have revealed to the firm before they started marketing the product?

   A. There was a significant amount of disposable income to support sales of the drink.

B. Indonesians preferred non-carbonated, coconut-based drinks.
C. The firm should have tried to plan to sell more drinks than they did.
D. Marketing research was not needed at all. The time saved from doing research could have been used to capture more of the market.
E. None of the above.

E. 20. Many of the inserts in this section showed that marketing research:

A. Can show cultural lifestyle differences and preferences of consumers in other countries.
B. Showed that the same advertisement in this country was not necessarily effective in another country.
C. Is an integral part of doing business overseas.
D. A and B only.
E. All of the above.

CHAPTER 2 — THE MARKETING RESEARCH BUSINESS

True - False

T   1. A successful career in marketing research usually pays less than a successful line career in marketing.

F   2. Effective coordination and control of the firm's research efforts are two of the major advantages to a decentralized organization.

T   3. The integrated organization of the marketing research function seeks to combine the best features of centralization and decentralization into one effective system.

F   4. The most important advantage gained by centralization of the research function is the research group's increased ability to react quickly to and focus its attention on areas where its information is needed most.

T   5. The marketing research function should reside where the marketing decision-power resides.

F   6. The first step in selecting a research supplier is to ask several firms to submit proposals for research.

F   7. Competitive bidding is widespread among suppliers of marketing research.

Multiple Choice

B   1. Which of the following organizations is prominent in undertaking research studies for their own planning purposes but also does a great deal of research on behalf of clients (users/doers)?

         A. Manufacturers.
         B. Advertising agencies.
         C. Trade associations.
         D. Retailers.
         E. Universities.

E   2. Which of the following organizations undertakes marketing research solely to provide information for the use of other institutions?

         A. Syndicated data sources.
         B. Universities.
         C. Research institutes.
         D. Research supplier firms of ad hoc studies.
         E. All of the above.

A   3. _____ data sources collect certain types of data and then sell these data on a subscription basis to any organization that will buy them.

         A. Syndicated.
         B. University.

C. National.
D. Secondary.
E. Primary.

B 4. Of the following marketing research positions, which would do the bulk of the designing and supervision of actual marketing research studies?

A. Research directors.
B. Analysts.
C. Technical specialists.
D. Clerical workers.
E. A and C above.

B 5. Of the following marketing research positions, which is the same as a "research generalist's?"

A. Research directors.
B. Analysts.
C. Technical specialists.
D. Clerical workers.
E. None of the above.

C 6. Which of the following is **not** an organizational alternative for the marketing research function?

A. Decentralized organization.
B. Centralized organization.
C. Operational organization.
D. Integrative organization.
E. A and C above.

E 7. The centralized organization of the marketing research function:

A. Increases duplication of effort.
B. Increases coordination and control of the firm's marketing research effort.
C. May be disadvantageous if divisional problems are quite diverse.
D. A and B above.
E. B and C above.

C 8. Decentralization of the marketing research function:

A. Adversely affects the ability of the marketing research group to react to divisional problems.
B. Creates a situation in which research findings receive less attention.
C. May cause research findings to be biased toward the short-run, divisional point of view.
D. Would not be appropriate if divisional problems were diverse.
E. C and D above.

E 9. Suppliers of marketing research:

A. May not be as familiar as need be with the particular problems of the company and/or industry.
B. May offer special skills not available internally.

C. Invariably charge more for a particular project than would a firm's own marketing research group.
D. All of the above.
E. A and B only.

E 10. A supplier of marketing research may be evaluated on such criteria as:

A. The capabilities of personnel.
B. Facilities of the supplier.
C. Location of the supplier.
D. A proposal outlining the supplier's research design.
E. All of the above.

E 11. Which of the following would a buyer of research not be expected to provide a supplier of research?

A. A timetable.
B. A statement of the management problem.
C. A statement of the research problem and objectives.
D. A range of budget available for the project.
E. All of the above would be provided.

C 12. Tybout and Zaltman suggest that respondents should have several basic rights when participating in a research study. Which is **not** a right suggested by them?

A. The right to choose whether or not to participate in a study.
B. The right to safety.
C. The right to know the sponsor of the study.
D. The right to be informed as to the purpose of the study either before or after its completion.
E. C and D above.

B 13. Which of the following government agencies most likely could bring a questionable marketing research practice under close legal examination?

A. Commerce Department.
B. Federal Trade Commission.
C. Census Department.
D. Internal Revenue Service.
E. Justice Department.

CHAPTER 3 — THE MARKETING RESEARCH PROCESS: CONCEPT AND EXAMPLE

True - False

F   1. Each stage of the research process is largely independent of the other stages.

F   2. In specifying research objectives and listing information needs, the researcher should concentrate on this phase and not be overly concerned with anticipating the remaining steps in the research process.

T   3. A large proportion of the total error in the research results typically occurs in the process of data collection.

F   4. Types of sampling errors include faulty population definition, nonresponse, and measurement errors.

T   5. Nonsampling errors create a bias in research results of unknown direction and magnitude.

F   6. Nonsampling error is measurable and it decreases as the sample size increases.

Multiple Choice

E   1. Which of the following is the initial step in the research process?

    A. Specify research objectives and information needs.
    B. Design the sample.
    C. Determine the sources of data.
    D. Develop the data collection forms.
    E. None of the above.

B   2. _____ may be thought of as a detailed listing of research objectives.

    A. Statement of the decision problem.
    B. Statement of information needs.
    C. Statement of problem definition.
    D. All of the above.
    E. None of the above.

A   3. Which of the following are controllable independent variables?

    A. Marketing mix variables
    B. Behavioral response variables
    C. Situation factors
    D. Performance measures
    E. A and C

C 4. Nonsampling errors:

   A. Decrease with sample size.
   B. May be dealt with statistically.
   C. Include all the errors that may occur in the marketing research process except the sampling error.
   D. Do not affect the accuracy of study results.
   E. A and C only.

E 5. Which of the following is **not** a nonsampling error?

   A. Nonresponse error.
   B. Measurement error.
   C. Improper causal inference.
   D. Auspices bias.
   E. All of the above are nonsampling errors.

E 6. Auspices bias:

   A. May inhibit people from revealing their true feelings.
   B. May be measured and the data adjusted accordingly.
   C. May result from the sponsor of the study being identified.
   D. All of the above.
   E. A and C only.

B 7. Total error is equal to:

   A. Two times the sampling error.
   B. Sampling error plus nonsampling error.
   C. Sampling error minus nonsampling error.
   D. Sampling error times nonsampling error.
   E. Square root of the sampling error.

The following question relates to the "Global Marketing Research Dynamics" titled "SPI Marketing Research: Selected Country Specific Differences"...

C 8. Which of the following countries put the highest values on the solid structure of plastics, according to marketing research results:

   A. France
   B. Japan
   C. Germany
   D. Canada
   E. Austria

The following question relates to the "Marketing Research in Action" insert about Hertz and Avis car rental companies...

D 9. The conflict between the two companies revolved around what important theme in marketing research:

A. Small marketing research firms can not compete with larger marketing research firms.
B. Exploratory research allows quantitative research to be designed more effectively.
C. Global marketing research must take into account the varied perceptions of research in different countries.
D. A lack of integrity and ethics can have the potential to do damage to a marketing research firm and its client.
E. None of the above.

CHAPTER 4 — THE DECISION TO UNDERTAKE RESEARCH

True - False

T 1. The decision-making process and the management process are often considered synonymous.

T 2. Recognition that a unique marketing problem exists or that an opportunity is present is the first stage of the decision-making process.

F 3. The terms symptom, problem, and opportunity are all used interchangeably in marketing management.

T 4. A symptom can be viewed as the result of a problem or opportunity.

F 5. Hypotheses are most readily formulated through the application of fixed and rigid procedures.

T 6. Since case histories represent an analysis of past situations which may have limited relevance to future situations, conclusions so derived should be viewed as tentative and suggestive of hypotheses to be tested with conclusive research methodology.

F 7. Exploratory research is not particularly useful in identifying alternative courses of action.

T 8. Generally, the more specific the statement of research objectives, the lower the risk that management will misperceive the purpose of the study.

T 9. The evaluation of marketing research is inherently subjective.

Multiple Choice

C 1. The analysis preceding the decision to undertake marketing research is:

　　A. Necessary only where the marketing research staff does not work closely with management.
　　B. Desirable but not essential.
　　C. The key determinant of the success of any subsequent research project undertaken.
　　D. More important with exploratory research than conclusive research.
　　E. A and D above.

D 2. In which ways do problems and opportunities differ?

　　A. Means by which detected.
　　B. Necessity for managerial response and attention.
　　C. Problems are less related to symptoms than opportunities.
　　D. Both A and B.
　　E. None of the above--problem and opportunity are synonymous.

A 3. The failure of sales volume to reach a forecasted level is most correctly termed:

   A. A symptom.
   B. A problem.
   C. An opportunity.
   D. An inadequacy.
   E. None of the above.

D 4. Performance monitoring research:

   A. Alerts management to a potential decision situation.
   B. Can be continuous and/or ad hoc.
   C. May concern both dependent and independent variables in the marketing system.
   D. All of the above.
   E. Only A and B above.

C 5. Which of the following is **not** an integral component of a decision problem?

   A. An objective.
   B. Alternatives.
   C. Inexperience.
   D. Uncertainty.
   E. A and B above.

D 6. The success of a research study is dependent upon a clear understanding of the decision objectives. Why is this a potential sore spot for marketing researchers?

   A. Organizational objectives may not be explicit.
   B. Personal objectives of the decision maker may be present which conflict with organizational objectives.
   C. The decision may be the responsibility of a group of individuals, each having personal objectives which may conflict with those of the other members of the group.
   D. All of the above.
   E. A and B only.

B 7. _____ is designed to bring ideas and insights to a decision situation where limited knowledge exists.

   A. Conclusive research.
   B. Exploratory research.
   C. Performance monitoring research.
   D. Experimental research.
   E. Survey research.

C 8. By _____ we refer to a conjectural statement about the relationship between two or more variables.

   A. Problem definition.
   B. Decision problem.
   C. Hypothesis.
   D. Opportunity statement.
   E. Symptom.

C 9. Which of the following is **not** associated with a situational analysis?

   A. Identification of problems and opportunities.
   B. Diagnosis and prognosis.
   C. Evaluation of alternative courses of action.
   D. Analysis of the marketing program as well as the situational variables in the marketing system.
   E. C and D above.

E 10. Why is a literature search of secondary sources a logical starting point in decision problem formulation?

   A. Secondary data is often inexpensive to acquire.
   B. Secondary data may be gathered relatively quickly.
   C. Such an analysis typically generates hypotheses which obviate the need for further exploratory work.
   D. All of the above.
   E. A and B above.

B 11. To be effective, a researcher must view the problem situation from the perspective(s) of which of the following individuals.

   A. His/her own.
   B. The decision maker.
   C. A representative of the decision maker.
   D. All of the above.
   E. Either B or C.

B 12. _____ provides information which helps the decision maker evaluate and select a course of action.

   A. Performance monitoring research.
   B. Conclusive research.
   C. Case history research.
   D. Secondary data.
   E. Exploratory research.

C 13. The marketing researcher is seldom given explicit objectives when requested to assist a decision maker. How might the researcher most effectively determine the relevant objectives?

   A. By directly confronting the decision maker as to the relevant objectives.
   B. By formulating objectives which in his or her judgment represent the objectives relevant to the decision situation.
   C. By confronting the decision maker with possible solutions to the decision problem, determining which would be unacceptable and why they would be unacceptable.
   D. Both A and B.
   E. All of the above.

B 14. How should research objectives be stated?

   A. In some situations, broadly, to permit flexibility in the implementation of the research.
   B. Precisely, to communicate the specifics of why the study is being conducted.
   C. It does not matter as long as the researcher is aware of the objectives.
   D. A and B above.
   E. All of the above.

D 15. Which of the following guide the specification of information needs?

   A. Research objectives.
   B. Decision maker.
   C. Ability of the marketing research system to gather the information.
   D. All of the above.
   E. A and B only.

D 16. Mocking-up potential research findings prior to conducting the project:

   A. Is a very expensive exercise, but generally worthwhile.
   B. May decrease the total cost of the project.
   C. Involves simulating the research presentation in order to identify voids in the original list of information needs.
   D. Both B and C.
   E. All of the above.

A 17. Ideally, decision criteria should be developed:

   A. Well before the results from the research project are obtained.
   B. After the research results are obtained.
   C. Before or after, depending on the particular situation.
   D. Since decision making is the responsibility of management, the researcher is not concerned with specifying decision criteria.
   E. None of the above.

B 18. Why is it difficult to evaluate a particular research project on a cost-benefit basis?

   A. Because it is difficult to quantify the costs associated with a research project.
   B. Because it is difficult to quantify the benefits associated with a research project.
   C. Because most managers are reluctant to have such an analysis conducted.
   D. Both B and C.
   E. All of the above.

E 19. In general, it is easier to justify the cost of research:

   A. As the market size increases.
   B. As the ratio of variable cost to selling price increases.
   C. As the ratio of variable cost to selling price decreases.
   D. A and B above.
   E. A and C above.

C 20. Solutions which might minimize the conflict between marketing research and management include:

   A. Delegating decision-making responsibility to researchers.
   B. Placing the marketing research department within the organizational structure so that management can call on its services whenever management feels the need to do so.
   C. Utilization of a "research generalist" to coordinate research and management.
   D. All of the above.
   E. None of the above.

D 21. Which of the following factors strain the relationship between marketing research and marketing management?

   A. Marketing researchers tend to be specialized, technique-oriented people.
   B. The failure of some researchers to recognize their role as an advisory one.
   C. The view by some marketing managers of research as limited in its usefulness.
   D. All of the above.
   E. B and C only.

B 22. The manager may view research as a way to satisfy needs other than those related to decision making. This has been called _____.

   A. Ego-research.
   B. Pseudo-research.
   C. Motivation research.
   D. Personal research.
   E. All of the above.

E 23. Several barriers to the effective management utilization of marketing research were identified. Which was not one identified in the text?

   A. Some managers view research as a threat to their personal status as decision makers.
   B. The lack of common organizational objectives may involve research in the internal struggle for power of various managers.
   C. The interdisciplinary training of specialists makes communication difficult.
   D. The isolation of marketing research personnel from managers.
   E. The lack of having "project teams" composed of managers and researchers.

The following question relates to the "Sanctioning International Marketing Research" section of the chapter...

B 24. The following are all characteristics mentioned in the text of doing international marketing research:

   A. International research is cheaper than domestic marketing research.
   B. Interviewing is more complicated than interviewing a domestic audience.
   C. Lack of formal infrastructure for marketing research in many non-U.S. countries.
   D. Smaller markets, in general, outside of the U.S., thus resulting in potential revenue and profit outcomes less than in the U.S. market.

The following question relates to the "Global Marketing Research Dynamics" insert...

C 25. Based on types of exporters mentioned in the example, how would a company that was familiar with exporting rules and regulations, but not proficient in exporting, be classified?

   A. Reactive/opportunistic exporters
   B. Active exporters
   C. Experimenting exporters
   D. Proficient exporters
   E. None of the above

CHAPTER 5 — RESEARCH DESIGN AND DATA SOURCES

True - False

F 1. Exploratory research uses formal and rather structured research designs.

T 2. Descriptive research typically makes use of a cross-sectional research design.

T 3. A cross-sectional research design is frequently called the survey research design.

F 4. Exploratory research presupposes that a sound causal model of the marketing system exists in the mind of the decision maker.

F 5. The vast majority of marketing research studies involve causal research.

F 6. Determining the causal relationships within a set of variables necessarily precedes prediction.

T 7. Despite its inability to establish causal relationships, descriptive research plays an important role in marketing research.

T 8. Descriptive research is useful only to the extent that a sound causal model exists in the mind of the decision maker.

T 9. Performance monitoring research may involve a special (ad hoc) study or a continuous research program.

F 10. The traditional panel is a fixed sample of respondents measured over time; however, the variables measured are different each time.

F 11. The omnibus panel is a fixed sample in which the same variables are measured over time.

T 12. A respondent may be a consumer, an industrial buyer, a wholesaler, or any knowledgeable person who can provide data useful to a decision situation.

T 13. A valid simulation means that the model's behavior corresponds to the system it is designed to represent.

T 14. An experiment is a valuable source of data in that it yields relatively unambiguous conclusions regarding cause and effect relationships.

F 15. Secondary data are collected specifically for purposes of the research needs at hand.

F 16. Starch Reports measure retail orders from manufacturers' warehouses.

T 17. Accounting data are inputs in a marketing decision support system.

F 18. The most complex (advanced) phase of an MDSS is the linkage system, where association among variables can be studied.

F 19. The main problem with the idealized MDSS concept is managers' reluctance to accept the modeling stage in the MDSS evolution.

F 20. Large, multinational corporations rely heavily on foreign governmental and public sources of secondary data for each country they are involved in.

Multiple Choice

C 1. Which of the following statements is (are) false?

   A. The research design is a framework which guides the data collection and analysis phases of the research project.
   B. The research design specifies the type of information to be collected and the data collection procedure.
   C. The ideal research design is usually exactly determined by the research objectives.
   D. The characteristics desired in the research design are determined (at least indirectly) by the information needs of the decision maker.
   E. Both C and D.

C 2. Descriptive research is inappropriate given which of the following objectives:

   A. To portray the characteristics of marketing phenomena and the frequency of occurrence.
   B. To determine the degree to which marketing variables are associated.
   C. To make predictions regarding the occurrence of marketing phenomena.
   D. A and B above.
   E. All of the above.

E 3. A cross-sectional design:

   A. Is also known as a survey research design.
   B. Involves taking a fixed sample of population elements which is measured repeatedly over time.
   C. Assures internal validity.
   D. Involves taking a sample of population elements at one point in time.
   E. Both A and D.

E 4. Which of the following sources of data may **not** be used in a descriptive research design?

   A. Secondary data.
   B. Experimentation.
   C. Simulation.
   D. Interrogation of respondents.
   E. None of the above.

E 5. The main source(s) of data for causal research include:

   A. Simulation.
   B. Experimentation.
   C. Interrogation of respondents through surveys.
   D. All of the above.
   E. B and C only.

D   6. The mode of research whose primary purpose is to signal the presence of potential problems or opportunities is:

   A. Exploratory research.
   B. Descriptive research.
   C. Causal research.
   D. Performance monitoring research.
   E. None of the above.

C   7. Which of the following is most **unlikely** to qualify as a data source for performance monitoring research?

   A. Interrogation of respondents.
   B. Secondary data.
   C. Simulation.
   D. Experimentation.
   E. Observation.

B   8. A longitudinal design:

   A. Involves taking a sample of population elements at one point in time.
   B. Involves taking a fixed sample of population elements which is measured repeatedly over time.
   C. Is not inherently analytical by nature.
   D. All of the above.
   E. None of the above.

D   9. A _____ design is where a fixed sample of population elements is measured repeatedly.

   A. Longitudinal design.
   B. Cross-sectional design.
   C. Panel design.
   D. A and C above.
   E. B and C above.

C   10. Which of the following is **not** an advantage of the longitudinal design over the cross-sectional design?

   A. The longitudinal is more analytical.
   B. Longitudinal designs yield more accurate data.
   C. Longitudinal designs are free from response bias.
   D. The cost of longitudinal data can be lower than the cost of comparable data collected through a survey.
   E. A and B above.

E   11. A _____ design is a fixed sample where the same variables are repeatedly measured.

   A. Omnibus panel.
   B. Causal.

237

C. Longitudinal.
D. Cross-sectional.
E. Traditional panel.

E 12. The fundamental difference(s) between qualitative and quantitative research pertain(s) to:

A. Number of respondents involved.
B. The usefulness of the findings.
C. The time span over which respondents are interviewed.
D. All of the above.
E. A and C above.

D 13. Which of the following does not constitute a basic source of marketing data?

A. Respondents.
B. Analogous situations.
C. Secondary data.
D. Nielsen reports.
E. Experimentation.

C 14. Depth interviews:

A. Span a relatively brief time period.
B. Involve a large sample of respondents.
C. Attempt to determine the "why" of past and future behavior.
D. All of the above.
E. None of the above.

A 15. Which of the following is **not** an advantage of simulation over other data sources?

A. Development of the model is relatively easy.
B. It allows evaluation of alternative marketing strategies.
C. Simulation can be conducted in complete secrecy.
D. It can be used as a training device within the organization.
E. Simulation encourages creativity since radical strategy changes can be evaluated.

B 16. A classification scheme of simulation models based on the management purpose served by the simulation includes all **but** which of the following?

A. Descriptive models.
B. Probabilistic models.
C. Predictive models.
D. Prescriptive models.
E. None of the above.

E 17. What characteristics should a simulation model possess?

A. Easy manipulation by the user.
B. Simple enough for comprehension.
C. Reasonably representative of the marketing system it represents.
D. A and C.
E. A, B, and C.

D 18. Which of the following statements is **not** correct?

   A. Secondary data may be obtained from internal or external sources.
   B. Secondary data may be obtained at a minimal (if any) cost.
   C. Secondary data can be quite expensive to purchase.
   D. None of the above.
   E. All of the above.

C 19. The distinction between primary and secondary data relates to:

   A. The source from which the data are obtained.
   B. The relative importance of the two types of data.
   C. The purpose for which the data are collected.
   D. None of the above.
   E. A and B only.

E 20. Inputs to the marketing information system may include:

   A. Accounting data.
   B. Salespersons' reports.
   C. Syndicated data.
   D. Data from library sources.
   E. All of the above.

B 21. MDSS output, if it is to be useful, must be all but which of the following?

   A. Inclusive.
   B. Standardized.
   C. Timely.
   D. Accurate.
   E. Convenient.

C 22. The MDSS concept:

   A. Has gained widespread acceptance among organizations.
   B. Has entirely replaced its predecessor, the marketing research system.
   C. Has encountered some difficulty in its implementation.
   D. Has been integrated into the decision-making framework of managers, particularly those at the highest levels.
   E. A, B, and D above.

A 23. Which of the following is **not** a component of MDSS?

   A. Standardized data inputs and outputs.
   B. Database management.
   C. Display formats.
   D. Statistical analysis.
   E. Modeling.

A 24. The following are factors in the implementation of research designs in various countries:

   A. Variations in available technology

239

B. Research institutions
C. Culture variations
D. Availability of data sources
E. All of the above

The following questions relate to the Global Marketing Research Dynamics insert, "International Data Sources"...

D 25. The following are preliminary screening techniques for determining attractive country markets:

A. Participation in overseas trade fairs and shows
B. Scrutiny of news media and trade publications
C. Trend analysis - domestic production plus imports minus exports
D. A and B
E. All of the above

E 26. The following techniques are used in determining company sales potential and profitability analysis in foreign markets:

A. Surveys of end users and distributors
B. Customized market research
C. Trade audits
D. Competitive intelligence gathering
E. All of the above

CHAPTER 6 — SECONDARY DATA

True - False

F   1. Primary data are already published data collected for purposes other than the specific research needs at hand.

F   2. The central advantage of primary data is the saving in cost and time in comparison with secondary data.

T   3. A serious limitation of secondary data is the difficulty in evaluating its accuracy.

F   4. The marketing researcher is **not** responsible for assessing the accuracy of secondary data.

F   5. The largest single source of statistical data is the A. C. Nielsen Company.

T   6. Census data are available at many different levels, ranging from city blocks to the nation as a whole.

F   7. Most census data are published only down to the "block" level.

T   8. A block is the smallest area for which census data are available.

F   9. A tract is the smallest area for which census data are available.

F   10. The SIC code is based on the geographic locale of manufacturers.

F   11. The SRDS (Standard Rate and Data Service, Inc.) provides data on production, prices, and consumption for approximately 100 individual commodities.

F   12. Due to the wealth of relatively inexpensive information available for strategic and tactical information on foreign competitors, there is no need to take the time to actually take a trip to the country being researched.

Multiple Choice

C   1. Which of the following statements are **not** true?

     A. Secondary data should be considered the initial source to explore in the research process.
     B. Internal secondary data are typically preferred to external secondary data.
     C. Secondary data usually fulfill the data requirements of a research project.
     D. Syndicated sources provide external secondary data.
     E. C and D above.

E   2. Which of the following are advantages of secondary data when compared to primary data?

   A. Available at a lower cost.
   B. Available in less time.
   C. More up-to-date.
   D. All of the above.
   E. A and B only.

D   3. The degree of fit between secondary data and information needs of the research project is a function of which of the following?

   A. Units of measurement.
   B. Definition of classes.
   C. Publication currency.
   D. All of the above.
   E. A and B only.

B   4. Criteria useful in assessing the accuracy of secondary data **do not** include which of the following?

   A. Source of the data.
   B. The rating of the data in **Statistical Abstracts**.
   C. Evidence regarding quality.
   D. Purpose of the publication.
   E. B and D above.

B   5. Which of the following does **not** characterize data from the Bureau of the Census?

   A. The data have a reputation of high quality.
   B. The data typically are not detailed enough for marketing information needs.
   C. The data are accessible on computer tape.
   D. Some census data are collected through the use of samples.
   E. B and D above.

C   6. Which of the following geographic units of the Census Bureau is lowest in terms of level of aggregation?

   A. MSA.
   B. Region.
   C. Tract.
   D. State.
   E. Division.

E   7. What are the limitations associated with Census data?

   A. Definitions have been changed from census to census.
   B. Little assistance is available on how to use the data.
   C. Definitions can have different meanings within a Census.
   D. All of the above.
   E. A and C only.

C   8. The publication which serves as an abstract and reference to data available in other published sources is:

A. *Survey of Current Business.*
B. *County and City Data-Book.*
C. *Statistical Abstract of the United States.*
D. *International Directory of Marketing Research.*
E. *Standard Rate and Data Service, Inc.*

D 9. Data useful for developing and updating industry and company forecasts are available from which of the following?

A. *Economic Indications.*
B. *Business Conditions Digest.*
C. *U.S. Industrial Outlook.*
D. All of the above.
E. A and B only.

D 10. Data pertaining to the major industries of the United States may be obtained from:

A. *Standard and Poor's Industry Surveys.*
B. *Survey of Current Business.*
C. *U.S. Industrial Outlook.*
D. All of the above.
E. A and C only.

A 11. Which of the following is not done by the Bureau of the Census?

A. Publication of most data all the way down to block level.
B. Industrialized computer runs.
C. Collection of data such as income, occupation, and marital history.
D. Selling unpublished data contained on census computer tapes.
E. Publish the *Statistical Abstract of the United States* as a base reference.

E 12. Company data and facts may be obtained from all but which of the following sources?

A. *Moody's Manuals.*
B. *Corporate Records.*
C. *Trade and Securities Statistics.*
D. *Fortune Double 500 Directory.*
E. *Company Reports.*

D 13. The following are all potential sources of information for research on companies in foreign countries:

A. Foreign brokerage houses.
B. Library of Congress.
C. *Statistical Abstract of the United States.*
D. A and B only.
E. All of the above.

243

CHAPTER 7 — THE MEASUREMENT PROCESS

True - False

T   1. The objective of the measurement process is to develop a correspondence between the empirical system and the abstract system.

F   2. Use of the characteristics of the number system in data analysis is not affected by the relationships which actually exist in the empirical system being modeled.

F   3. The empirical system includes the numbers used to represent the marketing phenomena of the abstract system.

T   4. The only restrictive rule imposed on the assignment of numbers from the nominal scale is: do not assign the same number to different objects or events or different numbers to the same object or event.

T   5. Numbers from the nominal scale serve only as labels to identify or categorize objects or events.

F   6. The nominal scale of measurement is not very useful in representing marketing phenomena.

T   7. The rule governing the assignment of numbers with ordinal measurement is simply that any series of numbers can be assigned that preserves the ordered relationships present in the empirical system.

T   8. The measurement of attitudes, opinions, preference, and perception often involves the ordinal scale.

F   9. The mean is an appropriate descriptive statistic for ordinal data.

F   10. The zero point on an interval scale corresponds to the absence of the characteristic being measured in the empirical system.

T   11. An absolute zero point on the ratio scale simply corresponds to the absence of the characteristic being measured in the empirical system.

T   12. A ratio scale implies that equal ratios among the scale values correspond to equal ratios among the marketing phenomena being measured.

F   13. Very few marketing phenomena are appropriately measured on the ratio scale.

F   14. The methods used to measure validity involve determining the extent of agreement between attempts to measure the same characteristic through maximally similar methods.

F   15. Concurrent validity is so named because it is appropriate only in conjunction with one or more of the other means of assessing validity.

T   16. For a measure to be valid it must be reliable.

F 17. The methods used to measure reliability involve determining the degree of agreement between attempts to measure the same characteristics through maximally different methods.

T 18. Test-reliability assumes that the greater the discrepancy in scores the greater the random error present in the measurement process and the lower the reliability.

T 19. Split-half reliability involves dividing a multi-item measurement device into equivalent groups and correlating the item responses to estimate reliability.

F 20. Based on evidence to date, measures are not highly reliable for hard variables, like demographics, across different countries.

Multiple Choice

C 1. Which of the following is **not** an element of the definition of measurement?

   A. The assignment of numbers
   B. to characteristics of objects or events,
   C. or to the objects or events themselves,
   D. according to rules.
   E. None of the above.

A 2. The number system has four characteristics. Which of the following is **not** one of them?

   A. Each number in the system is divisible.
   B. Ordering of the numbers is given by convention.
   C. Equal differences can be defined.
   D. Equal ratios can be defined.
   E. None of the above.

C 3. Which of the following is **not** a scale of measurement?

   A. Nominal.
   B. Ordinal.
   C. Linear.
   D. Interval.
   E. Ratio.

D 4. If we were to arrange the measurement scales in order of complexity (simplest to most complex), which of the following would be correct?

   A. Nominal, interval, ordinal, ratio.
   B. Interval, ratio, nominal, ordinal.
   C. Ratio, interval, ordinal, nominal.
   D. Nominal, ordinal, interval, ratio.
   E. Interval, nominal, ordinal, ratio.

E   5. Why is measurement so difficult a task in marketing?

    A. Because the phenomena measured typically involve the behavior of people.
    B. Because of the lack of appropriate scales of measurement.
    C. Because of the relatively crude measuring devices available.
    D. All of the above.
    E. A and C only.

D   6. The ordinal scale of measurement:

    A. Defines the ordered relationship among objects or events.
    B. Measures whether an object or event has more or less of a characteristic than some other object or event.
    C. Does not provide information on how much more or less of the characteristic various objects or events possess.
    D. All of the above.
    E. A and B only.

D   7. Which of the characteristics of the number system are associated with the ordinal scale of measurement?

    A. Uniqueness and equality of differences.
    B. Uniqueness, order, and equality of ratios.
    C. Equality of differences and equality of ratios.
    D. Uniqueness and order.
    E. Order and equality of differences.

A   8. The numbers used to identify basketball players are representative of which measurement scale?

    A. Nominal.
    B. Ordinal.
    C. Interval.
    D. Ratio.
    E. B and C above.

E   9. On an ordinal scale, which of the following series of numbers represent a permissible substitution for the series 1, 2, 3?

    A. 1, 3, 30
    B. 5, 10, 15
    C. 3, 2, 1
    D. All of the above.
    E. A and B only.

E   10. What conclusions can be drawn regarding the following series of numbers on the ordinal scale of measurement 1, 2, 3?

    A. 2 represents twice as much of the characteristic as does 1
    B. 3 represents three times as much of the characteristic as does 1.
    C. 3 represents 1-1/2 times as much of the characteristic as does 2.
    D. All of the above.
    E. None of the above.

C 11. The interval scale involves which of the characteristics of the number system?

   A. Equality of numerals.
   B. Equality of numerals and order of numerals.
   C. Equality of numerals, order of numerals, and equality of differences.
   D. Equality of numerals, order of numerals, and equality of ratios.
   E. Equality of numerals and equality of ratios.

D 12. Suppose three brands are rated on an **interval scale** regarding degree of preference. Brand X receives a 6 (most preferred), Brand Y a 3, and Brand Z a 2. What conclusions can be drawn from this data?

   A. Brand X is three times as preferred as Brand Z.
   B. Brand Y is more preferred than Brand Z.
   C. The difference between Brand X and Brand Y is three times greater than the difference between Brand Y and Brand Z.
   D. B and C above.
   E. All of the above.

D 13. Which of the following characteristics of the number system distinguish the ratio scale from the other measurement scales?

   A. Equality of numerals.
   B. Order of numerals.
   C. Equality of differences.
   D. Equality of ratios.
   E. C and D above.

C 14. Which of the following statements is incorrect?

   A. Measurement error consists of two components: systematic error and random error.
   B. Measurement error is difficult to avoid in practice.
   C. Measurement error is minimized by minimizing random error.
   D. Measurement error is at the minimum when a direct correspondence exists between the number system and the phenomena being measured.
   E. C and D above.

B 15. If the measurement process involves no systematic error and low random error, we say the measurements are:

   A. Valid but not reliable.
   B. Valid and reliable.
   C. Reliable but not valid.
   D. Neither valid nor reliable.
   E. None of the above.

C 16. If the measurement process involves high systematic error and low random error, we say that the measurements are:

   A. Valid but not reliable.
   B. Valid and reliable.

C. Reliable but not valid.
D. Neither valid nor reliable.
E. None of the above.

D 17. If the measurement process involves no systematic error and high random error, we say that the measurements are:

A. Valid but not reliable.
B. Valid and reliable.
C. Reliable but not valid.
D. Neither valid nor reliable.
E. None of the above.

D 18. Which of the following is **not** a means of estimating the validity of measurements?

A. Construct validity.
B. Content validity.
C. Concurrent validity.
D. Incidental validity.
E. Test-retest validity.

A 19. _____ validity involves understanding the theoretical rationale underlying the obtained measurements.

A. Construct.
B. Content.
C. Concurrent.
D. Pragmatic.
E. Predictive.

E 20. Content validity:

A. Involves a subjective judgment by an expert as to the appropriateness of the measurements.
B. Is primarily used to determine the validity of new measuring techniques.
C. Is commonly used in marketing research to determine the validity of measurements.
D. All of the above.
E. A and C only.

C 21. _____ validity involves correlating two different measurements of the same marketing phenomenon which have been administered at the same point in time.

A. Construct.
B. Content.
C. Concurrent.
D. Pragmatic.
E. Predictive.

E 22. _____ validity involves the ability of a measured marketing phenomenon at one point in time to predict another marketing phenomenon at a future point in time.

A. Predictive.
B. Content.
C. Pragmatic.
D. Criterion-related.
E. A, C and D above.

D 23. If the correlation between a measure of some marketing phenomena (brand preference) and other marketing phenomena (share of market) is high, the measure is said to have:

A. Construct validity.
B. Content validity.
C. Concurrent validity.
D. Predictive validity.
E. A and C above.

C 24. Which of the following is **not** a method of estimating the reliability of a measure?

A. Test-retest.
B. Alternative forms.
C. Repeated scale.
D. Split half.
E. A and D above.

D 25. _____ reliability involves repeated measurement using the same scaling device under conditions which are judged to be very similar.

A. Alternative forms.
B. Similar forms.
C. Repeated scale.
D. Test-retest.
E. Split-half.

A 26. _____ reliability involves giving the subject two forms which are judged equivalent but are not identical.

A. Alternative forms.
B. Similar forms.
C. Repeated scale.
D. Test-retest.
E. Split-half.

E 27. _____ reliability involves dividing a multi-item measurement device into equivalent groups and correlating the item responses to estimate reliability.

A. Alternative forms.
B. Similar forms.
C. Repeated scale.
D. Test-retest.
E. Split-half.

The following question relates to the Global Marketing Research Dynamics "Measurement in International Marketing Research" insert...

B 28. There is limited reliability of soft variables, such as life style or product involvement, in a research study across different countries. This can be mainly attributed to:

   A. Poor design of questionnaires
   B. Differing expectations and perspectives across cultures
   C. Insufficient resources to conduct the study
   D. Invalid construct in the research design
   E. None of the above

CHAPTER 8 — ATTITUDE MEASUREMENT

True - False

T   1. Attitude measurement is important in determining a segmentation or positioning strategy.

F   2. The cognitive component of an attitude concerns a person's feelings about the object or event.

T   3. The attitude construct is typically measured at the nominal or ordinal scale level.

F   4. The hierarchy-of-effect model hypothesizes a sequence resulting from marketing effort, the order of which does not vary according to the specific marketing situation.

F   5. The most widely used technique in attitude measurement in marketing involves performance of objective tasks.

T   6. As a method of measuring attitudes, responses to unstructured or partially structured stimuli can be classified as a communication technique.

F   7. A balanced scale always has an even number of categories.

F   8. An unbalanced scale always has an odd number of categories.

F   9. The rank order scaling approach, which results in an interval scaling of objects, involves the ranking of objects concerning the attitude under consideration.

F   10. Data from the paired comparison scaling technique are commonly analyzed by the method of profile analysis.

T   11. The Q-sort technique can be used at times when the experimenter is concerned by the accuracy of direct scaling approaches.

T   12. An advantage of the semantic differential is that it allows measurement of an image, defined as the average of separate attitudes.

T   13. The semantic differential uses rating scales bounded by bipolar adjectives or phrases.

T   14. The scale uses a unipolar 10-point nonverbal rating scale.

F   15. A single segmentation can be applied cross-culturally, thus making these types of attitude based segmentation systems very useful.

Multiple Choice

E 1. Attitude measurement plays a key role in marketing in:

    A. Evaluating advertising effectiveness.
    B. Segmentation/positioning strategy development.
    C. Predicting product acceptance.
    D. A and B above.
    E. All of the above.

C 2. Measurement in marketing, by comparison to the physical sciences, typically involves:

    A. Less difficulty and lower scales of measurement.
    B. Less difficulty and higher scales of measurement.
    C. More difficulty and lower scales of measurement.
    D. More difficulty and higher scales of measurement.
    E. Any of the above, depending on the circumstances.

B 3. Attitude measurement in marketing typically involves data at the:

    A. Nominal level.
    B. Nominal or ordinal level.
    C. Ordinal level.
    D. Ordinal or interval level.
    E. Interval level.

E 4. The hierarchy-of-effect model hypothesizes which of the following sequences concerning attitudes?

    A. Cognitive-affective-behavioral.
    B. Cognitive-behavioral-affective.
    C. Behavioral-affective-cognitive.
    D. None of the above.
    E. All of the above, depending upon the situation.

E 5. Research on the hierarchy-of-effects model suggests that the stages can occur in different sequences depending on:

    A. The degree of family interaction regarding the purchase.
    B. The degree of buyer involvement with the purchase.
    C. The degree of differentiation among alternatives.
    D. All of the above.
    E. B and C only.

D 6. The affective component of the hierarchy-of-effects model can be described by which of the following terms?

    A. Liking.
    B. Knowledge.
    C. Preference.
    D. A and C above.
    E. B and C above.

B 7. The most common tool of attitude measurement is:

   A. Performance of objective tasks.
   B. Self-report method.
   C. Overt behavior.
   D. Physiological reactions.
   E. Responses to unstructured or partially structured stimuli.

B 8. The simplest kind of self-reporting scale is the:

   A. Rating scale.
   B. Nominal scale.
   C. Graphic scale.
   D. Verbal scale.
   E. None of the above.

E 9. Which of the following are important issues in constructing graphic rating scales?

   A. Odd or even number of categories.
   B. Category numbering.
   C. Forced vs. nonforced scales.
   D. All of the above.
   E. None of the above.

C 10. Treating the data from rating scales as interval data suggests the experimenter should be sensitive to:

   A. Utilizing sufficient categories.
   B. Balancing the scale.
   C. Measurement error.
   D. Forcing the scale.
   E. None of the above.

D 11. A rating scale without a "no opinion" or "no knowledge" category is an example of what kind of scale?

   A. Balanced.
   B. Unbalanced.
   C. Noncomparative.
   D. Forced.
   E. Invalid.

D 12. Which of the following scales is often used when it is felt that self reporting through direct measurement may be inaccurate?

   A. Nominal scale.
   B. Staple scale.
   C. Semantic differential.
   D. Likert scale.
   E. None of the above.

A 13. A rating scale which results in data commonly displayed in matrix format is the:

A. Paired comparison scale.
B. Semantic differential.
C. Likert scale.
D. Rank order scale.
E. None of the above.

B 14. The semantic differential utilizes:

A. Unipolar ten-point scales.
B. Bipolar adjectives.
C. [n(n-1)/2] comparisons.
D. All of the above.
E. None of the above.

E 15. The profile analysis method:

A. Calculates a mean or median among observations.
B. Allows evaluation of an image.
C. Plots summary measures on the same scales as used for data collection.
D. A and C above.
E. All of the above.

C 16. An example of a scale designed to simultaneously measure the intensity and direction of attitudes is the:

A. Semantic differential.
B. Nominal scale.
C. Ratingscale.
D. Paired comparison scale.
E. Rank order scale.

A 17. Overt behavior and physiological reactions are examples of:

A. Observation techniques.
B. Self-reporting techniques.
C. Communication techniques.
D. Task performance behavior.
E. None of the above.

The following questions relate to the Global Marketing Research Dynamics insert "International Attitude Measures Help Identify Segments"...

B 18. The following are not segments consistently identified over various countries through Global Scan, an attitude based segmentation system available to international marketers:

A. Pressured
B. Innovators

C. Strivers
D. Unassigned
E. None of the above

B 19. The Japan VALS program, developed by SRI International, determines the consumer effect of changing values and social attitudes in Japan. What did SRI believe about segmentation systems?

A. Segmentation systems are only limited in their use.
B. One segmentation system can not be applied cross-culturally.
C. Segmentation systems can be used to replace marketing research by individual firms.
D. A segmentation system must have at least five segments to be useful.
E. None of the above.

A 20. Segmentation systems provide:

A. Valuable starting points for international market development decisions.
B. Sufficient data to avoid marketing research.
C. Data that can not be collected in any other way.
D. B and C.
E. None of the above.

CHAPTER 9 — CAUSAL DESIGNS

True - False

F 1. One can conclusively prove cause-and-effect relationships through the demonstration of concomitant variation.

T 2. Deterministic causation is essentially "common sense" causality, i.e., the cause precedes the effect.

F 3. Deterministic causation suggests that several events occurring together (causes) may result in another event occurring (effect).

F 4. It is impossible for two events to be both a cause and an effect of each other.

F 5. Observing the effect and searching for a cause is called **ex post facto** experimental research

T 6. History and maturation effects are similar extraneous variables.

T 7. Instrumentation could result in inconclusive results for either of the following designs, both of which are examples of one-group pretest-posttest designs:

$$O_1 \ X \ O_2; \quad R \ O_1 \ X \ O_2$$

T 8. In the static-group comparison design, the second group serves as a control since it does not receive the treatment.

T 9. In a true experimental design, no uncontrolled extraneous variables remain as possible confounding influences.

Questions 10 through 14 refer to an experimental design which can be represented as:

$$R \quad O_1 \quad X_1 \quad O_2$$
$$R \quad O_3 \quad \quad O_4$$

T 10. Such a design is known as a pretest-posttest control group design.

F 11. In this case, $O_4 - O_3 = TE + H + M + T + I + R + TM$.

F 12. $TE = (O_4 - O_3) - (O_2 - O_1)$

T 13. One major problem of this design concerns the interactive testing effect.

T 14. This design controls all sources of internal invalidity.

Questions 15 and 16 refer to the following design: R X O_1

   R O_2

T   15. One assumption of this design, if confounding is not to be a problem, is that test unit mortality affects each group the same way.

F   16. With this design, one need not be concerned by whether the groups are approximately equal on the dependent variable prior to the presentation of the treatment to the experimental group.

F   17. Laboratory settings in general offer lower control over confounding variables than other studies but do offer greater generalizability.

F   18. In a completely randomized design, treatments are randomly assigned to groups of test units, based on an external criterion variable.

F   19. In a randomized block design, the dependent variable must be of at least ratio scale.

T   20. Latin Square design allows the experimenter to control for the impact of two blocking factors.

T   21. A Latin Square design allows for the effects of two external criterion variables to be blocked.

F   22. Factorial design allows the analysis of main effects of more than one independent variable, but is ineffective in separating the effects of interaction among independent variables.

F   23. As it is with many international issues, the causal studies and their designs as presented in the text are not applicable for international research purposes.

Multiple Choice

E   1. Under which of the following conditions may causal inferences be made?

   A. Concomitant variation.
   B. Elimination of other causal factors.
   C. Time order of occurrence of variables.
   D. A and B above.
   E. A, B, and C above.

C   2. The variables which in an experiment distort measures such that one's ability to make causal inferences is impaired are known as:

   A. Independent variables.
   B. Exogenous variables.
   C. Extraneous variables.
   D. Dependent variables.
   E. None of the above.

E   3. Which of the following is a method of dealing with confounded variables?

        A. Randomization.
        B. Design features.
        C. Analysis of covariance.
        D. Physical control.
        E. All of the above.

C   4. _____ are the alternatives or independent variables that are manipulated and whose effects are measured.

        A. Test units.
        B. Options.
        C. Treatments.
        D. Main effects.
        E. All of the above.

A   5. _____ validity is concerned with the "generalizability" of experimental results.

        A. External.
        B. Construct.
        C. Content.
        D. Internal.
        E. Pragmatic.

D   6. _____ validity is the basic minimum that must be present in an experiment before any conclusion about treatment effects can be made.

        A. External.
        B. Construct.
        C. Content.
        D. Internal.
        E. Pragmatic.

B   7. The question of whether the observed effects on the test units could have been caused by variables other than the treatment refers to:

        A. External validity.
        B. Internal validity.
        C. Instrumentation errors.
        D. Concomitant variation.
        E. None of the above.

E   8. In an experimental design, _____ indicates that individuals have been assigned at random to separate treatment groups or that groups themselves have been allocated at random to separate treatments.

        A. X
        B. P
        C. O
        D. T
        E. R

C   9. In an experimental design, _____ refers to the process of observation or measurement of the dependent variable on the test units.

   A. X
   B. P
   C. O
   D. T
   E. R

A   10. In an experimental design, _____ represents the exposure of a test group to an experimental treatment, the effects of which are to be determined.

   A. X
   B. P
   C. O
   D. T
   E. R

E   11. What does the following experimental design mean?

$$O_1 \quad X_1 \quad O_2$$
$$O_1 \quad X_2 \quad O_2$$

   A. One group of subjects was exposed to two different treatment effects, with four measurements taken.
   B. Two groups of subjects were randomly assigned, with each measured twice at different points in time.
   C. Two groups were assigned; the first being measured, exposed to the treatment, remeasured; followed by the same procedure for the second group.
   D. Two groups were assigned; the first being exposed to the treatment, measured, re-exposed; followed by the same procedure for the second group.
   E. None of the above.

A   12. The situation in an experiment in which the test unit's pre-treatment measurement affects the reaction to the treatment is known as the:

   A. Reactive effect.
   B. Direct effect.
   C. Main effect.
   D. Maturation effect.
   E. None of the above.

B   13. Effects which occur where test units have been selected on the basis of an extreme pre-treatment score are known as:

   A. Selection bias.
   B. Statistical regression.
   C. Testing effects.
   D. Both A and B above.
   E. Both A and C above.

E 14. Which of the following constitutes an alternative explanation of what is observed in an experiment?

    A. Maturation.
    B. Instrumentation.
    C. Test unit mortality.
    D. Both A and C above.
    E. All of the above.

C 15. Which of the following is **not** an example of a pre-experimental design?

    A. One-group pretest-posttest design.
    B. Static group comparison.
    C. Pretest-posttest control group design.
    D. All of the above.
    E. None of the above.

D 16. The following experimental design is known as:

$$X \quad O_1$$
$$O_2$$

    A. Posttest-only control group design.
    B. Non-equivalent control group design.
    C. One-group pretest-posttest design.
    D. Static-group comparison.
    E. None of the above.

Questions 17 through 21 refer to an experimental design which can be represented as:

$$R \quad O_1 \quad X \quad O_2$$
$$R \quad O_3 \quad \quad O_4$$
$$R \quad \quad X \quad O_5$$
$$R \quad \quad \quad O_6$$

D 17. Such a design is known as the:

    A. Multiple time series design.
    B. Pretest-posttest control group design.
    C. R-O 4 x 4 design.
    D. Solomon design.
    E. None of the above.

D 18. TE + EXT =

    A. $O_5 - 1/2(O_1 - O_3)$
    B. $O_5 - O_1$
    C. $O_5 - O_3$
    D. All of the above.
    E. None of the above.

B 19. TE =

   A. $O_6 - 1/2(O_1 + O_3)$
   B. $[O_5 - 1/2(O_1 + O_3)] - [O_6 - 1/2(O_1 + O_3)]$
   C. $[O_6 - 1/2(O_1 + O_3)] - [O_5 - 1/2(O_1 + O_3)]$
   D. $(O_6 - O_5) + 1/2(O_1 + O_3)$
   E. None of the above.

D 20. IT =

   A. $[O_5 - 1/2(O_1 + O_3)] - [O_6 - 1/2(O_1 + O_3)]$
   B. $[O_2 - O_1] - [O_6 - 1/2(O_1 + O_3)]$
   C. $[O_2 - O_1] + [O_6 - 1/2(O_1 + O_3)]$
   D. $[O_2 - O_1] - [O_5 - 1/2(O_1 + O_3)]$
   E. $[O_2 - O_1] + [O_5 - 1/2(O_1 + O_3)]$

A 21. This design controls for problems with:

   A. Both internal and external validity.
   B. Internal but not external validity.
   C. External but not internal validity.
   D. Neither internal nor external validity.
   E. The interactive testing effect.

A 22. In a quasi-experiment, the researcher has control over:

   A. Data collection procedures.
   B. Scheduling of the treatments.
   C. Randomization of test units' exposure to treatments.
   D. A and B above.
   E. B and C above.

Questions 23 and 24 refer to the following experimental design:

   O X_1 O X_0 O O O X_1 O O X_0 O

B 23. This design is known as a (an):

   A. Multiple time series design.
   B. Equivalent time-sample design.
   C. Nonequivalent control sample design.
   D. Time trial design.
   E. External regression design.

C 24. By comparison to the field study, the laboratory experiment offers:

   A. High internal and external validity at a low cost.
   B. Low internal but high external validity at a high cost.
   C. High internal but low external validity at a low cost.
   D. Low internal and external validity at a low cost.
   E. None of the above.

A 25. Which of the following is not a limitation of experimentation:

   A. Extraneous variables that are easily controlled.
   B. Lack of cooperation in field experiments.
   C. Lack of knowledge of experimental procedures by marketing personnel.
   D. Cost and time considerations.
   E. Experimental bias of test unit responses.

B 26. An experimental design involving a single independent variable, a single dependent variable, with random assignment of treatments and in which all extraneous variables are assumed constant over all treatment groups is an example of a:

   A. Factorial design.
   B. Completely randomized design.
   C. Randomized block design.
   D. Latin square design.
   E. None of the above.

C 27. A Latin Square design allows consideration of which of the following combinations of variables?

   A. 1 dependent, 1 independent, 1 extraneous.
   B. 1 dependent, 2 independent, 1 extraneous.
   C. 1 dependent, 1 independent, 2 extraneous.
   D. 2 dependent, 2 independent, 1 extraneous.
   E. None of the above.

A 28. A _____ design is the simplest type of designed experiment.

   A. Completely randomized.
   B. Randomized block.
   C. Latin Square.
   D. Factorial.
   E. Stratified block.

D 29. A _____ design measures the simultaneous effects of two or more independent variables.

   A. Completely randomized.
   B. Randomized block.
   C. Latin Square.
   D. Factorial.
   E. Stratified block.

A 30. Blocking in experimental design results in:

   A. More homogeneous groups and smaller sampling error.
   B. More homogeneous groups and larger sampling error.
   C. Less homogeneous groups and smaller sampling error.
   D. Less homogeneous groups and larger sampling error.
   E. Either A or B above.

The following question relates to the Global Marketing Research Dynamics "Causal Studies in International Marketing Research" insert...

C 31. The various examples of causal studies in an international context showed that:

    A. Casual studies principles applied domestically can only be applied to one or two other countries at most.
    B. Only quasi-experiments could be used in international causal studies.
    C. Casual studies principles could be applied internationally as equally well as they are applied domestically.
    D. A and B
    E. None of the above

CHAPTER 10 — DATA COLLECTION: EXPLORATORY RESEARCH

True - False

F   1. Qualitative techniques are noted for their ability to provide statistical or scientifically accurate data.

T   2. One key use of focus groups is to develop hypotheses for further testing.

F   3. To provide a good mixture of people, a focus group should consist of various age groups, races, and economic backgrounds of people.

F   4. Focus group participants who have already done a session make good candidates for another session due to their expertise in the process.

F   5. The person who leads and manages the focus group session is called a facilitator.

F   6. The first step in the analysis of focus group data is to thoroughly study the group discussion.

T   7. Mini-groups are modified focus groups which consist of fewer participants than the standard focus group.

T   8. Depth interviews are especially useful for sensitive or confidential issues.

T   9. Focus group and depth interviews are both very flexible in terms of how questions are asked of respondents.

F   10. Focus group interviews are often used for conclusive research purposes.

T   11. The discussion in the text regarding focus groups in other countries shows that focus groups are conducted similarly in the United Kingdom, Asia, and the U.S.

Multiple Choice

E   1. Data obtained from respondents useful in predicting market behavior include:

     A. Attitudes.
     B. Respondent characteristics.
     C. Past behavior patterns.
     D. A and B above.
     E. All of the above.

E   2. Which of the following are not characteristics of qualitative techniques:

     A. Data collection format is open-ended.
     B. Approach is not intended
     C. Past behavior patterns.
     D. A and B above.
     E. All of the above.

D 4. Which of the following is the best composed focus group?

   A. 20 women, 2 hours in length, set in a living room.
   B. 20 men, 3 hours in length, set in a living room.
   C. 10 men and 10 women, 2 hours in length, set in a living room.
   D. 10 men, 2 hours in length, set in a living room.
   E. 10 women, 3 hours in length, set in a laboratory.

D 5. Synergism, one of the advantages of focus group interviews, refers to which of the following:

   A. Ideas are generated spontaneously.
   B. Ideas are freely expressed by group members.
   C. Ideas are more likely to be expressed once the general level of excitement over the topic increases.
   D. A wider range of information is expressed as a group than accumulation of separate individual responses.
   E. An idea expressed by one member triggers a series of responses from the rest of the group.

D 6. The depth interview differs from the focus group interview in that:

   A. It is less focused.
   B. It lasts longer.
   C. It interviews more people simultaneously.
   D. It attempts to gain more complete understanding of a respondent's position.
   E. It requires less direction by the moderator/interviewer.

A 7. Key qualifications for a moderator include:

   A. Incomplete understanding.
   B. Rigid structure.
   C. Separation from the group, no involvement.
   D. A and B above.
   E. None of the above.

B 8. The purpose of a moderator's guide is to:

   A. Provide the participants an outline to follow along with.
   B. Serve as memory aid for the moderator.
   C. Serve as a key component in the analysis of the focus group session.
   D. A and B above.
   E. All of the above.

E 9. Which of the following is a good cost estimate (as mentioned in the text) for a standard focus group session with 10 participants and with two researchers per session:

   A. $500-$1000
   B. $1000-$2500
   C. $2500-$4000
   D. $4000-$5500
   E. more than $5500

C 10. The discussion of qualitative technique implementations outside the United States showed that:

A. Focus groups are performed the same way in all countries.
B. In Asia, focus groups vary significantly from the U.S.'s method of conducting focus groups.
C. In the United Kingdom the majority of focus groups are rarely attended by clients.
D. Differences in focus group implementations are a result of the lack of knowledge of marketing research techniques in countries outside the U.S.
E. None of the above.

CHAPTER 11 — DATA COLLECTION: CONCLUSIVE RESEARCH

True - False

T 1. A questionnaire is a formalized schedule for collecting data from respondents.

F 2. An observational form should force the observer to summarize rather than list in detail the behavior observed.

F 3. Respondent data can be classified into three types: Past behavior, attitudes, and future behavior.

T 4. Communication and observation are the two commonly used methods of collecting data from respondents.

T 5. The influence of the questioning process can bias the data obtained by communication methods.

T 6. The communication method offers advantages to researchers in terms of both versatility and cost.

F 7. The potential for bias as a result of the interviewing process is reduced if communication techniques are used.

T 8. Controlling nonresponse rates is an important concern in choosing among communication media.

T 9. Quantity and quality of data likely obtained are two criteria used in determining among alternate communication media.

F 10. Personal, mail, and telephone interviews are all appropriate for use with unstructured data techniques.

T 11. Its lack of reliance on respondents' willingness to provide data is a prime advantage of the observation method.

F 12. One of the main disadvantages of the observation method is respondent's unwillingness to provide data.

T 13. The inability to observe certain behavior patterns and constructs is a limitation of observation methods of data collection.

F 14. One way of classifying communication techniques is as human versus mechanical methods.

F 15. The psychogalvanometer can be used to measure reactions to stimuli presented, as indicated by changes in the diameter of the pupil of the eye.

F 16. Although children spend more than $2 million yearly on personal purchases, researchers have not yet found an effective means of obtaining data from children.

F 17. The international discussion on performing marketing research overseas showed that one way to provide an incentive in most east Asian countries is through the offering of cash for cooperation.

Chapter 11--Multiple Choice

E 1. Data obtained from respondents useful in predicting market behavior include:

A. Attitudes.
B. Respondent characteristics.
C. Past behavior patterns.
D. A and B above.
E. All of the above.

D 2. Which of the following could be classified as a respondent characteristic variable?

A. Purchase behavior.
B. Family size.
C. Education level.
D. B and C above.
E. All of the above.

A 3. A disadvantage of the communication method of data collection is the:

A. Influence of the questioning process.
B. Cost.
C. Lack of versatility.
D. A and C above.
E. All of the above.

C 11. The potential source of bias resulting from an incomplete target population listing is most serious in which of the following types of interviewing?

A. Personal.
B. Mail.
C. Telephone.
D. B and C above.
E. All of the above.

A 12. Which of the following is **not** a characteristic of mail interviews?

A. Relatively inflexible.
B. Low in cost.
C. Low potential bias from interview-respondent interaction.
D. High potential nonresponse error.
E. None of the above.

E 13. Increasing the response rate of mail surveys can be accomplished by:

A. Using first class postage in mailings.
B. Using telephone calls to respondents prior to mailings.
C. Using monetary incentives.
D. A and C above.
E. All of the above.

A 14. On sensitive issues, which ordering of communication media listed below is likely to result in data **quality** ranging from lowest to highest?

    A. Personal interviews, telephone interviews, mail interviews.
    B. Telephone interviews, personal interviews, mail interviews.
    C. Mail interviews, telephone interviews, personal interviews.
    D. Mail interviews, personal interviews, telephone interviews.
    E. Personal interviews, mail interviews, telephone interviews.

E 15. Which of the following is not a relevant criterion in selecting among communication media?

    A. Sample control.
    B. Response rate.
    C. Quantity of data.
    D. Versatility.
    E. None of the above.

E 16. A low response rate always implies:

    A. High nonresponse error.
    B. Low nonresponse error.
    C. Either a very high or very low nonresponse error.
    D. Some intermediate level of nonresponse error.
    E. None of the above.

C 17. The method of estimating the degree of nonresponse error by determining how different each successive call-back group is from the previous one is known as:

    A. Subjective estimation.
    B. Subsample measurement.
    C. Sensitivity analysis.
    D. Trend projection.
    E. None of the above.

B 18. Personal interviews typically provide:

    A. High versatility at a low cost.
    B. High versatility at a high cost.
    C. Low versatility at a low cost.
    D. Low versatility at a high cost.
    E. Intermediate levels of versatility and cost.

B 19. Given normal levels of involvement, which technique can collect the greatest amount of data?

    A. Mail interviews.
    B. Personal interviews.
    C. Telephone interviews.
    D. Any of the above dependent upon the situation.
    E. Either A or C above.

C 20. Which of the following is **not** an advantage of the observation method over the communication technique?

- A. The respondent's willingness to cooperate is not a factor.
- B. Interview bias is reduced.
- C. Certain behavior patterns are of long duration.
- D. Certain types of data can be collected only by observation.
- E. None of the above.

B 20. Which are key differences in the way marketing research must be performed in Asia, the Pacific Rim, and the Middle East as compared to the U.S.?

- A. In the Middle East the culture promotes time sharing of simultaneous tasks, including meetings--whereas in the U.S. meetings are generally held to one-on-one when possible.
- B. In Japan the giving of cash is considered an insult--whereas in the U.S. many promotions have a cash incentive.
- C. Bankers in Malaysia, due to their knowledge of English, can communicate between Malays and Chinese nationals, but language becomes more of a problem between the two groups when dealing with small shop owners. In the U.S. the dominance of one single language (with only pockets of multi-lingual areas) removes most language barriers.
- D. All of the above.
- E. None of the above.

CHAPTER 12 — DESIGNING DATA COLLECTION FORMS

True - False

T   1.   A questionnaire is a formalized schedule for collecting data from respondents.

F   2.   Under no circumstances should a question be included in the questionnaire unless it addresses a specific information need.

T   3.   A question should be phrased so as to permit the respondent to admit a lack of knowledge.

F   4.   The aided recall approach, as the name implies, is intended to overcome respondents' unwillingness to respond to particular questions.

F   5.   The counterbiasing statement approach involves asking a nonsensitive question prior to and immediately after a sensitive question.

T   6.   Open-ended questions are most appropriate for exploratory research purposes.

T   7.   A dichotomous question is an extreme form of the multiple-choice question.

T   8.   The issue of whether to include a neutral response alternative in a dichotomous question is best decided on the basis of the proportion of the respondent group who are truly neutral.

T   9.   The questionnaire should be comprehensible to that segment of the population with the least vocabulary skills.

F   10. Leading questions are often needed to accurately assess respondents' feelings.

T   11. The split-ballot technique should be used to remove position bias.

T   12. The questionnaire should be pretested in the manner in which it is to be used in the final study.

F   13. An observational form should force the observer to summarize rather than list in detail the behavior observed.

F   14. International marketing research, due to expense, should not include pretesting of questionnaires that are determined to be translated (from one language to another) without error.

Multiple Choice

E   1.   Measurement error in the design of questionnaires:

   A. Is easily detected.
   B. May be of unknown direction and magnitude.

C. Does not require the degree of concern that is typically associated with sampling error.
D. Results from questions which measure something other than what they are intended to measure.
E. B and D above.

C 2. Which of the following is typically **not** a component of the questionnaire?

A. Classification data.
B. Request for cooperation.
C. A disclaimer.
D. Identification data.
E. None of the above.

D 3. Classification data:

A. Involve the characteristics of the respondent.
B. Are typically collected at the end of the interview.
C. May be collected at the beginning of the interview to determine whether the person qualifies as part of the sampling plan.
D. All of the above.
E. A and B above only.

E 4. Questionnaire design must be preceded by all but which of the following?

A. Selection of target population.
B. Specification of research design.
C. Determination of mode of data analysis.
D. Specification of the sampling plan.
E. All of the above must precede the design of the questionnaire.

E 5. What factors influence the content of questions?

A. Respondents' ability to answer accurately.
B. The sequence of the questions.
C. Respondents' willingness to respond accurately.
D. All of the above.
E. A and C only.

D 6. What factors affect a respondent's ability to remember a particular event?

A. Recency of the event.
B. Importance of the event.
C. Repetition of the event.
D. All of the above.
E. A and B only.

C 7. Questions which do not give cues regarding the event of interest are called:

A. Open-ended questions.
B. Task-specific questions.
C. Unaided recall questions.
D. Itemized questions.
E. A and B above.

E 8. The recognition method:

   A. Is a form of unaided recall.
   B. May create suggestion bias.
   C. Involves presenting to the respondent the actual event.
   D. All of the above.
   E. B and C only.

D 9. A respondents willingness to answer questions depends upon:

   A. The content of the interview.
   B. The perceived legitimacy of the interview.
   C. Personal sensitivity to potentially embarrassing questions.
   D. All of the above.
   E. A and B above.

B. 10. An approach which lists alternative responses to a sensitive question by letters or numbers and permits the respondent to answer with a letter or number is known as:

   A. Randomized response technique.
   B. Labeled response categories.
   C. Counterbiasing statement.
   D. Indirect statement.
   E. None of the above.

E 11. Open-ended questions:

   A. Are costly.
   B. Reduce interviewer bias.
   C. Permit diverse responses which may not have been anticipated.
   D. All of the above.
   E. A and C only.

C 12. Relative to open-ended questions, multiple-choice questions:

   A. Increase interviewer bias.
   B. Are more difficult to administer.
   C. Reduce the time and cost associated with data processing.
   D. All of the above.
   E. None of the above.

E 13. Responses to a multiple-choice question should be:

   A. Mutually exclusive.
   B. Presented in fixed, unvarying order.
   C. Collectively exhaustive.
   D. All of the above.
   E. A and C only.

A 14. Dichotomous questions:

   A. Assume that the respondent group approaches the topic of interest in dichotomous terms.
   B. Are notably free from measurement error.

C. Provide a valid means of reducing the response set to a particular issue.
D. All of the above.
E. B and C only.

D 15. Which of the following is **not** a guideline in designing the wording of a question?

A. Use simple words.
B. Avoid leading questions.
C. Avoid implicit alternatives.
D. Utilize estimates where possible.
E. All of the above are legitimate guidelines.

E 16. Which of the following should **not** be relied upon in determining question sequence?

A. Arrange questions in logical order.
B. Ask general questions last.
C. Place uninteresting and difficult questions early in sequence to make the rest of the questionnaire seem easier.
D. Use a simple and interesting opening question.
E. B and C only

C 17. Which of the following is not an issue in the design of questionnaires for international use?

A. Increased cost.
B. Increased complexity.
C. Lack of sufficient number of samples.
D. Varying perceptions of adequate forms of compensation for respondents.
E. The need for flexibility in choosing the different interviewing modes of personal, telephone, and mail.

CHAPTER 13 — THE BASICS OF SAMPLING

True - False

F   1.   Many marketing research studies do not require the selection of a sample.

F   2.   A sample cannot be more accurate than taking a census.

F   3.   A study population is a list of all the sampling units in the population.

F   4.   The first step in the sampling process is to identify the sampling frame from which the sample will be selected.

F   5.   The sampling unit and the element are identical in all but the most simple type of sampling, single-stage sampling.

T   6.   One of the major difficulties with convenience sampling is the uncertainty as to what population the actual sample is drawn from.

F   7.   Judgment sampling is superior to convenience sampling because the sampling error of the former can be ascertained.

F   8.   As long as the quota sample and the population match on known characteristics, sample error does not pose a problem.

T   9.   The telephone, due to lack of infrastructure, is not the most reliable or accurate method of conducting marketing research surveys in countries outside of the United States.

Multiple Choice

E   1.   Which of the following is an advantage of sampling over the alternative of taking a census?

       A.   Sampling is not as expensive.
       B.   Sampling takes less time.
       C.   A sample may be more accurate.
       D.   Sampling does not contaminate the entire population of interest.
       E.   All of the above are advantages.

B   2.   The unit about which information is sought is known in sampling terms as the:

       A.   Sampling unit.
       B.   Element.
       C.   Sampling frame.
       D.   Item.
       E.   None of the above.

E 3. The population and study population are closely related. Which of the following statements correctly distinguishes between the two?

   A. The population is defined prior to selection of the sample.
   B. The study population is the aggregation of elements from which the sample is actually drawn.
   C. The population is the aggregation to which we are legitimately generalized.
   D. All of the above.
   E. A and B only.

E 4. Which of the following could **not** qualify as a sampling frame?

   A. A mailing list.
   B. A telephone book.
   C. The "Fortune 500" list of corporations.
   D. A map.
   E. All of the above might conceivably be used as a sampling frame.

A 5. In sampling, the _____ is the list of all sampling units available for selection at a stage of the sampling process.

   A. Frame.
   B. Population.
   C. Element.
   D. Item.
   E. None of the above.

E 6. A properly designated population is fully defined in which of the following terms?

   A. Sampling units and extent.
   B. Elements and time.
   C. Extent and time.
   D. Sampling units, extent, and time.
   E. None of the above.

A 7. Having defined the population of interest, a number of steps remain before the researcher actually selects the sample. Which of the following is **not** one of them?

   A. Specify the sampling unit.
   B. Identify the sampling frame.
   C. Determine sample size.
   D. Select a sampling procedure.
   E. All of the above are essential intervening steps.

E 8. Which are the key differences between probability sampling and nonprobability sampling?

   A. In probability sampling the likelihood of each element of the population being selected for the sample is known; this is not the case with nonprobability sampling.
   B. A measure of sampling error is possible with probability sampling.
   C. The results from a probability sample are more accurate than those obtained by a nonprobability sample.
   D. All of the above.
   E. A and B only.

B 9. In _____, each element of the population has a known chance of being selected for the sample.

   A. Sample random sampling.
   B. Probability sampling.
   C. Judgment sampling.
   D. Convenience sampling.
   E. Quota sampling.

A 10. The "person-on-the-street" interviews by the news media may be classified as what type of sampling procedure?

   A. Convenience sampling.
   B. Judgment sampling.
   C. Direct sampling.
   D. Quota sampling.
   E. None of the above.

C 11. Selecting elements on the basis of expert opinion regarding those particular elements' potential contribution to the study at hand is called:

   A. Selective sampling.
   B. Instructive sampling.
   C. Judgment sampling.
   D. Convenience sampling.
   E. A and D above.

D 12. To insure the representativeness of a quota sample, the researcher must:

   A. Specify a list of relevant control characteristics.
   B. Know the distribution of these characteristics across the population.
   C. Minimize the divergence between the sample and the population on specified and unspecified characteristics.
   D. All of the above.
   E. A and B above.

The following question relates to the Global Marketing Research Dynamics, "Zhirinovsky Success Surprises Pollsters"...

E 13. The poor prediction by Russian President Boris Yeltsin and his pollsters could have been attributed to:

   A. A bias in the geographic selection of the samples.
   B. The use of country quota samples.
   C. The use of telephone polling.
   D. A and B only.
   E. All of the above.

CHAPTER 14 — SIMPLE RANDOM SAMPLING AND SAMPLE SIZE

True - False

F 1. A statistic is a summary description of a measure in the defined population.

T 2. The variance of a population dichotomous variable is simply

$$\pi(1-\pi)$$

F 3. Degrees of freedom equal the number of observations on the variable of interest.

T 4. A shorthand notation for the sample variance is SS/df.

T 5. Regardless of the shape of the population distribution, the sampling distribution of the mean is normal when $n \geq 30$.

T 6. The calculation of a confidence interval yields a measure of sampling error.

F 7. The standard error of the mean varies directly with the square root of the sample size; $s_{\bar{x}}$ increases by the square root of the sample size as sample size increases.

T 8. All things equal, the larger the sample size the smaller the confidence interval about the statistic.

F 9. For any given sample size, the value of the standard deviation of the sampling distribution of the mean of a dichotomous variable is at a minimum when p = .5.

F 10. A confidence interval accounts for both sampling and nonsampling errors.

T 11. An increase in sample size may reduce sampling error but at the expense of nonsampling error, e.g., the latter may increase.

F 12. Small sampling error implies an accurate survey result.

T 13. Nonsampling error increases with sample size.

T 14. Sample size can be determined by the use of statistical formulas alone.

Multiple Choice

D 1. The population mean of a continuous variable is denoted by which of the following symbols?

   A. $\bar{X}^2$
   B. σ^2

C. π
D. μ
E. X

C 2. The mean of the population (or sample) consisting of the values 1, 2, 3, 4, 5, 6, 7, 8, 9, and 10 is:

A. 4.5
B. 5.0
C. 5.5
D. 5.75
E. 6.25

C 3. The variance of the sample consisting of the values 2, 4, 6, 8, 10 is:

A. 6
B. 8
C. 10
D. 12
E. None of the above.

Calculation:

$$\Sigma X_2 = 220 \quad (\Sigma X)^2 = 900 \quad (\Sigma X)^2/n = 900/5 = 180$$

$$SS = 220 - 180 = 40$$

$$SS/df = 40/(5-1) = 10$$

A 4. What is the variance of a population of N = 9 elements whose sum of squared deviations is 72?

A. 8
B. 9
C. 9.5
D. 10
E. None of the above.

Calculation:

$$\sigma^2 = SS/N = 72/9 = 8$$

A 5. If the variance of a population is equal to 9, what is the standard deviation of the population?

A. 3
B. 9
C. 4.5
D. 81
E. Cannot determine from the information provided.

C 6. If sample size is equal to 100, and the sampling fraction is .2, what is the size of the population?

A. 20
B. 100
C. 500
D. 1000
E. None of the above.

E 7. The Central Limit Theorem is basic to statistical inference. Which of the following statements is **not** contained therein?

A. The sampling distribution of the mean of a measure whose population distribution is normal will be normal for all sample sizes.
B. The sampling distribution of the mean of a measure whose population distribution is not normal approaches normality as the sample size increases.
C. The mean of the sampling distribution of the mean is an unbiased estimate of the population mean.
D. The standard deviation of the sampling distribution of the mean is the population standard deviation divided by the square root of the sample size.
E. All of the above comprise the Central Limit Theorem.

B 8. Approximately 95% of all cases comprising a normal curve will be within how many standard deviations from the mean?

A. 1
B. 2
C. 3
D. 4
E. 5

B 9. What does a 95% confidence interval mean?

A. The probability that the parameter is contained in the interval is .95.
B. If we select 100 different random samples and calculate a 95% confidence interval for each of these samples, the parameter would be contained within the 95% confidence interval in 95 out of the 100 so computed.
C. The decision maker can have 95% confidence that a decision based on this interval will be correct.
D. Both A and B.
E. All of the above.

C 10. A statistic that approaches the population parameter in value as the sample size increases is what type of estimator?

A. Unbiased.
B. Efficient.
C. Consistent.
D. Valid.
E. None of the above.

B 11. An estimator whose distribution about the corresponding population parameter is characterized by minimum variance is known as:

A. An unbiased estimator.
B. An efficient estimator.

280

C. A consistent estimator.
D. A precise estimator.
E. The best estimator.

C 12. Which of the following is essential to the derivation of meaningful confidence intervals?

A. Large sample size.
B. Heterogeneous population.
C. Probability based sampling.
D. B and C above.
E. None of the above.

E 13. The finite population correction (or finite correction factor):

A. May take on any value between O and 1.
B. Approaches 1 as N gets bigger relative to n.
C. When multiplied times the standard error lowers the size of the standard error, unless it equals 1 or 0.
D. Is zero when N = n.
E. All of the above.

D 14. Sample size is best determined by considering:

A. The cost involved.
B. The type of data analysis planned.
C. The "statistically optimal" sample size.
D. All of the above.
E. A and C only.

C 15. Absolute precision is:

A. 2 times the standard deviation from the mean.
B. A measure of total study error.
C. The width of the confidence interval about a mean.
D. Totally related to sample size.
E. A and C only.

A 16. Which of the following is **not** needed to calculate the optimal sample size for a continuous variable?

A. An estimate of nonsampling error.
B. A specified required precision.
C. The coefficient of variation.
D. A specified level of confidence.
E. All of the above are needed.

CHAPTER 15 — MORE COMPLEX SAMPLING PROCEDURES

True - False

F   1. Stratified sampling typically will not yield more efficient estimators than simple random sampling.

F   2. Stratification ideally produces strata that are more heterogeneous than the population on the variable of interest.

F   3. In proportionate stratified sampling the number of elements selected from each stratum is in direct proportion to the relative variability on the stratification variable within each strata of the population.

T   4. The overall standard error of the mean in stratified sampling does not depend on the variability across strata.

F   5. A stratified sampling procedure is typically less efficient than a non-stratified procedure.

T   6. In general, to obtain more efficient estimates using stratification, within strata variability is minimized.

T   7. In stratified sampling, the overall sample mean is simply a weighted average of the within strata means.

F   8. The overall standard error in stratified sampling is simply a weighted average of the within stratum standard errors.

F   9. In proportionate stratified sampling, the sample sizes selected from each stratum are equal.

F   10. An optimal allocation of a fixed sample size among strata is one which maximizes the standard error of the overall estimate.

T   11. One-stage cluster sampling involves sampling from the set of groups composing the population and then using all of the elements in those groups selected.

T   12. In most cases, cluster sampling is less efficient statistically than is simple random sampling.

T   13. If the frame is ordered on what might be a stratification variable, then selection of a systematic sample will automatically provide a stratified sample.

T   14. Sampling error occurs at each stage of a multistage area sample.

F   15. The "equal probability" in equal probability area sampling refers to the fact that clusters have an equal probability of being selected.

T   16. Data gathered via complex sampling procedures are appropriate for statistical inference.

F 17. The available census demographic data in most countries outside of the U.S. makes probability based area samples very feasible.

Multiple Choice

D 1. Stratified sampling may enable the researcher to:

A. Increase the precision of estimates relative to that of estimates derived from an unstratified sample of the same size.
B. Obtain the same precision as an unstratified sample might yield, but with a smaller sample size and therefore at a lower cost.
C. Obtain the same precision as a simple random sample might yield, but with a larger sample size and therefore at a higher cost.
D. Both A and B.
E. None of the above.

E 2. Stratified sampling may result in:

A. An increase in the standard error of the estimator.
B. A decrease in the standard error of the estimator.
C. A smaller confidence interval.
D. A and B above.
E. B and C above.

D 3. Which of the following does **not** correspond to stratified sampling?

A. Mutually exclusive strata.
B. Two-stage process.
C. Collectively exhaustive strata.
D. Nonprobability procedure.
E. Random sampling from strata.

C 4. Confidence intervals about statistics constructed from a stratified sample:
A. Include the parameter approximately 95% of the time.
B. Are wider than the corresponding confidence intervals constructed on the basis of a random sample.
C. Are more narrow than the corresponding confidence intervals constructed on the basis of a random sample.
D. A and C above.
E. None of the above.

D 5. Which of the following statements is **incorrect**?

A. Each population element has an equal chance of being selected in both stratified and random sampling procedures.
B. All possible combinations of elements are equally likely in both stratified and random sampling.
C. The number of possible samples is substantially greater in simple random sampling than in stratified sampling.
D. A and B above.
E. None of the above.

B 6. Which variables may serve most effectively as stratification variables on the measure of interest, X?

    A. Variables whose correlation with X is low.
    B. Variables whose contribution to the variability in X is great.
    C. Variables that are statistically independent of X.
    D. Both A and C above.
    E. None of the above.

E 7. Why might one sample at a disproportionately high level in stratum j?

    A. Stratum j is smaller than the other strata.
    B. Stratum j exhibits greater variability on the measure of interest than the other strata.
    C. To minimize the standard error of the overall estimate.
    D. All of the above.
    E. B and C above.

E 8. The feature which distinguishes cluster sampling from other forms of probability sampling is that in cluster sampling:

    A. All possible combinations are not equally likely.
    B. Each population element has a known chance of being included in the sample.
    C. The population must be divided into mutually exclusive and collectively exhaustive groups.
    D. A and C above.
    E. None of the above.

E 9. How does the standard error corresponding to a cluster sample compare to the standard error corresponding to a simple random sample?

    A. The former is larger than the latter.
    B. The former is smaller than the latter.
    C. The former is approximately the same size as the latter.
    D. The former is exactly the same size as the latter.
    E. It depends on the heterogeneity of the clusters compared with the population.

E 10. The statistical efficiency of a sampling procedure:

    A. When combined with its cost yields a measure of the overall efficiency.
    B. Is the sole criterion by which alternative procedures are selected.
    C. Is a relative measure.
    D. All of the above.
    E. A and C only.

D 11. The criterion used in forming groups in cluster sampling:

    A. Is exactly opposite that used in stratified sampling.
    B. Involves maximizing within group homogeneity.
    C. Is in practice an ideal which is rarely attained.
    D. A and C only.
    E. B and C only.

D 12. Which of the following correctly characterize(s) the relationship between cluster sampling and simple random sampling?

   A. For a given sample size, cluster sampling is less costly.
   B. Cluster sampling is generally less efficient statistically.
   C. Cluster sampling is higher in terms of total efficiency.
   D. All of the above.
   E. A and C only.

C 13. In systematic sampling, if the sampling fraction is 1/5, the sampling interval is:

   A. .20
   B. 1.00
   C. 5.00
   D. 10.00
   E. Cannot be determined from the information provided.

E 14. Systematic sampling:

   A. Is a type of cluster sampling.
   B. Yields a biased estimate of the population mean.
   C. Is a close substitute for simple random sampling, if periodicity is not present.
   D. All of the above.
   E. A and C above.

D 15. Which of the following samples might have been generated by systematic sampling (the numbers correspond to the positions of elements within the sample frame)?

   A. 2, 4, 8, 16, 32
   B. 1, 2, 4, 16, 256
   C. 3, 5, 7, 9, 11
   D. 8, 18, 28, 38, 48
   E. C and D only.

D 16. Periodicity:

   A. Biases estimates derived through systematic sampling.
   B. May be removed from a sample frame by rearranging the elements.
   C. Is said to exist if the list of elements forming the frame contains a cyclical pattern that coincides with a multiple of the size of the sampling interval.
   D. All of the above.
   E. B and C only.

A 17. Area sampling:

   A. Does not require a complete and accurate listing of the elements of the population.
   B. Is not used in practice very extensively.
   C. Is not a probability sampling procedure.
   D. May not involve more than three stages.
   E. A and C above.

A 18. Multistage area sampling:

   A. Is less statistically efficient than simple random sampling.
   B. Is more statistically efficient than simple random sampling.
   C. May be more or less statistically efficient than simple random sampling.
   D. And simple random sampling cannot be compared on the basis of statistical efficiency.
   E. Insufficient information to answer.

B 19. Given a set sample size, to minimize the sampling error in multistage area sampling, a researcher should:

   A. Select a small number of clusters and a small number of elements from each cluster.
   B. Select a large number of clusters and a small number of elements from each cluster.
   C. Select a small number of clusters and a large number of elements from each cluster.
   D. Select a large number of clusters and a large number of elements from each cluster.
   E. B and C above.

E 20. An equal probability area sample may be drawn by means of:

   A. The "Weighted Factor Method."
   B. The "Equal Chance Selection of Clusters--Equal Proportion Selection of Elements Within Clusters Method."
   C. The "Probability Proportionate to Size Method."
   D. A and B above.
   E. B and C above.

C 21. Given 100 city blocks containing 1000 households, what would be the appropriate probability proportionate to size for block A which contains 50 households?

   A. .10
   B. 20
   C. .05
   D. .01
   E. 2
          Calculation: 50 / 1,000 = .05.

E 22. In unequal probability area sampling:

   A. Each element has an unknown chance of being selected.
   B. Elements may have different probabilities of being selected.
   C. Only subgroup analyses are valid.
   D. Each element must be assigned a weighting factor in proportion to the inverse of its probability of being selected prior to overall sample computations.
   E. B and D only.

The following questions relate to the international discussion of sampling in the text...

C 23. Which of the following is NOT feasible in countries without census demographic data and a lack of adequate lists to draw samples from:

   A. Probability based area samples.
   B. Stratified samples.
   C. Quota and judgment samples.
   D. Probability proportionate to size.
   E. Proper sample size selection.

D 24. In the Global Research Dynamics insert, the major international marketing research firm encountered the following difficulties in Saudi Arabia:

   A. Lack of private listings of households.
   B. Inaccurate maps of cities and towns.
   C. Incomplete and inaccurate telephone directories.
   D. A,B, and C
   E. None of the above.

CHAPTER 16 — FIELD OPERATIONS

True - False

F   1. The number of interviews to be completed is a sufficient performance measure for field operation personnel.

F   2. Mail surveys are less likely to meet time schedules and budgets than other data collection methods.

F   3. Probability sampling procedures eliminate the potential for sample selection errors by interviewers during the field process.

F   4. A callback program is the least effective means of increasing response rates.

F   5. Rapport between interviewer and respondent should be minimized in order to gain more complete and accurate data.

T   6. Field operation efficiency relies heavily on the infrastructure of technology and an acceptance of such practices in various cultures. Due to this dependence, it is often difficult to conduct accurate and quick field operations in countries outside of the U.S.

Multiple Choice

D   1. Performance measures for field operations personnel may include all but which of the following?

     A. Number of refusals.
     B. Number of contacts.
     C. Number of interviews completed.
     D. All of the above are legitimate performance measures.
     E. A and B above.

A   2. The training of interviewers:

     A. Has as its objective to establish a high degree of commonalty in the data collection process among interviewers.
     B. Is absolutely necessary for only the most complex studies.
     C. Is not necessary if a firm uses its own research organization.
     D. A and C above.
     E. None of the above.

D   3. An incentive pay scheme for interviewers:

     A. May cause the interviewer to hurry through an interview or even falsify questionnaires.
     B. May encourage the interviewers to plan their activities more efficiently.

C. Is best used in conjunction with specified standards for acceptable interviews.
D. All of the above.
E. A and C above.

C. 4. Sources of error in field operations include all but which of the following:

A. Sample selection errors.
B. Nonresponse errors.
C. Sampling errors.
D. Interviewing errors.
E. B and C above.

E 5. Nonresponse error:

A. Is declining in importance as more sophisticated statistical techniques evolve.
B. Is a problem only if those who respond to the survey are different from those who do not.
C. Can result from respondents being unavailable or unwilling to respond to the survey.
D. All of the above.
E. B and C above.

D 6. In general, the interviewer:

A. Should ask only those questions in the questionnaire which the respondent is likely to answer.
B. Should ask the questions in the order with which the interviewer and respondent are most comfortable.
C. Should not use probing techniques to get the respondent to answer the questions.
D. Should ask the questions exactly as they are worded in the questionnaire.
E. None of the above.

B 7. Which of the following would **not** be a neutral probing technique?

A. Repeating the question.
B. Rephrasing the question.
C. Reassuring the respondent.
D. An expectant pause.
E. Repeating the respondent's reply.

B 8. The interviewer should record:

A. The respondent's answers by paraphrasing wherever possible.
B. The respondent's answers during the interview.
C. What was said but not how it was said.
D. A and B above.
E. B and C above.

The following question is based on the Global Marketing Research Dynamic, "This Field Work is not Like Omaha!"...

C   9. From the various examples of international field operations, it can be concluded that:

   A. The relative ease of finding qualified interviewers abroad, makes field operations easier than in the U.S.
   B. Foreign government intervention is not a problem with field operations due to their research nature.
   C. Conducting a field operation must be done only after extensive research into the legal, political, and cultural ramifications have been defined for the study.
   D. Mall intercept interviews are the best way to reach many people, even in countries outside of the U.S.
   E. Due to wide accessibility, telephone surveys are the cheapest and most accurate way of reaching most respondents in countries outside of the U.S.

CHAPTER 17 — DATA PROCESSING

True - False

T   1. Editing and coding are two functions included in the traditional data processing approach.

T   2. A data codebook typically defines both relevant spreadsheet (matrix) columns and category definitions, if any.

T   3. One method of dealing with multiple responses is to treat them as missing data.

F   4. Response clarification is a major part of the data entry function.

F   5. The wild code check is part of the verifying function in data processing.

T   6. In constructing codes, one should establish mutually exclusive and collectively exhaustive categories.

F   7. The degree of complexity of the data instrument is not an issue to be considered in selecting a processing track.

F   8. In general, the more complex the data collection instrument, the more data processing types 4, 5, and 6 tend to be used.

T   9. Index creation is a valid circumstance resulting in the need for new variables in a dataset.

F   10. Removing a particular questionnaire from those to be processed is not justifiable solely because a key element of that questionnaire was not answered.

F   11. Due to the complexity of coding, coding at the international level is limited to only one or two methods.

Multiple Choice

A   1. Regarding an editor's function, the issue of interviewer bias or cheating is part of which of the following concerns:

    A. Accuracy.
    B. Completeness.
    C. Consistency.
    D. Legibility.
    E. Response clarification.

B   2. Edge coding, which eliminates the step of transferring codes to coding sheets, is part of which processing track?

    A. One
    B. Two

C. Three
D. Four
E. Five

E 3. Which of the following is a reason for excluding a data instrument from processing?

   A. The fact that a respondent misunderstood the instructions.
   B. A significant question was unanswered.
   C. The instrument was not physically complete.
   D. The wrong sample element completed the instrument.
   E. All of the above.

B 4. The codebook typically contains all of the following except:

   A. The variable name.
   B. The respondent number.
   C. The format.
   D. The variable number.
   E. The relevant matrix columns.

D 5. If a single response was anticipated to a question at the time the codebook was developed, what is an appropriate method of handling multiple responses?

   A. Designate as missing data.
   B. Select the first answer listed.
   C. Assign each response to a separate matrix column.
   D. A and B above.
   E. All of the above.

D 6. Which of the following is typically part of the verifying function?

   A. Consistency check.
   B. Extreme case check.
   C. Wild code check.
   D. None of the above.
   E. All of the above.

C 7. Which of the following represents a circumstance in which a new variable may **not** be created?

   A. Adding data not originally collected.
   B. Forming new variables as combinations of other variables.
   C. Forming interval variables from categorical ones.
   D. Creating indices from other variables collected.
   E. None of the above.

E 8. Which of the following factors must be considered in selecting a data processing track?

   A. Time and cost constraints.
   B. Availability of hardware.
   C. Complexity of the collection instrument.
   D. A and B above.
   E. All of the above.

The following question relates to the Global Marketing Research Dynamics insert "Complexities of International Coding"...

E   9. Which of the following is NOT a basic method of international coding:

    A. Code on the assumption that the world thinks like the native country conducting the study.
    B. Code on the assumption the world thinks in the English language.
    C. Allow local agencies to perform the bulk of the coding process, with a home office coordinating the final results.
    D. Computerized coding.
    E. None of the above (all are methods of international coding).

CHAPTER 18 — UNIVARIATE DATA ANALYSIS

True - False

F 1. Descriptive statistics allow the researcher to make summary judgments about a population.

F 2. The mean and median can both be appropriately used as measures of central tendency for ordinal data.

F 3. The mean can be appropriately calculated as a central tendency measure for nominal data.

T 4. Relative and absolute frequencies are appropriate measures of dispersion for nominal data.

F 5. The standard deviation is appropriate as a measure of dispersion for ordinal data.

T 6. The mean and standard deviation are measures of central tendency and dispersion for interval data.

F 7. Inferential statistics are commonly used to provide summary measures about a sample.

T 8. The probability of a type I error is the significance level of the hypothesis test.

T 9. A type II error, which occurs with a probability of β, results from the non-rejection of a false null hypothesis.

F 10. The expression $(1 - \beta)$ is known as the level of confidence.

T 11. The cost of a type II error may be even greater than that of a type I error, from a managerial viewpoint.

T 12. The power of the test is equal to the probability of rejecting a false null hypothesis.

T 13. The first step in hypothesis testing is to formulate a null and alternative hypothesis to be evaluated.

F 14. In hypothesis testing, if the calculated statistic is less than the critical value for the given α level, the null hypothesis is rejected.

F 15. If the alternative hypothesis is rejected, this would imply that the null hypothesis is accepted.

T 16. The t test is an appropriate test of inference concerning means of interval data, no matter what the sample size.

F 17. The z test should only be used when σ is known.

F   18. The chi square test can be used as a descriptive test for the distribution of subjects across a nominal variable.

Multiple Choice

B   1. An appropriate measure of central tendency for nominal scale data is the:

   A. Median.
   B. Mode.
   C. Mean.
   D. All of the above.
   E. None of the above.

C   2. For interval data, the appropriate measures of central tendency and dispersion are, respectively, the:

   A. Mode and median.
   B. Median and relative frequencies.
   C. Mean and standard deviation.
   D. Median and standard deviation.
   E. Correlation coefficient and median.

D   3. Two samples are drawn, each with a mean of 50. If the first sample has a coefficient of variation of 10 and the second has a standard deviation of 50, which of the following statements is/are true?

   A. $CV_1 < CV_2$
   B. $s_1 < s_2$
   C. $CV_1 = CV_2$
   D. $s_1 > s_2$
   E. None of the above or more information needed.

E   4. In the situation that H_o is false but it is not rejected, what type of error is made?

   A. Type I.
   B. Type II.
   C. β
   D. A and C above.
   E. B and C above.

D   5. The power of the test is given by:

   A. α
   B. $1 - \alpha$
   C. β
   D. $1 - \beta$
   E. The confidence level.

C 6. The significance level of a test is also known as:

   A. The confidence level.
   B. A correct decision.
   C. α
   D. $1 - \beta$
   E. A Type II error.

A 7. The expression $(1 - \alpha)$ gives the probability that:

   A. A true H_0 is not rejected.
   B. A false H_0 is not rejected.
   C. A true H_0 is rejected.
   D. A false H_0 is rejected.
   E. A Type II error is made.

B 8. In hypothesis testing, the hypothesis which is accepted is:

   A. The null hypothesis.
   B. The alternative hypothesis.
   C. Either the null or alternative hypothesis, depending upon the α level.
   D. Either the null or alternative hypothesis, depending upon the β level.
   E. Always correct.

D 9. Given the null hypothesis H_0: $\mu = 10$, which of the following would indicate a two-tailed test is appropriate?

   A. $\mu = 50$
   B. $\mu > 10$
   C. $\mu < 10$
   D. $\mu \neq 10$
   E. None of the above.

A 10. Which of the following is an example of a two-tailed test?

   A. H_0: $\mu = 65$; H_1: $\mu = 65$
   B. H_0: $\mu > 65$; H_1: $\mu < 65$
   C. H_0: $\mu \geq 65$; H_1: $\mu < 65$
   D. H_0: $\mu > 65$; H_1: $\mu < 65$
   E. None of the above.

E 11. The t test and z test are statistics which are appropriately applied to what levels of data, respectively?

   A. Ordinal and interval.
   B. Nominal and ordinal.
   C. Nominal and interval.
   D. Interval and ordinal.
   E. None of the above.

C 12. If is unknown, what test is appropriate for interval data, given any size sample?

 A. Chi square
 B. F
 C. t
 D. z
 E. None of the above.

E 13. Which of the following is the correct formula for a z test?

 A. $(\overline{X} - \mu) / (s_{\overline{X}} / \sqrt{n})$
 B. $(\overline{X} - \mu)^2 / (\overline{X})^2$
 C. $(\overline{X} - \mu) / (s_{\overline{X}} / n)$
 D. $\Sigma(\overline{X} - X)^2 / (\overline{X})^2$
 E. None of the above.

E 14. The z test is appropriate under which of the following conditions?

 A. σ unknown, n = 20.
 B. σ unknown, n = 35.
 C. σ known, n = 20.
 D. A and B above.
 E. B and C above.

Questions 15 through 19 refer to the following situation:

A product manager is concerned with whether or not her product's share is equal to 25% of the market. A sample of 35 data points yields a sample proportion equal to 38%.

D 15. What is the proper hypothesis specification, given the situation outlined?

 A. $H_0: \pi = .38; H_1: \pi \neq .38$
 B. $H_0: \pi \geq .38; H_1: \pi < .38$
 C. $H_0: \pi \leq .25; H_1: \pi > .28$
 D. $H_0: \pi = .25; H_1: \pi \neq .25$
 E. None of the above or indeterminate.

D 16. What test is appropriate for interference-making?

 A. Chi-square
 B. F
 C. t
 D. z
 E. None of the above.

A 17. What would the numerator of this test equal?

   A. .13
   B. -.13
   C. $(.13)^2$
   D. $1 - (.13)^2$
   E. None of the above.

B 18. Given the following abbreviated table of critical values,

α	One-Tail Test	Two-Tail Test
.05	1.64	1.96
.025	1.96	2.24
.01	2.33	2.47

What is the appropriate critical value if one wants a 95% confidence level?

   A. 1.64
   B. 1.96
   C. 2.24
   D. 2.33
   E. 2.47

A 19. Given the problem, hypothesis, and test procedure are as stated, a calculated test value of 1.78 is obtained. What conclusion is possible, assuming, as in the previous question, a 95% confidence level?

   A. H_o is not rejected.
   B. H_o is rejected.
   C. π in reality equals neither .25 nor .32.
   D. No statement is possible; more information required.
   E. None of the above.

B 20. The chi square test is appropriate for what level(s) of data?

   A. Ordinal.
   B. Nominal.
   C. Interval.
   D. A and C above.
   E. All of the above.

CHAPTER 19 — BIVARIATE DATA ANALYSIS

True - False

F 1. Linear correlation, r, is the amount of variation in one variable that can be explained by knowledge of the other.

F 2. Simple regression is appropriate for use with ordinally-scaled variables.

T 3. In the simple regression equation, b can be thought of as representing the slope of the line.

T 4. In regression, $r^2 = SS_{explained}/SS_{total}$

F 5. The simple regression model is given by the following expression:

$$SS_{total} = SS_{explained} - SS_{unexplained}$$

F 6. The null hypothesis for a chi square test used in bivariate statistics is that two nominal variables are dependently related.

F 7. The Kolmogorov-Smirnov test is appropriate for drawing inferences about two nominal variables.

F 8. The best way to cast percentages in crosstabulation tables is as row percentages.

T 9. Control variables are often used in crosstabulation tables as a method of elaboration.

F 10. One possible conclusion of elaboration, in the case in which no total sample relation was previously found, is that the original relationship was spurious.

T 11. Interaction is a possible conclusion of elaboration, given that a total sample relationship was found in the original crosstabulation.

F 12. The biggest advantage of the banner format is its ability to cast percentages in two directions for several variables at once.

Questions 13 and 14 are from the Appendix.

F 13. When performing a t test on the b coefficient of a regression equation, the null hypothesis is that the population coefficient differs from zero.

T 14. A z test can be used in bivariate analysis to test whether two population means are really different.

Multiple Choice

A   1. A bivariate descriptive statistic appropriate when dealing with two interval variables is:

     A. Correlation coefficient.
     B. Chi square test.
     C. z test.
     D. Contingency coefficient.
     E. Mann-Whitney U test.

B   2. In regression analysis, the predicted value of the ith observation of the dependent variable is:

     A. Y_i
     B. $\hat{Y}_i$
     C. $\overline{Y}_i$
     D. X_i
     E. $\overline{X}_i$

D   3. In regression analysis, the coefficient of determination equals:

     A. R_{xy}
     B. $\Sigma(Y_i - \overline{Y}_i)^2 / \Sigma(Y_i - Y)^2$
     C. $SS_{unexplained}/SS_{total}$.
     D. Explained variation/total variation.
     E. None of the above.

A   4. Given the regression equation $\overline{Y}_i = 352.69 + .003\ X_i$, which of the following statements is/are true?

     A. b = .003.
     B. An increase of .003 units in the independent measure would result in an increase of 1 unit in the predicted Y value.
     C. The intercept of this equation is .003.
     D. All of the above.
     E. A and B above.

B   5. A bivariate inferential statistic appropriate when dealing with two nominal variables is:

     A. Correlation coefficient.
     B. Chi square test.
     C. z test.
     D. Contingency coefficient.
     E. Mann-Whitney U test.

C   6. In bivariate applications, the data input to a chi square test are of what form?

   A. Means.
   B. Percentages.
   C. Raw frequencies.
   D. All of the above.
   E. None of the above.

A   7. A chi-square test, applied to bivariate statistics, can tell us:

   A. That two variables are not independent.
   B. That one cell size is significantly different from another.
   C. That two means are significantly different.
   D. All of the above.
   E. A and B above.

E   8. Which of the following methods of presentation is preferable when using crosstabulation tables?

   A. Row percentages.
   B. Column percentages.
   C. Cell percentages
   D. Raw frequencies.
   E. A generalization cannot be made without further information.

E   9. Assuming that a zero-order association is originally found, which of the following is/are possible conclusions of elaboration?

   A. Retaining the original conclusion of a relationship not existing.
   B. Specifying a different relationship by control categories.
   C. Identifying the original finding as spurious.
   D. All of the above.
   E. B and C above.

B   10. Assuming that no zero-order association is originally found, which of the following is/are possible conclusions of elaboration.

   A. Retaining the original conclusion of a relationship existing.
   B. Identifying a relationship.
   C. Identifying the original finding as spurious.
   D. All of the above.
   E. A and B above.

A   11. Which of the following is **not** a characteristic of the banner format:

   A. Better chance of detecting covariation.
   B. Allows presentation of many variables at once.
   C. Categories are often collapsed, making it more difficult to infer results.
   D. they are easily understood by management.
   E. All of the above are characteristics of the banner format.

Questions 12 through 15 are from the Appendix.

C 12. The standard error of the estimate:

    A. Has (n - 1) degrees of freedom.
    B. Measures the standard deviation of Y_i about $\bar{Y}_i$.
    C. Is a measure of the scatter of Y_i values about the regression line.
    D. All of the above.
    E. B and C above.

E 13. The appropriate test in simple regression to determine whether it has explained a statistically significant portion of the variation in Y is the:

    A. Chi square test.
    B. F test.
    C. t test.
    D. z test.
    E. B and C above.

C 14. A bivariate inferential statistic appropriate when dealing with two interval variables is:

    A. Correlation coefficient.
    B. Chi square test.
    C. z test.
    D. Contingency coefficient.
    E. Mann-Whitney U test.

E 15. The expression, $[(X_1 - X_2) - (\mu_1 - \mu_2)] / \sigma_{\bar{X}_1 - \bar{X}_2}$

    A. Is a t statistic.
    B. Is a z statistic.
    C. Is used to test that two population means are equal.
    D. A and B above.
    E. B and C above.

CHAPTER 20 — MULTIVARIATE DATA ANALYSIS I: INTERDEPENDENCE METHODS

True - False

F 1. Interdependence methods designate one or more variables as being predicted by a set of independent variables.

F 2. Dependence methods are interested in the relationships among all the variables taken together.

T 3. In factor analysis, a large number of variables or objects are analyzed to determine a smaller set of common factors.

F 4. R-type factor analysis considers correlations between objects.

T 5. Q-type factor analysis is analogous to cluster analysis.

F 6. Factor analysis output always yields uncorrelated factors.

F 7. Cluster analysis is commonly applied for purposes of data transformation and data reduction.

T 8. Cluster analysis algorithms exist for any of the four scale levels of variables.

T 9. Multidimensional scaling and factor analysis are examples of interdependence methods.

T 10. Nonmetric multidimensional scaling takes ordinal input measures and generates a set of relationships among the objects which is intervally-scaled.

Multiple Choice

E 1. Which of the following is not an example of an interdependence method?

　　A. Factor analysis.
　　B. Nonmetric multidimensional scaling.
　　C. Metric multidimensional scaling.
　　D. Cluster analysis.
　　E. None of the above.

B 2. The principal reason for rotating a factor analysis solution is to:

　　A. Increase the amount of "explained" variance in the variables.
　　B. Aid in the interpretation of the factors.
　　C. Maintain the orthogonal solution.
　　D. A and B above.
　　E. B and C above.

C 3. In factor analysis, H is a measure of:

   A. The proportion of a variable's total variation that is involved in the factors.
   B. Uniqueness.
   C. The common variance explained by the factors.
   D. The amount of variation in the data accounted for by one factor.
   E. None of the above.

Questions 4 and 5 refer to the following matrix:

Variable	Factor 1	Factor 2	Factor 3
1	.90	.04	-.21
2	.77	.11	.11
3	.79	.24	-.09

C 4. Given the factor loading matrix above, what is the h^2 communality measure, for variable 2?

   A. .39
   B. .99
   C. .62
   D. .01
   E. .38

B 5. What percentage of the total variation is accounted for by factor 1?

   A. .82
   B. .68
   C. .18
   D. .24
   E. None of the above.

E 6. Which of the following is **not** a common dimension of the various cluster analysis algorithms?

   A. Natural clusters are assumed to exist in the data.
   B. An input matrix of associations between objects or variables is used.
   C. The input matrix may take on any scale level.
   D. Subgroupings are formed and objects or variables assigned to these groups.
   E. None of the above.

E 7. The type of multidimensional scaling which takes ordinally-scaled input and generates rank order relationships is referred to as:

   A. Nonmetric.
   B. Partially metric.
   C. Fully metric.
   D. Metric.
   E. Fully nonmetric.

B 8. A multivariate procedure which could be used to identify viable segments existent in a market or to identify "holes" in a market that could support a new product venture is:

   A. Factor analysis.
   B. Nonmetric multidimensional scaling.
   C. Metric multidimensional scaling.
   D. Cluster analysis.
   E. None of the above.

D 9. A goodness of fit measure inversely related to the number of dimensions is:

   A. h^2
   B. $1 - h^2$
   C. An eigenvalue
   D. Stress
   E. H

D 10. The type of multidimensional scaling which takes interval or ratio-scaled input and generates interval or ratio relationships is called:

   A. Nonmetric.
   B. Partially metric.
   C. Fully metric.
   D. Metric.
   E. Fully nonmetric.

CHAPTER 21 – MULTIVARIATE DATA ANALYSIS II: DEPENDENCE METHODS

True - False

F   1. In multiple regression, R equals the proportion of the variation in Y explained by the regression.

F   2. The coefficient of multiple determination can be calculated as $SS_{explained}/SS_{unexplained}$.

F   3. ANCOVA is appropriate for use with a set of intervally-scaled dependent variables and a set of nominally-scaled independent variables.

T   4. Dummy variable discriminant analysis is designed to be used with nominally-scaled data.

F   5. An-category nominal variable is properly represented in a dummy variable multiple regression by n + 1 binary variables.

T   6. AID shares the same level requirements of data input as does ANOVA.

T   7. One technique designed for use with an ordinal level dependent variable and nominally-scaled independent variables is conjoint measurement.

T   8. If one is dealing with more than one dependent variable, either canonical correlation or MANOVA may be an appropriate technique.

F   9. The primary difference between ANOVA and MANOVA is that the latter is able to handle covariates.

T   10. The fixed effects model does not allow interpolations between treatments to be made.

F   11. ANOVA is a calculation of difference variances, df/SS.

T   12. In ANOVA, MS_{TR} is an estimate of the treatment variance.

F   13. In ANOVA, a treatment error equals the difference between the treatment mean and the grand mean.

F   14. MS_{TR} is obtained by dividing the SS_T by the relevant number of degrees of freedom (df).

F   15. Interaction is the result of a relationship between a dependent and an independent variable which differs for different categories of another dependent variable.

T   16 The relevant statistic for testing a one-way ANOVA is the F statistic.

T   17. The basic composition of a CRD analysis of variance is $SS_T = SS_{TR} + SS_E$

F   18. The total number of degrees of freedom in an RBD ANOVA table is n - 1.

F   19. In an RBD ANOVA, (t - 1)(n - 1) is the appropriate number of degrees of freedom for the blocking term.

T   20. In the ANOVA designs, the dependent variable is assumed to be of at least interval scaling, and the independent variable(s) nominally scaled.

F   21. The Latin Square R_i effect = $(M_{..k} - M)$.

F   22. The following represents a possible Latin Square treatment assignment:

$$\begin{array}{ccc} B & C & A \\ C & A & B \\ A & C & B \end{array}$$

F   23. The basic composition of an LS design analysis of variance is: $SS_T = SS_R + SS_C + SS_{TRA} + SS_E$.

T   24. The Latin Square column effect = the difference between the column mean and the grand mean, adding across all i's and k's.

F   25. In a factorial design, the B effect equals the difference between the column mean and the row mean.

Multiple Choice

E   1.   If one has a nominally-scaled dependent measure and several nominally-scaled independent measures, which of the following techniques should be considered?

   A. ANOVA.
   B. Conjoint measurement.
   C. Discriminant analysis.
   D. MANOVA.
   E. None of the above.

D   2.   Which of the following techniques is designed for use with one intervally-scaled dependent variable and a set of intervally-scaled independent variables?

   A. ANCOVA.
   B. MANOVA.
   C. Canonical correlation.
   D. Multiple regression.
   E. None of the above.

C   3.   Which of the following best describes the term R^2 in a multiple regression?

   A. The proportion of the variation in $\hat{Y}$ explained by the regression.
   B. The correlation between the Y_i's and the $\hat{Y}_i$'s.
   C. $SS_{explained}/SS_{total}$.

307

D. SS$_{explained}$/SS$_{unexplained}$.
E. None of the above.

A 4. Given nominally-scaled independent variables, which of the following techniques are likely to be appropriate?

A. ANOVA, AID.
B. AID, discriminant analysis.
C. Conjoint measurement, canonical correlation.
D. Discriminant analysis, ANOVA.
E. None of the above.

B 5. Which of the following techniques has as its objective to break down a total sample into a number of subgroups that are more homogeneous on the dependent variable than the sample as a whole?

A. Dummy variable multiple regression.
B. AID.
C. Discriminant analysis.
D. Conjoint measurement.
E. None of the above.

C 6. DVMR is to multiple regression as _____ is to discriminant analysis.

A. AID.
B. ANOVA.
C. Dummy variable discriminant analysis.
D. Conjoint measurement.
E. Canonical correlation.

E 7. Given two independent categorical variables, one with 10 categories and the other with 5 categories, how many dummy variables would be necessary to fully represent all categories in a DVMR?

A. 50
B. 15
C. 14
D. 16
E. 13

C 8. If one is dealing with intervally-scaled independent variables and a nominally-scaled dependent variable, which of the following techniques should be considered?

A. ANOVA.
B. Conjoint measurement.
C. Discriminant analysis.
D. MANOVA.
E. None of the above.

B 9. If one has an ordinally-scaled dependent measure and nominally-scaled independent measures, which of the following techniques should be considered?

   A. ANOVA.
   B. Conjoint measurement.
   C. Discriminant analysis.
   D. MANOVA.
   E. None of the above.

D 10. Given a set of intervally-scaled dependent variables, which of the following techniques should be considered?

   A. Multiple regression, discriminant analysis.
   B. AID, ANOVA.
   C. Conjoint measurement, canonical correlation.
   D. MANOVA, canonical correlation.
   E. None of the above.

Questions 11 through 24 are from the Appendix.

B 11. The ANOVA model in which the researcher is unwilling to interpolate between treatments is known as the:

   A. Random effects model.
   B. Fixed effects model.
   C. Mixed effects model.
   D. Noninteractive model.
   E. Factorial design model.

D 12. Using the ANOVA model, any individual score can be rewritten as a deviation from the:

   A. Treatment effect.
   B. Row effect.
   C. Column effect.
   D. Grand mean.
   E. Error term.

E 13. Experimental error in ANOVA is defined as the difference between:

   A. The grand mean and the treatment mean.
   B. The individual score and the grand mean.
   C. The treatment mean and between group sum of squares.
   D. The grand mean and the within group sum of squares.
   E. The individual score and the treatment mean.

E 14. Which of the following ratios is distributed as an F-statistic?

   A. MS_E/MS_{TR}.
   B. SS_{TR}/SS_E.

309

C. MS_T/MS_E.
D. $MS_{TR}/(tn - 1)$.
E. MS_{TR}/MS_E.

D 15. An ANOVA design which measures the effect of one independent variable without statistical control of extraneous factors is an:

A. RBD.
B. FD.
C. LS.
D. CRD.
E. None of the above.

A 16. When data previously analyzed by a CRD are reanalyzed by an RBD incorporating the same variables plus the addition of a blocking factor, which of the following is/are true?

A. SS_E decreases.
B. SS_{TR} increases.
C. SS_{TR} decreases.
D. SS_R decreases.
E. SS_C remains the same.

A 17. An ANOVA design which measures the effect of one independent variable and statistically controls one extraneous factor is an:

A. RBD.
B. FD.
C. LS.
D. CRD.
E. None of the above.

E 18. The design which is composed as $SS_T = SS_{TR} + SS_B + SS_E$ is best described as an:

A. CRD.
B. LS design.
C. FD.
D. FCD.
E. RBD.

C 19. This ANOVA design measures the effect of one independent variable and statistically controls two extraneous factors is an:

A. RBD.
B. FD.
C. LS.
D. CRD.
E. None of the above.

D 20. The basic composition of a factorial design ANOVA is:

A. $SS_T = SS_{TR} + SS_{INT(AB)} + SS_E$.
B. $SS_T = SS_{TR} + SS_R + SS_C + SS_E$.
C. $SS_T = SS_{TRA} + SS_{TRB} + SS_E$.
D. $SS_T = SS_{TRA} + SS_{INT(AB)} + SS_{TRB} + SS_E$.
E. $SS_T = SS_{INT(AB)} + SS_R + SS_C + SS_E$.

B 21. This ANOVA design measures the main and interactive effects of two or more independent variables:

A. RBD.
B. FD.
C. LS.
D. CRD.
E. None of the above.

D 22. The factorial design total sum of squares equals:

A. $\sum_i \sum_j \sum_k (Y_{ijk} - M)^2$

B. $SS_{TRA} + SS_{TRB} + SS_{INT(AB)} + SS_E$

C. $\sum_i \sum_j \sum_k (Y_{ijk} - M_{ij})^2$

D. A and B above.
E. B and C above.

A 23. The F-ratio for the interaction term in a factorial design ANOVA equals:

A. $\dfrac{SS_{INT(AB)}}{SS_E} \times \dfrac{ab(n-1)}{(a-1)(b-1)}$

B. $\dfrac{SS_{INT(AB)}}{SS_{TRB}} \times \dfrac{ab(n-1)}{(a-1)}$

C. $\dfrac{SS_E}{SS_{TRA}} \times \dfrac{(abn-1)}{ab(n-1)}$

D. $\dfrac{SS_{INT(AB)}}{SS_{TRB} - SS_{TRA}} \times \dfrac{(abn-1)}{(a-1)(b-1)}$

E. None of the above.

C 24. A technique which can handle extraneous variation after an experiment has been run is:

    A. FD ANOVA.
    B. CRD ANOVA.
    C. ANCOVA.
    D. LS ANOVA.
    E. RBD ANOVA.

CHAPTER 22 — REPORTING RESEARCH FINDINGS

True - False

T   1. The researcher should keep the needs of the audience in mind in preparing the research report and tailor the presentation accordingly.

F   2. Most decision makers are interested in the details of the research process and they should be included in the management summary.

F   3. The management summary is only an overview, thus conclusions and recommendations are not appropriate in this section.

F   4. The written report is typically used to support the oral presentation.

F   5. It is best to start the oral presentation by reviewing the research design and then turn to the research findings.

F   6. A good research report must include recommendations for action.

T   7. Technical details are better placed in an appendix as opposed to the body of a research report.

F   8. The tabular form involves the presentation of data in terms of visually interpreted sizes.

Multiple Choice

B   1. Which of the following would **not** be a characteristic of a well-written research report.

    A. Concise.
    B. Standardized.
    C. Objective.
    D. All of the above.
    E. A and B above.

E   2. The management summary of a research report:

    A. Is typically one or two pages in length.
    B. Provides the decision maker with the key research findings relevant to the decision problem.
    C. Is simply a miniature of the main report.
    D. All of the above.
    E. A and B above.

D   3. The introduction in the body of a research report:

    A. Should clearly explain the nature of the decision problem.
    B. Should not review previous research on the problem.

C. Should outline research objectives.
D. A and C above.
E. B and C above.

A 4. Limitations of the research project:

A. Should be pointed out in the research report.
B. Should not be pointed out in the research report.
C. May or may not be dealt with in the research report, depending upon the impact it may have.
D. Should focus mainly on sampling issues.
E. A and B above.

A 5. Several series compared on the same chart are best displayed via:

A. A line chart.
B. A pie chart.
C. A bar chart.
D. None of the above.
E. A and C above.

E 6. Graphic aids should always have all of the following:

A. Table or figure number.
B. Title.
C. Boxhead or stub head.
D. Footnotes.
E. All of the above.

314

CHAPTER 23 — DEMAND MEASUREMENT AND FORECASTING

True - False

F   1.   Measuring current demand is generally less accurate than forecasting demand.

T   2.   Market potential increases with increased levels of marketing effort.

T   3.   A company demand function expresses an estimate of company sales at alternate levels of marketing effort.

F   4.   Company sales potential is the maximum expected sales at a given level of marketing effort.

F   5.   Once a company's sales forecast has been prepared, the most desirable amount of marketing effort may be calculated.

F   6.   Methods for estimating current demand are more subjective for established products than for new products.

F   7.   The direct data method for determining current demand potential is used most frequently because of readily available data.

T   8.   The indirect data method logically relates a series of data to industry sales.

F   9.   A single factor index is the most accurate index to use in estimating market and/or sales potential.

T   10.   Multiple factor indexes weight and combine several factors that correlate to sales.

F   11.   The accuracy of a particular index may be determined before employing it.

T   12.   Use of the buildup method involves aggregating data from the customer or account level to the market or industry level.

T   13.   The Standard Industrial Classification (SIC) system classifies firms on the basis of their principal product or activity.

T   14.   The purpose of a sales forecast helps to determine the necessary accuracy.

F   15.   Once a specific forecasting technique has been perfected, it may be reused without amendment.

F   16.   Qualitative methods are the least popular type of sales forecasting technique.

F   17.   Time series forecasts are especially useful when the sales environment is changing.

F   18.   The accuracy of a moving average forecast is decreased by the effect of seasonally.

F   19.   Causal methods sacrifice accuracy for technical sophistication.

F   20. Consumer product and service sales forecasts make extensive use of consumer surveys.

F   21. Since marketing research is a well established field, the techniques and data sources developed over the decades in the U.S. can also be used in lesser developed countries.

Multiple Choice

B   1. Which dimension is not used to estimate market demand?

   A. Product.
   B. Industry.
   C. Customer.
   D. Geography.
   E. Time.

D   2. Which statement relating to market demand is false?

   A. Market potential establishes an upper limit to market demand.
   B. The definition of market demand includes specification along four dimensions.
   C. Market demand is best expressed as a function.
   D. A market forecast is the level of market demand under various levels of marketing effort and a variety of environmental conditions.
   E. None of the above.

B   3. Which definition associated with a company's demand measurement is correct?

   A. A sales budget is an optimistic estimate of sales volume.
   B. A sales quota is the sales goal set for a product line, company division or sales representative.
   C. A company sales forecast is the expected level of sales as marketing effort increases relative to competitors.
   D. Both B and C are correct.
   E. All of the above are correct.

B   4. Which is not used in the breakdown method of estimating market and sales potential?

   A. General multiple-factor index.
   B. Time series decomposition.
   C. Total industry or market data.
   D. General single-factor index.
   E. Neither B nor D.

B   5. The buildup method for estimating market and sales potentials:

   A. Begins with aggregate industry and/or market data.
   B. Seeks to establish a relationship between product or service purchases and one or more statistical series.
   C. May use either single- or multiple-factor indexes.
   D. Both A and C.
   E. All of the above.

316

E 6. The Standard Industrial Classification (SIC) system:

   A. Covers all economic activity within the United States.
   B. Sub-classifies firms by their secondary product or business activity.
   C. Is widely used for developing sales potential estimates.
   D. Both B and C.
   E. Both A and C.

B 7. The accuracy of sales forecasts:

   A. May be predetermined so that errors can be minimized.
   B. Is enhanced by the use of qualified systematic and objective procedures.
   C. Is always improved when sophisticated models are employed.
   D. Both B and C.
   E. All of the above.

E 8. When preparing a sales forecast, guidelines include:

   A. Relate the forecast to company capabilities and objectives.
   B. Prepare an initial forecast.
   C. Review environmental trends.
   D. Both A and B.
   E. All of the above.

B 9. What should a manager require a sales forecast to include?

   A. Qualification and exceptions.
   B. A brief statement of the assumptions underlying the forecast.
   C. Different forecasts for different situations.
   D. Both A and D.
   E. All of the above.

C 10. Qualitative sales forecasting methods include:

   A. Direct data method.
   B. Leading indicators.
   C. Sales force estimates.
   D. Buildup method.
   E. Both C and D.

C 11. The Delphi method is an example of :

   A. A direct data method.
   B. A newly developed model for developing sales forecasts.
   C. A qualitative forecasting technique.
   D. A way to estimate market potential.
   E. Both C and D.

A 12. Salesforce-distributor forecasts:

   A. Take advantage of a salesman's or distributor's expertise in specific regions.
   B. Incorporate long-run economic trends.

C. Have proven to be very reliable.
D. Both A and C.
E. All of the above.

A 13. Which of the following characterizes consumer surveys?

A. They are most appropriate when data is needed for a large number of potential buyers.
B. Information may be obtained from various publications.
C. They are used more for industrial products than consumer products and services.
D. Information may be used as input for the executive opinion method.
E. Neither A nor C.

C 14. Examples of time series methods include:

A. Multiple-factor indexes.
B. Multiple regression models.
C. Exponential smoothing.
D. Both B and C.
E. All of the above.

C 15. Time series forecasting is appropriate:

A. When historical sales data is unavailable.
B. Only if sophisticated statistical techniques are available.
C. When the sales environment is relatively stable.
D. If there are no discernible patterns or trends in historical sales data.
E. Both C and D.

B 16. The moving average method:

A. Computes a sales forecast by the formula y = a + bx.
B. Can remove the effect of seasonally from a forecast.
C. Requires the identification of at least one causal relationship.
D. Both B and C.
E. All of the above.

C 17. Which statement about time series methods is true?

A. The moving average method utilizes a constantly decreasing set of weights.
B. The older a data point is, the more weight it receives.
C. The exponential smoothing method utilizes an exponentially decreasing set of weights.
D. In general, time series forecasting is more appropriate for long-term forecasts than short-term forecasts.
E. Both A and C.

C 18. What are the temporal components measured in time-series decomposition?

A. Cycle, variation, trend, error.
B. Season, month, year, cycle.

C. Cycle, season, trend, error.
D. Variation, month, cycle, trend.
E. None of the above.

E 19. Causal methods:

A. Are rarely worth the effort since the results are not very accurate.
B. Predict turning points more accurately than time series methods.
C. Can explain variation in sales data.
D. Require many in-depth interviews with consumers.
E. Both B and C.

B 20. Which statement about causal models is false?

A. Leading indicators can be used to forecast turning points in sales.
B. Regression models require at least two causal variables.
C. Regression models are used in a wide variety of sales forecasting situations.
D. Both A and C.
E. None of the above.

The following questions are from the International discussion in the text (including the Global Research Dynamics insert)...

B 21. Which of the following is NOT an alternative technique for measuring demand in LDC's (Lesser Developed Countries)?

A. Macro surveys.
B. Markup ratio method.
C. Chain ratio method.
D. Trade audits.
E. All are possible alternative techniques.

B 22. The forecast for the band-aids started with the first step as:

A. An investigation into government related sources.
B. Exploratory research with pharmaceutical company members.
C. Conclusive research.
D. Trade audits.
E. None of the above.

CHAPTER 24 — PRODUCT RESEARCH AND TEST MARKETING

True - False

F   1. The use of product research has decreased substantially in the last 10 years.

F   2. The repertory grid technique requires respondents to rate concepts using a standardized scale.

T   3. Small nonprobability samples are often used in concept testing.

F   4. Concept testing techniques attempt to predict sales on a national level.

F   5. An advantage of the monadic rating system is that the ratings may be compared across products.

T   6. Conjoint analysis allows researchers to examine the relative importance of product attributes.

F   7. If laboratory usage tests can be satisfactorily completed, consumer usage tests are unnecessary.

F   8. Since consumers have actually used the product, buy intention measures taken in home usage tests have been shown to be very accurate.

T   9. The research objective of a business analysis is to estimate a product's sales level and profitability.

F   10. Test markets are typically true experimental research.

F   11. The results of test markets are nearly always generalizable to the national market.

T   12. The predictive research function of test marketing may involve a new product or brand introduction.

T   13. The predictive research function of test marketing may involve the evaluation of alternative marketing programs for existing brands.

T   14. Panel methods are used in test marketing as a predictive research tool.

F   15. The sales income method may be used to project test market results to a national product.

F   16. The buying income method is an example of test marketing's managerial control function.

F   17. Test marketing is not really done if plant investment for national introduction is high.

F   18. Costs, both direct and indirect, of running a test market are typically rather low.

F 19. Special campaigns by the company running the test do not bias the test marketing results.

T 20. Competitive reactions of other firms can influence the outcome of test markets.

T 21. The number of cities to be used is an important issue in the designing of a test market.

F 22. The demographic profile of test cities is an important consideration in determining how long a test market should run.

F 23. Although simulated test markets are cheaper than standard test markets, they do require more time.

T 24. Simulated test market models acquire information about both triers and non-triers.

F 25. Respondents for simulated test markets are usually chosen by simple random sampling.

F 26. Market share is estimated in simulated test markets from the proportion of "triers" resulting from the simulated shopping exercise.

Multiple Choice

D 1. When are focus groups used in product testing?

    A. Idea generation.
    B. Concept testing.
    C. Business analysis.
    D. Both A and B.
    E. All of the above.

B 2. Consumer testing techniques include:

    A. Consumer panels.
    B. Monadic ratings.
    C. Canonical analysis.
    D. Omnibus panels.
    E. All of the above.

B 3. Major business analysis techniques include:

    A. Conjoint analysis.
    B. Test marketing.
    C. Consumer usage tests.
    D. All of the above.
    E. None of the above.

A 4. Which is **not** a product research technique?

    A. Idea generation.
    B. Concept testing.

C. Laboratory testing.
D. Both A and B.
E. None of the above.

E 5. Idea generation techniques include:

A. Synectic sessions.
B. Repertory grids.
C. Focus groups.
D. Both B and C.
E. All of the above.

B 6. The objective of concept testing is to:

A. Evaluate alternative marketing plans.
B. Select the most promising concepts for further development.
C. Test the effectiveness of different advertising campaigns.
D. Both A and C.
E. All of the above.

E 7. Concept testing occurs at what stage?

A. Before the product exists physically.
B. When both the product and advertising are in unfinished form.
C. When the product exists but the advertising is in rough form.
D. When a prototype has been developed.
E. All of the above.

E 8. Product usage tests:

A. Give researchers information about long-run product acceptance.
B. Provide researchers with accurate purchase intention data.
C. Allow researchers to predict sales.
D. All of the above.
E. None of the above.

E 9. Which of the following is a fundamental use of test marketing?

A. Allowing the gathering of information prior to national introduction.
B. Gaining experience with a product prior to national introduction.
C. Deciding whether or not to undertake national introduction.
D. A and C above.
E. All of the above.

C 10. Most test markets involve a:

A. Factorial design.
B. Random block design.
C. Quasi-experiment.
D. Latin Square design.
E. None of the above.

E 11. Which of the following methods is/are used in conjunction with test marketing's managerial control function?

   A. Buying income method.
   B. Sales ratio method.
   C. Share of market method.
   D. All of the above.
   E. None of the above.

E 12. The share of market method can be defined as:

   A. $\left[\dfrac{\text{Total U.S. Income}}{\text{Test Area Income}}\right] * \text{(test area sales)}$

   B. $\left[\dfrac{\text{Test Area Sales of New Brand}}{\text{Test Area Sales of Product Category}}\right] * \text{(test area sales of new brand)}$

   C. $\left[\dfrac{\text{National Sales of Other Product}}{\text{Test Area Sales of this Other Product}}\right] * \text{(test area sales of test product)}$

   D. $\left[\dfrac{\text{Test Area Sales of Product Category}}{\text{National Sales of Product Category}}\right] * \text{(test area sales of new brand)}$

   E. None of the above.

C 13. An example of an indirect cost of test marketing is:

   A. Commercials.
   B. Syndicated research information.
   C. Management's time on the test market.
   D. Customized research information.
   E. None of the above.

B 14. The diversion of the sales force activity from money-making products to the test-marketed item is an example of:

   A. Direct costs of test marketing.
   B. Indirect costs.
   C. Either direct or indirect costs, depending on the situation.
   D. Both direct and indirect costs.
   E. Neither a direct nor an indirect cost.

D 15. A test market in which the environment is controlled to allow for tight designs is called a:

   A. Standard market.
   B. Mini-market.
   C. Control market.
   D. B and C above.
   E. None of the above.

C. 16. Which of the following is **not** a consideration in determining when to test market?

   A. The likelihood and speed of competitors' reactions.
   B. The plant investment necessary to go national.
   C. The number of cities to be tested.
   D. The effects on the company name of a failure.
   E. All of the above.

E. 17. Which of the following is **not** a major issue in designing test markets?

   A. How cities should be chosen.
   B. How many cities to use.
   C. The cost of the test.
   D. How long the test should run.
   E. None of the above.

D 18. The average test market runs for:

   A. Less than 6 weeks.
   B. 6 weeks to 3 months.
   C. 3 months to 6 months.
   D. 6 months to 12 months.
   E. 1 to 2 years.

C 19. The major potential negative consequence of test marketing is:

   A. Salespeople are stimulated to greater activity by the test.
   B. Special introductory offers and promotions bias the results.
   C. The results may lack projectivity to the national level.
   D. Competitive efforts may bias the test results.
   E. All of the above.

D 20. Simulated test markets predict market share by:

   A. Utilizing estimates of trial levels and repurchase rates.
   B. Utilizing the results of focus group data.
   C. Utilizing consumer preference judgments.
   D. Both A and C.
   E. All of the above.

E 21. Simulated test markets include:

   A. Usage tests.
   B. Repurchase measures.
   C. Advertising measures.
   D. Both A and B.
   E. All of the above.

D 22. Simulated test markets:

   A. Are cheaper and shorter in duration than traditional test markets.
   B. Utilize simulated retail stores.

- C. Predict sales from actual product trials alone.
- D. Both A and B.
- E. All of the above.

C23. In the Marketing Research in Action insert, "Cyanamid Tests Combat", what was the "hot button" that Combat discovered through test marketing:

- A. The three month kill formula was the most successful and matched consumer reactions determined through research.
- B. Consumers wanted lower prices and were swayed by lower prices.
- C. Consumers were concerned about the odor and mess and safety of the product.
- D. A and B only.
- E. None of the above.

CHAPTER 25 — ADVERTISING RESEARCH

True - False

F 1. Advertising research represents a minor application of marketing research.

F 2. A media audience measure is generally smaller than the media distribution measure.

F 3. Media vehicle distribution data provide advertisers with highly controversial information.

F 4. Broadcast media vehicle distribution data is an important decision-making aid to advertisers.

T 5. The number of people exposed to an ad usually exceeds the number who actively perceive it.

T 6. The discrepancies between magazine audience measures taken by Simmons Market Research Bureau (SMRB) and Mediamark Research, Inc. (MRI) are due primarily to differences in the research design.

F 7. Newspaper audience readers data is provided by many syndicated devices.

F 8. Television audience data is considered relatively unimportant by advertisers.

F 9. The personal interview method provides accurate and inexpensive information about TV audiences.

F 10. Measures of advertising exposure do not provide advertisers with information about a specific ad's effectiveness.

F 11. Copy testing examines the effectiveness of only the written portion of an ad.

T 12. The most desirable measure of an ad's effectiveness is sales.

T 14. Rating scales for ads can be standardized and compared to norms.

F 15. Consumer juries evaluate ads in finished form.

F 16. Physiological measures provide explicit information about a respondent's reaction to an ad.

F 17. Meters provide accurate and inexpensive information about the number of individuals watching a particular show.

T 18. Inquiry tests are best used when the consumer response is directly measurable.

T 19. Trailer tests and theater tests are both affected by the artificiality of the test environment.

F 20. Recall tests tend to overstate an ad's impact.

F 21. Sales tests provide accurate measures of the direct impact of an ad on sales.

F 22. The RC Cola example in the Marketing Research in Action insert showed one example where marketing research was not effective.

Multiple Choice

C 1. Which type of media data is subject to the least controversy about its accuracy?

    A. Advertising exposure data.
    B. Sales response data.
    C. Media vehicle distribution data.
    D. Media vehicle audience data.
    E. Both C and D.

B 2. Which of the following methods is **not** used to collect television audience data?

    A. Meters.
    B. "Pass-along" studies.
    C. Personal interview recall.
    D. Diaries.
    E. All are used.

B 3. Media audience data is typically attained for which of the following types of data?

    A. Advertising perception.
    B. Vehicle distribution and vehicle exposure.
    C. Advertising exposure.
    D. All of the above.
    E. Both B and C.

D 4. Copy testing measures the effectiveness of which aspects of an ad?

    A. Color and graphics.
    B. Pictures and action.
    C. Message.
    D. All of the above.
    E. Both A and C.

B 5. Which of the following is **not** one of the PACT (Positioning Advertising Copy Testing) principles aimed at improving copy testing, which state that a good copy testing system:

    A. Demonstrates reliability and validity.
    B. May be standardized and used for any ad testing situation.
    C. Provides multiple measures.
    D. Provides controls to avoid the biasing effects of the exposure context.
    E. Is based upon a model of human response to communication.

E 6. At which phase does copy testing normally occur?

    A. Before any media dollars have been spent.
    B. When the ad is in rough form.

C. When the ad is merely a written concept.
D. When the ad is in finished form.
E. At any of the above phases.

B 7. The idealized copy testing procedure:

A. Measures communication, for one ad, in roughform.
B. Measures sales of an entire campaign, in finished form.
C. Measures attention, for one ad, in finished form.
D. Measures profits of an entire campaign, in finished form.
E. Measures attention, for one ad, in rough form.

E 8. Which statement is part of the Idealized Measurement Procedure (IMP)?

A. The exposure environment and advertising context should be natural.
B. Measurement should be taken for all relevant media planned for the campaign.
C. Data should be collected through in-depth personal interviews.
D. All of the above.
E. Both A and B.

E 9. Common pre-testing procedures include:

A. Inquiry tests.
B. Theater tests.
C. Consumer juries.
D. All of the above.
E. Both B and C.

D 10. Consumer juries:

A. Judge a set of finished ads.
B. Have been proven to be a reliable and valid method for copy testing.
C. Consist of 500 consumers who fill out mail questionnaires.
D. Often use a numeric rating scale to evaluate ads on specific dimensions.
E. View ads in a natural advertising context.

C 11. Which copy-testing procedure does not involve an artificial testing environment?

A. Portfolio tests.
B. Theater tests.
C. On-the-air tests.
D. Physiological tests.
E. Both B and D.

D 12. Portfolio tests:

A. Use respondent recall as a measure of ad effectiveness.
B. Differentiate ads on the basis of creative presentation.
C. Include test and control ads.
D. Both A and C.
E. Both B and C.

D 13. Which of the following is true about physiological tests?

   A. They measure the physical reaction caused by an ad.
   B. They are totally reliable.
   C. Interpreting test results is often difficult.
   D. Both A and C.
   E. All of the above.

D 14. A major purpose of copy testing is to:

   A. Measure product interest.
   B. Increase product awareness.
   C. Estimate sales.
   D. Compare various creative approaches.
   E. Obtain constructive criticism from respondents.

E 15. Inquiry tests:

   A. Require a laboratory testing environment.
   B. Are commonly used when a coupon return or direct sale is the advertising objective.
   C. Measure the effectiveness of an ad on the basis of consumer inquiry.
   D. Require respondent interviews.
   E. Both B and C.

E 16. On-the-Air-Tests:

   A. Measure responses to TV or radio ads shown in a lab or theater.
   B. May be influenced by the show environment.
   C. Are conducted by many companies in a variety of formats.
   D. All of the above.
   E. Both B and C.

C 17. Which is **not** an example of an on-the-air-test?

   A. AdTel cable system.
   B. Masked recognition test.
   C. Nielson television index.
   D. Day-after recall.
   E. Total prime time.

D 18. Major post-testing procedures include:

   A. Recall tests.
   B. Sales tests.
   C. Recognition tests.
   D. All of the above.
   E. Both A and C.

E 19. Which of the following statements is not true about recognition tests?

   A. Recognition tests may be limited by respondent's confusion, forgetfulness, or false claims.
   B. Recognition measures include noted, seen-associated, and read most.

C. Norms for product classes and periodicals are available.
D. Both B and C.
E. None of the above.

E 20. Recall tests:

A. Directly relate recall to buying behavior.
B. May understate an ad's impact.
C. Are used for ads shown during prime time TV shows.
D. Both A and B.
E. Both B and C.

The following question relates to the Marketing Research in Action insert, "Advertising Research Helps Royal Crown Cola in the USA and Brazil"...

A 21. What was Royal Crown's solution to finding advertising copy that worked well in Brazil?

A. Mirroring current campaigns launched by Pepsi and Coca-Cola.
B. Hiring an outside agency to develop a brand new campaign focusing on current success from campaigns launched in the United States.
C. Translate and convert currently used ad copies for use in Brazil.
D. Launch an ad copy contest with an advertisement campaign for the contest to get natives of the country to come up with their own ideas.
E. None of the above.

CHAPTER 26 — DISTRIBUTION AND PRICING RESEARCH

True - False

F 1. A firm's records of shipments to retailers are useful in determining consumers' sensitivity to price changes.

F 2. Conjoint analysis is rarely used to research price sensitivity.

T 3. UPC scanner data and demographic information are useful to both retailers and manufacturers in determining local marketing strategies.

T 4. Syndicated services are used to monitor the flow of competitors' products and determine market share at the retail level.

F 5. Research to determine channel members' attitudes towards a manufacturers' products, service, promotions, etc. is performed primarily by manufacturers themselves.

T 6. Among the advantages of using surveys for pricing research are low cost, fast data collection, and flexibility.

F 7. Intention-to-buy statements are very good predictors of actual purchase behavior.

T 8. A field experiment relies on actual purchase data collected when buyers are not aware of any experimental manipulation.

T 9. One problem with using syndicated data to assess consumers' sensitivity to changes in your price level is lack of control over confounding variables like competitors' pricing and promotional activity.

F 10. One advantage of laboratory experiments is their realistic settings.

T 11. Use of standard test market cities is common to determine trade reaction to a new product offering.

T 12. Retailers rarely use semantic differential scales to measure their image in the eyes of consumers.

T 13. Manufacturers often use observational methods to assess channel members use of cooperative advertising and display allowances, quality of retail sales personnel, and other indicators of retailer performance.

Multiple Choice

D. 1. Marketing research by manufacturers on channel activities often includes:

   A. Monitoring product flow at the retail and wholesale level
   B. Attitude and performance studies of channel members

C. Measuring channel's response to marketing activities
D. All of the above
E. B and C only

E 2. Marketing research undertaken by channel members often includes:

A. Attitude and image studies
B. Location studies
C. Conjoint studies
D. A and B only
E. All of the above

D 3. It is common for manufacturers to use survey methodology to

A. Measure customer responses to channel members' activities
B. Measure customers' price sensitivity
C. Analyze patterns within a given geographic area
D. A and B only
E. All of the above

C 4. "Defining the relevant trading area" for a retail outlet involves:

A. Defining and describing the industry in which a firm operates.
B. Analyzing demographic characteristics of a retail outlet's current and potential customers.
C. Analyzing purchase patterns for the relevant product or service in a given location.
D. None of the above.
E. All of the above.

A 5. "Centroids" are geographic points that mark the center of the 260,000 block groups and enumeration districts in the U.S. Census. They are used by marketing researchers to:

A. Redefine census tract data into other shapes.
B. Provide a graphic representation of populated areas.
C. Measure the radial distance from the center of a city to a suburban location.
D. B and C only.
E. None of the above.

B 6. Defining the demographic characteristics of a trading area is typically done by:

A. Surveying a random sample of homes in the area.
B. Matching defined zones to census tract information.
C. Purchasing audit data from syndicated research firms such as IRI and Neilsen.
D. Conjoint analysis.
E. None of the above.

A 7. In a typical store's patronage forecasting model, the most important variable is:

   A. Distance
   B. Number of competitors
   C. Advertising
   D. Product offerings
   E. Target market demographics

D 8. The advantages of highly controlled versus uncontrolled studies of price sensitivity include:

   A. More accurate and useful results.
   B. Lower cost and less time-consuming.
   C. Greater internal validity.
   D. Both A and C.
   E. All of the above.

B 9. A simulated purchase survey is classified as a(n) _____ , _____ procedure for measuring price sensitivity. (Fill in the blanks.)

   A. Direct measure, high control
   B. Indirect measure, high control
   C. Indirect measure, low control
   D. Direct measure, low control
   E. None of the above

D 10. Syndicated store panel data and retail audit data are classified as _____ , _____ procedures for measuring price sensitivity. (Fill in the blanks.)

   A. Direct measure, high control
   B. Indirect measure, high control
   C. Indirect measure, low control
   D. Direct measure, low control
   E. None of the above

A 11. A Field or laboratory experiment is classified as a(n) _____ , _____ procedure for measuring price sensitivity. (Fill in the blanks.)

   A. Direct measure, high control
   B. Indirect measure, high control
   C. Indirect measure, low control
   D. Direct measure, low control
   E. None of the above

C 12. Which of the following methods for pricing research is the most **internally** valid?

   A. Survey
   B. Company sales records

        C. Field experiment
        D. Retail store audit data
        E. Panel store audit data

B   13. Which of the following methods for pricing research is the most **externally** valid?

        A. Survey
        B. Field experiment
        C. Laboratory experiment
        D. Simulated purchase survey
        E. Retail store audit data

C   14. Which of the following is the most **direct** measure of consumers' price sensitivity?

        A. Survey
        B. Company purchase records
        C. Retail store audit data
        D. Conjoint study
        E. All of the above are direct measures

The following question is based on the Marketing Research in Action insert, "Hong Kong Bank uses Marketing Research to Locate Branches"...

C   15. Which of the following reason(s) was key in spurring the Hong Kong Bank to conduct a marketing research effort to evaluate the location of retail bank branches?

        A. There was no information previously available to help the bank locate new branches.
        B. The rising costs of construction and opening a new location forced the firm to evaluate new locations before doing anything else.
        C. The bank had found a correlation between the location of retail branches and the volume of business and the bank wished to use this knowledge to optimize locations of future branches.
        D. The bank was seeking to phase out its retail business and wanted only to setup a few token branches, but did not know where.
        E. None of the above.

PART IV

CASE TEACHING NOTES

The teaching notes for the cases in the textbook are divided into five sections. They are:

1. Introduction: This section provides an overview of the facts and issues in the case.

2. Objectives of the Case: Here, the learning objectives of each case are presented. The instructor may wish to share these with the students after the class discussion to reinforce the learning experience.

3. Questions to Be Assigned: This section repeats the questions given in the textbook.

4. Case Analysis: In this section specific answers to the questions assigned are given.

5. Teaching Strategy: Here, we suggest specific execution patterns for using the cases. These are based on our experiences in using these materials. Other approaches are of course possible.

CASE 1-1

NATIONAL MARKETS — NUTRITIONAL LABELING

INTRODUCTION

This case presents background information related to a request for a research proposal by the marketing department of National Markets, a grocery store chain in the Midwest. The request is a direct result of National's recent loss of market share.

This case also serves as a foundation for two other cases: 1) Case 3-8: Midwest Marketing Research Associates (A), and 2) Case 5-2: Midwest Research Associates (B).

OBJECTIVES OF THE CASE

1) To help students understand the relevance of the decision-making environment to the specification of marketing research.

2) To give students an introduction to the difficulties of problem definition.

3) To give students practice at specifying research objectives and information needs.

4) To introduce students to alternative research designs.

5) To have students recognize the components of a research proposal.

QUESTIONS TO BE ASSIGNED

1) Develop a statement of research objectives. Think about:
   - Why was the request for information made?
   - Who is (are) the decision maker(s)?
   - What are the goals or objectives of the decision maker(s).
   - What is the decision-making environment?

2) What are the key information needs? List the five you feel are most important, and be prepared to defend your reasons for listing each.

3) One possible research design would be to interview (either in person, by telephone, or through the mail) grocery store shoppers. What are other possible designs?

4) Make a detailed outline of the research proposal you would submit if you were Jose Martinez. (Think about the information that National will be looking for in a research proposal.)

5) Prepare a research proposal. Use the outline you developed in question 4.

CASE ANALYSIS

Decision Environment

Students should recognize that before adequately defining the problem and preparing the proposal, a researcher must understand the background of the problem and the nature of the decision-making environment.

In this case, the several points are relevant: 1) If the marketing department is to gain cooperation from other departments in implementing its plan for providing nutrition information, research results must support the adoption of the program; 2) Since National has already compiled nutrition information, management is probably looking for reinforcement of an already-made decision to go ahead with the plan. The research is not being contracted to help make the decision, rather it is being made to convince others of the plan's benefits.

Reasons for Request

It is helpful to get students to speculate as to why the request for information was made. Possible answers include: (1) verification of senior management's already-made decision, (2) to determine a method of presenting the information so that store managers and consumers will best accept it, (3) determine the usefulness of nutrition information to current and potential customers, and (4) to see if by posting nutrition information, National could gain a differential advantage over its competitors and increase its market share.

Research Objectives

There are many research objectives which could be deemed appropriate for National Markets. These might include:

1) To determine the use and importance of labels in the purchase decision process for food.
2) To determine whether present label information is satisfactory.
3) To determine what kind of nutritional information consumers would like to see.
4) To determine the percentage of consumers that would use additional nutritional information.
5) To determine the demographic/psychographic composition of those consumers who would use nutrition information.
6) To see if shoppers' perceptions about National would be changed if National posted nutrition information.
7) To determine whether posting information would change consumer food preferences.
8) To determine the level of cooperation that could be expected from grocery store managers.

It should be clear to students that Mr. Martinez cannot be sure of National's decision problem, or the management objectives, or the research objectives. National has not provided Mr. Martinez with enough of their thinking, and he did not dig enough for it. Thus, all of the research proposals should be viewed as discussion documents which help to further clarify the decision problem and to identify information needs.

It should be noted that posting nutrition information would not be a sustainable differential advantage over the competition because it could be easily copied by other grocery stores. It would only be a successful strategy if National created store loyalty among any new customers it gained as a result of the strategy.

Key Information Needs

Once the class has identified the potential research objectives, the students should recognize that a list of information needs flows directly from the statement of research objectives. The instructor should tie the one directly to the other by having students who gave a particular research objective, then give related information needs. Note that this is exactly what is done in Chapter 3 of the text. Many possible lists of information needs can be proposed. A beginning of one such list follows:

1) Determine the demographic characteristics of people that use or would use nutritional information (e.g., are they calorie conscious?, or medically restricted dieters?, etc.).
2) Identify the type of nutritional information consumers find most useful.
3) Determine whether or not this type of information is currently gathered by consumers.
4) Determine if consumers feel that existing information is adequate.
5) Determine the information sources currently available to shoppers (e.g., advertising, friends, salespeople, labels).
6) Determine the most effective way of presenting nutritional information to consumers.
7) Predict which products might lose sales and which might gain sales if nutrition information were posted on labels.

Possible Research Designs

Given that this case is used early in the course, one should not expect students to be able to present or critically evaluate alternative designs in great detail. However, an overview of possible approaches is within their expertise. Possible designs include:

1) **Examination of Secondary Data.** It is possible that this idea has already been tried by country. However, consulting with managers of chain stores which are in competition with National may not be wise. As mentioned before, National's strategy could easily be duplicated.

2) **Exploratory Research:** Group Interviews. It appears that neither National nor MMRA has a sufficient understanding of this decision problem. Focus group interviews may be a reasonable first step in determining consumer perception in order to identify hypotheses regarding the decision problem. It is interesting to note to the class that it usually costs about $1200 per focus group.

3) **Survey.** Another approach is to question grocery store shoppers (as suggested in the guide questions). Students should be able to give the specifics of their plan: sample population, selection method, sample size, etc. This is hard for them now, but helps set up the rest of the course by demonstrating the need for this material. By drawing out the specifics regarding the nature of the survey the instructor can put a cost estimate on this design. To do this in rough, multiply the sample size by a cost per interview. For example, telephone runs $5-$20 per interview, depending on the length; mail runs $3-$10 per complete interview; and personal runs $15-$50 per complete interview. Note this excludes other costs such as data processing, analysis and reporting (see Chapter 18).

4) **Experiment.** Some bright student might suggest that a survey cannot accurately measure how people will behave and suggest an experiment. This allows for better control of variables and measurement of actual behavior.

5) **Observation.** An additional approach is to observe shoppers purchasing products. Students should be asked to specify those behavior patterns to be observed and how they might be measured.

What is important at this point in the course is that students do recognize the existence of alternative design approaches and a bit about the nature of each.

Research Proposal

In preparing their proposal, students should have included:

1) Statement of research objective.
2) Explanation of research design and procedure (sample size, interviewing procedures, data analysis, etc.).
3) Justification of design details in (2) above.
4) Demonstration of how potential research findings can lead to action-oriented decisions.
5) Proposed research budget and complete documentation of costs by stage of the process (interviewing, analysis, etc.).
6) Timetable of activities and completion date.
7) Statement of professional qualifications of all key personnel.
8) Possibly a proposed questionnaire.

The actual proposal prepared by the students is not as important at this point as the recognition of what belongs in it.

TEACHING STRATEGY

This case easily fills an hour-and-twenty-minute class period. It allows for a discussion of the decision environment for marketing research and all the managerial necessities of good research; i.e., problem definition, research objective and information needs. These issues should be dealt with first.

Once the issues are dealt with, alternative research designs can be discussed as a way of setting up the rest of the course. The instructor may want to give a short overview lecture of the course after using this case. The focus can be on the steps in the research process.

Finally, the instructor may wish to tie the course together by using this case combined with the Midwest Marketing Research Associates (A), (B) and (C) cases. These cases provide experience in questionnaire design, coding, and data analysis respectively.

CASE 1-2

WESTON FOOD COMPANY

INTRODUCTION

This case presents five short situations that raise issues concerning the working relationship between marketing research and marketing management. Each situation occurs within the same multi-product, consumer goods company.

OBJECTIVES OF THE CASE

1) To acquaint students with some potential areas of conflict between marketing research and marketing management.
2) To allow students to develop possible solutions to these areas of conflict.
3) To allow students to define the responsibilities of marketing researchers and marketing managers in the undertaking of marketing research.
4) To show the nature of the jobs of research director and research "generalist."

QUESTIONS TO BE ASSIGNED

The discussion questions are given in the first paragraph of the case. To repeat, they are for each episode:

1) What is going on?
2) Is the research/management interface effective? Why? Why not?
3) How could the situations be improved?
4) What generalizations can be made about how to establish an effective research/management interface in an organization?

CASE ANALYSIS

Episode A

Clearly, this constitutes an ineffective job of marketing research. This conclusion is easily reached by the class. Having determined this, we have found it useful then to take a vote of the class to see who they think is responsible for the ineffective situation. Is it Jones, Murphy, or both?

Some class members will argue that Jones is at fault. It can be argued that she failed to clearly specify the purpose for collecting the data. She specified the type of information needed, but not the purpose. Her statement after seeing the research should have been communicated earlier to Murphy. Ms. Jones is responsible as the marketing manager to specify how the research will be used, and he should communicate this to the researcher. Jones has asked too broad a research question. It is not until later that she asks specific questions. It could have been that her strategy was to be vague in order to get more data for her money. Clearly, this did not work.

On the other hand, it can be argued that Ms. Murphy is at fault. She should not have expected Ms. Jones to clearly define a problem so easily. Managers generally need help in doing so. It is Murphy's responsibility to draw out a clear problem definition. She jumped at Jones' first statement when Jones said: "need to know customers...". Murphy assumed that he meant current users of Weston's product. Jones' second statement indicates that what she really meant was customers of competitors' products.

Also, Murphy should not have spent seven weeks without interacting with Jones regarding this project. After a week or so, he should have gone back to discuss the actual design and how the information can be used by Jones. Murphy could have mocked-up some possible types of research results to see if they represented what Jones wanted.

It may also be argued that the organizational arrangements are at fault. Research should be an ongoing activity with the research department, not a strictly ad hoc situation. Also, there should be a set of rules for defining when research needs to be undertaken. This is usually done by having a project form filled out jointly by the manager and researcher. This form should include: problem definition and background, information needs, alternatives being considered, suggested design, timing, cost, etc. A systematic process would help avoid the situation presented in this episode. To be effective, the marketing researcher must have the right to get answers to these types of questions, and to refuse to do the research until he or she does.

In our view, Jones, Murphy, and the organization are at fault.

Episode B

In general, it is the manager's responsibility to define the causes of a problem. In this instance, Ms. Phelps defined the problem as package design. Past research plus experience and judgment may enter into the statement of the problem definition.

The communication and statement of problem definition are much better here than in Episode A. The participants are going to meet again and discuss the research proposal. However, are we sure that package design is the problem? There are many other possible causes. Here the manager and researcher have jumped from problem statement to a conclusive research design (an experiment). Maybe exploratory research is more appropriate.

Another worry is that Barbara Kindle is just not busy and has a technique in search of any problem. She could end up in an awkward situation if experimental design proves inappropriate for the problem situation.

Again, Murphy is not challenging enough regarding the need for research and problem definition. Alternatively, he may be waiting for a second meeting to do this. Someone should press Phelps regarding how he formulated his problem statement.

Again, a systematic approach using the project form discussed in Episode A's teaching note is needed.

Episode C

There are a number of possible causes of this situation. It is possible that Sid has poor interpersonal skills and has just turned everyone off. He may have been too pushy too soon. It is his function to listen and become a part of the management team.

Alternatively, the management group may not understand or respect marketing research and its role. Marketing research cannot function properly without top management support. This organizational status may be missing and thus the marketing manager may feel free to keep research at arm's length. Consequently, there needs to be a generally accepted charter of marketing research's role and procedures. Also, research must be strong enough to refuse to do research until the right questions are answers.

Episode D

This episode describes a situation experienced at one time or another by all marketing researchers. It is a frustration that one must learn to live with in most organizations.

It could be that the research analyst has overstepped the limits of her job responsibility. One could argue that she is only familiar with the research results and not with the many other factors that bear on the management decision. The position can be argued that the role of the researcher is to relate meaningful information to the decision problem, but it is the domain of management to make the decision.

The research departments' charter must spell out the extent to which the researcher makes recommendations and participates in the final decision. For example, at Procter and Gamble the analyst can actively disagree in written form with the use made of his or her research results. It is just possible here that management is purposely misusing the results to suit their own purposes.

Episode E

This is a case of outright managerial bias and pressure on the researcher to reach a particular conclusion. This kind of political pressure is hard to resist unless Ms. Tod is in an organizationally secure position. This means that the research department must be positioned high enough in the organization so that the director can win this type of political war. Effective marketing research will be lost if this kind of pressure is allowed to succeed.

A good question to ask here is what the class would do next if they were Ms. Tod.

TEACHING STRATEGY

This class flows best by proceeding from episode to episode. The focus overall should be to build a list of rules and procedures to allow the research/management interface to work effectively. Try and get out the charter of the research department as you proceed through the episodes.

The case can use a whole class session or be pushed to allow a short lecture overviewing some of the issues raised. These include:

1) The use of project forms to direct research;
2) Symptoms vs. problems;
3) Exploratory vs. conclusive research;
4) Organization of marketing research; and
5) Charter of the marketing research department.

CASE 1-3

FIELD MODULAR OFFICE FURNITURE

INTRODUCTION

This case requires students to critically examine two research proposals and their relationship to a managerial problem. The context is the Sword Group's Field Division which has agreed to work with one of two student groups in an effort to investigate a new market for their modular office furniture and panel technology. Field will make their student group selection based on the proposal that best meets their business objectives.

OBJECTIVES OF THE CASE

1) To expose students to examples of research proposals and to a proposal's components.
2) To allow students the opportunity to critically evaluate competing research designs.
3) To consider the value of marketing research.
4) To examine potential sources in research data.

QUESTIONS TO BE ASSIGNED

1) Which proposal should Field use? To justify your selection, consider the following:

   A) Evaluate the needs of Field. What is the managerial problem? How does the managerial problem relate to the research problem?
   B) Evaluate each phase of the research proposal. Are the proposals comprehensive? Are the proposals relevant to the research problem at hand?

2) Identify the strengths and weaknesses of the selected proposal.

3) What are some relevant sources of errors? How does each proposal attempt to control these errors, if at all?

CASE ANALYSIS

Evaluation of Field's Needs.

Field is still in the exploratory stage of market development. The organization needs to better understand the ECI market to determine viability. Field has also stated that they want information to identify an unmet customer need through competitive product design and to identify the target market (i.e. market segment/decision maker).

Note that Field's overall goals are far reaching and include both exploratory and conclusive needs, requiring a two part study. Also, Field is operating on a "tight deadline," however the exact timing and budget is not disclosed.

Phase Evaluation--Content and Relevancy.

Generally speaking, both proposals lack elements of a complete proposal and would be easier to follow if they were more detailed and organized. Prior to analyzing each proposal, ask the class to identify a comprehensive checklist of the required elements:

1) Problem (or opportunity) definition
2) A statement of objectives
3) A list of alternative courses of action
4) The information needs
5) The qualifications of the personnel who will be assigned to the project
6) An evaluation of the project, including how data will be handled, the potential for duplicating the project in other parts of the company, and the likelihood of its success
7) A budget or cost estimate
8) An accurate timetable

Proposal of Group 1:

The problem definition is absent. The research objectives assume market acceptance and proceed directly to investigating the financial viability of a new product line. The issue of product design is reduced to "desirable product attributes" and market segmentation is not specifically addressed in the statement of objectives. Additionally, the wording of the group's objectives needs improvement (i.e. presentation style). Alternative courses of action are not provided. The research information needs are described in the research design through the use of focus groups for preliminary information to then be used in a survey, and a survey to gain more conclusive information. Much of the information being solicited by the focus groups and survey are not directly related to the stated objectives. The evaluation of the project is also not complete and no personnel qualifications are described. While Field's budget is not disclosed, this proposal does not offer a cost estimate nor a timetable.

Proposal of Group 2:

As with Group 1, the problem definition is absent. Unlike Group 1's proposal, the second proposal does not assume market acceptance but rather seeks to explore this area more thoroughly. The need for product design information is included in the "nature of demand" objective, yet is limited to "product attributes" along with other demand elements. The market segment identification are not included and alternative courses of action are not provided. The information needs for the research are presented in the "Research Design" part of the proposal and describe how and what information is expected from each phase. The proposal includes a reference to using the survey information to cross-sell their current adult/professional line of products. A limited description of how the data will be handled is included, but it lacks a prediction of the likelihood of success. Research personnel descriptions are included. No timetable or cost estimate is included.

Based on the current state of both proposals, Field should select the proposal from Group 2. However, both proposals have positive and negative elements and could be effectively argued, based on the student's suggestions for improvement.

Improving the Research Design - Strengths and Weaknesses.

Generate a list of strengths and weaknesses on a blackboard or overhead projector. Have the students explain why a strength supports the proposal, and how a weakness could be altered to improve the proposal. In general, elements of a standard research proposal are missing and need to be included. Defining Field's management problem at hand would better establish the group's understanding of the project and would help guide the research objectives. Alternative methods of design should be encouraged. The described design should show how the information will be related back to and used by the organization. While each proposal should be reviewed independently, much of the difficulty lies in the area of general presentation style. The information is difficult to identify and even when the needed information is present, it is often obscured by wordy description.

Errors--Sources and Controls.

Sampling errors include:
- Achieving the appropriate ECI size-of-organization mix -- if necessary the data should be weighted to account for varying levels of market importance.
- It is not known whether or not the information solicited from local ECIs in the focus groups and/or interviews is representative of nation-wide ECIs because the sample is limited to one area of the country.
- Group 1's sample size of 100 may be too small for statistically accurate information. The respondents may include very small ECIs that would not be a viable market segment, such as in-home or family-run ECIs as noted by Group 2.
- A phone description of the product (Group 1) may be interpreted differently vs. the presentation of a drawing of the product.

Non-sampling errors include:
- At all phases, answers may be inaccurate, usage inflated, etc. to reflect socially desirable responses. Question ordering can be sensitive to this issue so respondents are not intimidated or insulted.
- Non-response errors may result if a distinctive segment or group does not return the questionnaire (Group 2). Similar errors occur if there is a high refusal or no-answer rate with the Group 1's phone sample. Interviewers should be persistent in trying to contact ECIs. Incentives should be provided (as stated by Group 1) if necessary and confidentiality must be assured.
- The definition of user and non-user could be inaccurate if usage is inflated. The definitions should be clearly delineated. The questions designed to assess this must be carefully worded.
- Errors in the research design may result from a vague decision situation definition.
- An auspices bias which may result if the respondents are suspicious about how the results will be used and the true purpose of the research. The purposes should be made clear and the use of an independent research group should be emphasized. This is not a significant problem with this case; however, it should be noted for class discussion.
- Usual interviewer errors in verbalization, recording, etc. can occur. Competent interviewers should be trained in standardized procedures.
- Usual data coding, processing and interpreting errors can be avoided by quality control and the use of standardized procedures.

TEACHING STRATEGY

This case is an excellent vehicle for student presentations to the class. Assign one team/group to defend and improve the proposal of Group 1; have another defend and improve the proposal of Group 2; and have a third team/group serve as the Field management. This adds a great deal of life and realism to the class discussion.

Discussion flows nicely by proceeding question by question, considering each proposal alternatively. In each instance where students criticize a proposal, they should be pushed for **specific** changes. This will illustrate the difficulty of specifying all details of a study a priori.

CASE 1-4

UNITED WAY OF AMERICA

INTRODUCTION

This case illustrates the multiple issues related to the decisions involved in undertaking research by a nonprofit organization. The context is the United Way of America, a nonprofit membership organization for 2,300 local United Ways across the United States. The case describes United Way's customers, information needs, research designs and data sources. This case encompasses all elements of the first four chapters and introduces the students to the subject matter covered in Part Two of the text.

OBJECTIVES OF THE CASE

1) To give students an opportunity to examine the elements of a management's decision situation and how it coincides with the marketing research process.
2) To allow students to objectively identify, formulate, and understand a nonprofit organization's need for marketing research.
3) To introduce students to the use and value of varying research designs and data sources.

QUESTIONS TO BE ASSIGNED

1) What marketing management problems and opportunities form the basis for United Way of America's need for marketing research?
2) What research objectives might the United Way have for the marketing research that it implements?
3) What information needs might the United Way have for the marketing research that it implements?
4) Evaluate the research designs that the United Way utilizes.
5) Evaluate the appropriateness of each of the data sources that the United Way utilizes.

CASE ANALYSIS

Problems and Opportunities as Basis for Marketing Research

There is no activity more critical to the success of the formal research process than a clear and concise statement of problems and/or opportunities. Marketing managers need to be cautious to not merely react to symptoms or vague feelings regarding a problem or opportunity.

United Way's initial problem is a constantly changing customer base and marketing environment. The United Way serves broad numbers and types of customers, and as the parent organization it is sensitive to the fact that the services provided must keep pace with the organization's needs. In many situations, knowledge regarding the underlying cause of the decision situation is unknown. In these cases, the United Way uses exploratory research to help facilitate the development of its statement of problems and opportunities.

Class discussion should generate a list of problems and opportunities. United Way's markets include corporate donors, volunteers, people in need, and local United Way organizations. Some problem and opportunity examples include: (1) Donor contributions from large businesses have decreased while medium to small businesses' contributions have increased; (2) Total volunteer hours has increased; (3) Total population of homeless persons outside of metropolitan areas have increased; (4) Participation in recent training sessions has been declining. Once these have been clearly established and prioritized, specific research objectives and information needs can be addressed.

The United Way's research needs are broad and extensive, requiring the use of multiple data sources and specialized research projects.

Research Objectives

In general, research objectives define the purpose of the research project. Using the students' original list of problems and opportunities, a list of research objectives can be established. Some examples include: (1) To categorize corporations based on their likelihood of philanthropic contribution; (2) To compare philanthropic causes with regard to dimensions indicative of corporate preference and volunteer potential; (3) To evaluate the effectiveness of United Way donations to homeless communities; (4) To compare current and potential internal training sessions with regard to dimensions indicative of organizational acceptance and usefulness.

The more detailed the statement of research objectives, the more it coincides with the list of information needs.

Information Needs

Once the objectives of a research project are established, specific information is needed to facilitate decision making. The United Way's information needs are as varied as its objectives. Statements of information needs often are typified by the following phrases: (1) To rank markets...; (2) To classify programs...; and (3) To calculate break-even contributions ... illustrated over a period of five years.

From these initial statements, focus group guidelines, formal questionnaire questions, and interview questions can be established. Each line of questioning should correspond directly to the research objective and information need. It should also be stressed that many data collection processes impose limitations on the types of information that can be collected.

Evaluation of Research Designs

Analysis preceding the actual research determines the necessity of the research and insures that the research conducted satisfies the requirements of the decision process. Different types of research are most appropriately used at different stages of the decision process. A research design is the basic plan which guides the data collection and analysis and should be a function of the research objectives.

Exploratory

This type of research needs to be flexible and is best used when the decision maker(s) need(s) more information than is currently available. Since the United Way states that it is an information provider, exploratory research helps to tap into new areas for formalized research studies, as well as uncovers attitudes and trends for future use. Much of United Way's research is in this area. Tracking trends, performing focus groups, and collecting market information are all examples of exploratory research. By providing this information, United Way is not conclusively telling or suggesting to its "customers" what to do, rather it is allowing them to use the information for their own purposes. One danger of this type of research is that information may be collected for "information's sake" instead of meeting a set objective. To ensure that this information is actually of value, the United Way should undertake performance monitoring research among its customer base.

Conclusive

Conclusive research is characterized by clearly defined research objectives and information needs, as well as formalized research procedures. Its purpose is to allow for the evaluation and selection between alternatives. The United Way undertakes national studies based on their exploratory research. It is important to understand who the decision makers are in this process. The Strategic Planning Committee makes recommendations based on the results of these studies to local United Ways and the United Way of America. This method may be effective; however, the decision makers should be involved in the process whenever possible.

Performance Monitoring

The purpose of this form of research is to signal the presence of potential problems or opportunities, similar to exploratory research. It involves monitoring performance measures, marketing mix variables, and situation variables. Much of the United Way's research falls in this category. While this information may give it a better understanding of its customer base, it should be conducted consistently and should be communicated back to the "customer."

Evaluation of Data Sources

There are four basic sources of marketing data: respondents, study of case histories and simulations, experimentation, and secondary data. The United Way relies on secondary data for much of its statistical information and on respondent data for much of its attitudinal information. The appropriateness of these data sources depends on how the information is used. Focus groups should only be used to guide future research or to gain insight into a subject, and can not be used to statistically generalize opinions to a population. Secondary information is fast and relatively inexpensive, however its value is limited since it was originally collected for a different objective. This limitation needs to be understood by the user.

Specific Data Sources - Statistical

Environmental Analysis - secondary information and analysis.

Comparative Cities - formal data collection

Performance Data on Local United Ways - formal data collection via surveys

Published Corporate Information - secondary data collected and maintained

Specific Data Sources - Attitudinal

National Polls - information gleaned from secondary data

Focus Groups - first hand information geared toward volunteers and to test their advertising effectiveness.

Tracking Local United Way organizations - observation and formal data collection.

TEACHING STRATEGY

Begin the class discussion by briefly reviewing the case facts and then asking the class for a list of the business decisions to be made. It would be helpful to write the list on a blackboard or overhead projector so that the class can refer back to it for analysis of the information needs and research designs to support each decision. More time should be spent discussing the decision process and information needs than the research design itself, since at this point students have not learned much about the details of doing the research.

CASE 1-5

ETHICAL DIMENSIONS IN MARKETING RESEARCH

INTRODUCTION

This case presents ten situations that occur in the real world of marketing research. Each raises one or more ethical issues that must be reconciled by a marketing research supplier or in-house marketing research department. While there are no precise "right" and "wrong" solutions, some cases may seem easier to resolve than others.

OBJECTIVES OF THE CASE

1) To give students an idea of some of the ethical concerns encountered in the marketing research world by both practitioners and managers.
2) To initiate class discussion and debate about very real issues that must be resolved in daily practice.
3) To show students, through discussion and debate, that while one may easily resolve a hypothetical issue individually, when more than one person has input the situation is much more complicated.

QUESTIONS TO BE ASSIGNED

For each situation and question, identify what you believe to be the ethical issue and indicate what you would do.

CASE ANALYSIS

The case analysis answers indicate what most practitioners would say in response to these questions.

Episode 1 - Competitive Proposals

Although some professional marketing research societies disagree, the firms submitting bids were not obligated to make proposals. Therefore, the practice is generally considered ethical. While the proposals would differ in many ways, hopefully the basic issues have been similarly identified by all bidders. Since guarantees have not been made, the client may feel free to use the ideas.

Episode 2 - Reuse of Questionnaire Questions

This practice is ethical when the appropriate questions have already been developed. Good questions belong in a researcher's inventory and should be used.

Episode 3 - Adding one client's questions to another questionnaire

Since the client assumes an exclusive study has been commissioned, this is unethical. To compromise at all on this is to open the door to significant abuse.

Episode 4 - Major error

When errors are discovered, suppliers have an ethical obligation to point them out to the client. Errors must be uncovered and discussed to maintain research quality. When a client is dependent upon a supplier for information, there is a clear responsibility to report errors since it may affect the resulting decisions.

Episode 5 - Studies for competing firms

While there is a moral and ethical obligation to keep the data sets and studies confidential and separate, the practice itself is ethical. The marketing community in a given area is often too small to expect exclusive arrangements on a large scale.

Episode 6 - Cannot make deadline

Knowingly accepting an assignment whose time constraints cannot be met is unethical. It happens often enough that a supplier must beg for extensions for truly unexpected delays.

Episode 7 - Entertainment and gifts

There is a fine line dividing what is and is not ethical. While expensive gifts and kickbacks are out of line, business-social lunches or tickets to sporting events are more difficult to judge. One rule is to treat clients or prospective clients as one would treat friends or social acquaintances. Clearly one rule is "one does not buy clients." Often either the client's or supplier's firm has policies that should not be violated. If either believes that their relationship revolves around continued favors, the relationship is unethical. But if neither expects favors or preferential treatment, it can be argued that the situation is ethical. Perceptions, expectations and assumptions, rather than a given behavior in every situation, determine what is and is not ethical behavior.

Episode 8 - Footnoting true author

Unless it was contracted that a particular person write the report, a report should represent a corporate product so footnoting is considered ethical. What is perhaps more important is that if the issue is raised, the main contributors should be given appropriate recognition.

Episode 9 - Professional/personal dilemma

If an individual feels he/she cannot objectively complete a research project, he/she has an obligation to refuse to accept it or request that it be assigned to another researcher. This is similar to an issue found in advertising where an account executive does not want to be assigned to a product such as a liquor or cigarette account. On the other hand, an individual should use this option with great discretion. For most cases an individual should be able to shelve his/her personal opinions and conduct an objective piece of research.

Episode 10 - Ultraviolet ink

At issue here is whether the practice of the ultraviolet ink is ethical and what the rights of the respondents are. In Crawford's research (Journal of Marketing, 1970), over 70 percent of the line marketers and research directors disapproved of this practice. When a respondent is assured that his/her response is confidential, that expectation should never be violated. Such a practice undermines the honesty and integrity of the research firm.

Episode 11 - Understanding length of interview

The issue at hand is whether it is ethical for an interviewer to lie about the interview length. This is common practice and some researchers feel that it is justified by the increase in response rates. Others, however, feel that any type of lie is unethical and should not be used in practice. By grossly understating the length of the interview, an interviewer runs the risk of irritating the respondent, which may reduce the quality of the responses near the end of the interview. Also, this practice may increase refusal rates in the long run if the respondent builds a mistrust of interviewers and the interviewing process. The instructor should encourage students to debate this issue during the class discussion.

Episode 12 - Hidden recording devices

Some researchers feel that recording people as they shop does not present an ethical problem, as long as the recording device does not tape conversations that could not be heard by the human ear alone. They argue that because the family is in public, the researcher is not being exposed to behaviors he or she should not be observing. On the other hand, many people feel that respondents have a right to know they are being recorded, and a right to refuse to be in the study. A middle ground opinion shared by many researchers is that hidden recordings are acceptable research tools as long as respondents are informed (after the fact) that they were recorded, and they are given the option of whether or not to be included in the study. As before, the instructor should foster debate among students regarding this issue.

Episode 13 - Sorting through trash

First, the researcher should check with the proper authorities about the legality of looking through peoples' trash. On the positive side, this is common practice in sociological research on culture. A precedent has been set for using trash-sorting as a research. On the other hand, many researchers would view this as an invasion of privacy, and thus an unacceptable research methodology.

TEACHING STRATEGY

Each episode should be discussed individually. Try to reach a consensus on each issue and examine them at the end of the period to see how the "policies" are related to one another and whether they are consistent. Additional current social issues may be examined. Role playing and/or encouraging different prospectives to be presented and supported is one way to view a given issue from its many angles. One should remember and point out that it is always easier to commit oneself in a hypothetical situation. Overall, let students say their piece no matter what.

CASE 2-1

AGT, INC.

INTRODUCTION

This case describes an international business problem and corresponding marketing research proposal. AGT, Inc. is a marketing research company located in Karachi, Pakistan, which has been asked by Jeff Sons Trading Company (JST) to research the validity and profitability of an amusement park in Karachi. The case recaps the learnings from Part One, introduces data collection procedures, and exposes the students to the complexities of conducting research in an international arena.

OBJECTIVES OF THE CASE

1) To introduce students to some of the issues involved in conducting marketing research in countries outside of the G-7 industrialized world (United States, Canada, Japan, Great Britain, France, Italy, and Germany).
2) To allow students to look at the effects of the elements of culture on the overall design of a marketing research study, specifically the data collection method and the selection of a sample.
3) To have students think about the relationship between the type of business decision to be made, information needs, and the type of research best studied to gather that information
4) To illustrate the variety of methods and sources of data available to aid in marketing decision making.

QUESTIONS TO BE ASSIGNED

1) What marketing management problems and opportunities form the basis for JST's need for marketing research?
2) What research objectives does JST have for the marketing research that it implements?
3) What information needs does JST have for marketing research that it plans to implement?
4) Evaluate the research designs that AGT proposes for JST.
5) Evaluate the appropriateness of each of the data sources that AGT proposes for JST.

CASE ANALYSIS

The case implies that the amusement park concept was a result of JST's understanding of the Karachi entertainment/recreation market. Research is needed to test this concept in order to reach a go/no go decision on the business proposal. There are two approaches that need to be taken: exploratory and conclusive. Exploratory and descriptive research will uncover unknown opportunities based on unmet market needs, while conclusive research will determine the profit potential and park design specifics. Complicating the issue is the presence of several cultural issues that need to be fully understood.

Problems and Opportunities

Opportunities:
- Current recreational facilities in Karachi are physically very small and crowded.
- There is not a sufficient number of parks for the size of the Karachi population.
- The higher social classes have the money and are willing to spend money on recreational vacations with their families.

Problems:
- Majority of population does not have the money to spend on leisure activities (low real per capita GDP).
- Unstable government situation
- Poor communication system: postal and telephone services
- A limited infrastructure with a lack of public and private transportation
- High crime rate
- Difficulties in data collection
- Wealthy class tends to leave the city for vacations

Research Objectives

The case states two objectives: (1) Identify the potential demand for this project and (2) Identify the primary target market and what they expect in an amusement area. AGT could have expanded these business needs/objectives by breaking them into more actionable statements by following the categories identified in their information needs section of the proposal.

Market/Consumer
- Is there a need for this project?
- Who are the target consumers?
- Is this a viable business?

Location
- Where should this project be located to attract the most visitors?
- What additional complications will arise due to the selected location? - transportation, security, accommodations, media options, etc.

Recreation Facilities
- What attractions are best suited to the target market?
- What should the pricing strategy be?
- What are the best hours of operations, capacity and public availability guidelines?

Information Needs

Similar to the limitations of the JST's stated research objectives, the information needs outlined in the case do not provide enough detail to effectively design the research. Some of the information needs statements are more accurately defined as objective statements. The problem and opportunity analysis identified a number of cultural difficulties involved in carrying out the research and also need to be considered when identifying the information needs. Consider whether or not this information can be obtained.

Market
- What are the different market segment(s)?
- What is the buying power of each of the market segments?
- What are the needs of each market segment?
- Do these needs support the concept of an amusement park?
- Which market segment(s) (if any) have the ability to support a profitable venture?
- What are the cultural differences and/or cultural faux pas issues?

Consumer
- Are the target segments satisfied with the existing facilities in the area? What unmet needs do these segments have?
- What pricing structure (one time admission fee, per ride fee) will most appeal to these segments? What price levels?
- Will these segments have a sufficient utilization rate to cover the cost of investment and operations?
- What media could be used to get the message across successfully to the potential customers?

Location
- Where should this project be built to attract the target segment(s)?
- Will transportation need to be arranged? Accommodations? Security?
- How does location affect the costs of the investment?

Recreation Facilities
- What attractions will most appeal to the target segment(s)?
- What should the hours of operation be?
- What food and entertainment should be available?
- What language(s) will the signs and park information be printed in?

Research Designs and Data Sources

A variety of research tools can and should be used to meet JST's information needs. The best research plan for this project would incorporate all of them: secondary information, exploratory research, descriptive research, and conclusive research.

Accurate and reliable secondary information may be difficult to obtain, but, it is a good starting point to determine the local demographics for market segmentation, researching optimal locations, and competitive options.

Exploratory research might provide interesting insights about the consumers' decision making process in choosing where and why they select a recreational location. Knowing this can be very helpful to the research process because it enables the information seeker to put more effort into the researching of areas that customers consider important, and less effort into the unimportant areas. Exploratory research could also be used to get feedback on the concept of an amusement park, stimulating ideas for the specific facilities and identifying unmet customer needs.

Descriptive research involves "listening to the customer" and would be useful for understanding the demographic, psychographic and physiographic characteristics, consumption patterns, and unmet needs of each potential market segment.

Conclusive research could be used to obtain quantitative information to verify the hypotheses developed through exploratory and descriptive research. It would also be helpful in determining potential sales, cost and, ultimately, profit figures. If the project is accepted, performance monitoring research could be conducted to track and adjust the marketing plans in place.

In AGT, Inc., the data collection method is affected by two elements of culture: (1) material culture, specifically the economics of the populace and the country's infrastructure, and (2) the belief system (i.e., the Islamic religion).

Social institutions affect the collection of the data, design of the questionnaire, and the selection of the sample. It also will affect the selection of the people to administer the questionnaire and where the data is to be collected. The issue is practicality in regards to getting the response needed while maintaining sensitivity to the caste system.

Language can have a unique effect on the research as only 7% of the population speaks Urdu, the official language. The rest of the population speaks a variety of dialects and regional languages. Pakistan is a former British colony (part of India until independence and partition) and English is understood by the educated population, which might alleviate the problem for this survey. However, this would offer a good discussion opportunity on how it might affect other research directed at a larger segment of the population.

A few questions to stimulate discussion and introduce future concepts include:

1) What types of survey method(s) will be most efficient for each information need?
2) How can you insure a random sample? Is it needed?
3) Will the results be free of bias? Does it matter?
4) Can the results be projected onto the general population?
5) How will the need to administer the surveys in multiple languages affect the results?

TEACHING STRATEGY

Begin class by briefly reviewing the case and then asking the students for a list of the business decisions needed to be made (i.e., market segment, location, facilities, financial viability, etc.). It would be helpful to write the list on a blackboard or overhead so that the class can refer back to it for discussion of the complexities of the international market, information needs and corresponding research design options. More time should be spent discussing the effects of the elements of culture (i.e., material culture, social institutions, belief systems, aesthetics, and language) on the design and how these cultural issues affect the information needs, rather than focusing on the details of the research plan.

Note: this case was derived from an actual market study commissioned in 1993. Recently, the political situation in Karachi has further eroded, disrupting many of the business and civilian functions.

CASE 2-2

TWIN PINES GOLF AND COUNTRY CLUB (A)

INTRODUCTION

This case presents: (1) the decision-making problem of the Twin Pines Golf and Country Club (TPG&CC) as it was given to the Capital Planning Committee of the TPG&CC by the club's president; (2) the research design utilized to provide information related to this decision; (3) the questionnaire used; (4) the results of a survey that were presented to the committee; and (S) a demographic profile of the committee members.

It is designed to be used early in the marketing research course in the section related to the managerial preliminaries to undertaking research. The results of the meeting are contained in TPG&CC (B) which appears at the end of this teaching note.

OBJECTIVES OF THE CASE

1) To show the research and decision-making difficulties arising from poor problem definition.
2) To show the need for firmly established decision criteria prior to undertaking research, and what can happen when this aspect is neglected.
3) To show the effect of personal background, interests, attitudes, etc. on the interpretation of research results (i.e., when the (A) case is used in conjunction with the TPG&CC (B) case as described below).
4) To give students early experience in interpreting one-and two-way tables and the specification of possible additional analysis.
5) To give students early experience in critically evaluating a questionnaire.

Due to the early positioning of this case in the course, objectives 1-4 above take priority over 5. Students as a way out of addressing "real" issues in the case will jump to a critique of the questionnaire. The instructor should stop this and force the discussion back to the other issues. See "Teaching Strategy" below for further discussion of this point.

QUESTIONS TO BE ASSIGNED

1) What action should the committee take?
2) Why?

Being any more specific than this will give too much away to the student. They should be expected to struggle mentally with the issues listed below as part of answering questions 1) and 2) above, and they should be knowledgeable about the issues from reading the introductory chapters of the text.

CASE ANALYSIS

Problem Definition

Exactly why and with what objectives has the president of TPG&CC asked this committee to examine possible new facilities for the club? It should be brought out in discussion that his letter to the committee provides little help. Let's examine his directive:

"We must be prepared to add new facilities to serve the current and future interests of our members and to attract new members..."

Note: (1) the new members issue is not being fully researched by the committee; they have only surveyed current members. (2) There is potential for major conflict between current and future interests of members; note from Exhibit 3 that if the future is given priority and the attitudes of intermediate members represent the wave of the future, then the pool appears a clear winner. However, if current interests are given priority, then the "correct" decision becomes more confused. (3) Just what does the president mean by "our members"? He implies that one position will satisfy all or most members. Clearly, a student in marketing should know by now that segments are likely to exist in the membership; Exhibit 3 shows this to be so. Which segment has priority or are we to deal with just the aggregate results as presented in Exhibit 2?

Possible causes of the president's request include: (1) the club is having trouble attracting new members; (2) intermediate members are not taking up senior membership on their 26th birthday to the degree necessary to keep membership at a proper level; (3) some senior members have made new facilities requests at the 19th hole (the bar) to the president from time to time; (4) there is no cause other than that the president himself thought a review was in order. Other causes are also possible.

What is important is that a different research design or no study at all should result from each possible cause. The problem has been poorly stated and the committee has failed to ask the right questions of the president. They are lost before they begin.

Decision-Making Criteria

The results in Exhibit 2 show that there is no clear winner or loser among the projects. How then does one decide what to do? In the absence of clearly stated criteria, the decision is likely to become caught up in the personal biases of those making the decision. All marketing managers (and committee members) have vested interests. Thus, it is absolutely essential to have established criteria. In this case, the committee has not done so. We would then predict that the meeting would be one of much subjective interpretation of the survey results. TPG&CC (B) shows this to be true.

Effects of Personal Background, Etc.

As noted above, the absence of criteria brings personal backgrounds, etc. very strongly into play in the decision situation. After the class discussion has run for some time on what decision to make and why (30-40 minutes) the instructor should ask the class to speculate on what decision the committee made and why. This should lead to a discussion of the backgrounds, attitudes, family situation, etc. of each member as presented in the case. The TPG&CC (B) case should then be handed out and have the class read it (reproduce it from this manual) or read it to the class if you prefer not to reproduce it for distribution.

After the class has read TPG&CC (B) ask them what has gone on at the May 15 meeting. The students should note that the committee members appear to be responding in relation to their own situations. For example, Johnston and Taylor, who favor the pool, are still at an age when they might use the pool themselves, plus their children are definitely potential users. In contrast, Robinson, Hains and Wecker, who are against the pool, have no children at an age to benefit from the pool.

The issue is how does one avoid this type of situation in dealing with research data. The need for decision criteria is obvious. Indeed, in the early discussion did the students interject their own biases into their arguments? Ask those who took certain positions what sports they are interested in.

Interpretation of the Data Presented

The tables are not complex. The following is a simple summary of what is in them:

(1) The response rate to the questionnaire varied by membership category; senior men were the highest (Exhibit 1).
(2) There was no project that was clearly preferred (Exhibit 2). Golf, swimming, and tennis club houses all seem possible. Interestingly, the latter project received no support in the committee meeting. We can only speculate why.
(3) Project preference varies greatly by membership category (Exhibit 3). The intermediates much prefer the pool and tennis club house. The senior preferences are more evenly spread across projects.
(4) The results of Exhibit 4 are much the same as Exhibit 2. Also note that this exhibit was never used by the committee in making a decision. It appears to be redundant information.

Possible Additional Analysis

The instructor should ask the students to suggest additional tables that would have proven useful to the committee. Some possible tables are listed below:

(1) A two-way table of the preferred projects by the preferred projects, i.e., this would show, for example, what other projects those favoring the golf holes also wanted.
(2) A table indicating how many members preferred no projects. Are the "no" answers the same people for each project?

The Questionnaire

Students will like to be critical of the questionnaire, but should only be allowed to do so near the end of the class. Other issues are more important here. Some criticisms of the questionnaire include:

(1) The effect of putting the total cost numbers in question 3: this is likely to confuse the respondent and possibly bias his responses to questions 3A and 3B.
(2) The effect of the projects on fees (question 4) is for senior members only; will they be paying the whole amount? An intermediate member would expect that he is getting a "free" ride, so why not answer "yes"?
(3) Questions 3 and 4 appear redundant.
(4) The committee did not use question 3 at all, so why ask it?
(5) Question 2 was not used, so why ask it?

Also, the instructor should ask the students what additional questions need to be asked.

A Census

The instructor should note to the class that this study involved the use of a census of the club membership. More typically, marketing research surveys make use of samples. It should be pointed out that a sample could have been used here. Because a census was taken, the concepts of estimation, confidence intervals, inference, etc., have no place. The errors that are likely to be active here are non-response error (some members did not respond) and measurement error (the question asked). These latter topics are dealt with in more detail in later sections of the text. The instructor may want to mention these aspects in passing at this time.

One other related problem is that the response rates of the various membership categories are different. The senior males have responded the most, etc. In the analysis presented, the responses of this group are thus overrepresented as compared to their true proportion of club members. Similarly, intermediate responses are underrepresented. The responses could be weighted to put them in their proper proportions. However, this assumes that the responses of those who did respond are representative of those who did not. Also, it could be argued that those responding are more interested and should have more voice.

TEACHING STRATEGY

The instructor should begin the class by asking what decisions the committee should make and why. Some students may try to duck this by starting an evaluation of the questionnaire or by being critical of some other aspect of the research. The instructor should stop this cold by pointing out that: "the committee has a deadline to meet, and it is a little late for them to attack these other issues. Decisions are made with incomplete information and usually some bad information. So let's have your decision."

When this is done, a diversity of options with respect to project selection usually occurs. In this way the personal differences of the class are allowed to come into play. The class will quite often mirror the discussions in the TPG&CC (B) case. Thus, the lesson of the need for better problem definition and decision criteria are brought home to the students much more so than any lecture can give. A later lecture could reinforce this class experience.

When the discussion on project selection and the underlying reasoning has run its course, the instructor should interject the TPG&CC (B) case. The discussion should then deal with what happened in the (B) case and why, then to the issues of problem definitions, decision criteria, data analysis, questionnaire construction, and the fact that this was a census.

Epilogue

As of the publication date of this text, no further action has been taken by the club in this regard.

TWIN PINES GOLF AND COUNTRY CLUB (B)

At 8:00 p.m. on May 15 the members of the Capital Planning Committee of the Twin Pines Golf and Country Club met to reach a decision concerning what capital project or projects to recommend to the Board of Directors of the club.

In making a decision, they intended to make use of the results of a survey of the membership that they had undertaken. The background of the survey and the associated results are presented in Twin Pines Golf and Country Club (A). A biographical description of the committee members is given in Appendix 1.

May 15 Meeting

The following is part of the discussion that occurred at the May 15 meeting.

Mr. Watts, the Chairman, opened the meeting.

J. B. Watts: Before we dig into the results of our membership survey, I want to thank Bruce, Bob and Ken for their hard and excellent work in polling the membership. It looks to me like they've done a great job....

All members banged on the large oak desk in the Twin Pines board room. Mr. Watts then continued.

J. B. Watts: ... Ken, perhaps...eh, you could pull your findings together and tell us what the membership wants.

K. L. Wecker: I'll try, Mr. Chairman, but it's not very clear cut to me, what the membership told us.... The swimming pool was most favored with...eh...about 35 percent saying yes to it; and...

B. A. Frederick: I guess to be exact, Ken, it should be noted that it was 37.1 percent, with the golf and tennis club house tied for second at 33 percent.

K. L. Wecker: Yes, that's it. Thank you, Bruce. I guess the members are saying they want a swimming pool. I must say, it is not the result I had expected. I'm not even sure I believe it.

L. G. Johnston: Well, times do change, Ken...the composition of the memberships, the popular recreation activities...maybe it's time for a pool. After all, we added tennis when the membership wanted it.

R. H. Robertson: Hold on! (banging table gently). It looks to me that the membership has said no to the swimming pool. Sixty percent to be exact. No other project got as many no responses. When close to two-thirds say no, I don't think we should proceed. Also, is 37 percent really a meaningful difference from the 33 percent for golf and tennis? These two are also looked upon less negatively. The new nine holes is almost as positive as the pool and the least negative. I think we should seriously consider recommending the golf alternative. After all, this organization was founded as a golf club.

The discussion went on for about half an hour on the issue of whether the positive or negative responses were the most important. At that point, Dr. Malcolm R. Richardson spoke for the first time.

M. R. Richardson: I don't think we're getting anywhere here. It seems to me that we can get a better feel for the membership's desires if we look at the preferences that each type of membership holds. I think this shows that it is the intermediates who want the pool...the seniors want the golf.

J. B. Watts: Maybe it comes down to which membership category should we try to please. You know the young people are very important to the long-run well-being of this club. What do you think about a pool to attract younger members?... Gary, what do you think about this idea?

L. G. Johnston: I guess by now everyone knows my position on this...let's recommend the pool...it was mot preferred overall and will surely allow the young people to use the club more, as you suggest, Mr. Chairman.

J. B. Taylor: I'm inclined to agree. Why not a pool? The club needs it.

R. H. Robertson: I think you've lost sight of one thing, eh... eh..., it's the senior members who pay most of the shot around here. I don't think they want all the trouble... eh, kids running around, etc., that a pool will bring.

W. L. Hains: That's certainty how I feel about it; and it seems to me that that's exactly what the senior members have told us in our pool. Just look at the numbers.

K. L. Wecker: Maybe the real answer in all this is that the membership wants us to do nothing. After all, no project was picked by a majority of the members. Doing nothing is a viable alternative for us...you know.

J. B. Watts: Perhaps you're right, Ken. I think we should have that point in mind. We can always undertake capital projects when the members really want them.

The discussion continued for an hour or so. The main topic was whether or not the members really wanted any of the projects, and if they want one whether it was golf holes or a pool. Finally, at 10:45 p.m., the chairman asked for a vote. All committee members voted to do nothing at this time.

APPENDIX 1

BIOGRAPHICAL DESCRIPTION OF CAPITAL PLANNING COMMITTEE MEMBERS

	Age	Family	Occupation	Club Activities
Mr. John B. Watts	62	Married, 2 boys ages 29 and 27	President, Exeter Tool Company	Golf
Dr. L. Gary Johnston	45	Married, 1 girl age 20; 2 boys ages 17 and 12	Dentist	Golf, Tennis
Mr. Joseph R. Taylor	35	Married, 1 boy age 7	Lawyer	Golf
Mr. Robert H. Robertson*	59	Married, 3 girls ages 32, 30 and 27	President, Robertson Advertising	Golf
Dr. Malcolm R. Richardson	42	Unmarried	Internal Medicine Specialist	Golf, Tennis
Mr. Kenneth L. Wecker	69	Widower, 2 girls, ages 42 and 38	Retired, President, Alpha Assoc., Management Consultant	Golf
Dr. W. Lloyd Hains	53	Married, no children	General Practitioner	Golf
Mr. Bruce A. Fredrick*	46	Married, 1 boy age 16	Sales Mgr., Beta Elect.	Golf

*Member research subcommittee.

CASE 2-3

AUTOMOTIVE SUPPLY, INC.

INTRODUCTION

The context of the case is an air conditioning and heating contractor, Automotive Supply, Inc., is experiencing a downturn in business. Automotive Supply has requested a proposal to help formulate a long-range growth strategy. The case requires students to appraise a statement of information needs and research objectives as it relates to the decision process. Students must evaluate the research design as it links back to the recognition of a situation calling for a decision and the subsequent decision to undertake research.

OBJECTIVES OF THE CASE

1) To show the importance of correctly defining the decision problem before undertaking a research project.

2) To demonstrate the importance of clearly identifying information needs and research objectives so that they accurately reflect the decision problem.

3) To illustrate the variety and availability of secondary data.

4) To illustrate the difference between information and data.

5) To give students exposure to and experience in evaluating a research design and data collection framework.

6) To examine the appropriateness of exploratory and conclusive research.

QUESTIONS TO BE ASSIGNED

1) Evaluate the stated research objective and the information needs presented in the proposal.

2) Are the data sources appropriate to the information needs and research objectives? Why or why not?

3) Evaluate the data collection framework.

4) What other possible research design and data sources could be used?

CASE ANALYSIS

Automotive's sales decline is a symptom of a problem, it is not a problem in itself. Douglass's assumption that the problem is caused by an influx of foreign imports is not necessarily true. Parts sales could be done for several reasons: a decline in domestic auto sale, an increase in the number of competitors, low company awareness, poor company reputation, or changing market needs. Students should recognize the need for a thorough situation analysis and exploratory research to uncover and better understand the real problem(s). Exploratory research would provide Douglass with additional insight and knowledge of the problems and opportunities. From this, hypotheses about the cause of the symptoms could be formulated from which conclusive research should be based.

Research Objective and Information Needs

The stated objectives relate to the information needs, to the ultimate research outcomes. The research objectives should include identification of the causes of the sales decline and alternative remedies. The statement of research objectives and information needs merely represents an ultimate goal of data collection for any marketer, but does not appear "customized" for meeting Automotive's needs. In other words, the objectives should indicate the need for both exploratory and conclusive research.

The stated information needs imply a causal link between (A) accurate demand forecasts and sufficient inventory and (B) success, as measured by sales. This is only a small part of the picture. Many other factors affect sales/success. Forecasts and inventory decisions may be accurate, yet Automotive may still experience flat or declining sales. The major problem here is that the stated information needs are not based on an accurate formulation of the decision problem.

Data Sources

The data sources are very general and will provide Douglass with information about trends in demand and consumer characteristics. Automotive may well benefit from research beyond the use of secondary data. For needed exploratory research, secondary data is appropriate. The use of interviews and case histories may yield useful information as well. The information must relate back to the decision problem and to Automotive and its problems. Large amounts of data can be collected without it having value. This is especially true when the problem is not clearly defined, or is defined incorrectly. During conclusive research, the data sources must provide information linking relevant variables to be of value. In summary, the proposed data sources can provide useful information if it is understood how to use the data. Overall, however, secondary data are insufficient for the task at hand.

Data Collection Framework

The data collection framework utilizes secondary data which is readily available from journals, government publications, and local sources. Some of the advantages of using secondary data include the ease of access and collection, low cost, and fast retrieval. However, it seldom suffices. Since the data is collected for other purposes, its accuracy is not guaranteed and there is rarely a complete fit. Therefore, while it is a good idea to include secondary data, a research project based entirely upon it may not provide adequate information.

Other Research Designs

Other possible research designs include the use of exploratory, conclusive, and performance monitoring research. Appropriate supplemental data sources include interviews with industry experts, the use of case histories, and internal company data. In this case, the causal model (that imports caused the sales decline) could be tested via causal research.

TEACHING STRATEGY

Direct the discussion so that students have clearly identified the major problems in the research design. The major issue is the failure to identify and specify the decision problem. If students do not recognize this at the onset, let the analysis proceed for a while and then bring up the issue. Once the major problems have been identified it is useful to discuss, in depth, the formulation of an appropriate research design.

CASE 2-4

NESTLÉ

INTRODUCTION

This case describes how Nestlé, an international packaged goods manufacturer and marketer, has incorporated information systems and creative marketing techniques to become more competitive. It requires students to understand the marketing situation that led to this need and to understand how databases can be used to enhance marketing strategies. It also raises the issues of ethical responsibilities and complications related to using customer databases and marketing decision support systems.

OBJECTIVES OF THE CASE

1) To demonstrate the value of a marketing information system within an organization.
2) To illustrate how technical advances in the field of marketing research can aid organizations in their need to adapt to competition.
3) To introduce students to the complexities of developing an effective Marketing Decision Support System (MDSS).
4) To introduce students to the ethical dilemmas associated with the use of customer databases.

QUESTIONS TO BE ASSIGNED

1) What marketing management problems have led Nestlé to establish these types of databases?
2) What types of marketing management questions may these types of databases help provide answers for?
3) What are the technical requirements and costs associated with the development of these types of databases?
4) How should a marketing decision support system (an MDSS) interface with these types of databases?
5) Are there any ethical question raised by Nestlé's having this database? If yes, what are they?

CASE ANALYSIS

Marketing Management Problems

Despite being a powerful name in consumer products, Nestlé was feeling the negative effects of strong competition. Nestlé was finding that its products were not well differentiated from copy-cat economy-priced products, yet the Nestlé products were significantly higher priced. In order to maintain and/or increase sales, Nestlé needed to implement more innovative marketing tactics than traditional mass advertising and distribution.

Marketing Management Questions and Answers via Databases

A database is only as good as the information contained within it. Nestlé was able to use information gleaned from the returned reply cards as well as their toll-free calls to build a relatively reliable, up-to-date customer/prospect database. Depending on how and what information is collected, a database like Nestlé's may be able to provide marketing answers to the following types of questions:

- Who are our current customers (i.e.. names, addresses, phone, etc.)
- What is our current customer profile (i.e. demographics, psychographics, buying habits, etc.)
- Who are our potential customers (Information found in the newspaper's birth announcements section)
- Who is not interested in our products
- Where our customers/noncustomers live (Are there clusters? Patterns?)
- The product life cycle related to the customer (Following the life stage of the child)
- Consumer opinions on our products or our competitor's products
- Response rates on promotions (i.e. return on investment)

Technical Requirements and Costs

The technical requirements and costs vary greatly depending on the size and configuration of the databases. In general, an organization will need a mainframe computer system that downloads information to a file server equipped with an Oracle graphic interface (or similar software interface). The basics system needs to be customizable to fit the organization's specific needs. The cost of such a combined software and hardware system ranges from $250,000 to over $5,000,000.

MDSS Interface with Databases

An MDSS is an integrated system of data, statistical analysis, modeling, and display formats using computer hardware and software to allow management to intelligently use the enormous amount of customer and product information available. These types of databases are simply the source of information for an MDSS. Connected via a computer network, the MDSS would use the data found within a database to statistically analyze and model the needed information based on predetermined methods programmed within the system.

Ideally, an MDSS provides the manager with easy-to-follow instructions, gives immediate results, provides flexibility, is and discovery-oriented. To establish an effective system, an organization needs to understand how it will use the information so that the MDSS can be programmed to manipulate the data when needed.

Ethical Questions

As in most situations, various practitioners will respond to this question in different ways. The purpose is to generate discussion and an understanding of the ethical dilemmas that surround the use of marketing databases. One should remember and point out that it is always easier to commit oneself to a hypothetical situation. Allow students to voice their differing opinions.

One ethical issue for discussion is whether or not Nestlé is misleading the consumer by disguising their sales tactics through offering consumer services intended to persuade the consumer. The toll-free number invites consumers to call the number in order to receive free baby nutrition counseling. Nestlé is able to obtain valuable customer information for future promotions and solicitations because the consumer called them first. It has been argued within the industry that this practice is ethical as long as Nestlé has identified themselves as the source of this information and is not trying to mislead the consumer into believing that the Nestlé product endorsements are coming from a third party. If the consumer information is obtained voluntarily and with the understanding that future mailing may result, the industry does not consider this to be unethical behavior.

A second issue is whether or not Nestlé is invading the consumer's privacy by obtaining their birth records through the newspaper announcements. In defense of this action, the records are public information and Nestlé does ask the consumer to either positively respond to their solicitation or they will drop the consumer from their mailing list. Again, industry experts agree that this is ethical as long as Nestlé is up-front as to how the provided information is used and that Nestlé does not mislead the consumer.

TEACHING STRATEGY

This case proceeds best if the instructor discusses each question sequentially. While this case introduces students to the use of databases in a specific marketing scenario, the customer database implementation can be applied to multiple marketing situations. As such, the questions are deliberately worded to be applied to many different organizations and environments.

CASE 3-1

THE NEW ENGLAND SOUP COMPANY

INTRODUCTION

This case describes a taste test for chowder that was conducted by a research supplier for the New England Soup Company. Background information about the company leading up to the taste test is presented along with a detailed description of the test, the results of the test, and the recommendation of the research supplier.

OBJECTIVES OF THE CASE

1) To facilitate a discussion of measurement problems in marketing research.

2) To show the importance of the correspondence between the numbers that are assigned to a characteristic of an object or event and the characteristic being measured.

3) To demonstrate the relationship between a scale of measurement used and the statistical procedures that may be applied to that scale.

4) To show the need for the measurement of reliability in marketing research.

5) To demonstrate that usefulness of measurement requires proper problem definition.

QUESTIONS TO BE ASSIGNED

1) What action should Mr. Kolander take based on the research findings?

CASE ANALYSIS

Begin the class by asking if anyone would accept the recommendation of the research supplier. If anyone wants to, ask them to state in brief overview why they would do so. Then ask what other actions people would take. Let each state why quickly. Do not let them dig into the details of the design or results at this point. This process helps position the class with respect to the research.

The instructor should then complete a list of alternatives by asking the class for possible alternatives. This list should include:

(1) Drop regular and add creamy.
(2) Drop regular and add extra creamy.
(3) Drop regular and add both.
(4) Keep regular and add creamy.
(5) Keep regular and add extra creamy.
(6) Keep regular and add both.
(7) Do nothing.
(8) Manipulate other marketing mix variables (leave a discussion of these until later).

The instructor should then direct the class to examine the way the study was executed. Again, the discussion of the resultant numbers should be left until later.

The Study Design

We note that the study design is a two-stage design. First, exploratory research was undertaken in the form of group interviews. Second, conclusive research was undertaken in the form of the taste test. This two-step process seems to make sense. The focus of the class discussion should be on the taste test.

Task of the Respondent

Students should recognize that the task of the respondent is a most difficult one. Three separate tests of five tastes each are required. The respondent has to be tired of the process by the time it is over. Can they really judge anything well at the end? This raises the question of reliability.

Reliability

With the same task being repeated three times, the opportunity exists to measure respondent taste test reliability. If significant unreliability exists, then all tabulated results are put in serious question. That is, results must be reliable to be valid. By combining the results of the three tests, the researchers have lost the opportunity to measure reliability.

The question might arise as to how the three rankings were combined to give the final ranking. The case does not state how. One might speculate, given the data analysis that follows in the case, that they add the rankings and then rerank them from 1 to 5. Given that the preference scale is ordinal, the addition is not allowed. More will be said of this below.

Scale of Measurement

If the students have read the text of Chapter 7, they should see that calculating an average chowder rating is inappropriate given ordinal preference data. Thus, the recommendation of the research company based on the averages is in question.

When a student points this out ask him or her what the appropriate measure is. The median will be forthcoming as the answer from someone in the class. This is in a sense a trap. If the median is calculated for each chowder, the conclusion based on the mean is not altered. The problem is more fundamental than this.

A closer look at the raw data reveals Kolander's regular gets a lot of 1's and 5's, as does Kolander's Extra Creamy. Also, the ranking for a subject often runs 1, 2, 3, 4, 5 and 5, 4, 3, 2, 1 across chowders (see subject 1 and 4, for example). That is, some people like chowder thin and others like it thick. The distribution of preference is bimodal, and no measure of central tendency can properly describe what is happening. In terms of product preference analysis, using a measure of central tendency is called the "majority fallacy."

Reanalyzing the Data

A useful way to reanalyze the case data is to calculate the proportion of first through fifth preference choice for each chowder. Teaching note Table 1 (TN) does this for all respondents. A further extension of this approach is to present these proportions for each brand user group. Teaching note exhibits do this as follows:

Table 2(TN): Kolander's Brand Users
Table 3 (TN): Cape Cod Brand Users
Table 4 (TN): Fisherman's Delight Brand Users.

By examining the proportions in these exhibits and even using the mean the pattern is clear. Current Kolander users prefer the thinner chowders, and constitute 45 percent of the sample. Thus, dropping the original Kolander's brand makes no sense. Cape Cod users prefer thicker formulations, and Kolander's Extra Creamy over Kolander's Creamy. They also constitute 45 percent of the sample. Thus, if a second brand is to be added, Extra Creamy seems to make more sense. Note that the mean is somewhat useful here as: (1) the data is not too far from being interval, and, more importantly, (2) by recasting the data by user brand groups the preference distribution for each is now unimodal.

When the discussion gets to this point, we suggest that you put teaching note Tables 1-4 up on the overhead to facilitate discussion (see section on Transparency Masters).

Problem Definition

It should be recognized that there are alternative explanations to taste being the problem here. Sales may be decreasing due to a loss of shelf space or price differences. Some discussion on this is appropriate, but it should be recognized that they did exploratory research to determine the problem. One hopes they did it well.

TEACHING STRATEGY

The case flows best if the instructor directs the discussion in order of the topics listed in the case analysis. Students have a tendency to want to jump into the middle of the numbers and point out that the mean is not acceptable given ordinal data. Often this blinds them to other issues such as reliability, appropriateness of any central tendency measure, problem definition, etc. It helps to have the exhibits in the teaching note available on overheads.

TABLE 1 (TN)

PROPORTION OF FIRST THROUGH FIFTH ORDER PREFERENCES FOR EACH CHOWDER

	Chowders				
	Kolander's Regular A	Fisherman's Delight B	Kolander's Creamy C	Cape Cod D	Kolander's Extra Creamy D
1st Order	.30	.10	.25	.10	.25
2nd Order	.05	.45	.10	.35	.05
3rd Order	.10	.05	.65	.10	.10
4th Order	.05	.40	.00	.45	.10
5th Order	.50	.00	.00	.00	.50
	1.00	1.00	1.00	1.00	1.00
N =	2.00	2.00	2.00	2.00	2.00
Mean =	3.4	2.8	2.4	2.9	3.6

TABLE 2 (TN)

PROPORTION OF FIRST THROUGH FIFTH ORDER PREFERENCES FOR EACH CHOWDER

(Kolander's Brand Users - 45% of Sample)

	Chowders				
	Kolander's Regular A	Fisherman's Delight B	Kolander's Creamy C	Cape Cod D	Kolander's Extra Creamy D
1st Order	.67	.11	.22	.00	.00
2nd Order	.11	.89	.00	.00	.00
3rd Order	.11	.00	.78	.11	.00
4th Order	.00	.00	.00	.89	.11
5th Order	.11	.00	.00	.00	.89
N =	1.00	1.00	1.00	1.00	1.00
Mean =	1.8	1.9	2.6	3.9	4.9

TABLE 3 (TN)
PROPORTION OF FIRST THROUGH FIFTH ORDER PREFERENCES FOR EACH CHOWDER

(Cape Cod Brand Users - 45% of Sample)

	Chowders				
	Kolander's Regular A	Fisherman's Delight B	Kolander's Creamy C	Cape Cod D	Kolander's Extra Creamy D
1st Order	.00	.00	.22	.22	.56
2nd Order	.00	.00	.11	.78	.11
3rd Order	.00	.11	.67	.00	.22
4th Order	.00	.89	.00	.00	.11
5th Order	1.00	.00	.00	.00	.00
	1.00	1.00	1.00	1.00	1.00
N =	90	90	90	90	90
Mean =	5.0	3.0	2.4	1.8	1.9

TABLE 4 (TN)
PROPORTION OF FIRST THROUGH FIFTH ORDER PREFERENCES FOR EACH CHOWDER

(Fisherman's Delight Brand Users - 10% of Sample)

	Chowders				
	Kolander's Regular A	Fisherman's Delight B	Kolander's Creamy C	Cape Cod D	Kolander's Extra Creamy D
1st Order	.00	.50	.50	.00	.00
2nd Order	.00	.50	.50	.00	.00
3rd Order	.50	.00	.00	.50	.00
4th Order	.50	.00	.00	.50	.00
5th Order	.00	.00	.00	.00	1.00
	1.00	1.00	1.00	1.00	1.00
N =	20	20	20	20	20
Mean =	3.5	1.5	1.5	3.5	5.0

CASE 3-2

CHRYSLER CAR LEASING SATISFACTION STUDY

INTRODUCTION

This case introduces a marketing need for understanding and tracking customer satisfaction in the marketing and manufacturing of cars and car leases. The case introduces the theory of customer satisfaction in relation to marketing research and allows students to explore the measurement process and debate the various attitude measurement methods available.

OBJECTIVES OF THE CASE

1) To facilitate a discussion of marketing management problems and opportunities related to the measurement of customer satisfaction.

2) To show the potential uses of marketing research in customer satisfaction studies (i.e., attitude measurement).

3) To debate the use, reliability and validity of various attitude measurement scales.

4) To discuss the use of various data in relation to management needs.

QUESTIONS TO BE ASSIGNED

1) How is customer satisfaction for the car and for the lease being measured?

2) What are the measurement scale characteristics of these customer satisfaction measures?

3) What attitude measurement approach is being taken to the measurement of customer satisfaction?

4) How should the reliability and validity of these customer satisfaction measures be measured?

5) What alternative measures of customer satisfaction could be utilized? Be specific, and be sure to consider the expectation-based approach described above.

6) What use should be made of the demographic and car description data that are also proposed to be collected?

7) How might trade-off data on attributes, which yield the importance of each attribute in forming overall satisfaction, be useful to Dodge managers?

CASE ANALYSIS

Measurement of Customer Satisfaction

The marketing research company's proposed measurement for the car and the lease has two parts. The attribute rating system follows a verbal rating scale. This is an ordinal scale, but would probably be close enough to an interval scale to be treated that way in data analysis. In effect, the attribute ratings have a 1 - 5 rating with distances among the numerals corresponding to the distances among the attitudes prescribed (i.e., excellent, very good, good, fair, and poor). These ratings can not be directly compared to one another to obtain a preference for one attribute over another.

The proposed overall satisfaction measurements for the car and lease is also a verbal rating scale. In effect, the opinion ratings have a 1 - 5 rating with distances among the numerals corresponding to the distances among the opinion prescribed (i.e., completely satisfied, very satisfied, somewhat satisfied, somewhat dissatisfied, and very dissatisfied). Satisfaction ratings can not be directly correlated to attribute ratings.

Measurement Scale Characteristics

Measurement is intended to develop a correspondence between the empirical system and the abstract system. Typically 5 or 6 categories are used in verbal interval rating scales. In theory, the more categories the scale has, the more precise they are. In practice, the trade-off to be considered is how the questionnaire is to be administered. While 10 categories may be more precise than 5, this scale differential is more difficult to communicate over the telephone, for example, than via a mail survey. A 5 or 6 category scale is easy to administer and maintains an acceptable level of precision in most cases. The rating scales (1 - 5) are verbally described, which clearly defines each category to avoid confusion by the respondent as well as management, and allows for the data to be treated as intervally scaled. The odd number of categories provides a "neutral" category, however; the corresponding category descriptions force the respondent to express a feeling.

Attitude Measurement Approach

An attitude is an individual's enduring perceptual, knowledge, evaluative, and action-oriented processes with respect to a product or phenomena. As the hierarchy of effects illustrates, the three components of attitude include cognitive, affective and behavioral. Clearly, a current customer of a product is cognitive of the product and has already reacted to that awareness. Customer satisfaction measures the affective component of an attitude relating to the customers liking and preferences.

Since the feeling to be measured is the "car satisfaction and lease satisfaction among recent leasees of their cars," a number of the techniques can be eliminated as not appropriate. In this case, the communication technique, rather than observation technique, is being followed via the measurement of self reports through a questionnaire.

Measuring Reliability and Validity

Because many managers today are being rewarded for achieving customer satisfaction objectives, both the measurement of overall satisfaction and the estimation of impact for controllable variables (i.e., product attributes) must be reliable and valid. From a customer's perspective, the measurement scale for overall satisfaction should be simple (i.e., easy to use, easy to relate to), understandable (i.e., the scale is interpreted in the intended manner), and consistent with the customer's language (i.e., the descriptions fit the customer's categorization of the product). If a measuring instrument does not meet these considerations, the reliability and validity of the data are likely to be reduced.

Reliability is a necessary but not sufficient condition for validity. Specifically, the reliability of measure indicates to what extent the process is free from random error. In practice, this measure tells the researcher how consistent the data will be. While the validity of a measure refers to the extent to which the process is free from both systematic and random error, in practice, validity tells the researcher how well the measurement system has been designed.

Reliability can be evaluated through a number of methods, such as test-retest, alternative forms method, and split-half reliability. To measure the reliability of customer satisfaction, the test-retest method – where the researcher repeats the measurement using the same measuring device under conditions which are judged to be very similar – would be effective. Low discrepancies imply higher reliabilities.

The validity of measuring customer satisfaction can be measured in two ways: construct and content. Construct validity involves understanding the theoretical rationale underlying the obtained measurements. Content validity involves a subjective measurement by an expert (i.e., marketing manager) as to the appropriateness of the measurements. In other words, the research needs to answer whether or not the results are in line with what was to be expected. While concurrent and prediction validity are two other ways in which validity is measured, they are not well suited to measuring customer satisfaction validity. The questionnaire would need to be given to a small sample of customers to test the reliability and validity before the it would be fully administered and used to base future marketing decisions.

Alternative Measures of Customer Satisfaction

The Dodge marketing managers wanted to consider measuring the difference between customer expectations and actual experiences. This would require a verbal interval rating scale rating of the respondents' expectations and then their actual experiences. The difference or "gap" would be either positive or negative denoting the respondents' satisfaction "level." Theoretically, it would give management insight into the customer's perceptions about certain attributes. However, measures of quality that depend on asking two questions – one about expectations and one about performance – and calculating the difference are notoriously unreliable. An alternative may be to directly question whether or not the product met their requirement for a specific attribute rather than their expectations of an attribute. Regardless, these ratings can not be directly compared to one another to obtain a preference for one attribute/opinion over another.

The attribute trade-offs could be measured via a rank order scale or a paired comparison scale. The trade-off measurements would allow for direct comparisons to one another to obtain an understanding of attribute preferences. However, this type of measurement does not tell the researcher how much an attribute is valued.

A rank order scale is merely ordinal and does not provide interval data. The number of attributes to be ranked must be limited to accommodate administration and respondent fatigue factors. In this instance, the attributes could be clustered (i.e., factored) in related groups to facilitate the technique.

With the paired comparison data method, the use is confined to a small number of objects to control respondent fatigue and the order of the attributes may bias results. In favor of the method, the task is simple and allows for comparisons to be made.

The choice of scales and measurement method is highly dependent on the research objectives and marketing problems. Dodge's managers appear to disagree on what is required for the research. As shown in previous cases, this issue must be clarified before a research methodology is selected.

Demographic and Car Description Data

Gathering data on the demographics of the customer and pairing that with the description of the car leased yields valuable information to marketing managers. It increases the depth of the information being gathered in the customer satisfaction surveys, by allowing researchers to cluster and analyze the data based on demographic, car, and lease differences. This increased depth of information allows management to adjust their marketing strategies and track them over time.

Trade-off Data

The data provided by the trade-offs made among attributes would be useful to Dodge managers for a variety of reasons. In the short term, knowing what attributes are most important to their customers would aid in the design of advertising campaigns and subsequent marketing efforts to current and potential customers (assuming potential customers would value product attributes similarly). Taking a more long term view, knowing what product attributes are most valued helps to guide management in product and service cost reduction efforts and product design of future cars and lease agreements.

Additionally, valuable strategic competitive positioning can be determined by comparing trade-off attributes of a competitor's product and lease attributes to Dodge attributes.

Related Issues

• **Tracking perceptual changes over time.** If a rating changes, the meanings may be somewhat ambiguous. Did perceived product performance remain the same and customer expectations increase? Did product performance decline and customer expectations stay constant? Or, did product performance decline and customer expectations increase? Regardless, a decrease in the customer's rating means the customer perceives quality to have decreased.

• **Handling ideal point attributes.** An ideal point attribute is one in which there is an "ideal amount" or "optimal" amount of an attribute. Receiving either less or more than the ideal amount of the attribute reduces perceptions of quality. With care, it is possible to word questions for such attributes that are logically sound and for which the attribute performance and expectations scales are appropriate.

• **Conceptual Definitions.** In conventional English, "expectation" carries the dual meaning of anticipation and obligation or requirement. It is this latter meaning that is usually desired in most questions about customer satisfaction. Extensive testing has shown that the "requirements" meaning of "expectations" can usually be invoked (thereby eliminating the ambiguity) by carefully introducing use of the scale with a phrase such as "Compared to what you think it should be, was attribute X much better than expected..." An option is to simply use the word "requirement" rather than "expectation."

TEACHING STRATEGY

The class proceeds easily through the topics in the case analysis, and can easily fill a whole class period. Just proceed one topic at a time.

When discussing alternative customer satisfaction measures, feel free to challenge the students to introduce other types of measurements that may extract similar information and how these measurements would have to be structured for the marketing problem (e.g., nominal, semantic differential, and stapel scales).

CASE 3-3

MAINLINE PACKAGE GOODS

INTRODUCTION

This case presents: (1) the history of Ice-Away window de-icer and its current market position; (2) a statement of problem definition by the brand manager, Mr. Ken Gibbs, i.e., "media decisions are the relevant area of decision making;" (3) a description of a market experiment developed in response to this problem definition; and (4) selected results from the experiment.

This case is designed to be used at the beginning of the section of the marketing research course dealing with experimentation and test marketing. However, the case also contains issues of problem definition and measurement.

OBJECTIVES OF THE CASE

1) To illustrate the use of and difficulties associated with marketing field experiments.

2) To show the need for "internal validity" in an experimental design as a prerequisite to meaningful decision making.

3) To show the need for "external validity" in an experimental design as a prerequisite to meaningful decision making.

4) To allow students to suggest possible superior experimental design for the problem as defined, as a way to improving their design skills.

5) To show the research and decision making difficulties arising from poor problem definition.

6) To set up the instructors' possible lecture on analysis of variance in an experimental design (ANOVA).

7) To illustrate possible measurement errors.

QUESTIONS TO BE ASSIGNED

1) Evaluate the experimental design used by Mainline Package Goods. Be sure to discuss the validity of the experiment.

2) Do you feel the design can be improved? If yes, indicate how you would do so. Be specific.

3) What conclusions can be drawn from the study? What action would you recommend if you were in Ken Gibbs' position?

CASE ANALYSIS

Experimental Design

The design in the case is an "after only with control group," without a random assignment of cities to treatments. In symbols:

December	March	City
X_1	O_1	Newark
X_2	O_2	Cleveland
X_3	O_3	Denver

where,

X_1 = spot TV only (control treatment).
X_2 = spot radio 50%, spot television 50%.
X_3 = newspapers 50%, spot television 50%.
X_1, X_2, and X_3 are the independent variables.

The measurement of the dependent variables are represented by O_1, O_2, and O_3 and are: (1) convenience, (2) effectiveness in melting ice, (3) speed in de-icing, (4) aesthetic appeal of the package, (5) ease in using the package, and (6) frequency of use. Note that ANOVA assumes nominal independent variables and an interval dependent variable.

Internal Validity

The design is suspect from an internal validity standpoint. It assumes that the values of a dependent variable would be the same in each of the three cities prior to the administration of the treatments. Were sales and attitude measures identical in each city prior to December? We do not know. Without premeasures the design is not internally valid. A better design from this standpoint would be:

Pre-December	December	March	City
O_1	X_1	O_4	Newark
O_2	X_2	O_5	Cleveland
O_3	X_3	O_6	Denver

Without these premeasures, the alternative hypothesis that there were differences to start with cannot be refuted.

As discussed in the text, other possible causes of significant differences include: history, maturation, testing, instrumentation, experimental mortality, selection, etc. The experiment is not internally valid.

As important as the premeasure issue is the possibility that something occurred in one or more but not all test cities during the experiment. For example, a competitor could have behaved differently among the test cities prior to or during the experiment. The present design just assumes that this has not happened. It makes no provision to measure or take account of such activity.

It should be noted that an "after only with control group" design can be internally valid if there is a random assignment of a large number of subjects (or cities) to treatment groups. This randomization assures statistically equal premeasures. In the case the cities were picked by and assigned by judgment.

External Validity

The question of external validity relates to the selection of the three cities. Clearly, they are not representative of the whole country on many dimensions even though their economic situations are similar. Other variables that could be important include: differences in weather, the tendency for ice to develop, the availability of covered parking in the city, etc. Some students are likely to suggest more or other cities. The costs ($22,000/3) and administrative complications of this should be discussed and the need for trade-offs among cost, administration and external validity clearly demonstrated to the students.

Measurement Issues

The timing of the measurement of the dependent variables is an issue. Is a three-month period the right amount of time between treatment execution and measurement? Both shorter-term and longer- term effects have been ignored. It seems that it is premature to judge the package change effects on such short notice.

The months of high and low purchase frequency should have been taken into account before the study. Do people buy de-icers in March? If not, are purchase intentions in March accurate indicators of purchase intentions the following winter?

The actual measurement instrument itself is also an issue. Brand purchase data was obtained by telephone interview. This type of reporting is suspect. They should have utilized a retail shelf movement procedure. This would likely raise the cost of the study. Again the cost/rigor tradeoff arises.

The brand attitude data is assumed to be interval in the experiment. Students should question the use of rating scales to collect the attitude data. Are the data truly interval? It should be noted that this is very common data collection procedure in marketing research.

A Possible Superior Design

By using a completely randomized design (simple one-way ANOVA design; see Appendix to Chapter 20) the potential for other useful information is lost. The combined effects of the media combinations are measured at the same time. Only the overall effected is available to be measured.

A factorial design would allow the separate effects of each package type plus their interactions to be measured. We must note, however, that additional cities would be required to implement this design. In this type of design, one must specify the number of levels of each factor. For example, one would have 3 factors (metal aerosol, metal non-aerosol, and plastic pump) and 3 levels of each. This is called a 3 x 3 design and requires $27(3^3)$ cells or cities. A 3 factor by 2 level design (3 x 2) requires 3^2 or 9 cells. Clearly again cost/information tradeoffs are involved.

The issue related to the differential effects among cities of competitors' actions, weather, etc. could be taken into account in the ANOVA if they were measured. Specifically, a covariance procedure could be utilized. This is a complex topic for beginning marketing research students. Therefore, it should just be mentioned without the unnecessary technical detail (i.e., "If we measure it, we can take it into account").

Problem Definition

All of the above technical issues are important for a student to understand in relation to experiments. However, a real issue in this case relates to whether or not the "real," "actionable" problem was researched.

Before conclusive research was ever attempted, exploratory research should have been conducted. The problem was never accurately ascertained. Loss of market shares is but a symptom of a problem, not the problem itself.

Also, are the alternatives he has tested actionable ones? We question whether he is really willing to make such radical changes in the package design or even whether he could sell these changes to his superiors. On both counts the answer is: "highly unlikely," no matter what the test results.

TEACHING STRATEGY

The instructor should begin the class by asking what package design the students would choose next year. Some students will try and duck this by questioning the technical aspects of the study. Do not let them do this. Say: "That's all very interesting and we will get into those issues later; however, we must make decisions even on very imperfect information; so, what's your decision?" This should lead to a discussion of the specific results of the study and whether "significant" differences are managerially meaningful.

After discussing these areas for a time then let the discussion go to the technical aspects of the experiment. Student criticisms should be forced to be specific, and suggestions for improvements in design should also be specific. Usually students find it easy to criticize but hard to suggest improvements.

Hopefully, some alert student will identify the problem definition problems. If this does not happen, the instructor should raise the issue after the design questions have been discussed.

CASE 3-4

UNILEVER'S PERSIL DETERGENT

INTRODUCTION

In this case, Unilever wants to determine the damage impact of their Pan-European detergent, Persil Power. Competition charged that Persil Power damaged clothes and Unilever management hoped to quiet critics and help relaunch the brand. It is interesting to note that this case is based on a real-world product situation faced by Unilever in 1994. Students are asked to design an experiment for this purpose. The case is intended to follow the material on causal research presented in Chapter 9.

OBJECTIVES OF THE CASE

1) To give students experience in designing experiments.
2) To apply the concepts of test units, dependent variables, extraneous variables, timing, selection of test units and assignment to treatment conditions.
3) To illustrate the fact that, while a true experiment is best in terms of pure statistical validity, "real world" factors often necessitate the use of less-than-ideal procedures.
4) To facilitate discussion about the pros and cons of various experimental design options.

QUESTIONS TO BE ASSIGNED

1) Prepare an experimental design that would allow management to determine the damage impact of Persil Power on clothes. Be sure to clearly identify: test units, dependent variables, methods of control of extraneous variables, timing of measurements taken, selection of test units and assignment of test units to treatments.

2) Display your design using the R, O, X symbols of experimental design.

3) Given the brand management's statement of purpose for the research, how should Unilever's marketing researchers state the objective for the research?

CASE ANALYSIS

Unilever needs to prove that their critics are wrong and that Persil Power is safe to use for a consumer's general washing needs. To quiet their critics, their research needed to be statistically correct so as to avoid critical claims of biasing the research. It should be assumed that product testing was performed in laboratory tests prior to the release of the product. The purpose of this marketing research is to prove causality through consumer experimental research. Unilever wants to prove that their new detergent formula (cause) is not responsible for damaging clothes (effect) when used by the average consumer.

Three types of experimental designs exist: pre-experimental, true experimental, and quasi-experimental. Essentially, any experimental design which does not include pre-treatment observation or does not test more than one group is not feasible in this situation. This eliminates all pre-experimental designs. In addition, quasi experiments, used when the researcher lacks control over the scheduling of the treatments, result in the possibility of obtaining confounded results. In this situation, treatment scheduling can be mostly controlled, and therefore a true experiment should be used. If this experiment is not conducted in a test laboratory, it may be argued that complete control of the treatment scheduling is not possible. However, it is possible to assign test units to washing their pre-determined clothes at a predetermined time, in a pre-determined washing temperature.

Experimental Design

The act of washing clothes in any form of detergent causes some damage to clothing. As a result, the optimal type of true experimentation design is the **pretest-posttest control group design**. Because testing the condition of the clothing can be performed objectively, the condition of interactive testing is limited. Additionally, a pretest measurement is desirable to establish a starting point for the initial condition of the clothing being tested.

The **test units** should be randomly selected European consumers of laundry detergent where Persil will be/is being sold. Similarity of the test units is not a critical issue because clothing conditions, not consumer attitudes, are being measured. As a result, the test units do not need to be confined to homemakers or to homes that own laundry machines, for example, due to the large number of male users and laundromat users in Europe. A random selection of test units is preferred over a non-random selection to account for real-world laundry conditions and machine usage. This selection may be solicited from telephone directories or city residential lists. This process will not, however, result in a purely random sample of consumers because not all consumers will be listed. Due to the time constraints and severity of the situation, this is an acceptable method. However, it may be argued by some students that a non-random sample of employee users or local residents may be justifiable to control costs and speed up the testing process.

The **assignment of test units** to treatment conditions should also be performed randomly to reduce the level of bias. Each group should have an equal number of test units and agree to a set number of washings between measurements.

The **dependent variable** (the one being measured) is the condition of the clothes. The **independent variable** (the one being manipulated) is the detergent used.

The **treatment conditions** (X_x) of the experiment groups is washing a predetermined amount and type of soiled clothes with Persil Power in varying laundry temperatures. The **control condition** (X_x) of the control groups is washing a predetermined amount and type of soiled clothes with original Persil detergent in varying laundry temperatures. By using the status quo as a control condition, we can control for the effects of extraneous variables such as history and instrumentation on the condition of the clothes.

The treatments should be administered concurrently in selected countries, to control for timing effects. Pre- and post-treatment observations of clothes conditions should be taken from each test unit. Multiple washing is needed to account for continued use and potential product build-up. Comparison of pre- and post-treatment results will allow Unilever to make inferences about the effects of Persil Power on clothing.

As mentioned previously, it is not possible to control for all **extraneous variables** in this type of experiment. For example, washing machine instrumentation, history effects, selection bias, or test unit mortality could all effect the study. The series of pre-and post experimental observations can be analyzed to determine a "baseline" level of the condition of the clothes. Then, because these variables will affect both the experimental and control groups, the effects of extraneous variables should be negated.

Symbolic Display of Experiment

In symbolic form, one version of the experiment would be represented as:

Experimental Group 1 (Whites in Warm)	R	O_1	X_1	O_2	X_2	X_3	O_3	Control
Group 1 (Whites in Warm)	R	O_{13}	X_{13}	O_{14}	X_{14}	X_{15}	O_{15}	
Experimental Group 2 (Colors in Warm)	R	O_4	X_4	O_5	X_5	X_6	O_6	Control
Group 2 (Colors in Warm)	R	O_{16}	X_{16}	O_{17}	X_{17}	X_{18}	O_{18}	
Experimental Group 3 (Whites in Cold)	R	O_7	X_7	O_8	X_8	X_9	O_9	
Control Group 3 (Whites in Cold)	R	O_{19}	X_{19}	O_{20}	X_{20}	X_{21}	O_{21}	
Experimental Group 4 (Colors in Cold)	R	O_{10}	X_{10}	O_{11}	X_{11}	X_{12}	O_{12}	
Control Group 4 (Colors in Cold)	R	O_{22}	X_{22}	O_{23}	X_{23}	X_{24}	O_{24}	

This experiment is the **pretest-posttest control group design**, with four treatment conditions and four control conditions. It gives Unilever multiple options to chose from in order to meet their objective of proving that the detergent is "safe." Students may argue for an alternative experiment with fewer or more than the four options.

Objective Statement for the Research

Research objectives answer the question "What is the purpose of the research project?" This study has the following objectives:

(1) To prove that Persil Power does not damage clothing when used in everyday washing situations.

(2) To obtain research information that is substantial enough to quiet Persil Power's critics.

TEACHING STRATEGY

This apparently simple case allows the instructor to touch on the full spectrum of issues in experimental design. One way to encourage class discussion of the case is to assign several students the responsibility of presenting an experimental design for the class to discuss. Let the first student present his/her design and briefly explain the reasons for choosing it. Then let the rest of the class identify test units, independent and dependent variables, extraneous variables, timing, selection of test units and assignment to treatment conditions. Repeat this process for another student's design if it seems appropriate, pointing out the pros and cons of the various designs.

Chances are that at least one student will mention the experimental designs discussed here. Just in case, the instructor should be prepared to discuss his/her suggested experimental design as outlined above.

What Actually Happened

The Unilever case is a prime example of the limitations of being "first to market." Sacrificing thorough research for speed to market gambles with the equity of a brand. In the spring of 1994, Unilever introduced Persil Power, basing their "power" stain cleaning abilities on the detergent's new additive "Accelerator," a manganese catalyst. Industry researchers had known for years that manganese was a stain remover, however the catalyst was known to remove dyes as well as stains. Unilever claimed to have patented a formula that allowed the catalyst to be used without damaging colored clothing. They then rushed a $300 million European product introduction to beat Proctor & Gamble's launch of their reformulated flagship brand, Ariel Future.

P&G's Ariel brand dominated the European market, and the new Persil Power brand had overtaken Ariel for the first time in the U.K. market. P&G response was to attack Unilever with an aggressive PR and advertising campaign that showed severely damaged clothing laundered in the Persil Power. Unilever reacted by claims that P&G's studies were generated under extreme conditions and then sought a court injunction to protect the launch in several European countries. While Unilever's product research did show that the product was "safe" on colored clothing, P&G's research proved that in certain conditions, the product was indeed not safe for colors. The court case was subsequently dropped.

Ten months after the first product introduction, Unilever had reformulated, added the additive to their other European brands, and then finally removed the catalyst from the products altogether. They then repositioned Persil Power as a niche stain-removal product for heavily soiled products. The entire incident reduced Unilever's European profits by 1% in 1994, despite strong sales from the company's ice cream and beverage categories.

CASE 3-5

EUROPEAN ALCOHOL RESEARCH FOUNDATION

INTRODUCTION

This case describes Young & Rubicam's Cross Cultural Consumer Characteristics (4Cs) approach to consumer classification in the research context of the European Alcohol Research Foundation, a nonprofit public service group. It challenges the student to consider alternative measurement systems and measurement constructs in regards to consumer behavior. It also examines how such systems should and should not be used.

OBJECTIVES OF THE CASE

1) To challenge students to look beyond traditional measurement scales and to consider the factors that influence consumer behavior.

2) To facilitate discussion about the uses and limitations of consumer classification systems.

3) To examine the appropriateness of consumer classifications across cultures

QUESTIONS TO BE ASSIGNED

1) What is the 4Cs approach to the consumer behavior measurement?

2) What are the measurement scale characteristics, and the reliability and validity of the 4Cs approach?

3) What conclusion for EARF can be drawn from this paper?

4) How could Y&R use the 4Cs approach with its clients who desire to market across borders in Europe?

5) On what basis should Y&R's clients be prepared to utilize these types of results in an advertising campaign?

CASE ANALYSIS

4Cs Measurement Approach

Similar to the SRI International Values and Lifestyles (VALS) Program, the 4Cs approach classifies the average international customer into one of seven different clusters of consumers. The approach is loosely based on Maslow's hierarchical classification of dominant motivation.

The case does not describe Young and Rubicam's research methodology; however, it may be assumed that they measured a large number consumers in various cultures on a wide number of variables. They then identified seven clusters from this research. (Cluster Analysis is described in Chapter 21.) Y&R defined the similarities across cultures, created the seven groups, described the groups, and then used them to simplify the world and make it more understandable. In effect,

Y&R combined several motivation and value items to measure a single construct: consumer behavior.

Instead of relying on the traditional method of classifying international consumers based on their geographical location, the 4Cs measures the consumer's pattern of behavior based on his or her value system. This allows the marketer to identify similarities and differences across, rather than within, cultures. Y&R does admit that consumer behavior is also affected by the context in which the behavioral decision is made.

Measurement Scale Characteristics

The idea of "measurement" assumes that there is something worth measuring, that is, to identify some underlying construct. In an effort to make these constructs understood and usable, there is a tendency to simplify them into a scale. In most cases, the construct is measured numerically. The 4Cs scale is not literally a number scale; however, it easily could be numbered if needed.

The 4Cs is not a metric scale, rather it has the qualities of both nominal and ordinal scales. In a purely nominal scale, there is no relation between the quantity of the construct being measured and the "value" assigned to it. On the other hand, in a purely ordinal scale, the higher the value, the more or less the construct exists. The 4Cs classifications combine these nonmetric scales. The identifying terms are organized around an arbitrary ranking (i.e., hierarchical motivations). The main effect of this type of scale is in its analysis. The 4Cs scale can only be used to compute frequencies, percentiles and medians. Because the scale is nonmetric, the mean and standard deviation may not be used.

Reliability and Validity

A measure is said to be reliable if it consistently obtains the same results, measure after measure. The reliability of a measurement can be assessed through the administration of alternative tests. In general, value-based classification systems have been investigated and found to be reasonably good (See Pessimier and Bruno 1971, Villani and Lehmann 1975). In other words, it has the ability to measure people's activities consistently. This does not mean that the measurement is valid. Validity is a much more difficult issue to resolve.

Validity revolves around the question, "What is being measuring?" Four types of validity should be examined: construct, content, convergent and predictive. One must question whether or not the test questions are logical and related to the measure in a predicted way. Perhaps the best assessment of the 4Cs measures comes from the extent to which test interpretations and conclusions provide marketers with useful and accurate appraisals of consumers.

EARF Conclusions

The EARF's goal is to reduce the abuse of alcohol and promote moderate rates of alcohol consumption. The paper has mapped out the consumption patterns of four main European markets in terms of their similarities and differences. What is clear is that alcohol consumption is deeply culturally based. Knowing that consumers in the French and UK markets are driven by transitional values, EARF should consider positioning their campaigns to appeal to the self-discovery nature of these consumers. In contrast, EARF should position their aspirer-driven Spanish and Italian campaigns to emphasize the negative status of alcoholic problems. Additionally, EARF may be able to save money by "recycling" the same theme for each of these market pairs.

4Cs Approach Across Borders

Traditional international management has developed the "country manager" style of marketing. The 4Cs approach indicates that in product categories, certain countries tend to cluster horizontally and are less geopolitically defined. Y&R could use the 4C approach to assist its clients in setting up a truly pan-European strategy for their products, prices, distribution patterns, and campaigns. This pan-European strategy would be based on a horizontal clustering to allow their client to minimize expenses and to better understand what drives their customers' behavior.

Y&R Uses in Advertising

The 4Cs approach offers companies opportunities to share brand names and advertising themes across borders. However, care needs to be taken in local advertising to account for cultural differences such as language, product usage, trends, etc.

TEACHING STRATEGY

This case proceeds best if the instructor discusses each question sequentially. While this case introduces students to the use of a value-based measurement scale in a specific marketing scenario, this implementation can be applied to multiple marketing situations. As such, the questions are deliberately worded to be applied to many different organizations and environments.

CASE 3-6

KELLOGG'S HEARTWISE CEREAL

INTRODUCTION

The case describes a clinical testing procedure upon which Kellogg based health claims for Heartwise cereal. It is designed to be used after the discussion of experimental design in Chapter 9.

OBJECTIVES OF THE CASE

1) To provide a broader understanding of experimental research methodology by using an example from a non-marketing discipline.
2) To provide student with another opportunity for practicing the identification of variables, treatments, sources of variation, and discussing the validity of an experiment.
3) To raise the ethical question of whether well-designed research used for a specific purpose can be equally valid when applied to another situation.

QUESTIONS TO BE ASSIGNED

1) Identify test units, dependent variable(s), independent variable(s), treatments, sources of extraneous variation, how control is obtained, timing of measurements, selection of test units, and assignment of test units to treatments.

2) Evaluate the internal and external validity of this study.

3) Is it a proper use of this research to make health claims for Heartwise cereal? Why or why not?

CASE ANALYSIS

The case describes a very well designed study of the effects of a low-fat diet and psyllium consumption on blood cholesterol level. The study was conducted at the University of Minnesota and was influential in Kellogg's decision to develop a cereal containing psyllium.

Experimental Design

The researchers utilized a pretest-postest control group design. It can be represented symbolically as:

Experimental Group	R	O_1	X	O_2
Control Group	R	O_3		O_4

Test units were individual participants in the study.

Dependent variables (measured) were levels of lipids, proteins, and cholesterol in subjects blood samples. The dependent variable of greatest interest was subjects' blood cholesterol levels.

The independent variable (manipulated) was the presence or absence of psyllium. One could also argue that since this study followed upon similar research where subjects were given a high fat diet, type of diet was an independent variable.

There were two treatment conditions; experimental (psyllium) and control (placebo.) The control group's pill was exactly the same as the treatment group's except for the absence of psyllium, so subjects could not tell whether or not they were receiving the real medication. Assignment to treatment conditions was random.

Experimental controls were numerous. The initial screening procedure resulted in a relatively homogeneous pool of subjects with initially high cholesterol levels who did not take any other medications that might somehow affect (interact with) the treatment medication. The second and third screenings further decreased the potential for extraneous error due to dietary factors. Random assignment to treatment conditions reduced the likelihood of systematic differences between groups. The "double blind" procedure eliminated potential errors resulting from the groups being treated differently by staff members. It also eliminated error that might result from subjects knowing they were in different groups and having different expectations about the outcome of the study.

Many potential sources of extraneous variation were eliminated through tight experimental control. These included differences between groups due to diet, age, gender, use of other medications, weight loss or gain during the study, pre-existing cholesterol level, experimenter bias, and other factors discussed in the previous paragraph.

Because potential sources of extraneous variation were so well controlled, internal validity was high. Researchers could be confident that differences in cholesterol level between groups were a result of the experimental manipulation and not some other factors. However, the external validity of the study is more questionable. One has to wonder whether psyllium in another form (e.g., in breakfast cereal) would have the same effect as the psyllium in Metamucil. That was not conclusively proven in this study. Kellogg and other cereal marketers incurred the wrath of the Food and Drug Administration for making claims that their psyllium-based cereals would reduce cholesterol level.

TEACHING STRATEGY

We suggest that the instructor begin with discussion of the experimental design, treatment conditions, and independent variables. From there, the discussion should progress to issues of experimental control, internal and external validity, and the appropriateness of Kellogg's use of the results. Students are usually quite stimulated by the ethical issues raised about the proper use of research as a basis for marketing claims.

CASE 3-7

PARKSIDE CORPORATION

INTRODUCTION

This case examines the use of the focus group as a data collection instrument in marketing research. Students are asked to design the study and develop the interviewer's guide. The context is Parkside Corporation, a manufacturer of recreation vehicles, who wishes to conduct exploratory research before doing more conclusive research concerning expanding into new markets.

OBJECTIVES OF THE CASE

1) To allow students to think through and develop an outline for a focus group.

2) To expose students to the level of detailed planning that must precede a focus group.

3) To demonstrate the necessity of preplanning a focus group in careful detail.

QUESTIONS TO BE ASSIGNED

1) Design the focus group study and develop the interviewer's guide.

CASE ANALYSIS

Focus group design should begin with the resolution of basic issues, with rationalization or justification where necessary. Some suggested guidelines follow.

a) Participant selection - some screening for ownership and/or experience is necessary to obtain desired information. Random selection could provide people who lack interest and the ability to give meaningful answers to questions.

b) Male or female - by using both, Parkside can gain the perspectives (often different) of both important users. This decision is made concurrently with the decision to ask couples to participate. Otherwise the group could be too heterogeneous.

c) Individuals or couples - since RV's are generally used by families together, their complimentary responses may prove insightful.

d) Age - although the group may flow best with a group of couples in the same general age group, some variation is necessary. Couples with children of different ages will have different needs and experiences to share. Some intra-group differences often provide more interaction.

e) Experience of respondents - since the information needs relate to gaining a better understanding of the travel trailer owner and their reaction to RV toilets, respondents with personal experiences will have a more useful basis for their attitudes and opinions. With more experience, users often can be prompted to provide valuable insight as to their needs and wants.

f) Recent or lifetime owners - again, owners with experience are preferable, but a mix of couples who have owned an RV for say 2 years to 15 years will provide diversity.

g) How many people per session - the optimal number of participants is 10-12, or 5-6 couples. in general, in selecting respondents, care should be taken to obtain a fairly homogeneous grouping in the respects mentioned above. Extremes or variations can be obtained by selecting different groups for different sessions. Interaction between the moderator and participants and amongst respondents is crucial for the session's success.

h) How many sessions - much of this decision is dictated by the budget. Ideally, adequate geographic representation would require 5-8 sessions. However, 3-4 would certainly be adequate for exploratory research. Regardless, the major requirement is that the sessions be replicated. If the potential market is seen as being clearly segmented, those seen as most critical should be included.

i) Where should sessions be held - the physical setting should provide a relaxed, comfortable atmosphere that facilitates spontaneous and congenial discussion. Either a "living room" or informal "board room" are appropriate for this. Rooms especially designed for this generally have the added amenities of a two-way mirror, etc.

j) Should session be taped - wherever this can be achieved inconspicuously through the use of a one-way mirror or other built-in facilities, it is highly desirable to tape sessions. This allows for later examination, analysis, and comparison with other groups. Clients can review sessions, too.

k) Who should moderate sessions - given the crucial nature of the moderator in determining the group's success, a professional is needed. Often it is an individual, trained as a psychologist, who has additional moderate skills and runs the session. Whether the moderator should be male or female is subject to debate.

l) How long should the sessions be - one-and-one-half to two hours is typical. There is enough time to establish rapport and explore the issues without infringing upon respondents' time or allowing the session to drag.

m) Questions for interviewer's guide - see the end of this note for the actual guide used in this study.

TEACHING STRATEGY

The instructor should ask a few students to present their focus group designs. Each should address the above issues as well as present their rationale if necessary. This should take about 30 minutes. Next the actual design may be presented, including the interviewer's guide. This is an excellent time to review points made in the chapter and to emphasize the importance of relating the information needs to the design and selection of data collection methods.

Parkside Corporation

Interviewer Guide
RV Group Study

A. Introduction

   Purpose of Session

   A leading manufacture of RV equipment is interested in listening to and understanding the ideas and opinions of experts such as yourself regarding RV ownership and travel.

B. Camping and Travel Experience and Current RV Usage

   - What type of RV do you currently own
   - First purchase or previous owner
   - Previous equipment owned
   - When do you use your RV (time of year)
   - How often
   - What types of trips (family vacation, clubs, etc.)
   - Who goes on these trips; how many people in your RV
   - How long have you been camping and traveling

C. RV Purchase Criteria

   - How did you come to buy present unit (word of mouth, personal experience, etc.)
   - What product attributes did you look for when purchasing - Why this type of RV as opposed to another (advantages/disadvantages of travel trailer vs. motor home)

D. Probe into Hassles of RV Ownership

   - Maintenance
   - Cleanup
   - Winterizing
   - The holding tank

E. Preliminary Discussion of Bathroom Facilities

   - How important to total RV purchase decision
   - What are key purchase decision attributes (size, location, color, others)

F. Discussion on Role of Toilet in RV Purchase Decision

   - Brand awareness
   - Importance of brand in RV purchase
   - Importance of color in RV purchase

G. Examination of Toilet Owned

   - Features included (flush mechanism, type of seal)
   - Features liked/disliked
   - Features of ideal toilet

CASE 3-8

MIDWEST MARKETING RESEARCH ASSOCIATES (A)

INTRODUCTION

This case presents the questionnaire designed by Midwest Marketing Research Associates for their client, National Markets. MMRA is researching the issue of providing additional nutritional information to supermarket shoppers. The case is designed to follow the material on questionnaire design in Chapter 11.

OBJECTIVES OF THE CASE

1) To give students practice at evaluating a questionnaire prior to field testing.
2) To facilitate discussion of alternatives for questionnaire design (wording, format, content, etc.)

CASE QUESTION

1) Read the National Markets - Nutritional Labeling case in part 1 of this book to develop an understanding of the decision situation related to the questionnaire in this case. Then read the questionnaire below and determine how it should be modified based upon the rules of questionnaire construction presented in Chapter 11. Record the needed changes on the worksheet at the end of this exercise. The worksheet is structured so as to facilitate your thinking regarding questionnaire changes. It asks you to address the following areas:

    a. Proposed changes in question format, wording, content, etc.
    b. Proposed changes in question sequence and general structure.
    c. General comments and concerns regarding the design of the questionnaire.

CASE ANALYSIS

There are significant questionnaire design issues raised in the exercise. We prefer to proceed through the questionnaire one question at a time asking for students to criticize the questions based upon their experience in the field and the Chapter 11 reading. Some specific points that usually are made include:

1) The location of respondent names, addresses, phone numbers, etc. at the start of the questionnaire is not a good opener; people may misread the purpose of the interview. This section should be moved to the back.

2) The term "nutrition information" in question 2 is not well defined. What exactly does it mean?

3) For questions 3 and 4, more and better information could be obtained by using some type of scale (5 or 7 point) for responses.

4) Question 4 is somewhat leading. Inclusion of the word "or" does not allow a clear answer to the question.

5) Question 5 is very limited in scope. There are many other places where nutrition information can be obtained, but respondents are limited to the choices provided. The phrase "type of information" is vague. The category "friends or relatives" should be split in two. Also, question 5 would be better asked as a scale (e.g., 1....7) than a simple yes or no; too much information is lost this way.

6) If a scale was used for question 5, question 6 would be redundant.

7) Question 7 assumes a priori that the respondent has a problem finding nutrition information. This may or may not be true.

8) Subjects who respond "no" to question 8 should skip to question 11. There is no need to ask people who are not on a special diet if they would like more nutritional information related to their special diets. In fact, doing so distorts responses to question 10.

9) Question 11 is worded so that it would be difficult for the respondent to say no. Question 12, because it immediately follows, has the same problem. A "don't know" option would be useful for both of these questions.

10) In question 13, the word "regularly" could easily be misinterpreted.

11) It might be easier to ask questions 13-16 about a specific product type before proceeding to the next one. Asking them all together tends to confuse the respondent.

12) In question 16, the interviewer must keep repeating the scale. A card should be handed to the respondent.

13) For question 18, a "don't know" option should be provided.

14) It would be difficult for a respondent to reply "no" to question 19.

15) Questions 10 and 20 are somewhat redundant.

16) For question 23, a "don't know" option should be provided.

17) For question 24, there is no space to check off the "least helpful" format.

18) A "don't know" option would be useful for the factual questions 28-31.

19) The response categories for question 32 are not exhaustive; all modern lifestyles are not captured. The same could be said for the life cycle classifications at the end of the questionnaire.

20) The response categories for question 33 should be given to the respondent on a card.

21) The income categories in question 40 overlap. A card listing these categories is also needed.

Students will easily find things to criticize about the questionnaire and the instructor should be flexible in the discussion to draw out those areas students deem important. Questions 11, 14, and 19, and the demographic questions are candidates for extensive discussion. Students should be asked to suggest how the questions can be improved through revision.

TEACHING STRATEGY

Students should be given a great deal of freedom to criticize the questionnaire using the guidelines outlined in Chapter 11. Many of their comments will prove to be "right on," but others will prove to be no problem later in the field test. Proceed one question at a time noting the comments made.

When the assignment is made, the instructor has the option of xeroxing and distributing copies of the Worksheet for Questionnaire Design included in this manual.

Name _____

WORKSHEETS FOR QUESTIONNAIRE DESIGN

1. Proposed changes in question format, wording, content, etc.

    A. Indicate question number and proposed change:

    B. Justification for change:

    A. Indicate question number and proposed change:

    B. Justification for change:

II. General suggestions on how to improve the questionnaire:

CASE 4-1

MILAN FOOD COOPERATIVE (A)

INTRODUCTION

This case presents a complete study population organized into a sampling frame. The case may be used by itself to facilitate a discussion of the pros and cons of alternative sampling procedures, plus a discussion of how exactly one would select a sample from this population using these procedures.

OBJECTIVES OF THE CASE

1) To facilitate a discussion of the pros and cons of alternative sampling procedures.

2) To facilitate a discussion of the mechanics of actually selecting sample elements under different sampling procedures.

QUESTIONS TO BE ASSIGNED

1) What alternative procedures are available to estimate weekly food expenditures?

2) Explain how each would be carried out?

3) Discuss the pros and cons of each.

CASE ANALYSIS

Nonprobability Sampling Procedures

There are three options available:

1) Convenience sampling;
2) Judgment sampling; and
3) Quota sampling.

Convenience Sampling

Here the researcher selects the number of elements desired, n, from anywhere in the frame based on personal convenience.

Pros	Cons
1) Easy to do 2) Fast 3) Inexpensive	1) The frame may be grouped, yielding a biased sample of the population. 2) Measurement of sampling error is not possible.

Judgment Sampling

Here the researcher selects sample elements based on expert knowledge about the situation and the population. Ms. Lauchner appears to have no such expertise to apply here, nor do the students. It is unclear a priori on what basis one element is any better than any other.

Pros	**Cons**
1) Fast 2) Inexpensive 3) Can be accurate if judgment is good	1) The judgment may be incorrect, yielding a biased sample. 2) Measurement of sampling error is not possible.

Quota Sampling

Here the researcher designates control characteristics deemed to be relevant to the variable being measured, and finds sample elements to fit the cells defined by control characteristics.

Pros	**Cons**
1) Likely more representative than the other nonprobability procedures if good control characteristics selected. 2) Inexpensive 3) Moderate skill involved	1) Identifying relevant control characteristics requires skill. 2) Finding elements to fit control cells 3) Measurement of sampling error is not possible.

A discussion of relevant control characteristics is useful. The alternatives are: 1) number of persons in household, 2) annual income, 3) education of head of household, and 4) age of head of household. The first characteristic is likely the best with income also useful. The last two seem of little value. The question to ask is what characteristics are likely to be correlated with the variable of interest, weekly food expenditures.

Once having determined the appropriate control characteristics, the task of the researcher is simply to find any elements that fit the defined cells of the control characteristics. This process continues until the required number of elements have been found for each cell.

Probability Sampling Procedures

Probability procedures form a legitimate option here. They are: 1) simple random sampling, 2) stratified sampling, and 3) the cluster sampling procedures of (a) systematic sampling, and (b) area sampling.

Simple Random Sampling

Here the researcher generates n, 3-digit random numbers in the range 001 to 500 from the table of random numbers in the appendix of the text. This identifies the elements that will form the sample.

Pros	Cons
1) Allows measurement of sampling error 2) Not too complex	1) Moderate level of skill required. 2) Slower than convenience sampling. 3) Jump back and forth in the sampling frame. 4) Possible benefits of stratification.

Stratified Sampling

Here the population must be divided in strata that are more homogeneous than the population as a whole on the variable of interest. Again, number of persons in household and annual income seem to make the most sense with education and age other possible options. Note that the population is organized by strata on the variable of education at the present time. On this basis stratum 1 has elements 1-104, stratum 2 has elements 105-206, stratum 3 has elements 207-386, and stratum 4 has elements 387-500. The relevant weights would be:

w1 = .208

w2 = .204

w3 = .360

w4 = .228

To save the students reorganizing the frame, you could ask them to explain how they would select a stratified sample if education were the stratification variable. Then ask why it is not the best variable to use.

Having defined the strata, one then simply selects the appropriate size simple random sample from each stratum.

Pros	Cons
1) Allows measurement of sampling error 2) Gives smaller standard error if stratification variable is correlated with variable of interest	1) High level of skill and understanding required 2) Very slow 3) More expensive than random sampling

Cluster Sampling: (a) Systematic Sampling

This procedure is easily done here. First one determines the sampling interval, k = N/n. Then one selects a random number within the range of 1 to k. This is the first element. The rest of the elements are then selected by successively adding k to the starting number.

Pros	Cons
1) Allows measurement of sampling error 2) Easily done 3) Fast 4) Inexpensive	1) Slower than convenience sampling error 2) Possible periodicity in the frame

Cluster Sampling: (b) Area Sampling

To make use of area sampling the frame must be divided into groups that are as homogeneous as the population, to the extent possible. There seems to be no a priori logical basis on which to do this in this population. Also, there is no real benefit since other probability procedures are so easily used here. This is not a situation where area sampling offers a benefit.

TEACHING STRATEGY

The instructor should keep a strong hold on this class and guide it through each sampling procedure. Some students may suggest a census of the 500 elements. Recognize this as a legitimate alternative and then push on to the sampling aspects.

CASE 4-2

CYNTHIA LU, STUDENT COUNCIL CANDIDATE

INTRODUCTION

This case involves polling for a student candidate to determine if Cynthia Lu will win the upcoming undergraduate business student council presidential election. The student task is to design all the steps in the sampling process. This case is designed to be assigned with the United Airlines and Ice Cream Castle cases to give students a diverse experience in sampling design.

OBJECTIVES OF THE CASE

1) To give students practice in designing all aspects of a sampling problem.
2) To demonstrate that a number of legitimate alternative designs are available for what seems like a straightforward sampling problem.

QUESTIONS TO BE ASSIGNED

1) Prepare a sampling plan. Be sure to designate a population definition, a sampling frame, a sampling procedure, and a method for determining the accuracy of the results.

CASE ANALYSIS

The discussion of this case should precede step-by-step through the steps in the sampling process outlined in Chapters 13 and 14. This teaching note is organized around these steps.

Step 1 – Define the Population

Ask a student to present a sampling design for the case. The student should begin with a definition of the population of interest. If the student does not begin there, stop the presentation and ask: "Is this where we should begin in the process of designing a sample?" Someone in the class will direct the discussion to population definition.

Population definition must include four components: (1) the elements, (2) the sampling units, (3) the extent, and (4) the time. Several examples of population definition are:

I. A. Elements - all undergraduate business students at Arizona State University.

   B. Sampling units - all undergraduate business students at Arizona State University.

   C. Extent - Tempe campus

   D. Time - last week in April, 1995.

II. A. Elements - all undergraduate business students at Arizona State University who have preregistered for fall term.

B. Sampling units - all undergraduate business students at Arizona State University who have preregistered for fall term.

C. Extent - Tempe campus.

D. Time - Tuesday before election day, 1995.

III. A. Elements - all undergraduates enrolled in the business school at Arizona State University.

B. Sampling units - all undergraduates enrolled in the business school at Arizona State University.

C. Extent - Arizona State University.

D. Time - full week preceding election day, 1995.

Other population definitions are possible. Note certain aspects of these definitions. The elements and sampling units are the same in each instance, indicating a one-stage sampling procedure will be used in sample selection. The major difference in the three population definitions relates to the elements/sampling unit definition. Students need to address the issue of the relevancy of the elements and what the best way to ensure that those sampled intend to vote. Since the case context is one week before election, the problem of assessing long-range voting intention is alleviated. A good discussion question would be "What if it were two months before the election?"

The possibility of a multistage sampling procedure exists here. The discussion of this point will be left until later.

Step 2 - Identify the Sampling Frame

The frame must be related to the population definition given by the student. If preregistered business students or currently enrolled business students constitute the element definition, then lists of preregistered business students or currently enrolled business students are meaningful sampling frames, respectively. With the designation "who intend to vote," then those on the student list would have to be "qualified" as to their intention. Unless there is a readily available list of this sort, or it is known that everyone will vote (highly unlikely) this is a two-stage sampling process and the sampling unit definition should reflect this.

Step 3 - Sample Size

The sample size question is one that is hard to be definitive about. However students must be prepared to give one, and defend it. In doing so, they should discuss: 1) sampling error, 2) nonsampling error, 3) study objective, 4) time constraints, 5) cost constraints, and 6) data analysis plans. All of these aspects are not laid out in the case. However, they should state their assumptions and be clear about certain aspects--for instance, time and cost constraints are likely severe, and data analysis will be of the simple one-way kind (re: the proportion favoring Cynthia Lu).

In a one-stage design, one might examine the question of sample size from a statistical point of view. Suppose that one designated: 1) absolute precision of $\pm .05$, 2) at the 95% level of confidence, 3) that X is estimated to be .33 and 4) that s is estimated to be .33. Then we solve the following equation for n, the required sample size.

$$0.05 * 0.33 = \pm 2 (0.33 \div \sqrt{n})$$

$$0.0165 = 0.66 \div \sqrt{n}$$

$$0.0165\sqrt{n} = 0.66$$

$$\sqrt{n} = 40$$

$$n = 1600$$

Students using this type of procedure should recognize that they had to specify a precision and a confidence level plus assume a mean level and standard deviation that is reasonable for a three person election. Also, cost and other factors should be discussed.

Step 4 – Select a Sampling Procedure

Simple random sampling is possible here given the existence of a voters list. However this procedure is inefficient in terms of work effort. The person selecting the elements would be jumping all over the list as random numbers were selected. A better procedure here would be to select a systematic sample, since there is no reason to expect a problem with periodicity in the list.

A two-stage sample might be more appropriate if, for example, it is known seniors tend to vote for seniors and juniors tend to vote for juniors. Here the first stage would be to list students by class. The second stage would be to randomly select respondents from each class category, maintaining the sampling frame proportions to class size.

Accuracy of the Results

Sampling error could be measured here using the confidence interval formula:

$$X \pm 2 (s \div \sqrt{n}) \quad \text{for the 95\% confidence interval.}$$

In the flow of the class, some student may suggest the use of a nonprobability sampling procedure, usually a quota sample. It should be made clear that this makes little sense given the ease with which one can select a probability sample here, and the problem of error measurement with a quota sample. Of course, the above equation only measures sampling error. Other sources of inaccuracies should be discussed but are generally not measurable (people change their minds, students absent on voting day, etc.).

TEACHING STRATEGY

This case proceeds best if the instructor directs the class through the steps in the sampling process. Have a discussion at each stage and then proceed to the next stage. It helps if one person speaks first at each stage. This gives continuity to the discussion. Given that the United Airlines and Ice Cream Castle cases are usually assigned for the same session, the instructor should expect this case to run from 20-35 minutes.

CASE 4-3

UNITED AIRLINES

INTRODUCTION

This case follows directly from the Cynthia Lu case. Though the issue is the same (namely, designing the required sample), the problems involved are more complex. Basically, what is required is a multi-stage area sample.

OBJECTIVES OF THE CASE

1) To give students practice in sample design with a problem covering a broad geographic area.
2) To facilitate a discussion of area sampling.
3) To demonstrate the practical problems of sample design when a frame is not readily available.

QUESTIONS TO BE ASSIGNED

1) Prepare a sampling plan. Be sure to designate a population definition, a sampling frame, a sampling procedure, and a method for determining the accuracy of the results.

CASE ANALYSIS

This case should proceed directly through the steps in the sampling process.

Step 1 – Define the Population

The center of debate concerning the population definition usually focuses on the choice of elements. Elements could be: (1) college students, or (2) college students who fly, or (3) college students who attend school within 50 miles of an airport. Other definitions are also possible.

Since a majority of college students do not generally travel by plane, and United does not serve many of the U.S. cities, just specifying college students is too broad.

The designation of elements requires a multi-stage design, since the cost (time and money) of preparing a complete population element list would be too great. Thus some multi-stage procedure is necessary. A possible population definition might be:

A. Elements: college students who attend school within 50 miles of an airport.

B. Sampling units: colleges within 50 miles of an airport, then students at these schools.

C. Extent: USA.

D. Time: Week of October 22, 1995.

Many other population definitions with merit are possible. Debate should be encouraged.

Step 2 – Identify Sampling Frame

The researcher must find or develop a list of sampling units for each stage of the sampling process. A list of colleges in the USA and their location relative to airports will have to be assembled to identify those schools within 50 miles of an airport. This process will yield a list of colleges to form the stage one sampling frame. Student directories at colleges selected in the first stage sample could form the second stage sampling frame.

If college students who fly are required, the students contacted would have to be "qualified" on this dimension as discussed in the Cynthia Lu case teaching note.

Step 3 – Sample Size

The factors to consider on sample size include: (1) sampling error, (2) nonsampling error, (3) study objective, (4) time constraints, (5) cost constraints, and (6) data analysis plan. Some of these points are ambiguous in the case and thus student assumptions should be made clear.

There are two points that should be made. First, statistical formulas presented in the text do not help in this situation, as none were presented for a multi-stage problem. In theory, one could derive the standard error for this sampling process and solve for sample size. The precision and confidence interval levels, expected mean and standard deviations on the attitude scales would have to be designated.

Second, the data analysis here will likely not be just simple univariate analysis. Cross tabulations among attitudes, usage and demographic (male-female, etc.) are likely. Thus, the sample size will have to be large enough to accommodate this process, say 400-500 people. If geographic differences are of interest, then the sample size will have to be even larger.

Step 4 – Select a Sampling Procedure

Clearly, based upon the discussion so far, this problem lends itself to a multi-stage area sampling procedure. The repeating cycle of listing sampling units and selecting them using a probability procedure will continue through as many stages as necessary. The time and cost of developing a complete list of population elements necessitates this sequential approach. Before discussing this section, it may add to the liveliness of the discussion if the instructor polls the class on what sampling procedure the students would use in this situation.

Some students may argue for a nonprobability sample due to cost considerations. However, the cost of obtaining class lists and team rosters will not be that great. Again, convenience sampling here seems to offer little advantage in cost and comes at the expense of measurement of sampling error.

Students suggesting a multi-stage area sample should be prepared to state how they are going to insure equal probability of element selection. Selecting an equal proportion of available sampling units at each stage may exclude some large schools deemed to be important. Thus, an argument can be made for using probability proportionate to size (PPS) at stage one of selection.

It also seems easier to select a systematic sample of students from the class directories. It is easier than simple random sampling. In addition, if the class directories are ordered by class level (freshman, sophomore, etc.), this procedure will yield a proportionate stratified sample.

Accuracy of the Results

A confidence interval could be calculated on the attitude measures if a probability sampling procedure is used. To do so one would have to use the relevant formulas available in more advanced sampling books. Also, cross tabular chi-square analysis would be possible to test for significant associations among variables. Neither procedure would be available if a nonprobability procedure was used. Again, these procedures would only measure sampling error, and other sources of inaccuracies should be discussed.

TEACHING STRATEGY

Like the Cynthia Lu case, this case should proceed step-by-step through the sampling process. Again it is useful to have one student begin the discussion of each new stage of the sampling process, except as noted in Step 4. This case usually takes about 25-40 minutes, depending on how much the instructor wants to dwell on various aspects of the case.

CASE 4-4

ICE CREAM CASTLE

INTRODUCTION

This case is designed to be used in conjunction with the Cynthia Lu and United Airlines cases. All three can be covered in an hour-and-twenty-minute class period or spread over two class periods if more lecturing on sample design is desired. The issue in this case is again to design a sample. This case in particular requires creative thinking and design on the students' part.

OBJECTIVES OF THE CASE

1) To give students practice in sample design when money and time constraints are high.
2) To demonstrate the practical problems of drawing meaningful samples in a situation where developing a sample frame ahead of time may be impossible.
3) To show that nonprobability procedures or a census may be useful to marketing researchers.

QUESTIONS TO BE ASSIGNED

1) Prepare a sampling plan. Be sure to designate a population definition, a sampling frame, a sampling procedure, and a method for determining the accuracy of the results.

CASE ANALYSIS

This case should proceed through the steps in the sampling process one step at a time, as was done in the Cynthia Lu and United Airlines cases. First, however, the question of measuring the influence of an advertisement might be raised.

The Influence of the Advertisement

Some student might suggest that the complexities of drawing a sample of customers is not necessary in this instance. The volume of total customers this week as compared to last week (or the last few weeks) is all that is necessary to measure the influence of the ad. This, of course, assumes that the across-week comparisons have equivalent environmental circumstances (rain, holidays, etc.).

Alternatively, one might argue that all that need be done is to place a coupon in the ad that can be redeemed on Monday and Tuesday. A count of coupons would then measure the effect of the ad. The problem with this approach is that there are some people who would have come without the ad and coupon, but who take advantage of the coupon. This procedure, then, does not provide a clear measure of the influence of the ad.

In summary, it is important for students to recognize that it is within the domain of the marketing researcher to suggest designs that differ from that requested by management. This case can be used to emphasize this point.

The rest of this teaching note assumes that some sort of interviewing of customers will take place.

Step 1 – Define the Population

There are several different possible designations of elements here. Some students usually suggest "all people entering Ice Cream Palace on Monday or Tuesday" as the appropriate elements. The problem is that families (any group living together) may come into the ice cream parlor together, including children. Do you actually want to consider each family member as an element or would it be wiser to define the elements as "families entering..."? An additional issue is that the influence of the ad may be indirect if only one family member saw the ad and sent another to go get ice cream, or accompanied the other to the store.

An alternative population definition of elements might be families entering the store. The family would then be interviewed to determine the influence of the ad. Even when an individual is in the store alone, he or she may be considered a representative of the family. An example of population definition might be:

- A. Elements - families entering Ice Cream Castle
- B. Sampling units - families entering Ice Cream Castle
- C. Extent - inside the store
- D. Time - Monday and Tuesday

Step 2 – Identify the Sampling Frame

It is impossible to identify the sampling frame ahead of time, since one does not know who will enter the store. Therefore, the frame must be developed as people arrive. Since people come and go all day, the frame cannot be listed all at once. The researcher must select sample elements from part of the frame before all of the elements have come in and been identified.

Step 3 – Sample Size

Again, the usual tradeoffs between time, cost, sampling error, etc. must be examined. It is important to note that simple univariate analysis is likely here since there is undoubtedly limited money to spend and the upper limit is determined by the number of people. Assuming there are 25 families per hour on average, for 10 hours a day, for 2 days, then the maximum population would be 25 x 10 x 2 = 500. A good argument could be made to take a census if it were possible to interview all incoming or outgoing families if there were enough interviewers and the interviews were brief.

Step 4 – Select a Sampling Procedure

Assuming that a sample, not a census, is taken, there is a clear recommendation for a systematic sample. Even though the frame is not known ahead of time, every fifth family could be interviewed. Note that the sample size cannot be predetermined since that depends upon the actual number of people. One would need to estimate population and sample size and designate $k = N/n$. This is not an arbitrary designation since interview length, available interviewers, etc. are factors to consider.

Given the nature of the research and low level of risk involved, some students might argue for a nonprobability example such as convenience or quota. Given the ease in drawing a systematic sample, there appears to be little effort saved over conducting a systematic sample.

Accuracy of the Results

Standard confidence interval procedures are again available to measure sampling error if systematic sampling is used. It cannot be estimated if nonprobability sampling is used. If a census were taken, estimates, confidence intervals, inferences, etc. are out of place.

TEACHING STRATEGY

This case usually proceeds quickly once the Cynthia Lu and United Airlines cases have been dealt with. Again, proceed step-by-step through the sampling process. Be sure to draw out alternative procedures to sampling as discussed in the note. This case can be compressed into 10-15 minutes if one pushes it, or stretched to 30 minutes if all bases are touched carefully.

CASE 4-5

COSMOPOLITAN

INTRODUCTION

This case requires students to evaluate a research project with respect to a variety of sampling issues, including population, sample size, and nonsampling errors. The context of the case is an actual survey conducted by **Cosmopolitan** magazine in 1980.

OBJECTIVES OF THE CASE

1) To illustrate the importance of accurately defining a sample population so as to generalize from the results.
2) To give students practice in critically evaluating sampling procedures.
3) To show some of the major problems associated with nonprobability samples.
4) To show the role of sample size in sampling error and its inability to help with nonsampling error.

QUESTIONS TO BE ASSIGNED

1) What is the population definition in this study? Does it differ from the study population?
2) What is the sampling frame used?
3) What sampling procedure was used?
4) Is the study superior to previous academic studies based upon the larger sample size? How was their sample size determined?

CASE ANALYSIS

Population Definition

The population definition in the study does not appear to be defined in detail beyond "American females." However, the actual study population, the aggregate of elements from which the sample is drawn, is quite different. The study sample is actually selected only from those readers of **Cosmopolitan**, January, 1980. Therefore, many elements of the desired population have been omitted.

Sampling Frame

The study never used a sampling frame. To have done so would have required listing all the sampling units in the population, or all readers of that issue. Clearly, a subscription list would not suffice since many readers buy issues off the newsstand or several readers may regularly read one issue. The use of area sampling can alleviate this difficulty.

Sampling Procedure

The sampling procedure used was a nonprobability convenience based one. Respondents are self selected. That is, anyone who had a copy of the magazine had the opportunity to respond.

As such, the size of the sample could not be determined in advance of the study since **Cosmopolitan** had no control over who would ultimately respond. Therefore, the differences between the population of interest and the sample values are unknown in terms of size and direction. Sampling error cannot be estimated. The use of a convenience sample prohibits making conclusive or definitive statements about the total population.

Issue of Study Superiority

Just because the sample size exceeded previous academic research, its results are not necessarily superior or more accurate. A well designed probability-based sample can be much smaller and still yield reliable results. Furthermore, sampling error may be estimated. **Cosmopolitan's** sample size was determined solely by the number who chose to respond. With the convenience sample, no matter how large, there is no guarantee that it will include representation of the population of interest. It is impossible to specify the characteristics of the sample. There are many possible nonsampling errors which may further invalidate the results. Nonsampling errors include: faulty population definition, the frame does not represent the population, nonresponse errors (there is a great probability that those who had the opportunity to respond and did not are significantly different from those who did), poor questionnaire design, interpretation errors, and auspices error. There may be little incentive for or guarantee that respondents answered truthfully or accurately.

TEACHING STRATEGY

Obviously the issues are interrelated. However, the best way to run the case is to go through the questions, discussing each one individually. As time allows, have students redesign the study using probability-based sampling. Also, the objectives of the study can be explored. Generalizations about the **Cosmopolitan** audience is quite different from making statements about American women.

CASE 4-6

GALLUP

INTRODUCTION

This case describes the multistage area sampling procedure used by Gallup for pre-election polling. It draws upon the concepts presented in Chapter 14.

OBJECTIVES OF THE CASE

1) To facilitate discussion about the multistage area sampling process.
2) To discuss pros and cons of Gallup's sampling procedure.
3) To demonstrate the usefulness of stratification in sampling.

QUESTIONS TO BE ASSIGNED

1) What is the study population? What sampling units were defined by this procedure? What were the sampling frames?
2) Are there any problems presented by the method used to define the study population, sampling unit or sampling frame?
3) Why was stratification used? Are there additional strata that should be considered?
4) What purpose was there in selecting PSUs and precincts with probability proportionate to census estimates of their respective household populations? How could this be accomplished?
5) What problems could result from sampling individuals who are not likely to actually vote in the election?

CASE ANALYSIS

We suggest that the instructor first discuss the sampling process and then answer the questions in order presented. In this case, Gallop used a three-stage area sampling process:

Step 1: 360 PSUs were stratified according to size and region.
A list of PSUs was made and a sample was drawn, with the probability of drawing each element proportionate to estimates of its population.

Step 2: One precinct was selected from each PSU with probability proportionate to the number of registered voters in that precinct.

Step 3: Each precinct was divided into ten equal parts (stratified). Interviewers were required to obtain one interview in each of the ten jurisdictions.

1) The **study population** consisted of all registered voters in the U.S. **Sampling units** were PSUs, precincts, and individuals. **Sampling frames** were lists of PSUs, precincts, and voting age individuals.

2) Potential problems could arise in Step 1 and Step 3. In Step 1, there could be a problem if the number of registered voters in a given PSU were not proportionate to population estimates. In Step 3, there could be a problem if non-voters were sampled.

3) Stratification was used in Step 1 to ensure that the sample of PSUs obtained would be representative of all regions and "sizes of place" within the U.S. It also allowed researchers to assess any differences in voting patterns based on region and size of place. One could also argue that stratification occurred in Step 3 when each precinct was divided into ten equal parts. This was done to ensure that a representative sample of all the neighborhoods within each precinct was selected.

Statistical efficiency is maximized by selecting a large number of clusters and a small number of elements within each cluster. The above stratification plan makes sense in light of that argument.

Other strata could have been utilized based on demographic variables such as age, gender, and party affiliation.

4) The purpose of selecting PSUs and precincts with probability proportionate to their household population was to ensure that large clusters were fully represented in the sample.

For any given PSU or precinct, the probability proportionate to size

$$\text{PPS} = \frac{\text{population of PSU or precinct}}{\text{total population}}$$

5) The problem that could arise from sampling individuals who are not likely to actually vote is that their opinions are obviously not included in or representative of the actual outcome of the election.

TEACHING STRATEGY

As mentioned above, we suggest that the instructor first discuss the sampling process and then answer the questions in the order in which they are presented in the text.

CASE 4-7

A DAY IN THE CAREERS OF PAMELA PALMERS AND SANDY SANDERS: PROFESSIONAL INTERVIEWERS

INTRODUCTION

This case presents partial transcripts of interviews for two professional field interviewers involved in the same study. The questionnaire used in the study, the background of the study, and a summary sheet of the respondent contacts for the day are also presented. The student task is to evaluate the two interviewers.

OBJECTIVES OF THE CASE

1) To show students the dynamics of actual field interviews.
2) To facilitate discussion of what constitutes "good" and "bad" interviewing.
3) To help prepare students for doing a future personal interviewing assignment.
4) To demonstrate the nature of field-related nonsampling errors.

QUESTIONS TO BE ASSIGNED

1) How would you evaluate the interviewing skills of Pamela Palmers and Sandy Sanders?
2) What specific suggestions would you make to improve their effectiveness?

CASE ANALYSIS

The student should proceed to evaluate the two interviewers using the rules of interviewing discussed in Chapter 15 under the heading "Interviewing Errors".

The instructor should review these rules by first drawing them out completely as discussed in the text under the section headings:

(1) Interviewer-respondent Rapport,
(2) Asking the Questions,
(3) Recording the Responses, and
(4) Cheating.

The list would be too long if all sections were done at once. We have found it useful to write the rules on the left side of the board by section in a column. The two interviewers' names could then be put in columns to the right of these rules. The evaluation of the interviewers is then done by filling in the resultant matrix.

Our interpretation of how the interviewers perform against these rules follows. Other interpretations are, of course, possible. A "+" sign indicates that the interviewer is rated as good on that dimension, a "-" sign indicates that the interviewer is rated as poor on that dimension, and a "?" indicates that the case does not allow a meaningful conclusion. In doing these ratings the student should be asked to cite specific examples from the case.

Rule	Pamela Palmers	Sandy Sanders
Section 1: Rapport		
1. Establish rapport.	+	-
Section 2: Asking the Questions		
2. Be thoroughly familiar with the questionnaire.	+	+?
3. Ask the questions exactly as they are worded in the questionnaire.	+	-
4. Ask the questions in the order in which they are presented in the questionnaire.	+	+
5. Ask every question specified in the questionnaire.	+?	+?
6. Use probing techniques; phrase in a neutral fashion.	+	-
7. Keep track of changes made in the questionnaire.	?	?
8. Provide a logical reason for collecting personal data.	?	?
Section 3: Recording Responses		
9. Record responses during the interview.	+	+
10. Use the respondent's own words.	+	-
11. Do not summarize or paraphrase the respondent's answers.	+	-
12. Include everything that pertains to the question objectives.	+	-
13. Include all probes and comments by entering them next to the question in parentheses.	+	+
14. Hold the respondent's interest by repeating the response as it is written down.	-	-
15. Find a place where you can write comfortably.	?	?

Rule	Pamela Palmers	Sandy Sanders
16. When the respondent starts to talk, begin to write immediately.	+	+
17. Abbreviate words and sentences. During the editing process, put these in along with punctuation.	−	−
18. Use a pencil.	? ?	
19. Writing must be legible.	+	−
20. Use parentheses to indicate the interviewer's words or observations.	+	+
21. Do not put anything the respondent says in parentheses.	+	+
22. Each question must have an answer or an explanation why it was not answered.	+	+
23. Be complete with identification data.	?	?

Section 4: Cheating

23. Do not cheat.	+	+

In summary, Pamela Palmers appears to be a very good interviewer, although she does have some weak points. This also shows up in her "contact sheet" for the day. She was able to complete 16 of 28 attempted interviews. The one major concern about her was that she was willing to interview a friend. She probably should not have done this.

On the other hand, Sandy Sanders is quite a poor interviewer overall. She has just too many negatives on important dimensions as indicated. Her contact sheet for the day provides further evidence of this. She was only able to complete 12 of 39 attempted interviews.

TEACHING STRATEGY

This case is not designed to fill an entire class period. It works best if used in conjunction with a "live" field interviewing assignment. Thus the first half hour of the class would be spent discussing Pamela Palmers and Sandy Sanders. The rest of the class would be spent discussing the experience (problems, success, temptations to lead respondents, etc.) of the students as "live" interviewers.

In discussing this case, it flows best if the two interviewers are examined on each dimension, taking one dimension at a time. It is important to force students to cite specific evidence from the case to support their evaluation.

Often students will want to critically evaluate the study design which is briefly described in the case. While this is a legitimate issue, it is not the purpose of the assignment and should be discussed only if the instructor desires to take class time for discussing research design.

CASE 5-1

THE ANN ARBOR METRO TIMES

INTRODUCTION

This case gives students experience in developing a coding manual for The Ann Arbor Metro Times reader survey. With this case, students are exposed to some of the issues facing coders. As the response choices to the various questions are generally ambiguous, issues may be highlighted and suggestions for improvements may be made.

OBJECTIVES OF THE CASE

1) To give students an opportunity to design a coding scheme for a questionnaire.
2) To emphasize the benefits of carefully planning a questionnaire and defining response categories.
3) To illustrate some of the prevalent issues surrounding coding.

QUESTIONS TO BE ASSIGNED

1) Prepare a coding manual for the AAMT's questionnaire.

CASE ANALYSIS

Column	Question	Variable	Description	Format	Coding Notes
1-3	–	1	Respondent Number	I3	3-digit number, 001-999
4	1	2	Number of issues read	I1	1- one 2- two 3- three 4- four 5- five 6- six 7- first time 0- no response (NR)/ don't know (DK)

**Be consistent with "no response" and "not checked" categories throughout coding manual.

5-19	2A	3	All regular features read	I1	Items 1 thru 15: 1- checked 0- not checked
20-21	2B	4	One feature most enjoyed	I2	01- "Ashes & Diamonds" 02- "Toni Swanger"

					03- "Letters" 04- "Rock & Roll Conf." 05- "What's Happening...AA" 06- "What's Happening...Detroit" 07- "Hot Dates" 08- "Pick of the Week" 09- "Flicks" 10- "Mondo Video" 11- "Real Astrology" 12- "The Comics Page" 13- "Detroit Live" 14- Classified Ads 15- Display Ads 00- NR; multiple responses
22-28	3A	5	Cover stories read	I1	Items 1 thru 7 1- checked 0- not checked
29	3B	6	Story enjoyed most	I1	0- NR; multiple responses 1- "U-M may Flunk" 2- "Motor City Gothic" 3- "EYF" 4- "The Greening of Valerie" 5- "Rob Tyner's Grande Days" 6- "Aggressing the Retina" 7- "A Hard Rain's Gonna Fall"
30-38	4	7	Stories read	I1	Items 1 thru 9: 1- checked 0- not checked
39-44	5	8	Preferred type of music	I1	Items 1 thru 6: 1- checked 0- not checked
45	5	9	Pref. type of music - other	I1	Open ended question: 0- NR/none/none listed/ not checked 1- Folk 2- Rap/Urban Black/Soul 3- Reggae 4- Ethnic/Imports/Latin 5- Local or Cover bands 6- Country 7- New age/Pop/Classic Rock 8- House/Dance/Industrial 9- Alternative/New/Punk

**Open-ended questions present a more complex problem for coding. This coding scheme could be prepared before or after the results have been returned. The major task of the research is to train coders so that they will convert the verbatim responses into the correct code categories.

Deleted   6

46-52	7	10	Preferred type of coverage	I1	Items 1 thru 7: 1- checked 0- not checked
53	7	11	Pref. coverage - other	I1	Open ended question: 0- NR/none/none listed/ not checked 1- Performing Arts/Theater 2- Book reviews/Literary 3- Letters 4- Health 5- Local Political Issues 6- Night Clubs
54-66	8	12	Publications looked/read	I1	Items 1 thru 13: 1- checked 0- not checked
175	9	13	Add anything to AAMT	I1	Open ended question: 0- NR/nothing 1- More like the Detroit MT 2- More comics 3- Movie or Theater coverage 4- Local music coverage 5- Record reviews 6- News/Detroit coverage 7- Columnists 8- Other
67	10	14	Gender	I1	0- NR 1- Female 2- Male
68-73	11	15	Household age categories	I1	Items 1 thru 6: 1- checked 0- not checked
74-75	12	16	Respondent's age	I2	01-99: actual response 00 - NR; other
76	13	17	Marital status	I1	0- NR 1- Single 2- Married 3- Separated/Divorced 4- Widowed
77	14	18	Employment Status	I1	0- NR 1- Unemployed 2- Full time 3- Part time 4- Retired 5- Homemaker 6- Volunteer 7- Full time student 8- Part time student

                                                                9- Multiple non-employed/
                                                                    Non-student responses
                                                                **code other responses into
                                                                1-7 when applicable, or 9
                                                                **Other multiple responses:
                                                                a) if full/part time
                                                                    employment, code as 2
                                                                b) if full/part time student and
                                                                    NOT employment, code as 7
                                                                c) if (b) and employed, code
                                                                    as 2 or 3

78-79   15   19   Income   I2   00- NR
                                                                01- under $10,000
                                                                02- 10,000 - 14,999
                                                                03- 15,000 - 19,999
                                                                04- 20,000 - 29,999
                                                                05- 30,000 - 39,999
                                                                06- 40,000 - 49,999
                                                                07- 50,000 - 59,999
                                                                08- 60,000 - 69,999
                                                                09- 70,000 - 79,999
                                                                10- 80,000 - 89,999
                                                                11- 90,000 or more

80-81   16   20   Area of Employment   I2   00- NR
                                                                01- Services
                                                                02- Artist/writer/entertainer
                                                                03- Student/unemployed
                                                                04- Homemaker/retired
                                                                05- Marketing/Sales/Advert.
                                                                06- Engineers/Computers/Tech.
                                                                07- Professional/Managerial
                                                                08- Educational/Counselors
                                                                09- Health or social prof.
                                                                10- Construction/agriculture/
                                                                    mechanics/postal/police/gov't
                                                                11- Other

82   17   21   Level of education   I1   0- NR
                                                                1- High school
                                                                2- College
                                                                3- Post graduate
                                                                4- Adv. degree: Masters
                                                                5- Adv. degree: Doctorate

83   18   22   Primary residence   I1   0-NR
                                                                1- own a private home
                                                                2- own a condo or co-op
                                                                3- rent a house
                                                                4- rent an apartment
                                                                5- student housing
                                                                6- cooperative housing

84   19   23   12-month home purchase   I1   0- NR

85	20	24	12-month rental plan	I1	1- Yes 2- No 0- NR 1- Yes 2- No
86-98	21	25	12-month activities	I1	Items 1 thru 13: 1- checked 0- not checked
99-100	22	26	30-day movie activity	I2	00- NR/DK/zero/other 01 - 99: actual response
101-102	23	27	60-day lecture activity	I2	00- NR/DK/zero 01 - 99: actual response
103-118	24	28	30-day activity attendance	I2	00- NR/DK/Checked 01 - 99: actual response
119-136	25	29	12-mo. purchase volume	I3	000- NR/DK/checked 001-999: actual number
137-150	26	30	12-month item purchases	I1	0- not checked 1- checked
151	27	31	Number of cars	I1	0- NR/DK 1-9: actual number
155-164	27	32	Make of car	I2	00- NR/DK/no car listed 01- Chrysler 02- Dodge 03- Plymouth 04- Buick 05- Cadillac 06- Chevrolet 07- Oldsmobile 08- Pontiac 09- General Motors (no specific make) 10- Ford 11- Mercury 12- Jeep 13- Toyota 14- Honda 15- Mazda 16- Nissan 17- Subaru 18- Suzuki 19- Acura 20- Lexus 21- Audi 22- BMW 23- Mercedes-Benz 24- Peugeot 25- Saab 26- Volvo

					27- VW
					28- Yugo
					29- Renault
					30- Other
165-174	27	33	Year	I2	00- NR/DK/no car listed
					01-99: actual year
152	27	34	New or Used	I1	0- NR/DK/no car listed
					1- New
					2- Used
					3- New & used (multiple purchases)
153	28A	35	12-month car purchase?	I1	0- NR/DK
					1- Yes
					2- No
154	28B	36	Type of car purchase	I1	0- No to Q28A/NR/DK
					1- New
					2- Used
					3- New & used (multiple expected purchases)

TEACHING STRATEGY

The importance of this case lies in the experience of actually editing and coding. This case may be used in conjunction with the case 5-2 "Midwest Marketing Research Associates (B)". Students may be asked to present their coding scheme for various questions. Class discussion may be directed to the different problems, issues, and alternatives. This case by itself should only require about 20-30 minutes of class time.

CASE 5-2

MIDWEST MARKETING RESEARCH ASSOCIATES (B)

INTRODUCTION

This case contains the coding manual proposed for the Midwest Marketing Research Associates questionnaire on nutrition information in grocery stores. It is designed for use with the material on Data Processing contained in Chapter 16.

OBJECTIVES OF THE CASE

1) To improve students' understanding of the editing and coding functions.
2) To provide opportunity to use a questionnaire in a personal interview.
3) To teach students how to edit and code a very open-ended questionnaire by having them actually go through the process.

QUESTIONS TO BE ASSIGNED

1) Use the questionnaire in case 3-8, Midwest Marketing Research Associates (A), in a personal interview, and use the coding manual to code it.
2) Critically evaluate the coding manual. Make specific recommendations for changes.

CASE ANALYSIS

Specific problems cited with the coding manual usually include:

1) For all questions: "other" should be given a standard code throughout the manual.

2) For question 5, columns 10-11, 13-14, 16-17, 19-20, 22-23, 25-26 and 28-29: this is really a multiple response question and should be given a larger number of columns to allow for several responses to each question. This would eliminate the necessity of combining categories, e.g. 14 = 5 and 9. If all possible combinations were coded in this manner, the number would be too great to handle. This point also applies to questions 25-27, columns 73-78.

3) Also regarding question 5 the "no response" category is potentially confusing. Does it mean "don't know," "refused to answer," or that the subject doesn't seek nutrition information from any source, which makes the question irrelevant. The coding scheme should pick up these differences. Also, the order of the categories in card column 21 is different from that in 22, and neither is the same as in the original question. This could create confusion in data analysis later.

5) For question 7, columns 32-33: "none" should be an option. Also, because there are fewer than 10 answer choices, only one digit / column is needed to code this question.

6) For questions 8 and 9, columns 34-35: As with the previous question, only one digit is needed to code responses.

7) The coding scheme for question 13 is missing. Each product should be coded as though it were a yes or no question. Thus a total of six columns are needed to code the question.

8) Regarding question 20, column 66: the two-digit response for "other" cannot fit in the one column allocated. It should be coded as 9, not 99.

9) Regarding question 19, column 65: the coding scheme should consistently use the same number for "yes" and not switch back and forth. Inconsistent coding could cause problems in data analysis later.

10) Regarding question 15, columns 45-50: the "no response" category is missing

11) Regarding question 17, columns 63, 65, 67: the categories do not match those in the original question.

12) Regarding question 34, columns 86-87: it is hard to fit some occupations into these categories.

13) Regarding question 37, columns 90-93: these categories are not exhaustive; they exclude children less than a year old.

14) Regarding questions 37 and 39, columns 90-93, and 96: it is good practice to have the code numbers assigned equal to the quantity of an attribute. Here the code "1" should equal one child (resident), "2" equal 2 children (residents), etc.

15) Regarding question 38, columns 94-95: the format F2.0 is not necessary. The number of children must be an integer, therefore 12 is the appropriate format.

16) Regarding question 40 column 97: income categories overlap.

17) Regarding question 42, column 99: the life cycle scheme does not allow all persons to be classified, nonmarried couples living together, separated, or divorced people without children are hard to classify. The concept of life cycle as described may now be outdated by new mores.

Based upon their use of the coding manual, students usually have no trouble finding fault with it.

TEACHING STRATEGY

The importance of this case lies in the experience of actually editing and coding. The class session serves to solidify the experience by sharing it with others.

We have designed worksheets that can be handed out to students for recording coded responses and criticisms about the questionnaire. Originals of these worksheets, located at the end of this case, can be duplicated and handed out when the assignment is made.

Class time should be spent identifying difficulties students had in using the coding manual, and discussing suggestions for improvements in the manual. This usually takes about half a class period. The remaining time is well served by a lecture on data processing or on introductory material in data analysis.

Name _____

WORKSHEET TO RECORD RESPONSE NUMBERS FOR KEYPUNCHING

Column	Response	Column	Response
1	_____	30	_____
2	_____	31	_____
3	_____	32	_____
4	_____	33	_____
5	_____	34	_____
6	_____	35	_____
7	_____	36	_____
8	_____	37	_____
9	_____	38	_____
10	_____	39	_____
11	_____	40	_____
12	_____	41	_____
13	_____	42	_____
14	_____	43	_____
15	_____	44	_____
16	_____	45	_____
17	_____	46	_____
18	_____	47	_____
19	_____	48	_____
20	_____	49	_____
21	_____	50	_____
22	_____	51	_____
23	_____	52	_____
24	_____	53	_____
25	_____	54	_____
26	_____	55	_____
27	_____	56	_____
28	_____	57	_____
29	_____	58	_____

Column	Response	Column	Response
59	_____	80	_____
60	_____	81	_____
61	_____	82	_____
62	_____	83	_____
63	_____	84	_____
64	_____	85	_____
65	_____	86	_____
66	_____	87	_____
67	_____	88	_____
68	_____	89	_____
69	_____	90	_____
70	_____	91	_____
71	_____	92	_____
72	_____	93	_____
73	_____	94	_____
74	_____	95	_____
75	_____	96	_____
76	_____	97	_____
77	_____	98	_____
78	_____	99	_____
79	_____		

Name _____

WORKSHEET TO RECORD IMPROVEMENTS IN THE
NUTRITIONAL LABELING CODING MANUAL

I. Suggested change in question coding

   A. Question number and coding change:

   B. Reason for change in coding:

   A. Question number and coding change:

   B. Reason for change in coding:

II. General suggestions on how to improve the coding manual.

CASE 5-3

MILAN FOOD COOPERATIVE (B)

INTRODUCTION

This case is a continuation of Milan Food Cooperative (A) from Part 4 of the text. Here results of regression and correlation analysis are presented and students are asked to interpret various relationships, determine a predictive function, determine statistical confidence intervals, and discuss analysis assumptions.

OBJECTIVES OF THE CASE

1) To expose students to an application of two common data analysis techniques, correlation and regression.
2) To give students practice in interpreting correlation and regression results while recognizing the various assumptions underlying the analyses.

QUESTIONS TO BE ASSIGNED

1) For the correlation results:

   a) What interpretation can you give to the results shown?
   b) What assumptions underlie your interpretations?
   c) How could these assumptions be tested?

2) For the regression results:

   a) What interpretations can you give to these results?
   b) What assumptions underlie your interpretations?
   c) How could these assumptions be tested?
   d) Does the low R^2 imply that our independent variables are poor predictors of food expenditures?
   e) Support your position.

CASE ANALYSIS

1. Correlation Matrix

   a) **Interpreting the results of the correlation matrix**

      Two types of associations should be examined. First, study the relationships between the dependent variable (weekly food expenditure) and the independent variables (number of persons, income, kids 6-18, kids under 6, education, and age). The conclusion is that there is a reasonably strong relationship between expenditures and 1) persons (.43); 2) income (.38); and 3) kids 6-18 (.40).

Second, examine relationships among independent variables. Correlation is strong between 1) persons and kids 6-18 (.70); 2) persons and kids under 6 (.56); 3) income and education (.48); and 4) kids 6-18 and kids under 6 (.25). Notice that there is no relationship between age of head of household and number of persons. Since this may be counterintuitive to many, students may seek to explain this. While there is no linear relationship, a nonlinear relationship is possible. The following crosstabs illustrate this point (see TN Figure 1).

This figure presents a frequency count of the number of respondents in each age/number of persons combination. This figure shows a very strong curvilinear relationship between age and number of persons in the household. Indeed, common sense would predict this. Younger people and older people should have smaller household sizes than those in the middle range ages. Linear correlation has failed to find a real relationship. This is an important lesson for students to learn.

TN Figure 1

Age

		25	34	44	54	64	74	75+
	9+			4	5	1		
	8			9	3			
	7		4	14	6			
No. of	6		6	19	8	1		
Persons	5		16	24	12	5		
	4	2	43	21	20	9	3	1
	3	13	28	22	21	9	1	1
	2	18	30	27	18	19	5	2
	1	9	10	6	6	10	8	1

b) **Assumptions underlying correlation matrix interpretations**

The major assumption is that linear relationships predominate amongst the variables. In most instances, this is probably all right, but exceptions do exist as noted above.

c) **Testing these assumptions**

The previous crosstab illustrates a violation of this assumption. Another way to examine whether relationships are linear is by graphing. For example, the relationship between weekly food expenditures and number of persons in household is also nonlinear (TN Figure 2). Other relationships display a great deal of linear association.

2. **Regression Results**

   a) **Interpreting regression results**

   It is possible to estimate a family's weekly food expenditure by plugging values into the regression formula. However, the levels of significance and the confidence intervals suggest that the coefficients for certain variables should not be taken at face value. These variables are: 1) kids less than 6; 2) education; and 3) age of head of household.

Conclusions include:

1) This estimation formula explains 29.6 percent of the total variability of weekly food expenditures; i.e., the variance of the true food expenditure about the regression line (plane) is about 70 percent of its variance about average food expenditures.

2) Standard error:

   Given a 5 percent probability of error, an estimation for expenditures by a particular sample household might be off by $35.30 or more.

3) Confidence intervals for the coefficients:

   The standard errors of the coefficients give the following 95 percent confidence intervals (2 standard errors) for the coefficients:

Persons	3.51 ± 1.42	Education	1.11 ± 1.52
Kids 0-6	-1.87 ± 4.46	Income	.77 ± .25
Kids 6-18	5.30 ± 4.60	Age	.025 ± .14

4) Coefficients

   a) Small children do not eat as much as teenagers and adults.

   b) In families where the head of household is elderly and more educated, expenditures tend to be higher.

   c) The significance of these three coefficients is weak. For example, using age there is a 71 percent chance of our saying that the age coefficient is different from zero when it is not.

5) a) **Using the regression equation:**

   13.78 constant
   +(3.51 * number persons)
   +(-1.87 if kids under 6)
   +(5.30 if kids 6-18)
   +(1.11 * education level)
   +(.768 * income in thousands)
   +(.025 * age in years)

For a family of four, with no children under 6, but children 6-18, where the head of household is a college graduate age 38 and the family income is $25,000 the food expenditure estimate is:

(13.78) + (3.41 x 4) + (-1.87 x 0) + (5.30 x 1) + (1.11 x 5) + (.768 x 25) + (.025 x 38) = $58.42/week

R2 = 0.296   Standard error of the estimate SSE = 17.65

Variable values are from Milan Food Cooperative (A).

b) **Assumptions underlying regression interpretations**

1) Multicollinearity is not present
2) Interactions are not present
3) Relationships between dependent and independent variables are linear

c) **Testing these assumptions**

TN Figures 1 and 2 illustrate tests for linear relationships. Similar analyses can be performed on other variables. TN Figure 3 illustrates the existence of multicollinearity between education and income while TN Figure 4 illustrates the effects of income interaction on the relationship between number of persons and weekly food expenditure. Thus, this data contains nonlinear relationships between the dependent variable and some independent variables, multicollinearity among predictor variables, and some interaction (nonadditive effects). This clearly demonstrates the risks of blindly running a canned regression package, and directly interpreting the coefficients.

d) & e) **Does the low R^2 value imply that the independent variables are poor predictors of food expenditures?**

Not necessarily. While there are other variables which relate to food expenditures and could possibly improve prediction, several points can be made about the variables used in this regression equation.

1) A transformation to a logarithmic scale might solve the problem of nonlinearity between expenditure and number of persons.
2) Interaction problems (food expenditure/number of persons/income) could be solved by the use of dummy variables.
3) Measurement errors are undoubtedly present. For example, a respondent incorrectly recalls actual food expenditure or fails to record a "quick pick up" purchase.
4) The multicollinearity problem may be solved by dropping out correlated variables, or forming indices.
5) It turns out that a three-variable equation using number of persons, income, and children 6-18 provides essentially the same estimate of food expenditure.

TEACHING STRATEGY

If Milan Food Cooperative (A) was not done, instruct students to read the case for background. If it was, a review is helpful. This is a good opportunity to review the principles, if not the mechanics of covariance, correlation, multicollinearity, interaction, multiple regression, etc. First, the correlation matrix can be examined with the instructor asking students to interpret various correlational relationships. Then the regression table can be similarly examined. This is a good opportunity for the instructor to explain or illustrate stepwise regression. Usually the instructor must take the lead in running this discussion. Students typically do not understand all the complexities of correlation and regression. It is also useful to have the material in TN Figures 1-4 available on overheads. Also note that the statistical tests performed imply that the data is from a sample, not a census. Students have no difficulty making this assumption for the case discussion.

TN FIGURE 2

RELATIONSHIP BETWEEN WEEKLY FOOD EXPENDITURE AND NUMBER OF PERSONS IN HOUSEHOLD

(NON-LINEAR RELATIONSHIP)

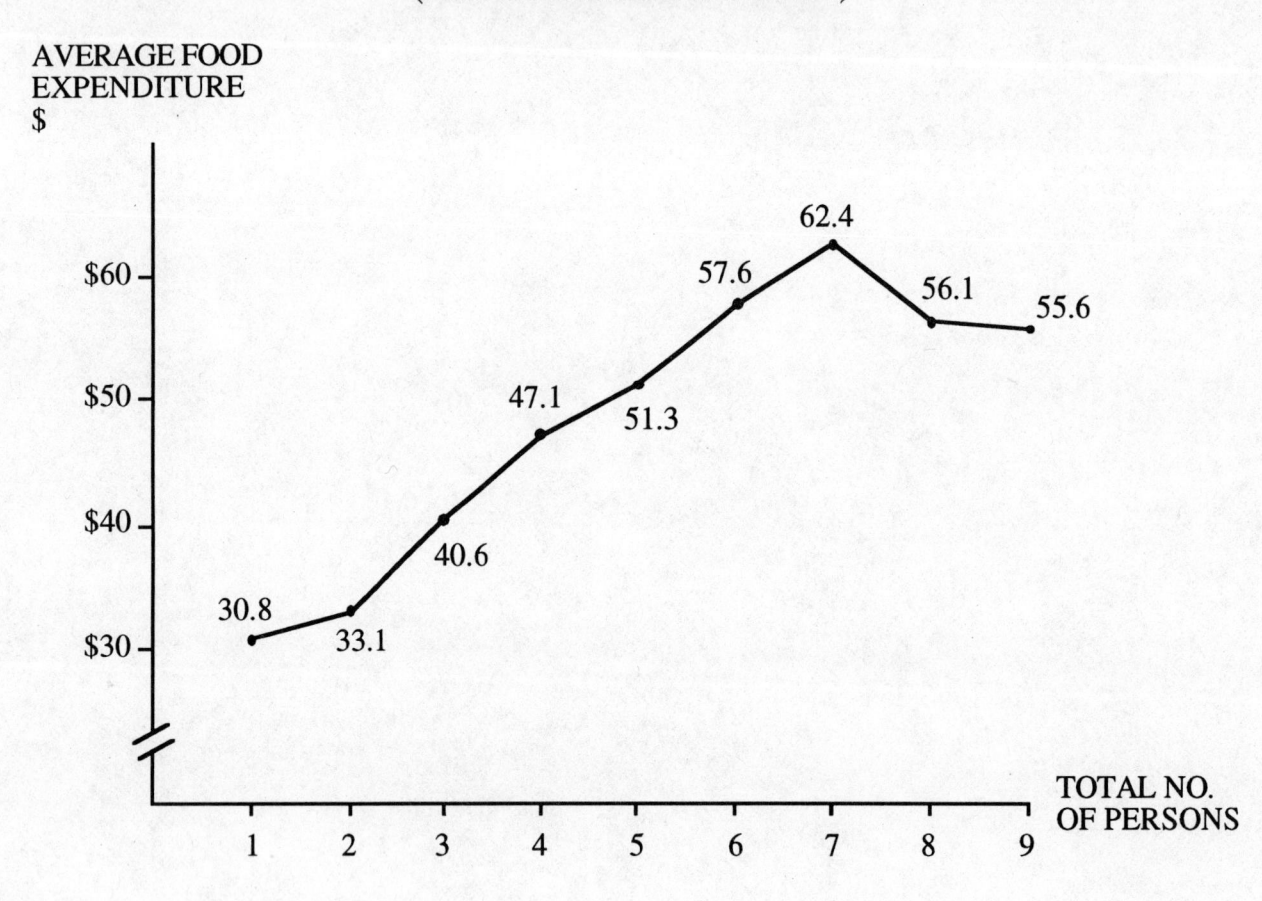

TN FIGURE 3

RELATIONSHIP BETWEEN HOUSEHOLD ANNUAL INCOME AND EDUCATION OF HOUSEHOLD HEAD

(MULTICOLLINEARITY)

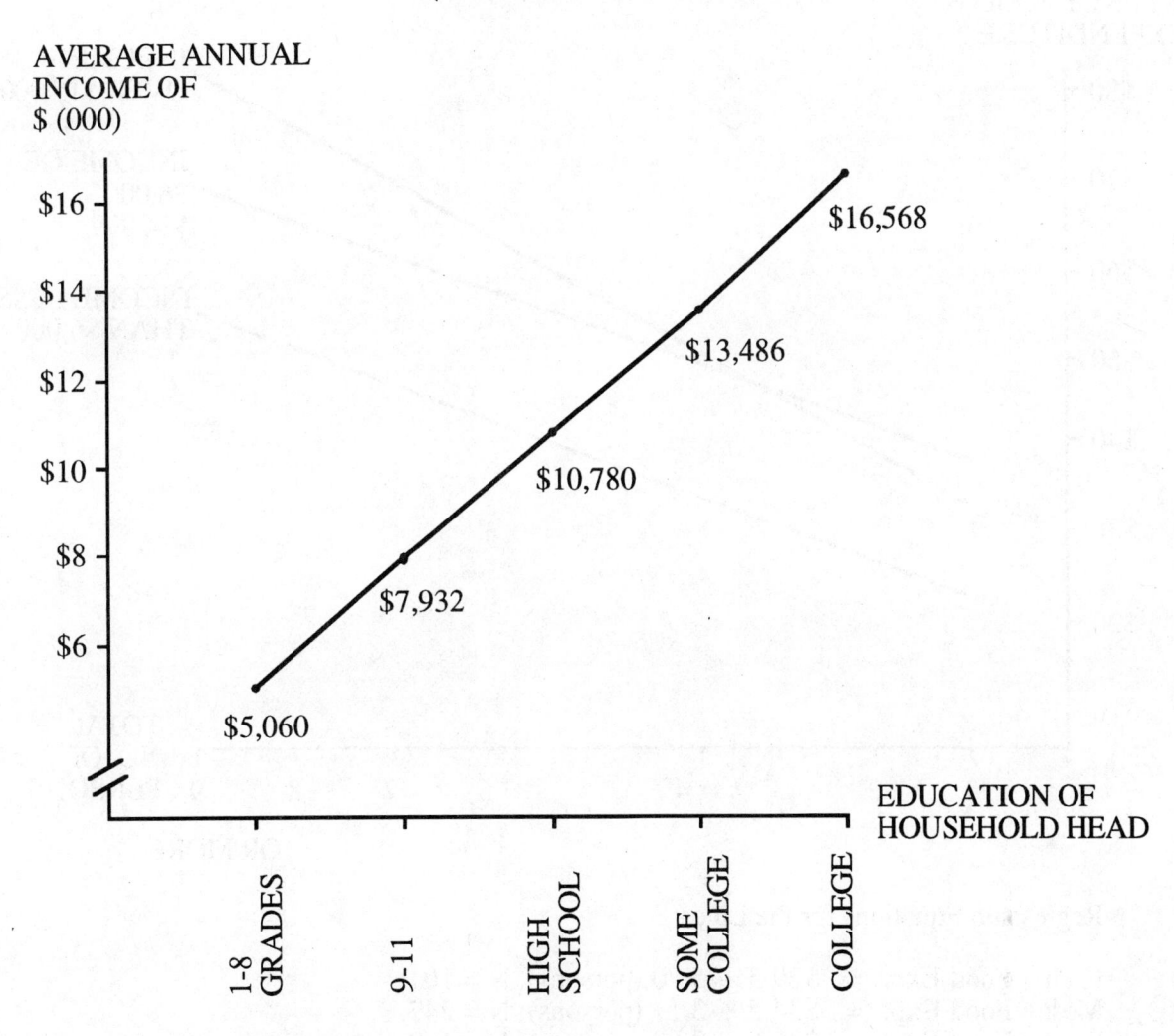

AVERAGE ANNUAL INCOME OF $ (000)

- $16,568 — COLLEGE
- $13,486 — SOME COLLEGE
- $10,780 — HIGH SCHOOL
- $7,932 — 9-11
- $5,060 — 1-8 GRADES

EDUCATION OF HOUSEHOLD HEAD

TN FIGURE 4

RELATIONSHIP BETWEEN FOOD EXPENDITURE AND NUMBER OF PERSONS IN HOUSEHOLD FOR THREE INCOME GROUPS

(INTERACTION)

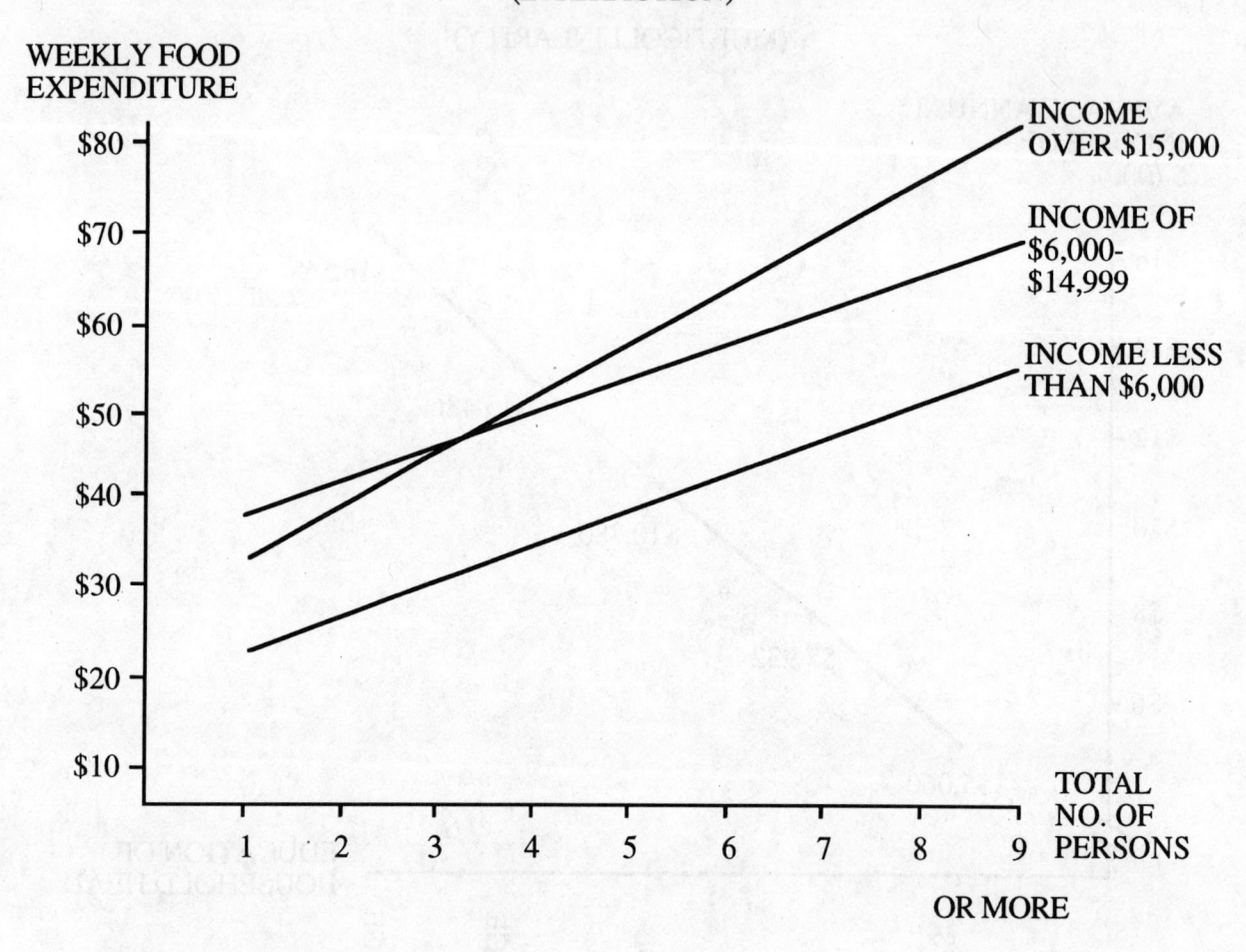

Regression Equations for the Lines:

High: Food Exp. = $29.5 + 5.70 (persons); N = 101
Med: Food Exp. = $34.5 + 3.17 (persons); N = 247
Low: Food Exp. = $20.0 + 3.88 (persons); N = 152

CASE 5-4

BERNIE'S STUDENT CAFETERIA

INTRODUCTION

This case presents some univariate and bivariate analyses performed on data collected for a survey on a university-run cafeteria. Students have an opportunity to interpret results and make conclusions. They also have to consider potential interaction between variables and suggest which bivariate tables need elaboration.

OBJECTIVES OF THE CASE

1) To give students an opportunity to interpret the results of bivariate and univariate analyses.
2) To demonstrate that data analyses can be potentially misleading without careful forethought about the relationships examined.
3) To provide students with a chance to examine bivariate relationships for instances where elaboration and the use of control variables can provide valuable insight into the results.
4) To require students to relate data analysis back to the objectives of the study.

QUESTIONS TO BE ASSIGNED

1) What conclusions can be drawn on the basis of the univariate analysis?
2) What conclusions can be drawn on the basis of the bivariate analysis? Be sure to write down the relevant conclusion for each crosstab table. Are all the percentages cast in the correct direction to aid in your interpretation?
3) Indicate which bivariate tables should be elaborated. Be specific with respect to the control variables you would use and to what effect the elaboration might have on the conclusions drawn from the bivariate table.
4) Write a management summary of the major findings of this study.

CASE ANALYSIS

Conclusions drawn from univariate analyses

TABLE 1:

This table indicates that the majority of students (55.6%) eat out between one and four times a month. Students should point out the confusion that may be associated with the phrase "eat out." The interpretation of this may vary by student. For some people "eating out" means "not eating at home," for others it is dinner at a restaurant. The table is presented correctly, but it is not very useful.

TABLE 2:

These results give an indication as to what college students feel is important when they purchase a mean (i.e., "eat out"). Food and price appear to be most important. The terms are vague, but questionnaire design was covered in the cases for part 5 and should not be dwelled upon here.

TABLE 3:

The results indicate that of those surveyed, 97.1 percent knew about Bernie's. However, given the wording of this question and the fact that a menu and two Bernie's coupons were included in the questionnaire, the results are not particularly meaningful. Students could have "learned" of the existence of Bernie's from the survey itself.

TABLE 4:

Although the figures show that 82.2 percent of the respondents nave eaten at Bernie's, one must again consider that a menu and coupons were included with the questionnaire. Also, freshmen had less opportunity than other students to eat at Bernie's (one semester vs. one year). As a result, any conclusions drawn from this table are extremely suspect.

TABLE 5:

This table lends some support to an argument that the coupon incentive may have induced some respondents to eat at Bernie's: note the large number of people in the first two groups.

TABLE 6:

This table presents a statistic that should not have been calculated. Means cannot be calculated for ordinal data. The data must be at least interval in nature before a mean can be calculated. In this case, however, one cannot say that the difference between "excellent" and "good" is the same as the difference between "good" and "fair". Thus, the data is only ordinal in nature and the appropriate measure of central tendency is the median.

TABLE 7:

The high number of people who answered "don't know" makes drawing any conclusion very difficult. One possible interpretation is that students are dissatisfied with Bernie's. Almost 80 percent of the students eat out once a month or more, yet even with the coupons, more people gave more definite "no" than "yes" answers. Another explanation is that the people who usually eat at Bernie's once a month already redeemed their coupons, and thus don't plan to eat there again until next month.

Conclusions drawn from bivariate analyses

TABLE 8:

The relevant interpretation of the data is this: of those who have knowledge of Bernie's, none has been on campus less than a year, 29.7 percent has been on campus for a year, 24.4 percent for two years, 18.9 percent for three years, 17.4 percent for four years, etc. One might be tempted to conclude that more first-year students than fourth-year students had heard of Bernie's. However, the crosstab percentages are cast the wrong way. As they are shown, one has no way of knowing how this relates to the population distribution by years on campus. The implied causality is that knowledge of Bernie's leads to year on campus. It would be better to examine what percent in each category had and had not heard of Bernie's. Column, rather than row, percentages should have been calculated.

TABLE 9:

Here the interpretation is that of those who have eaten at Bernie's once, 32 percent eat out less than once a month, 33.1 percent eat out 1-3 times a month, 29.3 percent eat out once a week, etc.; of those who have eaten at Bernie's more than 15 times, none eat out less than once a month, 5.4 percent eat out 1-3 times per month, etc. Some students might try to say that those persons who have not eaten at Bernie's more than once do not eat out very often. This, though, would be erroneous. The percentages are again cast in the wrong direction, implying that eating at Bernie's causes eating out.

TABLE 10:

The general conclusion that can be drawn from the table is that those students with meal contracts tend to eat at Bernie's more often. Of those students with meal contracts, 18.1 percent have eaten at Bernie's 11 or more times, compared to 13.7 percent of those without meal contracts. This crosstab is correct.

TABLE 11:

The crosstab is also correct. If it were cast in the other direction, it would imply that whether or not one has eaten at Bernie's causes the distance one lives from campus. From this data one can assert that those persons living close to campus eat at Bernie's more often. Because Burnett is interested in the **number** of people as well as their demographic characteristics, this is a situation where cell percentages might be informative. If, for example, it was discovered that 85 percent of the students lived in dorms, Burnett could build a better case for keeping Bernie's.

TABLE 12:

The appropriate interpretation is that the majority of those persons who ranked their overall experience at Bernie's as good or excellent plan to eat there in the next month. However, the table only refers to those persons who gave yes or no responses. The 57 percent who answered "don't know" were not included in the crosstab calculation.

TABLE 13:

One concludes here that of those who ate at Bernie's, 42 percent were male and 58 percent were female. Of those who did not, 26.4 percent were male and 73.6 percent were female. Because the crosstabs were cast the wrong way, one can conclude nothing, except perhaps that the sample had more women than men, since there was a greater percentage of women in both the yes and no categories. The percentages should be cast in the causal direction: i.e., by column.

TABLE 14:

The crosstabs are correctly cast here. One can conclude that for both males and females, pizza is the food eaten most when dining out. Hot entrees are also popular among both sexes.

3. **Elaborations**

A major objective of the survey is to assess student satisfaction with Bernie's and to determine awareness levels. A variety of variables could be used as controls to discover spurious relationships, suppressed relationships, and/or interactions. For example, having a University meal contract could be controlled for in Tables 9 and 11 under the hypothesis that if students have a meal contract, they would tend to eat at Bernie's more, since food eaten at Bernie's is partly considered as compensation for missed meals. Distance from campus could also be used as a control variable.

Other bivariate analyses could be done using similar control variables (years on campus, sex, etc.) for satisfaction about specific features of Bernie's.

TEACHING STRATEGY

One way to teach this case is to have students share their management summaries with the class. The tables can then be examined individually. If time permits, attention may be turned to an evaluation of the questionnaire and a discussion of sources of bias that may affect results. In particular, the method of obtaining respondents under what auspices and with what incentives are appropriate topics for discussion.

CASE 5-5

SOUTHERN ILLINOIS MEDICAL CENTER

INTRODUCTION

This case presents a factor analysis of quality-related attributes for health care. Southern Illinois Medical Center commissioned this study to determine the driving factors behind the choice of local rural hospitals versus urban hospitals.

OBJECTIVES OF CASE

1) To improve students' understanding of the value of factor analysis to survey analysis.
2) To provide the opportunity to interpret a factor analysis output and related correlation relevance.

QUESTIONS TO BE ASSIGNED

1) What overall managerial conclusions would you draw for the management of SIMC based upon the results of the factor analysis?
2) Which factors are the most important? Why do you conclude this?
3) How would you interpret the managerial relevance of the correlation among the factors?
4) How would you expect an orthogonal rotation of factors to change the results of the factor analysis?
5) How could these factor analysis results be utilized with the cost perceptions data, and hospital choice intentions data that were collected, to provide meaningful managerial conclusions?

CASE ANALYSIS

If hospital choice is to be affected by medical care managers and by public policy makers, the perceptions of quality that influence that choice and the attributes that contribute to those perceptions must be understood. The primary purpose of Factor Analysis is to group a large number of variables which are highly correlated and thus relatively redundant. The effect is to simplify data or to uncover the underlying structure of the data.

Overall Managerial Conclusions

The most obvious conclusion to be drawn is that attributes for both types of hospitals are loaded on similar factors. It would seem that similar factors contribute to consumers' perceptions of quality regarding both local and alternative hospitals. Factors 1 and 2's attributes may all be linked more closely to human involvement and interaction. Whereas Factors 3 and 4 may represent those attributes that consumers view as relatively fixed and unaffected by human elements.

When trying to improve the quality perceptions of consumers, administrators may consider the same attributes for both kinds of hospitals. With the application of additional marketing research techniques, administrators may be able to determine which quality-related attributes may be particularly troublesome for their institution.

Important Factors

The most important factors are Factor 1 and Factor 2. These two factors account for 56.5 percent of variance, 32.1 and 24.4 percent respectively, and each have eigenvalues (characteristic values) of greater than 1.0.

While the case implies that Factors 3 and 4 are "significant", their eigenvalues are both less than one. One criteria for determining the number of factors to include is to require any factor to explain at least the amount of variance which a truly independent variable would explain. If all the original variables were independent, then each component (which would be one variable) would explain 1/n percent of the total variance and have an eigenvalue equal to one. This criterion is often known as the eigenvalue-greater-than-one rule. This "rule" also provides a tip-off to the amount of collinearity in the data. If one third of the factors account for 85% of the variance, there is unusually high collinearity. If one third of the factors account for 50% of the variance, there is low intercorrelation among the original variables.

Managerial Relevance of the Correlation

Oblique rotation was performed because there was an expectation that the factors were correlated by their underlying dimensions. The higher the correlation, the greater the dependence. Squaring the correlation among factors indicates the percent of variance explained by the correlation. Not surprisingly, between Factors 1 and 2, only 2% of the variance is explained. As we would have suspected the "human involvement" factor of an alternative hospital is not very dependent on the "human involvement" factor of the local hospital. Between Factors 1 and 4, however, 37% of the variance is explained with the negative sign indicating that they are correlated in opposite directions. These two factors are not independent factors and are highly correlated. Between Factors 2 and 3, 23% of the variance is explained. Between 2 and 4, approximately 1% of the variance is explained. Between 3 and 4, less than 1% of the variance is explained, indicating that these factors are very independent of one another.

Orthogonal Rotation of Factors

Orthogonal rotation, which is performed when the factors are believed to be independent of one another, may indicate that fewer factors are needed. This would result in the formation of two factors rather than four.

Meaningful Managerial Conclusions

Factor analysis is often a means to an end. The factors derived can be used as input into other analyses (e.g. regression) or decisions (e.g. questionnaire design). By including data from cost perceptions and hospital choice intentions, the managers may have insight into actions they can take in order to control consumer quality perceptions. For example, if the cost of a service is very important to the consumer, prices may be adjusted to best attract these consumers. Additionally, the cost of traveling to an alternative hospital may prohibit consumers from using a different hospital regardless of quality perceptions.

Consumer intentions do not necessarily correspond with their actual behavior. Hospital choice intentions data compared with past choice data would indicate whether or not quality perceptions are shared by consumers who have and who have not recently used a hospital. This would testify to the strength of secondhand information.

TEACHING STRATEGY

The case can use a whole class session or be pushed to allow a short lecture overviewing some of the issues raised and discuss the uses and limitations of factor analysis in alternative environments.

CASE 5-6

THE SOPHISTICATED RESEARCH GROUP

INTRODUCTION

This case presents a multidimensional scaling map of U.S. candy brands. The Sophisticated Research Group prepared this map for a foreign candy manufacturer who was interested in entering the U.S. market.

OBJECTIVES OF CASE

1) To illustrate the type of information that one can obtain from a multidimensional scaling study.
2) To show students how to interpret axes, market segments and opportunities for a product group displayed on a perceptual map.
3) To illustrate the fact that multiple interpretations of any given perceptual map are possible.

QUESTIONS TO BE ASSIGNED

1) What interpretation would you give to the axes of the map?
2) What market opportunities for a new candy bar can be seen in the map?
3) What market segments do you think exist in this map? Hint: you must speculate, as no preference data is present.

CASE ANALYSIS

At first glance, the general logic to the spatial relationships on the map is apparent. Very similar products, such as Hershey's Plain and Almond, are grouped closely together. Likewise for M&M Plain and Peanut. In addition, the group of candy bars in the upper left quadrant (Three Musketeers, Mar's, Milky Way and Snickers) are similar: chocolate coated and containing multiple ingredients such as caramel, nuts, or nougat. Twix and Kit Kat, both of which are chocolate covered cookie bars, are located close together.

Interpretation of Axes

There are several ways that one could interpret the axes drawn on the map. The candy bars on the left of the diagram are all very sweet and somewhat sticky. Chocolate is not a predominant ingredient/flavor in those, while it is for the candy on the right side of the map. Thus one could argue that the east-west axis is sweet/sticky/non-chocolate vs. less sweet/non-sticky/more chocolate.

The north-south axis is more difficult to interpret. How are the candy bars on top systematically different from those on the bottom? One difference is that the candy bars on the bottom contain a larger amount of "non candy" ingredients such as cookie, puffed rice, and peanut butter. The candies on the top half are more "pure" candy - the only non-candy ingredient is nuts. When the interpretation is unclear, as in this case, further research must be done to determine what attributes serve to differentiate the brands evaluated.

Market Opportunities

Blank areas in the map can be interpreted as market opportunities. Some researchers like to call this technique "gap analysis." The most noticeable "gap" is found in the lower left quadrant of the map, between Twix and Snickers. One could infer that there might be potential for a candy bar that is a cross between Twix and Snickers (e.g. a Snickers-type bar with a cookie center, caramel, nuts, and/or nougat.)

While gap analysis is useful in generating ideas for products which are clearly different from existing brands, it does not provide any information about their market potential. Further research must be done to determine whether consumers actually **like** or perceive a need for the products.

Market Segments

Several distinct market segments can be identified on the map. Essentially, those brands that lie close together can be considered a segment. One can consider Three Musketeers, Mars, Snickers, and Milky Way a segment. They are all similar in taste, appearance, texture, and ingredients. One could also consider Twix and Kit Kat members of a segment, perhaps defined as "cookie bars."

There are several possibilities for segmenting the remaining brands. Nestlé's Crunch, Hershey's Plain and Almond could be considered members of the "chocolate bar" segment. One could argue that M&M Plain and Almond, Hershey's Plain and Almond could be considered a segment, perhaps defined as "classics" or "market leaders." Nestlé's Crunch and Reece's could be considered members of the same segment in that both consist of chocolate and one other main ingredient.

TEACHING STRATEGY

We have found it effective to present perceptual maps on an overhead projector for class discussion. This enables the instructor to write on the map as students make suggestions for interpretation of axes, etc. Axes can be labeled, segments circled, new brands drawn into the gaps, etc.

We suggest that general discussion proceed in the order indicated by the questions. First, ask the class how they would interpret the axes. Then, do the same for opportunities and segments.

Another possibility for stimulating discussion is to have product samples available for the class to examine and even taste.

CASE 6-1

TECHNO FORECASTS, INC.

INTRODUCTION

For each of three parts, the student is provided with a description of a business problem and one or more tables of secondary data. The student is then asked to solve the problem in each case, using the data and assumptions presented.

This case is designed to accompany the material on demand measurement and forecasting presented in Chapter 22, and to material on secondary data presented in Chapter 6.

CASE OBJECTIVES

1) To expose students to the type of data available from federal and state agencies.
2) To teach students to manipulate statistical secondary data to predict future market potential, establish sales quotas and determine the appropriate allocation for advertising dollars.
3) To lead students to develop a logical approach for using this type of data.

QUESTION TO BE ASSIGNED FOR PART A (Ready Made Containers, Inc.)

The sales manager for a manufacturer of corrugated and solid fiber boxes in one of the mountain states decided that he wanted to intensify the company's efforts in Arizona, one of the states which the firm served. In the Phoenix Standard Metropolitan Area (coextensive with Maricopa County), for example the firm's sales totaled $850,000 in 1990–$680,000, or 80 percent, to firms within the food and kindred products industry, and the remaining $170,000, or 20 percent, to firms manufacturing electrical equipment and supplies. The sales manager felt this was a very poor sales record, considering the diversity of industry in the Phoenix area.

In view of this preliminary analysis, he decided to determine the market potential for fiber boxes in the Phoenix area as the first step in establishing the firm's sales potential (or market share) and setting a realistic sales quota for the area.

Your task is to estimate the total market potential for corrugated and solid fiber boxes in a given area.

CASE ANALYSIS FOR PART A

READY MADE CONTAINERS, INC.

Solution Procedure

In order to estimate the total market potential for corrugated and solid-fibre boxes on an industry-by-industry basis, it was concluded that the initial analysis should be based on "end use" or consumption statistics as a means of determining the extent to which various industry groups use such products. Consumption per employee was determined by applying national employment data of each 2-digit SIC industry to the level of corrugated and solid fibre boxes used by each industry. The potential for Maricopa County was then determined by applying county employment data to arrive at the market potential for each using industry in the county. The 5-step procedure is shown below. The results appear in Table 6-1a of this note.

1) Value of the fibre container shipments by industry was arrived at by applying end-use percentage data from Source 1 to total U.S. shipments of the fibre box industry from Source 3. The resulting dollar values appear in column 1 of Table 6-1a.

2) Total U.S. and Maricopa County employment in each of the using industries were determined from Source 2. Columns 2 and 4 of Table 6-1a show these data.

3) Consumption per employee in each of the using industries were calculated by dividing data in column 1 by column 2. The results appear in column 3.

4) An estimate of the value of fibre box use by each industry in Maricopa County was then obtained by multiplying the consumption per employee data in column 3 by county employment in column 4. The resulting dollar estimate for each 2-digit industry in Maricopa County appears in column 5.

5) Total market potential in Maricopa County was obtained by adding the potential for individual industries.

Conclusion

With a market potential for corrugated and solid fibre boxes totaling $12,965,000 in the Phoenix, Arizona area, the sales manager concluded that his company sales of $850,000 in Phoenix constituted 6.6 percent of the total market potential and was considerably less than he had originally imagined.

More importantly, he learned that the firm had no sales in a number of 2-digit industries which used a considerable quantity of corrugated and solid fibre boxes. The lumber and wood products industry (SIC 24), for example, was consuming approximately $126,000 of such boxes, yet the firm had no sales in this industry group. The stone, clay, and glass products industry (SIC 32) was an even larger untapped market with a corrugated shipping container consumption of $1,407,000.

Table 6-1a. Estimated Market for Corrugated and Solid Fibre Box by Industry Group, Phoenix, Arizona Standard Metropolitan Statistical Area

SIC major group code	Consuming industries	Value of box shipments by end use[1] ($1,000)	Employment by industry group[2]	Consumption per employee by industry group (1/2) (dollars)	Maricopa County Employment by industry group[2]	Maricopa County Estimated share of the market (3 * 4) ($1,000)
		1	2	3	4	5
20	Food and kindred products	1,171,800	1,536,307	763	4,971	3,793
21	Tobacco manufactures	29,400	63,919	460	---	---
22	Textile mill products	121,800	935,925	130	---	---
23	Apparel and other textile products	54,600	1,349,000	40	3,158	126
24	Lumber and wood products	42,000	579,037	72	1,736	126
25	Furniture and fixtures	147,000	468,311	314	1,383	434
26	Paper and allied products	567,000	631,588	898	284	255
27	Printing and publishing	58,800	1,056,336	56	4,346	243
28	Chemicals and allied products	260,400	849,969	306	1,133	347
29	Petroleum and coal products	33,600	139,228	241	---	---
30	Rubber and miscellaneous plastics products	163,800	555,539	295	779	230
31	Leather and leather products	21,000	277,371	76	---	---
32	Stone, clay and glass products	365,400	588,897	620	2,270	1,407
33	Primary metal industries	42,000	1,144,327	37	2,036	75
34	Fabricated metal products	184,800	1,312,595	141	3,271	461
35	Machinery, except electrical	105,000	1,769,738	59	14,691	867
36	Electrical equipment and supplies	256,200	1,698,725	151	23,788	3,592
37	Transportation equipment	109,200	1,700,723	64	2,484	159
38	Instruments and related products	29,400	383,585	77	D	---
39	Miscellaneous manufacturing industries	403,200	411,967	979	868	850
90	Government	33,600	---	---	---	---
	Total	4,200,000				12,965

D Data withheld to avoid disclosure of individual reporting units.
1 Based on data reported in *Fibre Box Industry Annual Report*, Fibre Box Association
2 *Country Business Patterns*, U.S. Department of Commerce, Bureau of the Census
3 *U.S. Industrial Outlook, With Projections*, Bureau of Domestic Commerce, U.S. Department of Commerce

In light of these and other findings, the sales manager decided that his sales potential for the Phoenix area should be based upon the company's sales accomplishment in the food and kindred products industry where its market share was 17.9 percent ($680,000/$3,793,000). Thus, the initial sales quota for the Phoenix area was set at $2,320,735 ($12,965,000 * 17.9 percent) or about triple the sales of the preceding year. Each industry group in turn was assigned a sales quota equal to 17.9 percent of its market potential, e.g., the apparel group (SIC 23) was assigned a sales quota of $22,554 ($126,000 * 17.9 percent).

QUESTION TO BE ASSIGNED FOR PART B (XYZ Company)

The XYZ Company, which for many years had been estimating sales potential and quotas for battery replacements for automobiles based on past performance, decided to develop a mathematical procedure to project sales for replacement batteries by territory, since many of the company's sales managers felt their assigned quotas did not reflect the potential of their territory.

Your assignment is to establish national, state, and county sales quotas and a method for estimating potential market in 1992 for battery replacements for automobiles.

CASE ANALYSIS FOR PART B

THE XYZ COMPANY

Solution Procedure

(See calculations on Table 6-1b of this note which follows.)

1) Determine the total number of automobile registrations (column 1) in 1989 in the U.S., by states from Source 1, and for counties, when available, from Source 2 equivalent.

2) Estimate the potentials in 1989 for replacement batteries by multiplying column 1 by 31 percent, results shown in column

3) Multiply column 2 by $12, average price of battery FOB, to find the total estimated dollar value of replacement batteries, results shown in column 3.

4) Calculate the XYZ Company's state, county, and U.S. sales potential for 1989. This is done by applying the company's desired quota (14 percent) to 1989 total market potential, column 3. Thus, Alabama is given a sales quota of $860,160 (14 percent * $6,144,000).

5) Sales projections for 1992 were calculated on the basis of 3.8 percent average annual growth rate in automobile registration (column 4) + (column 4 * 3.8 percent cubed), results in column 5.

Sales quotas were established for the U.S., each state, and counties within states, using the above procedures. The company sales manager now has a more realistic goal than in prior years.

Table 6-1b. Automobile Registration and Company Battery Sales Quotas for Selected States, and by Counties for Pennsylvania, 1989 and Estimates for 1992

States and counties	Automobile registrations 1989[1] (1,000)	Estimated automobile replacement batteries in 1989 ($1,000)	Estimated value of replacement batteries in 1989 ($1,000)	XYZ Battery Company replacement quota 1989 ($1,000)	XYZ Battery Co. estimated replacement sales quota for 1992 ($1,000)
	(1)	(2)	(3)	(4)	(5)
Alabama	1,650	512	6,144	860	958
Arizona	885	274	3,288	460	512
Arkansas	747	232	2,784	390	434
California	10,166	3,151	37,812	5,294	5,898
Illinois	1,170	363	4,356	610	680
Missouri	4,686	1,453	17,436	2,441	2,719
New Jersey	1,944	602	7,224	1,011	1,126
North Carolina	3,337	1,034	12,408	1,737	1,935
Ohio	2,345	727	8,724	1,221	1,359
	5,328	1,652	19,824	2,775	3,091
Pennsylvania[2]	5,260	1,631	19,572	2,740	3,052
Allegheny	716	222	2,664	373	416
Berks	132	41	492	69	77
Erie	118	37	444	62	69
Jefferson	19	6	72	10	11
Montgomery	279	86	1,032	144	160
Philadelphia	896	278	3,336	467	520
Somerset	34	11	132	18	20
Westmoreland	168	52	624	87	98
All other counties	2,898	898	10,776	1,508	1,679
Total United States	92,301	28,613	343,356	48,070	53,548

[1] *Highway Statistics*, U.S. Bureau of Public Roads.
[2] *Pennsylvania Statistical Abstract*, Pennsylvania Department of Commerce.

QUESTION TO BE ASSIGNED FOR PART C (Ward Manufacturing Company)

Ward was introducing a new line of furniture and desired to construct a simplified model for allocating total introductory advertising budget, by state, so as to reach the customers who were most likely to be the prime buyers for their products.

Your assignment is to disperse advertising budget for 1991 in proportion to the potential markets, by state, in the South Atlantic Region.

TEACHING STRATEGY

There are worksheets provided at the end of this case which can be copied and distributed to students when the assignment is made.

For each problem assigned, we suggest that the instructor go through the solution procedure step-by-step. The solution tables should be displayed to students (overhead or photocopy, or both) so that they can compare their calculations to the correct ones. Time should be allocated for questions. All three parts of the case can easily be covered in one class session.

CASE ANALYSIS FOR PART C

WARD MANUFACTURING COMPANY

Solution Procedure

(See Table 6-1c for calculations.)

1) The company first determined the number of income tax returns with $45,000 or more adjusted gross income for the nine states in the South Atlantic Region, column 1.
2) The next step was to establish a market index for each state. This is shown in column 2 and is expressed as a percent of the total number of returns in the region.
3) The company allocated advertising appropriations for each state by multiplying the market index shown in column 2 by the introductory advertising budget of $150,000, e.g., Delaware 2.6 * $150,000 = $3,900.

Conclusion

Using the procedures described in the accompanying table, Ward allocated its introductory advertising budget by state. If so desired, the budget could be further allocated by major cities in the same manner as the state appropriations, by using census tract data which are available in the Census of Housing and Population.

TABLE 6-1c

NUMBER OF INDIVIDUAL INCOME TAX RETURNS WITH AN ADJUSTED GROSS INCOME OF $45,000 OR MORE IN 1990, AND ADVERTISING EXPENDITURES ESTIMATED BY STATE, 1992

South Atlantic Census Region	Number of Returns (1)	Market Index (2)	Distribution of Advertising Expenditures (3)
Delaware	39,406	2.6	$ 3,900
Maryland	323,217	21.1	31,650
Dist. of Columbia	44,123	2.9	4,350
Virginia	276,550	18.1	27,150
West Virginia	54,446	3.7	5,550
North Carolina	176,698	11.5	17,250
South Carolina	79,038	5.2	7,800
Georgia	195,907	12.8	19,200
Florida	337,954	22.1	33,150
TOTAL	1,527,339	100.0	$150,000

Source: *Statistics of Income: Individual Income Tax Returns.*
Internal Revenue Service, U.S. Department of Treasury.

Name _____

WORKSHEET FOR CASE 6-1a: READY MADE CONTAINERS, INC.

SIC major group code	Consuming industries	Value of box shipments by end use[1] ($1,000)	Employment by industry group[2]	Maricopa County Employment by industry group[2]		
		1	2	3	4	5
20	Food and kindred products	1,171,800	1,536,307	4,971		
21	Tobacco manufactures	29,400	63,919	---		
22	Textile mill products	121,800	935,925	---		
23	Apparel and other textile products	54,600	1,349,000	3,158		
24	Lumber and wood products	42,000	579,037	1,736		
25	Furniture and fixtures	147,000	468,311	1,383		
26	Paper and allied products	567,000	631,588	284		
27	Printing and publishing	58,800	1,056,336	4,346		
28	Chemicals and allied products	260,400	849,969	1,133		
29	Petroleum and coal products	33,600	139,228	---		
30	Rubber and miscellaneous plastics products	163,800	555,539	779		
31	Leather and leather products	21,000	277,371	---		
32	Stone, clay and glass products	365,400	588,897	2,270		
33	Primary metal industries	42,000	1,144,327	2,036		
34	Fabricated metal products	184,800	1,312,595	3,271		
35	Machinery, except electrical	105,000	1,769,738	14,691		
36	Electrical equipment and supplies	256,200	1,698,725	23,788		
37	Transportation equipment	109,200	1,700,723	2,484		
38	Instruments and related products	29,400	383,585	D		
39	Miscellaneous manufacturing industries	403,200	411,967	868		
90	Government	33,600	---	---		
	Total	4,200,000				

D Data withheld to avoid disclosure of individual reporting units.
1 Based on data reported in *Fibre Box Industry Annual Report*, Fibre Box Association
2 *Country Business Patterns*, U.S. Department of Commerce, Bureau of the Census
3 *U.S. Industrial Outlook, With Projections*, Bureau of Domestic Commerce, U.S. Department of Commerce

Name _____

WORKSHEET FOR CASE 6-1b: XYZ COMPANY

States and counties	Automobile registrations 1989[1] (1,000)				
	(1)	(2)	(3)	(4)	(5)
Alabama	1,650				
Arizona	885				
Arkansas	747				
California	10,166				
Illinois	1,170				
Missouri	4,686				
New Jersey	1,944				
North Carolina	3,337				
Ohio	2,345				
	5,328				
Pennsylvania[2]	5,260				
Allegheny	716				
Berks	132				
Erie	118				
Jefferson	19				
Montgomery	279				
Philadelphia	896				
Somerset	34				
Westmoreland	168				
All other counties	2,898				
Total United States	92,301				

[1] *Highway Statistics,* U.S. Bureau of Public Roads.
[2] *Pennsylvania Statistical Abstract,* Pennsylvania Department of Commerce.

Name _____

WORKSHEET FOR CASE 6-1c: WARD MANUFACTURING COMPANY

South Atlantic Census Region	Number of Returns (1)	Market Index (2)	Distribution of Advertising Expenditures (3)
Delaware	39,406		
Maryland	323,217		
Dist. of Columbia	44,123		
Virginia	276,550		
West Virginia	54,446		
North Carolina	176,698		
South Carolina	79,038		
Georgia	195,907		
Florida	337,954		
TOTAL	1,527,339		

Source: *Statistics of Income: Individual Income Tax Returns.*
Internal Revenue Service, U.S. Department of Treasury.

CASE 6-2

NO-SWEAT

INTRODUCTION

This case examines the concept testing phase of product research. The product being developed is a new antiperspirant/deodorant stick with a unique appearance. Students are asked to evaluate the concept statement and methodology, and to evaluate and interpret study results.

OBJECTIVES OF THE CASE

1) To expose students to a major application of marketing research.
2) To give students practice evaluating/interpreting concept tests.
3) To facilitate a discussion of the various procedures that can be used for product research and their applications.

QUESTIONS TO BE ANSWERED

1) Evaluate the concept statement.
2) Critique the methodology of the study.
3) What conclusions can be drawn from this study?
4) What further research needs to be done before this product is introduced? Be specific.

CASE ANALYSIS

Concept Evaluation

In early stages of product development, it is appropriate to rely upon verbal descriptions of the product. The description creates an image for the respondents. **How** the product is described and subsequently positioned determines their reaction. One criticism of the concept statement is that its use of technical jargon, i.e., "difficult to stabilize in stick form," makes the product appear somewhat dangerous.

Study Methodology

In this case, the objective is to "identify the potential market for "No-Sweat." This is a vague statement. Potential market can refer to many things: potential market segments or potential sales, for example. If it refers to potential market segments, the questions asked in the study are not appropriate (unless SFPG is segmenting by product type used). The questions measure consumer attitudes about product attributes more than they determine the product's appearance to any particular market segment. As for the other research objectives (investigating consumer attitudes, differentiating between spray, stick, and roll-on users), and the evaluation of the proposed package, it would have been better to separate these into several studies. Given the exploratory nature of the study, the attention paid to random sampling was unnecessary. Although personal interviews are preferable to telephone or mail questionnaires, SFPG may have benefitted from the focus group. They often provide a great deal of insight along with the added benefit of group interaction.

Study Conclusions

From the small amount of information contained in the concept statement, one must interpret the detailed results with some caution. At this stage of the research process, it is more important to get qualitative information than statistically significant percentages. Whether or not respondents understood the concept, liked the name, and were interested in the product as it was positioned should be primary concerns. Assessing physical characteristics of the product would be better accomplished when a formulation is available.

In the second table, there is not a great deal of difference between the various product users. Overall, if one wants to rely upon percentages, product characteristics were generally reacted to favorably. In interpreting these results, the possibility of biases from a desire to "cooperate" or appear positive must be acknowledged.

The third table gives more insight into the influence of several product characteristics or those who indicated they would and would not try the product. In making conclusions, the same cautions about interpreting percentages and possible response biases apply. At face value, it appears that indicated triers are more price-sensitive and less affected by product appearance than non-triers. Price acceptability, however, will have more meaning after product positioning is established. From the "reasons for trial" tables, one can see that curiosity is the major reason why "triers" would test the product. Brand satisfaction (loyalty) appears to be the major reason why non-triers would not try No-Sweat. The questions about packaging are narrow and do not allow the respondent any flexibility, and this freedom to make suggestions is important to exploratory research. Non-triers find the price objectionable and lack knowledge. Price acceptability will have more meaning after end-use positioning is established.

With all of these tables, the interpretations are quite vague and nondefinitive. The sample size is very small and the selection process was not true random sampling. Although random sampling is **not** necessary for exploratory research, given what SFPG **did** do, the statistical analyses were not appropriate with non-random sampling.

Studies to Undertake

As a product gets closer and closer to being brought to market, the more money is invested and hence the more expensive mistakes become. Therefore, a variety of marketing research studies would be appropriate. For example, when the product is available, use tests should be conducted. These could take on a variety of forms including having SFPG employees give their recommendations (laboratory usage tests), having consumers test No-Sweat at home (home usage tests), or conducting tests in special facilities. Up until this point, it is possible to only test the physical product. At some stage of the development process, the positioning, price, and other aspects of the marketing strategy must be included in the research. Additionally, economic or business analyses are necessary. This would include estimates of sales levels and profits. Two methods could be used to test No-Sweat. Test marketing and simulated test marketing can both provide information. SFPG could select several testing cities and introduce No-Sweat with a full marketing program while carefully monitoring sales response. Different cities might receive different marketing strategy treatments, including variations on price, product formulations, advertising, and other promotions.

As an alternative to test marketing, which can be long and expensive, SFPG could run simulated test markets. For this they could purchase the services of a research supply house such as Yankelovich, Skelly and White. The study is more confidential than a traditional test market.

Students should be prepared to be explicit about further research. Test duration, number of cities, test variations, sales projection method, etc. are all important decisions in the research project.

TEACHING STRATEGY

The discussion can move from an evaluation of the concept itself to a critique of the methodology and data interpretation. This case is a good opportunity to elaborate upon simulated test markets, a technique which students tend to be less familiar with.

CASE 6-3

EXECUTIVE EXPRESS

INTRODUCTION

This case deals with a small computer airline company that is considering expansion into a new market. Before understanding the expansion, company president Heather Clayton is examining the need for such a service. A brief description of the service, the cities involved in the proposed expansion, and the potential customers is given. Students are asked to determine the additional information Clayton will need in order to assess the feasibility of the service. They are also asked to suggest data collection methods, and to determine attributes and attribute levels for analysis using conjoint measurement.

OBJECTIVES OF THE CASE

1) To give students practice identifying information needs and ways of obtaining the needed information.
2) To demonstrate the usefulness of conjoint analysis through a "real-life" example.
3) To have students suggest attributes and the attribute levels which would be appropriate for conjoint measurement.

QUESTIONS TO BE ASSIGNED

1) Assume that Clayton has come to you for advice. What information will she need before deciding whether or not this service is feasible?
2) How would you obtain this information?
3) Assuming that part of this information would be collected by a conjoint measurement study, identify the appropriate attributes, attribute levels, and data instrument structure.

CASE ANALYSIS

In identifying information needs, students should point out that Clayton wants to know the demand for the proposed service. She needs to know if enough people would be interested in the service to make it profitable. This information could be obtained from mailed questionnaires or interviews of business travellers, travel agencies, and/or corporations. Clayton needs to know what customers would demand from such a service to determine whether Express Air could be a viable alternative.

Students should be creative when listing attributes which may be important to customers. The class can discuss which attributes are most important, and whether they can be categorized into different levels (a necessity for conjoint analysis). Attributes that could be mentioned include price, total travel time, type of plane, comfort, schedule, arrival and departure airports, availability of food and drinks, etc. Levels of these attributes should probably be limited to four or five to help minimize respondent burden and simplify data interpretation. Students should cite matrices (like those shown in Chapter 20) as the appropriate method of collecting the data for conjoint analysis.

TEACHING STRATEGY

While discussing which characteristics might be important to a customer, the instructor can lead students into suggesting tradeoffs. For example, to shorten total travel time, would a businessperson be willing to fly on a prop plane rather than a jet? Would comfort be sacrificed for lower prices? There are many such tradeoffs. From this discussion, conjoint analysis should emerge as an appropriate data analysis technique. This case flows directly into case 6-4, the Cupertino Group.

CASE 6-4

THE CUPERTINO GROUP

INTRODUCTION

This case should follow the Express Air case. Here, the students are asked to interpret data obtained from conjoint analysis of six variables. Students are presented with data from eight two-factor matrices which utilize the six variables. The figures given in the case are: (1) the utility values for each level of each of the two variables in a matrix, and (2) the relative importance of the two variables being analyzed. Both (1) and (2) provided for all eight matrices.

OBJECTIVES OF THE CASE

1) To give students practice in turning "information" into "data."
2) To integrate quantitative and qualitative analysis. When given a lot of numerical data, students often get caught up in "number crunching" (or become intimidated and quit), forgetting the importance of qualitative analysis.
3) To give students hands-on experience with multivariate analysis. In particular, students can practice analyzing conjoint measurement data.
4) To have students make a decision about the feasibility of the service by using both the cost data and the information obtained from the conjoint analysis.

CASE ANALYSIS

Data from conjoint analysis--calculation of average utilities

For their analysis, students should have used **average** utilities to calculate the **overall** utilities of different combinations of levels of the six factors (price, travel time, type of plane, airport, schedule, and comfort). A description of the planes is in the Express Air case.

Each average utility is a simple average of all two-factor matrix occurrences of the particular level of the variable of interest. For example, the average utility of a $170 price would be calculated as follows:

The utility of $170 in the price-travel time matrix is .16. This must be added to the utility values of $170 in Tables A through C. Thus, the average utility of $170 is the simple average of these four numbers: (.16 + .23 + .17 + .21)/4 = .19.

The average utilities for other levels and other variables are calculated similarly. The average utilities of all levels of all variables are in Appendix A. Several combinations of different levels of the six variables are presented in Appendix B. From the utilities of these combinations, the students should be able to make conjectures about the necessary "ingredients" for a proposed St. Andrew-Bayville service.

Obviously, this is but a few of the possible combinations which can be analyzed. These were chosen because they contain realistic attributes for a St. Andrew-Bayville service.

APPENDIX A

Average Utilities

Price	Average Utility	Travel Time	Average Utility
$ 70	.78	1 hour	.73
$120	.53	1 hour	.60
$170	.19	2 hours	.17

Sort of Plane	Average Utility	Airport	Average Utility
DC-9	.76	St. Andrew	.71
Metroliner	.51	Eastside	.29
CASA	.23		

Schedule	Average Utility	Comfort	Average Utility
Hourly	.90	Stand, rest room	.90
Leave St. Andrew 8 am, 1 pm, 5 pm	.50	Can't stand, rest room	.54
Leave St. Andrew 8 am, 1 pm, 7 pm	.41	Stand, no rest room	.45
Leave St. Andrew 8 am, 5 pm	.17	Can't stand, no room	.12

These average utilities are additive. For example, the combination of a DC-9 leaving hourly has a utility of 1.68, which is higher than the .68 utility of a Metroliner which leaves St. Andrew at only 8 am and 5 pm. By calculating utilities of various combinations of the six variables, one can determine which combinations are most preferred by customers.

APPENDIX B

Total average utility of six possible combinations of variables:

A. The existing services:

Level of Factor	Average Utility
$120	.53
2 hours	.17
DC-9	.75
Eastside Airport	.29
Flexible schedule	.93
Most comfort*	.90
TOTAL	3.57

B. CASA alternatives:

Level of Factor	Average Utility
$120	.78
1 hour	.73
CASA	.23
St. Andrew	.71
Leave St. Andrew 8 am, 1 pm, 5 pm	
Most comfort*	.90
TOTAL	3.60

C. Metroliner alternative:

Level of Factor	Average Utility
$120	.53
1 hour	.73
Metroliner	.51
St. Andrew	.71
Leave St. Andrew 8 am, 1 pm, 5 pm	.51
Mid-level comfort**	.54
TOTAL	3.52

D. CASA low-price alternative:

Level of Factor	Average Utility
$70	.78
1 hour	.73
CASA	.23
St. Andrew	.71
Leave St. Andrew 8 am, 1 pm, 5 pm	.50
Most comfort*	.90
TOTAL	3.85

E. Low-price existing services:

Level of Factor	Average Utility
$70	.78
2 hours	.17
DC-9	.75
Eastside Airport	.29
Flexible schedule	.93
Most comfort	.90
TOTAL	3.82

F. Low-price Metroliner:

Level of Factor	Average Utility
$70	.78
1 hour	.73
Metroliner	.51
St. Andrew	.71
Leave St. Andrew 8 am, 1 pm, 5 pm	.50
Mid-level comfort**	.54
TOTAL	3.77

*Passengers are able to stand while on the plane and rest room facilities are available.

**Passengers are unable to stand upright on the plane, but rest room facilities are available.

CASE 6-5

PARADISE FOODS

INTRODUCTION

This case examines the issue of whether or not the available market test results support the launch of a new product. Senior management was concerned that the new product would cannibalize current product sales and decided not to launch the product, despite the recommendation of the new product manager. An original version of The Paradise Foods case first appeared in the September-October 1988 issue of *Harvard Business Review* as "The Case of the Test Market Toss-up," and includes additional case evaluation commentary.

OBJECTIVES OF THE CASE

1) To expose students to common problems involved in product development and test marketing, such as competitive retaliation, research data analysis, and product line strategy.
2) To introduce students to database and electronic supermarket testing.
3) To introduce students to the political process of presenting and positioning marketing research information.

QUESTIONS TO BE ASSIGNED

1) Should management at Paradise Foods reevaluate the no-launch decision for Sweet Dream? Why or why not?
2) Assuming that the decision was to reevaluate the no-launch decision, which would you recommend – more test marketing or a national launch? Support your position.
3) Evaluate the performance of Bill Horton, Barbara Mayer, and Paradise Food's senior management.

CASE ANALYSIS

Reevaluate the No-launch Decision

Senior management should reevaluate their no-launch decision. Management is making 1988 decisions with the business mindset from the 1970s. In 1988, and even more so today, the market moves at breakneck speed. While Paradise Foods has control over Sweet Dream's cannibalization of LaTreat, they have no control over a successful product launch by the competition. If there is going to be cannibalization of one of a company's products, it should be from one of their own products, not the competition's. Paradise needs a coordinated strategy for its two products that will maximize the combined profits. With a good marketing plan execution, Paradise may effectively shut out other competitors from the high-margin segment of the frozen specialties market, thereby experiencing the benefits of the category growth.

In addition, a company that consistently dismisses new product introductions because retreating from the market is a safe decision is sending the message that it is not serious about new product development. In a highly political environment, such as at Paradise Foods, single employees who feel threatened by another employee's success can easily undermine an otherwise successful project. Paradise Foods needs a new product champion in its upper management ranks to convince the "no" proponents to listen to good ideas and proposals.

Properly researched and developed products are the future of a company operating in a highly dynamic and competitive market such as frozen specialty foods. A company that wants to maintain its market strength needs to introduce new products on a regular basis, so as to recapture consumers as they tire of existing products.

More Test Marketing or National Launch?

One issue presented with this question is whether or not current market tests actually do support the launch of the product. The other is whether or not there is time to conduct additional market tests.

Bill Horton's marketing efforts "generated a stack of computer printouts several feet high", and included year-long market testing of the product. What is not mentioned in the case is whether or not Bill or product researchers interviewed the actual consumer about how Sweet Dreams was perceived relative to LaTreat and other products on the market, which would have been helpful in addressing the cannibalization issue. If available, this research may provide Paradise with product characteristic information on Sweet Dream that could be promoted to clearly differentiate it from LaTreat.

With supermarket scanners and electronic test market facilities, it is easy for companies to get mounds of test data. What is more difficult is interpreting that data and understanding why there is a market opportunity for Sweet Dream. However, it appears that Paradise has all the data it needs to support the national launch of the product. The problem is not that Bill didn't supply enough data, but rather, how he presented the data. What is needed is the explanation of Bill's central assumptions and inputs which will allow the senior managers to use their real world experiences and judgment to appraise the research, especially when the group appears to be uncomfortable with technology. A list of discerning insights presented in a form familiar to senior management is more effective than a 70-page report full of complicated market research models.

The research data that Bill generated through market testing is unfortunately also available to the competition. Because the competition is relatively more advanced in using the technical database data than Paradise, Bill's concern that the competition will react to Paradise's successful test results by quickly introducing a competing product is valid. Knowing that Paradise has only a six month lead on the competition should be an incentive to launch nationally rather than continuing to test market the product in additional markets.

Bill Horton's Evaluation

Bill acted with the right intentions. However, he failed to properly execute his research findings and he underestimated the power of Barbara's political savvy. It does not appear that Bill consulted closely with the senior managers prior to his starting the research project. If he had, he may have been able to anticipate upper management's concerns regarding LaTreat's cannibalization. Bill should have realized that his research was to prove the better of two options: LaTreat alone, or LaTreat with Sweet Dream. One hard question that needed to be answered was where was Sweet Dream's sales coming from. Bill's 40-page report with a 30-page appendix borders on being ridiculous. In a committee environment, this type of report can only overwhelm, not provide useful information. If Bill did not have the experience of interpreting the data, nor the internal research staff to assist him, he should have solicited the help of his research supplier. He probably does not have the objectivity nor the perspective that comes from previous product launches to effectively make a useful presentation.

Bill obviously does not understand the culture of Paradise Foods. Nor does he seem to understand that launch decisions are made on more than just computer printouts of test market results. Attacking LaTreat with his data and then confronting Barbara directly was a mistake. History has shown that a conservative, non-challenging employee thrives at Paradise. Barbara Mayer will be climbing the Paradise corporate ladder despite a surprise new product introduction in the frozen novelty segment. She has learned how to protect herself and how to anticipate the concerns of senior management, while Bill has dug himself into a hole.

Barbara Mayer's Evaluation

Barbara is the perfect example of a political fighter. She may have made a number of sound business decisions in the past, but now she is fighting to protect her share of the corporate pie. She feels threatened by Bill's potential success and views Sweet Dreams as a career killer for her. She is bright and has learned to take advantage of senior management's insecurities. Barbara's weakness is that she does not act as a team player. By working with Bill, the health of the entire product line and the company itself would be improved. She is a short term thinker and has limited the company's future as a result.

Paradise Food's Senior Management's Evaluation

Paradise's senior management is guilty of not asking the right questions soon enough. Where were they when the new product project was first proposed? Why didn't they ask about cannibalization then? With all of their years of experience, they should have been able to anticipate this problem 18 months ago. Clearly they were not thinking strategically, and as a result, allowed themselves to be manipulated by the best presenter (i.e. Barbara Mayer), not the best proposal.

Management also needs to face up to its long-term problem with its corporate organization. The division between existing and new products can only result in continuing turf battles in the future. Established products are run by the most senior managers in the group, leaving new products to the most junior employees. In this type of environment, new products will lose to the established profit generators and growth of the entire organization will suffer. Instead, if Barbara were category manager, she would be much more of a new product champion, providing a more long-term perspective to the organization.

TEACHING STRATEGY

Begin the class discussion overviewing the case facts. Have the class outline the actions and motives of the principle players involved in the case: Bill Horton, Bob Murphy, Barbara Mayer, and senior management. From this, the case discussion flows best when the instructor moves directly through the assigned questions.

PART V

COMPUTER CASES – INSTRUCTIONS

INTRODUCTION

These cases are designed as exercises for the student to analyze data provided in its raw form. The student is expected to utilize statistical software programs to assist in organizing and analyzing the data provided for each case. Instructions for loading the file containing the data into SPSS/PC+, SAS, SYSTAT or MYSTAT are provided below. The disk (in DOS format) contains the data sets, along with source files containing program statements that may be utilized to load the entire data set into the statistical program with a minimum of effort.

DATA FILES: The collected data for each case is available as an ASCII file on the disk. The data is generally presented in order of the associated questionnaire, however, some question responses are not in exact order. The codebook for the particular case in question should be consulted to determine the exact location of the responses for the question of interest.

SOURCE FILES: For each case, a source file containing program commands that load the data file into SPSS/PC+, SAS, or SYSTAT statistical programs has been provided on the disk. There is one source file for each case, for all three of the above programs. The commands in these files are simple text commands, and can be edited to change filenames, etc., using any text editor.

The source files command the statistical program to read the associated ASCII data file, assign variables and labels (in some cases), and save the resultant work file on the current directory. If it is desired that the work file be saved on other than the current directory, the appropriate command in the source file may be edited in accordance with the syntax of the statistical program in use. Likewise, if it is desired to exclude certain variables from the analysis, the source file commands can be edited for this purpose. We suggest, however, that the data be read using the source files as provided, and then saving or altering the resultant work file, as necessary.

The time required to run the source files varies with the speed of the machine in use: from less than a minute for SPSS on the faster machines to almost five minutes for the SYSTAT program on slower machines.

OPTIONS: There are two options envisioned for the use of the source files:

   a. The instructor can run the source files, using the instructions below, and provide the student with a computer file containing the resultant work file.

   b. The instructor can provide the student with the data and source files, and require that student to run the source file him/herself.

MYSTAT: Due to the limitations of the MYSTAT program, only the Milan Food Cooperative case has the data files in the proper format for MYSTAT to correctly interpret the data. Instructions are provided for MYSTAT for the Milan case only. Instructors who wish to use MYSTAT for the other two cases would need to place delimiters (spaces) between variable values throughout the data file. Then the case could be inputted into MYSTAT using the same procedure as presented for the Milan case (reminder: every variable must be named in the Edit screen before the data can be read).

To make a copy of these instructions and the case descriptions that follow utilize the following command with the data disk in the A drive:

COPY A:INSTRUCS.DOC   PRN (return)

Other relevant files can also be copies to printer. These files are:

AAMTQUES.DOC	This file contains the Ann Arbor Metro Times questionnaire.
AAMTCODE.DOC	This file contains the Ann Arbor Metro Times codebooks.
NUTRQUES.DOC	This file contains the revised nutritional labeling questionnaire.
NUTRCODE.DOC	This file contains the revised nutritional labeling codebooks.

These files are also all reprinted in this section of the instructor's manual. The instructor can have them duplicated from this section if preferred.

COMPUTER CASE 1

MILAN FOOD COOPERATIVE

BACKGROUND: The background and introduction for this case is located in Case 4-1, Milan Food Cooperative (A).

DATA SET: The data file for this case is located in the file "MILASCII.DOC". The data consists of 500 cases, in 11 variables (as shown in Case 4-1).

SOURCE FILES & INSTRUCTIONS:

    SPSS/PC+: The source file for the SPSS/PC+ statistical program is "MILAN.SPS". This source file loads the data file, adds labels to the variables, and saves the resultant SPSS work file on the current directory.

Instructions:

    a. Start the SPSS/PC+ program. Ensure the current directory has at least 60,000 bytes of memory available to store the SPSS file.

    b. Place the data disk in the 3-1/2" disk drive, assumed here to be the A: drive. If your 3-1/2" drive is not your A: drive, perform the following:

        i) Edit the source file "MILAN.SPS", using any text editor, to tailor the commands to your system: on the first line of the file, replace the A: with the correct drive name (for instance, if your 3-1/2" drive is your E: drive, edit the first line to read "DATA LIST FILE 'E:MILASCII.DOC' . . .").

        ii) Save the source file, preferably under a different name. Use this new name, and the correct drive name, in the instructions below.

    c. Enter and run the following command: INCLUDE 'A:MILAN.SPS'

    d. The resultant work file is stored on the current directory under the name "MILSPSS.SYS".

    e. The data is now ready for analysis.

    SAS: The source file for the SAS statistical program is "MILREAD.SAS". This source file creates a library file named "OUT" for the root directory, loads the data file, adds labels to the variables, and saves the result as an SAS work file on the current directory.

Instructions:

    a. Start the SAS program. Ensure the current (root) directory has at least 50,000 bytes of memory available to store the SAS work file.

    b. Place the data disk in the 3-1/2" disk drive, assumed here to be the A: drive. If your 3-1/2" drive is not your A: drive, perform the following:

i) Edit the source file "MILREAD.SAS", using any text editor, to tailor the commands to your system: on the third line of the file, replace the A: with the correct drive name (for instance, if your 3-1/2" drive is your E: drive, edit the third line to read "INFILE 'E:MILASCII.DOC';").

ii) Save the source file, preferably under a different name. Use this new name, and the correct drive name, in the instructions below.

c. Enter and run the following commands:

i) AUTOWRAP ON

ii) INCLUDE 'A:MILREAD.SAS'

iii) Press F10 to submit the source program.

d. The resultant SAS work file is stored on the current (root) directory under the name "MILFOOD.SSD".

e. The data is now ready for analysis.

SYSTAT: The source file for the SYSTAT statistical program is "MILANFD.CMD". This source file loads the data file and saves the resultant SYSTAT file on the current directory.

Instructions:

a. Start the SYSTAT program. Ensure the current directory has at least 50,000 bytes of memory available to store the SYSTAT file.

b. Place the data disk in the 3-1/2" disk drive, assumed here to be the A: drive. If your 3-1/2" drive is not your A: drive, perform the following:

i) Edit the source file "MILANFD.CMD", using any text editor, to tailor the commands to your system: on the second line of the file, replace the A: with the correct drive name (for instance, if your 3-1/2" drive is your E: drive, edit the first line to read "GET 'E:MILASCII.DOC'").

ii) Save the source file, preferably under a different name. Use this new name, and the correct drive name, in the instructions below.

c. While in the DATA module, execute the following command:

SUBMIT 'A:MILANFD.CMD' /ECHO

The ECHO option displays the source file commands on the screen, and may be left off without affecting the program.

NOTE: A warning about a non-ASCII character on Case 1, if it appears, may be ignored as it does not affect the data in the SYSTAT file.

d. The resultant work file is stored on the current directory under the name "MILANFOO.SYS".

e. The data is now ready for analysis.

MYSTAT: Follow the instructions below to load the Milan Food data set into MYSTAT. A source file containing the commands below is not provided on the disk due to the limitations of MYSTAT working with variable names.

Instructions:

a. Start the MYSTAT program. At the menu prompt, type "EDIT" and <ENTER> to invoke the Edit module.

b. At the Edit screen, enter the variable names for the data set as follows (toggle between the prompt and the window by pressing the ESC key):

i) Place the cursor at the top left corner, and type: 'HOUSENUM". Then press <ENTER>. The cursor will move one cell to the right and the first column is now designated as variable HOUSENUM. The quotation marks around the variable name must be included for MYSTAT to recognize the input as a label instead of a number.

ii) Continue entering names for the rest of the variables in the following order (remember to surround the name with quotes): EXPENDIT, PERSONS, INCOME, EDUCATN, AGE, CODEDEXP, LESS6, SIXTO18, CODEDINC, CODEDAGE. [You may substitute your own variable names if you wish.]

iii) After you have entered all of the 11 variable names, press the ESC key to toggle to the prompt, and type:

GET 'A:MILASCII.DOC". Ensure the disk is in the A: drive (substitute the correct path name if the disk does not fit in your A: drive). Press <ENTER> to execute the command. MYSTAT now reads the data file on the disk and fills in the window with data.

iv) When the prompt reappears, type: SAVE path:filename to save the new MYSTAT file you just created. Press <ENTER> to execute.

c. The data is now ready for analysis.

d. NOTE: Due to memory requirements, calculations involving continuous variables such as EXPENDIT and AGE may use too much memory for MYSTAT to complete the computations. Asking MYSTAT to "TABULATE EXPENDIT" will usually cause an out of memory condition. The 'coded' variables (CODEDEXP, CODEDAGE) will allow analysis of these continuous variables, although admittedly with some loss of detail.

COMPUTER CASE 2

THE ANN ARBOR METRO TIMES

BACKGROUND: The Ann Arbor Metro Times is a weekly entertainment newspaper covering music, arts, and current events. It is distributed free throughout the Ann Arbor, MI metropolitan area, and generates revenue largely through the sale of advertising space to local merchants. The Ann Arbor Metro Times (AAMT) was established in 1988 to specifically address the needs of the Ann Arbor area in much the same manner as its parent publication, the Detroit Metro Times. AAMT issues include articles on a variety of subjects, music reviews, arts and theater reviews, classified ads, and a detailed current events calendar. Early in 1990, the AAMT decided to conduct a mail-in reader survey to identify and gauge its readership. This case has been developed using this survey and its data. This case does not appear in the text.

QUESTIONNAIRE: The questionnaire was printed in an April issue of the AAMT, and a record store contest was used as incentive to mail in the postage-free survey. Two hundred and twenty-two readers returned the survey by the deadline, and these make up the data set. The questionnaire design was based upon a similar reader survey conducted by the Detroit Metro Times. The questionnaire is reproduced later in this part of the Instructor's Manual, and can be reproduced to give to students.

CODEBOOK: The codebook was developed by the researchers, and is reproduced later in this part of the Instructor's Manual, and can be reproduced to give to students. The following notes apply to the codebook:

a. Variables were assigned on the basis of question number. For example, responses to Question 10 were coded under the variable Q10.

b. Questions with multiple parts were assigned a separate variable to each part. For instance, in Question 5, each music category in the question was assigned a variable: Q5A, Q5B, ..., Q5F. In addition, the 'Other' category was assigned its own variable, Q5G. Other multi-part questions include: Questions 2, 3, 4, 7, 8, 11, 21, 24, 25, and 26.

c. Due to the possibilities of multiple cars reported in Question 27, five variables were assigned to each of Make of Car, and Year of Car. This provides space to record almost all multiple responses; however for questionnaires with less than 5 cars listed, the remaining MAKE and YEAR variables were coded '00' to indicate no data. If complete analysis of Make or Year of cars owned is desired, a compilation of the five associated variables is required.

DATA SET: The data for this case is located in the file "AADATATX.DOC". The data set consists of 222 cases, and 137 variables; in an ASCII file without delimiters between variables.

SOURCE FILES & INSTRUCTIONS:

SPSS/PC+: The source file for the SPSS/PC+ statistical program is "AAA.SPS". This source file loads the data file and saves the resultant SPSS work file on the current directory.

Instructions:

a. Start the SPSS/PC+ program. Ensure the current directory has at least 255,000 bytes of memory available to store the SPSS file.

b. Place the data disk in the 3-1/2" disk drive, assumed here to be the A: drive. If your 3-1/2" drive is not your A: drive, perform the following:

   i) Edit the source file "AAA.SPS", using any text editor, to tailor the commands to your system: on the first line of the file, replace the A: with the correct drive name (for instance, if your 3-1/2" drive is your E: drive, edit the first line to read "DATA LIST FILE 'E:AADATATX.DOC' FIXED . . .").

   ii) Save the source file, preferably under a different name. Use this new name, and the correct drive name, in the instructions below.

c. Enter and run the following command:INCLUDE 'A:AAA.SPS'

d. The resultant work file is stored on the current directory under the name "AAMTSPSS.SYS".

e. The data is now ready for analysis.

SAS: The source file for the SAS statistical program is "AAMTREAD.SAS". This source file creates a library file named "OUT" for the root directory, loads the data file, and saves the result as a SAS work file on the current directory.

Instructions:

a. Start the SAS program. Ensure the current (root) directory has at least 260,000 bytes of memory available to store the SAS work file.

b. Place the data disk in the 3-1/2" disk drive, assumed here to be the A: drive. If your 3-1/2" drive is not your A: drive, perform the following:

   i) Edit the source file "AAMTREAD.SAS", using any text editor, to tailor the commands to your system: on the third line of the file, replace the A: with the correct drive name (for instance, if your 3-1/2" drive is your E: drive, edit the third line to read "INFILE 'E:AAMTREAD.DOC' . . .").

   ii) Save the source file, preferably under a different name. Use this new name, and the correct drive name, in the instructions below.

c. Enter and run the following commands:

   i) AUTOWRAP ON

   ii) INCLUDE 'A:AAMTREAD.SAS'

   iii) Press F10 to submit the source program.

d. The resultant SAS work file is stored on the current (root) directory under the name "AAMT.SSD".

e. The data is now ready for analysis.

SYSTAT: The source file for the SYSTAT statistical program is "AAREADTX.CMD". This source file loads the data file and saves the resultant SYSTAT file on the current directory.

Instructions:

a. Start the SYSTAT program. Ensure the current directory has at least 250,000 bytes of memory available to store the SYSTAT file.

b. Place the data disk in the 3-1/2" disk drive, assumed here to be the A: drive. If your 3-1/2" drive is not your A: drive, perform the following:

   i) Edit the source file "AAREADTX.CMD", using any text editor, to tailor the commands to your system: on the second line of the file, replace the A: with the correct drive name (for instance, if your 3-1/2" drive is your E: drive, edit the first line to read "GET 'E:AADATATX.DOC'").

   ii) Save the source file, preferably under a different name. Use this new name, and the correct drive name, in the instructions below.

c. While in the DATA module, execute the following command:

   SUBMIT 'A:AAREADTX.CMD' /ECHO

   The ECHO option displays the source file commands on the screen, and may be left off without affecting the program. NOTE: A warning about a non-ASCII character on Case 1, if it appears, may be ignored as it does not affect the data in the SYSTAT file.

d. The resultant work file is stored on the current directory under the name "AAMTSTAT.SYS".

e. The data is now ready for analysis.

COMPUTER CASE 3

MIDWEST MARKETING RESEARCH ASSOCIATES (C)

BACKGROUND: The background and introduction for this case is located in Case 3-8, and Case 5-2: Midwest Marketing Research Associates (A) and (B).

This case presents a data set of responses collected from a sample of major food buyers who completed the questionnaire for this case, titled "Nutritional Labeling Study".

QUESTIONNAIRE: The questionnaire is based directly on that presented in Case 3-8. The questionnaire was updated and improved from that in Case 3-8 to provide accurate and correct results. In addition, there were some items deleted or clarified to ease in administering the questionnaire. Interviews were conducted on a personal level. The revised questionnaire is reproduced later in this part of the Instructor's Manual, and can be reproduced to give to students.

CODEBOOK: The codebook is based directly on that presented as part of Case 5-2. Necessary corrections, clarifications, and other revisions were made to reflect the changes made to the questionnaire, and to provide an accurate codebook for use. The revised codebook is reproduced later in this part of the Instructor's Manual, and can be reproduced to give to students.

DATA SET: The data file for this case is located in the file "NUTRDATA.DOC". The data consists of 230 cases, in 88 variables.

SOURCE FILES & INSTRUCTIONS:

   SPSS/PC+: The source file for the SPSS/PC+ statistical program is "NUTRIT.SPS". This source file loads the data file, and saves the resultant SPSS work file on the current directory.

Instructions:

   a. Start the SPSS/PC+ program. Ensure the current directory has at least 220,000 bytes of memory available to store the SPSS file.

   b. Place the data disk in the 3-1/2" disk drive, assumed here to be the A: drive. If your 3-1/2" drive is not your A: drive, perform the following:

   i) Edit the source file "NUTRIT.SPS", using any text editor, to tailor the commands to your system: on the first line of the file, replace the A: with the correct drive name (for instance, if your 3-1/2" drive is your E: drive, edit the first line to read "DATA LIST FILE 'E:NUTRDATA.DOC' . . .").

   ii) Save the source file, preferably under a different name. Use this new name, and the correct drive name, in the instructions below.

   c. Enter and run the following command:

   INCLUDE 'A:NUTRIT.SPS'

   d. The resultant work file is stored on the current directory under the name "NUTRSPSS.SYS".

   e. The data is now ready for analysis.

SAS: The source file for the SAS statistical program is "NUTREAD.SAS". This source file creates a library file named "OUT" for the root directory, loads the data file, and saves the result as an SAS work file on the current directory.

Instructions:

a. Start the SAS program. Ensure the current (root) directory has at least 220,000 bytes of memory available to store the SAS work file.b. Place the data disk in the 3-1/2" disk drive, assumed here to be the A: drive. If your 3-1/2" drive is not your A: drive, perform the following:

   i) Edit the source file "NUTREAD.SAS", using any text editor, to tailor the commands to your system: on the third line of the file, replace the A: with the correct drive name (for instance, if your 3-1/2" drive is your E: drive, edit the third line to read "INFILE 'E:NUTRDATA.DOC';").

   ii) Save the source file, preferably under a different name. Use this new name, and the correct drive name, in the instructions below.

c. Enter and run the following commands:

   i) AUTOWRAP ON

   ii) INCLUDE 'A:NUTREAD.SAS'

   iii) Press F10 to submit the source program.

d. The resultant SAS work file is stored on the current (root) directory under the name "NUTRSAS.SSD".

e. The data is now ready for analysis.

SYSTAT: The source file for the SYSTAT statistical program is "NUTLABEL.CMD". This source file loads the data file and saves the resultant SYSTAT file on the current directory.

Instructions:

a. Start the SYSTAT program. Ensure the current directory has at least 210,000 bytes of memory available to store the SYSTAT file.

b. Place the data disk in the 3-1/2" disk drive, assumed here to be the A: drive. If your 3-1/2" drive is not your A: drive, perform the following:

   i) Edit the source file "NUTLABEL.CMD", using any text editor, to tailor the commands to your system: on the second line of the file, replace the A: with the correct drive name (for instance, if your 3-1/2" drive is your E: drive, edit the first line to read "GET 'E:NUTRDATA.DOC'").

ii) Save the source file, preferably under a different name. Use this new name, and the correct drive name, in the instructions below.

c. While in the DATA module, execute the following command:

SUBMIT 'A:NUTLABEL.CMD' /ECHO

The ECHO option displays the source file commands on the screen, and may be left off without affecting the program. NOTE: A warning about a non-ASCII character on Case 1, if it appears, may be ignored as it does not affect the data in the SYSTAT file.

d. The resultant work file is stored on the current directory under the name "NUTRSTAT.SYS".

e. The data is now ready for analysis.

QUESTIONNAIRE FOR
THE ANN ARBOR METRO TIMES
READER SURVEY

1. The Ann Arbor Metro Times comes out every Wednesday. Not including this issue, how many of the last six issues have you read or looked into?

   [ ] 6
   [ ] 5
   [ ] 4
   [ ] 3
   [ ] 2
   [ ] 1
   [ ] this is the 1st

2. Under column A, please check the features you read regularly. Under column B, check the one you enjoy the most.

A	B	
[ ]	[ ]	"Ashes & Diamonds"
[ ]	[ ]	"Toni Swanger"
[ ]	[ ]	"Letters"
[ ]	[ ]	"Rock & Roll Confidential"
[ ]	[ ]	"What's Happening in and Around Ann Arbor"
[ ]	[ ]	"What's Happening in and Around Detroit"
[ ]	[ ]	"Hot Dates"
[ ]	[ ]	"Pick of the Week"
[ ]	[ ]	"Flicks"
[ ]	[ ]	"Mondo Video"
[ ]	[ ]	"Real Astrology"
[ ]	[ ]	"The Comics Page"
[ ]	[ ]	"Detroit Live"
[ ]	[ ]	Classified Ads
[ ]	[ ]	Display Ads

3. Under column A, check the following Ann Arbor Metro Times cover stories of which you read some or all. Under column B, also please check one story you enjoyed the most.

A	B	
[ ]	[ ]	"U-M may Flunk" - A feature about the firing of three faculty members during the McCarthy era.
[ ]	[ ]	"Motor City Gothic" - An investigation into the Heinz architecture building in Detroit.
[ ]	[ ]	"EYE" - The fashion issue.
[ ]	[ ]	"The Greening of Valarie Ackerman" - A profile of a Green Party city council candidate.
[ ]	[ ]	"Rob Tyner's Grande Days" - A music feature on Tyner's new band and a look back at MC5.
[ ]	[ ]	"Aggressing the Retina" - A profile of Victor Vasarly, optical artist.
[ ]	[ ]	"A Hard Rain's Gonna Fall" - An exposition on Earth Day, environmental efforts and regional events.

4. Which of the following stories did you read?

   [ ] "Cyberpunk Packs Literary Punch" the fiction of Mark Leyner.
   [ ] "Radical Makeover for Ms." - changes at Ms. Magazine.
   [ ] "Still Faithfull" - Interview with Marianne Faithfull.
   [ ] "Dance: Encounter with a Diary" - People Dancing show at Michigan Theater.
   [ ] "Nicaraguan Election Surprises Ann Arbor" - Juigalpa, our sister city.
   [ ] "Film Fest Warms Up" - the 28th annual 16mm Ann Arbor Film Festival.
   [ ] "Are You Ready For 110 Decibels?" - a preview of the Chelsea band The Holy Cows.
   [ ] "Can't Play Without My Hair" - a preview of Ann Arbor band, Big Chief.
   [ ] "Activist Professor in Residence" - the proposal to establish a visiting 'activist' professorship at the University of Michigan.

5. What type of music would you like to see more Ann Arbor Metro Times coverage of?

   [ ] Jazz
   [ ] Classical
   [ ] Blues
   [ ] R & B
   [ ] Hard Rock
   [ ] Heavy Metal
   [ ] Other _____

6. Deleted

7. What type of coverage do you like the best?

   [ ] Music
   [ ] Visual Arts
   [ ] Investigative news
   [ ] Profiles
   [ ] Opinion/Essay
   [ ] Interviews
   [ ] Photo Stories
   [ ] Other _____

8. Which of the following publications have you looked into or read in the past 7 days?

   [ ] The Ann Arbor News
   [ ] The Ann Arbor Observer
   [ ] The Michigan Daily
   [ ] Current
   [ ] The Detroit Free Press
   [ ] The Detroit News
   [ ] Prospect Magazine
   [ ] The University Record
   [ ] Agenda
   [ ] The Michigan Review

[ ] The New York Times
[ ] Spotlight
[ ] Jam Rag

9. If you could add anything to the Ann Arbor Metro Times, what would it be?

_____

_____

10. Your gender:

[ ] Female
[ ] Male

11. Including yourself, please indicate where people in your household fall into the following categories?

[ ] 5 yrs or younger
[ ] 6-11 yrs
[ ] 12-17 yrs
[ ] 18-29 yrs
[ ] 30-49 yrs
[ ] 50 or older

12. What is your age? _____

13. What is your marital status?

[ ] Single
[ ] Married
[ ] Separated or Divorced
[ ] Widowed

14. Which best describes your current employment status?

[ ] Full time 30+ hours per week
[ ] Part time - 1-29 hours per week
[ ] Retired
[ ] Homemaker
[ ] Volunteer
[ ] Full time student - 12+ credit hrs
[ ] Part time student - 1-11 credit hrs
[ ] Other _____

15. Please check the box which describes your employment income:

    [ ] under 10,000
    [ ] 10,000 - 14,999
    [ ] 15,000 - 19,999
    [ ] 20,000 - 29,999
    [ ] 30,000 - 39,999
    [ ] 40,000 - 49,999
    [ ] 50,000 - 59,999
    [ ] 60,000 - 69,999
    [ ] 70,000 - 79,999
    [ ] 80,000 - 89,999
    [ ] 90,000 or more

16. In what kind of business, industry or profession are you employed?

    _____

17. What is your highest level of education?

    [ ] High School
    [ ] College
    [ ] Post Graduate
    [ ] Advanced Degree: [ ] Masters
                             [ ] Doctorate

18. Your primary place of residence, do you:

    [ ] Own a private home
    [ ] Own a condo or co-op
    [ ] Rent a house
    [ ] Rent an apartment
    [ ] Live in student housing
    [ ] Live in cooperative housing

19. Do you plan to purchase a house, condo or co-op in the next 12 months?

    [ ] Yes
    [ ] No

20. Do you plan to rent an apartment in the next 12 months?

    [ ] Yes
    [ ] No

21. Please indicate which of the following activities you actively participated in, within the last 12 months.

[ ] Adult education courses
[ ] Antique shopping
[ ] Aerobics
[ ] Bicycling (outdoor)
[ ] Cooking for leisure
[ ] Golf
[ ] Hiking / camping
[ ] Jogging / distance running
[ ] Outdoor gardening
[ ] Photography
[ ] Racquet sports
[ ] Sailing
[ ] Canoeing / kayaking

22. How many times have you gone to the movies in the last 30 days?

    _____

23. How many times have you attended a lecture/seminar open to the public in the last 60 days?

    _____

24. How many times have you attended the following in the last 30 days?

    _____ Art gallery
    _____ Dance performance
    _____ Live theater
    _____ Concert (pop, rock, other)
    _____ Concert (classical)
    _____ Bar in which you consumed an alcoholic beverage
    _____ Restaurant in which you ate lunch
    _____ Restaurant in which you ate dinner

25. Please indicate how many of the following items you have purchased in the past 12 months.

    _____ Compact disc
    _____ Hard cover book
    _____ Paper back book
    _____ Record album
    _____ Pre-recorded cassette
    _____ Pre-recorded video cassette

26. Please indicate which of the following items you or other members of your household bought in the last 12 months.

    [ ] Car stereo
    [ ] Home stereo system

[ ] CD player
[ ] Video cassette recorder
[ ] Video camcorder
[ ] Camera
[ ] Personal computer
[ ] Car phone
[ ] Small household appliance (toaster, blender, etc.)
[ ] Lamp
[ ] Blinds
[ ] Couch, sofa, loveseat
[ ] Health club membership
[ ] Bicycle

27. How many passenger cars are currently owned by all the people in your household?

_____

Please indicate make/year

_____

Purchased new [ ] or used [ ]

28. Do you or members in you household plan to purchase a new or used car for personal use only in the next 12 months?

[ ] Yes
[ ] No

If yes, will you purchase a new [ ] or used [ ] car?

CODEBOOK FOR
THE ANN ARBOR METRO TIMES
READER SURVEY

VARIABLE NAME	COL	CODE
RESP#	1-3	001-222 - CODE RESPONDENT NUMBER, 3-DIGITS
Q1	4	1-1 2-2 3-3 4-4 5-5 6-6 0-1ST TIME 9-No Response (NR) / Don't Know (DK)
Q2A:	5-19	Q2AA thru Q2AO: 1-CHECKED 0-NOT CHECKED
Q2B	20,21	1-"ASHES & DIAMONDS" 2-"TONI SWANGER" 3-"LETTERS" 4-"ROCK & ROLL CONFIDENTIAL" 5-"WHAT'S HAPPENING ... ANN ARBOR" 6-"WHAT'S HAPPENING ... DETROIT" 7-"HOT DATES" 8-"PICK OF THE WEEK" 9-"FLICKS" 10-"MONDO VIDEO" 11-"REAL ASTROLOGY" 12-"THE COMICS PAGE" 13-"DETROIT LIVE" 14-CLASSIFIED ADS 15-DISPLAY ADS 99-NR ** code multiple responses as 99 **
Q3A:	22-28	Q3AA thru Q3AG: 1-CHECKED 0-NOT CHECKED
Q3B	29	1-"U-M MAY FLUNK" 2-"MOTOR CITY GOTHIC" 3-"EYE" 4-"THE GREENING OF VALARIE ACKERMAN" 5-"ROB TYNER'S GRANDE DAYS" 6-"AGGRESSING THE RETINA" 7-"A HARD RAIN'S GONNA FALL" 9-NR ** code multiple responses as 9 **

VARIABLE NAME	COL	CODE
Q4:	30-38	Q4A thru Q4I: 1-CHECKED 0-NOT CHECKED
Q5:	39-44	Q5A thru Q5F: 1-CHECKED 0-NOT CHECKED
	45	Q5G: open ended: 0 - NR/NONE/NONE LISTED/NOT CHECKED 1 - FOLK 2 - RAP/FUNK/URBAN BLACK CONTEMPORARY/SOUL 3 - REGGAE 4 - INTERNATIONAL/ETHNIC/IMPORTS/LATIN 5 - LOCAL BANDS/COVER BANDS (LOCAL)/ OPEN MIC HOSTS SHOWS 6 - COUNTRY/ROCK-A-BILLY 7 - NEW AGE/POP/CLASSIC ROCK/OLDIES/ EASY LISTENING 8 - HOUSE/DANCE/INDUSTRIAL/MISC: SPIRITUAL,WOMENS,NON-COMMERCIAL 9 - NEW WAVE/NEW/ALTERNATIVE/ PROGRESSIVE/UNDERGROUND/PUNK
Q6	Deleted	
Q7:	46-52	Q7A thru Q7G: 1-CHECKED 0-NOT CHECKED
	53	Q7H: open ended: 0-NOT CHECKED 1-PERFORMING ARTS/THEATER 2-BOOK REVIEWS/LITERARY 3-LETTERS 4-HEALTH 5-LOCAL POLITICAL ISSUES 6-NIGHT CLUBS
Q8:	54-66	Q8A thru Q8M: 1-CHECKED 0-NOT CHECKED

VARIABLE NAME	COL	CODE
Q9	174	0-NR 1-MORE LIKE THE DETROIT METRO TIMES 2-MORE COMICS 3-MOVIE COVERAGE/THEATERS/FILM REVIEWS 4-LOCAL MUSIC COVERAGE/REVIEWS/PROFILES 5-RECORD REVIEWS 6-NEWS/DETROIT NEWS/DETROIT COVERAGE 7-COLUMNISTS 8-OTHER
Q10	67	1-FEMALE 2-MALE 9-NR
Q11:	68-73	Q11A thru Q11F: 1-CHECKED 0-NOT CHECKED
Q12	74,75	1 - 97-actual response 98- >98 YEARS 99-NR
Q13	76	1-SINGLE 2-MARRIED 3-SEPARATED OR DIVORCED 4-WIDOWED 9-NR

Q14	77	0-UNEMPLOYED
		1-FULL TIME
		2-PART TIME
		3-RETIRED
		4-HOMEMAKER
		5-VOLUNTEER
		6-FULL TIME STUDENT
		7-PART TIME STUDENT
		8-Multiple Non-employed/Non-student Responses
		9-NR
		** code 'other' responses into 1-7 or 9 **
		**** Multiple Response Precedence:
		If multiple responses are indicated, code as follows:
		
		a) if full/part time employment is
		    checked, code as 1 or 2.
		b) if full/part time student is checked,
		    and employment is not checked, code
		    as 6 or 7.
		c) if Retired/Homemaker/Volunteer only
		    multiple responses checked, code as 8.

VARIABLE NAME	COL	CODE
Q15	78,79	1-under $10,000 2-10,000 - 14,999 3-15,000 - 19,999 4-20,000 - 29,999 5-30,000 - 39,999 6-40,000 - 49,999 7-50,000 - 59,999 8-60,000 - 69,999 9-70,000 - 79,999 10-80,000 - 89,999 11-90,000 or more 99-NR
Q16	80	0-SERVICES 1-WRITERS/ARTISTS/MUSIC/ENTERTAINMENT 2-STUDENT/HOMEMAKER/RETIRED/DISABLED/ UNEMPLOYED 3-MARKETING/SALES/ADVERTISING/OFFICE/ CLERICAL 4-ENGINEERS/TECHNICAL/COMPUTER/SCIENCES/ MANUFACT. 5-EDUCATION/EDUCATORS/LIBRARIAN/ COUNSELORS 6-MANAGERIAL/ADMINISTRATION/ CONSULTANT/LAWYERS/DRAFTSMEN/ DESIGNERS/PRESERVATION/REAL ESTATE 7-HEALTH PROFESSIONALS/SOCIAL SERVICES/ACTIVISTS 8-CONSTRUCTION/AGRICULTURAL/ MECHANICS/GOVERNMENT/LAW ENFORCEMENT/POSTAL SERVICE 9-NR
Q17	81	1-HIGH SCHOOL 2-COLLEGE 3-POST GRADUATE 4-ADVANCED DEGREE: MASTERS 5-ADVANCED DEGREE: DOCTORATE 9-NR
Q18	82	1-OWN A PRIVATE HOME 2-OWN A CONDO OR CO-OP 3-RENT A HOUSE 4-RENT AN APARTMENT 5-LIVE IN STUDENT HOUSING 6-LIVE IN COOPERATIVE HOUSING 9-NR

VARIABLE NAME	COL	CODE	
Q19	83	1-YES 2-NO 9-NR	
Q20	84	1-YES 2-NO 9-NR	
Q21:	85-97	Q21A thru Q21M:	1-CHECKED 0-NOT CHECKED
Q22	98,99	00 - 98 code actual response 99-NR/DK	
Q23	100,101	00 - 98 code actual response 99-NR/DK	
Q24:	102-117	Q24A thru Q24H:	00 - 97 code actual response 98-DK/marked, no number 99-NR
Q25:	118-135	Q25A thru Q25F:	code actual response, in 3 digits (ie, 005) 888-DK/marked, no number 999-NR
Q26:	136-149	Q26A thru Q26N:	1-CHECKED 0-NOT CHECKED
Q27:	150	Q27A:	code actual # 8- >8 9-NR/DK
	154-163	MAKE:	MAKE1 through MAKE 5: code MAKE only from list below 00-Q27A = 0 or No Car Listed 99-NR/DK
	164-173	YEAR:	YEAR1 thru YEAR5: code YEAR 00-Q27A = 0 or No Car Listed 01 - 90 actual response 99-NR/DK

VARIABLE NAME	COL	CODE	
	151	Q27D:	0-Q27A = 0 1-NEW 2-USED 3-NEW & USED (multiple purchases) 9-NR/DK ** if 27A=0, then 27B,27C,27D must =0 **
Q28:	152	Q28A:	1-YES 2-NO 9-NR/DK
	153	Q28B:	0-28A = 2 (NO) or 9 (NR/DK) 1-NEW 2-USED 3-NEW AND USED (multiple expected purchases) 9-NR/DK

QUESTION 27B:

AUTOMOBILE MAKES

U.S. CARS
CHRYSLER: 01- Chrysler
02- Dodge
04- Plymouth

GM: 05- Buick
06- Cadillac
07- Chevrolet
08- Oldsmobile
09- Pontiac

FORD: 10- Ford
12- Mercury

TRUCKS: 13- Chevrolet
15- Ford
16- GMC
17- Jeep
18- Toyota

VARIABLE NAME	COL	CODE

AUTOMOBILE MAKES

IMPORTS

ASIA:
- 31- Honda
- 36- Mazda
- 38- Nissan
- 39- Subaru
- 40- Suzuki
- 41- Toyota
- 42- Acura

EUROPE:
- 51- Audi
- 52- BMW
- 55- Mercedes-Benz
- 57- Peugeot
- 59- Saab
- 61- Volvo
- 62- VW
- 63- Yugo
- 64- Renault
- 65- Other

REVISED QUESTIONNAIRE FOR
NUTRITIONAL LABELING STUDY

Hello, I'm [your name] from Midwest Marketing Research Associates. We're doing a survey to find our how shoppers go about getting nutritional information. Would you mind giving us a few minutes of your time to answer some questions? Are you the person who buys most of the groceries for the household?

If respondent refuses an interview, or doesn't purchase most of the groceries for the household, thank the person for his or her time, then call the next potential interviewee.

1. Where do you buy most of the food your family eats?
   - 1( ) Large supermarket chain
   - 2( ) Independent grocer
   - 3( ) Farmer's market
   - 4( ) Convenience store like 7-11 or Stop-N-Go
   - 5( ) Other _____

2. Is this store helpful in providing nutritional information?
   - 1( ) Yes
   - 2( ) No

3. Do you read the labels on packaged food?
   - 1( ) Yes
   - 2( ) No

4. Are you hesitant or uncertain about buying foods that don't have nutrition information provided on the label?
   - 1( ) Yes
   - 2( ) No

5. We're interested in finding out where you get information regarding nutrition, and what type of information you find. Do you get nutritional information from:

	Yes / No	What kind of information?
Food Labels	( ) ( ) 1 2	_____
Friends or relatives	( ) ( ) 1 2	_____
Advertisements	( ) ( ) 1 2	_____

Books   ( ) ( )   _____
                      1   2   _____
                                _____

Magazines   ( ) ( )   _____
                      1   2   _____
                                _____

Doctor   ( ) ( )   _____
                      1   2   _____
                                _____

Store Clerks   ( ) ( )   _____
                      1   2   _____
                                _____

6. Which of these sources do you use "Most Often"? (Read list.) "Second Most Often'?

	Most Often	Second Most Often
Advertisements	( )3	( )3
Books	( )4	( )4
Doctor	( )6	( )6
Food labels	( )1	( )1
Friends or relatives	( )2	( )2
Magazines	( )5	( )5
Store clerks	( )7	( )7

7. What problems do you have finding information about the nutritional content of your food?

8. In the past, the provision of nutritional information has been primarily for those on special diets. Do you have a special diet that requires you to restrict certain foods?

   1( )   Yes
   2( )   No   (Skip to question 10.)

9. Do you find that there is adequate information to meet your needs?

   1( )   Yes (Skip to question 11.)
   2( )   No

10. What other types of information would you like to see?

11. Most people feel that as consumers, we deserve detailed information about the nutritional content of all the foods we eat. Do you agree?

    1( ) Yes
    2( ) No

12. Would you like to have more nutritional information provided to you?

    1( ) Yes
    2( ) No

13. Which of these foods do you regularly purchase?

    ( ) Breakfast cereal
    ( ) Frozen vegetables
    ( ) Canned soup
    ( ) Canned or bottled fruit and vegetable juice
    ( ) Canned or bottled fruit
    ( ) TV (frozen) dinners

14. How often do you purchase _____?

	Don't	Every Week	Every 2-3 Weeks	Once a Month or Less
Breakfast cereal	( )1	( )2	( )3	( )4
Frozen vegetables	( )1	( )2	( )3	( )4
Canned soup	( )1	( )2	( )3	( )4
Canned/bottled fruit and vegetable juice	( )1	( )2	( )3	( )4
Canned or bottled fruit	( )1	( )2	( )3	( )4
TV (frozen) dinners	( )1	( )2	( )3	( )4

15. Do you look for nutritional information about _____? (Read list.)

	Yes	No
Breakfast cereal	( )1	( )2
Frozen vegetables	( )1	( )2
Canned soup	( )1	( )2
Canned or bottled fruit and vegetable juice	( )1	( )2
Canned or bottled fruit	( )1	( )2
TV (frozen) dinners	( )1	( )2

16. How easy do you find it to obtain nutritional information about _____? (Read name of specific item.) Is it "Very Easy", "Somewhat Easy", "Neutral", "Somewhat Difficult", or "Very Difficult"?

		Very Easy	Somewhat Easy	Neutral	Somewhat Difficult	Very Difficult
(a)	Breakfast cereal	( )1	( )2	( )3	( )4	( )5
(b)	Frozen vegetables	( )1	( )2	( )3	( )4	( )5
(c)	Canned soup	( )1	( )2	( )3	( )4	( )5
(d)	Canned or bottled fruit and vegetable juice	( )1	( )2	( )3	( )4	( )5
(e)	Canned or bottled fruit	( )1	( )2	( )3	( )4	( )5
(f)	TV dinners	( )1	( )2	( )3	( )4	( )5

17. Would readily available nutritional information influence your decision regarding which brand to buy?

    1( ) Yes
    2( ) No
    3( ) Not Sure

18. Would nutritional information influence you to try a new product?

    1( ) Yes
    2( ) No

19. Some people believe that grocery stores could help consumers by presenting nutritional information about the foods they sell in a format which is easy to read and understand. Do you think it would be helpful if, for example, a store posted the nutritional content of its products?

    1( ) Yes
    2( ) No   (Skip to question 21.)

20. What kinds of information would you like to see posted?

21. How would your opinions of a store that provided this type of information be affected? Would it be "much Higher", "Somewhat Higher", "The Same", "Somewhat Lower", or "Much Lower"?

    1( ) Much Higher
    2( ) Somewhat Higher
    3( ) The Same
    4( ) Somewhat Lower
    5( ) Much Lower

22. If a local grocer were to post these sheets for every type of food, would you be more likely to do your grocery shopping there?

    1( ) Yes
    2( ) No
    3( ) Don't Know

23. In general, if more nutritional information were provided, would you use it in making purchase decisions?

    1( ) Yes
    2( ) No

24. I'm going to hand you three formats* which present some nutritional information for TV dinners. Take a few seconds to glance at these. Which do you find "Most Helpful:? "Second Most Helpful?" "Least Helpful"?

	Most Helpful	Second Most Helpful	Least Helpful
Matrix (format no. 1)	( )1	( )1	( )1
Summary (format no. 2)	( )2	( )2	( )2
Complete (format no. 3)	( )3	( )3	( )3

25. Why do you find format number _____ "Most Helpful"?

---

*Note: MHRA utilized formats developed by J. Edward Russo of Cornell University. For a copy of these formats see Case 3-8: Midwest Marketing Research Associates (A).

26. Why do you find format number _____ "Second Most Helpful"?

27. Why do you find format number _____ "Least Helpful"?

For the next part of the questionnaire, we're trying to find out what shoppers do and don't know about nutrition.

28. Do you think too much of some vitamins can be harmful?

    1( )   Yes
    2( )   No

29. Do you think that eating a variety of foods ordinarily provides a sufficient intake of nutrients?

    1( )   Yes
    2( )   No

30. Do you think that fortification with seven vitamins and minerals provides all the essential nutrients?

    1( )   Yes
    2( )   No

31. Which of these foods do you feel is more nutritious:
    (a)   Beef or turkey?
           ( )1   ( )2

    (b)   Apple juice or tomato juice?
           ( )1   ( )2

Demographic Data

The following questions are for statistical purposes only. They are solely to help us analyze the data from the survey. In no way will you be identified with your answers.

32. What is your marital status?

    1( )   Single
    2( )   Married
    3( )   Widowed
    4( )   Divorced

33. Could you please tell us which age bracket you are in?

    18-24   ( )1   25-34   ( )2   35-44   ( )3
    45-54   ( )4   55-64   ( )5   65 or over ( )6

34. What is your occupation? _____

35. What is the highest grade of school or college that you have completed?

    1( )   Grade school
    2( )   Some high school
    3( )   High school (graduate)
    4( )   Some college, trade, or technical school
    5( )   College (graduate)
    6( )   Postgraduate

36. Do you have any children?

    1( )   Yes
    2( )   No   (Skip to question 39.)

37. What ages?

Age Range	Number
1-5	_____
6-12	_____
13-19	_____
20 or over	_____

38. How many of the children are at home? _____

39. Including children and all others (relatives, boarders, etc.), how many person live in your home? _____

40. Into which income category does your total family income fall?

Under $7500	( )1	$18,001-$27,000	( )4
$7501-$12,000	( )2	$27,001-$45,000	( )5
$12,001-$18,000	( )3	$45,001-$60,000	( )6
		Over $60,000	( )7

Thank you for your participation in our study.

REVISED CODEBOOK FOR NUTRITIONAL LABELING STUDY

Col#	Que#	Var#	Description	Codes
1-3	-	Q0	Respondent #	3 digit #
4	1	Q1	Where buy food?	0=no response 1=supermarket chain 2=independent grocer 3=farmer's market 4=convenience store 9=other
5	2	Q2	Store helpful	0=no response 1=yes 2=no
6	3	Q3	Read labels?	0=no response 1=yes 2=no 3=sometimes
7	4	Q4	Hesitant to buy without label info?	0=no response 1=yes 2=no
8	5a	Q5a	Info from labels?	0=no response 1=yes 2=no
9-10 11-12 13-14	5b	Q5b1 Q5b2 Q5b3	Kind of info from labels?	00=no response 01=ingredients 02=vitamins 03=minerals 04=additives/preservatives 05=warnings 06=calories 07=cholesterol 08=fat 09=sodium 10=sugar 11=carbohydrates 12=manufacturer's claims and reputation 13=general info 14=dietary guidelines 99=other

Col#	Que#	Var#	Description	Codes
15	5c	Q5c	Info from friends or relatives?	0=no response 1=yes 2=no
16-17 18-19	5d 5d	Q5d1 Q5d2	Kinds of info from friends and relatives?	same codes as question 5b
20	5e	Q5e	Info from advertisements?	0=no response 1=yes 2=no
21-22 23-24	5f 5f	Q5f1 Q5f2	Kinds of info from ads?	same codes as question 5b
25	5g	Q5g	Info from books?	0=no response 1=yes 2=no
26-27 28-29	5h 5h	Q5h1 Q5h2	Kinds of info from books?	same codes as question 5b
30	5i	Q5i	Info from magazines?	0=no response 1=yes 2=no
31-32 33-34	5j 5j	Q5j1 Q5j2	Kinds of info from magazines?	same codes as question 5b
35	5k	Q5k	Info from doctor?	0=no response 1=yes 2=no
36-37 38-39	5l 5l	Q5l1 Q5l2	Kinds of info from doctor?	same codes as question 5b
40	5m	Q5m	Info from store clerks?	0=no response 1=yes 2=no
41-42	5n	Q5n1	Kind of info from store clerks?	same codes as question 5b
43	6a	Q6a	Most often source of info?	0=no response 1=labels 2=friends/relatives 3=advertisements 4=books 5=magazines 6=doctors 7=store clerks

Col#	Que#	Var#	Description	Codes
44	6b	Q6b	Second most often source of info?	0=no response 1=labels 2=friends/relatives 3=advertisements 4=books 5=magazines 6=doctors 7=store clerks
45	7	Q7	Problems finding info?	0=no response 1=none 2=info not on label 3=info on label confusing/ambiguous; don't understand 4=conflicting sources 9=other
46	8	Q8	Special diet?	0=no response 1=yes 2=no
47	9	Q9	Adequate info for special diet?	0=no response 1=yes 2=no
48	10	Q10	What other types of info would you like to see?	0=no response 1=more detail 9=other
49	11	Q11	Deserve nutrition info?	0=no response 1=yes 2=no 3=don't know
50	12	Q12	Like to see more info?	0=no response 1=yes 2=no 3=don't know
51	13a	Q13a	Regularly purchase cereal?	0=no response 1=yes 2=no
52	13b	Q13b	Regularly purchase frozen veggies?	0=no response 1=yes 2=no
53	13c	Q13c	Regularly purchase soup?	0=no response 1=yes 2=no

Col#	Que#	Var#	Description	Codes
54	13d	Q13d	Regularly purchase juice?	0=no response 1=yes 2=no
55	13e	Q13e	Regularly purchase fruit?	0=no response 1=yes 2=no
56	13f	Q13f	Regularly purchase frozen dinners?	0=no response 1=yes 2=no
57	14a	Q14a	How often purchase cereal?	0=no response 1=don't purchase 2=every week 3=every 2-3 weeks 4=once a month or less 9=other
58	14b	Q14b	How often purchase frozen vegetables?	0=no response 1=don't purchase 2=every week 3=every 2-3 weeks 4=once a month or less 9=other
59	14c	Q14c	How often purchase soup?	0=no response 1=don't purchase 2=every week 3=every 2-3 weeks 4=once a month or less 9=other
60	14d	Q14d	How often purchase juice?	0=no response 1=don't purchase 2=every week 3=every 2-3 weeks 4=once a month or less 9=other
61	14e	Q14e	How often purchase fruit?	0=no response 1=don't purchase 2=every week 3=every 2-3 weeks 4=once a month or less 9=other

Col#	Que#	Var#	Description	Codes
62	14f	Q14f	How often purchase frozen dinners?	0=no response 1=don't purchase 2=every week 3=every 2-3 weeks 4=one a month or less 9=other
63	15a	Q15a	Look for info about cereal?	1=yes 2=no
64	15b	Q15b	Look for info about frozen vegetables?	1=yes 2=no
65	15c	Q15c	Look for info about soup?	1=yes 2=no
66	15d	Q15d	Look for info about juice?	1=yes 2=no
67	15e	Q15e	Look for info about fruit?	1=yes 2=no
68	15f	Q15f	Look for info about frozen dinners?	1=yes 2=no
69	16a	Q16a	Ease in finding info about cereal	0=no response 1=very easy 2=somewhat easy 3=neutral 4=somewhat difficult 5=very difficult
70	16b	Q16b	Ease in finding info about frozen vegetables	0=no response 1=very easy 2=somewhat easy 3=neutral 4=somewhat difficult 5=very difficult
71	16c	Q16c	Ease in finding info about soup	0=no response 1=very easy 2=somewhat easy 3=neutral 4=somewhat difficult 5=very difficult

Col#	Que#	Var#	Description	Codes
72	16d	Q16d	Ease in finding info about juice	0=no response 1=very easy 2=somewhat easy 3=neutral 4=somewhat difficult 5=very difficult
73	16e	Q16e	Ease in finding info about fruit	0=no response 1=very easy 2=somewhat easy 3=neutral 4=somewhat difficult 5=very difficult
74	16f	Q16f	Ease in finding info about frozen dinners	0=no response 1=very easy 2=somewhat easy 3=neutral 4=somewhat difficult 5=very difficult
75	17	Q17	Info influence brand decision?	0=no response 1=yes 2=no 3=not sure
76	18	Q18	Info influence trial?	0=no response 1=yes 2=no 3=not sure/maybe
77	19	Q19	Helpful if store posted info?	0=no response 1=yes 2=no
78-79	20	Q20	Kinds of info like to see	00=no response 01=ingredients 02=vitamins 03=minerals 04=additives/preservatives 05=warnings 06=calories 07=cholesterol 08=fat 09=sodium 10=sugar 99=other

Col#	Que#	Var#	Description	Codes
80	21	Q21	How would opinion of store be affected?	0=no response 1=much higher 2=somewhat higher 3=same 4=somewhat lower 5=much lower
81	22	Q22	More likely to shop there?	0=no response 1=yes 2=no 3=don't know
82	23	Q23	Would use info posted	0=no response 1=yes 2=no
83	24a	Q24a	Most helpful format	0=no response 1=matrix 2=summary 3=complete 4=no preference
84	24b	Q24b	Second most helpful format	0=no response 1=matrix 2=summary 3=complete 4=no preference
85	24c	Q24c	Least helpful format	0=no response 1=matrix 2=summary 3=complete 4=no preference
86	25	Q25	Why most helpful?	0=no response 1=most detailed info 2=quickest/easiest 3=has both detail and summary 4=don't like nutrient quotient (NQ) 9=other
87	26	Q26	Why second most helpful?	0=no response 1=has both detail and summary 2=next quickest 3=has detail 4=don't like NQ 5=like NQ 9=other

Col#	Que#	Var#	Description	Codes
88	27	Q27	Why least helpful?	0=no response 1=too much detail 2=too little detail 4=don't like NQ 9=other
89	28	Q28	Too many vitamins harmful?	0=no response 1=yes 2=no 3=don't know
90	29	Q29	Variety of foods sufficient nutrition?	0=no response 1=yes 2=no 3=don't know
91	30	Q30	Fortification sufficient?	0=no response 1=yes 2=no 3=don't know
92	31a	Q31a	Which is more nutritious?	0=no response 1=beef 2=turkey 3=don't know
93	31b	Q31b	Which is more nutritious?	0=no response 1=apple juice 2=tomato juice 3=don't know
94	32	Q32	Marital Status	0=no response 1=single 2=married 3=widowed 4=divorced
95	33	Q33	Age	0=no response 1=18-24 2=25-34 3=35-44 4=45-54 5=55-64 6=65+
96	34	Q34	Occupation	0=no response 1=professional/managerial 2=clerical/sales 3=technical/craft 4=other employed 5=not employed

Col#	Que#	Var#	Description	Codes
97	35	Q35	Education	0=no response 1=grade school 2=some high school 3=high school graduate 4=some college, trade, or technical school 5=college graduate 6=postgraduate
98	36	Q36	Children	0=no response 1=yes 2=no
99-100	37a	Q37a	Children ages 1-5	2-digit number (actual number)
101-102	37b	Q37b	Children 6-12	same as above
103-104	37c	Q37c	Children 13-19	same as above
105-106	37d	Q37d	Children ages 20+	same as above
107-108	38	Q38	Number of children at home	2-digit number (actual number)
109-110	39	Q39	Total residents	2-digit number (actual number)
111	40	Q40	Income	0=no response 1=under $7500 2=$7501-$12,000 3=$12,001-$18,000 4=$18,001-$27,000 5=$27,001-$45,000 6=$45,001-$60,000 7=over $60,000

PART VI

A DECISION THEORY APPROACH TO MARKETING RESEARCH

Thomas C. Kinnear
James R. Taylor

NOTE: This section of the manual provides a decision theory approach to the cost and value of information discussion presented in Chapter 4 of the text. Instructors who wish to supplement the text with this decision theory discussion have permission to duplicate the following pages for distribution to students. This material appeared as an appendix to Chapter 4 in earlier editions of the text.

A DECISION THEORY APPROACH TO MARKETING RESEARCH

In Chapter 4 it was noted that the value of research information is related to the degree of uncertainty held by the manager and the likely benefits of marketing activity (contribution per unit, market size, and market share). The more uncertainty, or the larger the market size or contribution margin, the more value would accrue to research information. In Chapter 4 we made no attempt to measure uncertainty or benefit. An approach to marketing research which allows the researcher to do this is called the *decision theory*, or *bayesian approach*, and it constitutes the topic of this note.

THE DECISION THEORY APPROACH

To use the decision theory, or bayesian approach, the decision maker must undertake the following steps:

1. Identify the objectives toward which the decision making should be directed.

2. Identify the alternative courses of action that should be considered.

3. Identify the possible events (environmental conditions) that would influence the payoff of each course of action.

4. Assign a numerical value to the payoff of each course of action, given each possible event.

5. Assign a subjective probability to the occurrence of each possible event.

6. Using the probabilities, compute the weighted average (expected value) of the payoffs assigned to each course of action.

7. Assess the exposure to both gain and loss associated with each course of action.

8. Choose among the alternative courses of action on the basis of the combination of (a) expected monetary value and (b) exposure to gain and loss that is most consistent with the decision maker's objectives and attitude toward risk, i.e., convert the payouts to utility values.

The decision theory approach is then based on the belief that a decision maker can assign meaningful subjective probabilities to events or outcomes. Instead of saying, for example "There is a good chance of S_1 occurring," the decision maker must be prepared to say, "There is a .70 probability of S_1 occurring," This probability is not based on relative frequencies, as in classical statistics, but on the belief of the manager.

The two decision criteria generally used in a decision theory analysis are (1) the expected monetary value criterion and (2) the expected utility criterion.

Expected Monetary Value Criterion (EMV)

According to the EMV criterion, one simply selects the alternative with the highest EMV. Table 1 presents the payoffs associated with the various combinations of two courses of action, A_1 and A_2, with three outcomes, S_1, S_2, and S_3. Note that the decision maker has assigned different probabilities, $P(S_i)$ to various outcomes depending on the alternative and that the sum of the probabilities for outcomes of any action equals 1.0. This latter point is true because the identified outcomes must be mutually exclusive and collectively exhaustive of all possible outcomes.

The EMV of an alternative is calculated by multiplying the probability of an outcome by the value of that outcome and adding this to the probability-multiplied values associated with other outcomes. In symbols,

$$\text{EMV}(A_j) = \sum_{i=1}^{k} S_i P(S_i)$$

where A_j is the jth alternative and k is the number of possible outcomes of an alternative. Here

$$\text{EMV}(A_1) = \sum_{i=1}^{3} S_i P(S_i)$$

$$= 115(.2) + 64(.5) + 15(.3) = 59.5$$

For A_2, the EMV is 73.0. Since the EMV (A_2) is greater than the EMV(A_1), the decision maker would select A_2.

TABLE 1 PAYOUT MATRIX AND SUBJECTIVE PROBABILITIES

Courses of action	S_1	$P(S_1)$	S_2	$P(S_2)$	S_3	$P(S_3)$
A_1	115	.2	64	.5	15	.3
A_2	101	.4	80	.4	3	.2

$$\text{EMV}(A_1) = 115(.2) + 64(.5) + 15(.3) = 59.5$$
$$\text{EMV}(A_2) = 101(.4) + 80(.4) + 3(.2) = 73.0$$

Expected Utility Value Criterion (EUV)

The EMV criterion assumes that the decision maker's utility function with respect to money is linear, but this may not be the case. For example the utility to a small company of a $100,000 loss may be much greater than the same loss to a giant corporation. Here the differences in exposure to gain or loss are large enough to be relevant to the decision and should be incorporated into the analysis. This can be done by converting the monetary payouts to utility values, a procedure which allows one explicitly to incorporate one's attitude toward risk into the analysis. One then selects the alternative with the highest EUV.

We will not make use of the EUV criterion in this note. All decision theory illustrations in this appendix will use the EMV criterion. We have now laid the necessary foundation to present the first type of decision theory analysis, namely, prior analysis, which is performed before additional information is collected.

PRIOR ANALYSIS

Prior analysis involves the application of the decision theory approach where the probabilities of outcomes are assessed on the basis of the manager's present judgments, without the benefit of additional information. Consider the situation faced by a marketing manager for a soft-drink company who is considering whether to undertake a special promotion. Table 2 represents the manager's structuring of the problem. On this table we note that (1) alternative A_1 is "run a special promotion" and alternative A_2 is "have no special promotion"; (2) the possible consumer reactions are considered to be "very favorable," "favorable," and "unfavorable"; (3) the associated probabilities of reactions are .4, .3, and .3, respectively; and (4) the associated payoffs are listed in the body of the table. The EMV (A_1) is $300,000(.4) + $100,000(.3) - $200,000(.3) = $90,000. The EMV (A_2) is $0. The manager would decide to run the special promotion.

TABLE 2   EXPECTED PAYOFFS: SOFT-DRINK SPECIAL PROMOTION

Possible consumer reactions	Alternative courses of action A_1	A_2	Probabilities of consumer reactions
Very favorable	$300,000	$0	.4
Favorable	100,000	0	.3
Unfavorable	−200,000	0	.3
Expected payoffs	$ 90,000	$0	1.0

Source: Joseph W. Newman, *Management Applications of Decision Theory* (New York: Harper & Row, 1971), p. 10. Used with permission.

Decision Trees

A decision situation can be much more complex than this example. It might have many more alternatives and possible outcomes. As an aid in understanding decision problems, we may use a decision tree. Figure 1 presents a decision tree for the soft-drink promotion problem. Basically a graphic representation of the problem, it is composed of a series of nodes and branches. Decision nodes are represented by square boxes, and outcome or event nodes by circles. The decision to be made is always to the leftmost node point. Event branches then appear as they are related to the alternatives in chronological order. Note that for alternative A_1, run the special promotion, the manager has identified the same three outcomes as in Table 2 and has assigned the same subjective probabilities. For alternative A_2, do not run the special promotion, the manager's judgment is that it is certain no change will occur. The associate monetary value of each end point has been assigned.

The tree is solved as follows: (1) Calculate the EMV of each node, beginning with the rightmost node; (2) adopt the alternative for the branch with the highest EMV. On Figure 1 the EMV of each alternative is presented at the outcome nodes following each alternative. Alternatives A_1 and A_2 have EMVs of $90,000 and $0, respectively, as before. The fact that we reject alternative A_2 is indicated by the fact that we have drawn double slash marks through the A_2 branch.

Alternative	Probability	Consumer reaction	Economic consequences
A_1 Run special promotion (EMV = $90,000)	(.4)	Very favorable	+$300,000
	(.3)	Favorable	+$100,000
	(.3)	Unfavorable	−$200,000
A_2 No special promotion (EMV = $0)	(1.0)	No change	$0

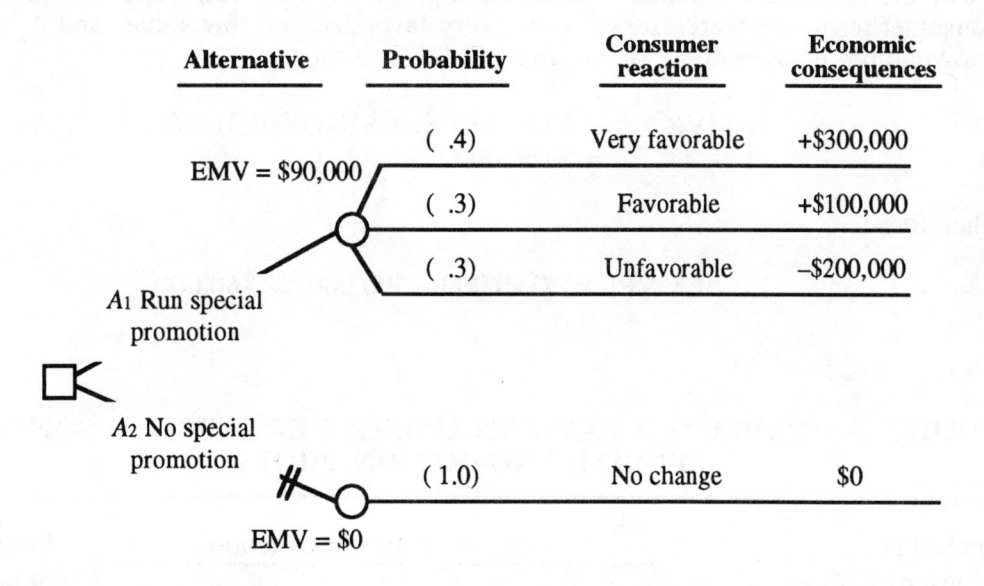

FIGURE 1 Decision tree: soft-drink promotion problem

Expected Monetary Value of Perfect Information

The structure of a prior analysis allows one to calculate the absolute theoretical limit to marketing research expenditures, known as the *expected monetary value of perfect information (EMVPI)*. To calculate this value we must subtract the EMV of the decision under uncertainty from the EMV of the decision in the situation where certainty about outcomes exists. In symbols,

$$EMVPI = EMV(C) - EMV(UC)$$

where EMV(C) is the EMV with certainty and EMV(UC) is the EMV with uncertainty. The rationale for this approach is that if we were certain about outcomes, we would make the correct decision in each outcome situation. The EMV of these correct decisions represents some gain over the EMV where outcomes are uncertain. The amount of the gain is the difference between EMV(C) and EMV(UC).

For the soft-drink promotion problem, we already calculated the EMV(UC) as $90,000. Table 3 presents the calculation of the EMV(C) for this problem, which is performed as follows: if one had perfect information that a particular outcome would occur, one would select the associated alternative with the highest payout. Thus one would select A_1 if consumer responses were known to be "very favorable" or "favorable" and A_2 if they were known to be "unfavorable." The resultant EMV(C) is then

$$\begin{aligned} EMV(C) &= \$300,000(.4) + \$100,000(.3) + \$0(.3) \\ &= \$150,000 \end{aligned}$$

Therefore

$$EMVPI = \$150,000 - \$90,000 = \$60,000$$

TABLE 3   EXPECTED PAYOFFS UNDER CERTAINTY – SOFT-DRINK SPECIAL PROMOTION PROBLEM

Possible consumer reactions	Alternative courses of action A_1	A_2	Probabilities of consumer reactions
Very favorable	$300,000	$0	.4
Favorable	100,000	0	.3
Unfavorable	0	0	.3
Expected payoffs	$150,000	$0	1.0

Source: Joseph W. Newman, *Management Applications of Decision Theory* (New York: Harper & Row, 1971), p. 18. Used with permission.

Under no circumstances should the manager making these judgments be willing to spend more than $60,000 on marketing research. Marketing research information is never perfect. Many errors are likely to be in the findings, so the amount this manager should in fact be willing to spend will be substantially less than $60,000; the exact amount depends on the value of imperfect information. We will develop procedures for valuing imperfect information later in this note. To understand this material properly, we must first grasp certain rules of probability theory.

THE NECESSARY PROBABILITY THEORY

We begin this section on probability theory by considering a number of definitions.

Some Definitions

Conditional Probability Conditional probability is the probability assigned to an event when another event is known or assumed to have occurred. In symbols we can write $P(A/B)$, which reads "the probability of A given B." For example, one might assign a probability of .9 that a certain football team will win the big game, given that the star quarterback is not injured.

Joint Probability Joint probability is the probability that two or more events will occur. In symbols we can write $P(A \text{ and } B)$, which reads "the probability of A and B." For example, one might assign a probability of .2 that both the football and basketball teams will win their weekend games.

Unconditional Probability Unconditional probability is the probability assigned to an event that is independent of other events. It is also called *marginal probability*. It can be calculated by adding the probabilities of all the joint events of which it is a part. For example, if $P(A \text{ and } B) = .2$ and $P(A \text{ and } C) = .3$, then $P(A) = .5$.

The decision theory approach makes use of relationships among all these probability concepts. To apply these concepts properly, we must be familiar with certain rules of probability theory.

Rules

Addition Rules The addition law states that given the two events A and B,

$$P(A \text{ or } B) = P(A) + P(B) - P(A \text{ and } B)$$

If the two events are mutually exclusive, then

$$P(A \text{ or } B) = P(A) + P(B)$$

Multiplication Rule The multiplication law states that given the two events A and B,

$$P(A \text{ and } B) = P(A/B) \cdot P(B) \qquad (1)$$

If the two events are independent, then

$$P(A \text{ and } B) = P(A) \cdot P(B)$$

Bayes' Rule We could rearrange Equation 1 to yield what is called Bayes' rule, which is that

$$P(A/B) = \frac{P(A \text{ and } B)}{P(B)}$$

In words, the conditional probability of A given B is equal to the joint probability of A and B divided by the unconditional probability of B. This formula could be rewritten in the following way:

$$P(A/B) = \frac{P(A) \cdot (B/A)}{P(A) \cdot P(B/A) + P(A') \cdot P(B/A')}$$

The numerator is simply the application of the multiplication rule for nonindependent events, and the denominator is simply the application of the fact that an unconditional or marginal probability is the sum of the joint probabilities where it occurs. In this latter formula A' represents events other than A.

We now have the necessary probability theory stated. We are ready to undertake the remaining two types of decision theory analysis.

POSTERIOR ANALYSIS

Posterior analysis requires the straightforward application of Bayes' rule: prior information is combined with additional information to provide revised probability estimates. Posterior analysis values both present and additional information. These posterior (revised) probabilities are then used to calculate a posterior EMV/(A_i).

An example will make this clear. Suppose that, on the basis of pretest results, we wish to revise our prior probabilities of A_1 in our soft-drink promotion problem. Table 4 presents the necessary information. In the first two columns of this table we have identified the three possible outcomes and their respective prior probabilities. Now suppose a pretest result on this promotion was "very favorable." To update the prior probabilities, the manager must assess the conditional probability of getting a very favorable pretest given the various possible outcomes. In symbols, the manager must assess $P(R/S_i)$, where R is the very favorable pretest. Column 3 of Table 4 presents one such assessment. For example, this manager has assigned a probability of .7 to getting the very favorable pretest, given that the true outcome is indeed very favorable. The joint probability of R and S_i, $P(R \text{ and } S_i)$, is obtained by multiplying columns 2 and 3. This is just an application of the multiplication rule. The unconditional probability of getting a very favorable pretest, $P(R)$, is equal to the sum of all the joint probabilities where R occurs, $P(R) = .370$ in this example. The posterior probabilities are obtained by applying Bayes' rule. Here we want the $P(S_i/R)$. That is, we want the probability of various outcomes given the test results. For example, to calculate $P(S_1/R)$ we use the formula

$$P(S_1/R) = \frac{P(R \text{ and } S_1)}{P(R)}$$

$$= .280/.370 = .757$$

Thus the posterior probability of S_1 given this pretest result is .757. The probabilities of the other outcomes are calculated in a similar manner.

TABLE 4 AN EXAMPLE OF POSTERIOR ANALYSIS

	Probabilities			
Outcome S_i (1)	Prior $P(S_i)$ (2)	Conditional* $P(R/S_i)$ (3)	Joint $P(R \text{ and } S_i)$ (4)	Posterior $P(S_i/R)$ (5)
S_1	.400	.700	.280	.757**
S_2	.300	.200	.060	.162
S_3	.300	.100	.030	.081
Totals	1.00		P(R) = .370	1.00

Posterior EMV(A_1) = $300,000(.757) + $100,000(.162) − $200,000(.081)
= $227,100

*R = very favorable pretest result.
**$P(S_1/R)$ = .280/.370 = .757.

The posterior EMV(A_1) = $300,000(.757) + $100,000(.162) − $200,000(.081) = $227,100. Thus, on the basis of the pretest the manager is able to recalculate the EMV of each alternative. At this point the EMV(C) will have changed to $300,000(.757) + $100,000(.162) + $0(.081) = $243,300. Therefore the new EMVPI = $243,300 − $227,100 = $16,200. Prior to doing the pretest the EMVPI was $60,000. This should make sense. New information has reduced the uncertainty and thus the value of additional information.

The decision theory approach may also be used to evaluate the worth of research before this research is undertaken. This type of decision theory analysis is called *preposterior analysis*, the topic to which we now turn our attention.

PREPOSTERIOR ANALYSIS

If one is willing to make certain probability assessments, *preposterior analysis* will allow the value of alternative research studies to be measured prior to the research being undertaken.

This value is referred to as the *expected monetary value of imperfect information* (EMVII). In our soft-drink example we know the EMVII must be less than $60,000, since this was the amount of the EMVPI. What follows is a simple example of how to calculate the EMVII for one specific study design. In performing this type of analysis we must recognize that a research study will cost money; thus, we also need to calculate this expected monetary value net of the cost of the research. We define this value as the expected monetary gain of imperfect information (EMGII). In symbols,

$$EMGII = EMVII - \text{cost of information}$$

In our example, we shall also calculate the EMGII. Actually, many alternative research designs could be considered in this fashion. We would select that design with the most positive EMGII. Clearly if the EMGII were negative, we would not undertake the research.

Preposterior analysis involves the following steps:

1. List the possible research outcomes and calculate their unconditional or marginal probabilities.

2. Assume, in turn, that each of the research outcomes has been obtained. For each research outcome: (a) calculate posterior probabilities; (b) calculate the expected payoff of each course of action under consideration and select the act with the highest expected payoff; (c) multiply the expected payoff of the best course of action by the marginal probability of the research outcome.

3. Sum the products of step 2c (taken for each research outcome) to get the expected payoff of the strategy that includes ordering research before taking final action.

4. Calculate the EMVII.

5. Calculate the EMGII.

6. Choose the strategy with the highest EMGII if at least one strategy has a positive EMGII; otherwise, choose the strategy without research that has the highest EMV.

An example should make these steps clear. Suppose that the manager was considering undertaking a market test of the special soft-drink promotion. The cost of this test would be $3,500. Figure 2 presents the structure of the problem in decision tree form. Note that the decision to be made is whether to market-test and that the internal branches of the tree contain the original decision problem about whether to run the special promotion. The sequence is in chronological order. The test market decision comes first, then the test market (if it is undertaken), then the choice of decision alternatives about the promotion, then the possible outcomes of this latter decision. Also note that the prior probabilities of various outcomes are assigned to the top fork of the tree and that the EMV of the best decision without research is $90,000, as calculated in our prior analysis. Now we shall proceed to go through the steps of a preposterior analysis.

	Test results	Decision		
Decision on	and their	on special		Payoffs
market test	probabilities	promotion	Probabilities	(ΔPBT)

```
                                                    ( .4)   $300,000
                                    $90,000         ( .3)    100,000
                                  A₁                ( .3)    200,000
                                  A₂                (1.0)          0
                                    $0
```

No market test

```
                                                    ( .73)  $300,000
                                    $219,000        ( .18)   100,000
                                  A₁                ( .09)  -200,000
                                  A₂                (1.0)          0
                                    $0
```

Market test

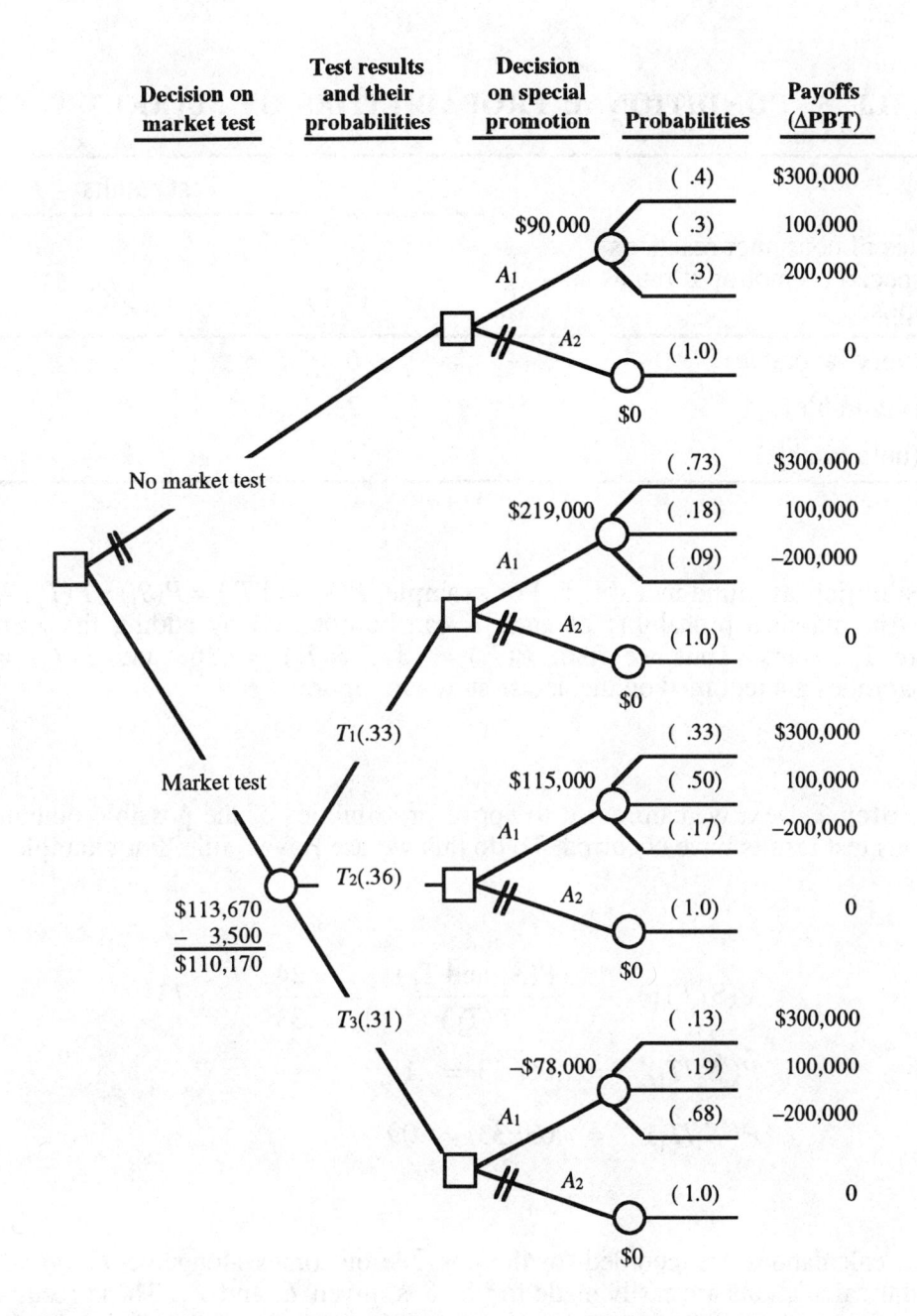

T₁(.33)
```
                                                    ( .33)  $300,000
                                    $115,000        ( .50)   100,000
                                  A₁                ( .17)  -200,000
                                  A₂                (1.0)          0
                                    $0
```

$113,670
− 3,500
─────────
$110,170

T₂(.36)

T₃(.31)
```
                                                    ( .13)  $300,000
                                    −$78,000        ( .19)   100,000
                                  A₁                ( .68)  -200,000
                                  A₂                (1.0)          0
                                    $0
```

FIGURE 2 Decision tree for soft-drink special promotion problem.

Step 1 Three market-test outcomes are thought possible: a 15 percent increase in sales (T_1), a 5 percent increase in sales (T_2), and no sales increase (T_3). To obtain the marginal probabilities of T_1, T_2, and T_3, one could reason as follows: if the promotion were run as planned and received a very favorable consumer reaction, what is the probability of T_1, T_2, and T_3 occurring? This is the $P(T_i/S_1)$. One such set of assessments is given in the first line of Table 5. For example, we note that the conditional probability of finding T_1 given that S_1 would be found is .6. The other two lines of this table present the conditional probabilities of various test results given other possible consumer reactions, S_2 and S_3. These assessments are in essence a judgment about the ability of particular research designs to find the true situation. These $P(T_i/S_i)$'s are multiplied by the prior probabilities, $P(S_i)$, to yield joint

TABLE 5 CONDITIONAL PROBABILITIES OF MARKET-TEST RESULTS

States of consumer reactions to special promotion if run as proposed	Test results		
	T_1 (+ 15%)	T_2 (+ 5%)	T_3 (± 0%)
S_1 (very favorable)	.6	.3	.1
S_2 (favorable)	.2	.6	.2
S_3 (unfavorable)	.1	.2	.7

probabilities, as found in Table 6. For example, $P(S_1 \text{ and } T_1) = P(S_1) \cdot P(T_1/S_1) = (.4)(.6) = .24$. The marginal probability of each T_i can be obtained by adding the joint probabilities where T_i occurs. Thus we find: $P(T_1) = .33$, $P(T_2) = .36$, and $P(T_3) = .31$. These probabilities are recorded on the decision tree in Figure 1.

Step 2 Next we can revise the prior probabilities of the possible outcomes given that various test results have occurred. To do this we use Bayes' rule. For example,

$$P(S_1/T_1) = \frac{P(S_1 \text{ and } T_1)}{P(T_1)} = \frac{.24}{.33} = .73$$

$$P(S_2/T_1) = .06/.33 = .18$$

$$P(S_3/T_1) = .03/.33 = .09$$

These calculations are recorded for the possible outcomes along the T_1 branch of the tree. Similar calculations are easily made for the S_i's, given T_2 and T_3. These results are recorded on the decision tree. The expected payout of each alternative is recalculated using the revised probabilities. Thus, if a 15 percent sales increase is observed in the market test (T_1), the expected payoff is $219,000; similarly for T_2, $115,000; and T_3, -$78,000. If T_1 or T_2 were observed, we would choose A_1, but if T_3 were observed we would choose A_2. Thus, the best courses of action and payoffs are $T_1 = \$219,000$, $T_2 = \$115,000$, and $T_3 = \$0$. These three best payoffs are then multiplied by their associated $P(T_i)$.

Step 3 The sum of the best outcomes, each multiplied by its respective $P(T_i)$, equals $113,670 [$219,000(.33) + $115,000(.36) + $0(.31)].

TABLE 6   CONDITIONAL PROBABILITIES OF MARKET-TEST RESULTS

States of consumer reactions to special promotion if run as proposed	T_1 (+15%)	T_2 (+5%)	T_1 (±0%)	Marginal probabilities
S_1 (very favorable)	.24	.12	.04	.4
S_2 (favorable)	.06	.18	.06	.3
S_3 (unfavorable)	.03	.06	.21	.3
Marginal probabilities	.33	.36	.31	1.00

Step 4   Now we are in a position to calculate EMVII:

$$\begin{aligned} \text{EMVII} &= \text{EMV (with test)} - \text{EMV (without test)} \\ &= \$113{,}670 - \$90{,}000 \\ &= \$23{,}670 \end{aligned}$$

This is the absolute maximum we would be willing to pay for this research.

Step 5   The net gain of the study can also be calculated:

$$\begin{aligned} \text{EMGII} &= \text{EMVII} - \text{cost of study} \\ &= \$23{,}670 - \$3{,}500 \\ &= \$20{,}170 \end{aligned}$$

Step 6   Since the EMGII is positive, we would choose to do the market test. It is possible that alternative designs for this test may be possible, each having different costs and conditional probabilities, $P(T_i / S_i)$. We could calculate the EMGII for each of these, just as we have done here, and select that study with the highest EMGII. Clearly if EMGII is negative, we are better off making the decision without research.

ADVANTAGES AND LIMITATIONS

The decision theory approach has a number of advantages, including (1) the rigor of requiring the manager to structure the problem completely; (2) the rigor of having to specify the value of each outcome; (3) the ability to determine the expected value of alternatives before and after research; and (4) the ability to determine the expected value of alternative research projects before undertaking the research. These are indeed major benefits of this approach. However, we must temper these positive aspects with some strong limitations—

for example, (1) the lack of knowledge among managers and researchers of the procedures of this approach; (2) the inability or unwillingness of managers to structure problems completely and identify outcomes; (3) the inability or unwillingness of managers to make the necessary conditional probability judgments; and (4) the general unwillingness of managers to expose their thinking in such an explicit manner. For the present, therefore, the decision theory approach remains a powerful theoretical tool that has obtained some usage in sophisticated organizations. It is for the future to judge its long-term practical value.

PART VII

TRANSPARENCY MASTERS

TEXTBOOK AND CASES

PART I   INTRODUCTION TO MARKETING RESEARCH IN MARKETING DECISION MAKING

Chapter 1   Marketing Research Role in Marketing Decision Making

    Figure 1-1   Model of the Marketing System

    Figure 1-2   Steps in the Decision-Making Process

    Figure 1-3   The Marketing Management Process

Chapter 2   The Marketing Research Business

    Figure 2-1   Institutional Structure of the Marketing Research Business

    Table 2-2   Responsibilities of the Research Generalist

    Table 2-5   Centralized Organization

    Table 2-6   Decentralized Organization

    Figure 2-3   General Foods' Marketing Research Organization

Chapter 3   The Marketing Research Process: Concept and Example

    Figure 3-1   Steps in the Research Process

Chapter 4   The Decision to Undertake Research

    Figure 4-2   Link Between the Decision Process and the Research Process

    Figure 4-3   Preliminary Steps in the Decision-Making Process

    Figure 4-4   Pyramid of Research Objectives and Information Needs

    Table 4-1   Research Value as Function of Contribution Margin and Market Size

    Exhibit 4-1   Research Request Form

PART II DETERMINE RESEARCH DESIGN AND DATA SOURCES

Chapter 5 Research Design and Data Sources

- Figure 5-2 Types of Research
- Figure 5-3 Research Design
- Table 5-1 Cross-Sectional Data May Not-Reflect Longitudinal Data
- Figure 5-10 Marketing Decision Support System

Chapter 6 Secondary Data

- Figure 6-2 Initial Steps in the Research Process
- Figure 6-3 Census Bureau Geographic Units and Their Hierarchical Relationships
- Figure 6-4 Geographic Subdivision of an MSA
- Figure 6-5 Washington, DC MSA

PART III DEVELOP THE DATA COLLECTION PROCEDURE

Chapter 7 The Measurement Process

- Figure 7-2 The Measurement Process
- Table 7-1 Characteristics of Measurement Scales
- Figure 7-3 Permissible Transformation by Scale Type
- Figure 7-4 Difficulty of the Measurement Process
- Figure 7-5 Reliability and Validity

Chapter 8 Attitude Measurement

- Figure 8-2 Model of Behavioral Response
- Figure 8-3 Graphic and Verbal Rating Scales
- Figure 8-4 Profile Analysis of Beer Brand Images
- Table 8-3 Staple Scale Format
- Figure 8-5 Staple Scale Comparative Profiles

Chapter 9   Causal Designs

    Figure 9-2   Some Possible Results of a Time-Series Experiment

    Table 9-2   Sources of Invalidity of Preexperimental and Experimental Designs

    Table 9-3   Sources of Invalidity of Quasi-Experimental Designs

    Table 9-4   Latin Square Design for Sales Training Experiment

    Table 9-5   3 x 2 Factorial Design for Sales Training and Compensation Experiment

    Figure 9-7   Navy Experimental Design

Chapter 10   Data Collection: Exploratory Research

    Figure 10-5   Sample Focus Group Session

    Figure 10-10   Demographic Profile

    Figure 10-12   Cross-Tabulation Analysis

Chapter 11   Data Collection: Conclusive Research

    Table 11-1   Life-Style Characteristics

    Table 11-4   Summary of Communication Approaches

Chapter 12   Designing Data Collection Forms

    Figure 12-2   Steps in Questionnaire Design

    Figure 12-3   Information Needs-Data Linkage

    Figure 12-4   Example of a Flow Chart Plan for a Draft Questionnaire

PART IV   SAMPLING PLAN AND DATA COLLECTION

Chapter 13   The Basics of Sampling

    Figure 13-2   Steps in Selecting a Sample

    Figure 13-3   Sampling Procedures

Chapter 14   Simple Random Sampling and Sample Size

> Figure 14-4   Nomograph to Determine Sample Size in Simple Random Sampling for Estimation Problems of the Mean
>
> Figure 14-5   Nomograph to Determine Sample Size for the Mean of a Proportion
>
> Figure A14-1   Demonstrates the Central-Limit Theorem: Four Different Populations
>
> Figure A14-2   Area Under the Normal Curve

Chapter 15   More Complex Sampling Procedures

> Figure 15-3   Disproportionate Stratified Sampling in Retail Store Audits
>
> Figure 15-6   An Illustration of Area Sampling
>
> Table 15-3   Managerial Summary of Sampling

Chapter 16   Field Operations

> Figure 16-2   Field Time Schedule Flow Diagram
>
> Table 16-1   Study Performance Measures: Expected and Actual

PART V   DATA ANALYSIS AND REPORTING RESEARCH FINDINGS

Chapter 17   Data Processing

> Figure 17-2   ASCII Data Matrix and Commercial Spreadsheet Representations of Marketing Research Data
>
> Figure 17-3   Classic Data Processing Flow
>
> Table 17-1   An Illustrative Codebook
>
> Figure 17-4   Creation of a Computer File for Analysis

Chapter 18   Univariate Data Analysis

> Figure 18-2   Overview of Data Analysis Techniques
>
> Figure 18-3   Overview of Univariate Data Analysis Procedure
>
> Table 18-4   Summary of Hypothesis-Testing Errors
>
> Table 18-5   Calculation of Chi-Square for Occupational Categories

Chapter 19   Bivariate Data Analysis

    Figure 19-2   Bivariate Data Analysis Procedures

    Figure 19-4   An Example of a Scatter Diagram and Associated Quadrants

    Figure 19-5   Scatter Diagram of Course Grades

    Figure 19-6   Partitioning of Deviations in Regression

    Table 19-5   Alternative Way of Presenting Cross-Tabular Results

    Table 19-6   Retain Original Conclusion of a Relationship Existing

    Table 19-7   Specification of Relationship

    Table 19-8   Identification of a Spurious Relationship

    Table 19-9   Retain Original Conclusion of No Relationship

    Table 19-10   Identification of a Relationship

Chapter 20   Multivariate Data Analysis I: Interdependence Methods

    Figure 20-2   Interdependence Versus Dependence Methods

    Figure 20-4   Development of R-type and Q-type Correlation Matrices

    Table 20-2   Factor Loadings

    Table 20-3   Interpretation of Factors

    Figure 20-6   Perceptual Space Solution Based on Data in Table 20-4

Chapter 21   Multivariate Data Analysis II: Dependence Methods

    Figure 21-2   Classification of Dependence Methods

    Table 21-1   Situation Where Dependence Methods Are Appropriate

    Figure 21-4   AID Tree for Use of Nonphosphate Laundry Products

Chapter 22   Reporting Research Findings

    Figure 22-2   Pie Chart of Weekly Traffic Count by Retail Stores (August 8-14, 1995)

    Figure 22-3   Exploding Pie Chart

Figure 22-4   Bar Chart of Traffic Count of Retail Stores by Day of Week (August 8-14, 1995)

Figure 22-5   Cluster Bar Chart

Figure 22-6   Line Chart of Traffic Count by Retail Stores by Day of Week (August 8-14, 1995)

PART VI   APPLICATIONS

Chapter 23   Demand Measurement and Forecasting

Table 23-1   Four Dimensions of Demand Management and Forecasting

Figure 23-1   Market Demand Concepts and Terminology

Table 23-5   Forecasting Methods

Chapter 24   Product Research and Test Marketing

Figure 24-2   Most Simulation Models Operate in the Same General Framework

Chapter 25   Advertising Research

Figure 25-1   A Model for Evaluating Advertising

Figure 25-2   What to Measure

Figure 25-3   What and How to Measure

Chapter 26   Distribution and Pricing Research

Figure 26-1   NPDC Data on Income and Locations for Dallas County

Figure 26-2   Illustration of the Centroid Method

Table 26-1   Classification of Procedures for Measuring Price Sensitivity

Decision Theory Approach to Marketing Research (from Part VI of instructor's manual)

Figure 1   Decision Tree: Soft-Drink Special Promotion Problem

Figure 2   Decision Tree for Soft-Drink Special Promotion Problem

Figure 1-1
Model of the marketing system.

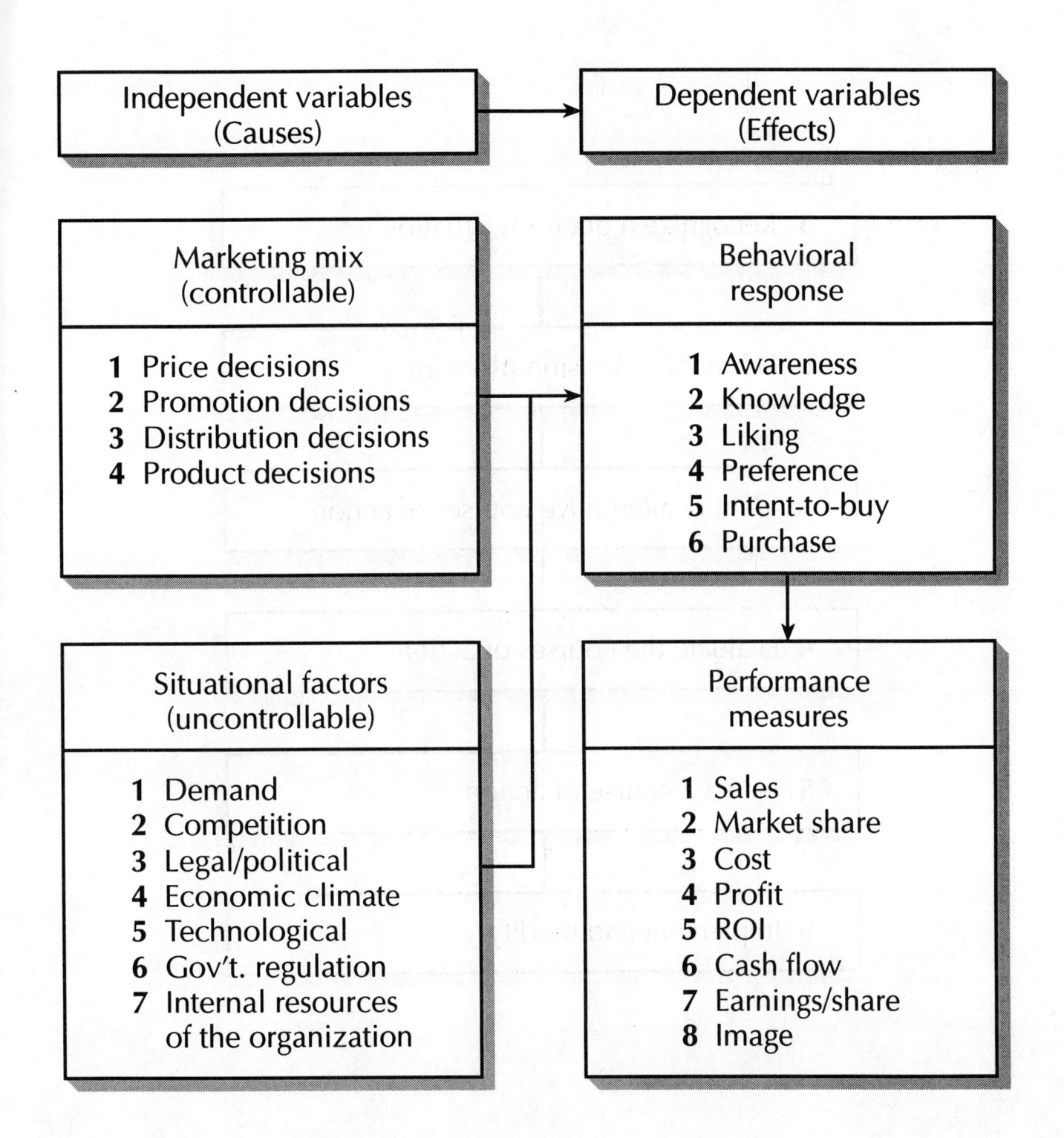

```
┌─────────────────────────┐      ┌─────────────────────────┐
│ Independent variables   │ ───▶ │  Dependent variables    │
│       (Causes)          │      │       (Effects)         │
└─────────────────────────┘      └─────────────────────────┘
```

Marketing mix (controllable)

1. Price decisions
2. Promotion decisions
3. Distribution decisions
4. Product decisions

Behavioral response

1. Awareness
2. Knowledge
3. Liking
4. Preference
5. Intent-to-buy
6. Purchase

Situational factors (uncontrollable)

1. Demand
2. Competition
3. Legal/political
4. Economic climate
5. Technological
6. Gov't. regulation
7. Internal resources of the organization

Performance measures

1. Sales
2. Market share
3. Cost
4. Profit
5. ROI
6. Cash flow
7. Earnings/share
8. Image

Copyright © 1996 by the McGraw-Hill Companies, Inc. All Rights Reserved.

Figure 1-2
Steps in the decision-making process.

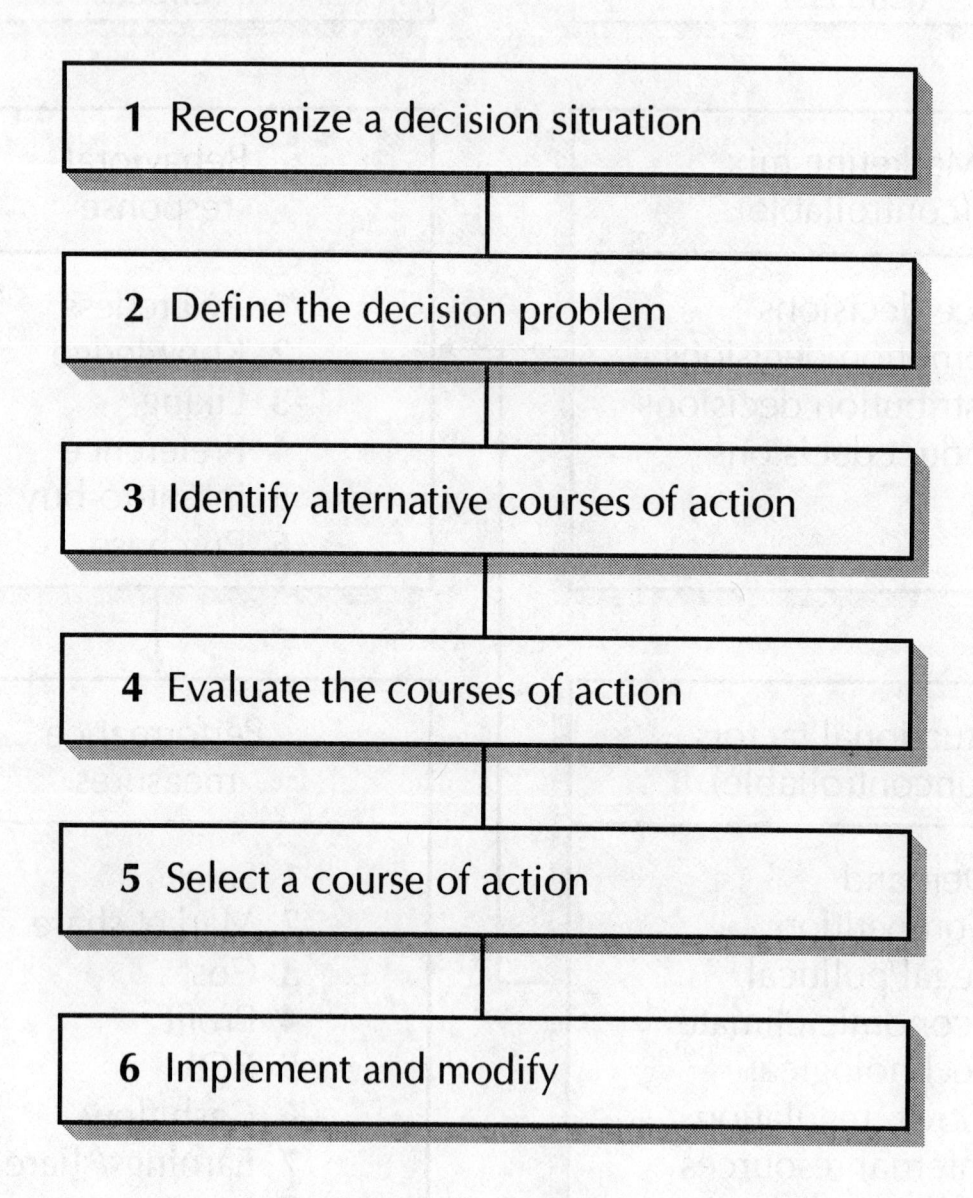

1. Recognize a decision situation
2. Define the decision problem
3. Identify alternative courses of action
4. Evaluate the courses of action
5. Select a course of action
6. Implement and modify

Copyright © 1996 by the McGraw-Hill Companies, Inc. All Rights Reserved.

Figure 1-3
The marketing management process.

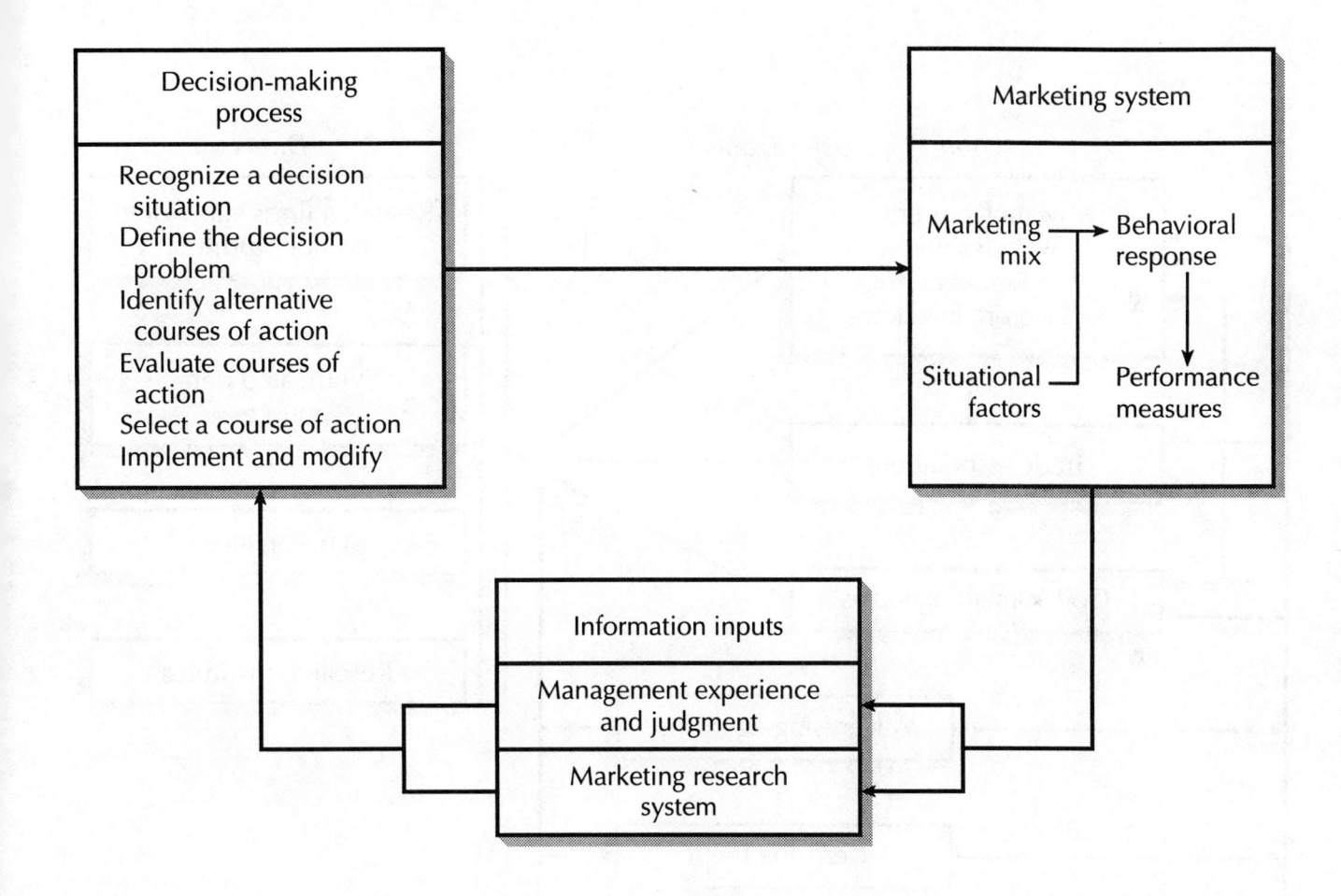

Decision-making process
- Recognize a decision situation
- Define the decision problem
- Identify alternative courses of action
- Evaluate courses of action
- Select a course of action
- Implement and modify

Marketing system
- Marketing mix → Behavioral response
- Situational factors → Performance measures

Information inputs
- Management experience and judgment
- Marketing research system

Copyright © 1996 by the McGraw-Hill Companies, Inc. All Rights Reserved.

Figure 2-1
The institutional structure of the marketing research business.

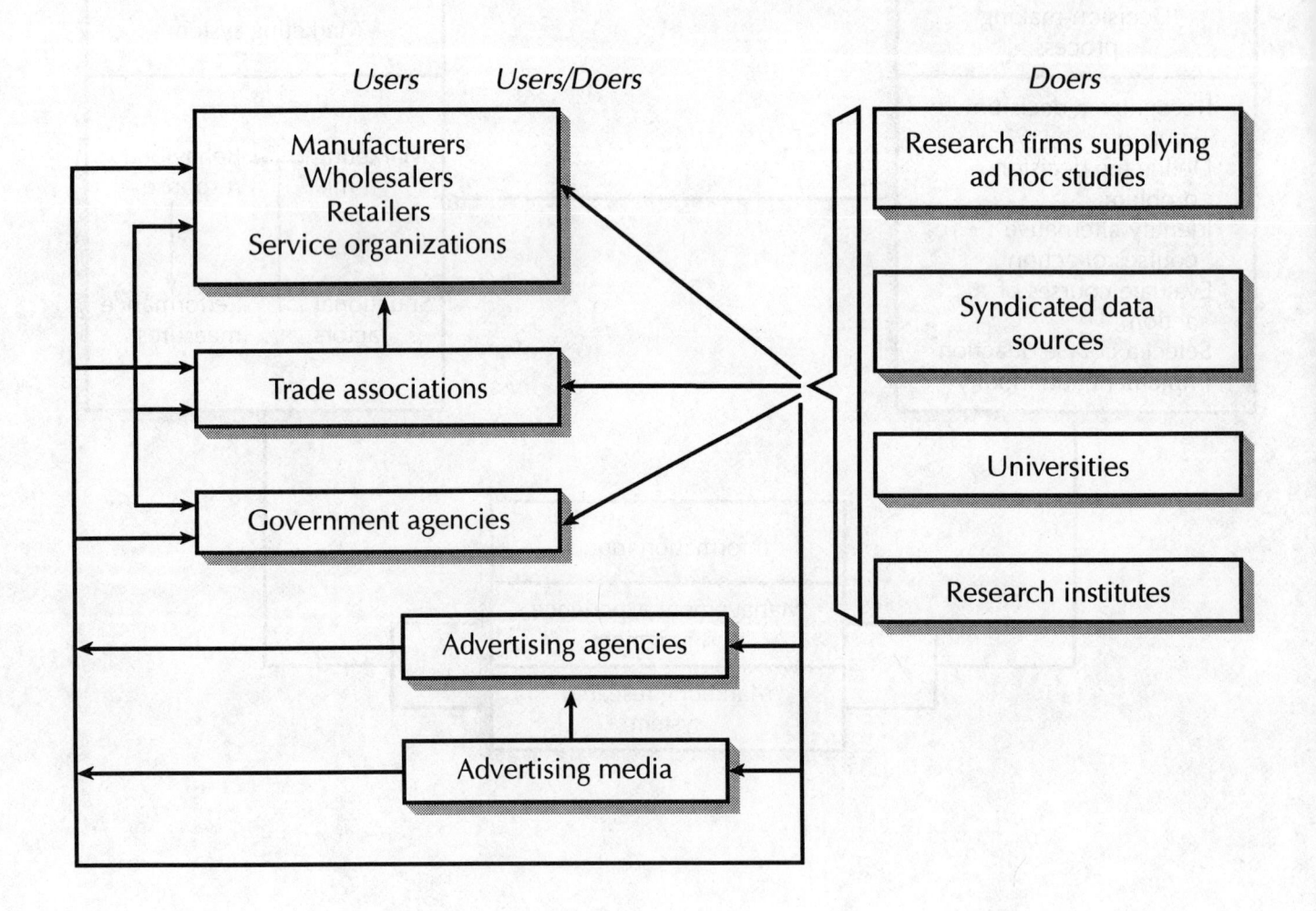

Table 2-2

RESPONSIBILITIES OF THE RESEARCH GENERALIST

1. Develop knowledge and judgment about various businesses.
2. Understand the research process and language.
3. Define problems and identify opportunities.
4. Identify management alternatives.
5. Marshall evidence to evaluate alternatives.
6. Propose profit-oriented research to close information gaps.
7. Balance decision risks and research costs to achieve high-payoff research projects.
8. Provide an element of entrepreneurial spirit in the planning of research.
9. Bring an element of creativity and insight to research findings and their implications for decision making.
10. Provide perspective on the long-range research needs for a business.
11. Be an educator, a liaison person, a communicator, and a counselor.

Table 2-5

CENTRALIZED ORGANIZATION

Advantages

1. Effective coordination and control of the research activity is possible.
2. Encouragement of economical and flexible use of facilities and personnel occurs.
3. Increased usefulness and objectivity of research results to corporate executives develops.
4. Greater prestige to marketing research occurs.
5. Better likelihood of attracting top-notch researchers is possible.
6. Cross-fertilization of ideas occurs.
7. Greater likelihood of obtaining an adequate budget is possible.

Disadvantages

1. Isolates researchers from day-to-day activities and problems.
2. Corporate problems receive all the time and attention, at the expense of the divisions.
3. Separates researchers from the action programs based on the research; takes no responsibility for their implemented recommendations.

Copyright © 1996 by the McGraw-Hill Companies, Inc. All Rights Reserved.

Table 2-6

DECENTRALIZED ORGANIZATION

Advantages

1. Researchers are close to the action of marketing problems and implementation of their recommendations.
2. More specialization is available on product, customers, or markets.
3. More attention will be paid by divisional managers to marketing research.
4. Breakdown of the corporate/divisional barriers can occur.

Disadvantages

1. Tendency to bias results in favor of the marketing group for which the researcher works.
2. Inadequate research controls, standards, and procedures.
3. Difficulty in finding qualified people.
4. High cost.
5. Duplication of effort.
6. Central management needs not attended to.

Copyright © 1996 by the McGraw-Hill Companies, Inc. All Rights Reserved.

Figure 2-3
General Foods' marketing research organization. (*Source:* "Marketing Research: Career Opportunities at General Foods," General Foods Corporation, White Plains, NY.)

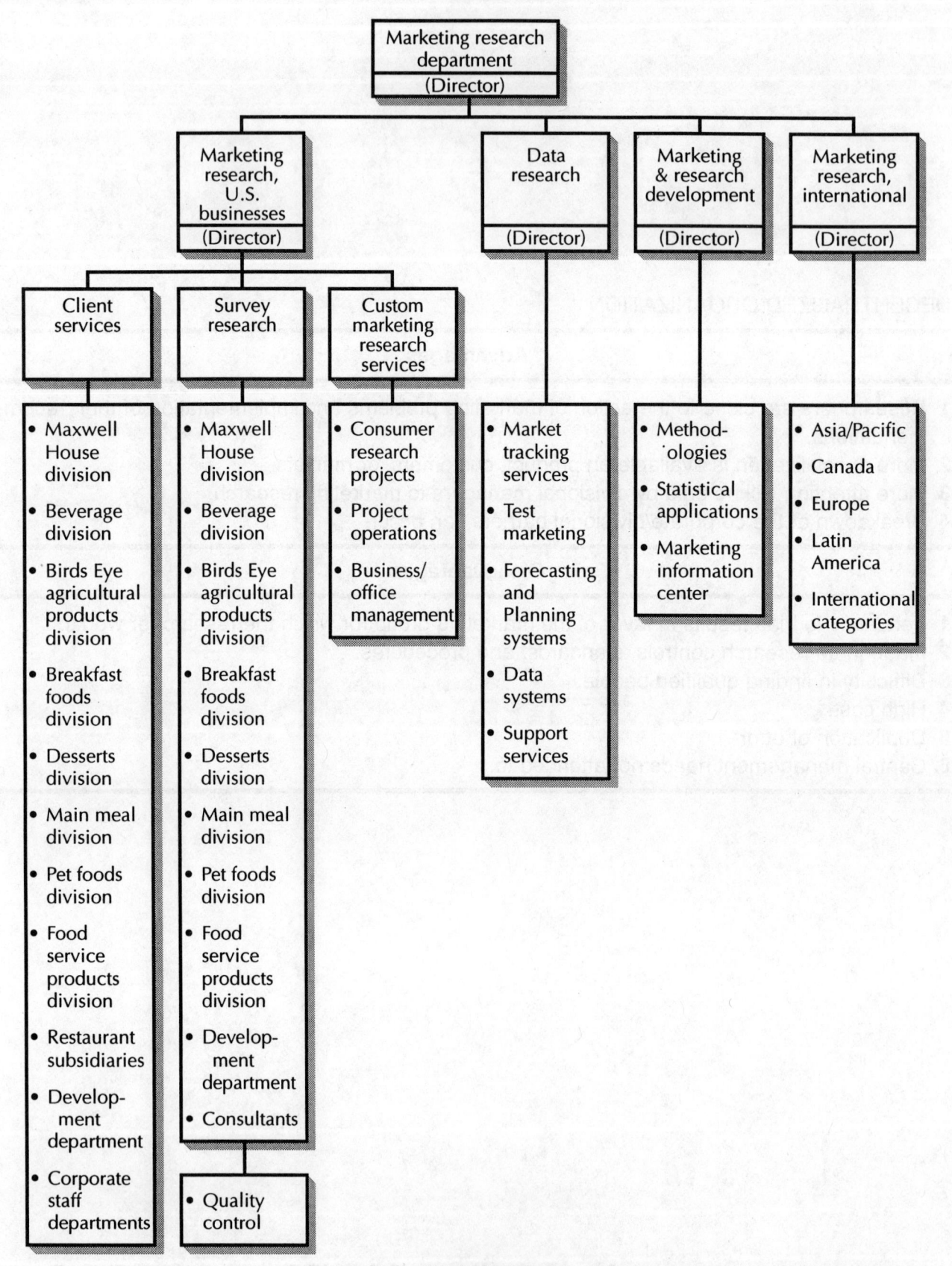

- **Marketing research department (Director)**
  - **Marketing research, U.S. businesses (Director)**
    - Client services
      - Maxwell House division
      - Beverage division
      - Birds Eye agricultural products division
      - Breakfast foods division
      - Desserts division
      - Main meal division
      - Pet foods division
      - Food service products division
      - Restaurant subsidiaries
      - Development department
      - Corporate staff departments
    - Survey research
      - Maxwell House division
      - Beverage division
      - Birds Eye agricultural products division
      - Breakfast foods division
      - Desserts division
      - Main meal division
      - Pet foods division
      - Food service products division
      - Development department
      - Consultants
      - Quality control
    - Custom marketing research services
      - Consumer research projects
      - Project operations
      - Business/office management
  - **Data research (Director)**
    - Market tracking services
    - Test marketing
    - Forecasting and Planning systems
    - Data systems
    - Support services
  - **Marketing & research development (Director)**
    - Methodologies
    - Statistical applications
    - Marketing information center
  - **Marketing research, international (Director)**
    - Asia/Pacific
    - Canada
    - Europe
    - Latin America
    - International categories

Figure 3-1
Steps in the research process.

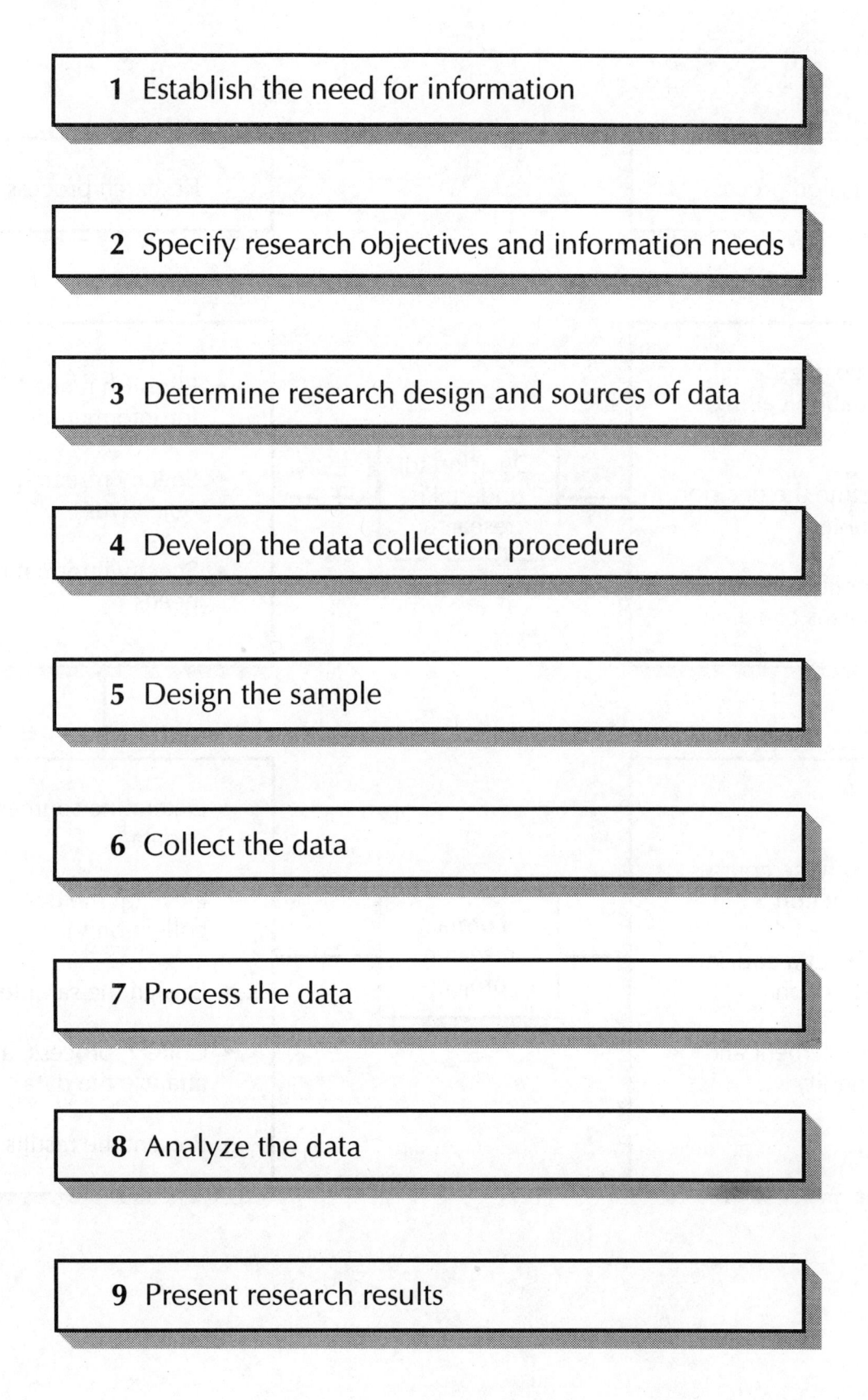

1. Establish the need for information
2. Specify research objectives and information needs
3. Determine research design and sources of data
4. Develop the data collection procedure
5. Design the sample
6. Collect the data
7. Process the data
8. Analyze the data
9. Present research results

Figure 4-2
Links between the decision process and the research process.

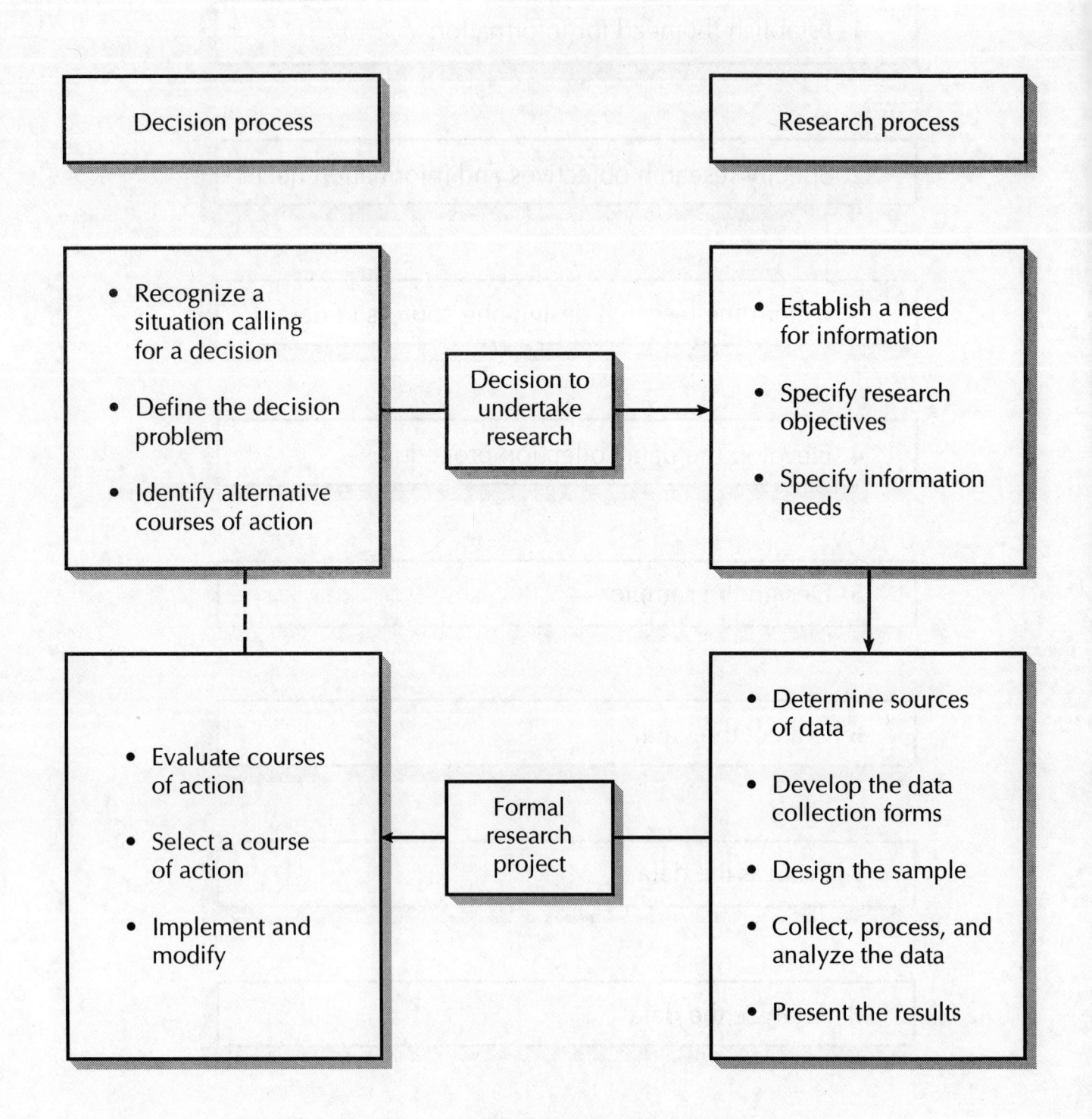

Decision process

- Recognize a situation calling for a decision
- Define the decision problem
- Identify alternative courses of action

→ Decision to undertake research →

Research process

- Establish a need for information
- Specify research objectives
- Specify information needs

- Determine sources of data
- Develop the data collection forms
- Design the sample
- Collect, process, and analyze the data
- Present the results

← Formal research project ←

- Evaluate courses of action
- Select a course of action
- Implement and modify

Copyright © 1996 by the McGraw-Hill Companies, Inc. All Rights Reserved.

Figure 4-3
Preliminary steps in the decision-making process.

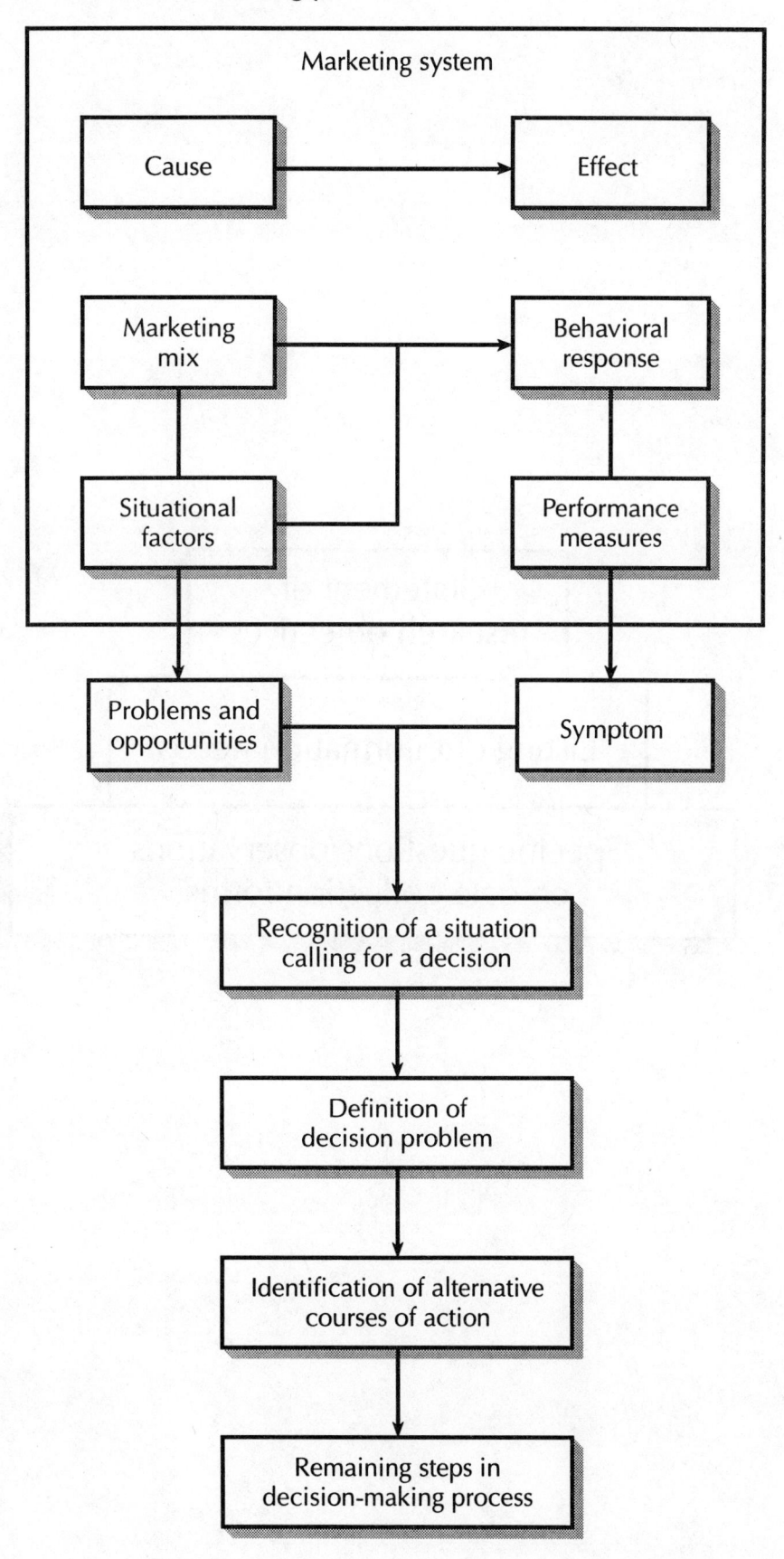

Figure 4-4
Pyramid of research objectives and information needs.

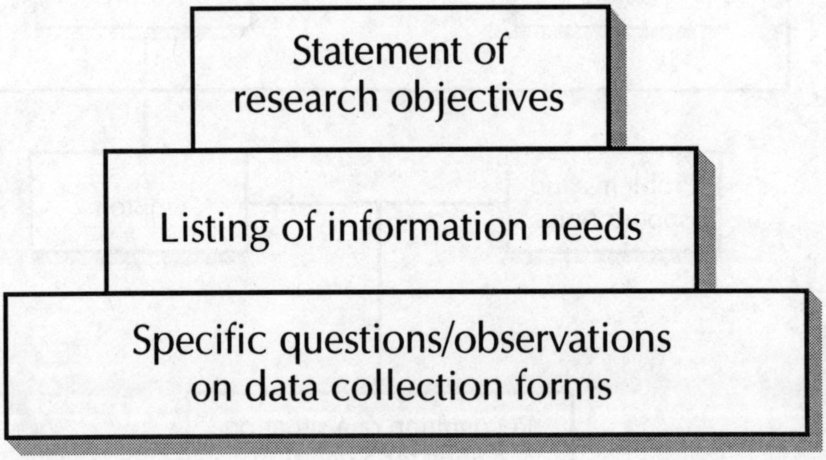

Statement of research objectives

Listing of information needs

Specific questions/observations on data collection forms

Copyright © 1996 by the McGraw-Hill Companies, Inc. All Rights Reserved.

Table 4-1

RESEARCH VALUE AS FUNCTION OF CONTRIBUTION MARGIN AND MARKET SIZE

Market size	Contribution margin	
	Small	Large
Small	Unlikely research can be supported, e.g., hobby glue (Elmers), nail clippers (Trim), screwdriver (Stanley)	Can support some small research, e.g., specialty tape (3M), specialty drugs (Upjohn), executive aircraft (Lear)
Large	Can support large amount of research, e.g., razor blades (Gillette), soap powder (Tide), soft drinks (Coca-Cola)	Easy to support large amount of research, e.g., automobiles (Ford), appliances (Hotpoint), long-distance calls (AT&T)

Exhibit 4-1

RESEARCH REQUEST FORM

Title:_____ Date prepared:_____
Requested by:_____ Start of project:_____
Approved by:_____ Report due:_____
Date approved:_____ Budget:_____
Project number:_____ Supplier:_____

1. *Background.* What led to the recognition that research was needed?
2. *Objectives.* What are the decision objectives?
3. *Problem/opportunity.* What are the underlying causes of the decision situation?
4. *Decision alternatives.* What are the alternative courses of action?
5. *Research objectives.* What is the purpose of the research?
6. *Information needs.* What type of information is needed?
7. *Example of questions.* What kind of questions should be asked?
8. *Decision criteria.* What criteria should be used to select the best alternative?
9. *Value of research.* Why is the research useful?

Copyright © 1996 by the McGraw-Hill Companies, Inc. All Rights Reserved.

Figure 5-2
Types of research.

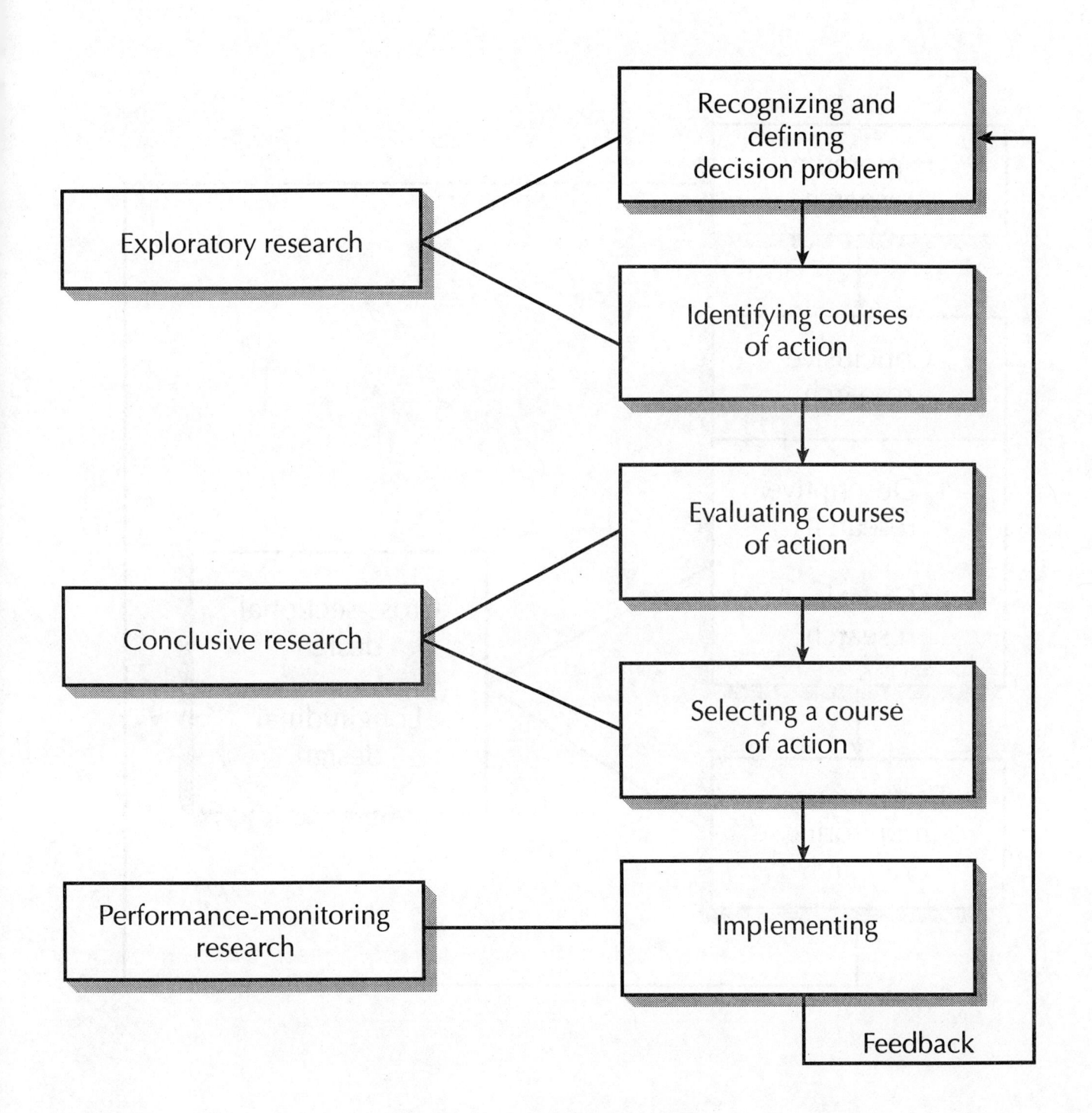

Figure 5-3
Research design.

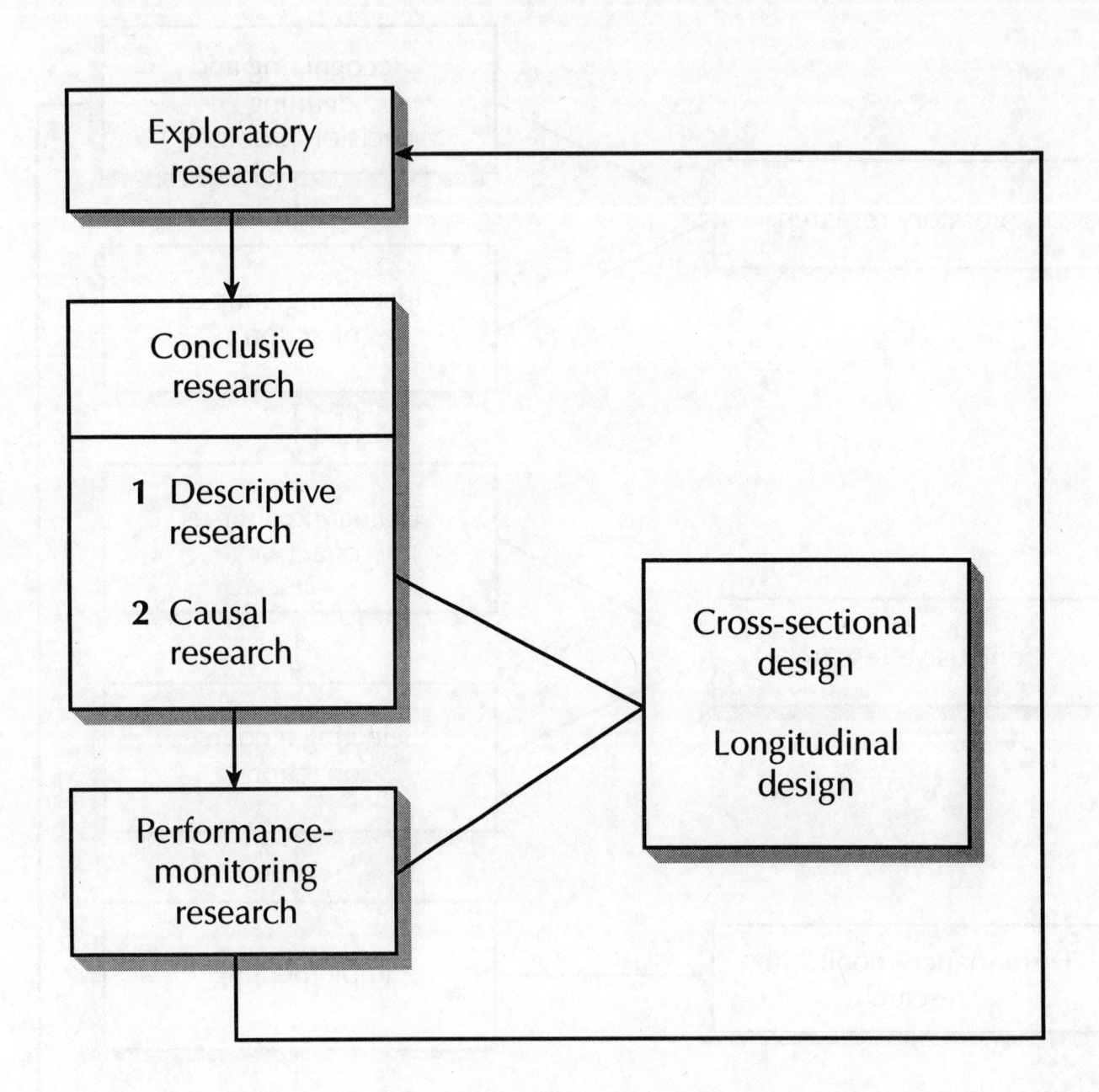

Table 5-1

CROSS-SECTIONAL DATA MAY NOT REFLECT LONGITUDINAL DATA

	Cross-sectional data	
	Period 1 survey	Period 2 survey
Brand A		
Purchase	100	100
No purchase	400	400
Total	500	500
Brand B		
Purchase	100	100
No purchase	400	400
Total	500	500

Longitudinal data

Period 1 panel reporting

Brand A

Period 2 panel reporting	Purchase	No purchase	Total
Brand A			
Purchase	100	0	100
No purchase	0	400	400
Total	100	400	500

Brand B

	Purchase	No purchase	Total
Brand B			
Purchase	0	100	100
No purchase	100	300	400
Total	100	400	500

Source: Adapted from Seymour Sudman and Robert Ferber, *Consumer Panels* (Chicago, Ill.: American Marketing Association, 1979), p. 5.

Copyright © 1996 by the McGraw-Hill Companies, Inc. All Rights Reserved.

Figure 5-10
Marketing decision support system.

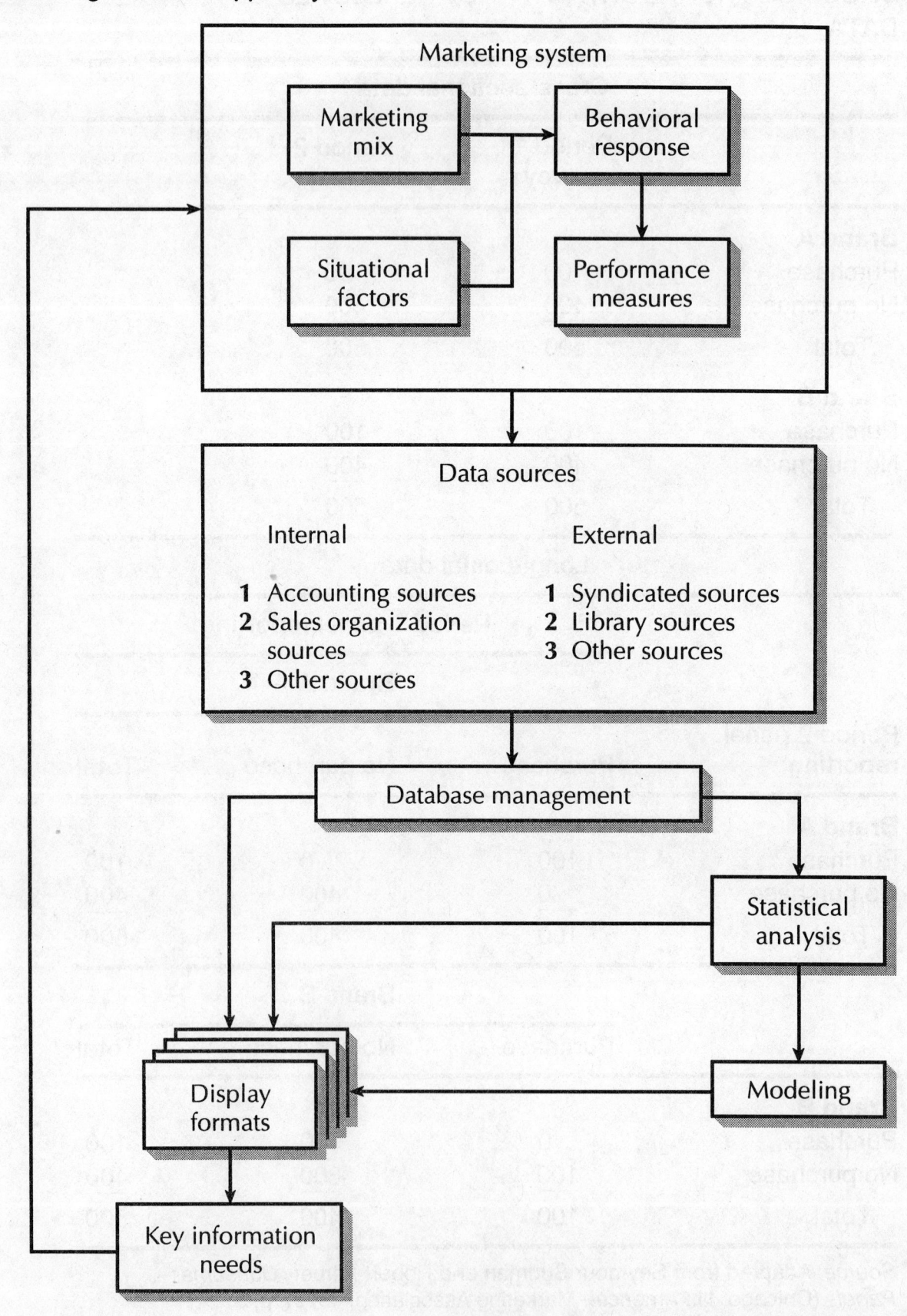

Figure 6-2
Initial steps in the research process.

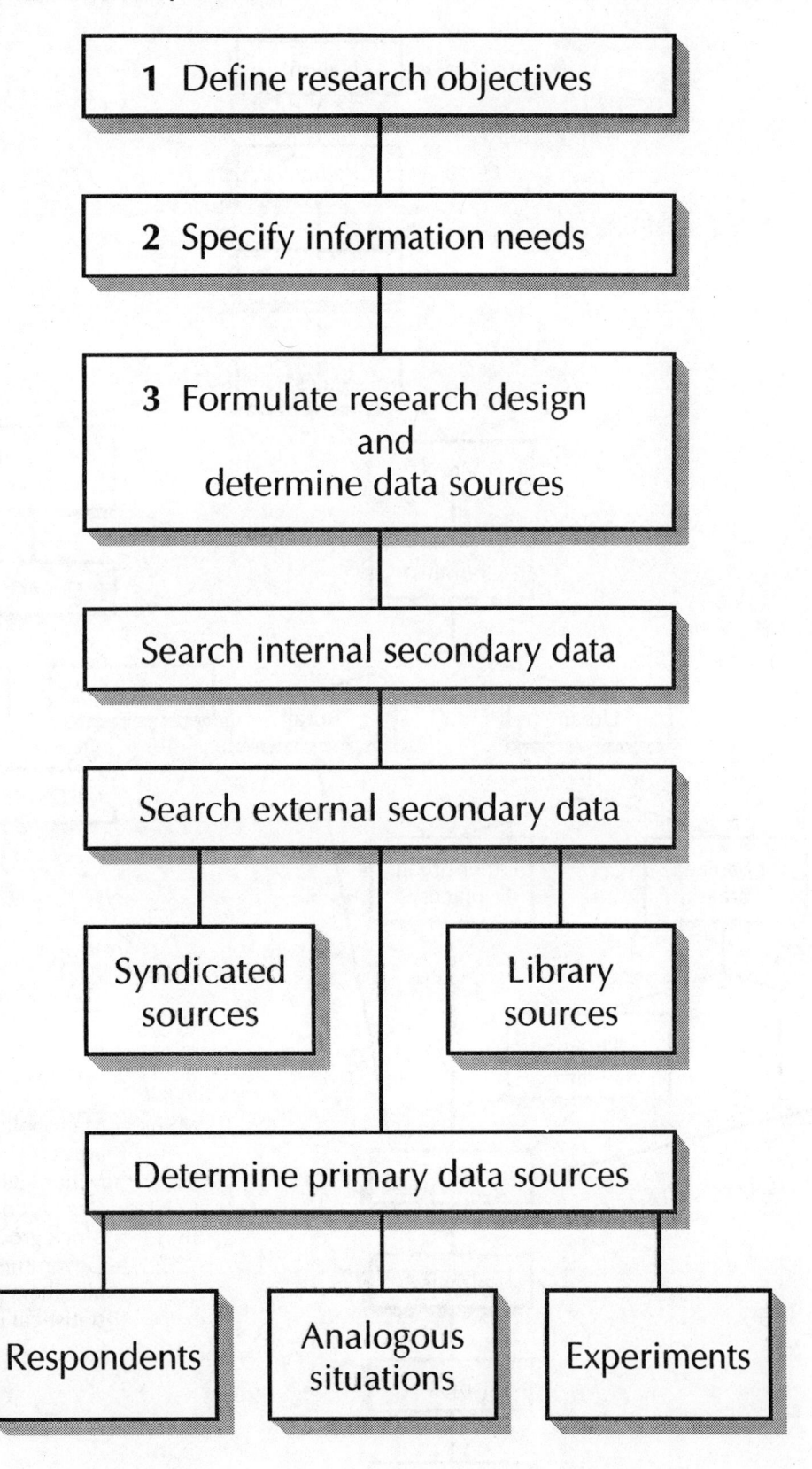

```
┌─────────────────────────────────────┐
│  1  Define research objectives      │
└─────────────────────────────────────┘
                 │
┌─────────────────────────────────────┐
│  2  Specify information needs       │
└─────────────────────────────────────┘
                 │
┌─────────────────────────────────────┐
│  3  Formulate research design       │
│             and                     │
│     determine data sources          │
└─────────────────────────────────────┘
                 │
┌─────────────────────────────────────┐
│    Search internal secondary data   │
└─────────────────────────────────────┘
                 │
┌─────────────────────────────────────┐
│    Search external secondary data   │
└─────────────────────────────────────┘
           │                │
   ┌───────────────┐  ┌───────────────┐
   │  Syndicated   │  │    Library    │
   │    sources    │  │    sources    │
   └───────────────┘  └───────────────┘
                 │
┌─────────────────────────────────────┐
│    Determine primary data sources   │
└─────────────────────────────────────┘
        │           │           │
 ┌─────────────┐ ┌──────────┐ ┌─────────────┐
 │ Respondents │ │Analogous │ │ Experiments │
 │             │ │situations│ │             │
 └─────────────┘ └──────────┘ └─────────────┘
```

Copyright © 1996 by the McGraw-Hill Companies, Inc. All Rights Reserved.

Figure 6-3
Bureau of the Census geographic units and their hierarchical relationships.

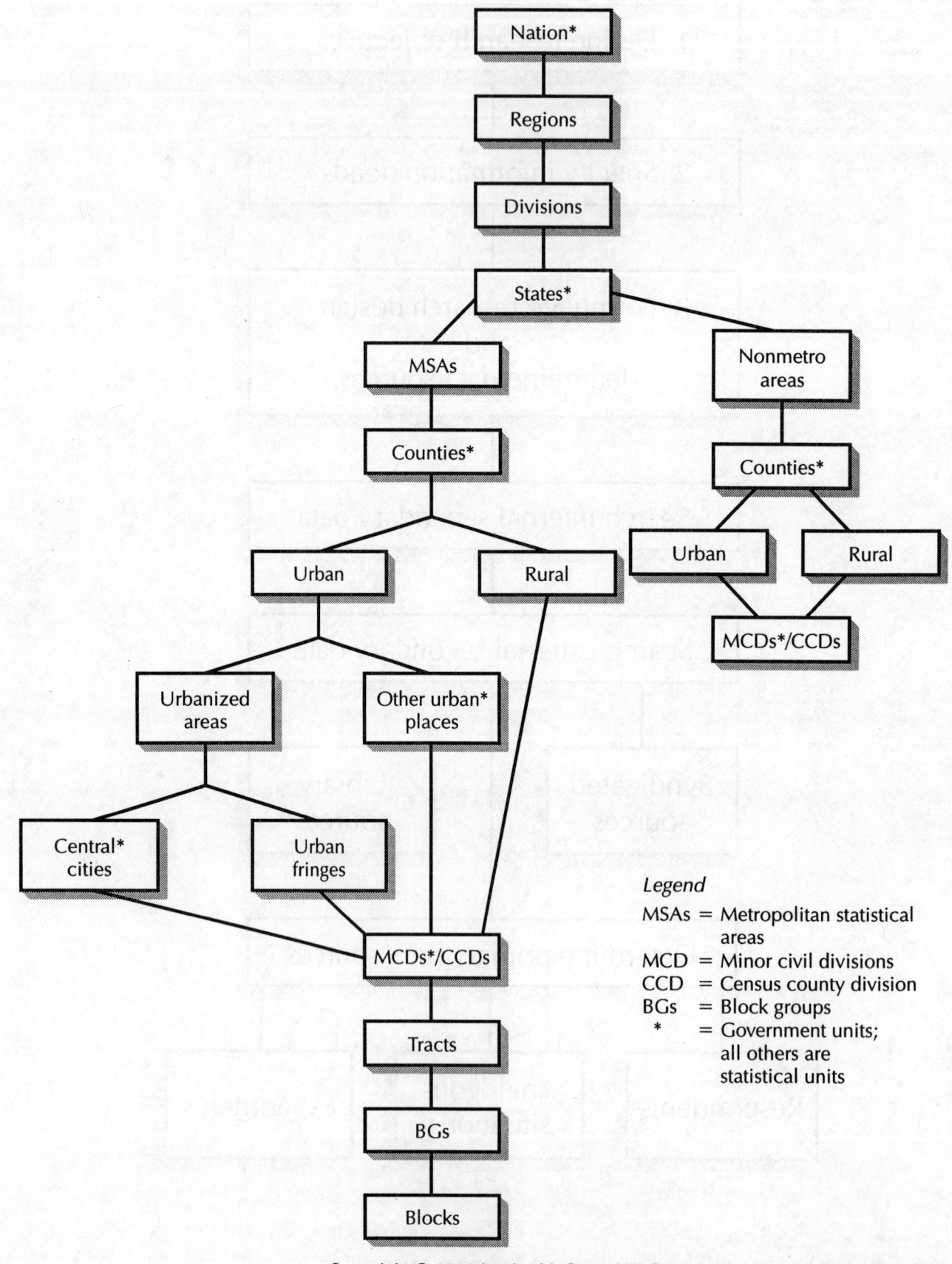

Legend
MSAs = Metropolitan statistical areas
MCD = Minor civil divisions
CCD = Census county division
BGs = Block groups
* = Government units; all others are statistical units

Copyright © 1996 by the McGraw-Hill Companies, Inc. All Rights Reserved.

Figure 6-4
Geographic subdivisions of an MSA.

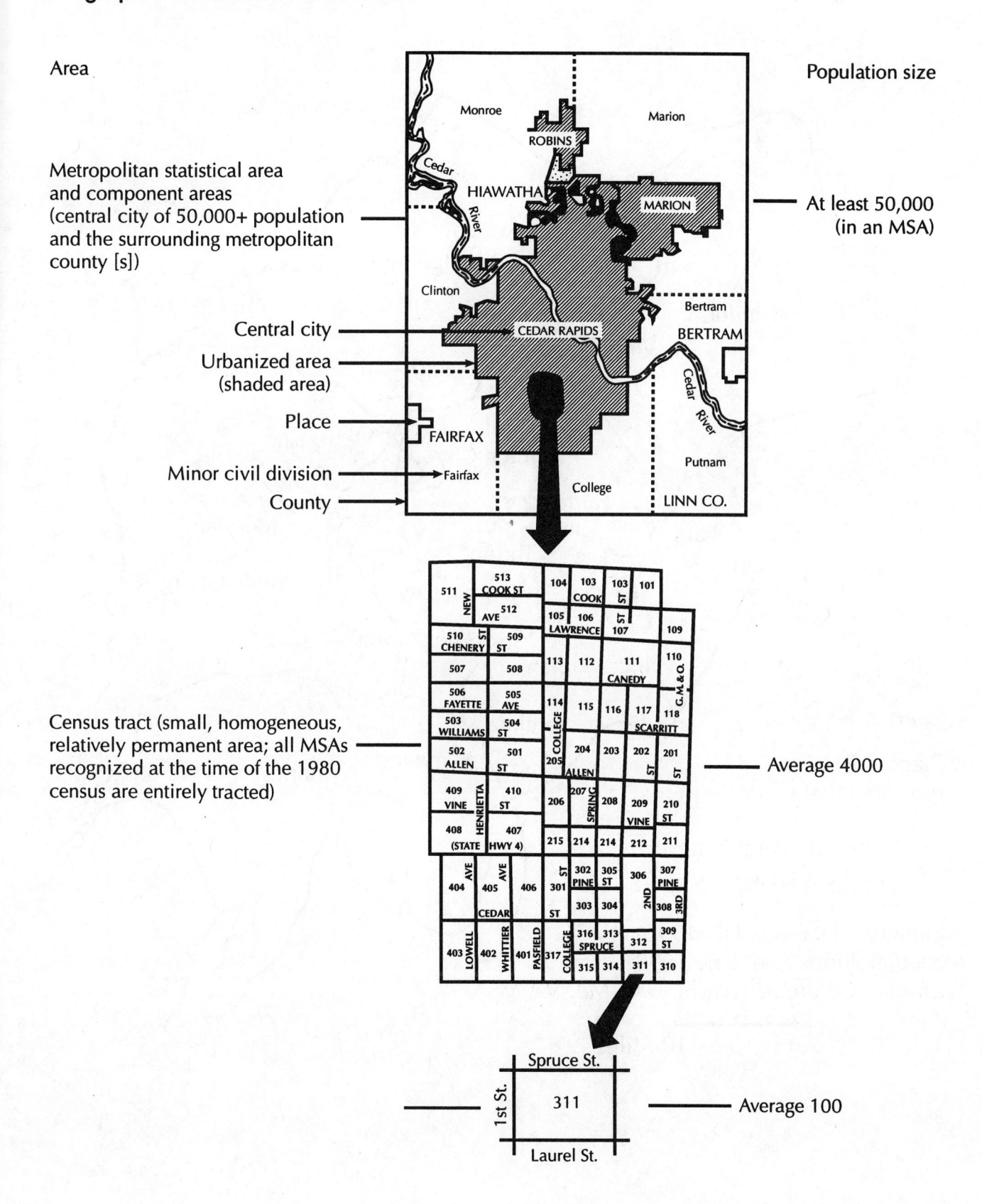

Area		Population size
Metropolitan statistical area and component areas (central city of 50,000+ population and the surrounding metropolitan county [s])		At least 50,000 (in an MSA)
Central city		
Urbanized area (shaded area)		
Place		
Minor civil division		
County		
Census tract (small, homogeneous, relatively permanent area; all MSAs recognized at the time of the 1980 census are entirely tracted)		Average 4000
		Average 100

Copyright © 1996 by the McGraw-Hill Companies, Inc. All Rights Reserved.

Figure 6-5
The Washington, DC, MSA.

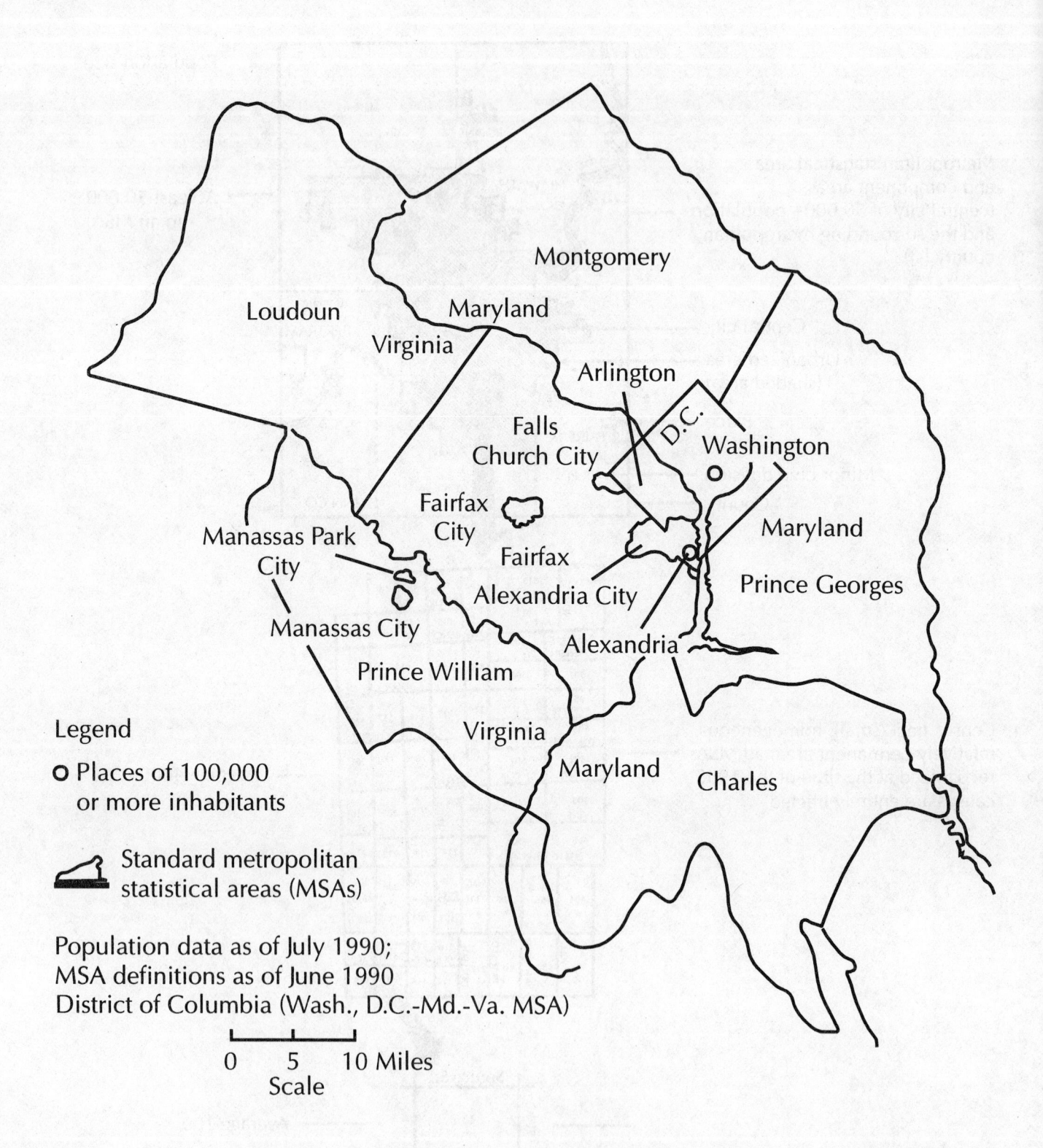

Legend
○ Places of 100,000 or more inhabitants

Standard metropolitan statistical areas (MSAs)

Population data as of July 1990;
MSA definitions as of June 1990
District of Columbia (Wash., D.C.-Md.-Va. MSA)

0　5　10 Miles
Scale

Copyright © 1996 by the McGraw-Hill Companies, Inc. All Rights Reserved.

Figure 7-2
The measurement process.

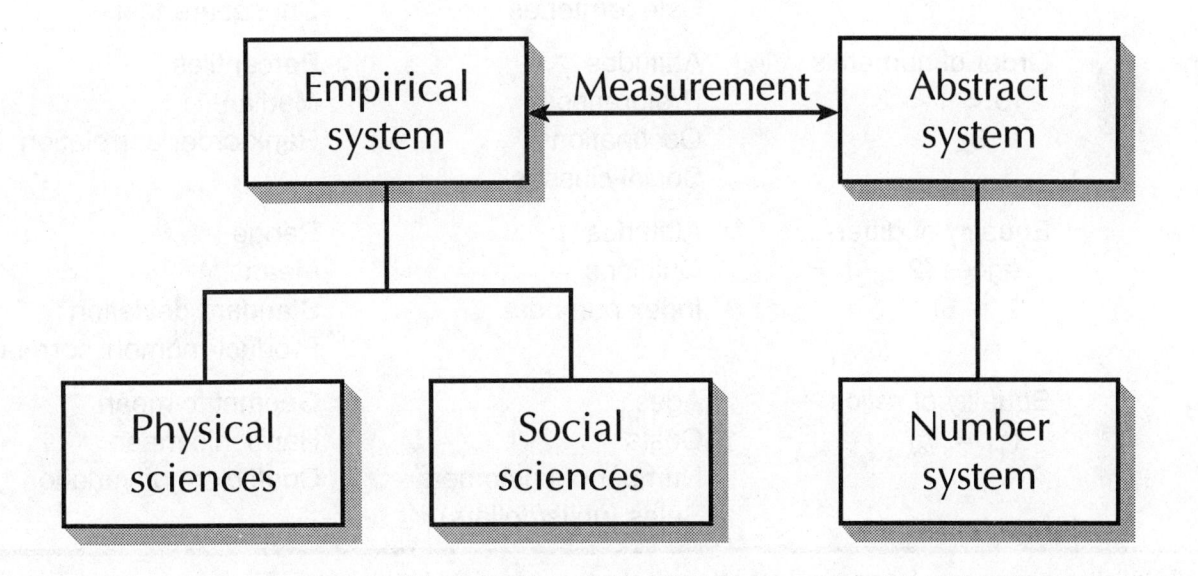

Table 7-1

CHARACTERISTICS OF MEASUREMENT SCALES

Scale	Number system	Marketing phenomena	Permissible statistics*
Nominal	Unique definition of numerals (0, 1, 2, . . . , 9)	Brands Male-female Store types Sale territories	Percentages Mode Binomial test Chi-square test
Ordinal	Order of numerals (0 < 1 < 2 . . . < 9)	Attitudes Preferences Occupations Social classes	Percentiles Median Rank-order correlation
Interval	Equality of differences (2 − 1 = 7 − 6)	Attitudes Opinions Index numbers	Range Mean Standard deviation Product-moment correlation
Ratio	Equality of ratios ($\frac{2}{4} = \frac{4}{8}$)	Ages Costs Number of customers Sales (units/dollars)	Geometric mean Harmonic mean Coefficient of variation

*All statistics appropriate for nominal measurement are appropriate for higher scale measurement. The same is true for ordinal- and interval-scale measurements.

Copyright © 1996 by the McGraw-Hill Companies, Inc. All Rights Reserved.

Figure 7-3
Permissible transformation by scale type.

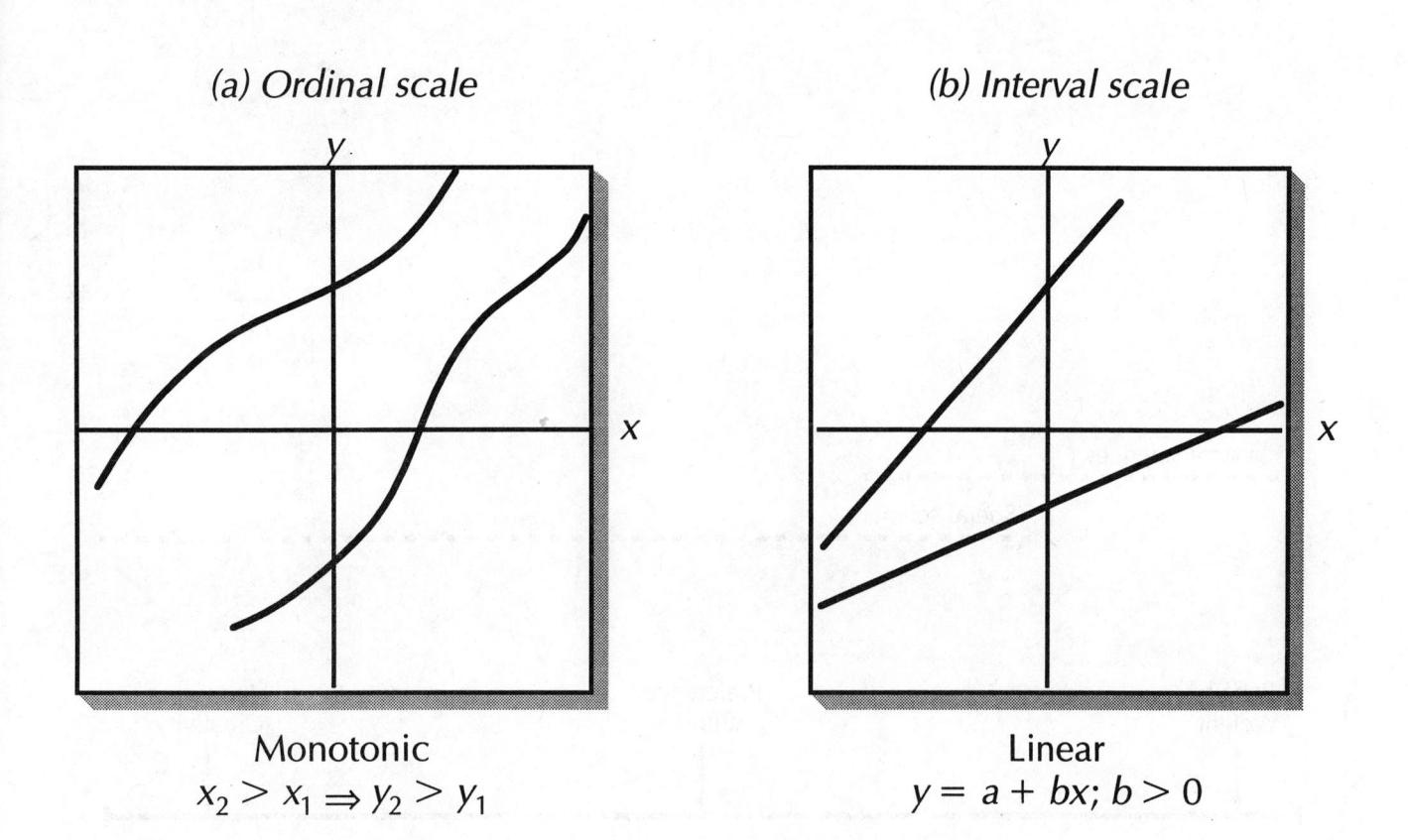

(a) Ordinal scale

Monotonic
$x_2 > x_1 \Rightarrow y_2 > y_1$

(b) Interval scale

Linear
$y = a + bx; b > 0$

(c) Ratio scale

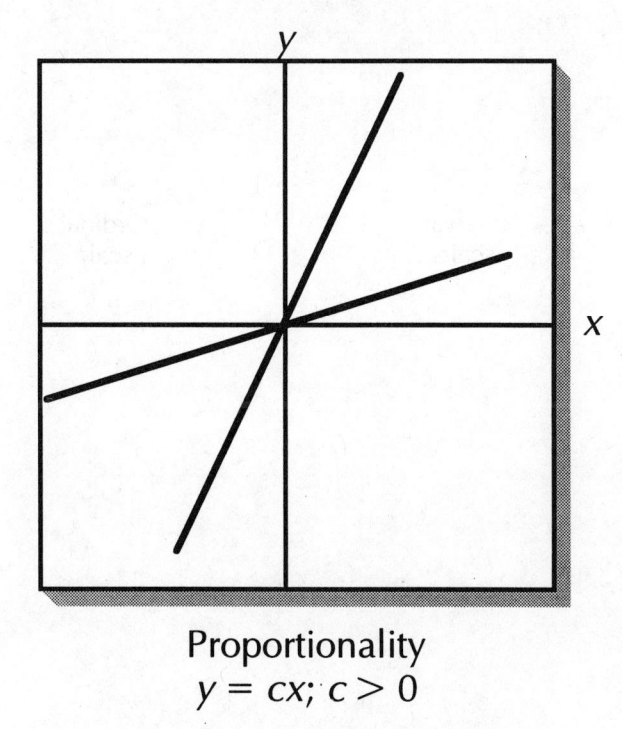

Proportionality
$y = cx; c > 0$

Copyright © 1996 by the McGraw-Hill Companies, Inc. All Rights Reserved.

Figure 7-4
Difficulty of the measurement process.

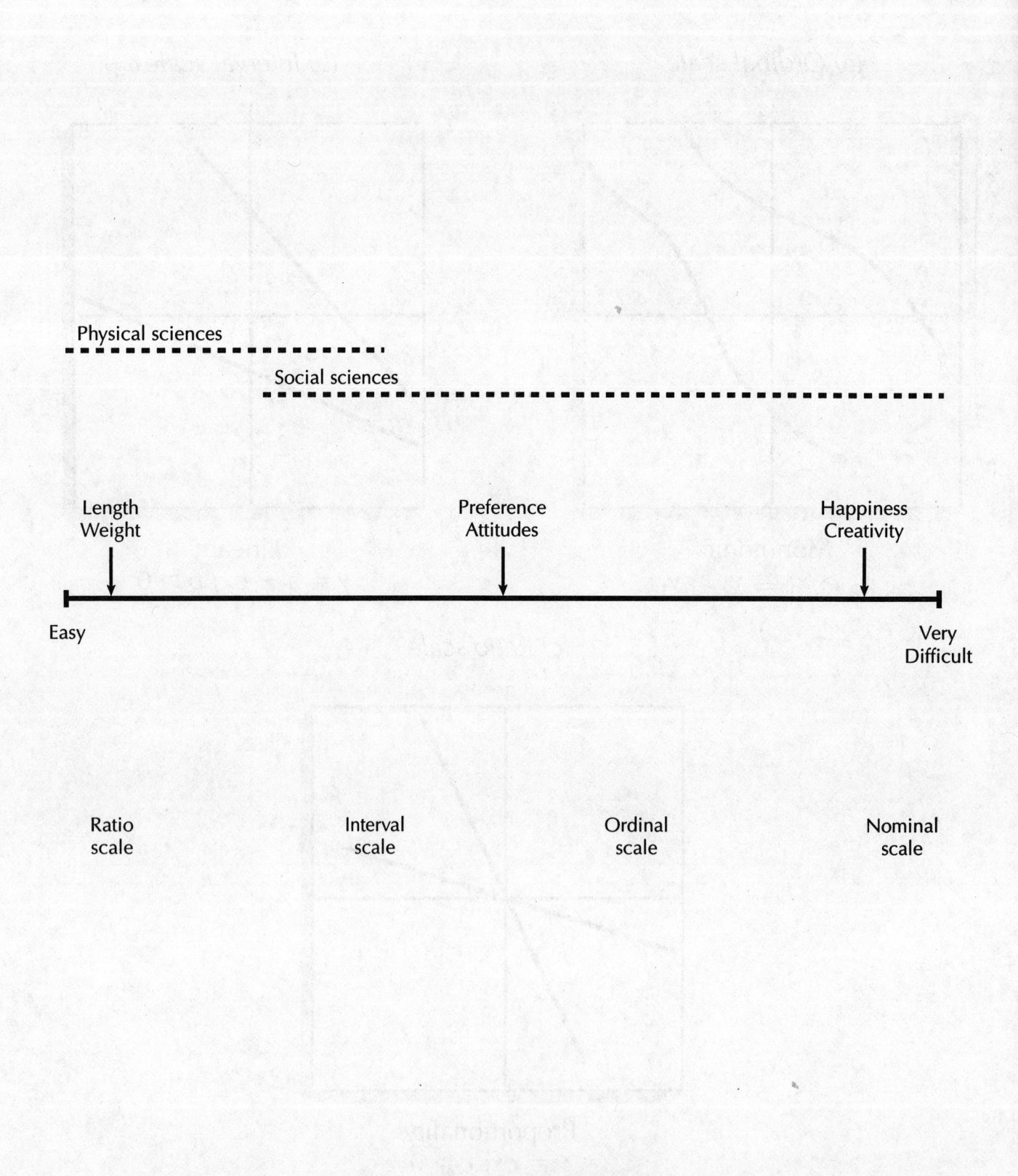

Physical sciences
- - - - - - - - - - - - - - - - - - -
            Social sciences
            -

Length   Preference   Happiness
Weight   Attitudes   Creativity
  ↓   ↓   ↓
|——|
Easy   Very
                                          Difficult

Ratio   Interval   Ordinal   Nominal
scale   scale   scale   scale

Copyright © 1996 by the McGraw-Hill Companies, Inc. All Rights Reserved.

Figure 7-5
Reliability and validity.

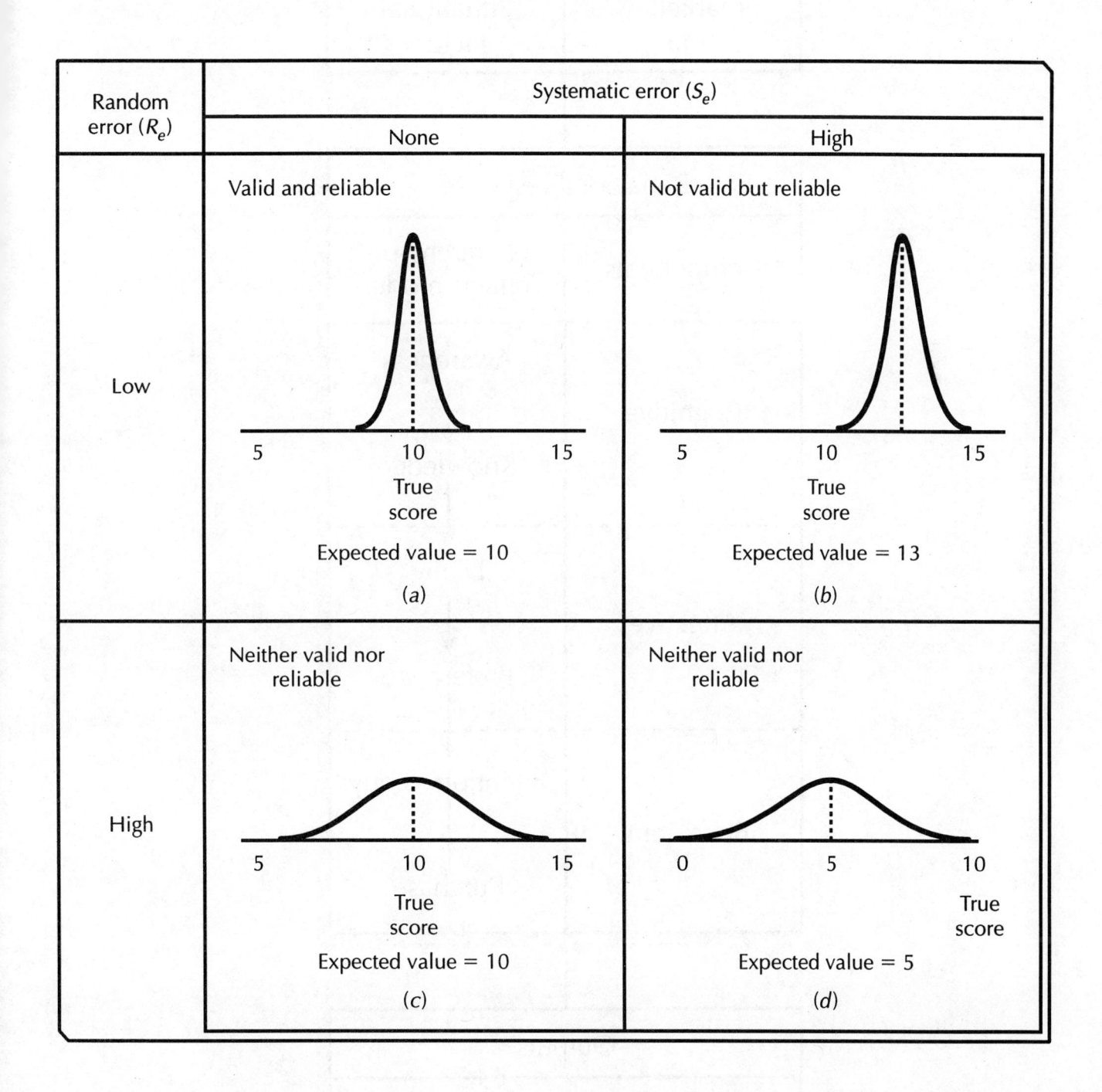

Random error (R_e)	Systematic error (S_e)	
	None	High
Low	Valid and reliable Expected value = 10 (a)	Not valid but reliable Expected value = 13 (b)
High	Neither valid nor reliable Expected value = 10 (c)	Neither valid nor reliable Expected value = 5 (d)

Copyright © 1996 by the McGraw-Hill Companies, Inc. All Rights Reserved.

Figure 8-2
Model of behavioral response.

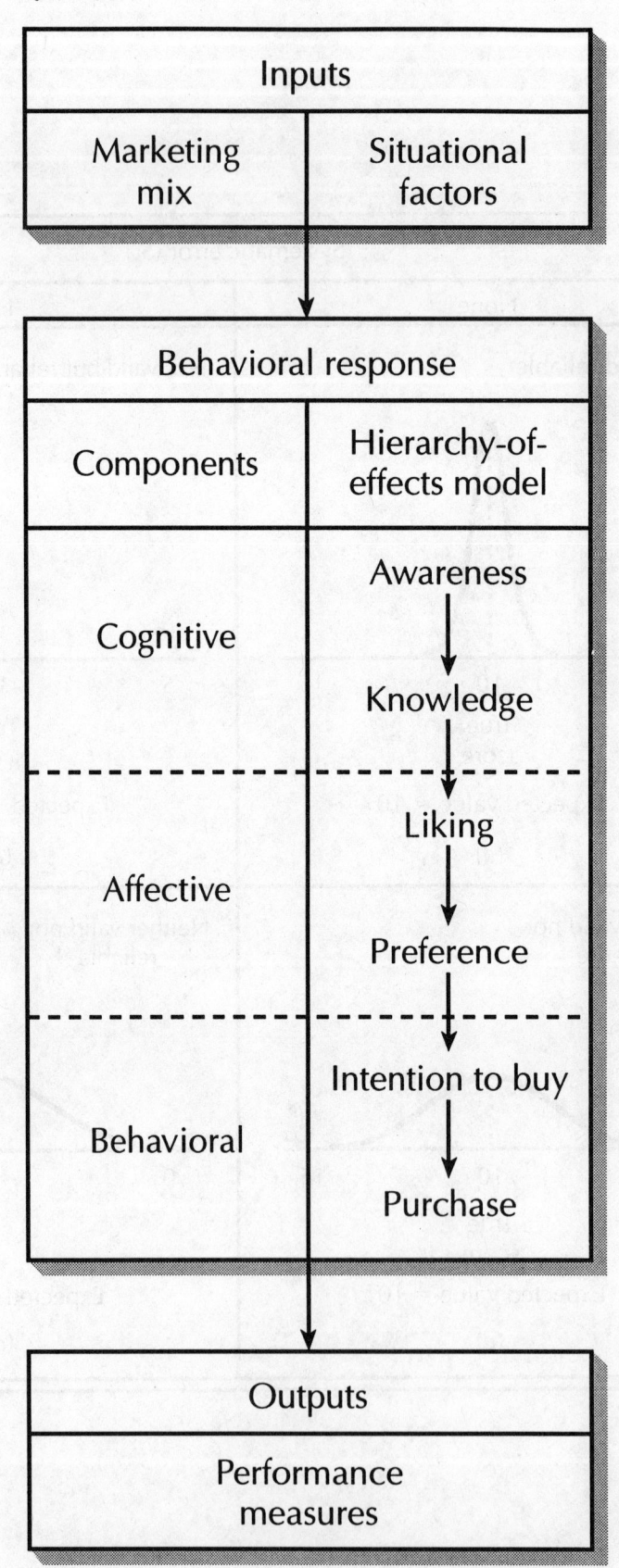

Figure 8-3
Graphic and verbal rating scales.

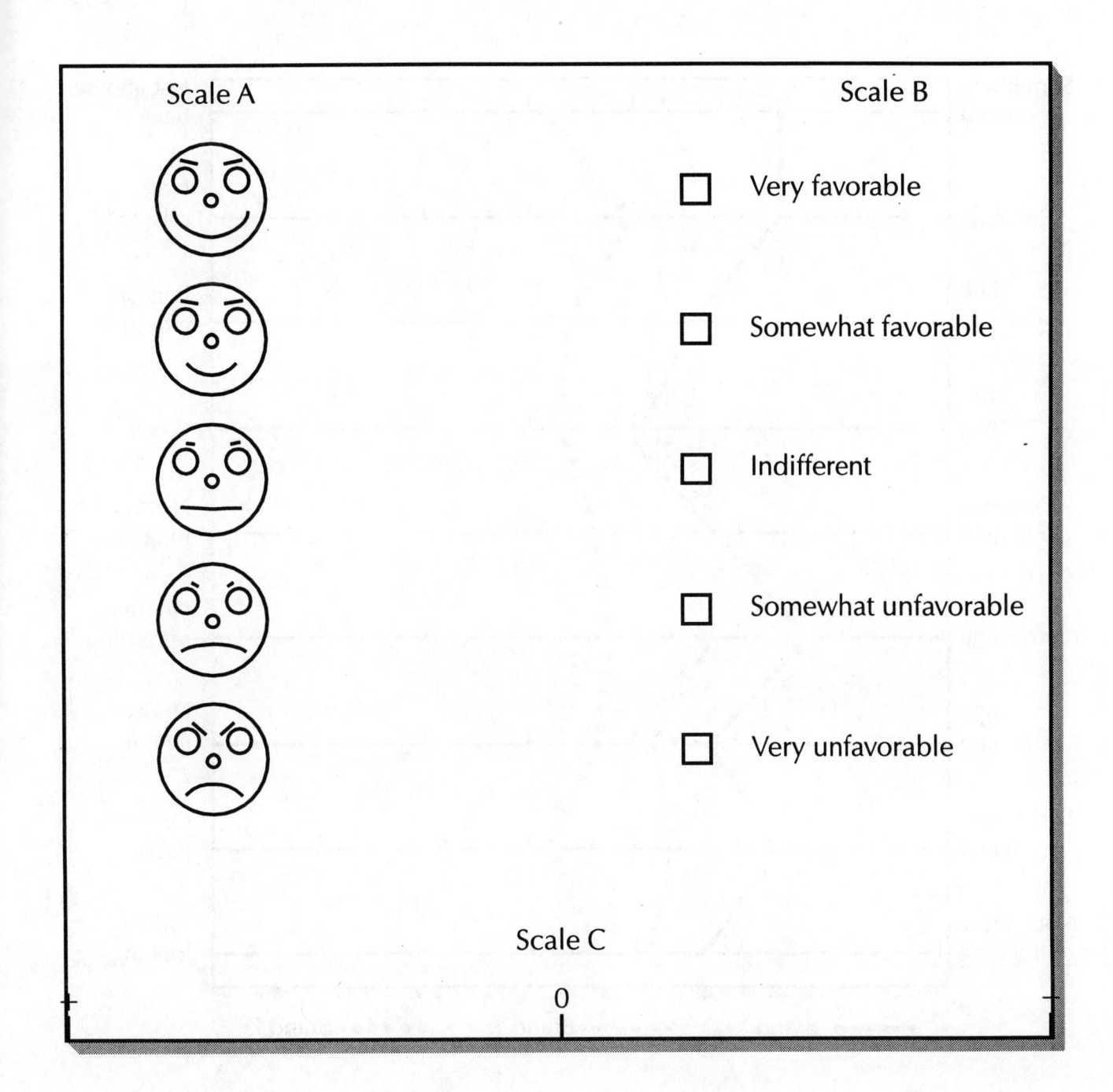

Scale A

Scale B

☐ Very favorable

☐ Somewhat favorable

☐ Indifferent

☐ Somewhat unfavorable

☐ Very unfavorable

Scale C

0

Copyright © 1996 by the McGraw-Hill Companies, Inc. All Rights Reserved.

Figure 8-4
Profile analysis of beer brand images.

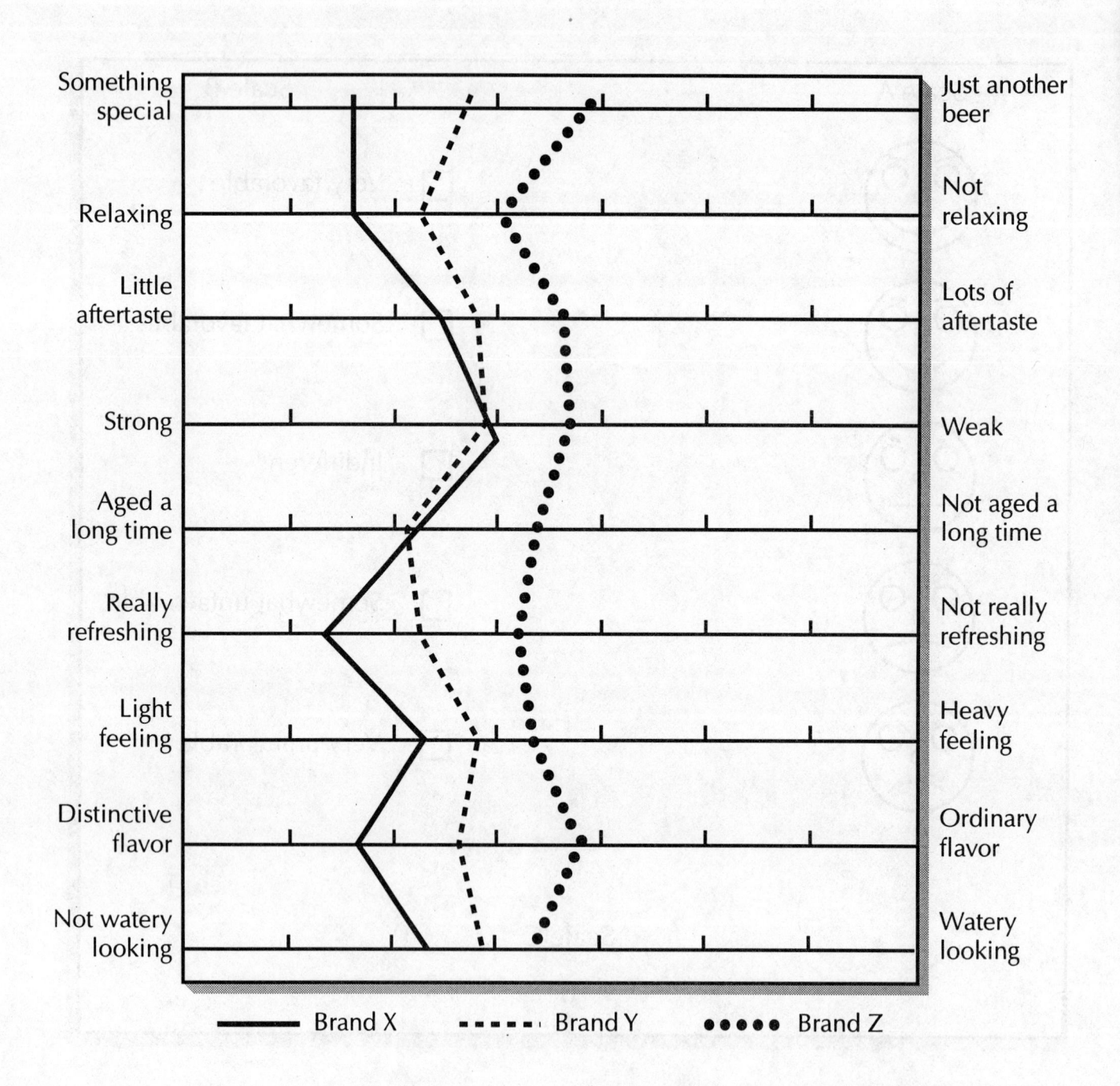

Copyright © 1996 by the McGraw-Hill Companies, Inc. All Rights Reserved.

Table 8-3

STAPEL SCALE FORMAT

	Bank	
	5	5
	4	4
	3	3
	2	2
	1	1
Fast service		Friendly
	−1	−1
	−2	−2
	−3	−3
	−4	−4
	−5	−5

Copyright © 1996 by the McGraw-Hill Companies, Inc. All Rights Reserved.

Figure 8-5
Stapel scale comparative profiles.

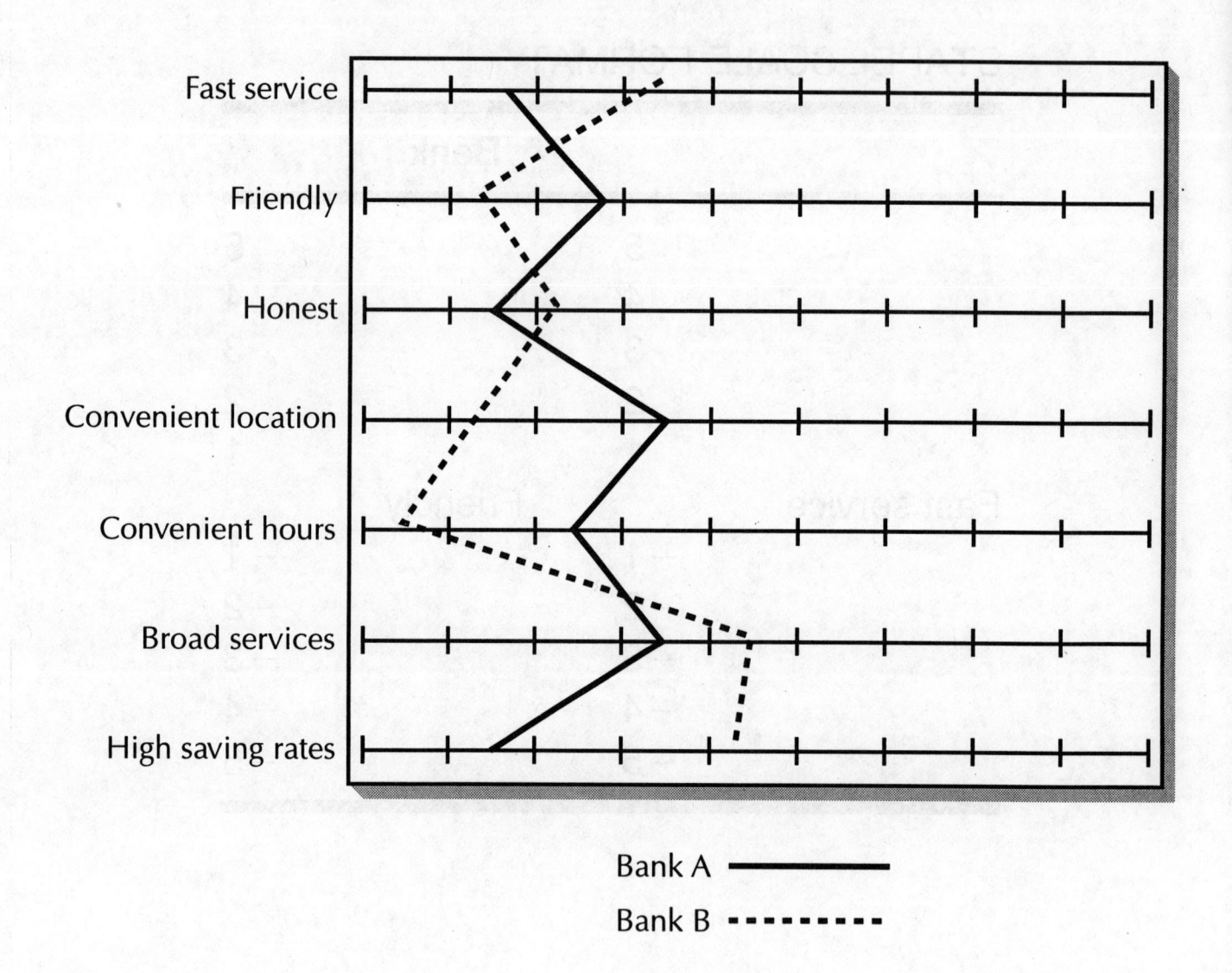

Bank A ———
Bank B - - - - -

Copyright © 1996 by the McGraw-Hill Companies, Inc. All Rights Reserved.

Figure 9-2
Some possible results of a time-series experiment.

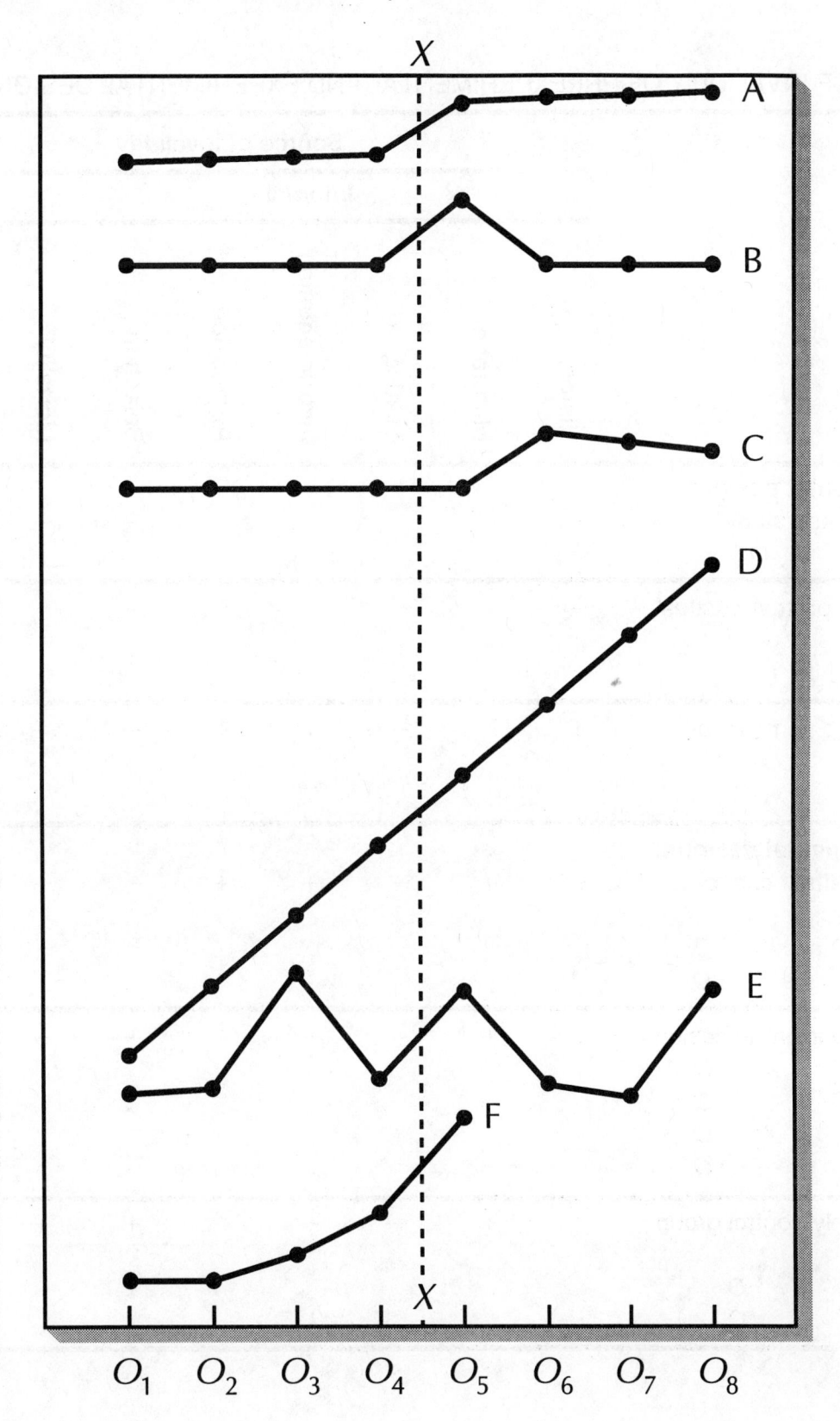

Table 9-2

SOURCES OF INVALIDITY OF PREEXPERIMENTAL AND EXPERIMENTAL DESIGNS

	\multicolumn{8}{c	}{Source of invalidity}
	\multicolumn{7}{c	}{Internal}	External
Design	History	Maturation	Testing	Instrumentation	Regression	Selection	Mortality	Interaction of testing and X
Preexperimental designs:								
One-shot case study X O	–	–				–	–	
One-group pretest-posttest design O X O	–	–	–	–	?			–

Static-group comparison
    X O
    O
	+	?	+	+	+	–	–	

True experimental designs:								

Pretest-posttest control group design
  R O X O
  R O   O
	+	+	+	+	+	+	+	–

Solomon four-group design
  R O X O
  R O   O
  R   X O
  R   O
	+	+	+	+	+	+	+	+

Posttest-only control group design
    R X O
    R   O
	+	+	+	+	+	+	+	+

Copyright © 1996 by the McGraw-Hill Companies, Inc. All Rights Reserved.

Table 9-3

SOURCES OF INVALIDITY OF QUASI-EXPERIMENTAL DESIGNS

Design	\multicolumn{7}{c	}{Source of invalidity}	
	\multicolumn{7}{c	}{Internal}	External
	History	Maturation	Testing	Instrument decay	Regression	Selection	Mortality	Interaction of testing and X
Times series O O O X O O O	−	+	+	?	+	+	+	−
Multiple time series O O O X O O O O O O O O O	+	+	+	+	+	+	+	−
Equivalent time sample O X_1O X_0O X_1O	+	+	+	+	+	+	+	−
Nonequivalent control group O X O O O	+	+	+	+	−?	+	+	−

Copyright © 1996 by the McGraw-Hill Companies, Inc. All Rights Reserved.

Table 9-4

LS DESIGN FOR SALES TRAINING EXPERIMENT

	Sales potential per year (in thousands)		
Ages of salespersons	$200–$999	$1000–$1999	$2000–$2999
18–25	A	B	C
26–30	B	C	A
Over 30	C	A	B

A = no sales training, B = head office lectures, for sales training, C = on-the-job sales training.

Table 9-5

3 × 2 FACTORIAL DESIGN FOR SALES TRAINING AND COMPENSATION EXPERIMENT

			B	
			B_1 Straight salary	B_2 Straight commission
A	A_1	No sales training	A_1B_1	A_1B_2
	A_2	Head office lectures	A_2B_1	A_2B_1
	A_3	On-the-job training	A_3B_1	A_3B_2

Copyright © 1996 by the McGraw-Hill Companies, Inc. All Rights Reserved.

Figure 9-7
Navy experimental design.

	Recruiters −20%	Recruiters same	Recruiters +20%
ADV +100%		Davenport–Rock Island	
ADV +50%	Tulsa Roanoke Syracuse	Washington Indianapolis Richmond	Boston St. Louis Charleston–Huntington
ADV same	Baltimore Cheyenne, WY Laurel, MS	Providence Terre Haute Springfield, IL*	Harrisburg South Bend Grand Junction, CO
ADV −50%	Wilkes Barre Phoenix Odessa–Midland	Chicago Pittsburgh Columbus, OH	Dallas Louisville Lansing
ADV −100%		Johnstown–Altoona	

* Additional control markets:

Nashville	Des Moines	Waco
Los Angeles	Youngstown	Sioux City
Charlotte	West Palm Beach	McAllen
Greenville	Chattanooga	Anniston
Knoxville	Huntsville	

Copyright © 1996 by the McGraw-Hill Companies, Inc. All Rights Reserved.

Figure 10-5
Sample focus group session.

In this focus group session, 10 people are being asked questions about what they think about a new cereal, Kellogg's Raisin Squares. The participants are white, male, fortyish, and in the lower-middle to upper-middle income classes. Here are sample segments of that session.

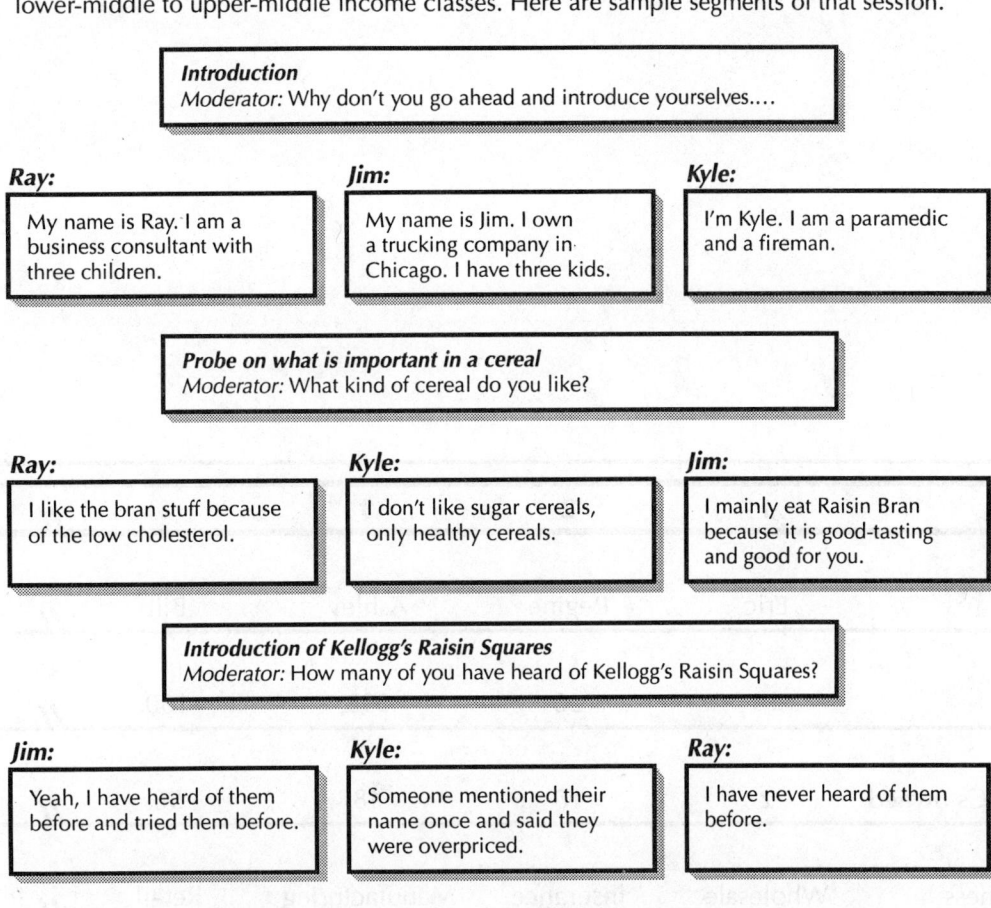

Introduction
Moderator: Why don't you go ahead and introduce yourselves....

Ray:
My name is Ray. I am a business consultant with three children.

Jim:
My name is Jim. I own a trucking company in Chicago. I have three kids.

Kyle:
I'm Kyle. I am a paramedic and a fireman.

Probe on what is important in a cereal
Moderator: What kind of cereal do you like?

Ray:
I like the bran stuff because of the low cholesterol.

Kyle:
I don't like sugar cereals, only healthy cereals.

Jim:
I mainly eat Raisin Bran because it is good-tasting and good for you.

Introduction of Kellogg's Raisin Squares
Moderator: How many of you have heard of Kellogg's Raisin Squares?

Jim:
Yeah, I have heard of them before and tried them before.

Kyle:
Someone mentioned their name once and said they were overpriced.

Ray:
I have never heard of them before.

Moderator gives each participant a sample of Kellogg's Raisin Squares to taste-test.

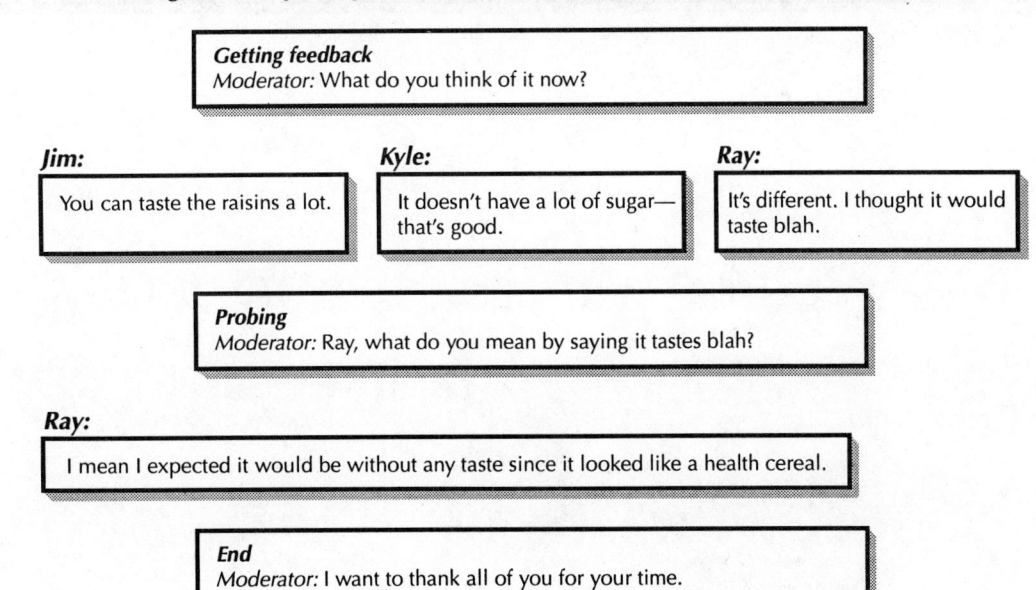

Getting feedback
Moderator: What do you think of it now?

Jim:
You can taste the raisins a lot.

Kyle:
It doesn't have a lot of sugar—that's good.

Ray:
It's different. I thought it would taste blah.

Probing
Moderator: Ray, what do you mean by saying it tastes blah?

Ray:
I mean I expected it would be without any taste since it looked like a health cereal.

End
Moderator: I want to thank all of you for your time.

Copyright © 1996 by the McGraw-Hill Companies, Inc. All Rights Reserved.

Figure 10-10
Demographic profile.

Number	1	2	3	4	//	48
Respondent	Eric	Regine	Ashley	Bill	//	Samir
Firm size	14	20	993	180	//	330
Number of PCs owned	2	10	48	56	//	125
Type of business	Wholesale	Insurance	Manufacturing	Retail	//	Insurance

Copyright © 1996 by the McGraw-Hill Companies, Inc. All Rights Reserved.

Figure 10-12
Cross-tabulation analysis.

Compatibility, frequency (%)

	High	Medium	Low	Total
Large	8 (50)	6 (38)	2 (12)	16 (100)
Medium	6 (38)	6 (38)	4 (24)	16 (100)
Small	3 (19)	5 (32)	8 (50)	16 (100)
Total	17	17	14	48

Hypothesis: Large businesses are more concerned with compatibility than are small and medium businesses

Service, frequency (%)

	High	Medium	Low	Total
Large	5 (32)	4 (25)	7 (44)	16 (100)
Medium	4 (25)	8 (50)	4 (25)	16 (100)
Small	9 (56)	4 (25)	3 (19)	16 (100)
Total	18	16	14	48

Hypothesis: Small businesses are more concerned with service and support than are large and medium businesses

Copyright © 1996 by the McGraw-Hill Companies, Inc. All Rights Reserved.

Table 11-1

LIFE-STYLE CHARACTERISTICS

Activities	Interests	Opinions
Work	Family	Themselves
Hobbies	Home	Social issues
Social events	Job	Politics
Vacations	Community	Business
Entertainment	Recreation	Economics
Club membership	Fashion	Education
Community	Food	Products
Shopping	Media	Future
Sports	Achievements	Culture

Copyright © 1996 by the McGraw-Hill Companies, Inc. All Rights Reserved.

Table 11-4

SUMMARY OF COMMUNICATION APPROACHES

Criteria	Personal interview	Phone interview	Mail	Computer disk
Versatility	High[1]	Fair[1]	Very little	Fair
Cost	$50–100/interview	$25–40/interview	$20–30/interview	$10–25/interview
Time	Months	Days	Weeks to months	Weeks to months
Sample control	Highest	High	High	Fair
Quantity of data	Highest	High	High	N/A (no history)
Quality of data	High	High	Fair	High
Response rate[2]	Fair	Fair	Fair	Fair

[1]Varies greatly depending on whether computer-assisted software packages are being used; with the use of these software tools, the versatility increases tremendously.
[2]Varies greatly based on length of interview, callbacks (or number of mailings), and selection of respondents; the typical business interview is about 20 minutes, with two callbacks and a random selection of respondents.

Copyright © 1996 by the McGraw-Hill Companies, Inc. All Rights Reserved.

Figure 12-2
Steps in questionnaire design.

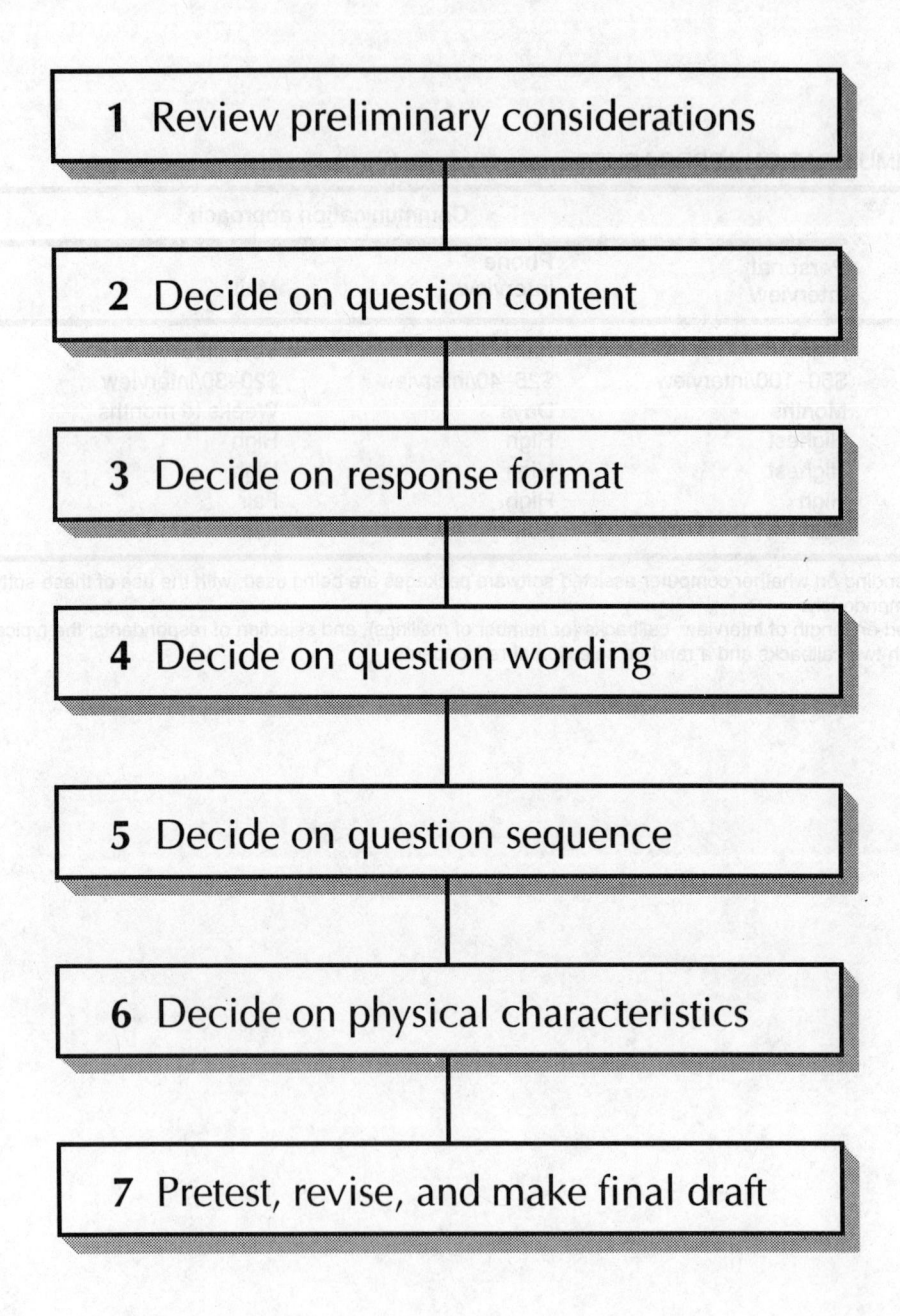

1. Review preliminary considerations
2. Decide on question content
3. Decide on response format
4. Decide on question wording
5. Decide on question sequence
6. Decide on physical characteristics
7. Pretest, revise, and make final draft

Figure 12-3
Information needs—data linkage.

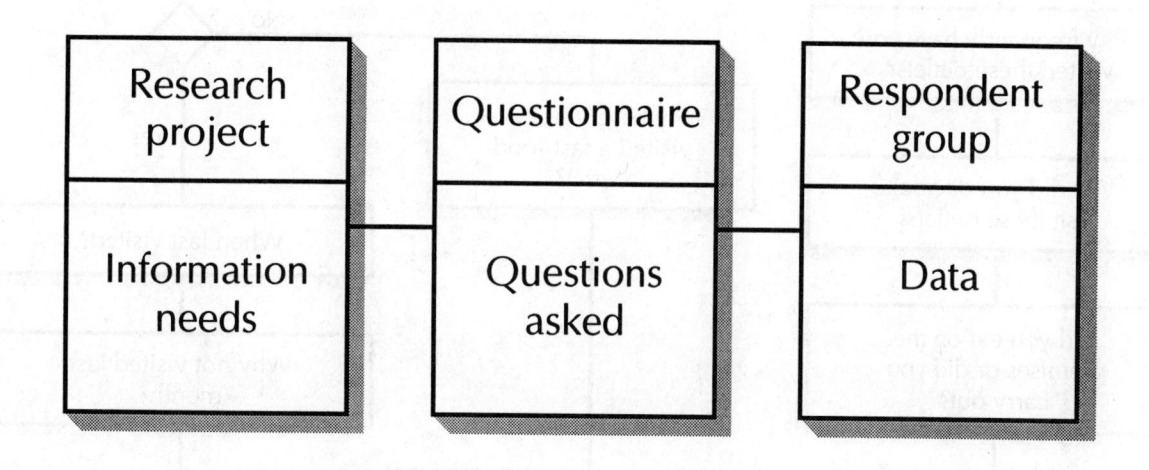

Research project	Questionnaire	Respondent group
Information needs	Questions asked	Data

Copyright © 1996 by the McGraw-Hill Companies, Inc. All Rights Reserved.

Figure 12-4
Example of a flowchart plan for a draft questionnaire.

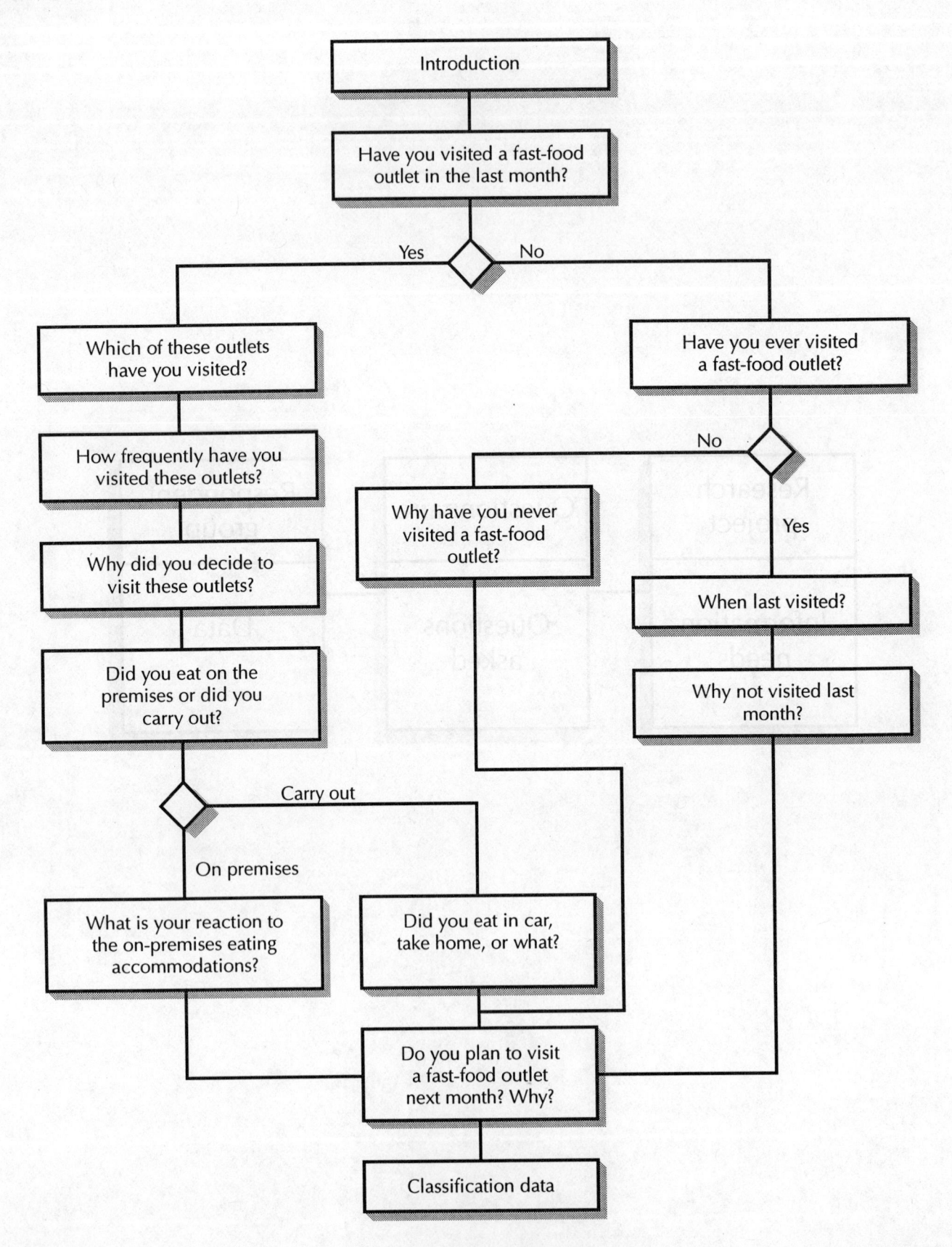

```
                    ┌──────────────┐
                    │ Introduction │
                    └──────┬───────┘
                           │
              ┌────────────┴────────────┐
              │ Have you visited a      │
              │ fast-food outlet in     │
              │ the last month?         │
              └────────────┬────────────┘
                           ◇
                   Yes ───┘ └─── No
```

- Which of these outlets have you visited?
- How frequently have you visited these outlets?
- Why did you decide to visit these outlets?
- Did you eat on the premises or did you carry out?
  - Carry out → Did you eat in car, take home, or what?
  - On premises → What is your reaction to the on-premises eating accommodations?

- Have you ever visited a fast-food outlet?
  - No → Why have you never visited a fast-food outlet?
  - Yes → When last visited? → Why not visited last month?

- Do you plan to visit a fast-food outlet next month? Why?
- Classification data

Copyright © 1996 by the McGraw-Hill Companies, Inc. All Rights Reserved.

Figure 13-2
Steps in selecting a sample.

Step 1 — Define the population:
1. Elements
2. Units
3. Extent
4. Time

Step 2 — Identify the sampling frame

Step 3 — Determine sample size

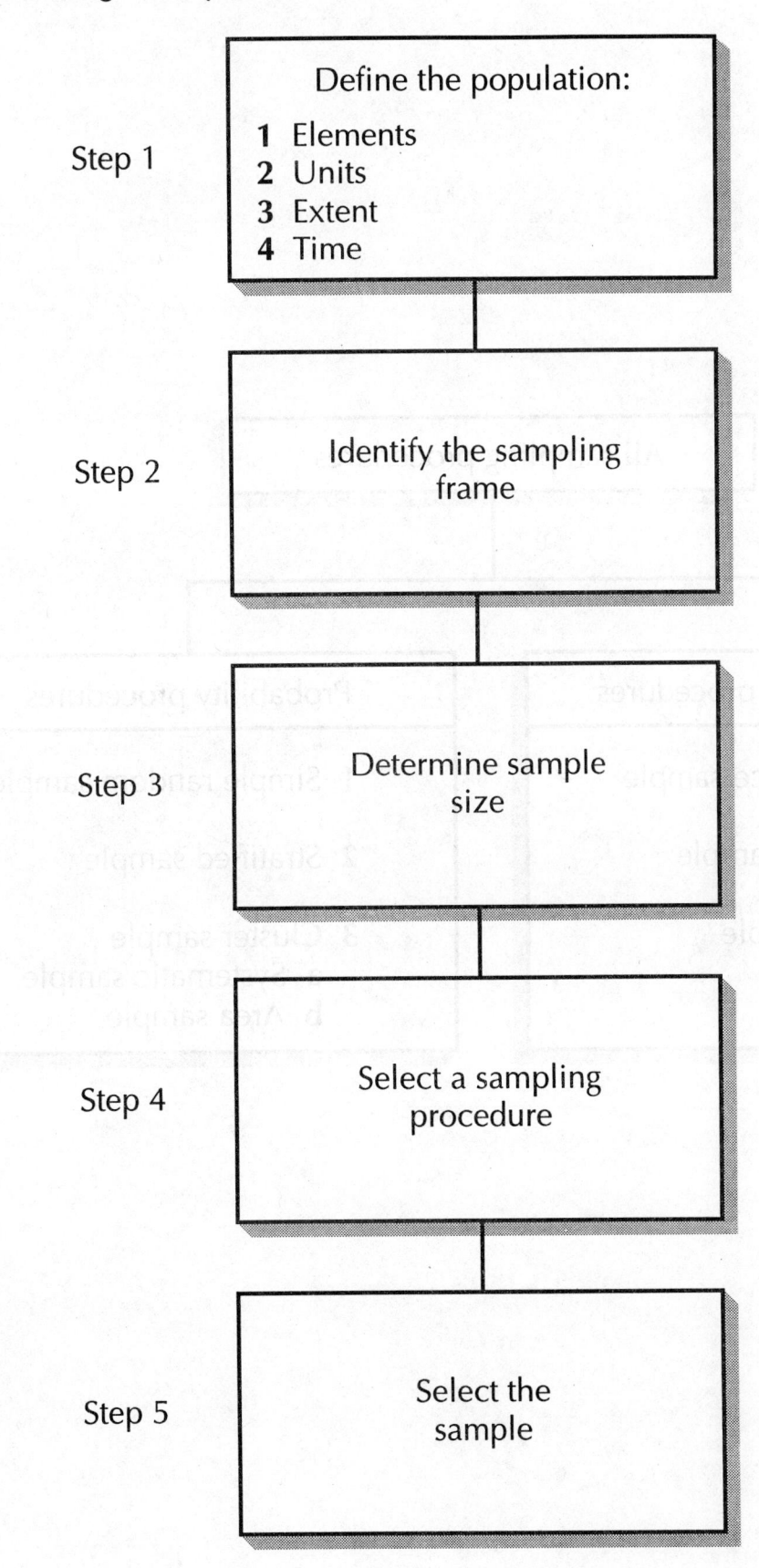

Step 4 — Select a sampling procedure

Step 5 — Select the sample

Copyright © 1996 by the McGraw-Hill Companies, Inc. All Rights Reserved.

Figure 13-3
Sampling procedures.

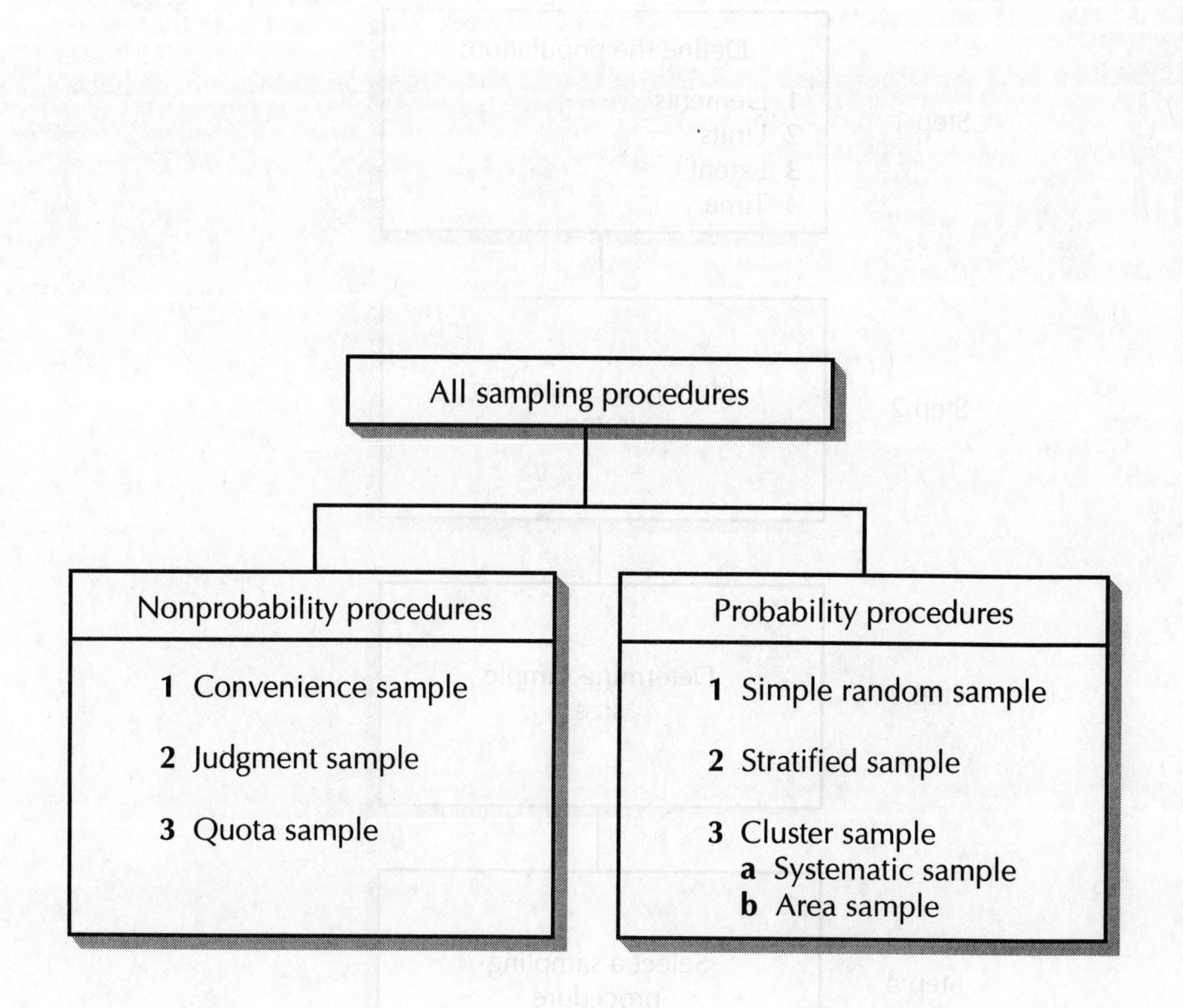

All sampling procedures

Nonprobability procedures
1. Convenience sample
2. Judgment sample
3. Quota sample

Probability procedures
1. Simple random sample
2. Stratified sample
3. Cluster sample
   a. Systematic sample
   b. Area sample

Copyright © 1996 by the McGraw-Hill Companies, Inc. All Rights Reserved.

Figure 14-4

Nomograph to determine sample size in simple random sampling for estimation problems of the mean for an infinite population. (*Source:* Audits and Surveys, Inc. Used with permission.)

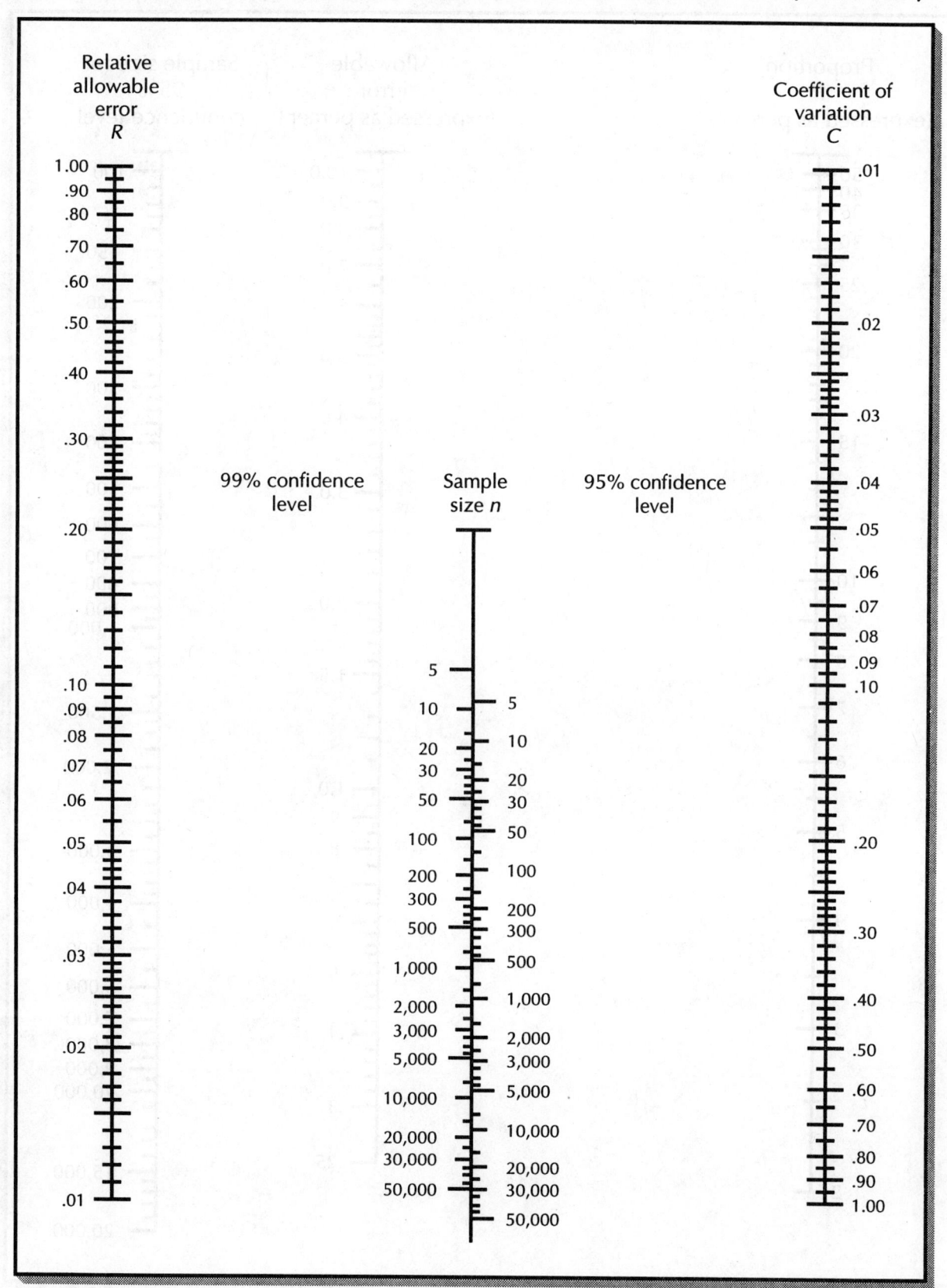

Figure 14-5

Nomograph to determine sample size in simple random sampling for estimation problems of the mean for an infinite population. (*Source:* Audits and Surveys, Inc. Used with permission.)

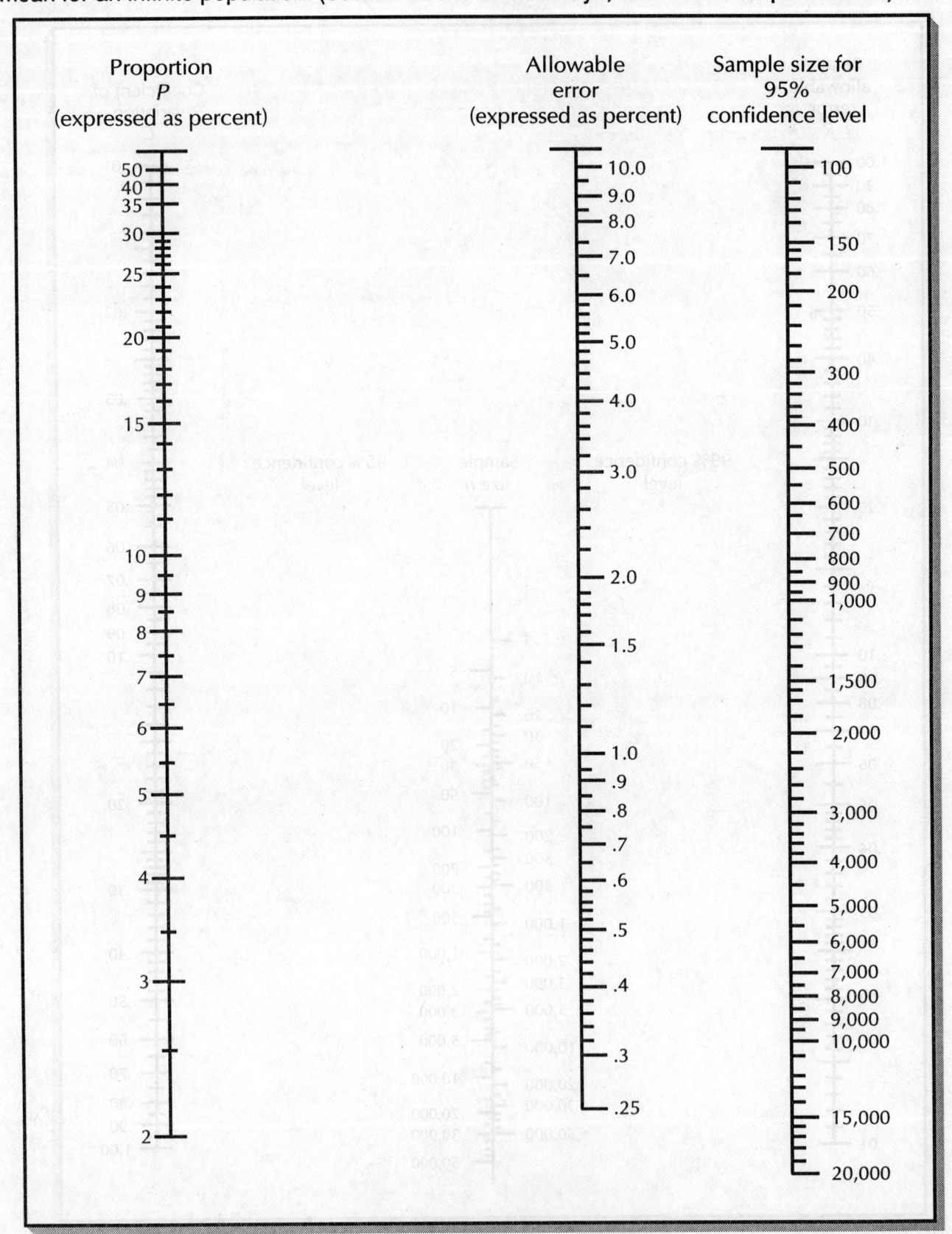

Copyright © 1996 by the McGraw-Hill Companies, Inc. All Rights Reserved.

Figure A14-1

Distribution of sample means for samples of various sizes and different population distributions. (*Source:* Ernest Kurnow, Gerald J. Glasser, and Frederick R. Ottman, *Statistics for Business Decisions*, Homewood, IL: Irwin, 1959, pp. 182–183. Reproduced with permission.)

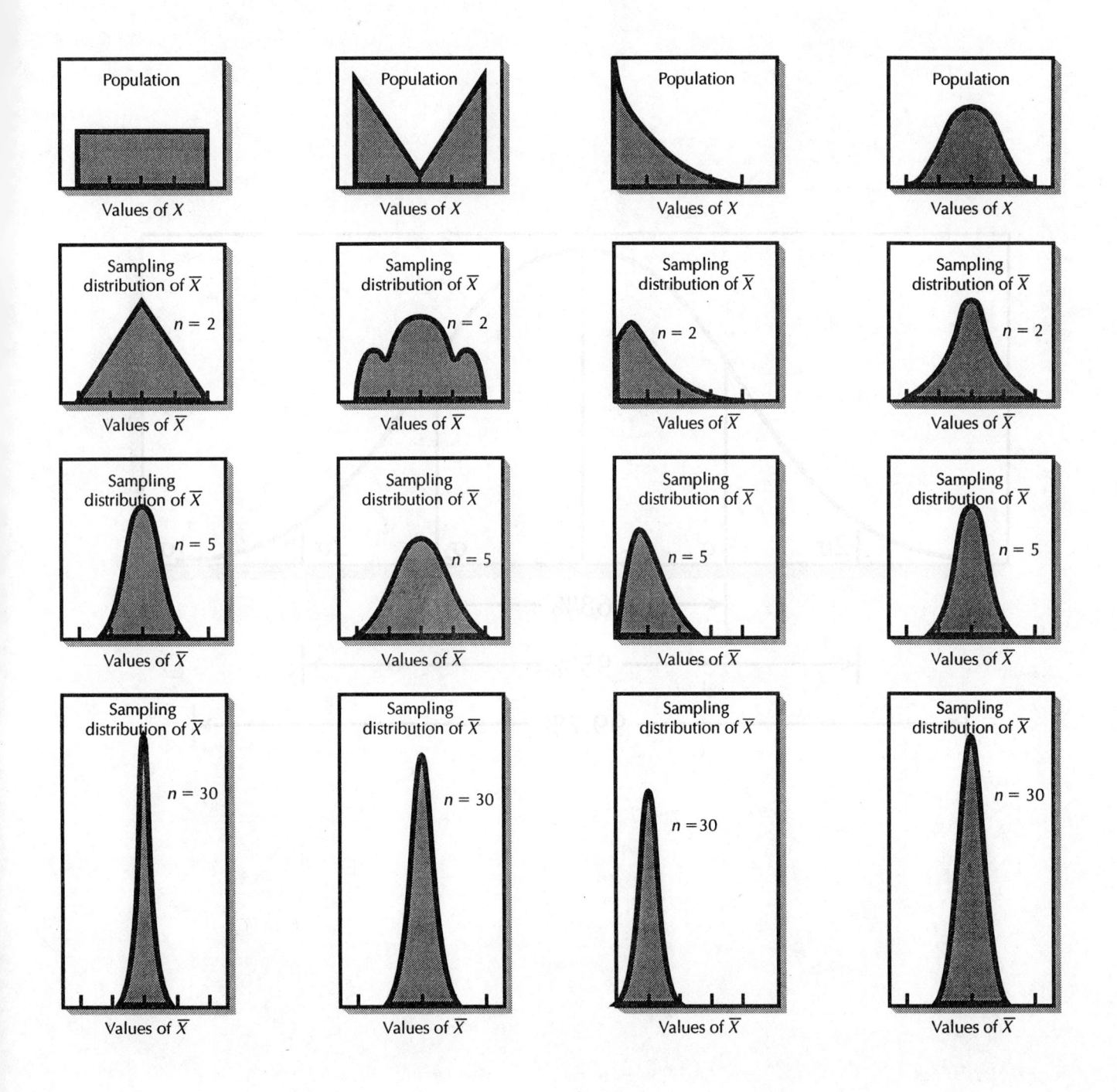

Copyright © 1996 by the McGraw-Hill Companies, Inc. All Rights Reserved.

Figure A14-2
Area under the normal curve.

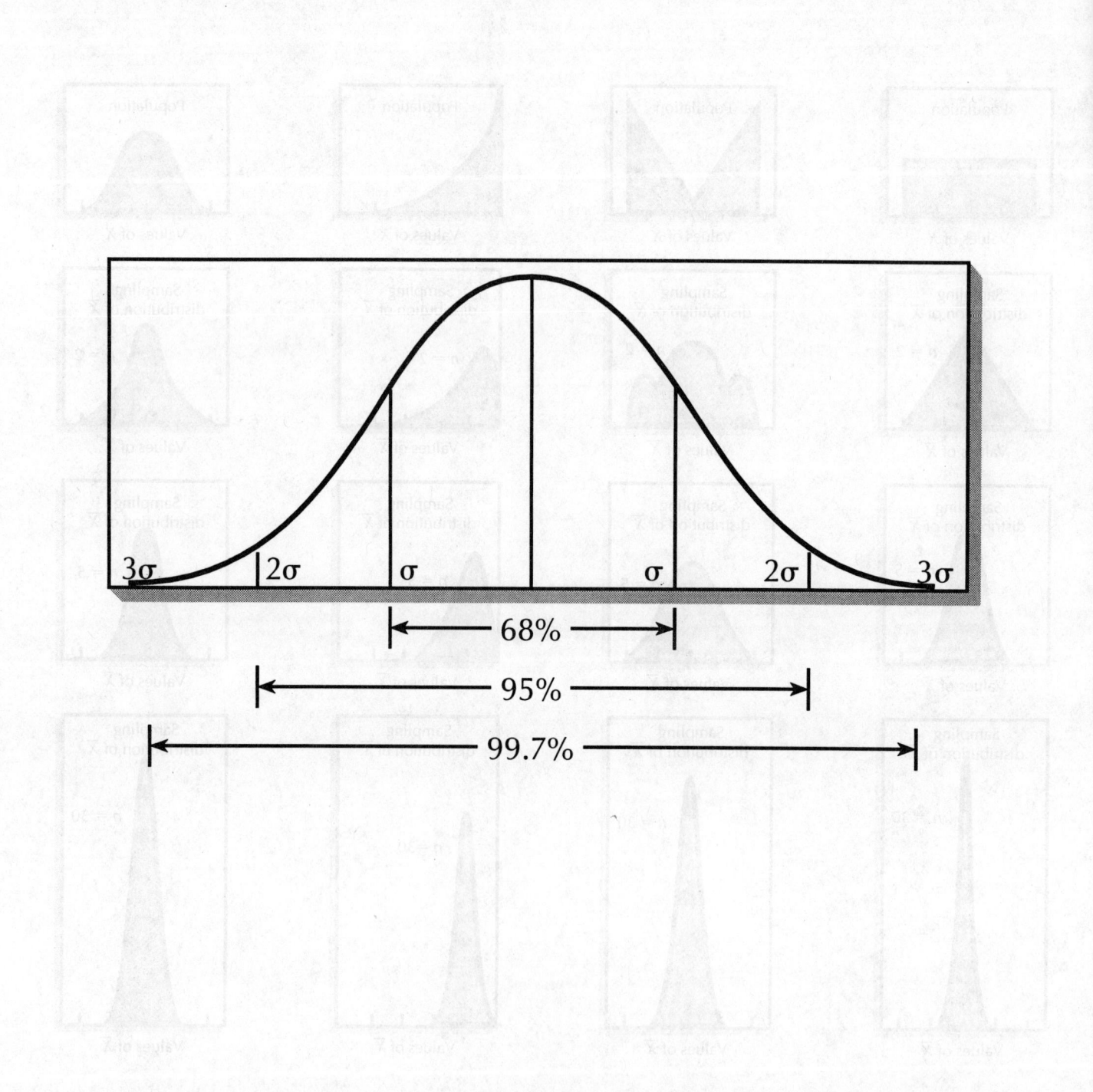

Figure 15-3
Disproportionate stratified sampling in retail store audits. (*Source:* Nielson Retail Index Services A. C. Nielson Company, Northbrook, IL, 1983. Reprinted with permission.)

DEMONSTRATION OF DISPROPORTIONATE SAMPLING CONCEPT
DRUG STORES

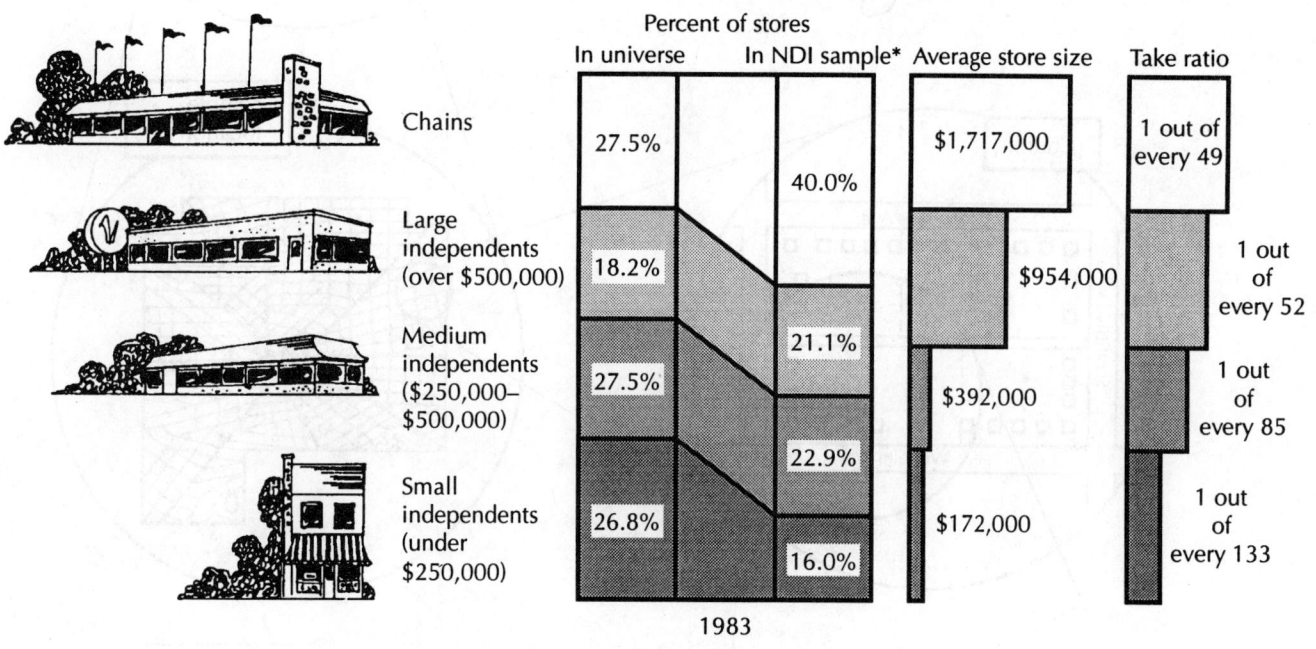

Store Type	In universe	In NDI sample*	Average store size	Take ratio
Chains	27.5%	40.0%	$1,717,000	1 out of every 49
Large independents (over $500,000)	18.2%	21.1%	$954,000	1 out of every 52
Medium independents ($250,000–$500,000)	27.5%	22.9%	$392,000	1 out of every 85
Small independents (under $250,000)	26.8%	16.0%	$172,000	1 out of every 133

1983

*NDI = Nielsen Distribution Index

Copyright © 1996 by the McGraw-Hill Companies, Inc. All Rights Reserved.

Figure 15-6
An illustration of area sampling. [*Source:* Adapted from *Interviewer's Manual*, rev. ed. (Ann Arbor: Survey Research Center, Institute for Social Research, University of Michigan, 1976), p. 36.]

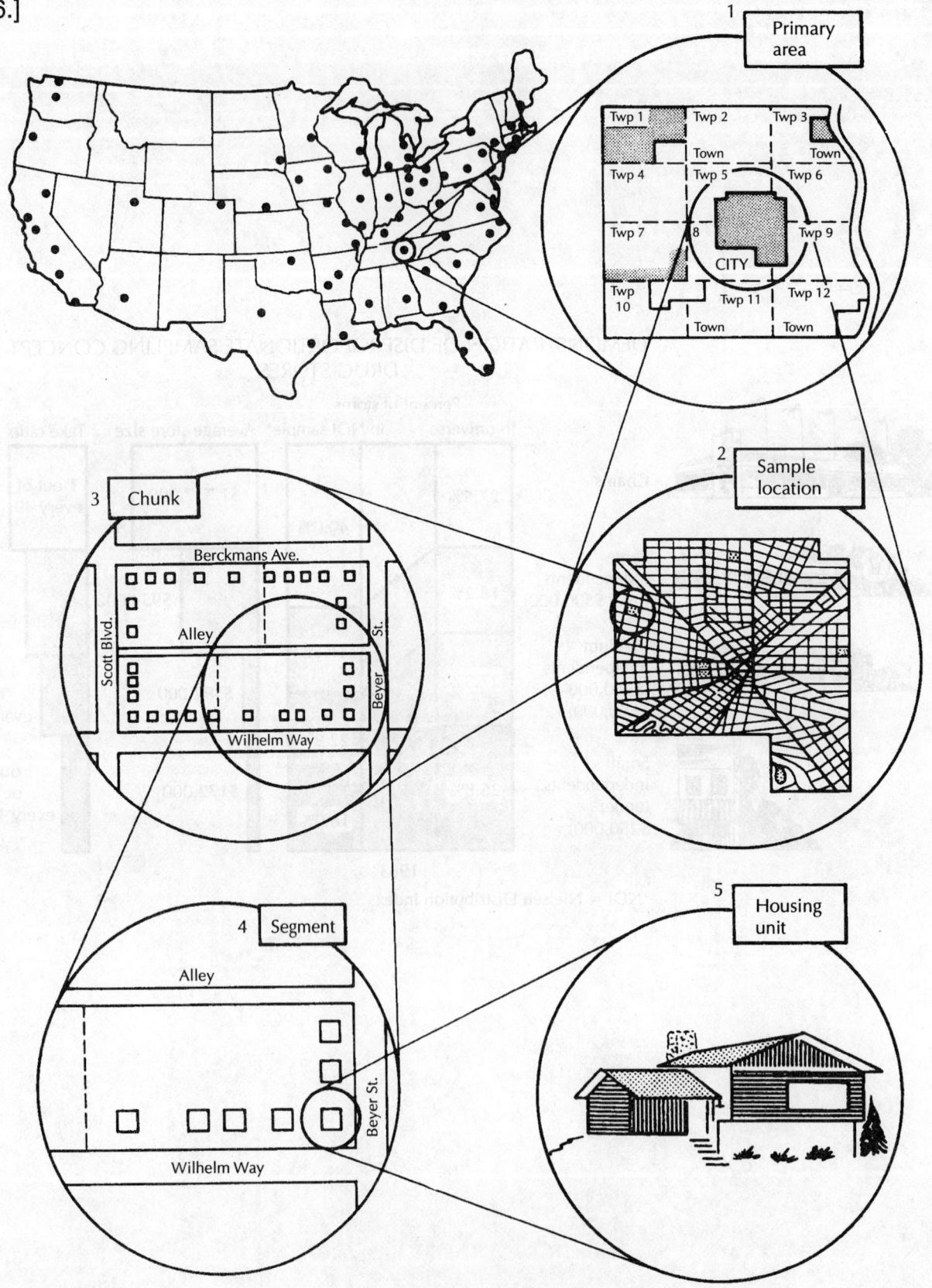

Table 15-3

MANAGERIAL SUMMARY OF SAMPLING

| Dimensions | Census | Nonprobability samples |||| Probability samples ||||
		Convenience	Judgment	Quota	Simple random	Stratified	Systematic	Area
1 Generation of sampling error	No	No	No	No	Yes	Yes	Yes	Yes
2 Statistical efficiency		—No measurement—			The level compared to	High when stratification variables work	Somewhat low	Low
3 Need for population list	Yes	No	No	No	Yes	Yes	Not necessary in all applications	Only for selected clusters
4 Cost	Very high	Very low	Low	Moderate	High	High	Moderate	Moderate to high
5 Frequency of use in practice	Low	53%	49%	86%	90%	85%	49%	52%

Copyright © 1996 by the McGraw-Hill Companies, Inc. All Rights Reserved.

Table 16-1

STUDY PERFORMANCE MEASURES: EXPECTED AND ACTUAL

Performance measure	Expected	Actual
1 Total eligible respondents	_____	_____
1.1 Interviews	_____	_____
1.2 Refusals	_____	_____
1.3 Noncontacts (assumed eligible)	_____	_____
1.4 Other (specify) _____		
2 Total ineligible respondents	_____	_____
2.1 Moved	_____	_____
2.2 Other (specify) _____	_____	_____
3 Total sample	_____	_____
Response rate (1.1 ÷ 1)	_____	_____
Refusal rate (1.2) ÷ (1.1 1.2)	_____	_____
Contact rate [(1 − 1.3) ÷ 1]	_____ %	_____ %
Eligibility rate (1 ÷ 3)	_____ %	

Copyright © 1996 by the McGraw-Hill Companies, Inc. All Rights Reserved.

Figure 17-2
ASCII data matrix and commercial spreadsheet representations of marketing research data.

Part A ASCII Format

```
                                    Column numbers
                                1 2 3 4 . . . . . . . . . . 90
                                ⌣
         Variables (1 to m)    1   2                        m
                               ─────────────────────────────
                               2 6 2 5 . . . . . . . . . . 4
                               3 7 1 0 . . . . . . . . . . 1
                               1 5 2 1 . . . . . . . . . . 3
           Cases       Row     1 6 0 1 . . . . . . . . . . 2
          (1 to n)   numbers   4 7 0 6 . . . . . . . . . . 1
                               3 5 0 7 . . . . . . . . . . 5
                               2 4 2 9 . . . . . . . . . . 1
                               . . . . . . . . . . . . . .
                               1 7 6 4 . . . . . . . . . . 2
```

Part B Commercial Spreadsheet Format

```
                                    Variables (1 to m)
                                    Column numbers
                                   1   2   .   .   .   m
                                   ─────────────────────
                              1  │ 2   625              4
                              2  │ 3   710              1
                              3  │ 1   521              3
                              4  │ 1   601              2
           Cases      Row     5  │ 4   706              1
          (1 to n)  numbers   6  │ 3   507              5
                              7  │ 2   429              1
                              .
                              .
                              .
                              n  │ 1   764              2
```

Variable 1 = year in college
               (1 = 1st year, 2 = 2nd year, 3 = 3rd year, 4 = 4th year)
Variable 2 = SAT score (out of 800)
Variable m = region of the country in which parents live
               (1 = Northeast, 2 = Southeast, 3 = Southwest,
               (4 = Northwest, 5 = Midwest)

Copyright © 1996 by the McGraw-Hill Companies, Inc. All Rights Reserved.

Figure 17-3
Classic data processing flow.

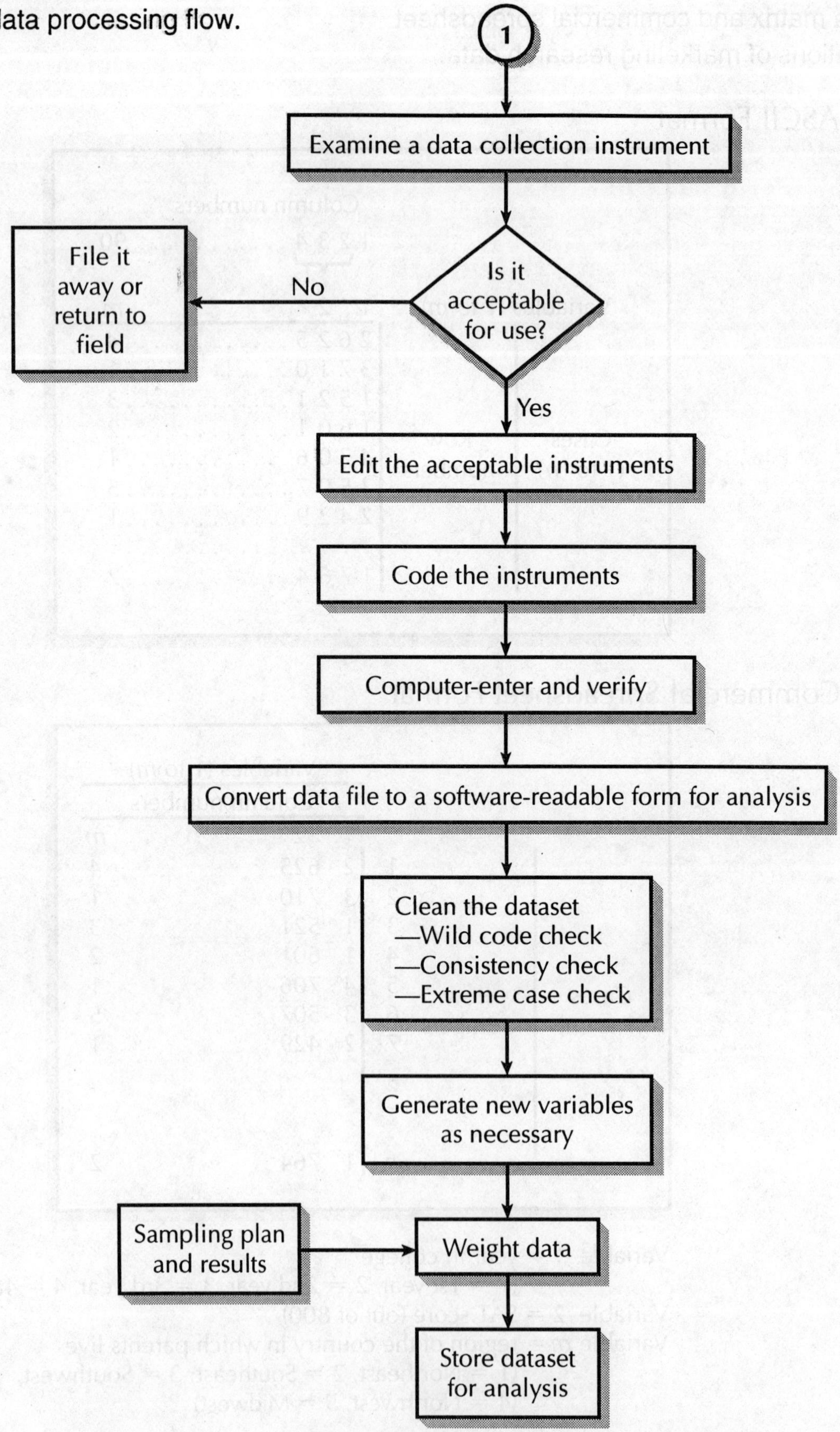

```
                                    ( 1 )
                                      │
                                      ▼
                      ┌───────────────────────────────┐
                      │ Examine a data collection instrument │
                      └───────────────────────────────┘
                                      │
                                      ▼
   ┌──────────┐                    ◇ Is it ◇
   │ File it  │       No         ◇ acceptable ◇
   │ away or  │◄─────────────── ◇   for use?  ◇
   │ return to│                   ◇          ◇
   │ field    │                      │
   └──────────┘                      │ Yes
                                      ▼
                      ┌───────────────────────────────┐
                      │   Edit the acceptable instruments   │
                      └───────────────────────────────┘
                                      │
                                      ▼
                      ┌───────────────────────────────┐
                      │       Code the instruments         │
                      └───────────────────────────────┘
                                      │
                                      ▼
                      ┌───────────────────────────────┐
                      │     Computer-enter and verify      │
                      └───────────────────────────────┘
                                      │
                                      ▼
        ┌────────────────────────────────────────────────────────┐
        │ Convert data file to a software-readable form for analysis │
        └────────────────────────────────────────────────────────┘
                                      │
                                      ▼
                         ┌──────────────────────┐
                         │   Clean the dataset   │
                         │   —Wild code check    │
                         │   —Consistency check  │
                         │   —Extreme case check │
                         └──────────────────────┘
                                      │
                                      ▼
                         ┌──────────────────────┐
                         │  Generate new variables │
                         │      as necessary       │
                         └──────────────────────┘
                                      │
   ┌──────────────┐                   ▼
   │ Sampling plan │        ┌──────────────────┐
   │  and results  │───────►│    Weight data    │
   └──────────────┘        └──────────────────┘
                                      │
                                      ▼
                             ┌──────────────────┐
                             │  Store dataset    │
                             │   for analysis    │
                             └──────────────────┘
```

Copyright © 1996 by the McGraw-Hill Companies, Inc. All Rights Reserved.

Table 17-1

AN ILLUSTRATIVE CODEBOOK

Question number	Variable number	ASCII file column	Format*	Variable name	Category definitions
35	46	52	I1	Sex	1 = female 2 = male 9 = missing data
36 . . .	47 . . .	53–54 . . .	I2 . . .	Age . . .	Two-digit number 00–98 99 = missing data
74	121	91–93	F3.2	GPA	Three-digit number 000–400 with decimal place two places to left in field given

*The use of "I" refers to an integer value in card column(s). The number after the I indicates the number of digits in the variable. For example, I1 indicates a one-digit integer variable and I6 indicates a six-digit integer variable.

The use of "F" indicates that other variables in the card column or columns can take on real values. That is, the variable with an F can have a decimal place. The position of the decimal is given by the number after the decimal place, and the number of digits is given by the number before the decimal. For example, F3.2 indicates a real variable containing three digits with the decimal place position before the second digit. That is, the decimal is two places from the end of the field.

Copyright © 1996 by the McGraw-Hill Companies, Inc. All Rights Reserved.

Figure 17-4
Creation of a computer file for analysis.

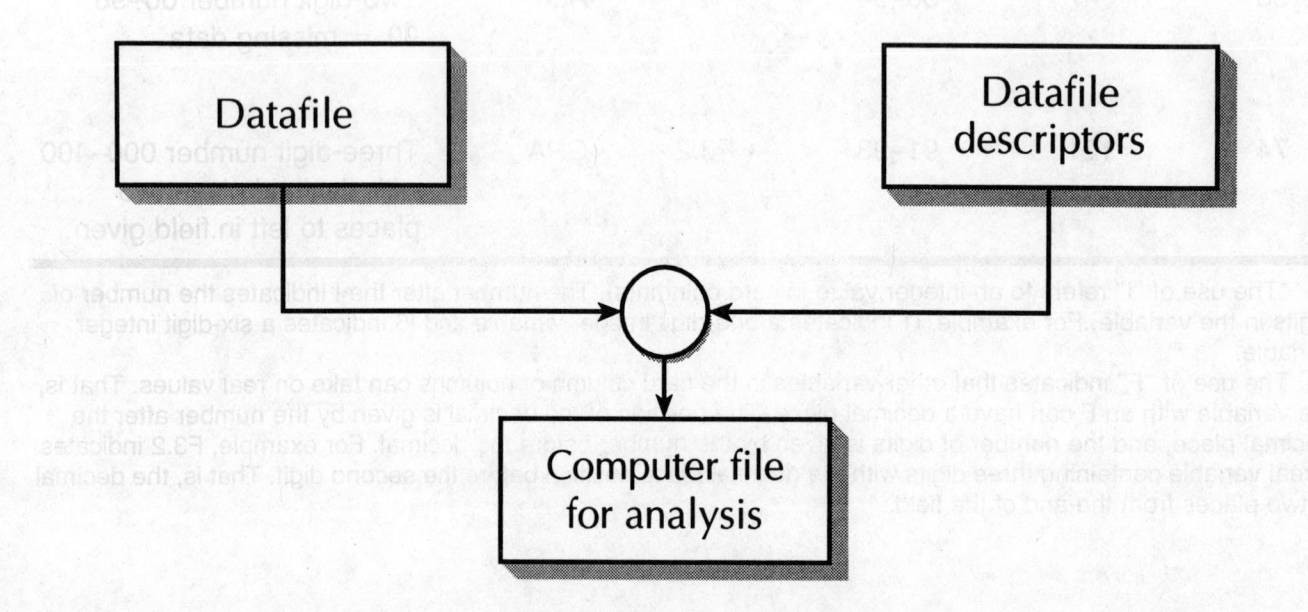

Figure 18-2
Overview of data analysis techniques.

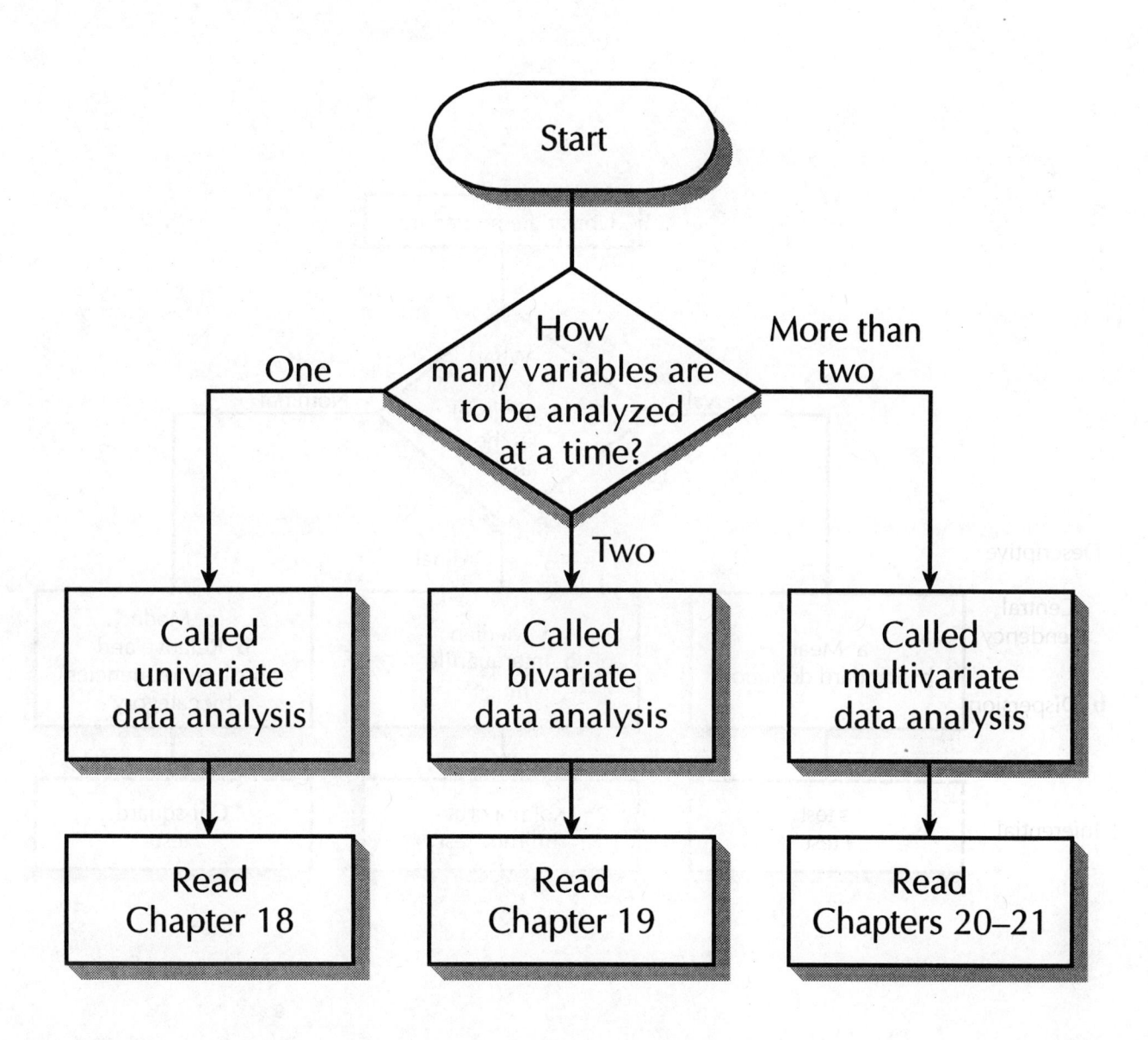

```
                    ┌─────────┐
                    │  Start  │
                    └────┬────┘
                         │
              ╱──────────────────╲
              ╲    How many       ╱
     One   ╱───  variables are  ───╲  More than two
       ╱───    to be analyzed       ───╲
              ╲    at a time?     ╱
              ╱──────────────────╲
                         │ Two
    ┌──────────┐   ┌──────────┐   ┌──────────┐
    │  Called  │   │  Called  │   │  Called  │
    │univariate│   │ bivariate│   │multivariate│
    │data      │   │data      │   │data      │
    │analysis  │   │analysis  │   │analysis  │
    └────┬─────┘   └────┬─────┘   └────┬─────┘
         │              │              │
    ┌────┴─────┐   ┌────┴─────┐   ┌────┴─────┐
    │  Read    │   │  Read    │   │  Read    │
    │Chapter 18│   │Chapter 19│   │Chapters  │
    │          │   │          │   │  20–21   │
    └──────────┘   └──────────┘   └──────────┘
```

Copyright © 1996 by the McGraw-Hill Companies, Inc. All Rights Reserved.

Figure 18-3
Overview of univariate data analysis procedures.

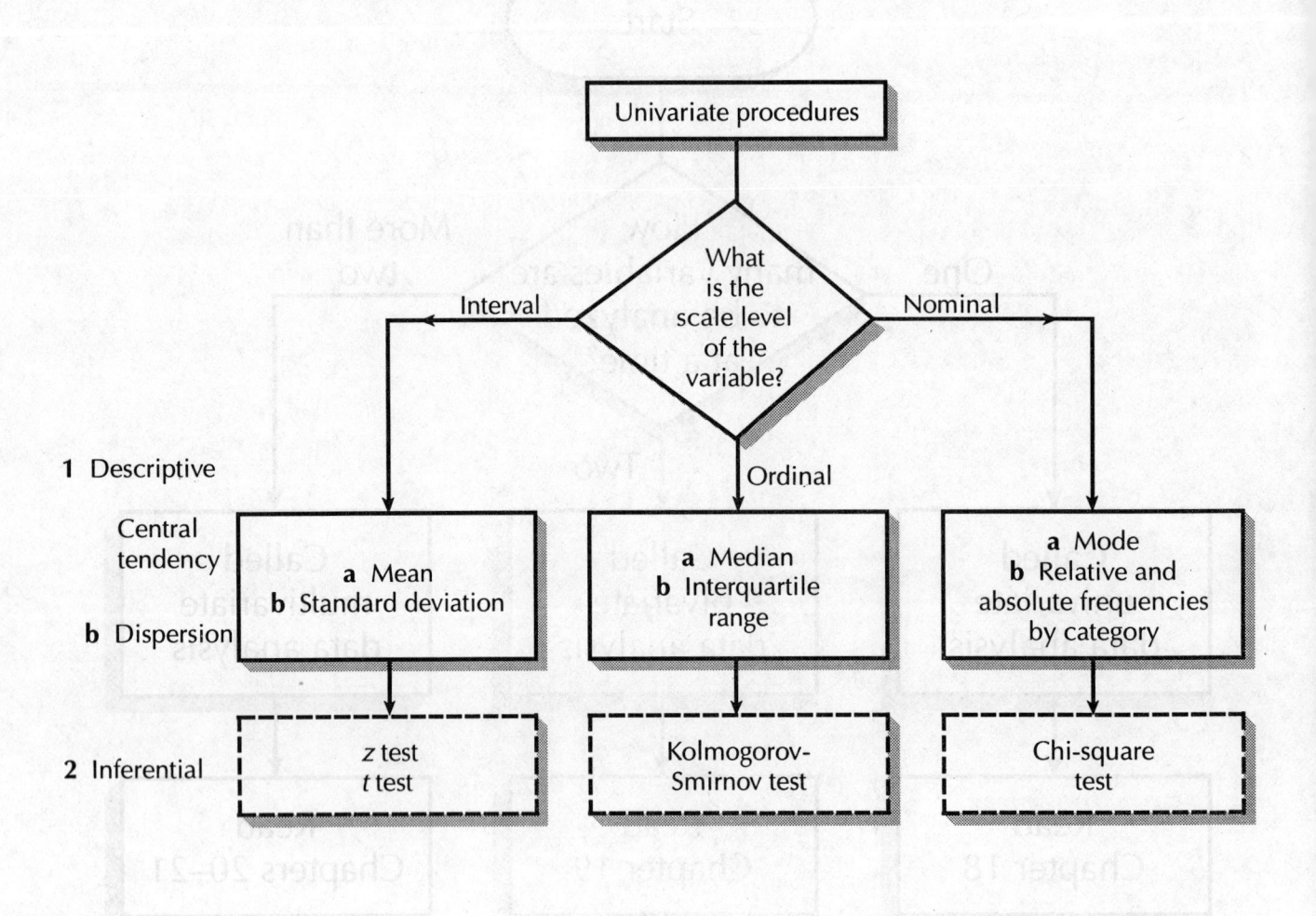

```
                        ┌──────────────────────┐
                        │ Univariate procedures│
                        └──────────┬───────────┘
                                   │
                              ╱─────────╲
                             ╱  What is  ╲
                   Interval ╱ the scale   ╲ Nominal
             ┌─────────────╱  level of the ╲──────────────┐
             │             ╲   variable?   ╱              │
             │              ╲─────────────╱               │
             │                     │ Ordinal              │
             │                     │                      │
```

1 Descriptive

Central tendency

a Mean   a Median   a Mode
b Standard deviation b Interquartile range   b Relative and absolute frequencies by category

b Dispersion

2 Inferential

| z test / t test | Kolmogorov-Smirnov test | Chi-square test |

Copyright © 1996 by the McGraw-Hill Companies, Inc. All Rights Reserved.

Table 18-4

SUMMARY OF HYPOTHESIS TESTING ERRORS

Sample conclusion	True condition	
	H_0 is true	H_0 is false
Do not reject H_0	1 Correct decision 2 Confidence level 3 Probability = $1 - \alpha$	1 Type II error 2 Probability = β
Reject H_0	1 Type I error 2 Significance level 3 Probability = α	1 Correct decision 2 Power of the test 3 Probability = $1 - \beta$

Table 18-5

CALCULATION OF CHI SQUARE FOR OCCUPATIONAL CATEGORIES

Occupational category	O_i	E_i	$O_i - E_i$	$(O_i - E_i)^2$	$(O_i - E_i)^2/E_i$
Labor	15	25	−10	100	4
Clerical	20	25	−5	25	1
Managerial	30	25	5	25	1
Student	35	25	10	100	4
Total	100	100			10

$df = k - 1 = 3$; calculated $\chi^2 = 10$; critical χ^2 at 3 df and $\alpha = .1 = 6.25$.

Figure 19-2
Bivariate data analysis procedures.

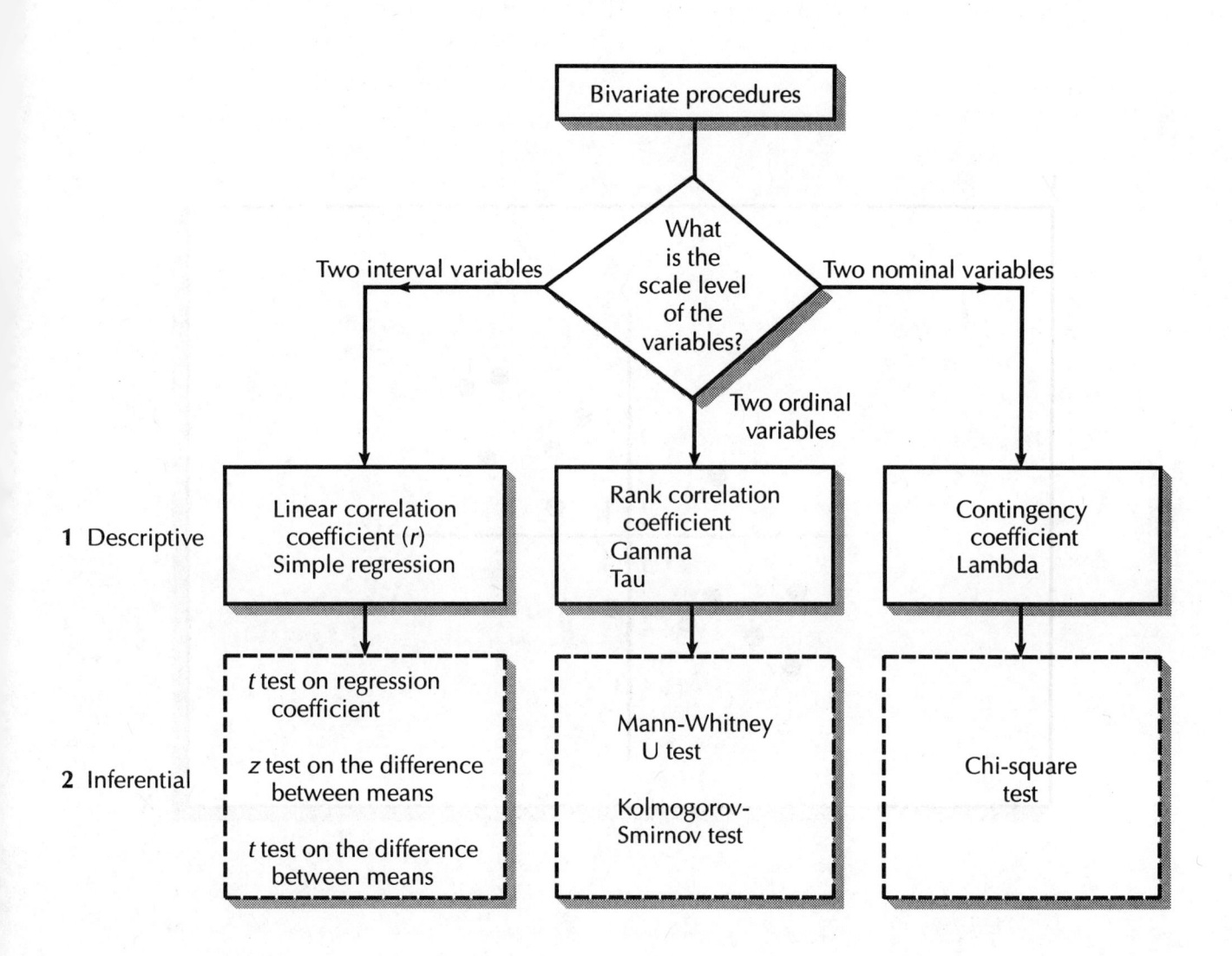

```
                        ┌─────────────────────┐
                        │ Bivariate procedures│
                        └──────────┬──────────┘
                                   │
                              ╱What is the╲
          Two interval      ╱  scale level  ╲    Two nominal
          variables   ◄────╱  of the         ╲────►  variables
                           ╲   variables?    ╱
                            ╲               ╱
                             ╲      │      ╱
                                Two ordinal
                                 variables
```

1 Descriptive	Linear correlation coefficient (r) Simple regression	Rank correlation coefficient Gamma Tau	Contingency coefficient Lambda
2 Inferential	*t* test on regression coefficient; *z* test on the difference between means; *t* test on the difference between means	Mann-Whitney U test; Kolmogorov-Smirnov test	Chi-square test

Copyright © 1996 by the McGraw-Hill Companies, Inc. All Rights Reserved.

Figure 19-4
An example of a scatter diagram and associated quadrants.

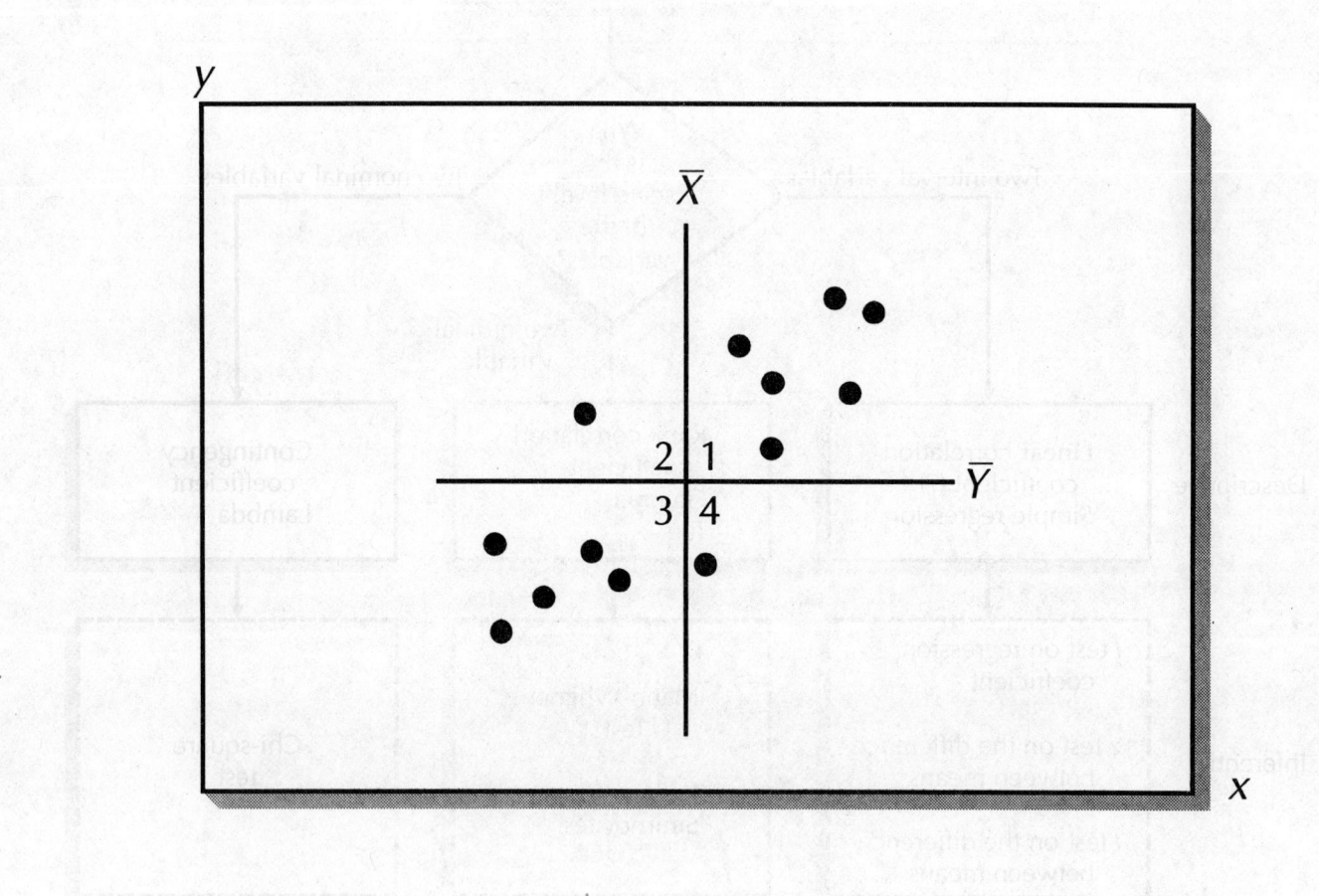

Figure 19-5
Scatter diagram of course grades.

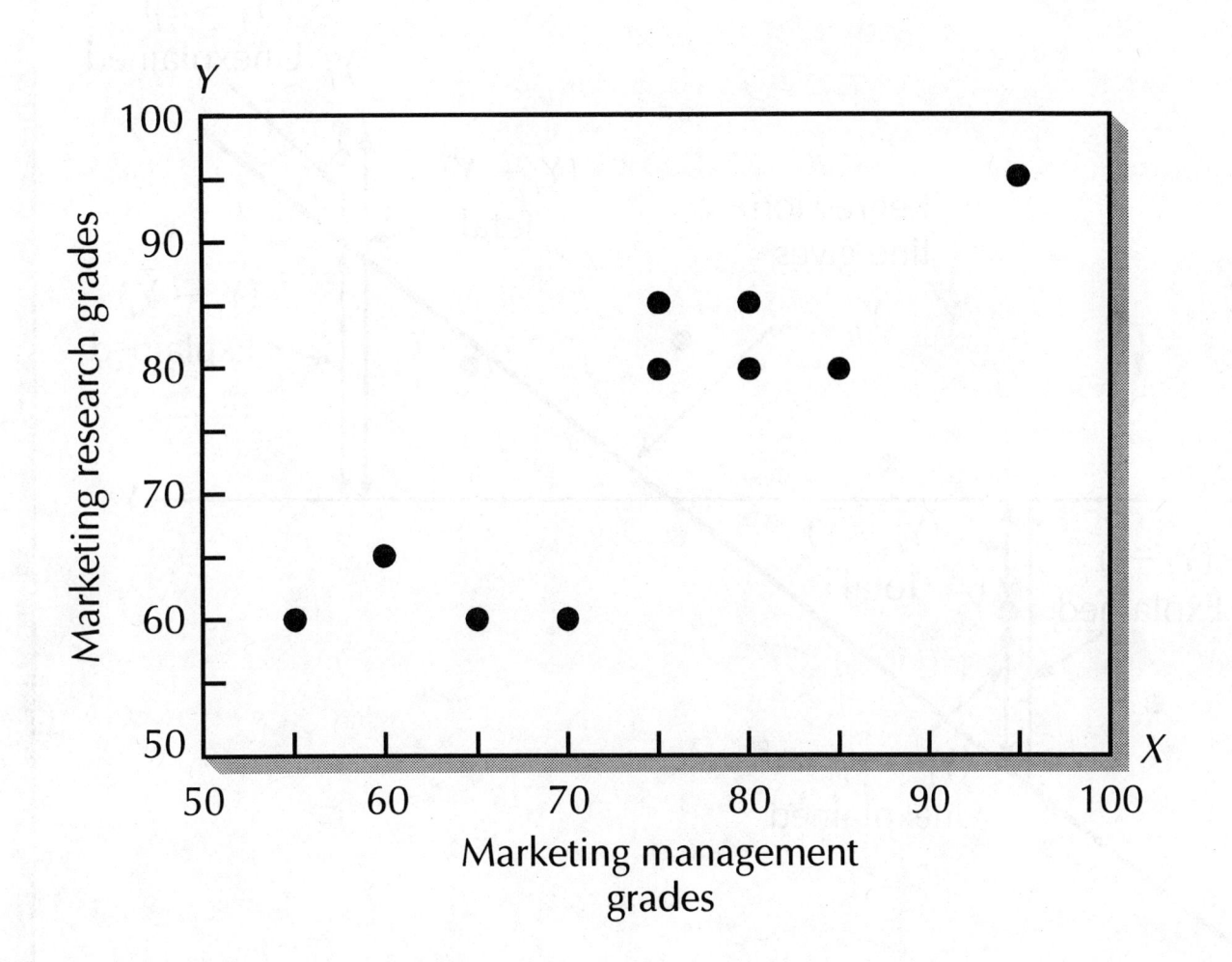

Figure 19-6
Partitioning of deviations in regression.

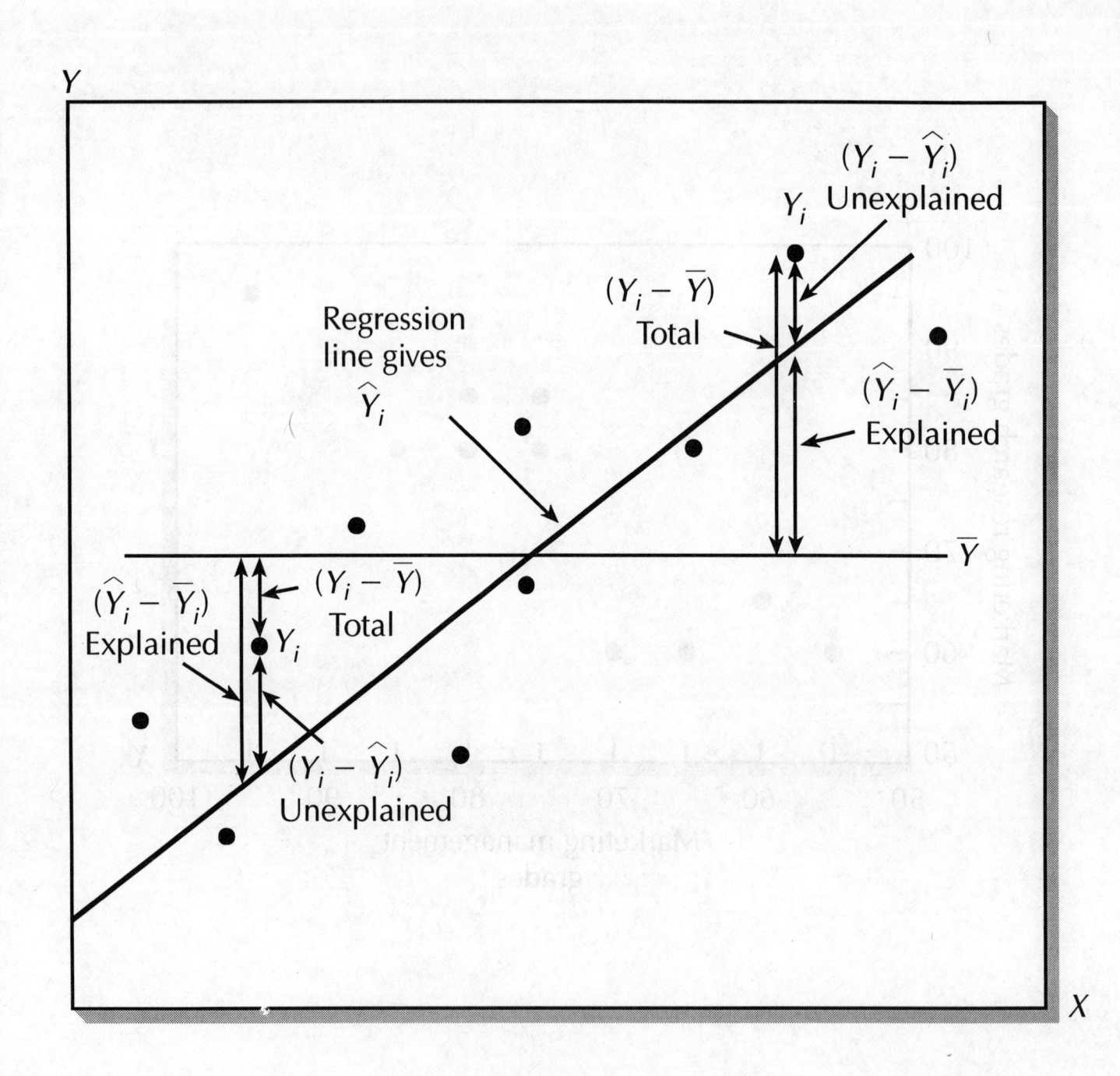

Table 19-5

ALTERNATIVE WAYS OF PRESENTING CROSS-TABULAR RESULTS

A Raw frequencies

Income	Type of wine consumed		Total
	Cheap	Premium	
Less than $25,000	75	10	85
$25,000 and over	40	80	120
Total	115	90	205

B Row percentages

Income	Type of wine consumed		Total
	Cheap	Premium	
Less than $25,000	88.2%	11.8%	100.0
$25,000 and over	33.3	66.7	100.0

C Column percentages

Income	Type of wine consumed	
	Cheap	Premium
Less than $25,000	65.2%	11.1%
$25,000 and over	34.8	88.9
Total	100.0%	100.0%

D Cell percentages

Income	Type of wine consumed	
	Cheap	Premium
Less than $25,000	36.6%	4.9%
$25,000 and over	19.5	39.0
	Total 100.0%	

Copyright © 1996 by the McGraw-Hill Companies, Inc. All Rights Reserved.

Table 19-6

RETAIN ORIGINAL CONCLUSION THAT A RELATIONSHIP EXISTS

A Total sample (n = 1000)

Use credit cards	Income Under $25,000		Income $25,000 and over	
Yes	(100)	25.0%	(500)	83.3%
No	(300)	75.0	(100)	16.7
Total	(400)	100.0%	(600)	100.0%

B Conditional on age

B-1 For ages 18–35 (n = 350)

Use credit cards	Income Under $25,000		Income $25,000 and over	
Yes	(34)	29.6%	(199)	84.7%
No	(81)	70.4	(36)	15.3
Total	(115)	100.0%	(235)	100.0%

B-2 For ages over 35 (n = 650)

Use credit cards	Income Under $25,000		Income $25,000 and over	
Yes	(66)	23.2%	(301)	82.5%
No	(219)	76.8	(64)	17.5
Total	(285)	100.0%	(365)	100.0%

Copyright © 1996 by the McGraw-Hill Companies, Inc. All Rights Reserved.

Table 19-7

SPECIFICATION OF RELATIONSHIP

A Total sample (n = 1000)

Use credit cards	Income Under $25,000		$25,000 and over	
Yes	(175)	43.8%	(350)	58.3%
No	(225)	56.2	(250)	41.7
Total	(400)	100.0%	(600)	100.0%

B Conditional on age

B-1 For ages 18–35 (n = 350)

Use credit cards	Income Under $25,000		$25,000 and over	
Yes	(100)	76.9%	(150)	68.2%
No	(30)	23.1	(70)	31.8
Total	(130)	100.0%	(220)	100.0%

B-2 For ages over 35 (n = 650)

Use credit cards	Income Under $25,000		$25,000 and over	
Yes	(75)	27.8%	(230)	60.5%
No	(195)	72.2	(150)	39.5
Total	(270)	100.0%	(380)	100.0%

Copyright © 1996 by the McGraw-Hill Companies, Inc. All Rights Reserved.

Table 19-8

IDENTIFICATION OF A SPURIOUS RELATIONSHIP

A Total sample (n = 1430)

Attendance at theater movies	Television ownership			
	No		Yes	
Yes	(240)	36.4%	(610)	79.2%
No	(420)	63.6	(160)	20.8
Total	(660)	100.0%	(770)	100.0%

B Conditional on income

B-1 For income under $25,000 (n = 550)

Attendance at theater movies	Television ownership			
	No		Yes	
Yes	(40)	9.1%	(10)	9.1%
No	(400)	90.9	(100)	90.9
Total	(440)	100.0%	(110)	100.0%

B-2 For income $25,000 and over (n = 880)

Attendance at theater movies	Television ownership			
	No		Yes	
Yes	(200)	90.9%	(600)	90.9%
No	(20)	9.1	(60)	9.1
Total	(220)	100.0%	(660)	100.0%

Source: Adapted from Herman J. Loether and Donald G. McTavish, *Descriptive Statistics for Sociologists* (Boston: Allyn and Bacon, 1974), pp. 276–287.

Table 19-9

RETAIN ORIGINAL CONCLUSION OF NO RELATIONSHIP

A Total sample (n = 1000)

Home ownership	Region of the country			
	East		West	
Yes	(205)	41.0%	(201)	40.2%
No	(295)	59.0	(299)	59.8
Total	(500)	100.0%	(500)	100.0%

B Conditional on income

B-1 For income under $25,000 (n = 300)

Home ownership	Region of the country			
	East		West	
Yes	(60)	40.0%	(63)	42.0%
No	(90)	60.0	(87)	58.0
Total	(150)	100.0%	(150)	100.0%

B-2 For income $25,000 and over (n = 700)

Home ownership	Region of the country			
	East		West	
Yes	(145)	41.4%	(138)	39.4%
No	(205)	58.6	(212)	60.6
Total	(350)	100.0%	(350)	100.0%

Copyright © 1996 by the McGraw-Hill Companies, Inc. All Rights Reserved.

Figure 20-2
Interdependence versus dependence methods.

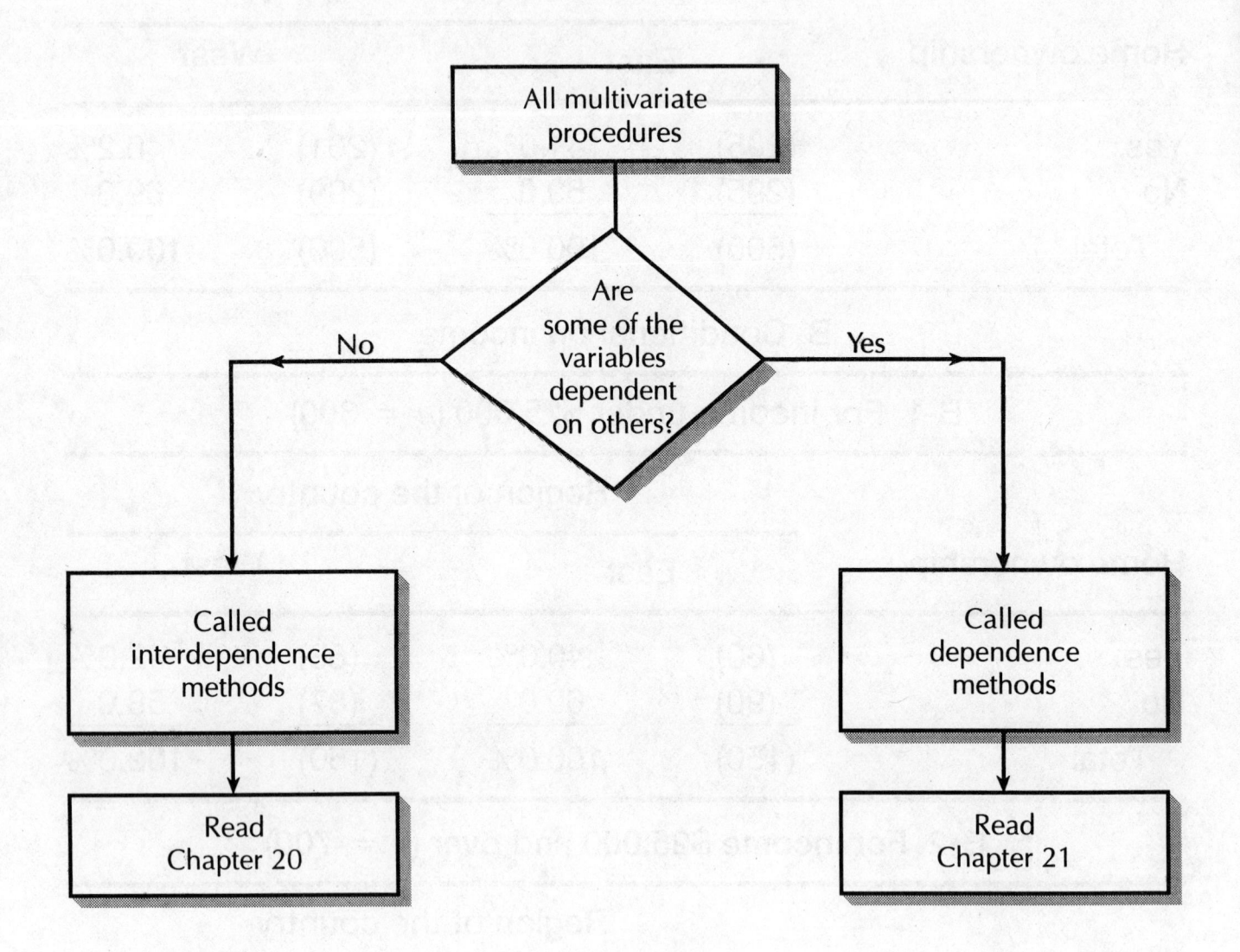

Figure 20-4
Development of *R*- and *Q*-type correlation matrices.

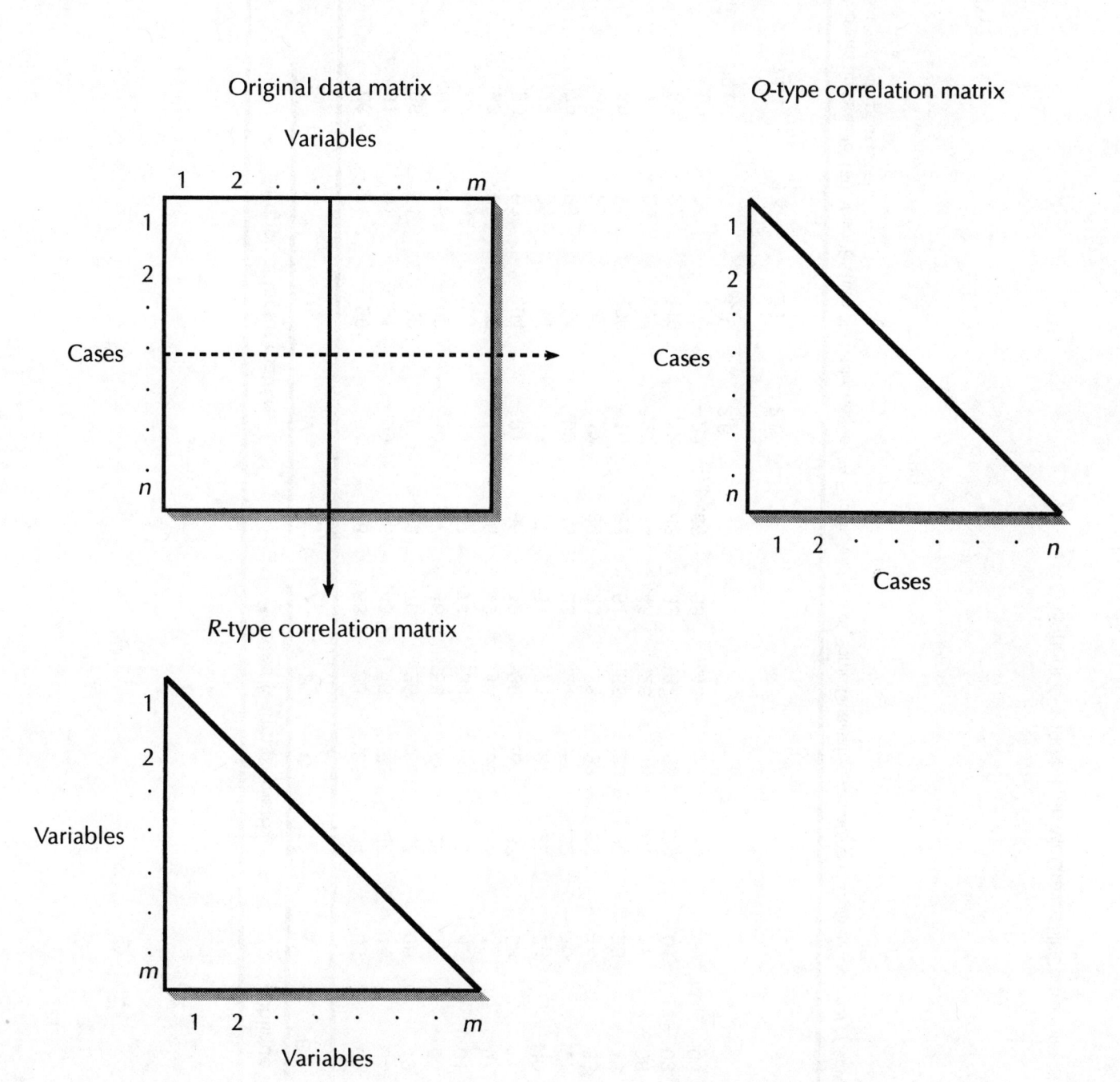

Table 20-2

FACTOR LOADINGS

	Principal factor matrix					Rotated (varimax) matrix				Oblique factor matrix			
	I	II	III	IV	h^2	A	B	C	D	A	B	C	D
1	.86	−.01	−.20	.04	.78	.63	.38	.36	.34	.34	.01	.07	−.03
2	.91	−.01	−.01	−.09	.83	.48	.43	.53	.38	.14	.04	.23	.04
3	.86	.11	.28	.002	.83	.70	.26	.38	.36	.36	.13	−.003	−.01
4	.91	.15	−.001	−.10	.87	.46	.53	.54	.29	.16	−.05	.34	−.07
5	.87	−.002	−.31	.10	.74	.74	.38	.30	.32	.47	.01	−.004	−.08
6	.93	.03	−.02	−.16	.90	.49	.43	.59	.35	.12	.07	.30	−.01
7	.90	−.02	−.04	−.21	.86	.42	.38	.64	.37	.03	.11	.33	−.04
8	.77	.36	.11	.16	.77	.31	.27	.52	.22	.24	−.40	.32	−.37
9	.79	−.28	.24	−.09	.76	.23	.74	.24	.62	−.15	.11	.14	−.10
10	.87	.25	.22	.17	.89	.28	.75	.33	.39	.14	.38	.31	−.07
11	.89	.11	.05	.10	.82	.51	.55	.36	.36	.28	−.15	.17	−.01
12	.76	−.29	.04	.27	.74	.43	.28	.16	.67	.18	−.08	−.18	.38
13	.84	−.27	.19	.12	.83	.33	.32	.36	.70	.01	−.03	−.001	.41
14	.90	−.04	.08	−.23	.86	.38	.43	.65	.34	.002	−.08	.39	.01
Percent common variance	90.0	4.1	3.3	2.6									
Percent total variance	74.4	3.4	2.7	2.6									

Source: Adapted and updated to 1995 from Bishwa Nath Mukherjee, "A Factor Analysis of Some Qualitative Attributes of Coffee," *Journal of Advertising Research*, vol. 5, p. 37, March 1965. Used with permission.

Copyright © 1996 by the McGraw-Hill Companies, Inc. All Rights Reserved.

Table 20-3

INTERPRETATION OF FACTORS

Variable	Attribute	Varimax	Oblique
Factor A (comforting quality)			
1	Pleasant flavor	.625	.340
3	Mellow taste	.698	.359
5	Comforting taste	.736	.465
11	Pure clear taste	.512	.283
Factor B (heartiness)			
8	Deep distinct flavor	.742	.396
10	Hearty flavor	.745	.380
Factor C (genuineness)			
2	Sparkling taste	.524	.232
4	Expensive taste	.541	.334
6	Alive taste	.594	.301
7	Tastes like real coffee	.636	.328
8	Deep distinct flavor	.268	.323
10	Hearty flavor	.332	.310
14	Overall preference	.653	.387
Factor D (freshness)			
9	Tastes just brewed	.621	.359
12	Roasted taste	.670	.465
13	Fresh taste	.698	.238

Source: Updated to 1995 from Bishwa Nath Mukherjee, "A Factor Analysis of Some Qualitative Attributes of Coffee," *Journal of Advertising Research,* vol. 5, p. 37, March 1965. Used with permission.

Copyright © 1996 by the McGraw-Hill Companies, Inc. All Rights Reserved.

Figure 20-6
Perceptual space solution based on data in Table 20-4.

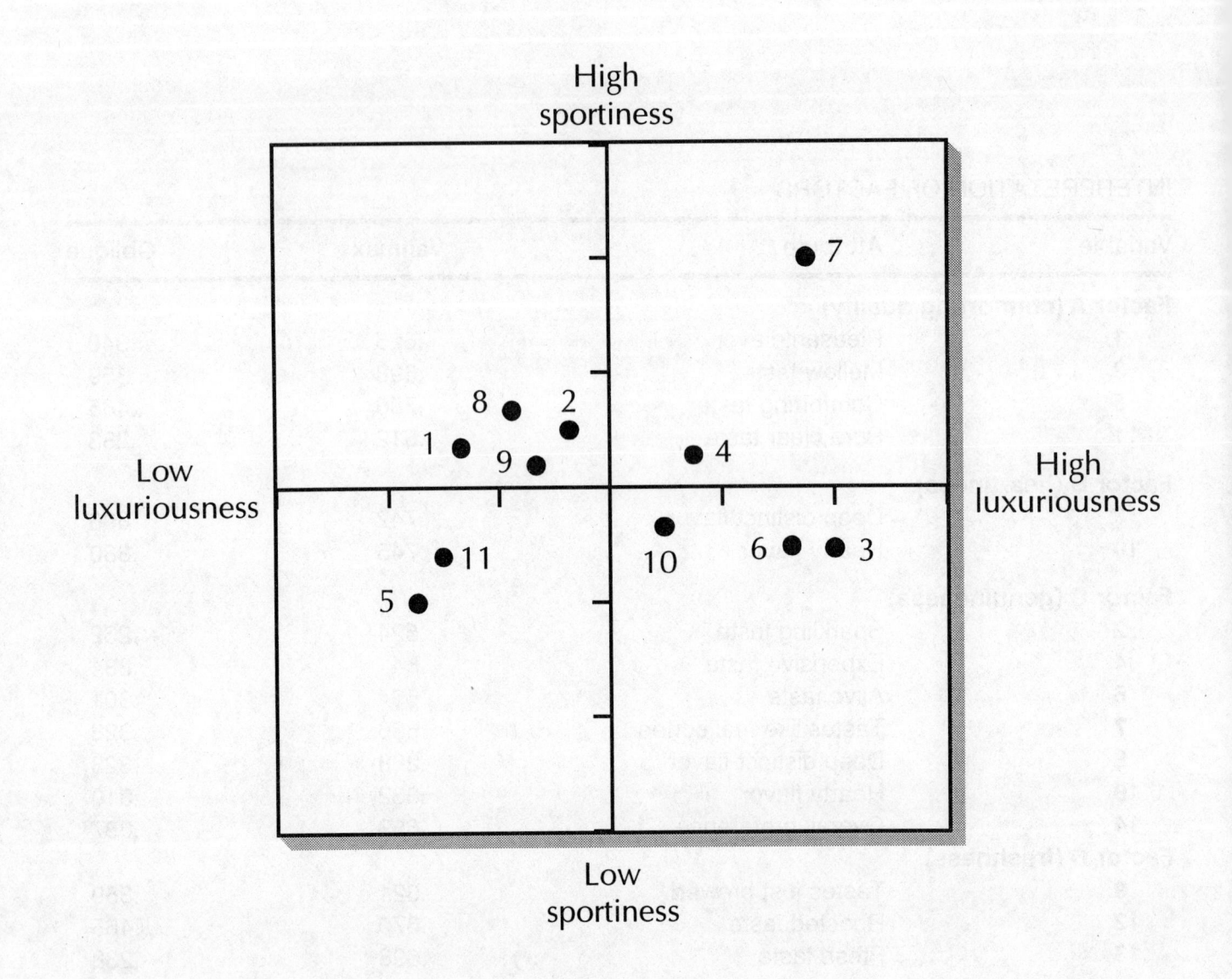

High sportiness

Low luxuriousness — High luxuriousness

Low sportiness

1994 Car Models

1 Ford Taurus
2 Mercury Sable
3 Lincoln Continental
4 Ford Thunderbird
5 Ford Escort
6 Cadillac Eldorado
7 Jaguar XJ Sedan
8 Mazda 626
9 Dodge Intrepid
10 Buick Le Sabre
11 Chevrolet Cavalier

Copyright © 1996 by the McGraw-Hill Companies, Inc. All Rights Reserved.

Figure 21-2
Classification of dependence methods. (*Source:* Adapted from a scheme presented in Thomas C. Kinnear and James Taylor, "Multivariate in Marketing Research: A Further Attempt at Classification," *Journal of Marketing*, vol. 35, pp. 56–59, October 1971.)

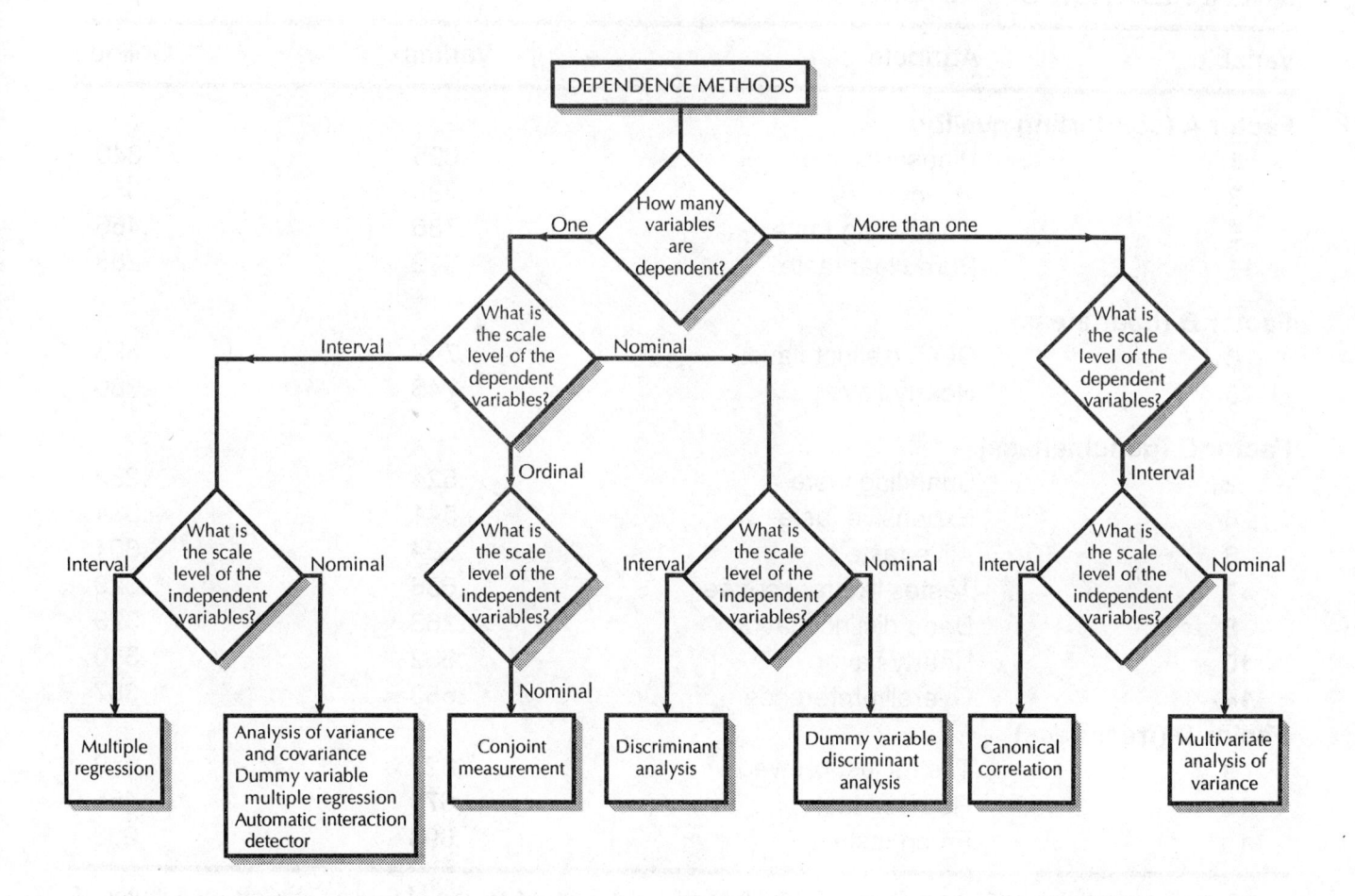

Copyright © 1996 by the McGraw-Hill Companies, Inc. All Rights Reserved.

Table 21-1

INTERPRETATION OF FACTORS

Variable	Attribute	Varimax	Oblique
Factor A (comforting quality)			
1	Pleasant flavor	.625	.340
3	Mellow taste	.698	.359
5	Comforting taste	.736	.465
11	Pure clear taste	.512	.283
Factor B (heartiness)			
8	Deep distinct flavor	.742	.396
10	Hearty flavor	.745	.380
Factor C (genuineness)			
2	Sparkling taste	.524	.232
4	Expensive taste	.541	.334
6	Alive taste	.594	.301
7	Tastes like real coffee	.636	.328
8	Deep distinct flavor	.268	.323
10	Hearty flavor	.332	.310
14	Overall preference	.653	.387
Factor D (freshness)			
9	Tastes just brewed	.621	.359
12	Roasted taste	.670	.465
13	Fresh taste	.698	.238

Source: Updated to 1995 from Bishwa Nath Mukherjee, "A Factor Analysis of Some Qualitative Attributes of Coffee," *Journal of Advertising Research,* vol. 5, p. 37, March 1965. Used with permission.

Figure 21-4
AID tree for use of nonphosphate laundry products.

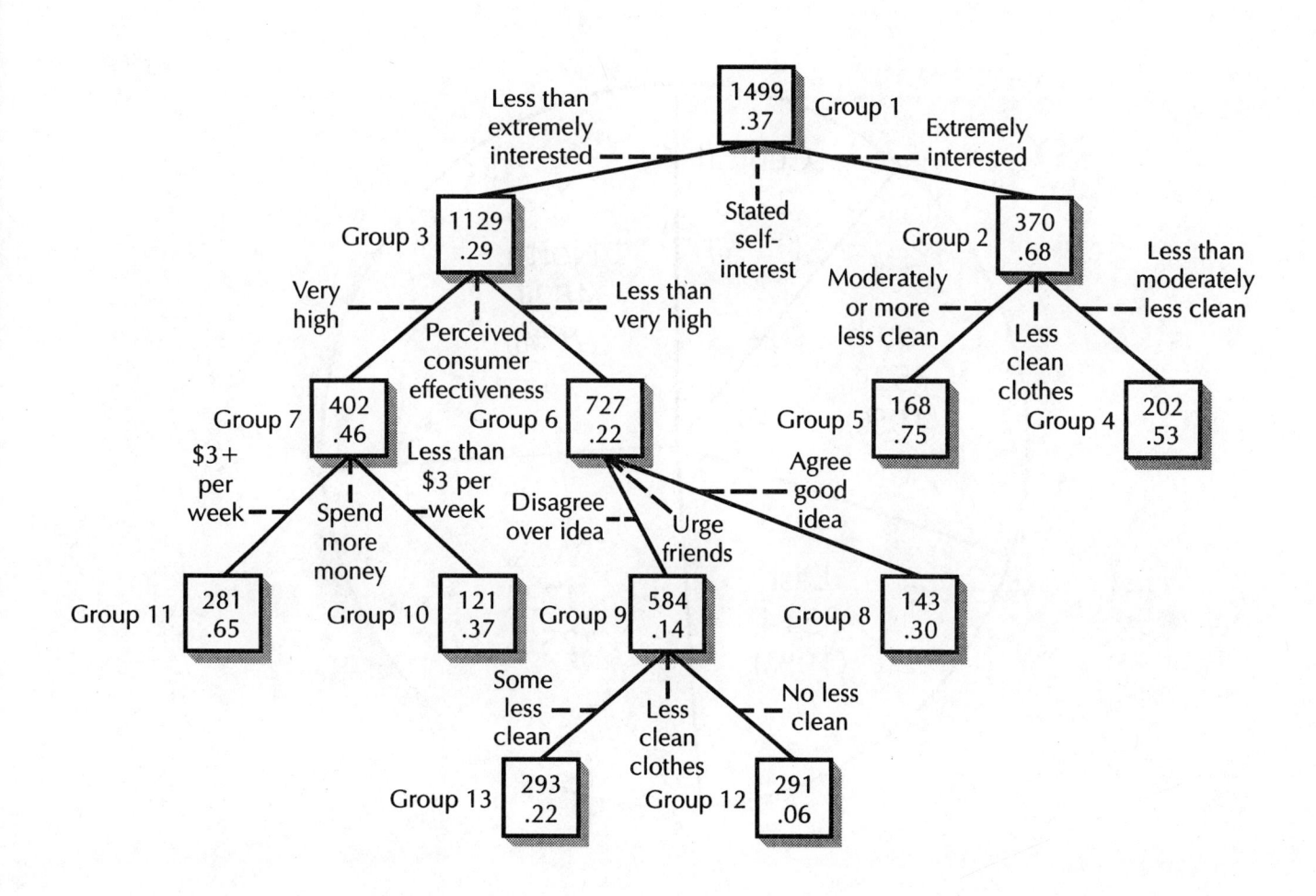

Figure 22-2
Pie chart of weekly traffic count by retail stores (August 8–14, 1995).

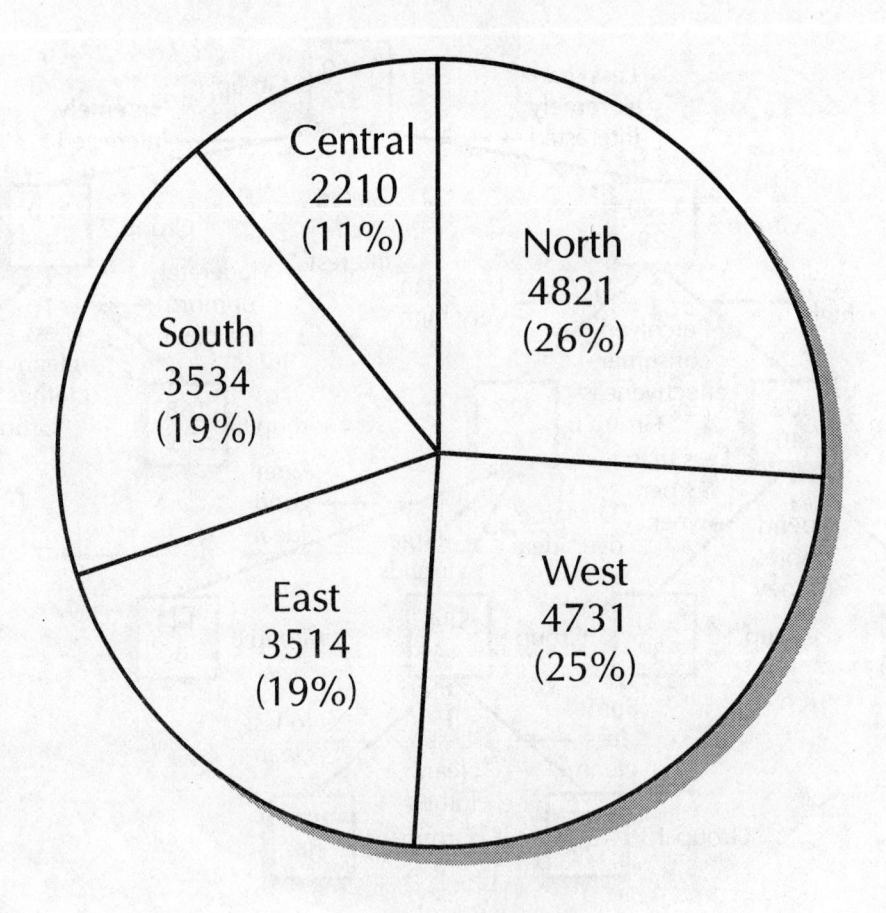

Store	Count	Percent
Central	2210	11%
North	4821	26%
West	4731	25%
East	3514	19%
South	3534	19%

Copyright © 1996 by the McGraw-Hill Companies, Inc. All Rights Reserved.

Figure 22-3
Exploding pie chart.

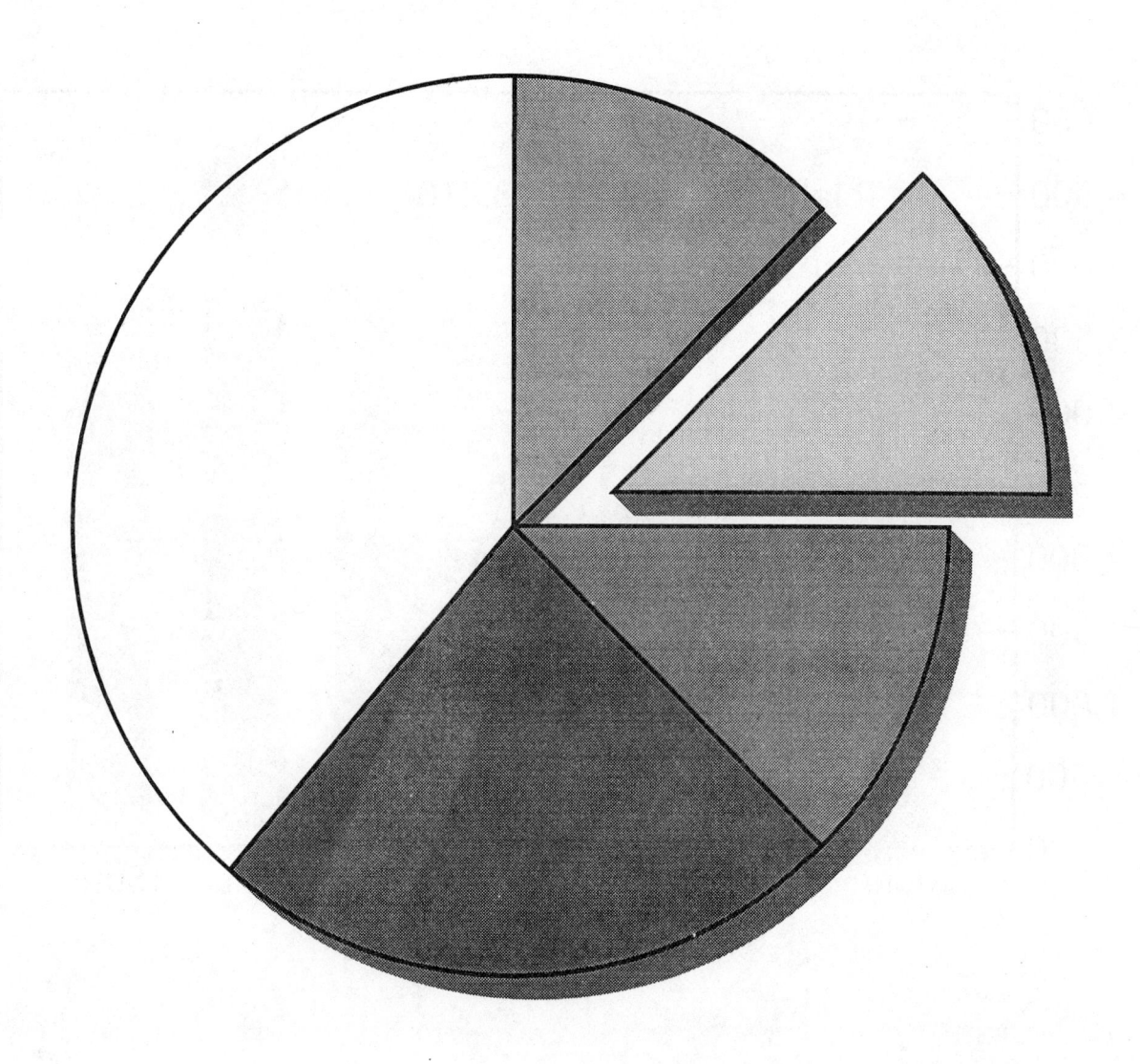

Figure 22-4
Bar chart of traffic count of retail stores by day of week (August 8–14, 1995).

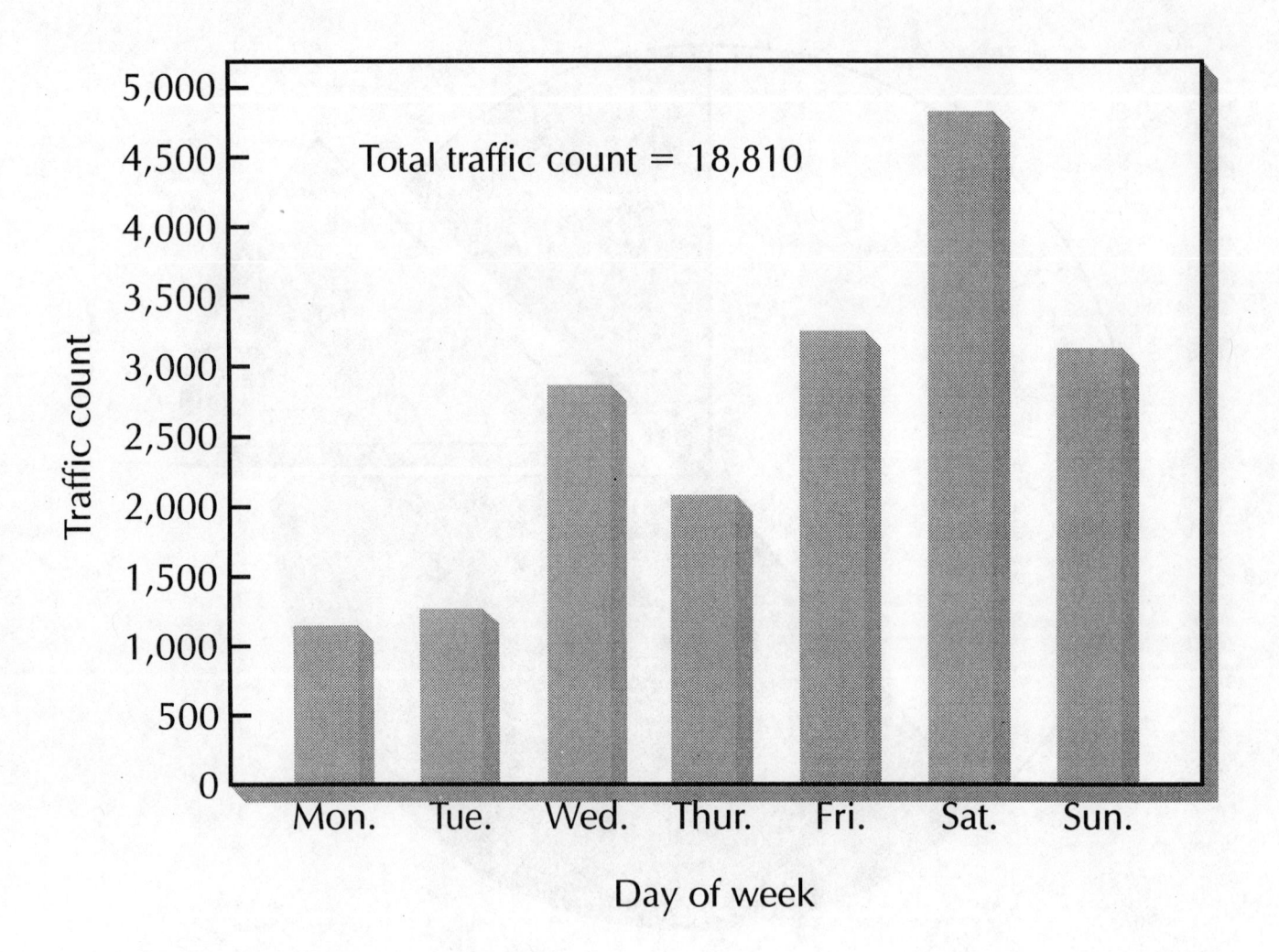

Copyright © 1996 by the McGraw-Hill Companies, Inc. All Rights Reserved.

Figure 22-5
Cluster bar chart.

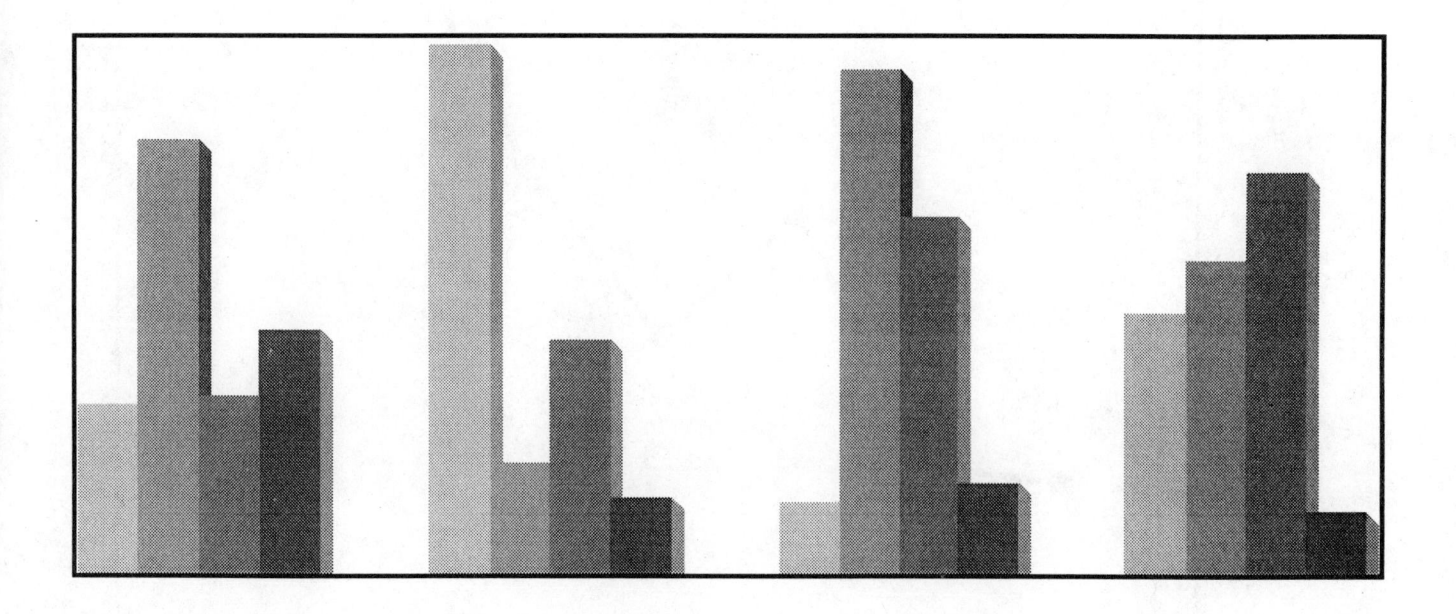

Copyright © 1996 by the McGraw-Hill Companies, Inc. All Rights Reserved.

Figure 22-6
Line chart of traffic count of retail stores by day of week (August 8–14, 1995).

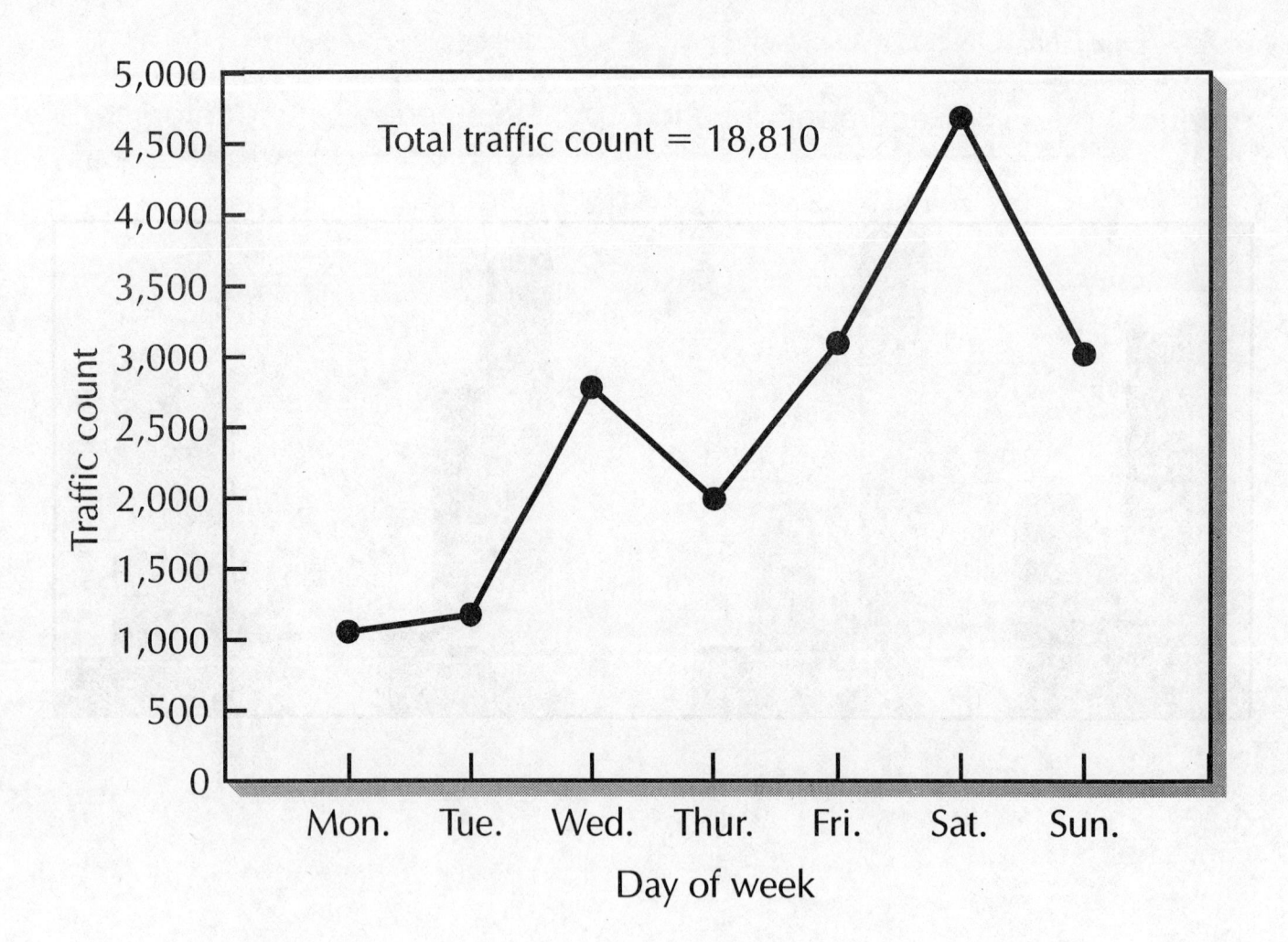

Total traffic count = 18,810

Copyright © 1996 by the McGraw-Hill Companies, Inc. All Rights Reserved.

Table 23-1

FOUR DIMENSIONS OF DEMAND MEASUREMENT AND FORECASTING

Product	Geographic location	Time period	Customer
Industry	World	Current	Consumer
Company	United States	Short-range	Business
Product line	Region	Long-range	Government
Product class	Territory		
Product item			

Figure 23-1
Market demand concepts and terminology. (*a*) Market demand as a function of industry marketing effort (assumes a particular marketing environment. (*b*) Market demand as a function of industry marketing effort (two different environments assumed). [*Source:* Philip Kotler, Marketing Management, 4th ed. (Englewood Cliffs, NJ: Prentice-Hall, 1990), p. 216.]

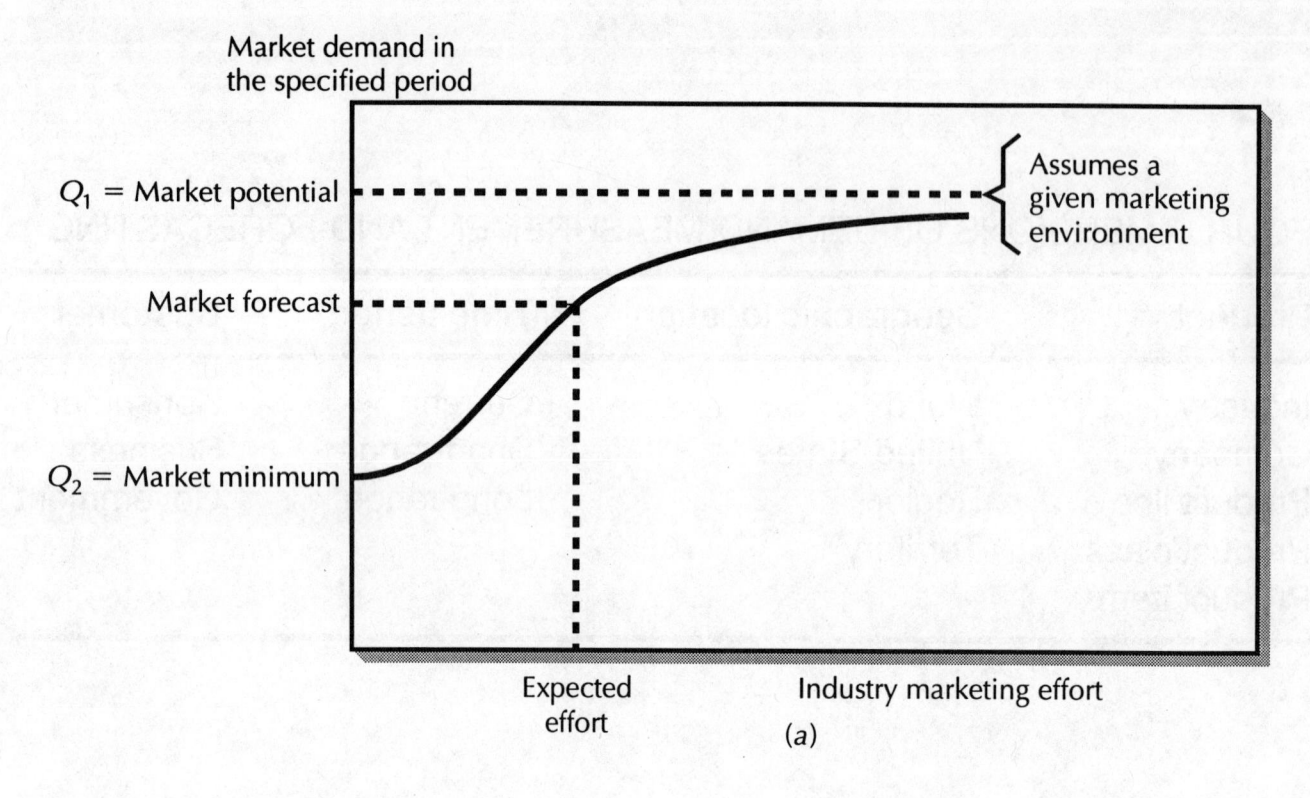

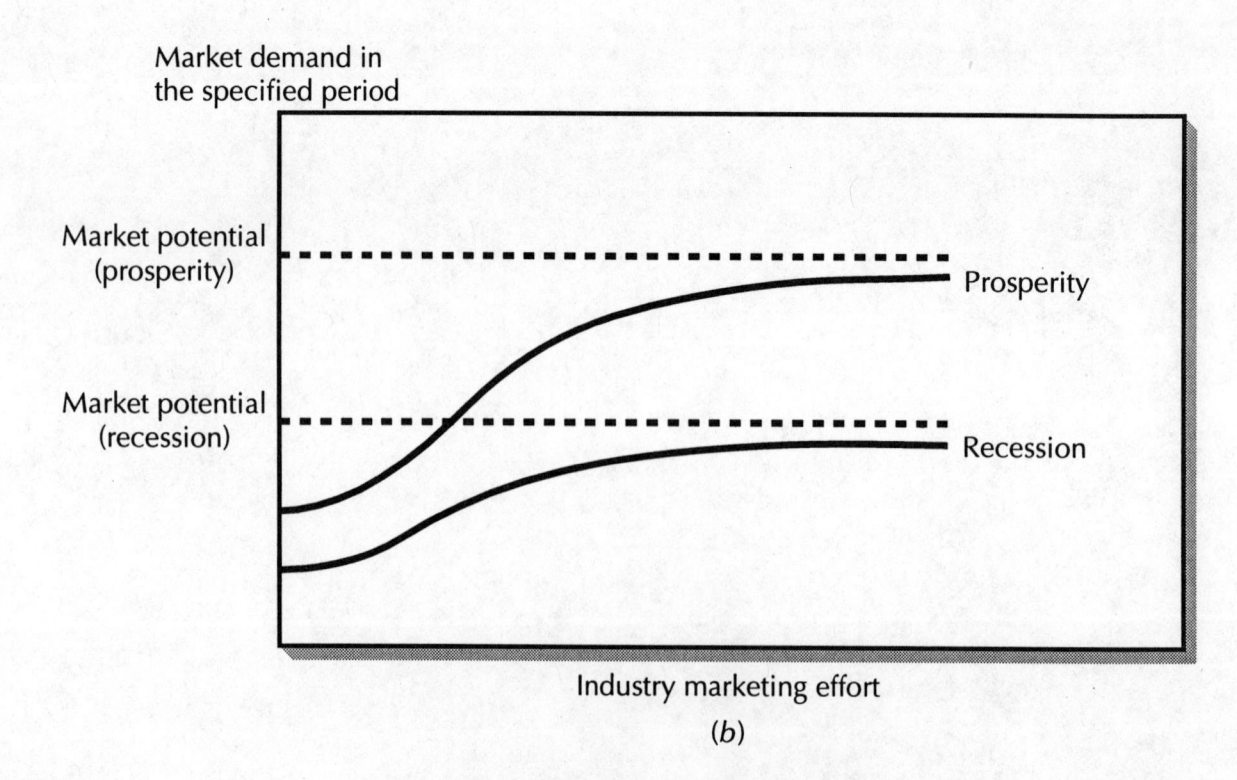

Copyright © 1996 by the McGraw-Hill Companies, Inc. All Rights Reserved.

Table 23-5

FORECASTING METHODS

Qualitative methods	Time-series methods	Causal methods
Executive opinion	Moving average	Leading indicators
Sales force—distributor estimates	Exponential smoothing	Regression models
Buyer or consumer surveys	Time-series decomposition	

Figure 24-2
Most stimulation models operate in the same general framework. (*Source: Advertising Age*, p. M-11, Feb. 22, 1982. Reprinted with permission of Crain Publications, Inc.)

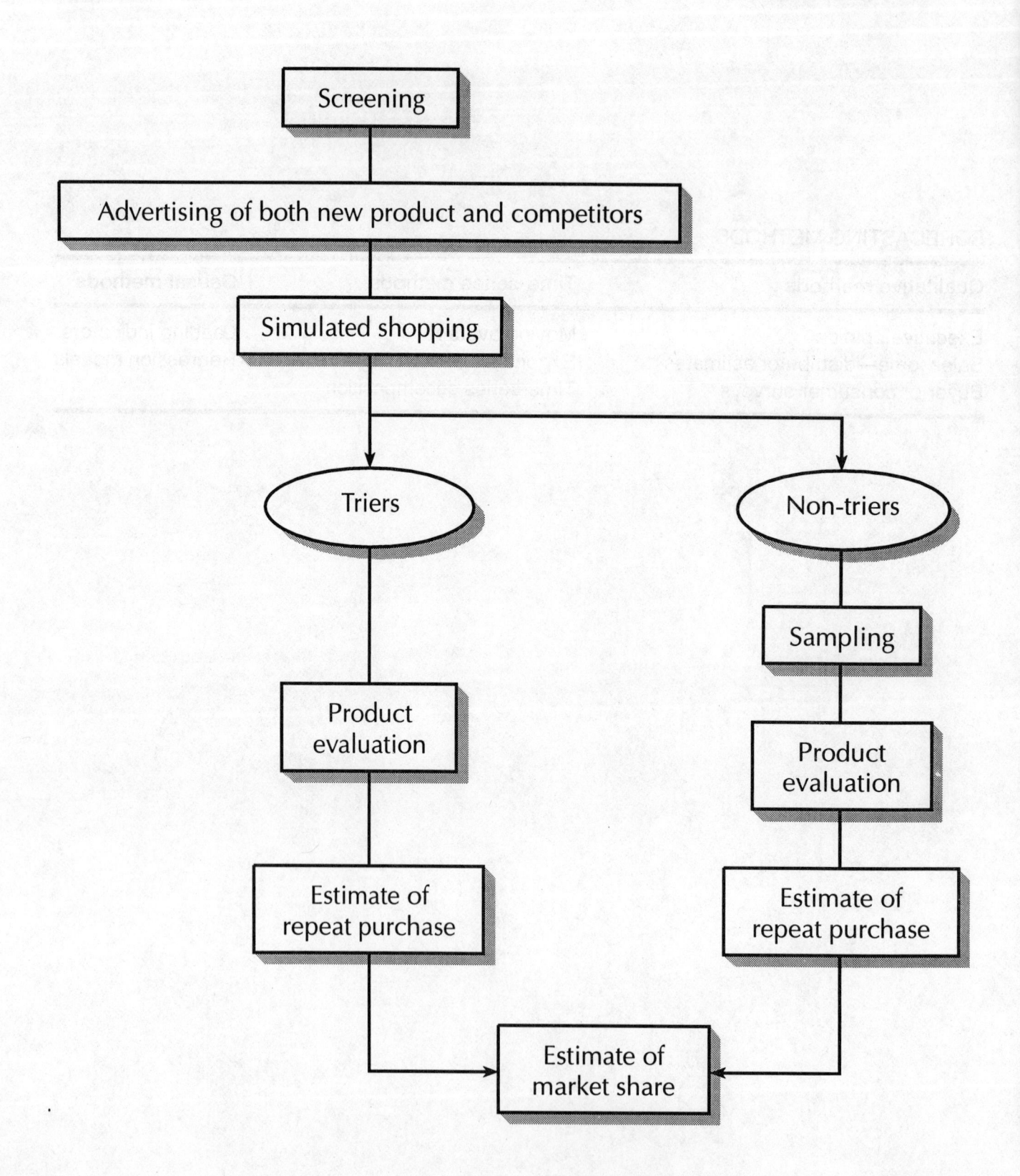

Copyright © 1996 by the McGraw-Hill Companies, Inc. All Rights Reserved.

Figure 25-1
A model for evaluation advertising.

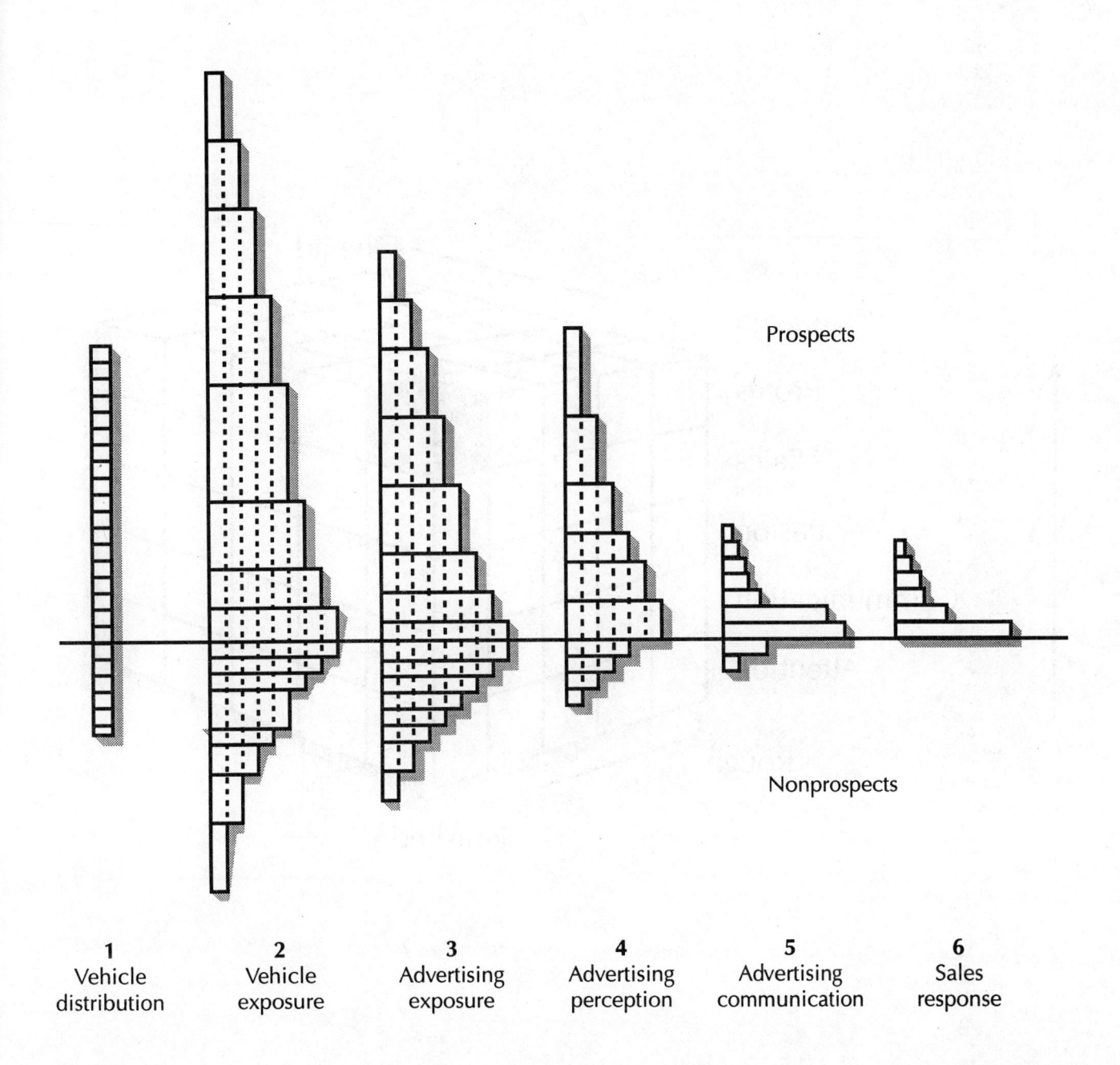

1 Vehicle distribution
2 Vehicle exposure
3 Advertising exposure
4 Advertising perception
5 Advertising communication
6 Sales response

Prospects

Nonprospects

Copyright © 1996 by the McGraw-Hill Companies, Inc. All Rights Reserved.

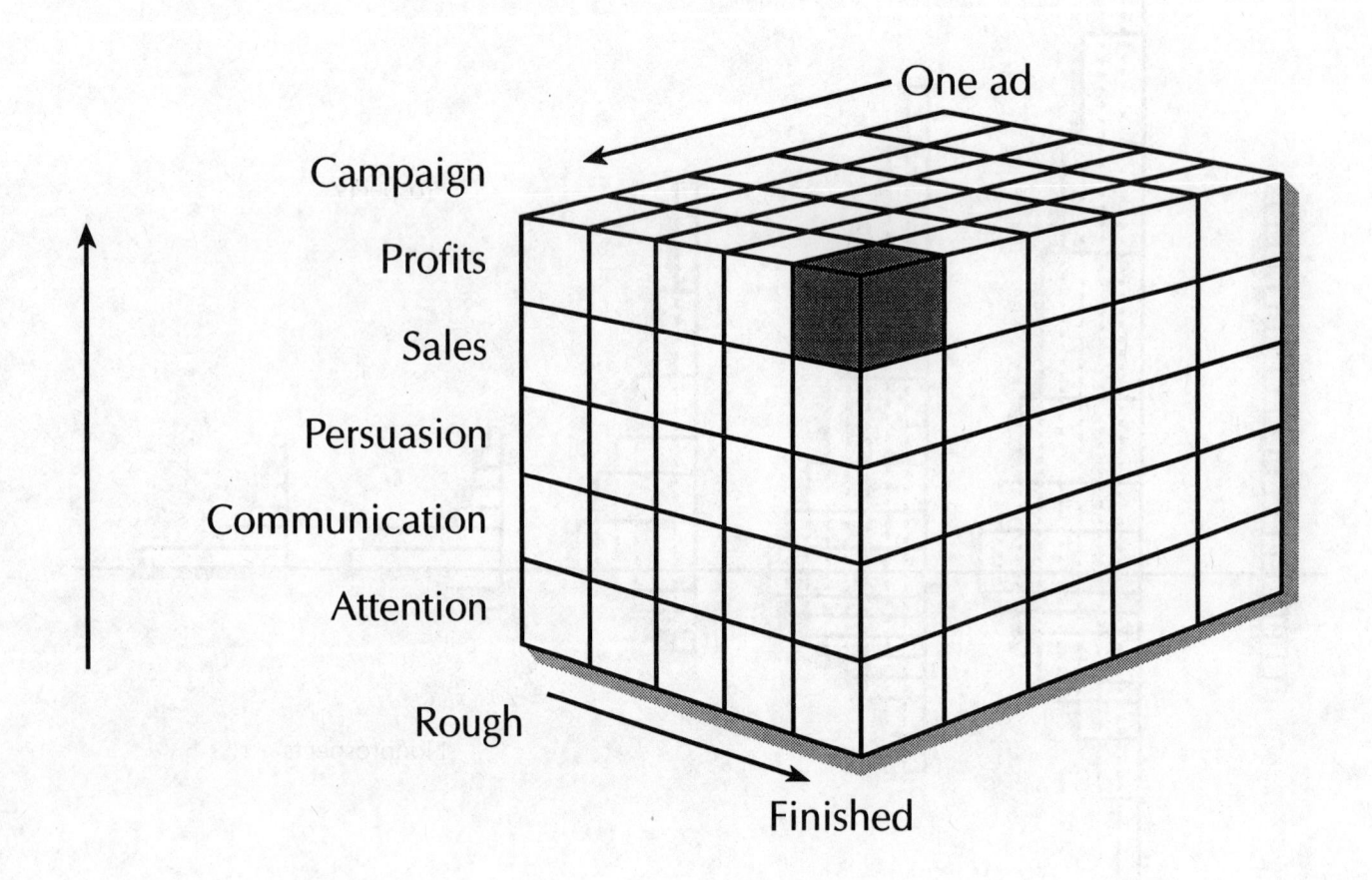

Figure 25-2
What to measure. (*Source:* Eugene C. Pomerance, "How Agencies Evaluate Advertising," in *Reflections on Progress in Marketing*, American Marketing Association, pp. 167–172, December 1964.)

Figure 25-3
What and how to measure. (*Source:* Eugene C. Pomerance, "How Agencies Evaluate Advertising," in *Reflections on Progress in Marketing*, American Marketing Association, pp. 167–172, December 1964.)

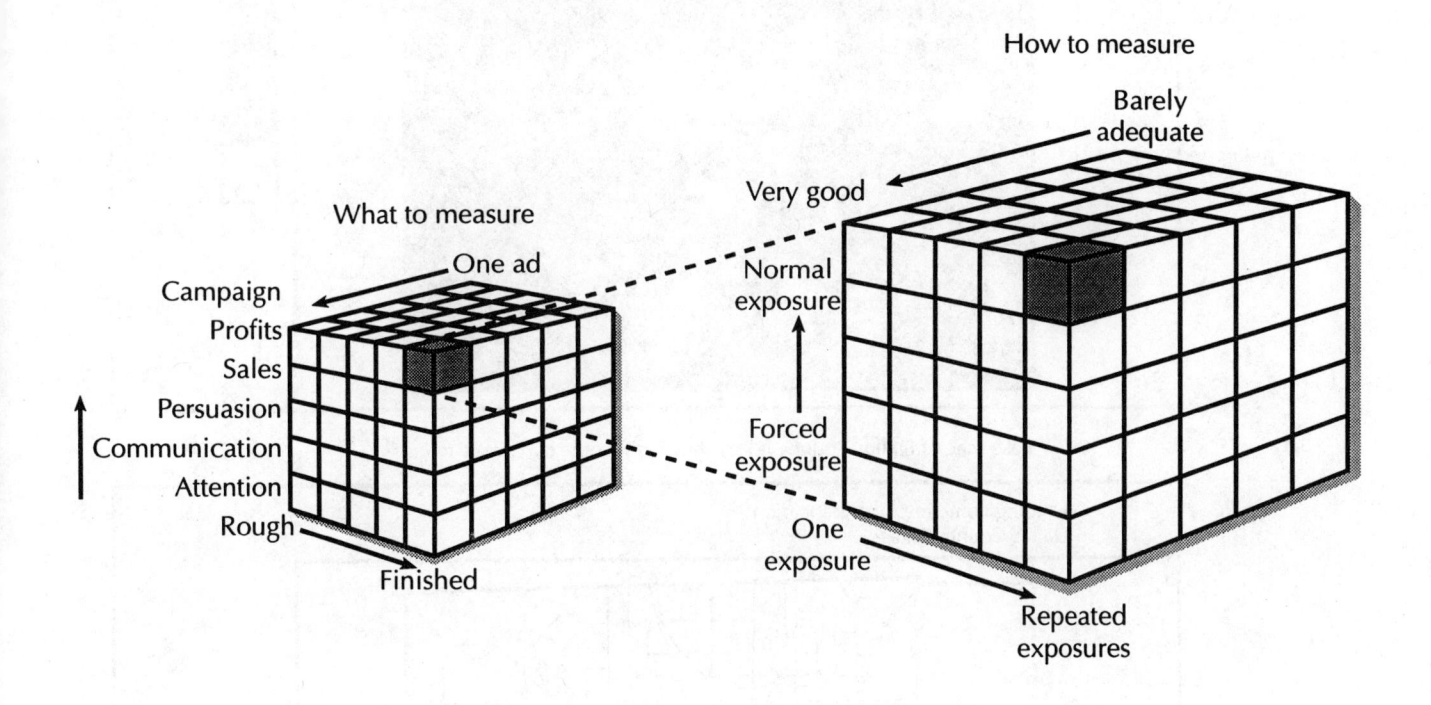

Figure 26-1
NPDC data on income and locations for Dallas County. (*Source:* P. K. Skipper, "Prospecting for Deposits with MAX and Map Analysis," *Demometrics*, vol. 6, no. 4, p. 4, Autumn 1989.)

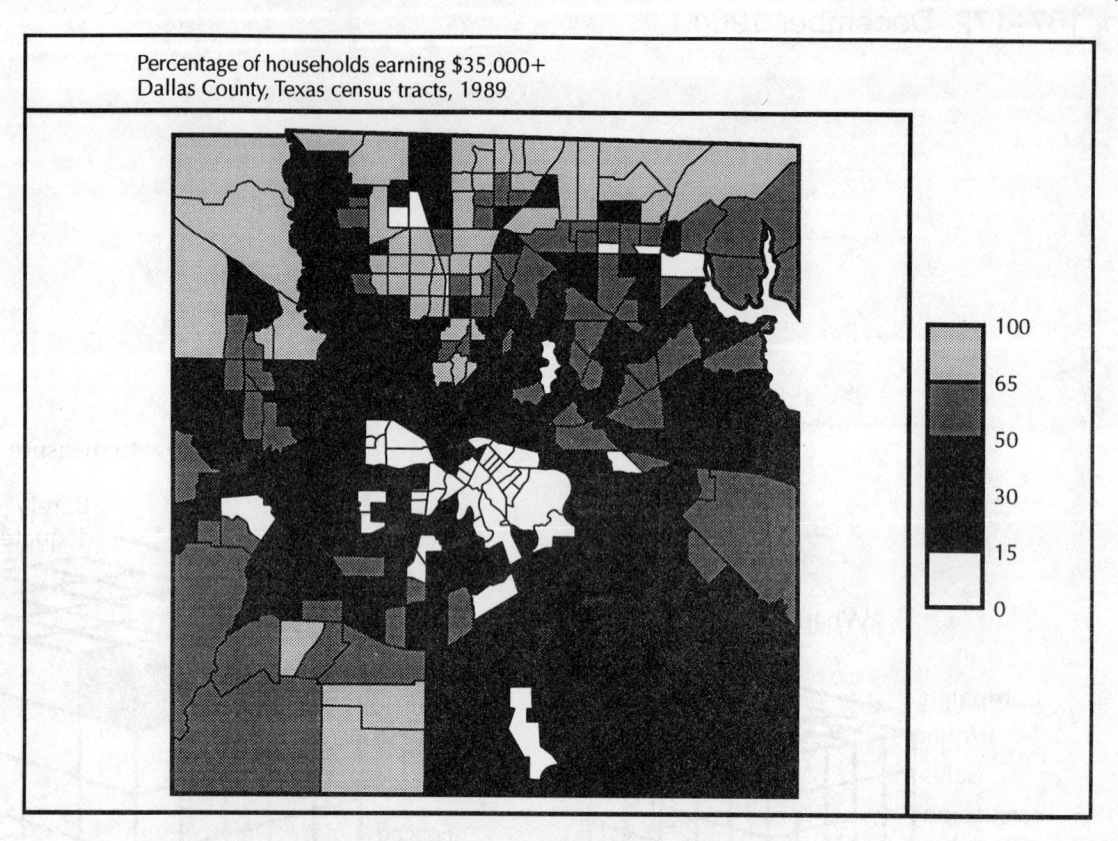

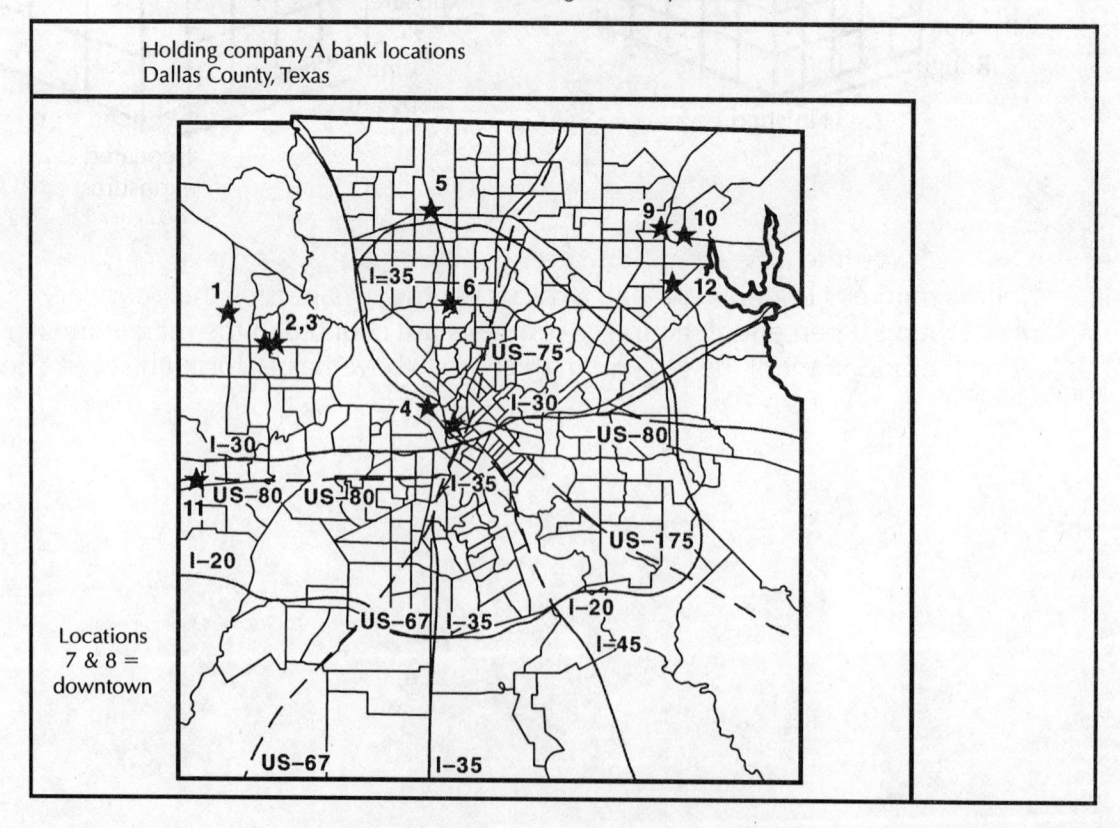

Figure 26-2
Illustration of the centroid method. (*Source:* Stephen J. Tordella, "How to Relate to Centroids," *American Demographics*, vol. 9, iss. 5, p. 50, May 1987.)

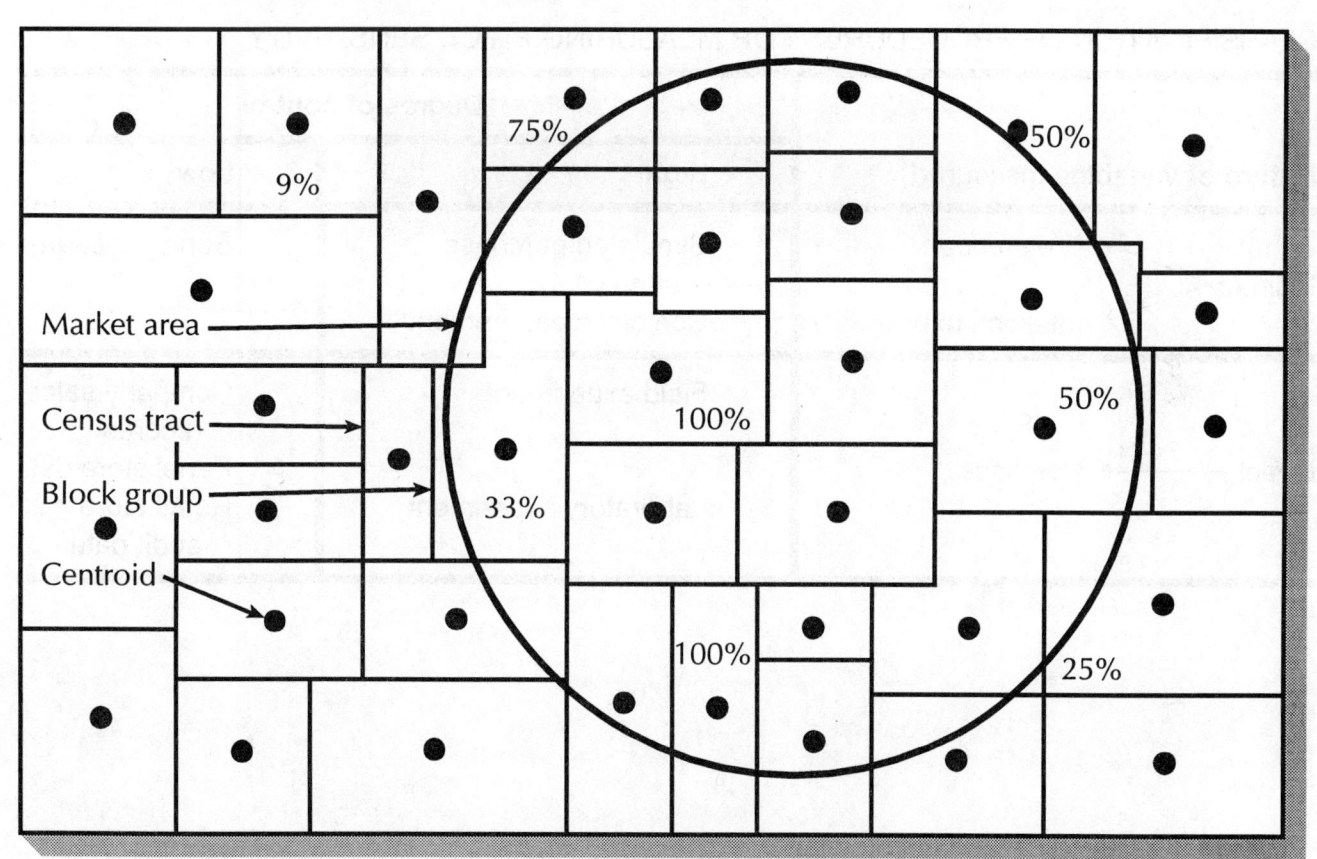

The residents of a census tract are counted as living in a market area in proportion to the number of centroids (the geographical centers of block groups that make up tracts) that fall within the market's boundary. If half a tract's centroids fall inside the boundary, for example, then 50 percent of the tract's residents are counted in the market area's population. The boundary of the circular market area above passes through seven census tracts. The proportion of the residents who will be included in the market's population are indicated within each tract.

Copyright © 1996 by the McGraw-Hill Companies, Inc. All Rights Reserved.

Table 26-1

CLASSIFICATION OF PROCEDURES FOR MEASURING PRICE SENSITIVITY

Nature of variables measured	Degree of control	
	High	Low
Indirect → Preference / Intention to buy	Simulated purchase survey Conjoint measurement	Survey research
Direct → Purchase	Field experiment Laboratory experiment	Company sales records Panel store data Retail store audit data

Copyright © 1996 by the McGraw-Hill Companies, Inc. All Rights Reserved.

NOTES

NOTES

NOTES

NOTES

NOTES

NOTES